Superfast Computer Course

Superfast Computer Course

Mrinal Talukdar

PRABHAT
PRAKASHAN

Image Credit goes to Short India

Published by
PRABHAT PRAKASHAN PVT. LTD.
4/19 Asaf Ali Road,
New Delhi-110 002 (INDIA)
e-mail: prabhatbooks@gmail.com

ISBN 978-93-5186-625-1
SUPERFAST COMPUTER COURSE
by Mrinal Talukdar

Edition
2025

Price
₹ 800.00 (Rupees Eight Hundred only)

Printed at
Narula Printers, Delhi

Preface

We live in the age of computer, or better we can say, the information age. This period could equally be called 'the age of learning'. The rate of change in the workplace is not the only factor giving increased importance to the ability to learn. The global scale of the consequences of human actions makes it ever more urgent for us to understand what we are doing. Computer has become the basic requirement of life. The computers have become so common and important that many of us will be incomplete without them. Today, computers are found practically in every household.

To become acquainted with computer, there are certain basic skills to be mastered. While these skills might seem obvious at first, the fact is that many people never take the time to learn these very important basics. By studying them now, you will both save time later and also improve your daily computer productivity. Once you have understood these basics, you will have a clear understanding on which to build your future knowledge of and skill with computers. With the objective to give you a precise and specific set of computer knowledge, here we present the book ***Superfast Computer Course***. This book is designed in a unique and exceptional style so as to make the learning of basic computer and handling of the same swift and easy. The contents covered in the book are imperative towards learning the basics of computer.

It is a fact that each year, new technologies hold the promise to alter the way we think and learn. Computers are prevalent everywhere and they are used for everything; and in every type of work and business, we become too dependent on computers. The younger generation particularly has seized on the strange communication through the Internet. Computers are appearing in almost every aspect of our lives, and in most cases, they are making things very easy for us. Hence, to match with the new technologies and innovations in information technology, the book is bequeathed with all the latest versions of the programs so that the learners can cope up with the most up-to-date updates available on different programs and applications. In this way, the book can be a great advantage to the learners.

It is our high hope that this book ***Superfast Computer Course*** will do wonder in teaching and educating people who crave to stand on the platform of information technology and make the most of it. The CD offered with this book will surely make the learning more pleasurable and enjoyable as you can get to know about the functions and procedures of the programs in an interactive way. However, we agree that there could be some shortcomings. We request readers to send their invaluable feedbacks so as to help us overcome those deficiencies and make this book more instructive as well as informative in the future editions.

Enjoy learning through reading!

Contents

1
An Introduction to Computers

The invention of computer is one of the most important events in human history of the 20th century. It has added to develop and improve the effectiveness and accuracy of all the scientific machines of the present world. It has helped in bringing the distance closer with respect to information and development taking place all around the globe. A computer is an electronic device for storing and processing data, making calculations or controlling machines. It can process at a very high speed with remarkable accuracy. It can also perform all arithmetic and logical functions to solve any problem and produce processed information.

The word 'computer' was first recorded as being used in 1613 and was originally used to describe a human who performed calculations or computations. The definition of a computer remained the same until the end of the 19th century when people began to realise machines that never get tired and can perform calculations much faster and more accurately than human. Nowadays, most of the people know how to use computers. Therefore, computers become more and more popular and important to our society. We can use computers everywhere and it is very useful and helpful to our life.

The first electronic computer, the Electronic Numerical Integrator And Computer (ENIAC), was developed in 1946. It took up 1,800 square feet and weighed 30 tons.

Evolution of Computers

Computers have evolved in a gradual process. Its history is vast. In 1822, Charles Babbage conceptualized and began developing the 'Difference Engine', considered to be the first automatic computing machine that was capable of computing several sets of numbers and making hard copies of the results. Babbage received some help with development of the Difference Engine from Ada Lovelace, considered by many to be the first computer programmer for her work and notes on the Difference Engine. In 1837, Charles Babbage proposed the first general mechanical computer, the 'Analytical Engine'. The Analytical Engine contained an Arithmetic Logic Unit (ALU), basic flow control and integrated memory and is the first general-purpose computer concept.

The Analytical Engine

First Programmable Computer

The Z1, created by Germany's Konrad Zuse between 1936 and 1938, is considered to be the first electro-mechanical binary programmable computer.

The Z1

First Electric Programmable Computer

The Colossus was the first electric programmable computer, developed by Tommy Flowers in 1943. The Colossus was created to help the British code breakers read encrypted German messages.

The Colossus

First Digital Computer

ENIAC

The ENIAC was invented by J. Presper Eckert and John Mauchly at the University of Pennsylvania in 1946. It occupied about 1,800 square feet and used about 18,000 vacuum tubes, weighing almost 50 tons. It is considered to be the first digital computer.

The ENIAC

First Stored Program Computer

The early British computer, known as the EDSAC, is considered to be the first stored program electronic computer. The computer performed its first calculation on May 6, 1949 and was the computer that ran the first graphical computer game, nicknamed 'Baby'.

The EDSAC

Around the same time, the Manchester Mark 1 was another computer that could run stored programs. Built at the Victoria University of Manchester, the first version of the

Mark 1 computer became operational in April 1949 and ran a program to search for Mersenne primes for nine hours without error on June 16 and 17 that same year.

First Stored Program Computer

The UNIVAC 1101 or ERA 1101, developed in 1950 is considered to be the first computer that was capable of storing and running a program from memory.

The UNIVAC 1101

First Computer with RAM

The Whirlwind machine was the first digital computer with magnetic core RAM and real-time graphics introduced in 1955.

The Whirlwind

First Transistor Computer

The TX-O (Transistorized Experimental computer) is the first transistorized computer to be demonstrated at the Massachusetts Institute of Technology in 1956.

Transistor

First Minicomputer

The PDP-1 was the first minicomputer, developed by Digital Equipment Corporation in 1960.

First Microprocessor

The first microprocessor, Intel 4004, was introduced by Intel on November 15, 1971.

First Personal Computer

In 1975, Ed Roberts coined the term 'personal computer' when he introduced the Altair 8800. The computer relied on a series of switches for inputting data and output data by turning on and off a series of lights.

The Altair 8800

First Laptop or Portable Computer

The IBM 5100, released on September 1975, is the first portable computer. The computer weighed 55 pounds and had a five inch CRT display, tape drive, 1.9 MHz PALM processor, and 64KB of RAM.

The IBM 5100

However, the first truly portable computer or laptop is considered to be the Osborne I, developed by Adam Osborne and released on April 1981. It weighed 24.5 pounds, had a 5-inch display, 64 KB of memory, two 5 1/4" floppy drives, ran the CP/M 2.2 operating system and included a modem.

First IBM Personal Computer

IBM introduced its first personal computer called the IBM PC in 1981. The computer was code named and still sometimes referred to as the 'Acorn' and had a 8088 processor, 16 KB of memory, which was expandable to 256 and utilized MS-DOS.

The IBM PC

GENERATION OF COMPUTERS

First Generation (1940-1956): Vacuum Tubes

The first computers used vacuum tubes for circuitry and magnetic drums for memory, and were often enormous, taking up entire rooms. They were very expensive to operate and in addition to using a great deal of electricity, generated a lot of heat, which was often the cause of malfunctions.

The first generation computers relied on machine language, the lowest-level programming language understood by computers, to perform operations, and they could only solve one problem at a time. Input was based on punched cards and paper tape, and output was displayed on printouts.

The UNIVAC and ENIAC computers are examples of first-generation computing devices.

Second Generation (1956-1963): Transistors

Transistors replaced vacuum tubes and ushered in the second generation of computers. The transistor was invented in 1947 but did not see widespread use in computers until the late 1950s. The transistor was far superior to the vacuum tube, allowing computers to become smaller, faster, cheaper, more energy-efficient and more reliable than their first-generation computers. The transistor also generated a great deal of heat but was a vast improvement over the vacuum tube. The second generation computers too relied on punched cards for input and printouts for output.

High-level programming languages like COBOL and FORTRAN were developed during this time. Second generation computers were also the first computers that stored their instructions in their memory, which moved from a magnetic drum to magnetic core technology.

Third Generation (1964-1971): Integrated Circuits

The development of the integrated circuit was the hallmark of the third generation of computers. Transistors were miniaturized and placed on silicon chips, called semiconductors, which drastically increased the speed and efficiency of computers.

Instead of punched cards and printouts, users interacted with third generation computers through keyboards and monitors and interfaced with an operating system, which allowed the device to run many different applications at one time with a central program that monitored the memory.

Fourth Generation (1971-Present): Microprocessors

The microprocessor brought the fourth generation of computers, as thousands of integrated circuits were built onto a single silicon chip. The Intel 4004 chip, developed in 1971, located all the components of the computer – from the central processing unit and memory to input/output controls – on a single chip. In 1981, IBM introduced its first computer for the home user, and in 1984, Apple introduced the Macintosh. Fourth generation computers saw the development of Graphical User Interface (GUI), the mouse and handheld devices.

Fifth Generation (Present and Beyond): Artificial Intelligence

The fifth generation computing devices, based on artificial intelligence, are still in development, though there are some applications, such as voice recognition, face recognition, etc. that are being used today. The use of parallel processing and superconductors is helping to make artificial intelligence a reality. The goal of fifth generation computing is to develop devices that respond to natural language input and are capable of learning and self-organization.

TYPES OF COMPUTERS

According to the principles of operation, there are three different types of computers.

Analog Computer

An analog computer is a computing device that works on continuous range of values. The results given by the analog computers will only be approximate since they deal with quantities that vary continuously. It generally deals with physical variables, such as voltage, pressure, temperature and speed.

Digital Computer

A digital computer operates on digital data, such as numbers. It uses binary number system in which there are only two digits, 0 and 1. Each one is called a bit. The digital computer is designed using digital circuits in which there are two levels for an input or output signal. These two levels are known as logic 0 and logic 1. Digital computers can give more accurate and faster results.

Hybrid Computer

A hybrid computer combines the desirable features of analog and digital computers. It is mostly used for automatic operations of complicated physical processes and machines. Nowadays, analog-to-digital and digital-to-analog converters are used for transforming the data into suitable form for either type of computation.

There are four different types of computers when we classify them based on their performance and capacity.

Supercomputers

Supercomputers are the best in terms of processing capacity and also the most expensive ones. These computers can process billions of instructions per second.

Normally, they are used for applications which require intensive numerical computations, such as stock analysis and weather forecasting. Other uses of supercomputers are scientific simulations, (animated) graphics, fluid dynamic calculations, nuclear energy research, electronic design and analysis of geological data.

Mainframe Computers

Mainframe computers can also process data at very high speeds, i.e., hundreds of millions of instructions per second and they are also quite expensive. Normally, they are used in banking, airlines and railways, etc. for their applications.

Mini Computers

Mini computers are lower to mainframe computers in terms of speed and storage capacity. They are also less expensive than the mainframe computers.

Micro Computers

The invention of microprocessor (single chip CPU) gave birth to the much cheaper **micro computers.**

Micro computers are further classified into:

- Desktop Computers
- Laptop Computers
- Handheld Computers (PDAs)

Desktop Computers

Desktop computers are the most popular computer systems today. They are also known as personal computers or simply PCs. They are usually easier to use and are more affordable.

Laptop Computers

Laptop computers are portable computers. They are light-weight computers with a thin screen. They are also called notebook computers because of their small size.

Handheld Computers

Handheld computers are highly mobile and compact computers, which are also called Personal Digital Assistants (PDAs). These are originally built to function as a personal scheduling assistant. Today, handheld computers frequently provide a convenient connection to the Internet using wireless technology.

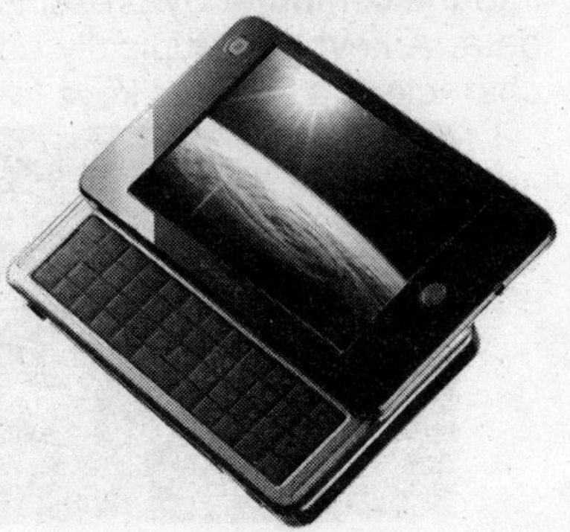

A **server** is a computer that 'serves up' information to other computers on a network. Servers play an important role in making the Internet work. They are where web pages are stored. When you use your browser to click on a link, a web server delivers the page you requested.

A server can look like a regular desktop computer, or it can be much larger.

Today, there are many everyday devices that are basically specialised computers, even though we don't always think of them as computers.

Tablet Computers

These small devices use a touch-sensitive screen for typing and navigation. They don't require a keyboard or mouse and are even more portable than laptops.

Mobile Phones

Many mobile phones can do a lot of things which computers can do, such as browsing the Internet and playing games. These phones are often called smartphones.

Game Consoles

A game console is a specialised kind of computer, used for playing video games.

PARTS OF A COMPUTER

A computer is a system of many parts working together. The physical parts, which you can see and touch, are collectively called **hardware**.

Let's now know about the parts of a computer. There are mainly four parts of a computer:

1. Keyboard 2. Mouse 3. System Unit 4. Monitor

Keyboard

The keyboard is the main input device used to enter characters and functions into the computer by pressing buttons, or keys. It is the primary device used to enter data. A keyboard typically contains keys for individual letters, numbers and special characters, as well as keys for specific functions. A keyboard has more than 100 keys.

Numeric Keys

The numeric keys are used to type numbers.

Alphabetic Keys

The alphabetic keys are used to type letters of the alphabet.

Mathematical Keys

The keys having the symbols +, –, /, *, =, %, ?, <, >, ^, { }, [ ], ( ) are called mathematical keys. These keys are used to input mathematical signs.

Numeric Keypad

The numeric keypad contains a set of keys that contain the numbers 0 through 9 arranged as an adding machine.

Function Keys

The function keys are labelled F1 through F12. Some programmes use these keys as shortcuts for common tasks. For example, in many programmes, F1 opens the Help file.

Cursor Movement Keys

To move the cursor, where you want to type, the directional arrow keys are used, which are called cursor movement keys.

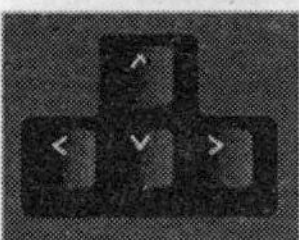

Special Keys

The various kinds of keys found in the keyboard used to do several operations are called special keys. Special keys include Enter, Ctrl, Esc, Insert, Delete, Shift, Tab, Backspace, Alt, Caps Lock, Spacebar and Print Screen.

Mouse

A mouse is a small device used to point to and select items on your computer screen. It is also known as a pointing device. It lets you point to objects on the screen, click on them, and move them.

A mouse usually has two buttons: a primary button (usually the left button) and a secondary button.

There are two main types of mice: optical and mechanical. The optical mouse uses an electronic eye to detect movement and is easier to clean. The mechanical mouse uses a rolling ball to detect movement.

System Unit

The system unit is the core of a computer system. It is a rectangular box placed on or underneath the desk. Inside this box are many electronic components that process information.

CPU (Central Processing Unit)

The central processing unit (CPU), also called a processor, is located inside the computer case on the motherboard. It is also called the brain of the computer, and its job is to carry out commands. Whenever you press a key, click the mouse, or start an application, you are sending instructions to the CPU.

A processor's speed is measured in megahertz (MHz), or millions of instructions per second, and gigahertz (GHz), or billions of instructions per second. A faster processor can execute instructions more quickly.

A microprocessor is a tiny electronic chip found inside a computer's central processing unit. Its basic function is to take input, process it and then provide appropriate output.

Basing on the brand and version of the microprocessor, computers are also known as Pentium I, Pentium II, Pentium III, Pentium IV, Celeron, etc. The latest version of microprocessor available now in the market is i7, manufactured by Intel.

RAM (Random Access Memory)

RAM or Random Access Memory is the system's short-term memory. Whenever the computer performs calculations, it temporarily stores the data in the RAM until it is needed. This short-term memory disappears when the computer is turned off. RAM is measured in megabytes (MB) or gigabytes (GB). The more RAM a computer has, the more things the computer can do at the same time.

Motherboard

The motherboard is the computer's main circuit board. It is a thin plate that holds the CPU, memory, connectors for the hard drive and optical drives, expansion cards to control the video and audio, and connections to your computer's ports (such as USB ports). The motherboard connects directly or indirectly to every part of the computer.

Hard Disk

The hard drive is the data centre of the computer. This is where the software is installed, and it is also where the documents and other files are stored. The hard drive is a long-term storage, which means the data is still saved even if you turn the computer off or unplug it.

Power Supply Unit

The power supply unit in a computer converts the power from the wall outlet to the type of power needed by the computer. It sends power through the cables to the motherboard and other components.

CD-ROM

Compact Disc-Read Only Memory (CD-ROM) is a type of optical disk capable of storing large amount of data in the form of text or graphic.

Monitor

The monitor displays the computer's user interface and open programmes, allowing the user to interact with the computer, typically using the keyboard and mouse. The monitor displays video and graphics information generated by the computer. Monitors are very similar to televisions but usually display information at a much higher resolution.

DIFFERENCE BETWEEN INPUT AND OUTPUT DEVICES

Both input and output devices are components of the computer hardware.

An input device is a kind of component being used to provide data or feed the information into the computer. Input devices are physically interacted with by the user and have buttons, keys, a lens or some other component that is responsible for the actual data input. Input device works before output device. It converts commands to Binary digit. The most common input devices are mouse, keyboard, webcam, scanner, joystick and microphone.

Any device that outputs information from a computer is called an output device. The output device provides the processed information back into the user. Output devices are never contacted and typically have a screen or set of speakers for data output. Output device works after input device. It converts binary result to our language. The output devices usually include the speaker, the printer and the monitor.

Storage Devices

A storage device is any hardware capable of holding information on a computer. The storage device may hold or save the information temporarily or permanently. There are two types of storage devices used in computers: (i) Primary storage device, such as RAM; and (ii) Secondary storage device, like a hard drive. Secondary storage device is removable and can be used as internal or external storage.

Types of Storage Devices

The following are some of the different types of storage devices used with computers.

Magnetic Storage Devices

The magnetic storage is one of the most common types of storage used with computers.

(i) Floppy diskette

A Floppy Disk Drive (3½") is a computer disk drive that enables a user to save data to removable diskettes. Because of the limited capacity and reliability of floppy diskettes, many computers no longer come equipped with floppy disk drives and are being replaced with CD-R, other writable discs and flash drives.

(ii) Hard drive

A hard disk drive or simply hard drive is a data storage device. The hard disk was first introduced on September 13, 1956 and consists of one or more platters inside of an air-sealed casing.

(iii) Tape cassette

It is a magnetically thin coated piece of plastic wrapped around wheels capable of storing data. Tape is much less expensive than other storage mediums, but a much slower solution that was typically used only for backup.

(iv) Zip diskette

A Zip drive and Zip disk is a hardware data storage device that functions like a standard 1.44" floppy drive and diskette. It can hold up to 100 MB of data or 250 MB of data. These drives became very popular in late 1990s but quickly became less popular as users needed larger storage capabilities.

Optical Storage Devices

Another common storage is optical storage, which uses lasers and lights as its method of reading and writing data.

(i) Blu-Ray disc

A Blu-ray Disc or a BD-ROM is an optical disc introduced on January 4, 2006. It is capable of storing up to 25 GB on a single-layer disc and 50 GB on a dual-layer disc, each disc being the same size as a standard CD.

(ii) CD-ROM disc

A Compact Disc-Read Only Memory or a CD-ROM is an optical disc which contains audio or software data whose memory is read only. A CD-ROM Drive or optical drive is the device used to read them. These drives are capable of playing audio CDs and reading data CDs.

(iii) CD-R and CD-RW disc

A CD-R (CD-Recordable) is a writable disc and drive that is capable of having information written to the disc once and then having that disc read many times after that.

Flash Memory Devices

Flash memory is a non-volatile computer memory. This type of memory is an integrated circuit that does not need continuous power to retain the data and is much more expensive than magnetic storage.

(i) Jump drive or flash drive

Alternatively referred to as a USB flash drive, data stick, pen drive, memory unit, keychain drive and thumb drive, a jump drive is a portable drive that is often the size of your thumb that connects to the computer USB port. Today, flash drives are available in sizes such as 256 MB, 512 MB, 1 GB, 5 GB and 16 GB and are an easy way to transfer and store information.

(ii) Memory card

Alternatively referred to as a flash memory card, a memory card is a type of storage media that is most commonly used in digital cameras, digital camcorders, handheld computers, MP3 players, PDAs, cell phones, game consoles and printers, to store pictures, videos, music and other data.

(iii) SSD

A Solid-State Drive or Solid-State Disk (SSD) is a drive that uses non-volatile memory as a means of storing and accessing data, much like computer RAM. Unlike other storage devices, such as hard drives, an SSD has no moving parts, which gives it advantages, such as accessing stored information faster, produces no noise, often more reliable and consume much less power than the traditional hard drive (HDD) found in computers.

Online and Cloud

Storing data online and in cloud storage is becoming popular as people need to access their data from more than one device.

(i) Cloud storage

Cloud storage is a term used to describe services over a network by a collection of servers. These computers or cloud of computers enable the users visiting to have access to much faster computers or servers, be able to access programs and services from anywhere with Internet access often without having to install other software, and get access to the services from any device capable of reaching the network or Internet.

Some examples of cloud services –

Amazon Web Services (AWS) and Amazon EC2: Amazon.com provides a variety of different cloud computing services.

Dashlane: Online password service to synchronize and manage passwords between all devices.

Google App Engine: A service that provides users the ability to create scalable web services that employ Google's resources.

Google Calendar: A way to organize your schedule, synchronize, and share events with your friends.

Google Docs: A free solution from Google that allows you to open Microsoft Office documents as well as share them with other users with Internet access.

Online backup: There are dozens of online backup services to store your important information offsite in the cloud. For example, Mozy and Dropbox are two good examples of cloud storage and online storage backup solutions that store information in the cloud.

Windows Azure: A cloud computing solution by Microsoft that allows companies to develop and run services from their cloud.

Websites: Many popular social networking sites, such as Facebook, Picasa and YouTube are also often considered parts of cloud computing.

(ii) Network media

Network media is any audio, video, images or text, used on a computer network, like the Internet. It almost always requires a computer to send and receive, as well as a community of people to create and consume the content. Network media are decentralized and contributed by many people, who not only provide it to others, but are also recipients and users of the media.

Paper Storage

Early computers had no method of using any of the above technologies for storing information and had to rely on paper. Today, these forms of storage are rarely used or found.

(i) OMR

OMR, short for Optical Mark Reading or Optical Mark Recognition, is the process of gathering information from human beings by recognizing marks on a document. OMR is accomplished by using a hardware device (scanner) that detects a reflection or limited light transmittance on or through piece of paper.

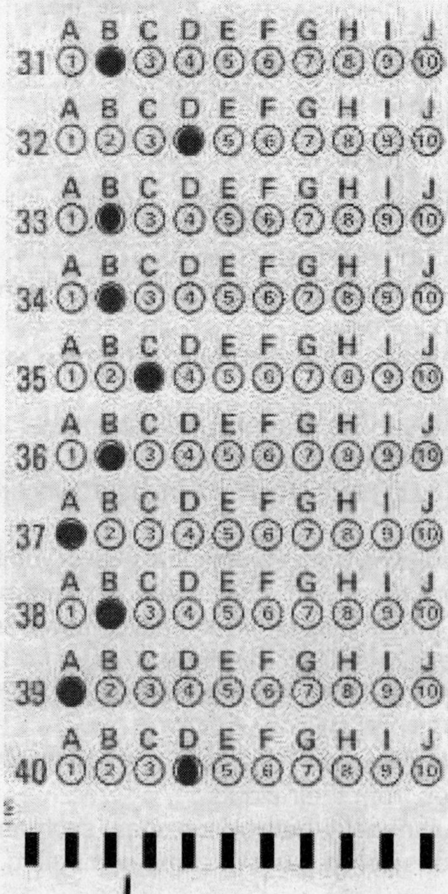

(ii) Punch card

Punch cards are paper cards containing several punched holes that were punched by hand or machine to represent data. These cards allowed companies to store and access information by entering the card into the computer. Using a punch card is an early method of data storage used with early computers.

80 column numeric punch card

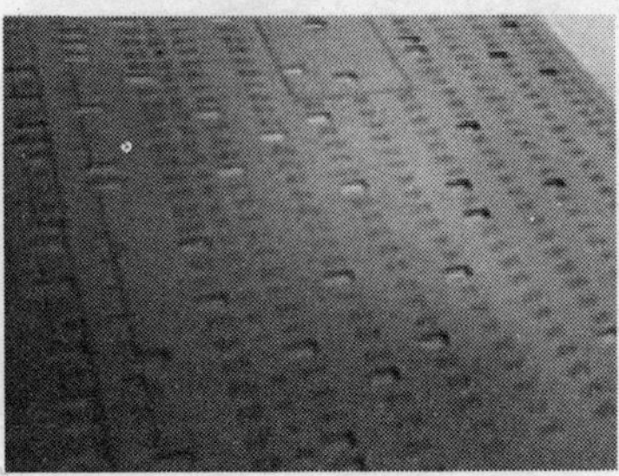

Read Only Memory (ROM)

Read-Only Memory is a type of 'built-in' memory that is used with computers and other electronic devices. As the name indicates, data stored in ROM can only be read and not modified. A simple example of ROM is the cartridge used with video game consoles; which allows one system to run multiple games. Another example of ROM is EEPROM, which is a programmable ROM used for the computer BIOS.

Expansion Slots and Expansion Cards

An expansion slot, also referred to as a bus slot or expansion port, is an opening located inside a computer on the motherboard that allows additional boards to be connected to it.

Here is a list of some of the expansion slots commonly found in computers.

AGP - Video card
AMR - Modem, Sound card
CNR - Modem, Network card, Sound card
EISA - SCSI, Network card, Video card
ISA - Network card, Sound card, Video card
PCI - Network card, SCSI, Sound card, Video card
PCIe - Video card
VESA - Video card

An expansion card, also referred to as an add-on card, expansion board, internal card, or interface adapter is an electronic board or circuit added into the expansion slot of a desktop computer or other non-portable computer to give that computer a new ability, such as the ability to connect to another computer using a network cable.

Here is a list of some of the types of expansion cards used in computers.

Interface card (ATA, Bluetooth, EIDE, Firewire, IDE, Parallel, RAID, SCSI, Serial and USB)

Modem

MPEG Decoder

Network Card

Sound Card

Video Card

Video capture card

Ports

A port is a physical docking point using which an external device can be connected to the computer. A port has the following characteristics:

- External devices are connected to a computer using cables and ports.
- Ports are slots on the motherboard into which a cable of external device is plugged in.
- External devices attached via ports are mouse, keyboard, monitor, microphone, speakers, etc.

Power Supply

The Power Supply Unit (PSU) is an internal hardware component used to suppiy the components in a computer with power by converting potentially lethal 110-115 or 220-230 volt alternating current (AC) into a steady low-voltage direct current (DC) usable by the computer. A power supply is rated by the number of watts it generates.

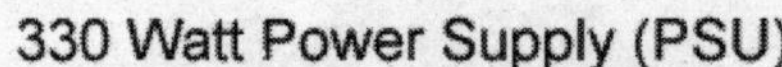

330 Watt Power Supply (PSU)

INPUT DEVICES

An input device is any hardware device that sends data to a computer, allowing you to interact with and control the computer. The most commonly used input devices on a computer are the keyboard and mouse. However, there are dozens of other devices that can also be used to input data into the computer.

Here is a list of the common input devices that can be used with a computer:

Barcode Reader

A barcode reader is a hardware device capable of reading a barcode and printing out the details of the product or logging that product into a database.

Biometrics

Microsoft Fingerprint scanner

Biometrics is the identification of a person by the measurement of their biological features. For example, users identifying themselves to a computer or building by their finger print or voice is considered a biometric identification.

The following are the types of biometric devices: Face scanner; Hand scanner; Finger scanner; Retina or iris scanner; and Voice scanner.

Business Card Reader

Business Card Reader

A business card reader allows a user to scan business cards into their computer for digital storage. Computer scanners are capable of scanning and converting text documents to typed text by use of Optical Character Recognition (OCR) software. Business card readers work on a similar principle, reading the text on the business card and converting to typed text on the computer.

Digital Camera

A digital camera is a camera that stores the pictures and video it takes in electronic format instead of to film.

Joystick

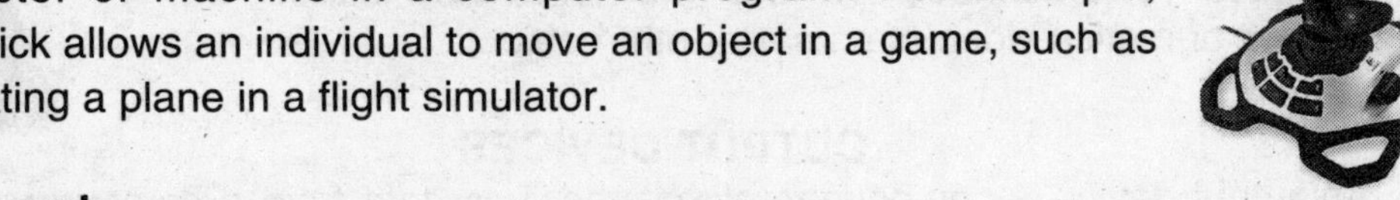

Joystick is an input device that allows the user to control a character or machine in a computer program. For example, a joystick allows an individual to move an object in a game, such as navigating a plane in a flight simulator.

Keyboard

A computer keyboard is one of the primary input devices used with a computer that looks similar to those found on electric typewriters, but with some additional keys. Keyboards allow the user to input letters, numbers and other symbols into a computer that often function as commands.

Microphone

A microphone or simply a mic is a hardware peripheral that allows computer users to input audio into their computers.

Mouse

A mouse is a hardware input device that allows an individual to control a pointer in a graphical user interface (GUI) and manipulate on-screen objects, such as icons, files and folders.

Stylus

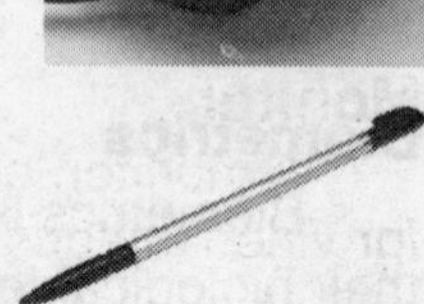

A stylus is a pen-shaped instrument used with graphics tablets or touch screen input devices to write or draw on the computer screen, similar to a sheet of paper.

Remote

A remote is a hardware device that allows a user to control a device or object in another location. For example, the TV remote allows a person to change the channel, volume, or turn on and off the TV without having to get up and press the buttons on the front of the TV.

Scanner

A scanner is a hardware input device that allows a user to take an image or text and convert it into a digital file, allowing the computer to read or display the scanned object.

Touchscreen

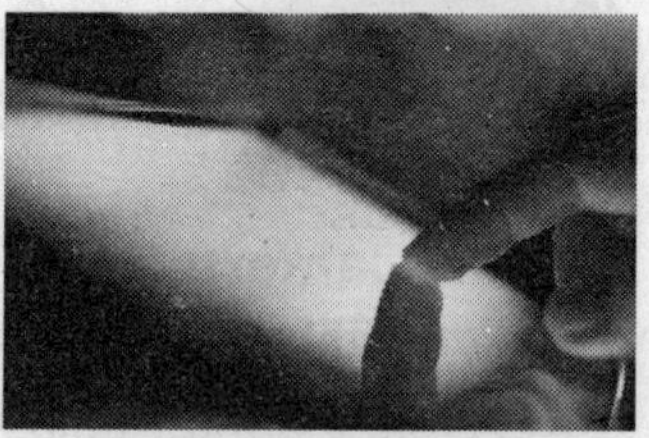

A touchscreen is a monitor or other flat surface with a sensitive panel directly on the screen that registers the touch of a finger as an input. A touchscreen allows the user to interact with a device without a mouse or keyboard and is used with smartphones, tablets, computer screens and information kiosks.

Webcam

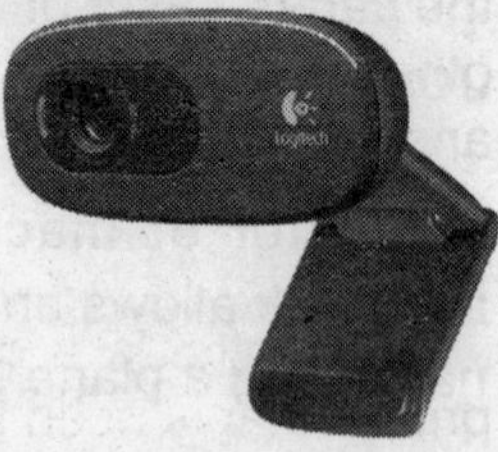

A webcam is a hardware camera connected to a computer that allows anyone connected to the Internet to view either still pictures or motion video of a user or other object.

OUTPUT DEVICES

An output device is any peripheral that receives data from a computer, usually for display, projection, or physical reproduction. The most commonly used output devices on a computer are monitors and printers. However, there are many other devices that can also be used to output data from a computer.

Here is a list of some common output devices that can be used with a computer:

GPS

GPS stands for Global Positioning System. It is a network of satellites that helps users to determine a location on Earth. A common example of GPS is to find locations while driving cars.

Headphones

Headphones, sometimes called earphones, are a hardware device that you can either plug into your computer (line out) or your speakers which allow you to privately listen to audio without disturbing anyone else.

Monitor

A monitor, also called a video display unit (VDU), encompasses a display screen for video images and casing that holds it.

Printer (Dot matrix printer, Inkjet printer, Laser printer and Plotter)

A printer is one of the most used peripherals on computers that are commonly used to print text, images and photos.

Dot matrix printer:

The term 'DOT matrix' refers to the process of placing dots to form an image; the quality of the image being determined by the dots per inch. Today, Dot matrix printers are rarely used or found because of the low quality print outs when compared to ink jet printers and laser printers.

Inkjet printer:

An inkjet printer is the most popular printer for home computer users that prints by spraying streams of quick-drying ink on paper.

Laser printer:

A laser printer utilizes laser technology to print images on the paper. Laser printers are often used in corporate, school and other environments that require print jobs to be completed quickly and in large quantities.

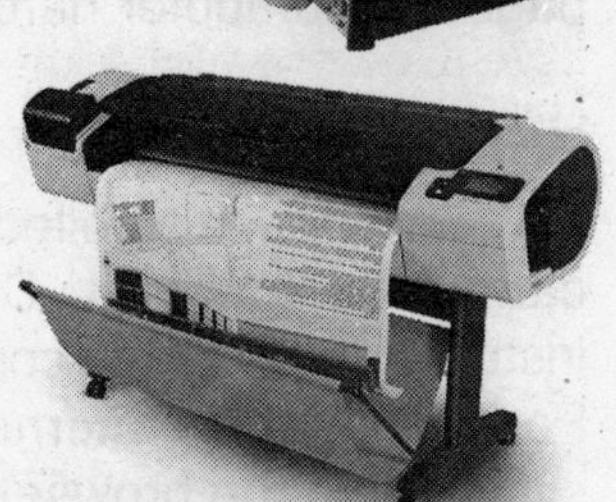

Plotter:

A plotter is a computer hardware device much like a printer that is used for printing vector graphics. Plotters use a pen, pencil, marker, or other writing tool to draw a design onto paper.

Projector

A projector is an output device that can take images generated by a computer and reproduce them on a large, flat surface. For example, projectors are used in meetings to help ensure that all participants can view the information being presented.

Sound Card

A sound card is an expansion card or integrated circuit that provides a computer with the ability to produce sound that can be perceived by the user through a peripheral device, like speakers or headphones.

Speakers

A speaker is a hardware device connected to a computer's sound card that outputs sound generated by the computer.

TV

A TV (short for television) is an electronics device that receives a visual and audible signal and plays it to the viewer.

Video Card

Alternatively referred to as a display adapter, graphics card, video adapter, video board, or a video controller, a video card is an internal circuit board that allows a display device, such as a monitor, to display images from the computer.

HARDWARE AND SOFTWARE

All types of computers consist of two basic parts: **Hardware** and **Software.**

Hardware

The physical components that make up a computer system are called hardware. Different types of hardware include monitor, mouse, keyboard, hard disk drive, system unit, etc., all of which are physical objects that can be touched. For example, the computer monitor you use to read a text and the mouse you use to navigate a web page are computer hardware.

Software

Software is a collection of instructions and codes installed into the computer that cannot be touched. Computer programmes and related data that provide the instructions for telling computer hardware what to do and how to do are called software. For example, the Internet browser that allows you to visit a website and the operating system that the browser runs on is a software.

USE OF COMPUTER IN MODERN DAYS

The use of computers in modern life is immense. Undoubtedly, we can say that modern world will be incomplete without computers and their applications. It has become so common in our daily lives that it is almost impossible to imagine life without the use of computers. The uses of computers in different fields are described below.

Marketing

Computers are an integral part of today's marketing world. Marketing professionals use computers in every aspect of their jobs. Companies use computers to boost their online marketing efforts that strengthen their organisation's brand and increase their visibility and influence in the marketplace. Computers are regarded as the powerful tool for assisting small companies in many aspects of marketing new products and services.

Banks

Computers are used in banks for various purposes. They help bank personnel operate more efficiently and effectively. Computers are used to track certain transactions and they help process other customer information as well. Without computers, it would be very hard for a bank to offer good customer service day in and day out. The introduction of computerised banking and automated teller machines (ATMs) have paved a great way towards helping customers save time and do several transactions at their convenience without physically coming to the banks. Computers help a bank save time and money, and can be used as an aid to generate profits.

Offices

Computers are used in different offices to do different kinds of jobs. The management and administrative tasks performed in an office, which are the five general categories of activities, like decision-making, data manipulation, document handling, communication and storage are all done using computers. Offices have used advance computer technologies to perform various tasks in an office system, such as for document management system, message handling system and office support systems.

Medical

Computers are commonly used in some areas of medical fields, such as laboratories, researches, scanning, monitoring and pharmacy, which help doctors to diagnose and treat illness. Computers are used in hospitals to monitor critically ill patients in intensive care units. The patients have sensors attached to them, which detect changes in heart rate, pulse rate, blood pressure, breathing and brain activity.

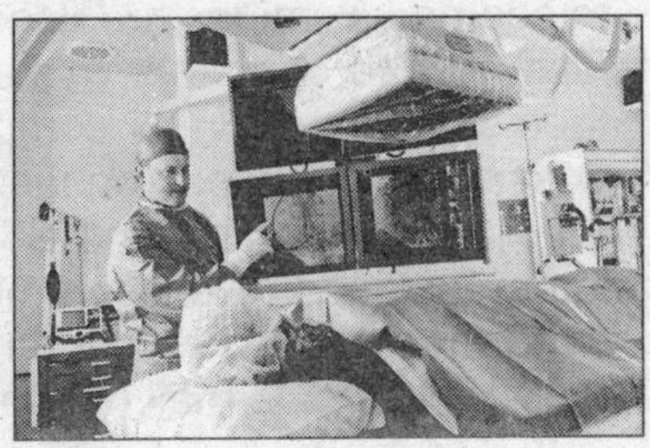

Computers are also used to store databases which contain information about patients, doctors, medicines and other chemicals and equipment. It also stores information in proper order to provide the convenient way of arrangements for hospital staff.

Engineering

Computers can be used in every aspect of the engineering process, from design through to production and distribution. Multi-storeyed buildings, bridges, electronic items, automobiles, etc. are all designed by computers. Earlier, engineers used to draw designs of these items on paper and if there was any mistake, the design had to be redrawn. But now, the designs could be changed or corrected number of times with the help of certain engineering and drawing software. Thus, computers can speed up the flow of information and make everything work more efficiently.

Education

Computers are used in schools to provide the methods of teaching in different ways. Learning through computers is getting very familiar and rapidly increasing nowadays. There are a number of methods in which educational institutions use computers to teach the students. Various educational software are available, which help students to study different subjects, like Maths, Science, English, Physics and Chemistry, and even learn to speak foreign languages. Another most important use of computer in education is e-Learning. The introduction of this technology has enabled people to learn anytime and anywhere. e-Learning can include training, the delivery of just-in-time information and guidance from experts.

Telecommunication

The electronic transmission of information over distances, called telecommunication, has become greatly possible due to computers. Telecommunications are the means of electronic transmission of information over distances. The information may be in the form of voice telephone calls, data, text, images or videos. Today, telecommunications are used to organize more or less remote computer systems into telecommunication networks. These networks themselves are run by computers. Due to advancement in telecommunications, it is possible to call a person instantly living in another country or in a different city within a country using ISD and STD facilities, respectively. Today, mobile phones are the latest instance of telecommunication. Not only this, computers have enabled us to send messages or documents from one location to other location through facsimile (FAX), electronic mail (E-mail), Voice mail, etc. by means of telecommunication.

Transport System

With Internet on computers, we can know the details of the buses or trains or the flights available to our desired destination. The timings and even the updates on the delay can also be known through the computers. We can book our tickets online. Staffs of the transport system keep a track of the passengers, trains or flights details, departure and arrival timings by using computers. Mainly in airline system, computers are used to control aircrafts. Earlier, aircrafts were controlled by moving parts attached to the controls using cables. Nowadays, computers are embedded in the pilot's controls and electronic signals from the cockpit are sent to the control towers to adjust the flight movement.

Defence

Computers are the main tools which help in developing missiles and other equipment in the defence system. Their designing and maintenance are wholly done through computers. Computer builds the links between the soldiers and commanders through the satellite. Construction of weapons and controlling their function is not possible without the aid of computers. The list of the criminals and the records of the cops are maintained regularly in the system.

Weather Forecasting

Computer-based weather forecasting depends on accurate collection of data from weather stations, airports, satellites, different sensitive devices all around the world. Computer depends on building a model of hot, cold air, dry and humid air interaction, and how these interactions are effected by land and sea temperature, season and so on. Once this is done, the data are collected on atmospheric phenomena over a region. The computer model then generates a forecast of how the air will change. However, the necessary parameters can never be measured with total accuracy and it is impossible to make a perfect representation of all the factors that affect weather.

Industry

Computers are used in industry in different types of systems. Computer-controlled robots are used to perform many complicated jobs in the manufacturing industry, military, space exploration, transportation and medical applications. Robots are computer-controlled programmable machines. They can perform mechanical jobs, like pick and place different parts, welding or painting cars, etc. Today, computer-controlled robots are used to assemble cars, spray paint and in industrial welding. Computers are also used to control manufacturing system and continuous running of the machinery. These also help in monitoring temperature, pressure and also check the quality and accuracy, measurement needed in the manufacturing process.

E-commerce

E-commerce or electronic commerce describes the buying, selling and exchanging of products, services and information via computer network. There are many applications of e-commerce, such as home banking, shopping, buying stocks, finding a job, conducting an auction, collaborating electronically with business partners around the globe, marketing and advertising and providing customer service. Electronic mail is the revolutionary service that transports text messages (with attachments of videos, audio, documents) from sender to one or more receivers via computer. Video conferencing is a type of conferencing in which video transmits over networks. It is an advanced form of teleconferencing. Almost all businesses now have websites that allow Internet users to buy their goods or services. Electronic shopping can take place using a computer from anywhere in the world working 24 hours a day. Electronic banking, also known as cyber-banking or online banking, includes various banking activities conducted from home, a business, or on the road instead of a physical bank location.

Home

Nowadays, computers have become a necessary electrical home appliance. Children play games, draw pictures, play music, watch movies and do some sorts of reading and writing according to their needs. People also utilise computers for keeping records, making home budgets, using electronic mail and Internet services.

POSITIVE EFFECTS OF COMPUTER IN MODERN DAYS

The prevalence of computer and technology has drastically affected many areas of society in positive ways. There can be no denying the fact that we derive many benefits by using computers.

1. Computers have made computational and clerical work easy to a great extent.
2. Computers have made many tasks of modern life, like buying, selling, banking, etc. more easy and convenient.
3. Computers have given easy access to a lot of useful information through the Internet.
4. Computers have made it easy for us to communicate and keep in touch with others.

5. Computers have made available to us many new forms of entertainment, like computer games.

Apart from this, modern-day students not only have computers to help them with their schoolwork, they also use the Internet for research while teachers use technology to enhance their lessons.

Research

If a school's library lacks in a selection of titles, a student might find it difficult to compile the necessary research for an essay or research paper. In this case, the students can use the Internet and digital encyclopedias to obtain the research they need.

Globalization

When schools in different parts of the state, country or world connect, students can meet their counterparts through video conferencing without leaving the classroom.

Educational Games

In younger grades, teachers expose children to computers through educational games. Instead of playing board games that focus on education, students can learn the basics of spelling, counting and other early educational lessons through computer games that make learning fun.

Distance Education (no need)

In the past, students could take distance or continuing education classes, also called correspondence courses, at community colleges and universities. After enrolling in a course of this style, a student would receive course documents in the mail and would be required to mail assignments to his teacher at the educational institution.

Web Seminars

Due to scarcity of resources and budget when students could not attend field trips related to the course of study, they can use the Internet to virtually attend Web seminars, put on by museums and other educational institutions. For example, NASA offers a program that allows students to talk to astronauts in space.

□

2
An Introduction to Windows

The most important piece of software on any computer is the operating system. The operating system gives the framework upon which all other services and applications run. The most popular operating system is Microsoft Windows.

Microsoft Windows is extremely popular in schools and colleges, offices and businesses. Most of today's applications and games are designed to run solely on Microsoft Windows.

The Windows family is the most widely used Operating System.

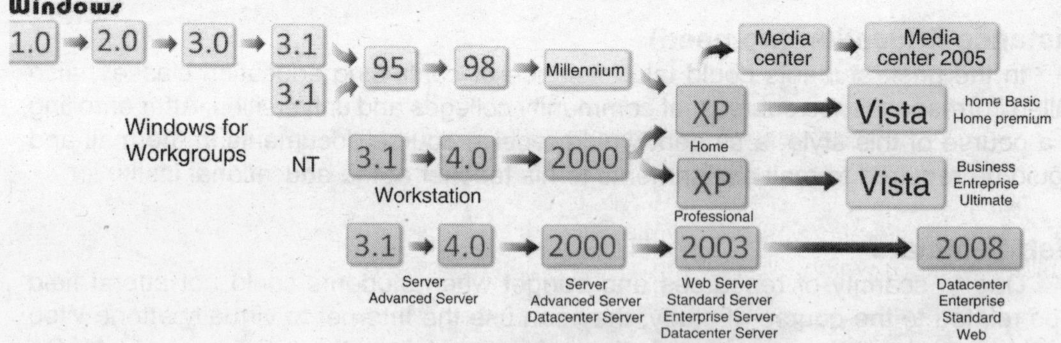

The oldest of all Microsoft's operating systems is MS-DOS (Microsoft Disk Operating System).

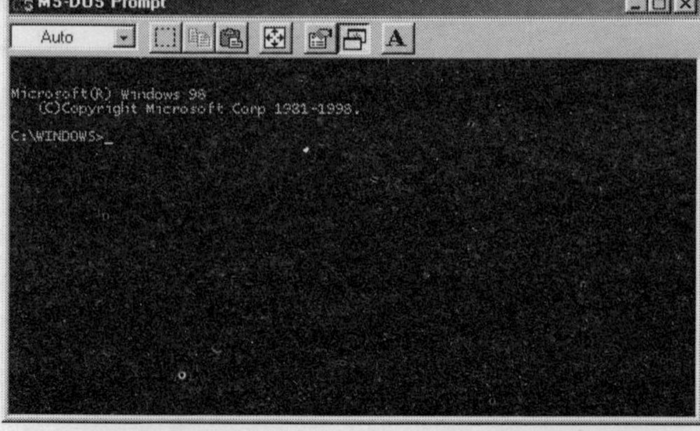

MS-DOS is a text-based operating system. Users have to type commands rather than use the more friendly graphical user interfaces (GUIs) available today.

Despite its very basic appearance, MS-DOS is a very

powerful operating system. There are many advanced applications and games available for MS-DOS. A version of MS-DOS fortifies Windows. Many advanced administration tasks in Windows can only be performed using MS-DOS.

The history of Microsoft Windows dates back to 1985, when Microsoft released Microsoft Windows Version 1.01.

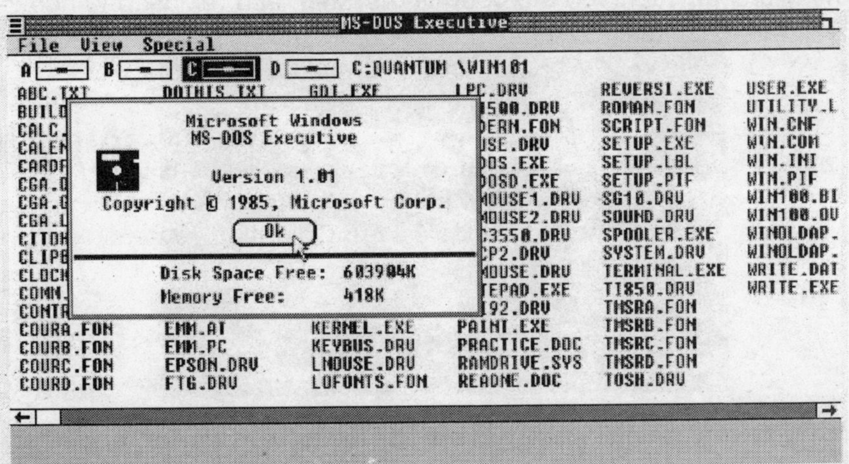

Microsoft's aim was to provide a friendly user-interface known as GUI (graphical user interface) which allowed for easier navigation of the system features.

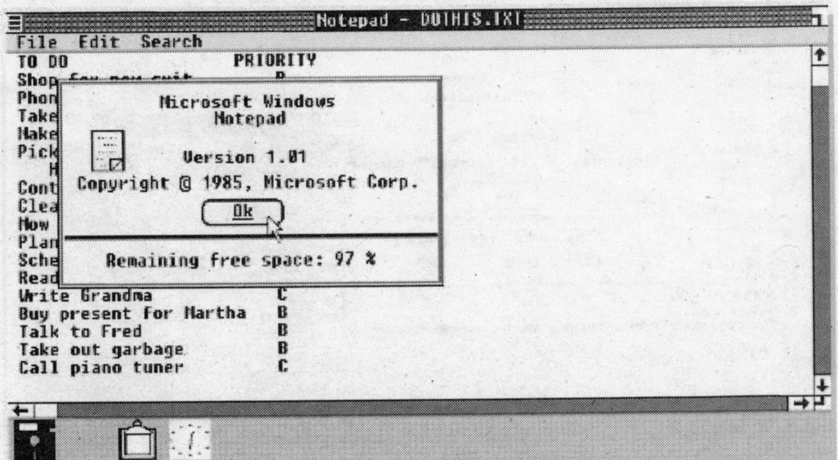

Windows 1.01 never really became popular. The amazing thing about Windows 1.01 is that it fitted on a single floppy disk.

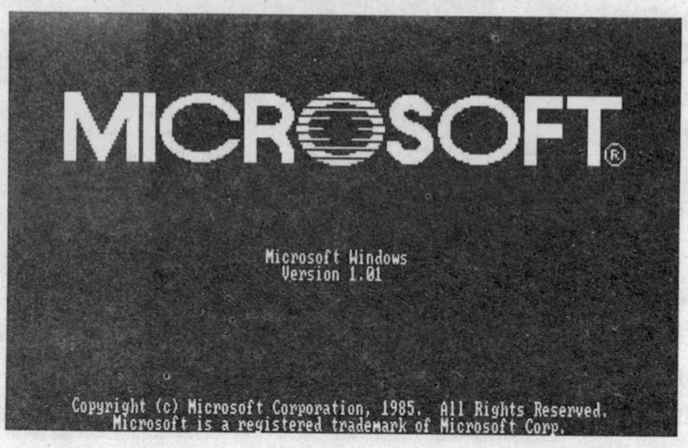

In 1987, Microsoft improved the operating system and released Windows 2.03.

The GUI was very slightly improved but still looked too similar to Windows 1.01. The operating system again failed to capture a wide audience.

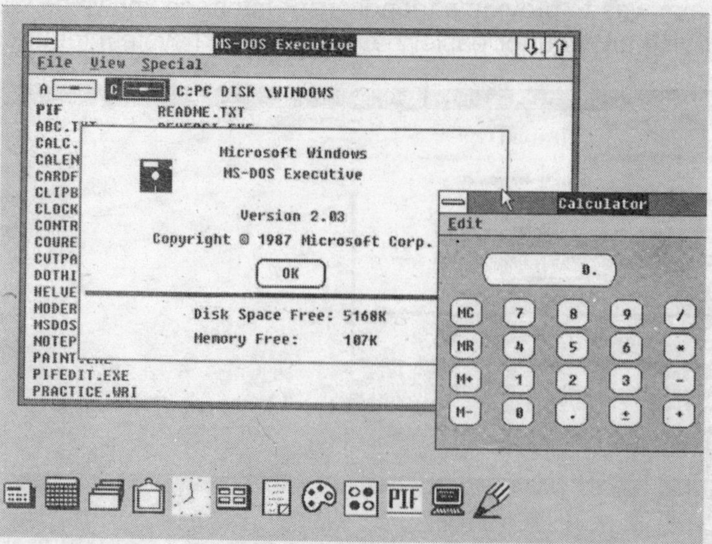

Microsoft made an enormous impression with Windows 3.0 and 3.1. Graphics and functionality were drastically improved in this version.

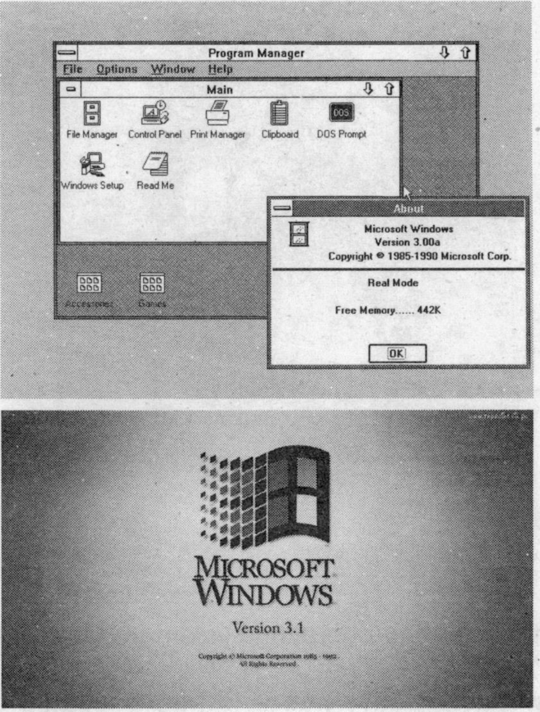

The Windows 3.x family provided multimedia capabilities as well as vastly improved graphics and application support.

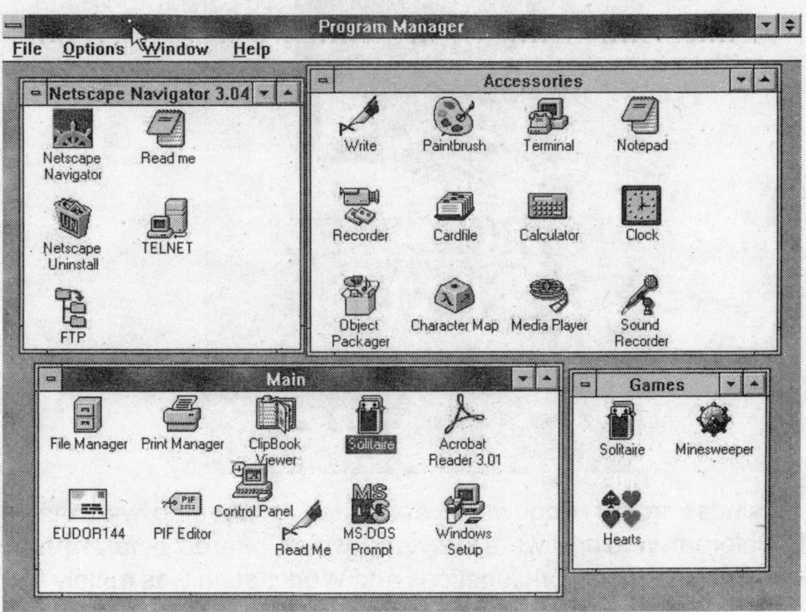

Building on the success of Windows 3.x, Microsoft released Microsoft Windows for Workgroups 3.11. This gave Windows the ability to function on a network. It is not uncommon to find companies still using Windows 3.11.

In 1993, Microsoft divided the operating system into two categories – business and home user.

WindowsNT (New Technology) was a lot more reliable than Windows 3.x. WindowsNT provided advanced network features.

On the business front, WindowsNT continued to develop with the release of version 3.51. Different versions were provided which offered different functionality. Server provided the higher network functions and Workstation was mainly for the client machines.

In 1995, Windows went through a major revamp and Microsoft Windows 95 was released. This provided greatly improved multimedia and a much more polished user interface.

The now familiar desktop and Start Menu appeared. Internet and networking support was built in. Although Windows 95 was a home user operating system, it proved to be very popular in schools and businesses.

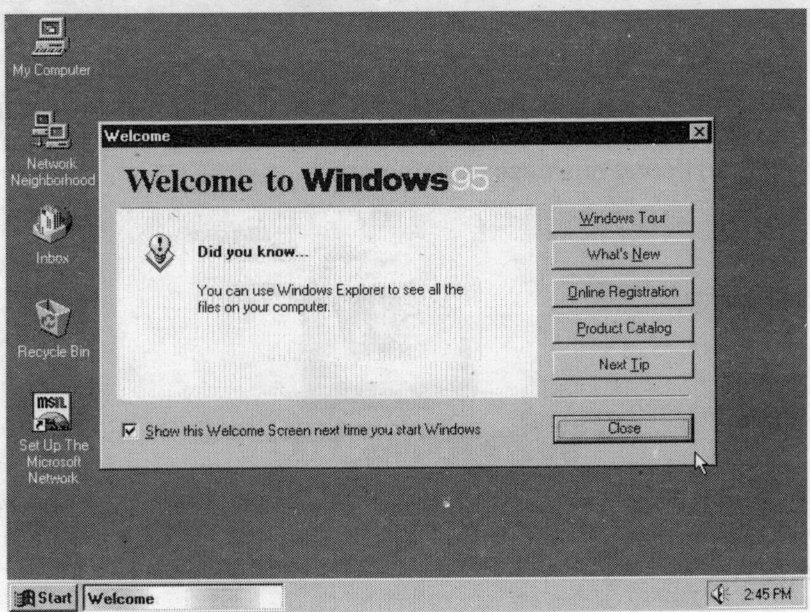

After the success of Windows 95, Microsoft improved the GUI interface of WindowsNT and released WindowsNT 4.0.

NT4.0 could be tailored to the size of the business, NT4.0 Server for small-to medium-sized businesses and Enterprise Server for larger networks.

Microsoft continued to improve the Windows format. Although Microsoft Windows 98 was very similar to Windows 95, it offered a much tidier display and enhanced multimedia support.

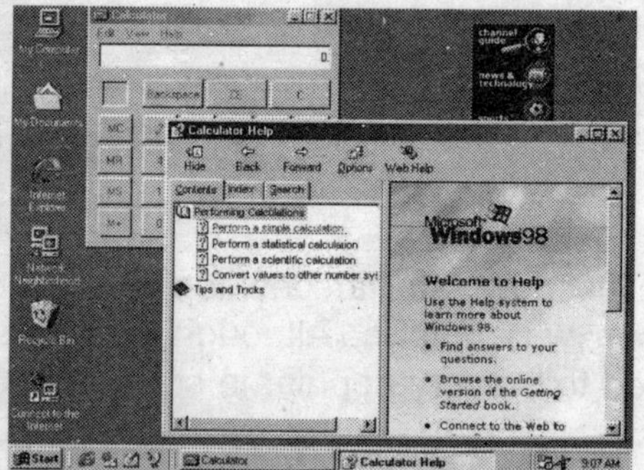

Breaking with its own naming conventions, Microsoft released Windows 2000 (initially called NT 5.0) for the business market. It appeared in four models: Professional – which replaced Workstation, Server, Advanced Server and Datacenter Server, catered for differing business requirements.

Although Windows 2000 had a greatly improved user interface, the best of the enhancements appeared on the server side. Active Directory was introduced which allowed much greater control of security and organisation. Improvements to the overall operating system allowed for easier configuration and installation.

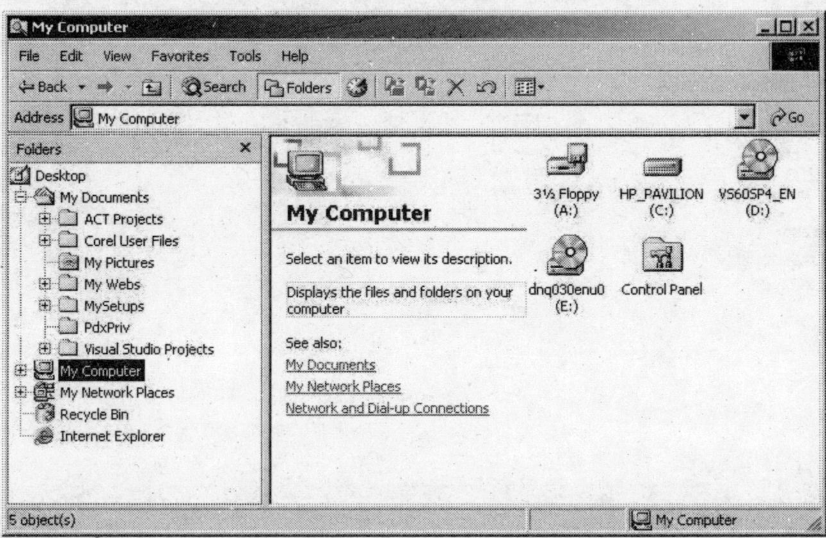

One big advantage of Windows 2000 was that the operating system settings could be modified easily without the need to restart the machine.

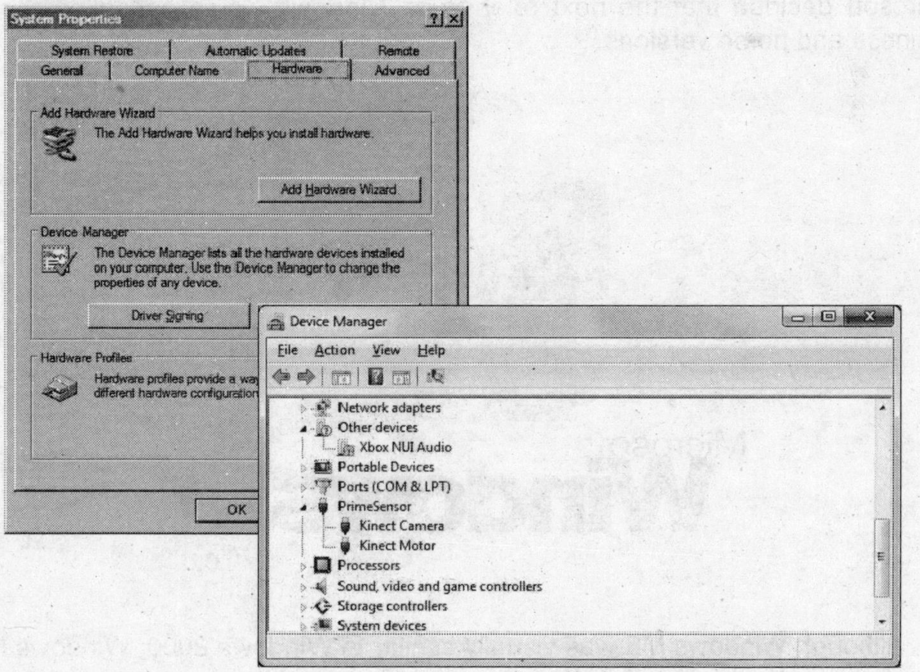

Windows 2000 proved to be a very stable operating system that offered enhanced security and ease of administration.

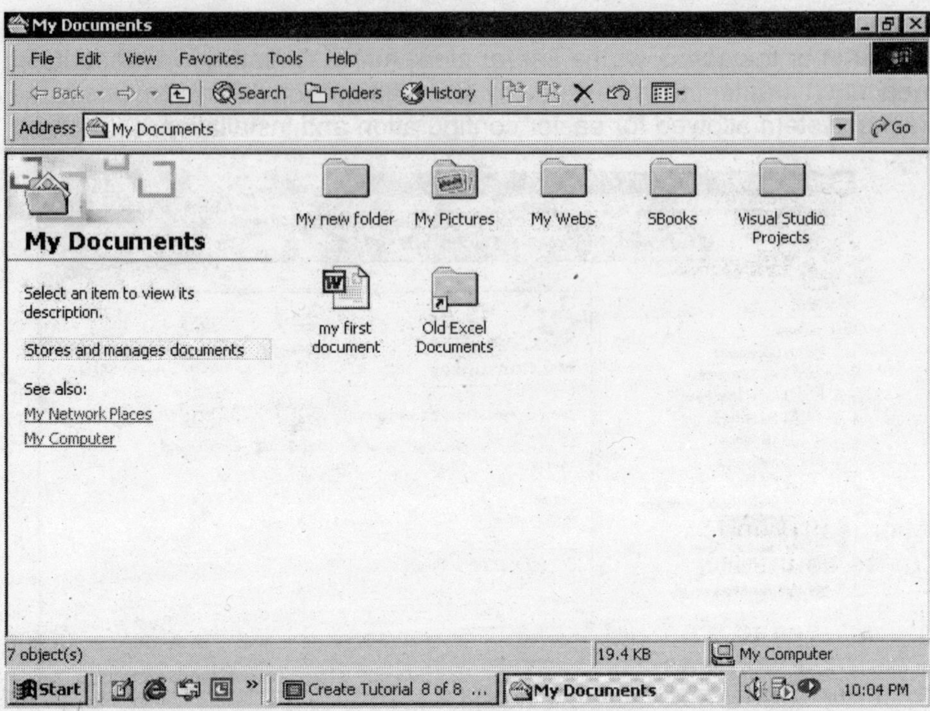

The last incarnation of the Windows 9x family was Windows Millennium Edition (ME). There were so many versions of Windows floating around at this stage that Microsoft decided that the next release of Windows would consolidate both the business and home versions.

Although Windows ME was visually similar to Windows 2000, Windows ME was based on the Windows 9x line. Windows 9x/ME systems are not as secure and stable as WindowsNT and 2000 systems.

Because of the stability of WindowsNT/2000, Microsoft decided to end the development of the Windows 9x line, and merge both the consumer and business products.

Microsoft Windows XP comes as the Home Edition and Professional; each is based on Windows 2000. Windows 2000 Server has been upgraded to Windows 2003. This appears in four variants: Web Server, Standard Server, Enterprise Server and Datacenter Server, each fulfilling a different business role.

Windows XP has a very polished look, but the overall functionality is very similar to Windows 2000.

Then came Windows Vista, released in 2006. It was widely considered a flop in technology circles as it had high system requirements and suffered issues with performance and security. The version lasted only for three years, during which some users downgraded back to XP to avoid the pitfalls of Vista.

Windows 7 closely resembled its predecessor Windows Vista. The major change found in this version is the launch of the new taskbar, which has a whole lot of features. For this current release of Windows, Microsoft learned its mistakes with Vista and created an operating system with speed, stability and minimal system requirements. This version was released in 2009.

Windows 8 is the latest release from Microsoft which is getting a lot of attention. With its redesigned Metro-style user interface and Windows Store, this version is, once again, redefining what Windows is. It also comes with integrated antivirus protection, a virtual hard disk and a new platform based on HTML 5 and JavaScript. It promises faster boot time, touch screen compatibility and the ability to create a bootable USB flash drive.

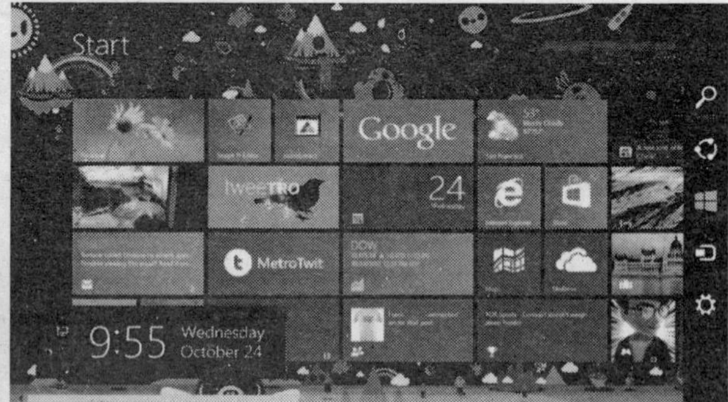

OTHER OPERATING SYSTEMS

There are other operating systems in the computing world, and some are a lot older than Microsoft Windows. But most operating systems can interoperate with each other. Many of today's larger networks contain a variety of operating systems.

UNIX

The UNIX operating system is one of the oldest and most powerful operating systems. It was developed by Bell Laboratories. There are many variants of UNIX available.

A big advantage of UNIX is that it can be run on nearly every computer hardware platform including Apple Macintosh machines.

Novell NetWare

Novell NetWare is an advanced network operating system. It has an advanced directory service structure similar to Microsoft's Active Directory.

Linux/FreeBSD

Two of the most popular variations of UNIX come in the form of Linux and FreeBSD. A big advantage of both Linux and FreeBSD is that they are both open-source, that is, any user can contribute to the development of the OS.

Linux and FreeBSD can easily take the role of a server or client machine. However, they are considered to be more difficult to master as both utilise the command line rather than a user-friendly GUI.

Apple Macintosh machines offer high performance sound and graphics editing and are, therefore, extremely popular in the design industry. Apple have developed their own operating system, the newest version of which is the Mac OS X 10.9.4 Mavericks, which is based on UNIX.

□

3
An Introduction to Windows 8

There have been many different versions of Windows over the years, including Windows XP (2001), Windows Vista (2006) and Windows 7 (2009). While previous versions of Windows mainly ran on desktop and laptop computers, Windows 8 is also designed to run on tablets.

Windows 8 is a personal computer operating system developed by Microsoft as part of WindowsNT family of operating systems. It was released in 2012. There are many new features and changes in Windows 8. These changes include a redesigned interface, online features and improved security.

INTERFACE CHANGES

The first thing you will notice about Windows 8 is that it looks totally different from previous versions of Windows. The all-new interface includes features like the Start screen, Live tiles and Hot corners.

Start Screen

The main screen is called the Start screen. It displays all of the apps as tiles. You can personalize your Start screen by changing the colour scheme, choosing a background image and rearranging your tiles.

Live Tiles

Some apps use Live tiles, which let you see information without even clicking on the app. For example, the Weather app displays the current weather on its tile, and you can click on it to see more details.

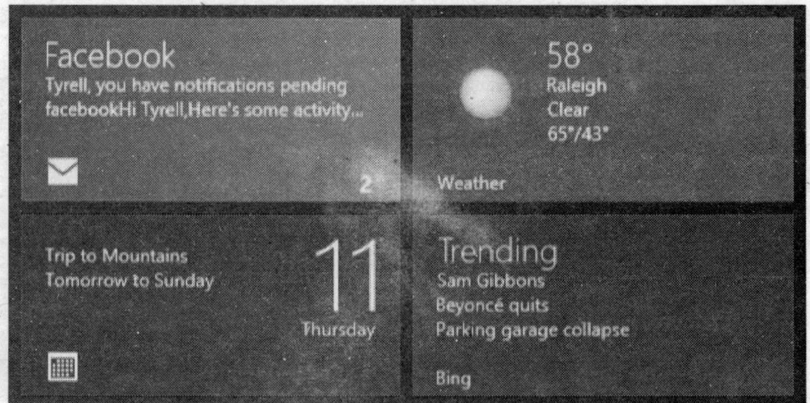

Hot Corners

You'll navigate through Windows 8 by using Hot corners. To use a Hot corner, just hover the mouse in the corner of the screen, and it will open a toolbar or tile that you can click. For example, to switch to another open app, you can hover the mouse in the top-left corner and then click.

Charms Bar

Many of the computer's settings are found in a toolbar called the Charms bar. You can access it by hovering in the top-right or bottom-right corner of the screen.

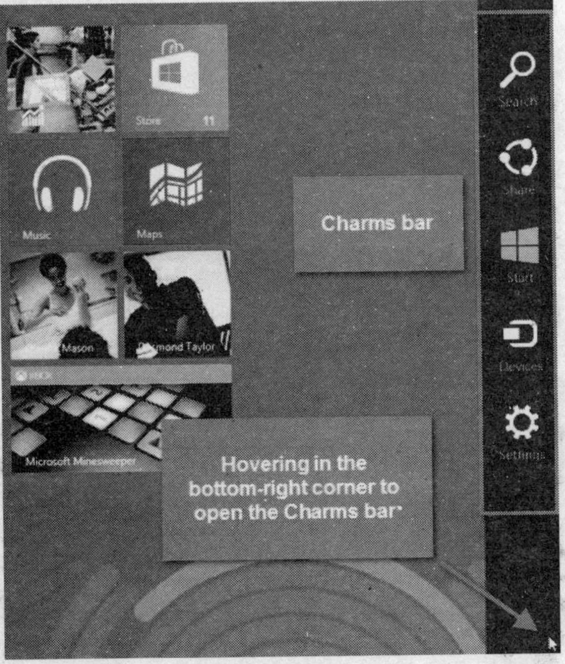

ONLINE FEATURES IN WINDOWS 8

In order to save files and other information online, you can use Microsoft's OneDrive service (previously call SkyDrive). This is also known as **cloud**.

Windows 8 is designed to connect seamlessly to OneDrive, as well as to other online services like Facebook and Twitter. Instead of creating an account on your computer, you can sign in with your free Microsoft account. This will bring all of your OneDrive files, contacts and more into your Start screen.

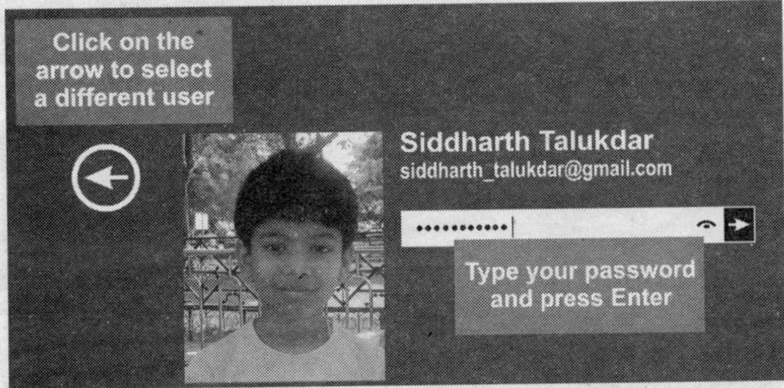

You can also connect your Facebook, Twitter and Flickr accounts to Windows 8, which allows you to see your friends' updates directly from your Start screen or from the built-in People app.

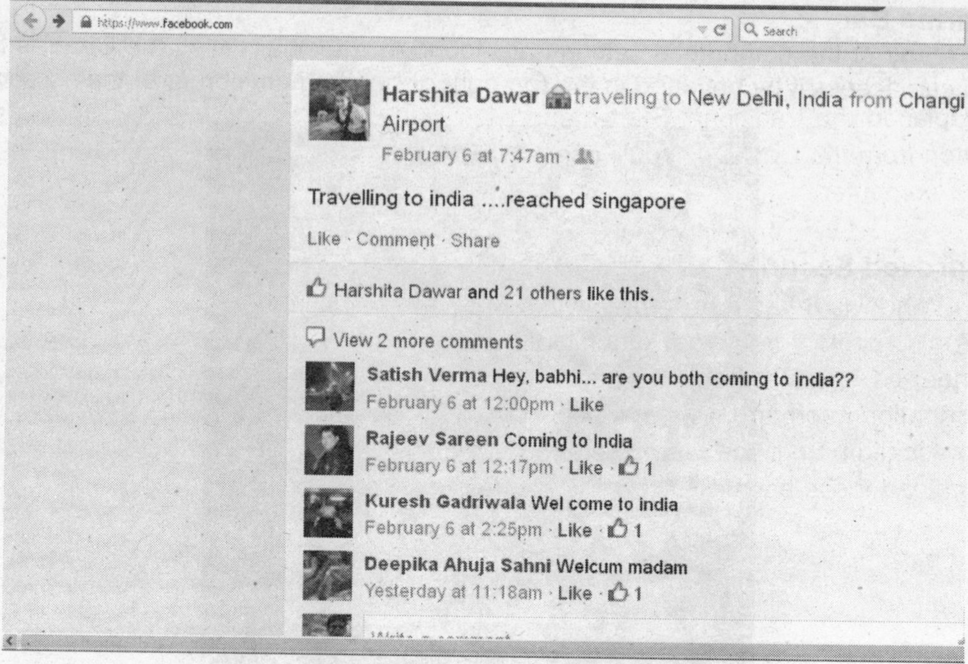

OTHER FEATURES OF WINDOWS 8

Simplified Desktop

Microsoft hasn't removed the Desktop, and you can still use it to manage your files or open many of your existing programmes. However, it has removed some of the transparency effects that often caused Windows 7 and Vista to run slowly.

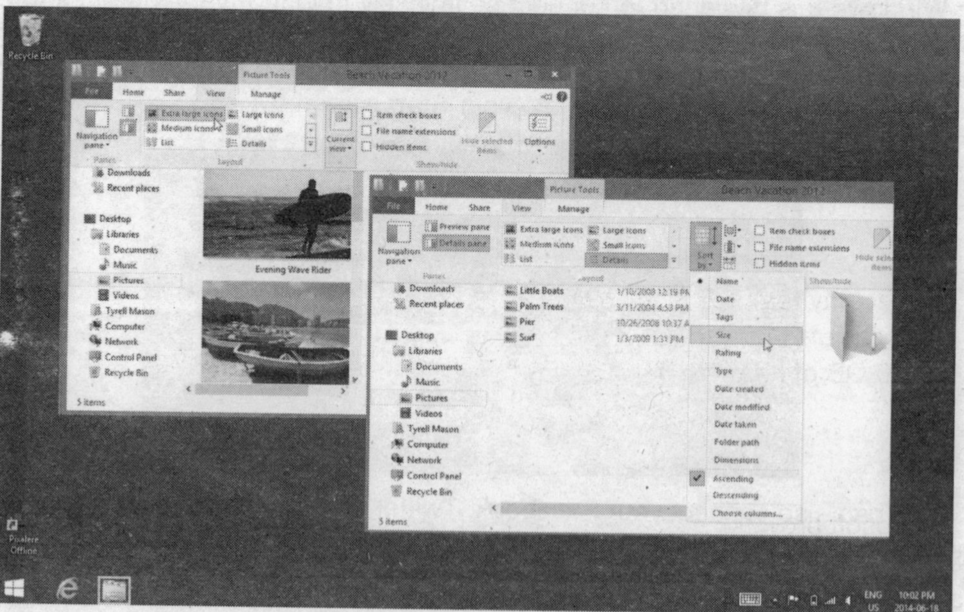

Start Button

The Start menu was an important feature in earlier versions of Windows. Windows 8 replaced the traditional Start menu with the Start screen and removed the Start button from the Desktop. You'll use the Start screen to open programmes or search your computer.

Improved Security

Windows 8 has a built-in antivirus programme called Windows Defender, which can also protect you from other types of malware, such as spyware. The built-in Windows Store also helps to keep you and your computer safe by showing you what information each app will have access to. For example, some apps have access to your location. So if you're uncomfortable sharing your location, you can decide not to download those apps.

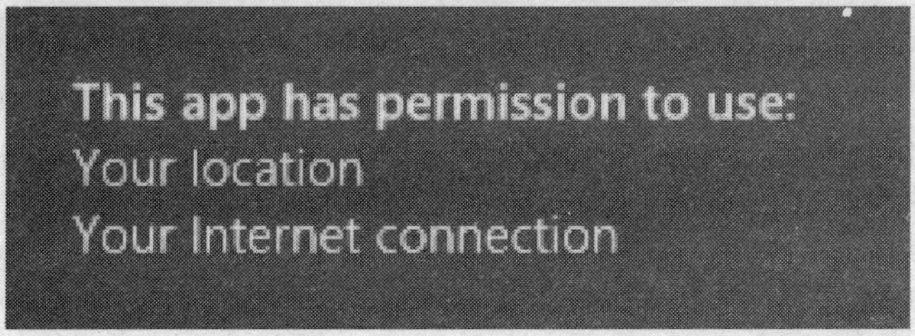

This app has permission to use:
Your location
Your Internet connection

Snap Start Screen Apps

Windows 8 introduced full-screen apps for the Start screen, but it did not allow you to view more than two apps at once. Traditional desktop apps still work the way they did in earlier versions of Windows. They'll appear in individual windows that you can move and resize.

WINDOWS 8 SYSTEM REQUIREMENTS

To install Windows 8, you require the following features:

- 1 GHz or faster CPU
  It also needs to support PAE or PAE-NX Physical Address Extension for new security features in the Windows 8 kernel.
- 1 GB of RAM (or 2GB for 64-bit systems)
- 20 GB of hard drive space
- A DirectX 9 graphics card with WDDM driver

INSTALLING AND UPGRADING

Microsoft provides step-by-step guide to download and install Windows 8 online. However, if you are upgrading your system from Windows 7 to Windows 8, you get most of the options with an upgrade from Windows 7.

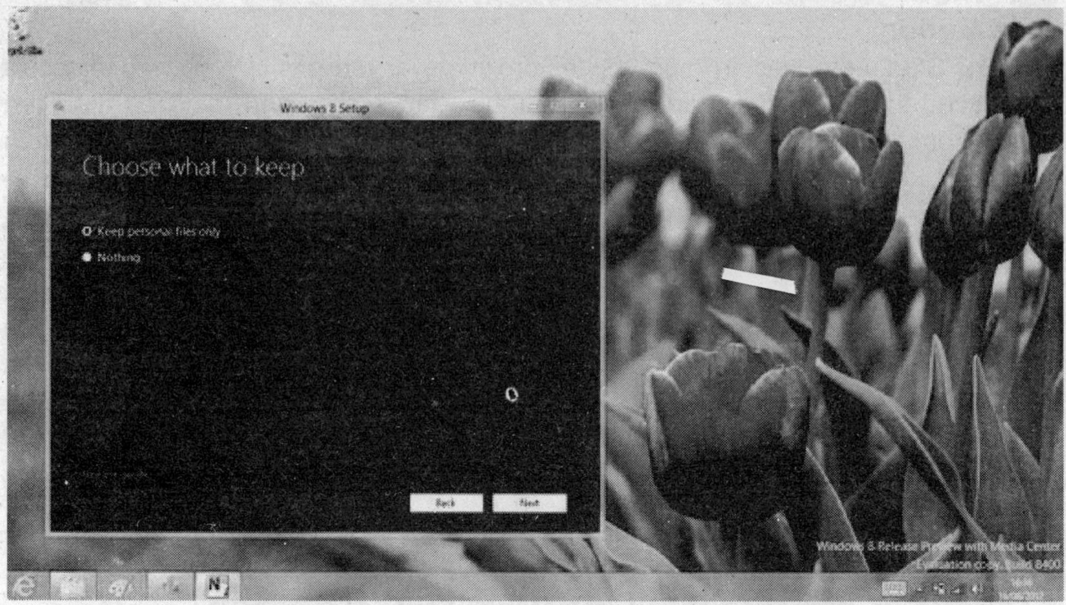

It takes 10 to 15 minutes from starting the installation and entering the license key to get to pick the colour scheme and customise the set-up.

While Windows 8 finishes the set-up, which takes a couple more minutes, you get a brief onscreen tutorial that shows you how to move your mouse into the corners of the screen to open the charm bar.

□

4
General Functions of Windows 8

Getting Started with Windows 8

Windows 8 can be confusing at first, since the interface has changed so much. You'll need to know how to navigate the Start screen, as well as the Desktop. Although the Desktop looks very similar to previous versions of Windows, it has one major change: The Start menu has been removed.

To Sign in to Windows 8

When you're setting up Windows 8, it will require you to create an account name and password that you will use to sign in. You can also create additional accounts, and you'll have the option of associating each one with a Microsoft account.

1. Click anywhere on the **lock screen** to unlock the computer.

2. Your user account name and picture will appear. Type your **password** and then press **Enter** to sign in.
   - Alternatively, you can press the **back arrow** to select a different user.

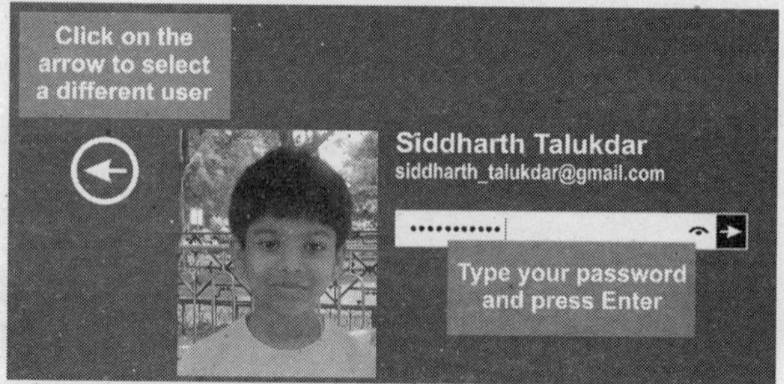

3. The **Start screen** will appear.

Navigating Windows 8

There are several ways to navigate through Windows 8, including hot corners and keyboard shortcuts.

Using Hot Corners

Whether you're in the Start screen or the Desktop, you can navigate through Windows 8 by using hot corners. To use a hot corner, just hover the mouse in the corner of the screen, and it will open a toolbar or tile that you can click.

Each corner performs a different task.

- **Lower-left:** When you're using an app, you can click on the lower-left corner to switch back to the Start screen.

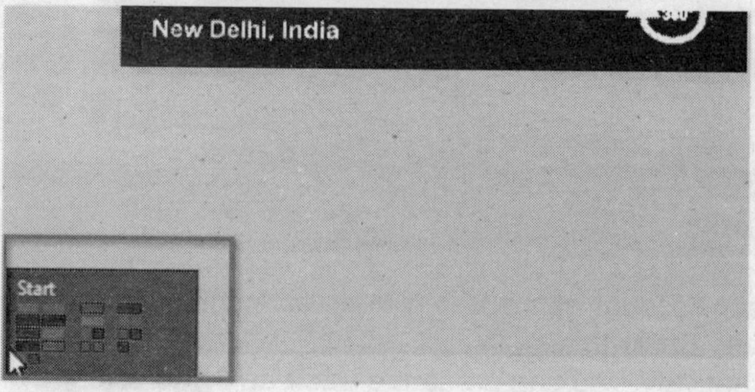

- **Upper-left:** If you click on the upper-left corner, it will switch to the previous app you were using.

- **Upper-right or Lower-right:** You can hover the mouse in the upper-right or lower-right corner to open the Charms bar, which you'll use to adjust your computer's settings and manage printers.

If you have several apps open, you can switch between them by hovering the mouse in the upper-left corner and then moving the mouse down. This displays a list of all of your open apps, and you can click on the desired app to switch to it.

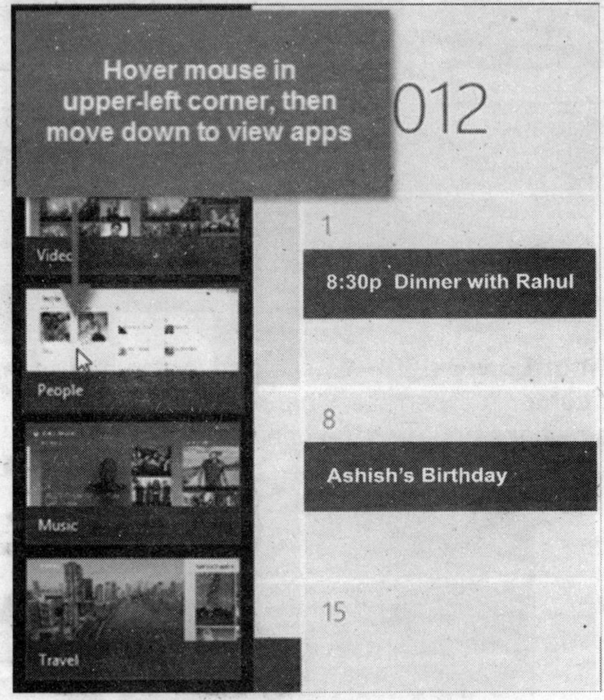

Using Keyboard Shortcuts

Windows 8 has several keyboard shortcuts that you can use to navigate more easily.

- **Alt+Tab**

You can hold down the Alt key and then press the Tab one or more times to switch between your open apps. This feature is called Flip, and it works in both Desktop view and the Start screen.

- **Windows**

When you have an app open, you can press the **Windows key** to switch to the

Start screen. This shortcut also lets you switch back to the Start screen when you are in Desktop view.

- **Windows+D**

You can hold down the **Windows key** and press **D** to switch to Desktop view.

The Charms Bar

The Charms bar is a toolbar that lets you access your computer's settings, along with other options. You can access the Charms bar by hovering the mouse in the top-right or bottom-right corner.

The Charms bar contains several icons, which are called charms, and each one contains different options.

Search

The Search charm lets you find apps, files or settings on your computer. However, a simpler way to search is to go to the Start screen and type the name of the file or app that you're looking for.

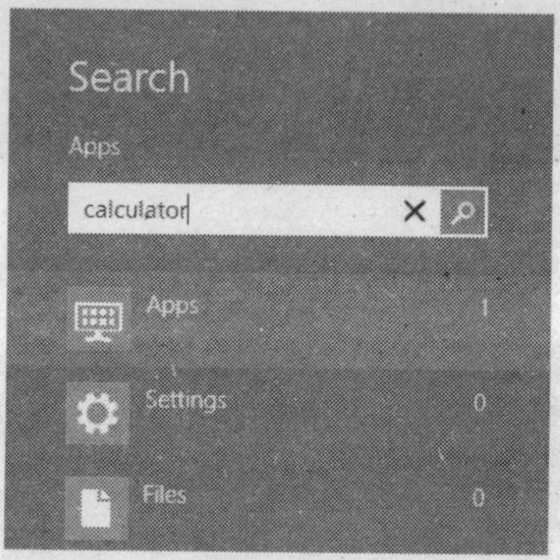

Share

The Share charm is basically a copy and paste feature that is designed to be as convenient as possible. It allows you to copy information (such as a photo or web address) and paste it into another app. For example, if you're viewing a photo in the Photos app, you can share it with the OneDrive app, which will upload the photo to your OneDrive. If you are reading an article online, you can share the address with the E-mail app, which lets you e-mail the article to a friend.

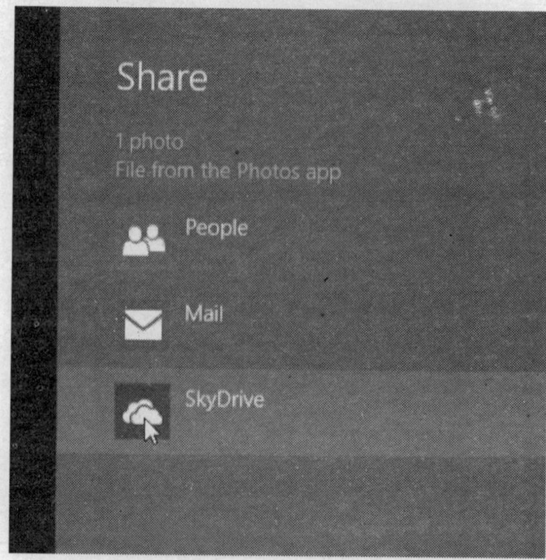

Start

This switches to the Start screen. If you are already on the Start screen, it will open the most recent app.

Devices

This shows any hardware devices that are connected to your computer, such as printers or monitors.

Settings

This lets you access general settings for your computer, as well as settings for the app you are currently viewing. For example, if you're in Internet Explorer, you can go to the Settings charm to access your Internet Options.

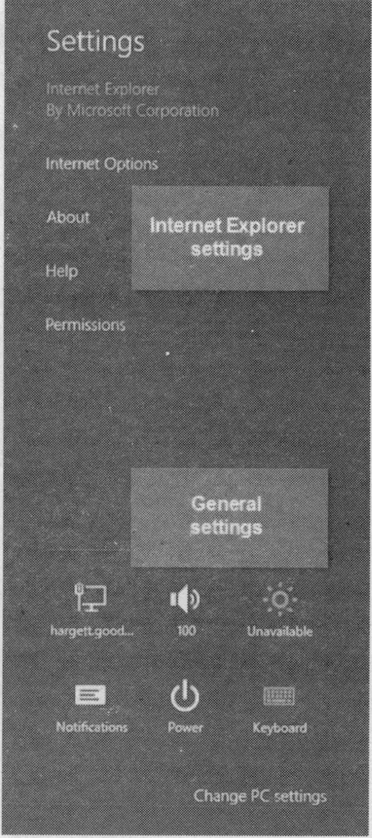

Working with Start Screen Apps

Start screen apps are different from the 'classic' Windows apps you may be used to. Apps fill the entire screen instead of opening in a window. However, you can still multi-task by opening two apps side by side.

To Open an App

1. On the Start screen, locate and click on the app you want to open.

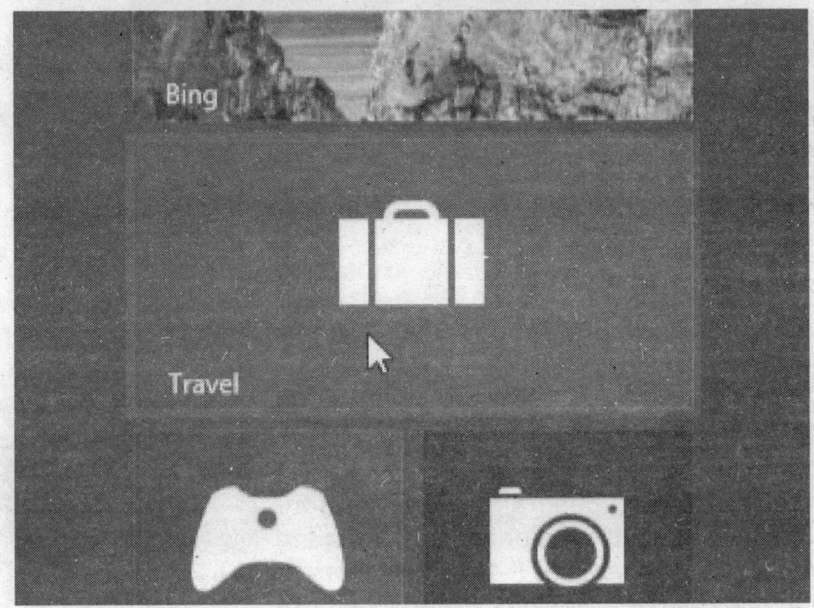

2. The app will open and fill the entire screen.

To Close an App

1. Hover the **mouse** at the top of the app. The cursor will change to a **hand icon**.

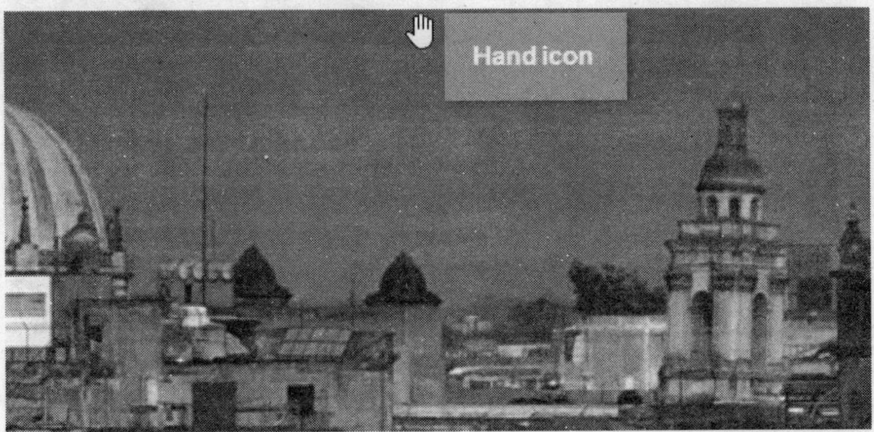

2. Click, hold and drag the top of the app all the way down to the bottom of the screen and then release. The app will close and you'll return to the Start screen.

3. When dragging the app down, it may look like it is 'stuck'. However, just keep moving the mouse down until the cursor gets to the bottom of the screen, and the app will then close.

Viewing Apps Side by Side

Although apps usually fill up the entire screen, Windows 8 lets you snap an app to the left or right side and then open other apps next to it. For example, you might want to keep your calendar visible while you're using another app.

To View Apps Side by Side

1. From the Start screen, click on the first app to open it.

2. Click, hold and drag the top of the app all the way to the right or left side of the screen.

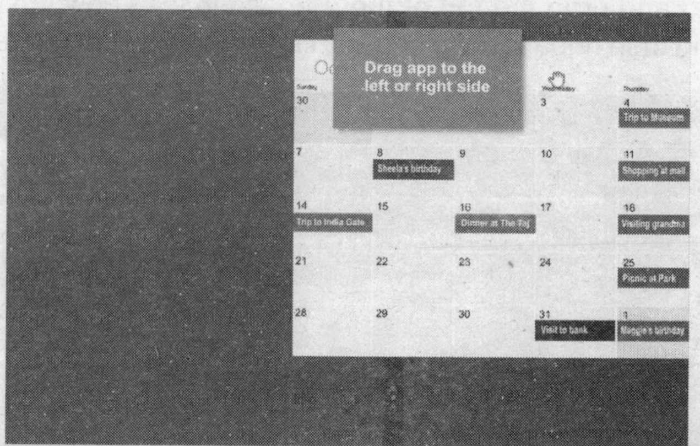

3. Release the mouse, and the app will snap to the side of the screen.

4. Click anywhere on the empty part of the screen to return to the Start screen.

5. Click on an app to open it.

6. The apps will now appear side by side. Drag the bar to change the size of the apps.

7. Snapping is designed to work with widescreen monitors. You will need a screen resolution of at least 1366 × 768 pixels to use this feature. If you have a larger monitor, you'll be able to snap more apps at once.

Coping Without the Start Menu

Windows 8 doesn't have a Start menu. The Start menu was a very important feature in previous versions of Windows, as it was used to launch apps, search for files, open the Control Panel and shut down the computer. You can still do all of these things in Windows 8, but they're now found in different places.

To Launch an App

There are several ways to open an app in Windows 8:

1. Click on the app icon on the taskbar.

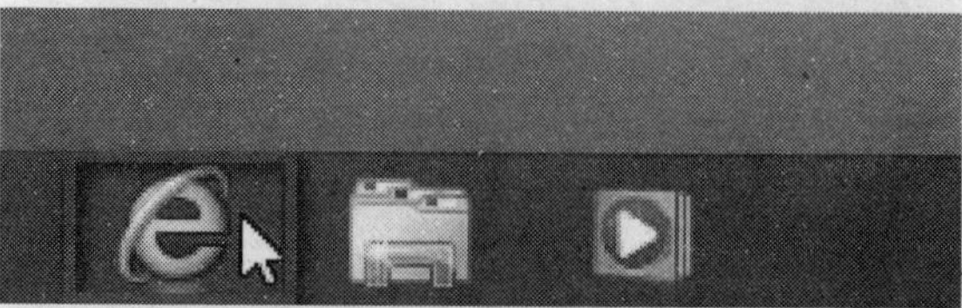

2. Double-click on the app shortcut on the Desktop.

3. Click on the app tile in the Start screen.

4. To view all of your apps, click on the arrow in the bottom-left corner of the Start screen.

Personalising Your Start Screen

There are different ways to personalise your Start screen.

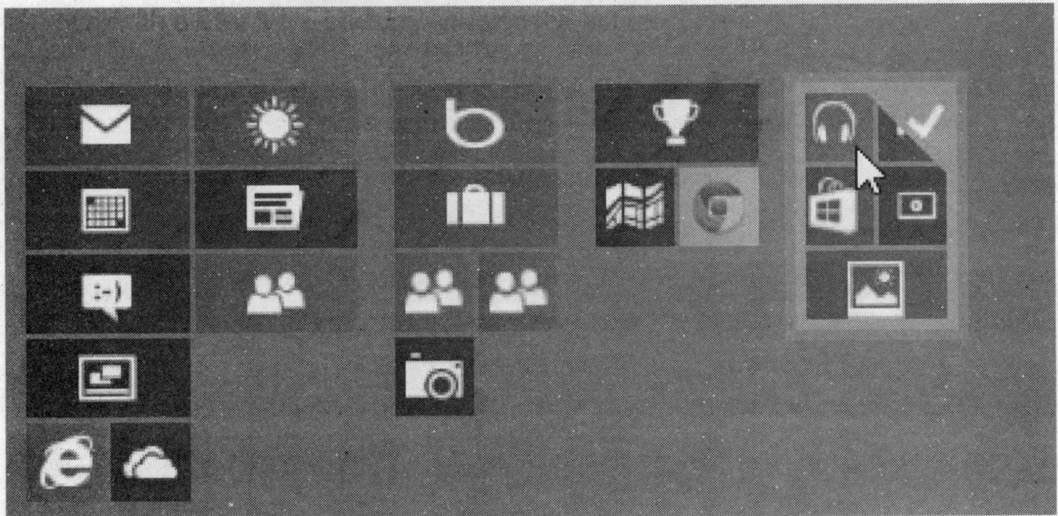

To Change Your Start Screen Background

1. Hover the **mouse** in the lower-right corner to open the Charms bar and then select the **Settings charm**.

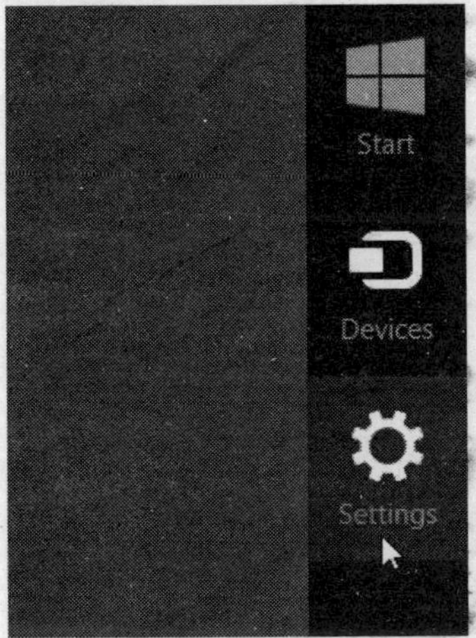

2. Click on **Personalize**.

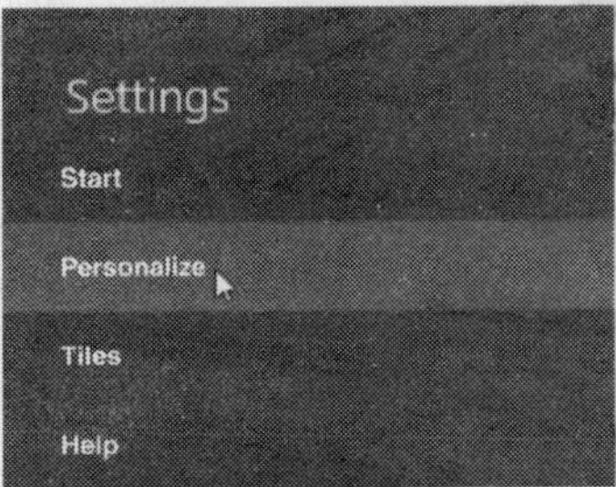

3. Select the desired **background image** and **colour scheme**.

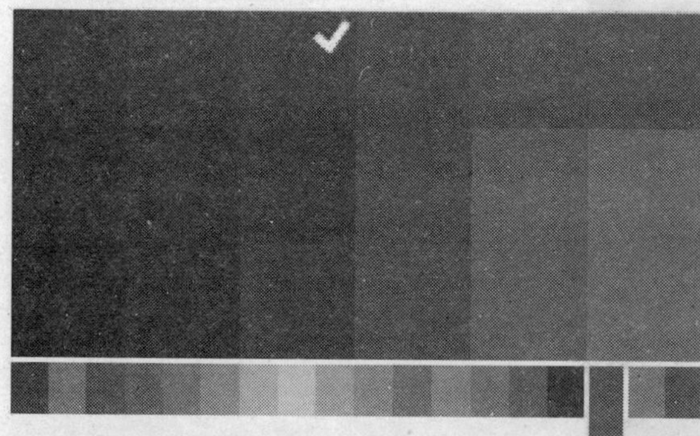

To Change Your Lock Screen Picture

1. Hover the **mouse** in the lower-right corner to open the **Charms bar** and then select the **Settings charm**. Click on **Change PC** settings.

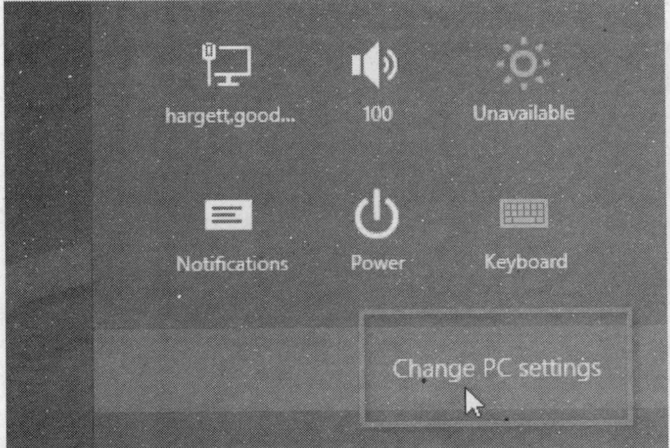

2. Select **Lock screen** near the top of the screen.

Personalize

View recently used settings

3. Select the desired picture from the list of thumbnails. Alternatively, you can click on **Browse** to select one of your own pictures.

4. The **lock** screen will appear whenever your computer is locked, which happens automatically after a few minutes of inactivity. You can also lock your computer by clicking on your **account name** and selecting **Lock**.

To Change Your Account Picture

1. Hover the **mouse** in the lower-right corner to open the **Charms bar** and then select the **Settings charm**. Click on **Change PC settings**, and then select **Account picture**. Then click on **Browse**.

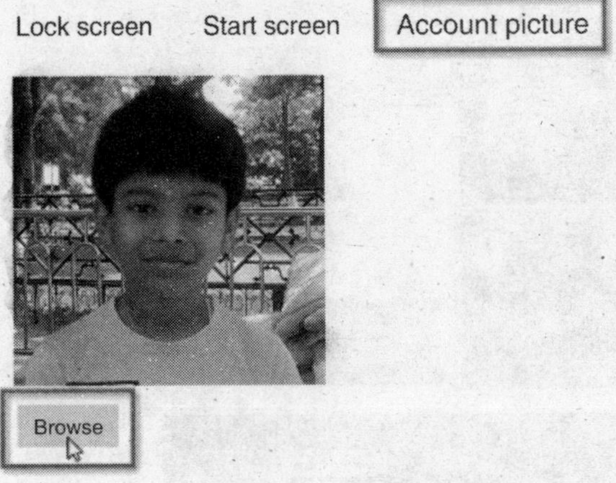

Create an account picture

2. A list of folders will appear. Select the desired photo on your computer, or click on the **drop-down arrow** at the top of the screen to select a different location. Let us take an example to add a photo from our SkyDrive.

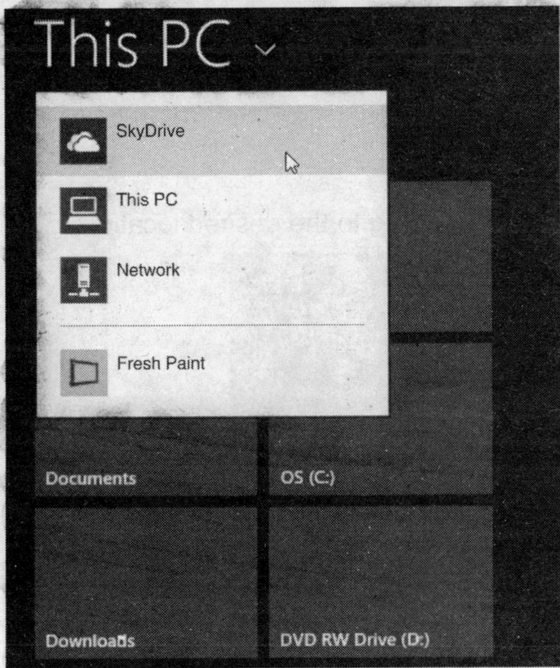

3. When you have selected a photo, click on **Choose image**.

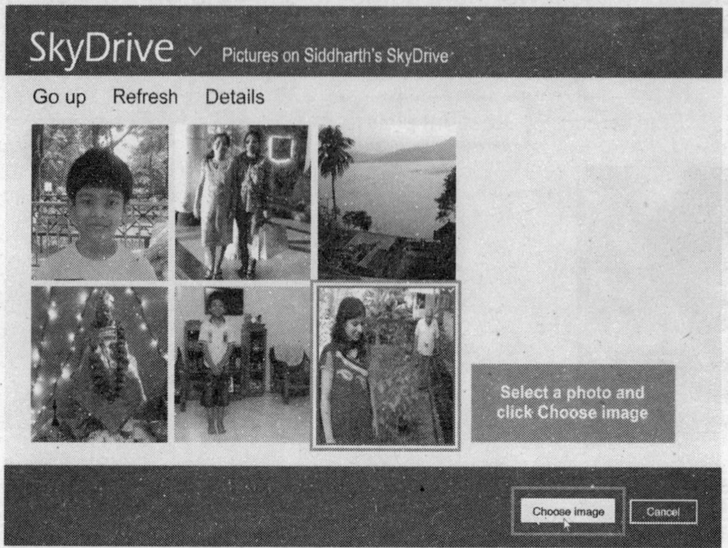

4. If your computer has a built-in camera, you can click on **Camera** to take a picture of yourself.

Create an account picture

Customising Your Start Screen Apps

If you do not like the way your apps are arranged on the Start screen, you can rearrange them by moving them wherever you want. You may also find that the animated live tiles are too distracting, and you can easily turn them off so they will display a plain background with no animation.

To Move an App

1. Click on the app and then hold and drag to the desired location.

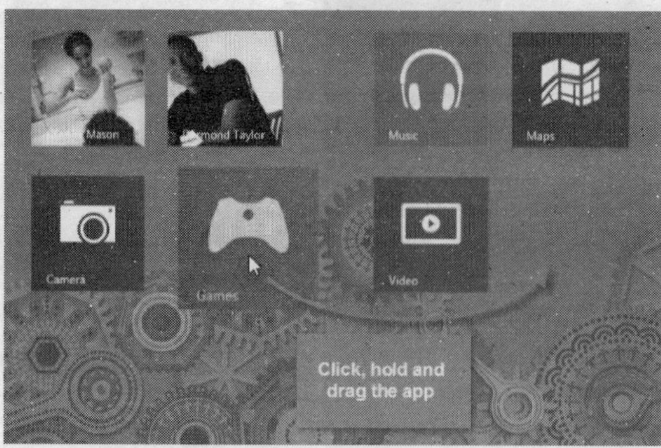

2. **Release** the mouse. The app will move to the new location.

To Turn a Live Tile Off

1. **Right-click** on the app you want to change.

2. A **toolbar** will appear at the bottom of the screen. Click on **Turn live tile off** and the tile will change to a plain background.

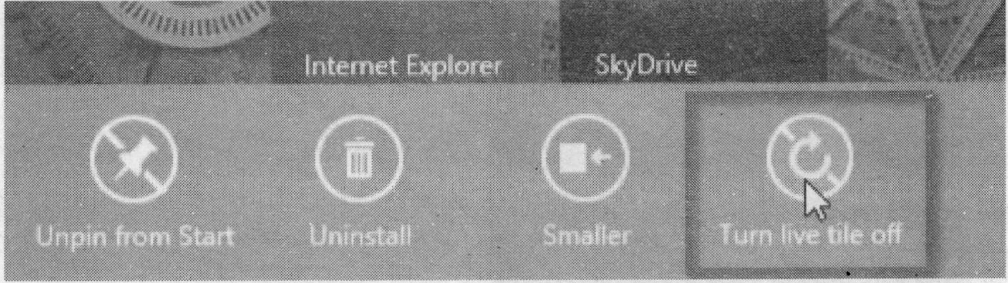

Pinning Apps to the Start Screen

By default, the Start screen does not show all of the apps on your computer. However, it is easy to pin your favourite apps to the Start screen so that you can open them quickly.

To Pin an App to the Start Screen

1. Click on the **arrow** in the bottom-left corner of the Start screen to view all of the apps installed on your computer.

2. Locate and **right-click** on the desired app.

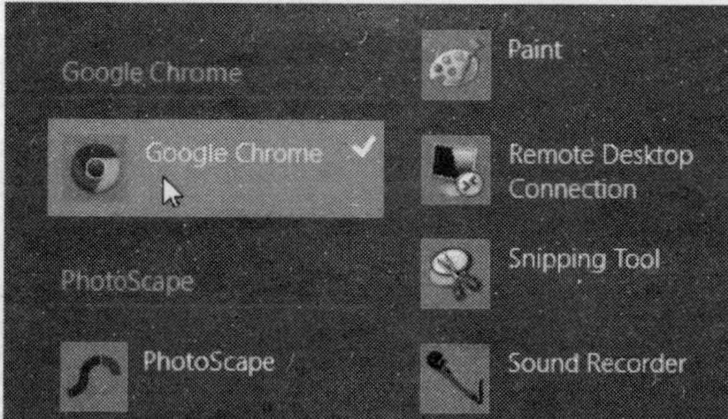

3. At the bottom of the screen, click on **Pin to Start**.

4. Click on the lower-left corner to return to the Start screen. Your app will now appear on the **Start screen**.

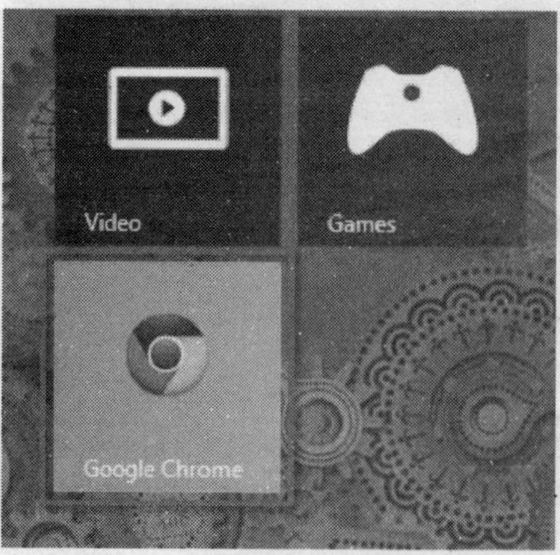

To Unpin an App from the Start Screen

1. From the Start screen, **right-click** on the desired app.

2. At the bottom of the screen, click on **Unpin from Start**. The app will disappear from the Start screen.

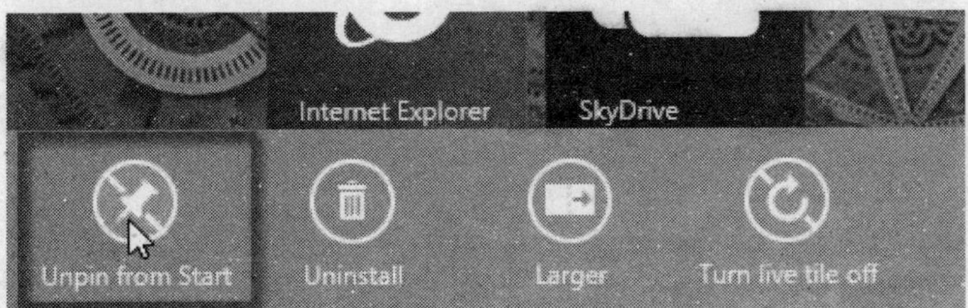

Creating App Groups

To further organise your apps, you can put related apps into groups. You can also name your groups, and each group will display its name at the top.

To Create a New App Group

1. Click on an app and then hold and drag to the right until it is on an empty area of the Start screen.

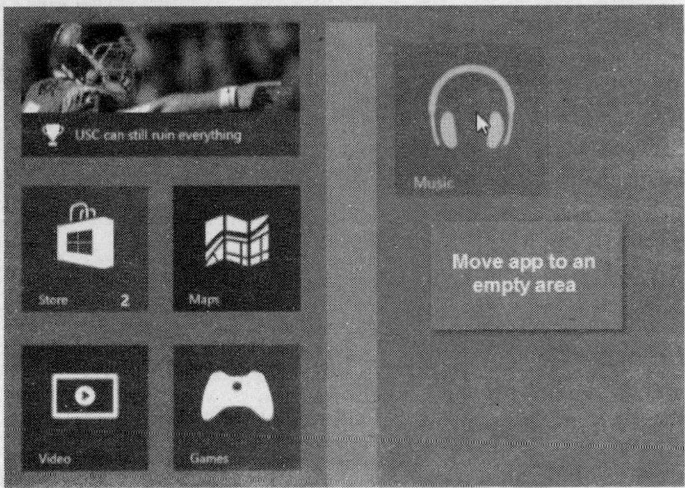

2. **Release** the mouse. The app will now be in its own app group, and you should see a space between the new group and the other groups. This space helps to visually separate the different groups.

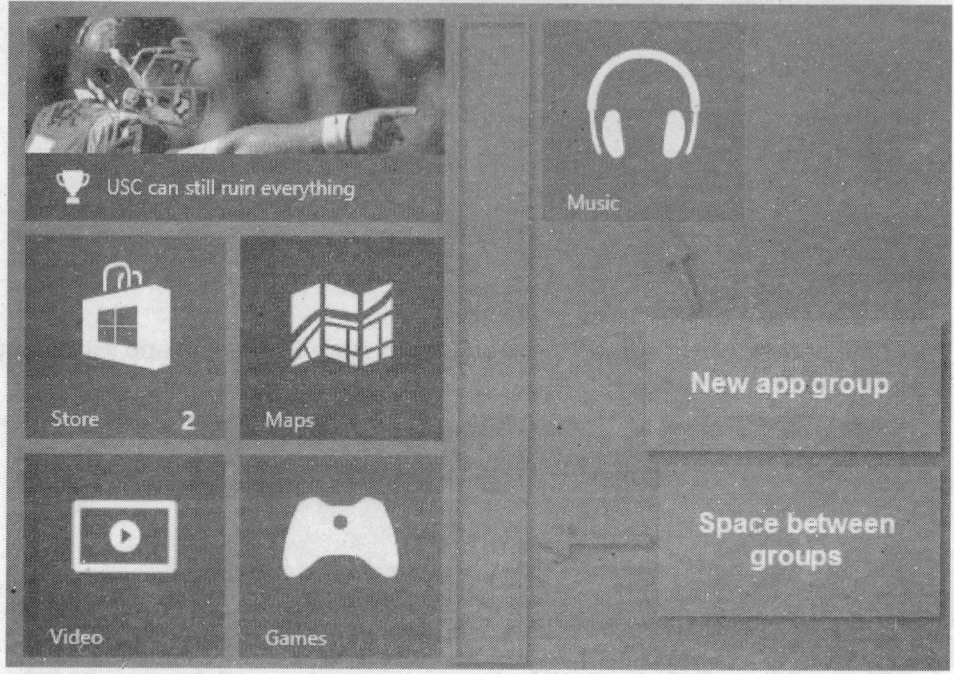

3. You can now move more apps into the new app group.

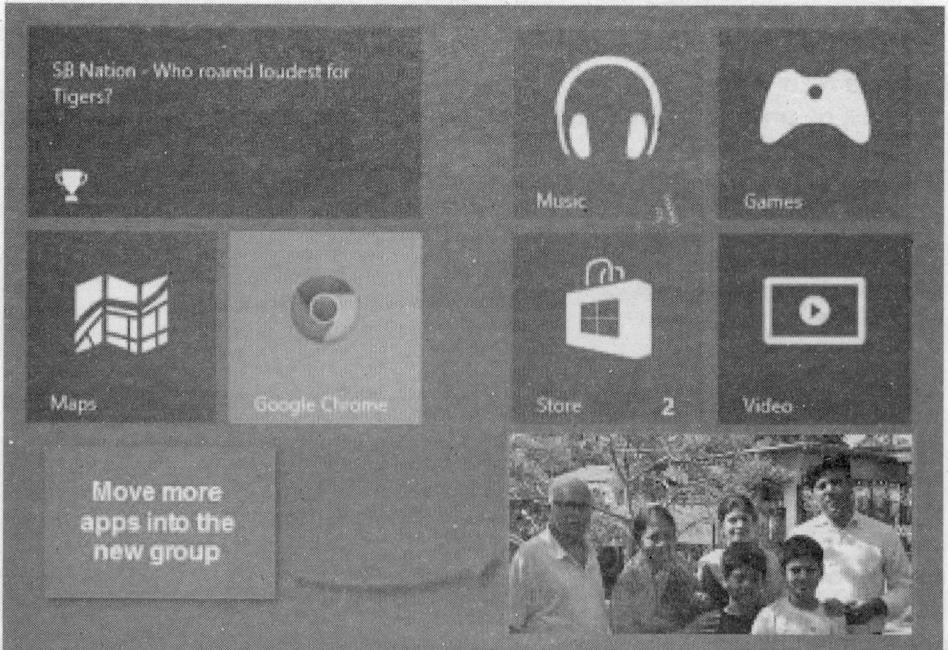

To Name an App Group

1. **Right-click** on any app on the Start screen, and then click on **Name group** above the desired app group.

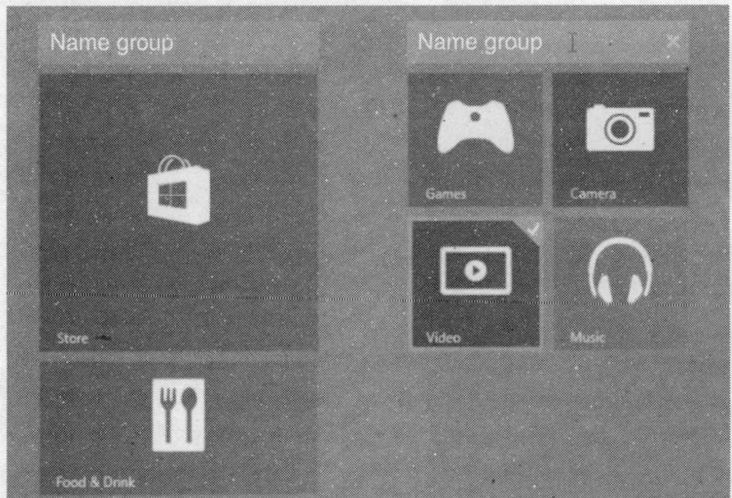

2. Type the desired name. Shorter names usually work best, so try to use a single word, if possible. When you're done, press **Enter**.

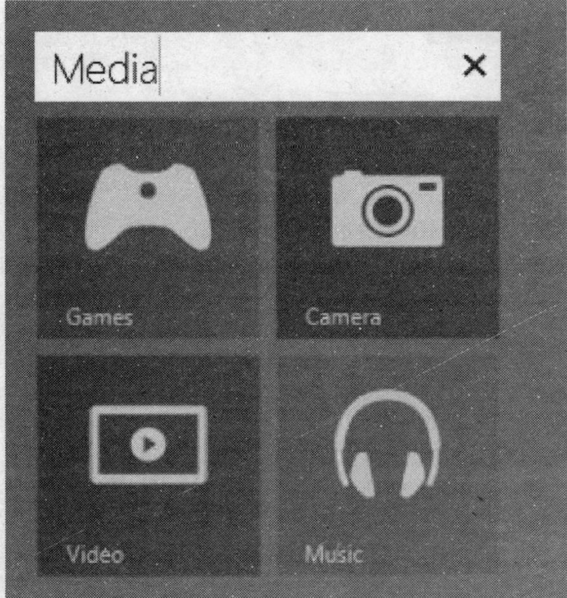

3. Click anywhere on the **Start screen** to return to the normal view. The new name will appear above the app group.

Using the Search Feature

Windows 8 has a built-in search feature, which can help you find files, apps, or almost anything else on your computer.

To Search from the Start Screen

From the Start screen, type what you are looking for. Your search results will instantly appear below the search bar. A list of suggested web searches will appear below the results.

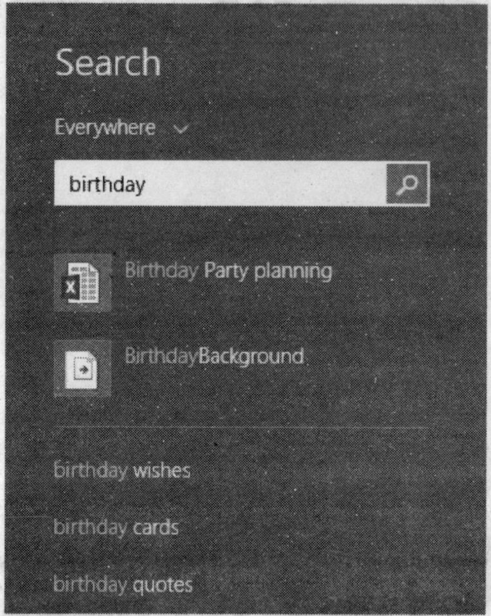

Using Different Search Options

You can select different search options to help find specific files and settings. Just click on the **drop-down arrow** above the search box, and then select the desired option:

- Select **Settings** or **Files** to search for a setting or file.
- Select **Web images** or **Web videos** to search the Web.

Searching from the Desktop

If you are on the Desktop, you will first need to press the Windows key to switch to the Start screen and then type what you're looking for.

To Open the Control Panel

1. From the Desktop view, hover the **mouse** in the lower-right corner to access the **Charms bar** and then select **Settings**.

2. Locate and select **Control Panel** from the Settings Pane.

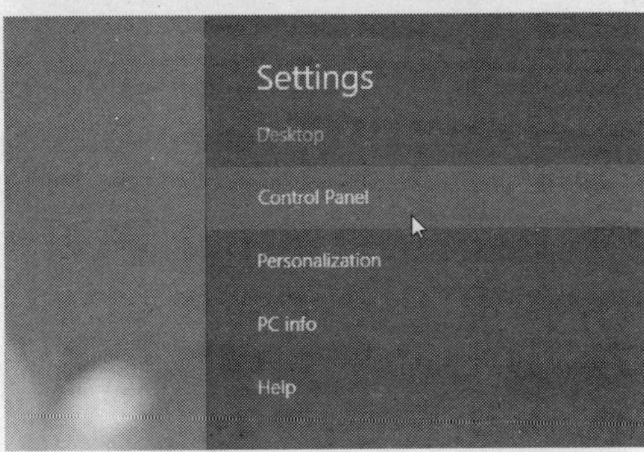

3. The **Control Panel** will appear. You can then select the desired setting to change it.

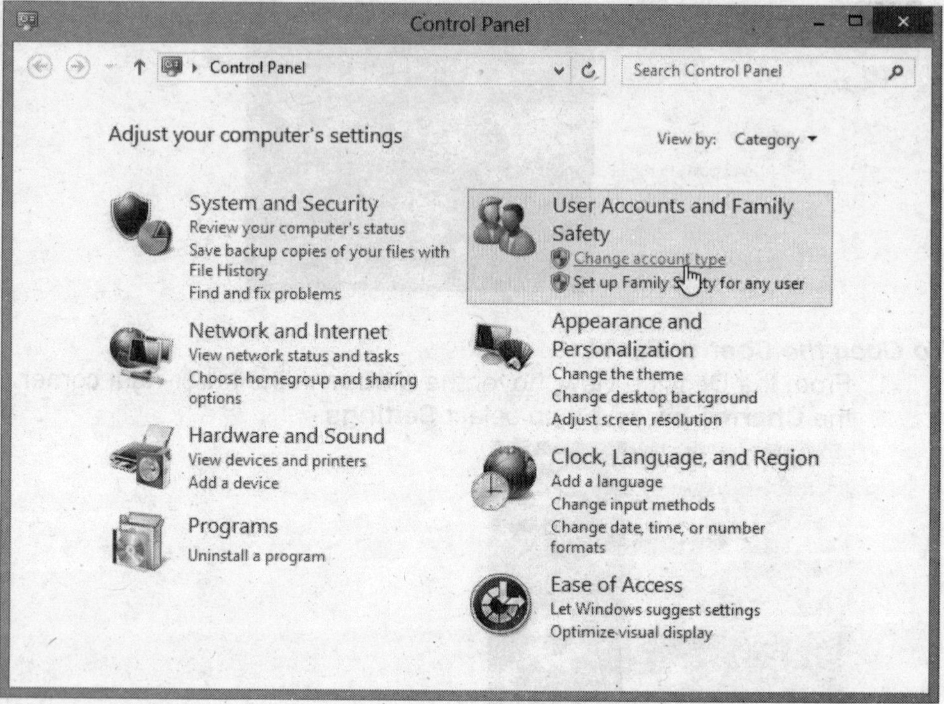

Start Screen Options

Windows 8 introduces a lot of new features, but you may be annoyed and frustrated by the Start screen. If you are not interested in using the Start screen very often, there are a few options that can make your computer function more like older versions of Windows. This includes the option to boot your computer directly to the Desktop instead of the Start screen.

To Modify Your Start Screen Options

1. Go to the **Desktop**.
2. **Right-click** on the **taskbar** and select **Properties**.

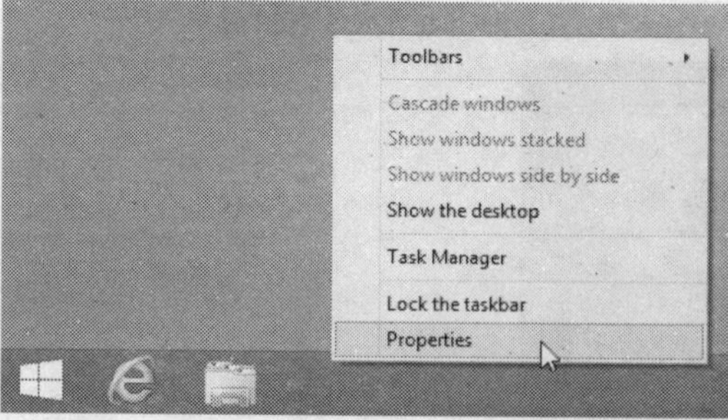

3. A dialog box will appear. In the interactive below, we will review a few options that you may want to customize.

4. Click on the **buttons** in the interactive below to learn about different **Start screen** options.

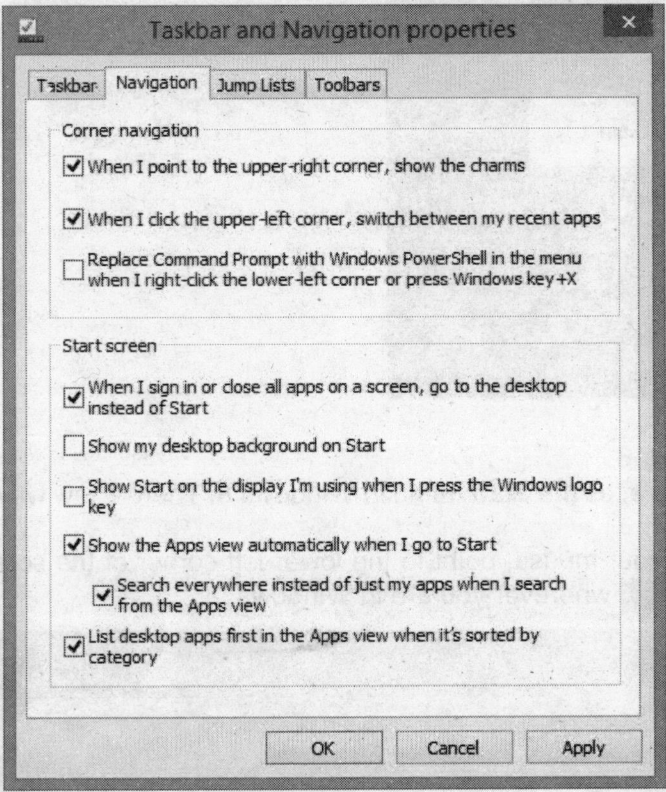

To Shut Down Your Computer

1. Hover the **mouse** in the lower-right corner to access the **Charms bar** and then select **Settings**.

2. Click on **Power**, and select **Shut down**.

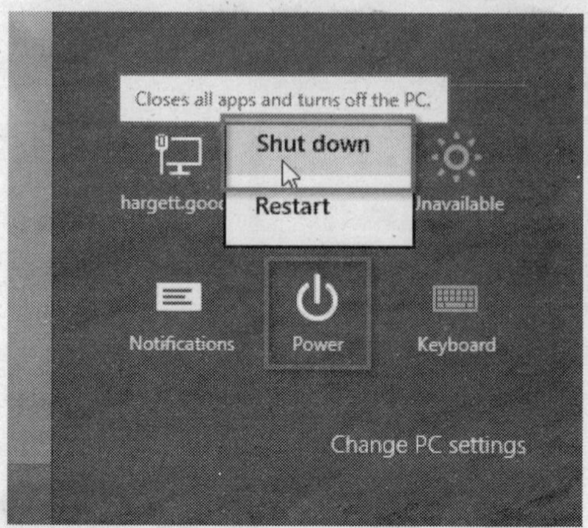

How to start Windows 8

The Start screen replaces the Start menu in Windows 8. There a few ways to get to Start in Windows 8:

1. With the help of your mouse, point to the lower-left corner of the screen and click on the Start button wherever you are in Windows.

2. Press the Windows key on your keyboard.

3. Open the charms and then click on Start button ⊞.

Getting help from Windows 8

You can get to know about different aspects of operation in Windows 8 from the inbuilt Windows Help and Support. The benefit of using Windows Help and Support is that you can launch applications or commands directly from within the search results.

To use Windows Help and Support, select **Settings** ! **Help** from Charms Bar in desktop mode, as shown below.

Now, move the mouse cursor to the upper right corner until the Charms Bar appears. Type in the search box what you are looking for, e.g. 'shortcut keys'. Click on the item from the search results, e.g. "Mouse and keyboard: What's new in Windows 8 Consumer Preview".

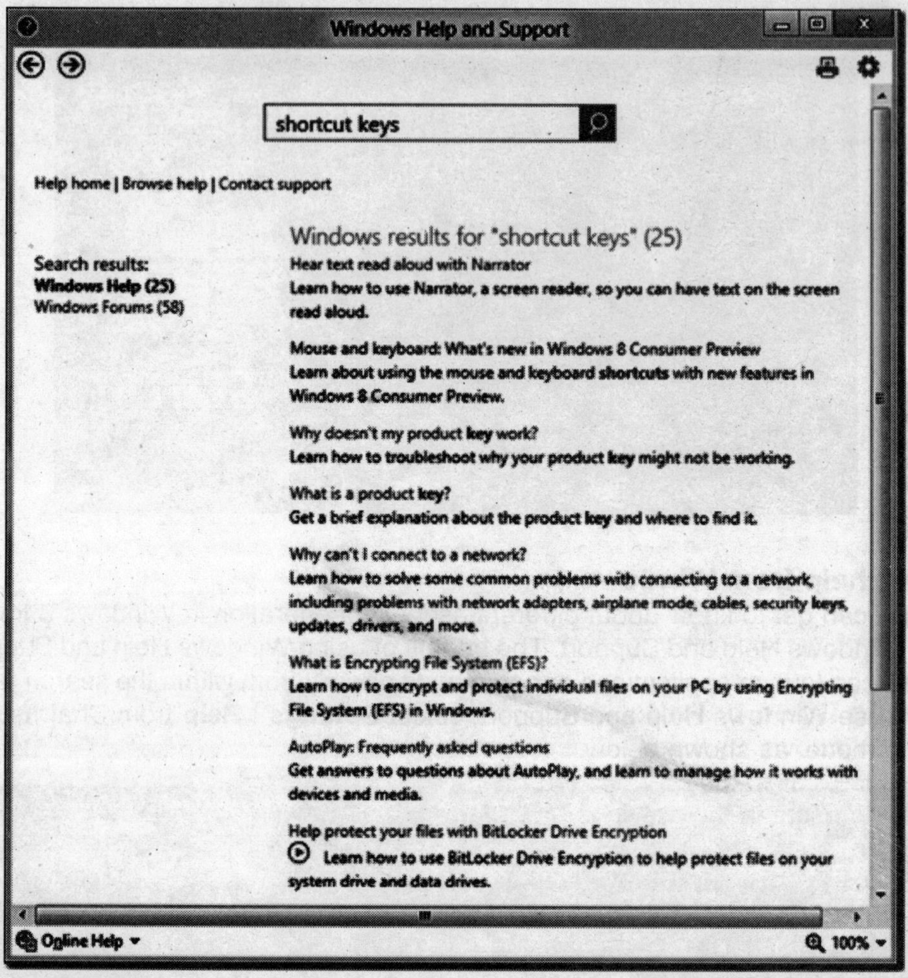

Windows Help and Support
shortcut keys
Help home | Browse help | Contact support
Search results:
Windows Help (25)
Windows Forums (58)
Windows results for "shortcut keys" (25)
Hear text read aloud with Narrator
Learn how to use Narrator, a screen reader, so you can have text on the screen read aloud.
Mouse and keyboard: What's new in Windows 8 Consumer Preview
Learn about using the mouse and keyboard shortcuts with new features in Windows 8 Consumer Preview.
Why doesn't my product key work?
Learn how to troubleshoot why your product key might not be working.
What is a product key?
Get a brief explanation about the product key and where to find it.
Why can't I connect to a network?
Learn how to solve some common problems with connecting to a network, including problems with network adapters, airplane mode, cables, security keys, updates, drivers, and more.
What is Encrypting File System (EFS)?
Learn how to encrypt and protect individual files on your PC by using Encrypting File System (EFS) in Windows.
AutoPlay: Frequently asked questions
Get answers to questions about AutoPlay, and learn to manage how it works with devices and media.
Help protect your files with BitLocker Drive Encryption
Learn how to use BitLocker Drive Encryption to help protect files on your system drive and data drives.
Online Help
100%

Windows Help and Support
Search
Mouse and keyboard: What's new in Windows 8 Consumer Preview

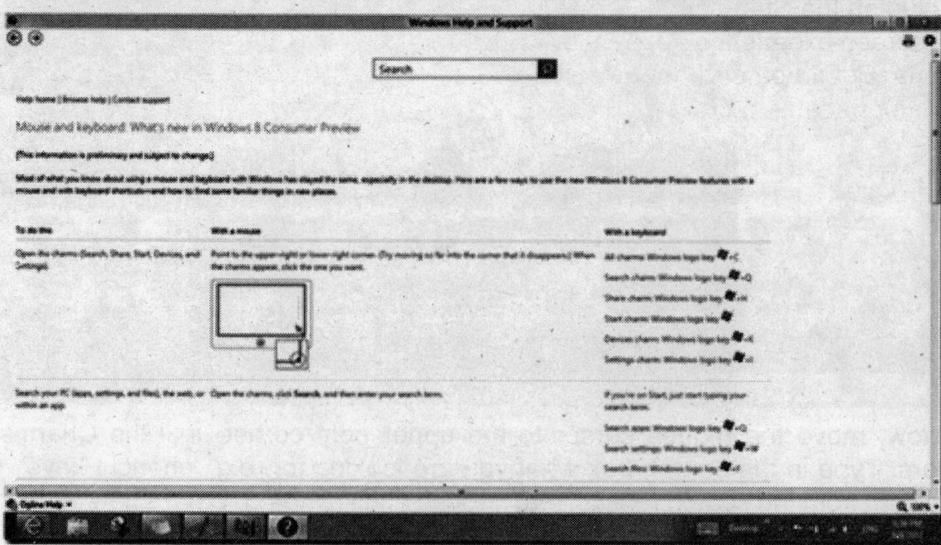

Note that if you often use Windows Help, you can pin the app to the Taskbar.

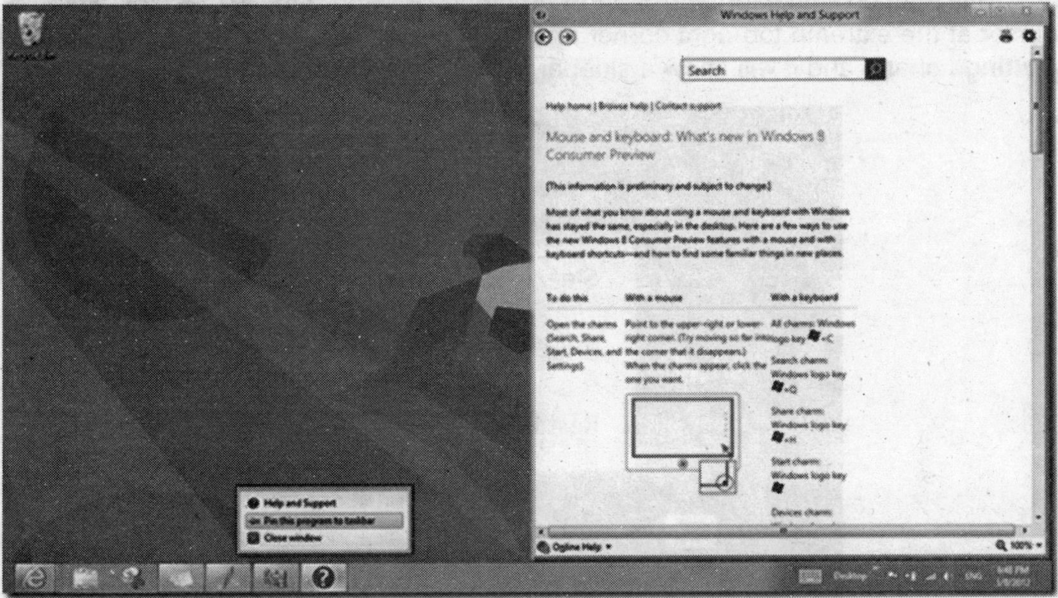

Shutting Down or Rebooting in Windows 8

In Windows 8, the interface has been replaced by a new full-screen Start experience, called the Start screen; and those Start Menu-based power management options, present in the previous MS Windows, are no longer available there.

There are a few ways to lock, log off, restart and shut down in Windows 8.

1. Using Ctrl+Alt+Del Key Combination

The easiest and simplest way to turn down a computer in Windows 8 is by pressing the **CTRL + ALT + DEL** keyboard shortcut. This will work from anywhere in Windows 8, including the Start screen, any Metro-style app, or the desktop. When you do this, a full-screen experience appears, with Lock, Switch User, Sign Out and Task Manager Options. But if you click that **Power** icon in the bottom right, you'll see a menu with power management options: **Sleep**, **Shut down** and **Restart**.

2. Using New Charms Bar

This method works for both Start Screen and Desktop. Simply move your mouse cursor at the extreme top-right corner and it will show the new Charms bar. Click on **Settings** charm and it will show a sidebar in right-side of screen.

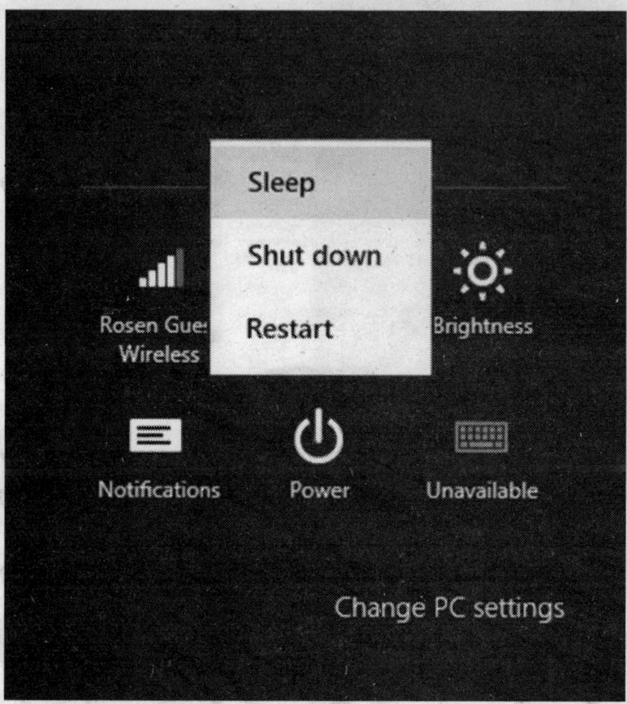

There you can click on **Power** button and select the desired option.

3. Using Alt + F4 Key Combination

Click on **Taskbar** and press **Alt+F4** keys together. It will show following dialog box:

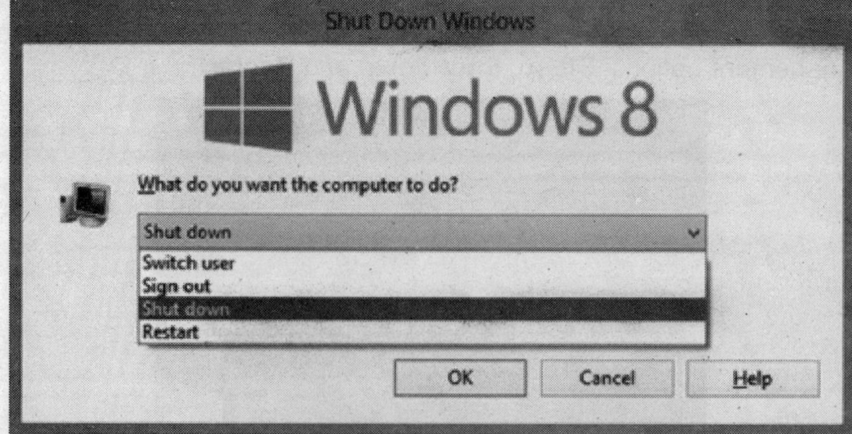

Now you can select the desired option from drop-down menu and click on **OK** button.

Install (Add) or Uninstall (Remove) a program in Windows 8

Install a program

You can install a program either from a CD /DVD or the internet.

To install a program from a CD or DVD

Insert the disc into your computer, and then follow the instructions on your screen. If you're prompted for an administrator password or confirmation, type the password or provide confirmation.

- Many programs installed from CDs or DVDs, open an installation wizard for the program automatically. In these cases, the AutoPlay dialog box appears and you can choose to run the wizard.
- If a program doesn't begin installation automatically, check the information that came with the program. This information will likely provide instructions for installing the program manually. If you can't access the information, you can also browse through the disc and open the program setup file, usually called Setup.exe or Install.exe.

To install a program from the Internet

In your web browser, click on the link to the program and do one of the following:

- To install the program immediately, click on **Open** or **Run**, and then follow the instructions on your screen. If you're prompted for an administrator password or confirmation, type the password or provide confirmation.
- To install the program later, click on **Save**, and then download the installation file to your computer. When you're ready to install the program, double-click on the file, and then follow the instructions on your screen.

Uninstall a Program

The process of uninstalling a program from the computer is very easy.

Uninstall a Program on the Start screen

- On the Start screen, press and hold or right-click on the program tile.
- Click on **Uninstall**.

If you'd rather not uninstall a program, but want to remove it from your Start screen, instead of clicking on **Uninstall**, click on **Unpin** from Start.

Uninstall a Desktop Program

- With the help of your mouse, point to the upper-right corner of the screen, move the mouse pointer down, and then click on **Search**.
- Enter **Control Panel** in the search box, and then click on **Control Panel**.
- Under **View by:** select **Large Icons**, and then click on **Programs and features**.
- Click on the program, and then click on **Uninstall**.
- Follow the instructions on the screen.

Change a Program

Some programs can be changed – adding or removing features.

- With you mouse, point to the upper-right corner of the screen, move the mouse pointer down, and then click on **Search**.
- Enter **Control Panel** in the search box, and then click on **Control Panel**.
- Under **View by:** select **Large Icons**, and then click on **Programs and features**.
- Click on the program, and then click on **Change**.
- Follow the instructions on the screen.

Repair a Program

If a program isn't working properly, you might be able to repair it.

- Point to the upper-right corner of the screen with the mouse and move the mouse pointer down, and then click on **Search**.
- Enter **Control Panel** in the search box, and then click on **Control Panel**.
- Under **View by:** select **Large Icons**, and then click on **Programs and features**.
- Click on the program, and then click on **Repair**.

  – Or –

  If you don't see the **Repair** option, click on **Change**, if available, and see if repair is offered as an option.
- Follow the instructions on the screen.

Creating and Applying Themes

A theme is a combination of pictures, colors and sounds. Themes include:

Desktop Background
Slide Show

Color
Automatic

Sounds
Windows Default

Screen Saver
None

You can find all of your themes in **Personalization** in Control Panel. Click on any theme to apply it to your desktop.

Open **Personalization** by pointing to the upper-right corner of the screen, moving the mouse pointer down, and then clicking on **Search**, enter **Personalization** in the search box, click on **Settings**, and then click on **Personalization**.

In **Personalization** in Control Panel, there are four types of themes: *My Themes, Windows Default Themes, Installed Themes, and High Contrast Themes.*

You're not limited to the themes that come with Windows – you can create customized themes using your own pictures and screen savers, and choose the colors and sounds that go along with them. To get started, click on any theme to apply it to your desktop. Then change each part of the theme until the desktop background, window border color, sounds and screen saver are just how you want them to be. All of your changes will appear under **My Themes** as an unsaved theme.

Creating a Theme

- Open **Personalization** by pointing your mouse to the upper-right corner of the screen, moving the mouse pointer down, and then clicking on **Search**, enter **Personalization** in the search box, click on **Settings**, and then click on **Personalization.**
- To change the desktop background, click on **Desktop Background** at the bottom of the page, browse to the pictures you want to use, select the check boxes for the pictures that you want to include in your slide show, and then click on **Save changes.**
- To change the color of your window borders and taskbar, click on **Color** at the bottom of the page, and then do one of the following:
  - ➢ Click on **Automatic** to let Windows choose a color automatically based on the colors in your desktop background picture, and then click on **Save** changes.

    Or,

  - ➢ Click on the color that you want to use, and then click on **Save changes.**
- To change the sounds you hear when something happens on your computer, click on **Sounds** at the bottom of the page, click on an item in the **Sound Scheme** list, and then click on **OK.**
- To add or change a screen saver, click on **Screen Saver** at the bottom of the page, click on an item in the **Screen Saver** list, change any settings to suit your preference, and then click on **OK.**

Thus your theme will be applied to your desktop.

Maximize and Minimize a Window

To Maximize a Window

- Drag the title bar of the window to the top of the screen. The window's outline expands to fill the screen.
- Release the window to expand it to fill the entire desktop.

To return the window to its original size, drag the title bar of the window away from the top of the screen.

To Minimize a Open Window

- **Using the mouse**
  - ➢ Click the **Show desktop** button at the end of the notification area on the taskbar.
  - ➢ To restore minimized windows, click on the **Show desktop** button again.
- **Using the keyboard**
  - ➢ Press the Windows logo key + D.
  - ➢ To restore minimized windows, press the Windows logo key + D again.

Move or Resize a Window

There are two ways to move or resize a window:

- **Using keyboard shortcut**

Press **ALT+SPACEBAR** keys together and it'll open the System Menu which shows **minimize**, **maximize**, **restore**, **close**, **size** and **move** options.

Once you get the menu, you can use arrow keys to go to the desired option and press the **Enter** key.

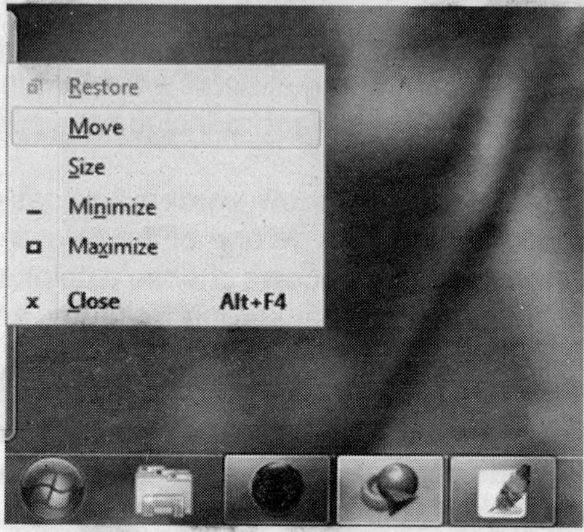

For example, to move the window select **Move** option and then you can use arrow keys to move the program window to left, right, top or bottom.

Similarly, to resize a large and wide window, select **Size** option and then use arrow keys to resize it.

- **Using mouse**

If you don't want to use keyboard shortcut, you can use your mouse to access system menu. Just, right-click on the **Program** button present in Taskbar.

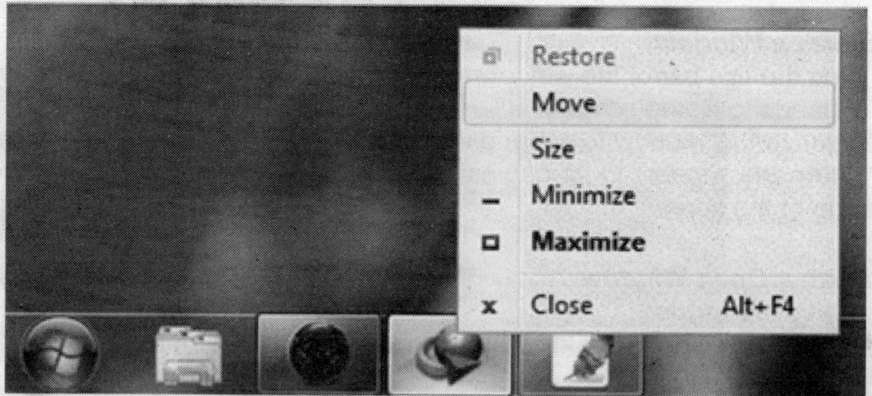

Right-clicking on the program button will show the same system menu and then you can click on the desired option but you will still need to use arrow keys to move or resize the program window.

Adding and Removing a Program in Start Menu

To Pin (Add) a Program Icon

If you use a program regularly, you can create a shortcut to it by pinning the program icon to the Start menu. Pinned program icons appear on the left side of the Start menu.

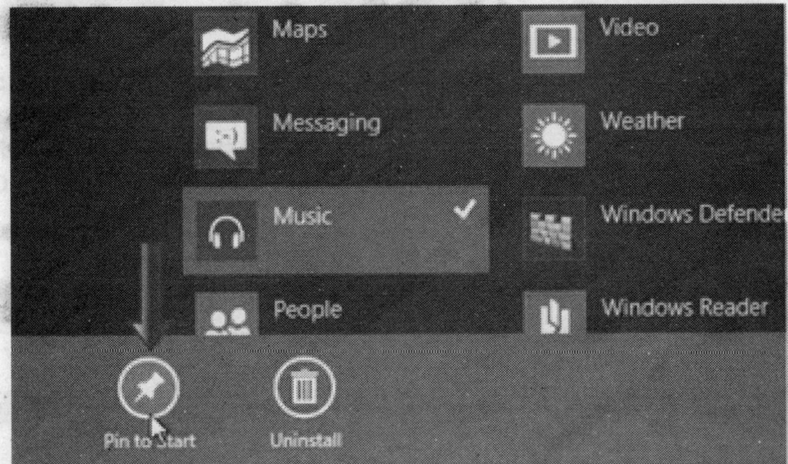

- With the new right click option in Windows 8; it is easier to add programs you would like to automatically start up after you log in.
- Right-click on the program icon you want to pin to the Start menu, and then click on **Pin to Start**.

To Unpin (Remove) a Program Icon

Removing a program icon from the Start menu doesn't remove it from the All Programs list or uninstall the program.

- Click on the **Start** button.
- Right-click on the program icon you want to remove from the Start menu, and then click on **Unpin from Start** in the bottom option bar.

- To change the order of a pinned item, drag the program icon to a new position in the list.

Managing Files and Folders

In Windows 8, Microsoft has renamed Windows Explorer to File Explorer, and added in a tool, the Ribbon, from MS Office to help make new features accessible. File Explorer is where you can access all the content you have stored on your computer and manipulate it. You can copy it, move it, rename it, or delete it and so on.

How to Use Windows 8 File Explorer

1. If you don't find it simple to use the new Ribbon, you have the option to put it out of sight. There's a small arrow on the far right of the menu bar, and you can use this to hide the Ribbon when you don't need it.

2. Libraries are a bit easier to manage in Windows 8 via the Ribbon. You can easily add folders to a library. Folders themselves don't move, nor do their contents, but they are displayed when a library is selected.

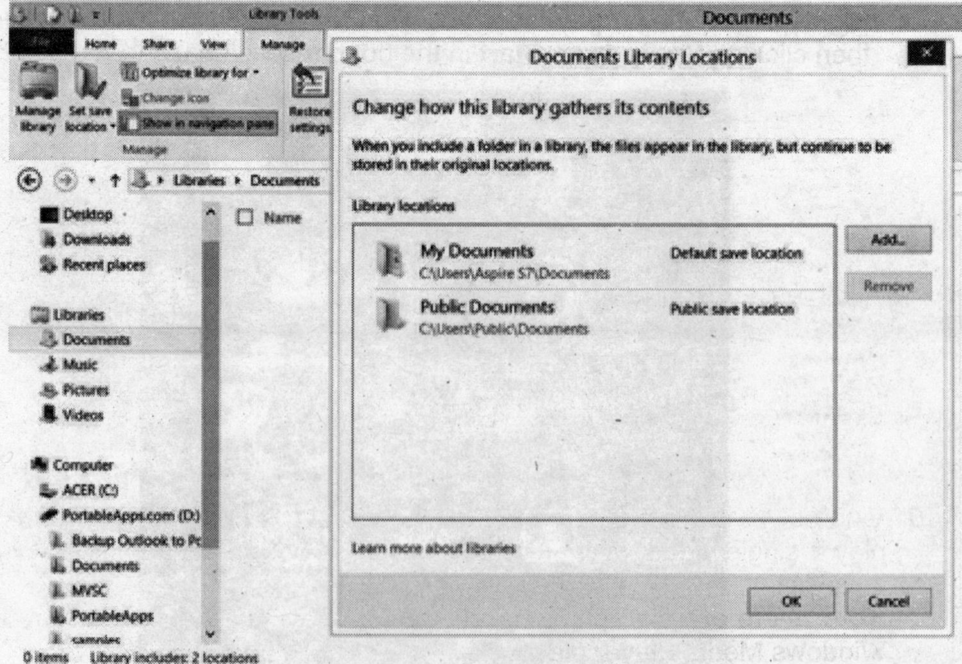

3. There are functions dedicated to music on the Windows 8 File Explorer. You can play single tunes or the contents of a folder, and even manage playlists. Note, the music options are only available when a music file is selected.

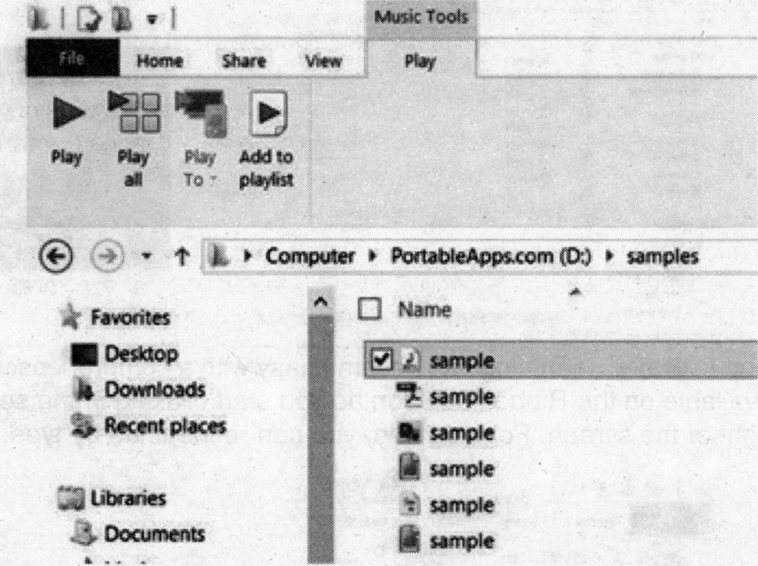

4. When you select an image file you can access a range of features from within Windows 8 File Explorer. Rotation is useful for viewing in the Preview Pane, and you can set a photo as the desktop background image or view multiple images in a slide show.

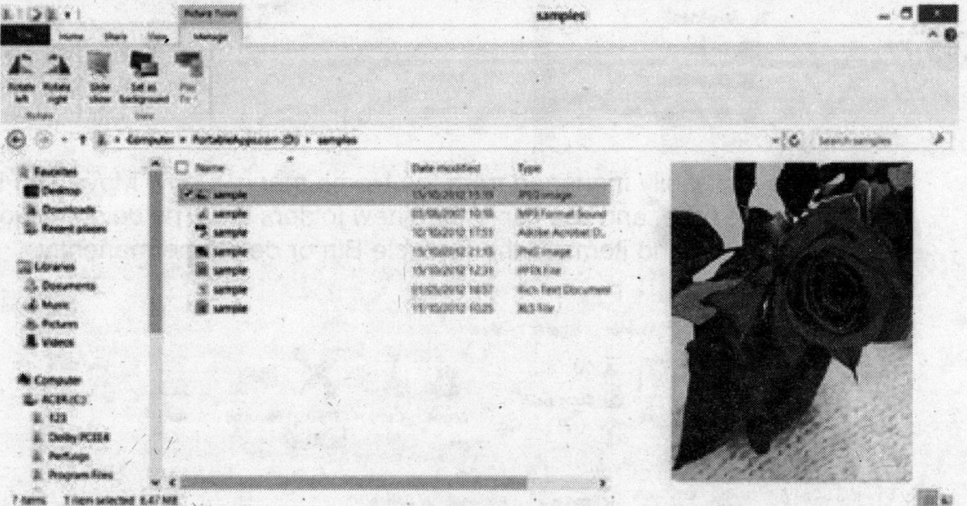

5. Video files also get their own controls in Windows 8 File Explorer. You can play a single video, play all videos in a folder, or add any particular video to a playlist.
   Note: there are also playback controls in the Preview Pane for preview or Windows Media Player playback.

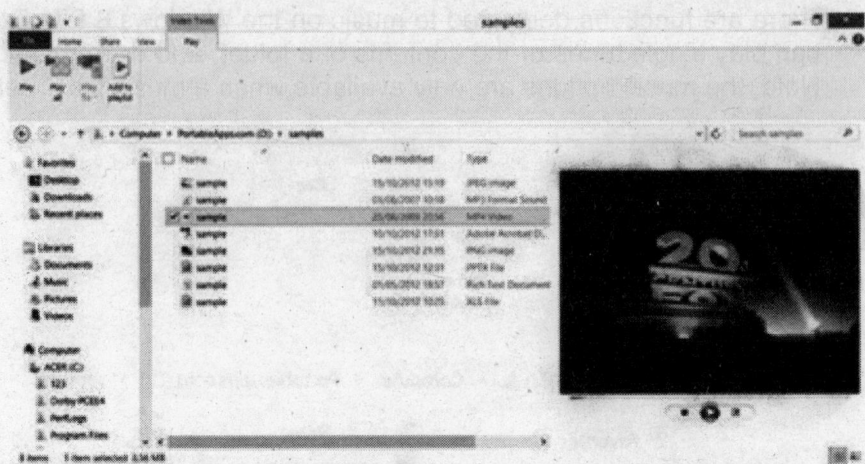

6. Sophisticated searching has become easy with a comprehensive set of options available on the Ribbon as soon as you start clicking in the search box to the right of the screen. For example, you can refine finds by type, date and size.

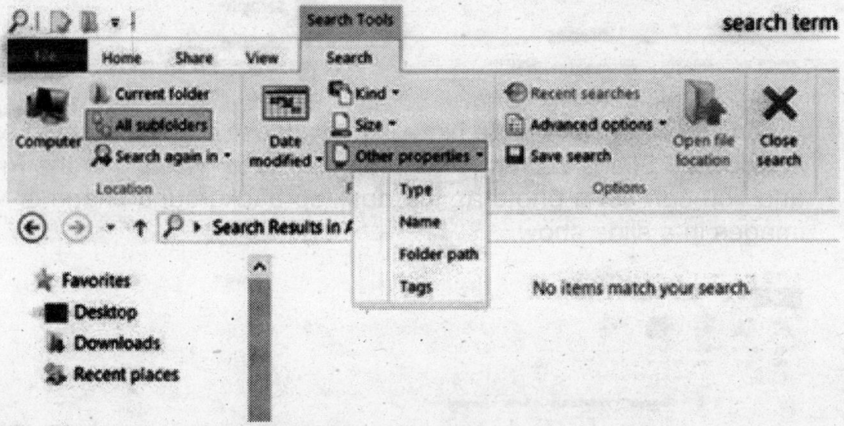

7. Folders are easily managed from the Home menu. Copy, Move and Rename options are here, and you can create new folders too. The delete option allows you to either send items to the Recycle Bin or delete permanently.

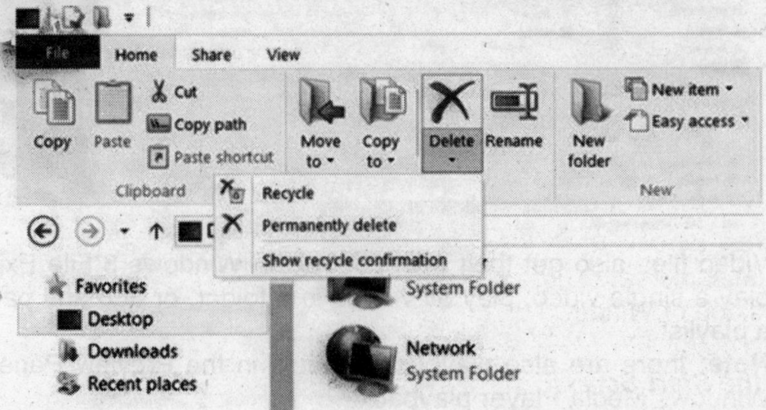

8. There are some very useful file sharing options on the Ribbon allowing you to email, print and even fax files as well as burning them to disc and sharing them wirelessly with selected people or groups.

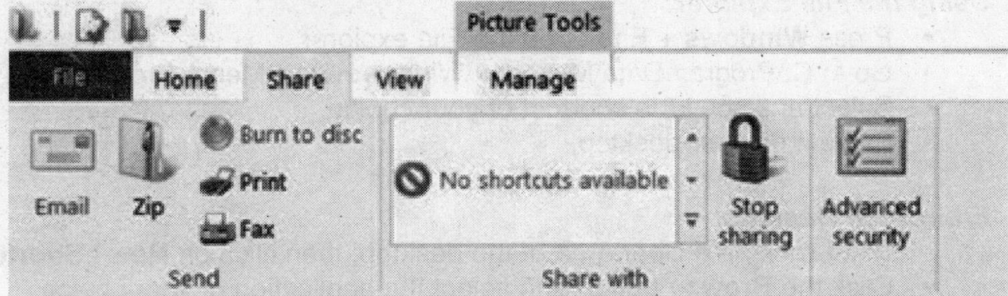

9. The Preview Pane has been joined by the 'Details Pane'. You can access these in the View Menu. Use the Details pane to see file information. What you get varies depending on the file format. For example, for videos you get frame rate, bitrate, frame size, video length and more.

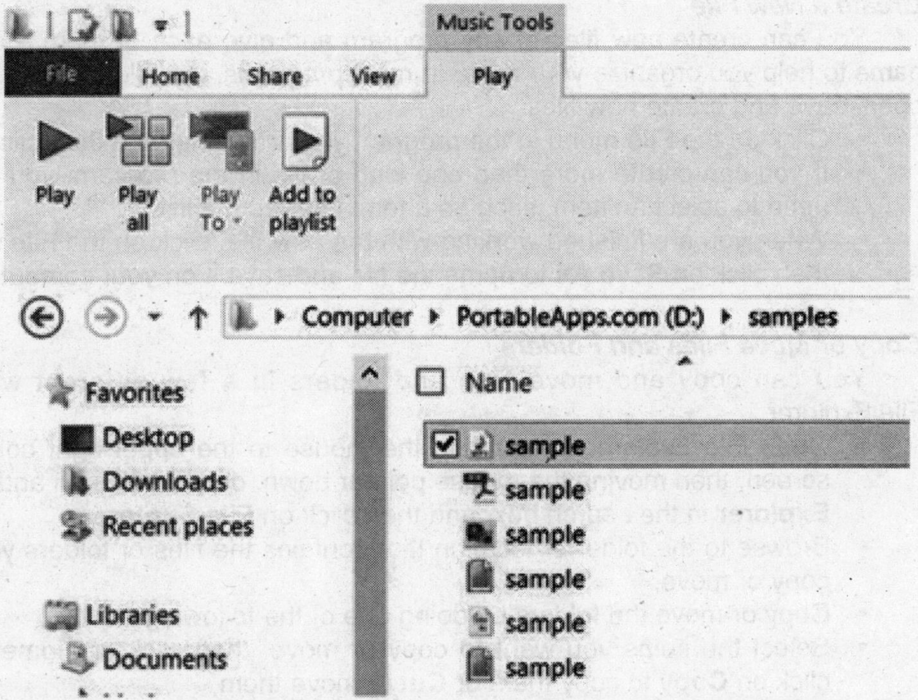

Creating Shortcut

You can create shortcuts from the Start Screen, the File Explorer or directly from the desktop of Windows 8.

From the Start Screen:

- Type the name of the program.

- Right-click on the program tile and select **Open File Location**.
- Copy/paste the program shortcut on your desktop.

Using the File Explorer:

- Press **Windows + E** to open the File explorer.
- Go to C:\ProgramData\Microsoft\Windows\Start Menu\ Programs.
- Select and copy the shortcut of your choice.
- Paste it on your desktop.

From Your Desktop:

- Right-click on a clear area of the desktop; then click on **New ! Shortcut**.
- Click the **Browse** button and select the application of your choice.
- Give it a name and click on **OK**.

Create, Copy and Rename File in Windows 8

Create a New File

You can create new files in any program and give each of them a meaningful name to help you organize your work. In most programs, the File menu is where you open, save and create new files.

- Click on the **File** menu in the program you are using, and then click on **New**.
- If you can create more than one kind of file in the program, you might also need to select an item, such as a template, from a list.
- When you are finished working with the new file, click on the **File** menu, and then click on **Save As** to name the file and save it on your computer.

Copy or Move Files and Folders

You can copy and move files and folders in a few different ways using File Explorer.

- Open File Explorer by pointing the mouse to the upper-right corner of the screen, then moving the mouse pointer down, click on Search and enter **File Explorer** in the search box, and then click on **File Explorer**.
- Browse to the folder or location that contains the files or folders you want to copy or move.
- Copy or move the folders by doing one of the following:
- Select the items you want to copy or move, then click on Home, and then click on **Copy** to copy them or **Cut** to move them.

(Clipboard options in File Explorer)

- Browse to the new place where you want the files or folders to go, click on **Home**, and then click on **Paste**.
- Open two File Explorer windows side by side, and then drag items from one window to the other. To open a new File Explorer window, click on **File**, and then click on **Open new window**.

Rename a File

Option 1:

- Open the program that was used to create the file, open the file, and then save it with a different name.

Option 2:

- Right-click on the **file** that you want to rename, and then click on **Rename**.
- Type the **new name**, and then press **Enter**.

To Restore a Deleted File

- Point to the upper-right corner of the screen with the mouse and move the mouse pointer down, and then click on **Search**. Press Enter to **restore your files** in the search box, and then click on **Restore your files with File History**.
- Enter the name of file you're looking for in the search box, or use the left and right arrows to browse through different versions of your folders and files.
- Select what you want to restore to its original location, and then click on the **Restore** button.
- If you want to restore your files to a different location than the original, press and hold or right-click on the **Restore** button, and click on **Restore To**, and then choose a new location.

Searching Files

To access File Explorer for searching files from the Start screen, perform any of these three steps:

- Type **file**, then click on the **File Explorer**.
- Move your mouse to the lower-left corner of the screen, right-click, and then choose **File Explorer** from the pop-up menu.
- Press **Win-E** (i.e. the Windows key and E key).

By default, File Explorer points to Libraries, but you can make it search more broadly by clicking your desired drive or folder in the navigation pane at left, then typing your search parameters in the **Search** field.

Empty Recycle Bin

To permanently remove files from your computer, you need to delete the files from the Recycle Bin. You can delete individual files from the Recycle Bin or empty the entire Recycle Bin at once, or you can use (Alt+Ctrl+Delete) to completely delete a file without being sent to Recycle Bin.

- Open the Recycle Bin by double-clicking on the **Recycle Bin** on the desktop.

Now, do one of the following:

- To permanently delete one file, click on it, press **Delete**, and then click on **Yes**.
- To delete all of the files, click on **Empty the Recycle Bin** on the toolbar, and then click on **Yes**.

To Open Picture Using Photos App

You can use the Photos app to view or edit photos and videos in your Pictures library and on OneDrive, and to import photos and videos in Windows 8.

There are a few different ways to open the Photos app.

If you're on Start

- Click on the Photos tile.

If you're using another app or the desktop

- With the help of your mouse, point to the lower-right corner of the screen, move the mouse pointer up, and then click on Search.
- Enter **Photos** in the search box, and then click on **Photos** in the results.

If you're using File Explorer

- Go to the photo you want to see in the Photos app.
- Right-click or press and hold it, click on **Open with**, and then click on **Photos**.

View and Import a Picture

There are a few ways to see your photos in Windows 8. The way you view and edit photos is the same in several apps, so you can use the app that is most convenient for you. The Photos and OneDrive apps show all of the photos in your Pictures library and in your OneDrive. You can also use those apps to import photos from your camera or phone.

These apps are great for looking at your photos. Photos are displayed full screen, and you can quickly switch between editing and viewing. Open these apps by clicking on their tiles on the Start screen or by searching and then opening the app.

Photos App

- You can use this app to view photos that are in your Pictures library and in your OneDrive. If you want to switch between your OneDrive folders and your Pictures library folders, click on the toggle in the upper-left corner.
- If you have photos on your camera or phone, you can use this app to import them.

OneDrive App

- You can use this app to view photos that are on your OneDrive and in your Pictures library. If you want to switch between your OneDrive folders and your Pictures library folders, click on the toggle in the upper-left corner.

- If you automatically upload photos you take with the Camera app to OneDrive, you'll find them in the **Camera roll** folder.

Camera App

- You can see photos you've taken with the Camera app in the camera roll. Swipe up from the bottom edge or right-click to see the app commands, and then click on **Camera roll**.

Edit a Picture

The Photos app is used to make automatic corrections in images in Windows 8, or you can experiment with lighting and color adjustments, effects and touch ups, plus cropping and rotating.

Here are some options to get you started:

- Let the app make the adjustments for you.
- Make basic fixes, such as remove red eye and retouch blemishes.
- Adjust the light, such as changing brightness, contrast, highlights, and shadows.
- Adjust the color, such as changing temperature, tint and saturation. You can also pick a color and use **Color Enhance** to adjust that color everywhere in the photo.
- Add effects, such as darken or lighten the corners with **Vignette** and change the focus area with **Selective focus**.
- Rotate your photos.
- Crop your photos. You can choose from a list of options or adjust the size manually.

Basic Photo Editing

These steps will get you started and help you save your changes. Once you start editing, you can experiment with different adjustments and effects.

- Open a photo.
- Right-click within the app.
- Click on **Edit**.

- Click on a category on a left, and then click on an editing option on the right.
- Make your edits.
- If you want to zoom in or out in the photo, use the + and - in the lower right or pinch and stretch fingers on the screen.
- Right-click to use other editing options, which might include:
  - ➢ Undo
  - ➢ Redo
  - ➢ View original (click and hold to see the original photo)
  - ➢ Cancel
- When you're done making changes, right-click, and then save your photo. You can save a copy or update the original photo.

Print a Picture

Windows Photo Viewer is a desktop app that provides a great way to print photos. You can print a single picture or multiple pictures at once.

To Print by Using Windows Photo Viewer

- Point to the lower-right corner of the screen with your mouse, move the mouse pointer up, and then click on Search.
- Enter **File Explorer** in the search box, and then click on **File Explorer**.
- Double-click on the **Pictures** folder.
- If the pictures you want to print are stored somewhere other than the Pictures folder, go to that place instead.
- If you want to print a single picture, right-click on the picture you want to print, and then click on **Print**.

– or –

- If you want to print more than one picture, press and hold the Ctrl key, click on each of the pictures you want to print, and then click on **Print**.
- In the **Print Pictures** dialog box, choose a printer, paper size, print quality, print style and the number of copies.

- When you're done with your selection, click on **Print**.

Creating a Restore Point

A restore point is a representation of a stored state of your computer's system files. You can use a restore point to restore your computer's system files to an earlier point in time. Restore points are automatically created by System Restore weekly and when System Restore detects the beginning of a change to your computer, such as when you install a program or a driver.

To Create a Restore Point

- Open System by clicking on the Start button, right-click on Computer, and then click on Properties.
- In the left pane, click on **System protection**.
- Click on **System Protection** tab, and then click on **Create**.
- In the System Protection dialog box, type a description, and then click on **Create**.

How to Set and Change a Screen Saver

Screen savers can help protect your monitor from wear by showing a constantly changing display when your computer is not being used.

- Open **Personalization** window.
- Right-click on any blank area on the desktop and select **Personalize** to open it.

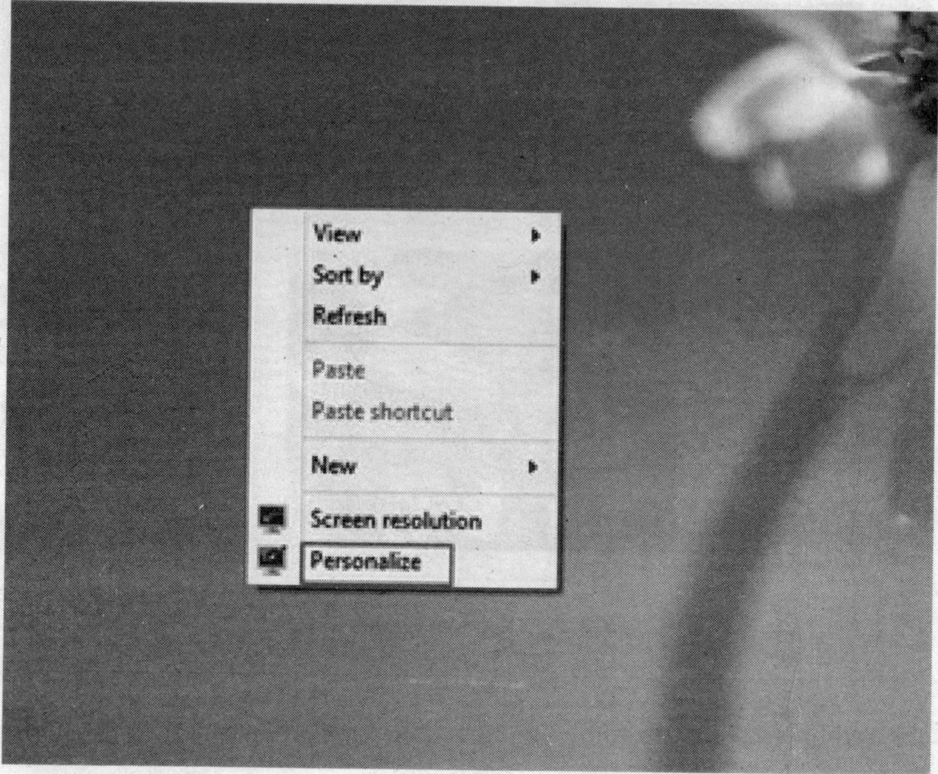

- Or, on the desktop, press **Windows+I** keys to open the Settings panel and choose **Personalization** on it.

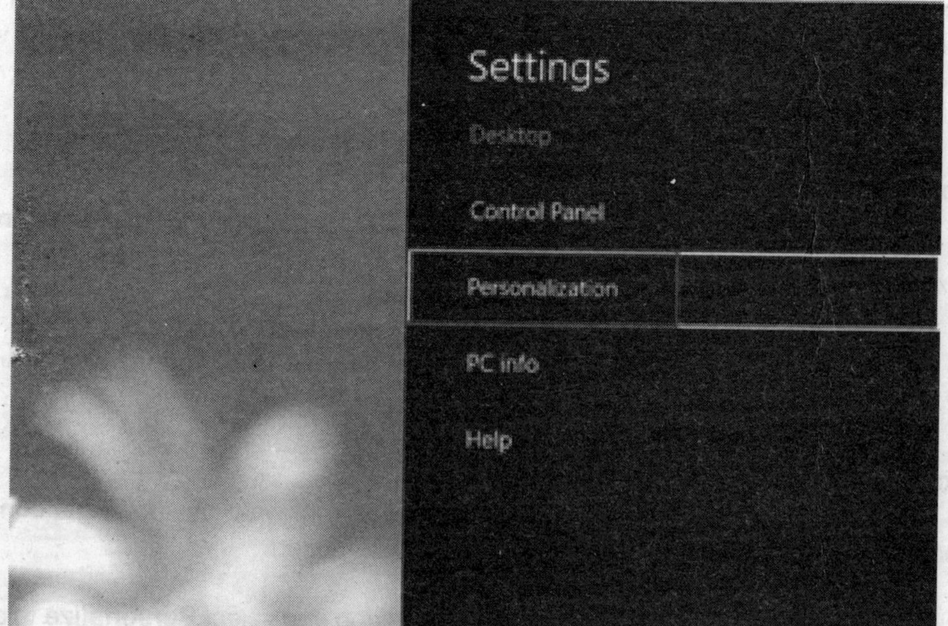

- In the Personalization window, find and click on **Screen Saver** on the bottom right corner.

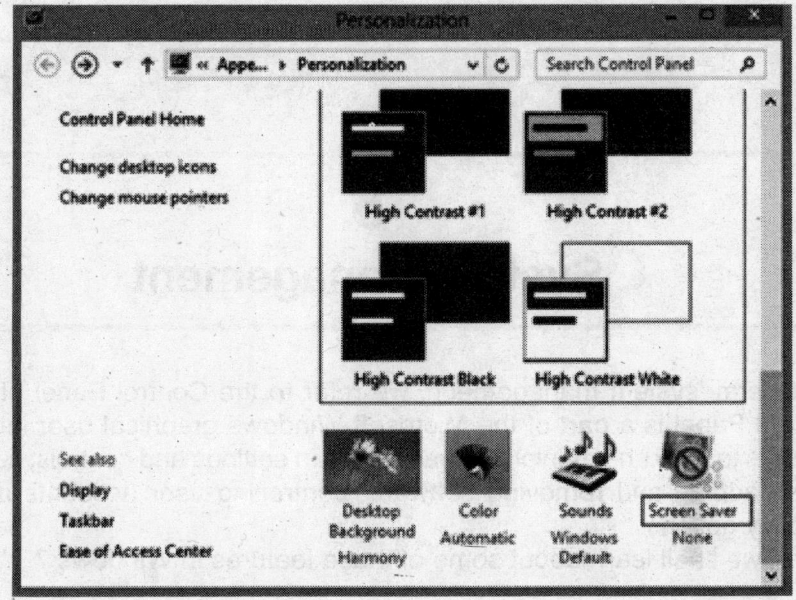

□

5
System Management

By the term 'system management', we refer to the Control Panel of a computer. Control Panel is a part of the Microsoft Windows graphical user interface which allows users to view and manipulate basic system settings and controls, such as adding hardware, adding and removing software, controlling user accounts and changing accessibility options.

Here, we shall learn about some of these features in Windows 7.

Opening the Control Panel

The Control Panel is opened by clicking on **Start ➢ Control Panel**.

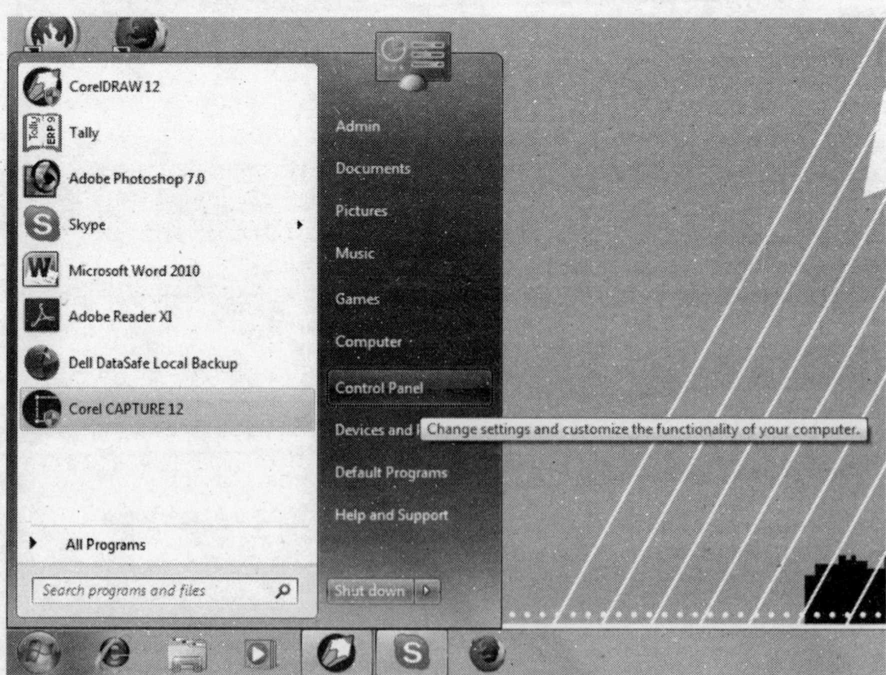

The Control Panel contains an address bar and search box like many other folders. The different commands are categorised into eight groups.

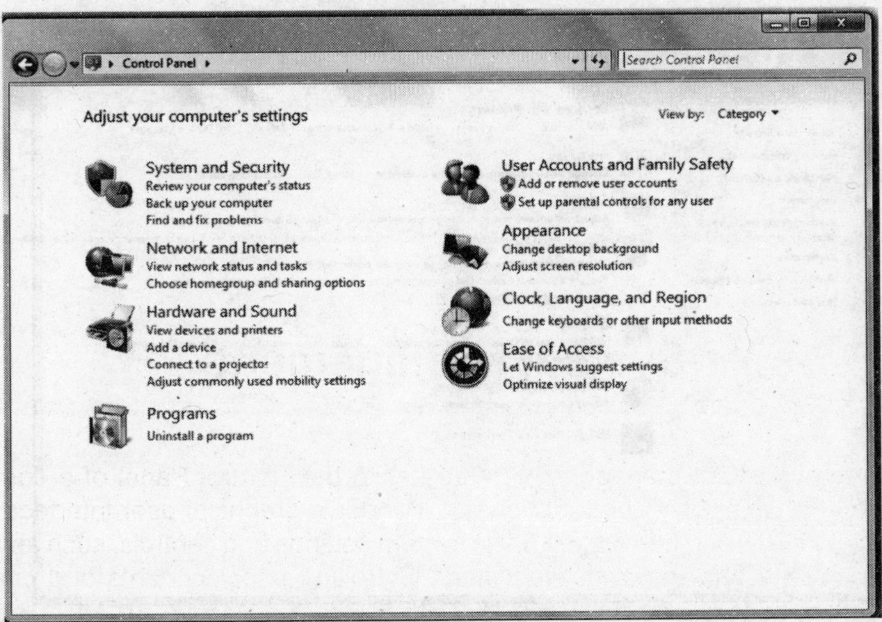

When you open the Control Panel, all of the primary categories of options are listed in green, with the most commonly used category options in blue. For example, consider the Hardware and Sound options.

Hardware and Sound
View devices and printers
Add a device

When you click on a category, a navigation pane will appear on the left side of the window. This pane shows you where you are in relation to the other categories.

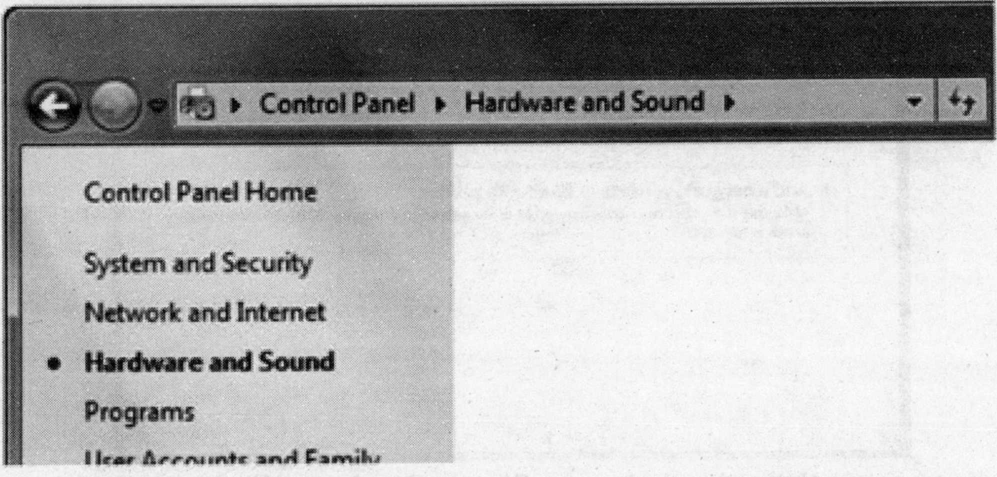

When you click on the **Hardware and Sound**, a link will open all category options, as shown below. If you click on **Add a device** link, you would be taken directly to the sub-option (in the box).

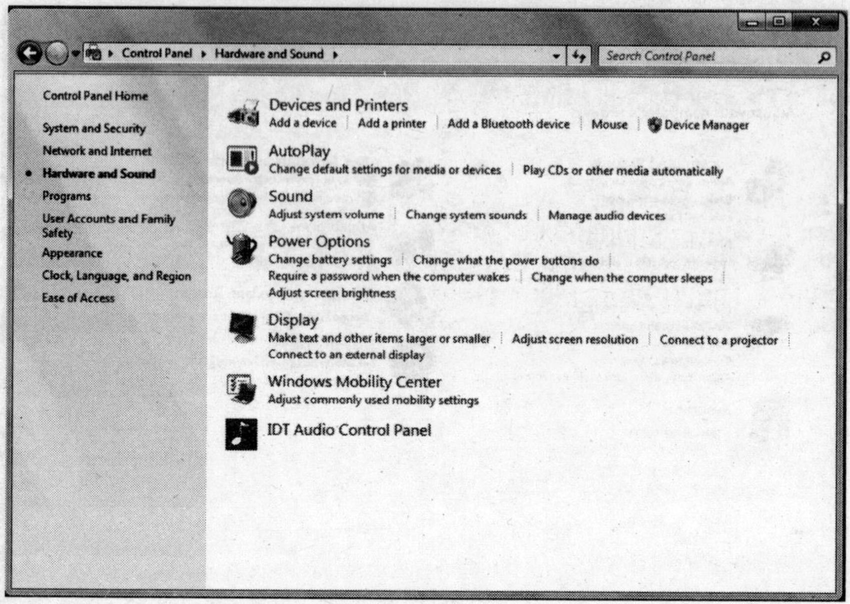

Installing a Printer

- Go to **Start ➢ Devices and Printers**
- Click on **Add a printer**.

Now you will be asked to confirm whether it is a Local printer or a Network, Wireless or Bluetooth printer.

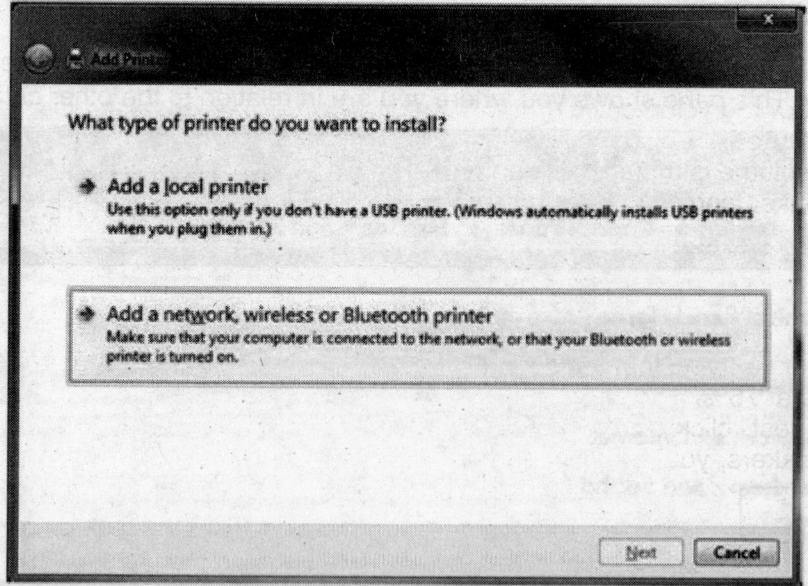

If you select **Network, wireless or Bluetooth printer**, Windows will scan your network and display a list of devices. Select the printer you want and click on **Next**. If it is not listed, then click on the **printer** that you want to install. Add the device by using its name or IP address, then press **Next**.

Windows will now begin connecting to the printer. You will be alerted once it has been successfully connected. Press **Next**. Now you will be given the opportunity to set the device as your default printer, and **print a test page**. Press **Finish** to complete the action.

Installing a Media Device

- Click on **Start** and then click on **Control Panel**.
- Click on **Hardware and Sound**. Under **Sound**, click on **Adjust system volume**. The **Volume Mixer window** opens.

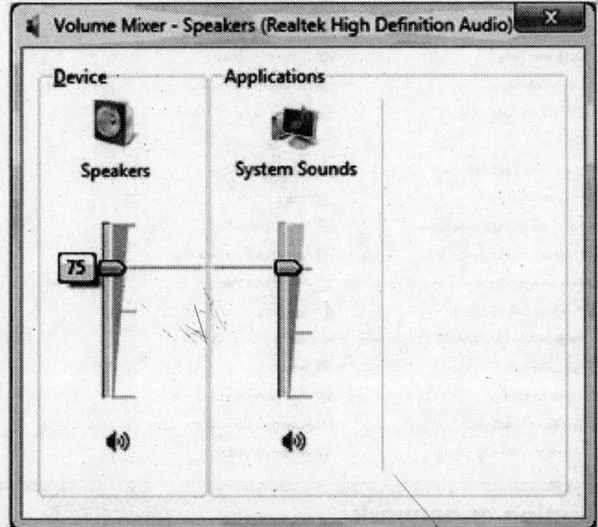

- Check that the volume is not muted by looking at the square Mute buttons below the volume slider. If the button displays a small **red circle**, the volume is **muted.**

If the volume is muted, click on the **Mute button** to enable sound. The red circle on the speaker icon disappears when sound is no longer muted.

- After verifying that the sound is not muted, drag the **volume adjuster up** until it is at 75%.
- To test, click on the **volume slider** bar. If you hear a ding sound from all speakers, you are finished troubleshooting.

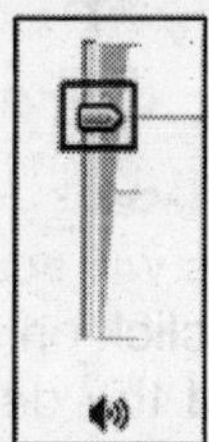

If you still do not hear any sound, set your default speakers and test them.

Configuring a Modem

- Click on **Start** and then on the **Control Panel**.
- In the Control Panel window, select **Network and Sharing Center**.

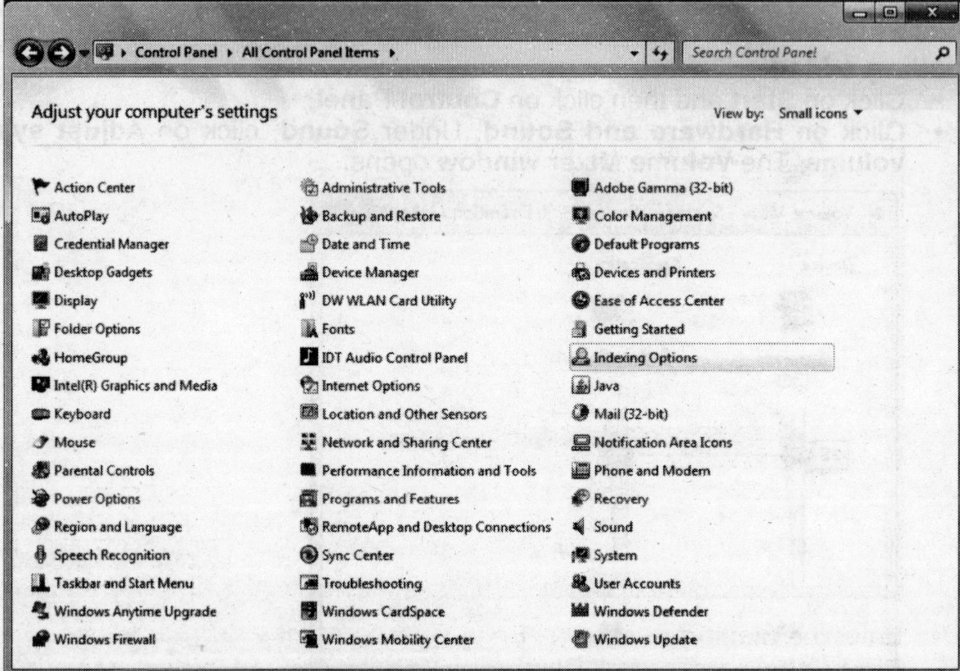

- Select **Set up a connection** or **network**.

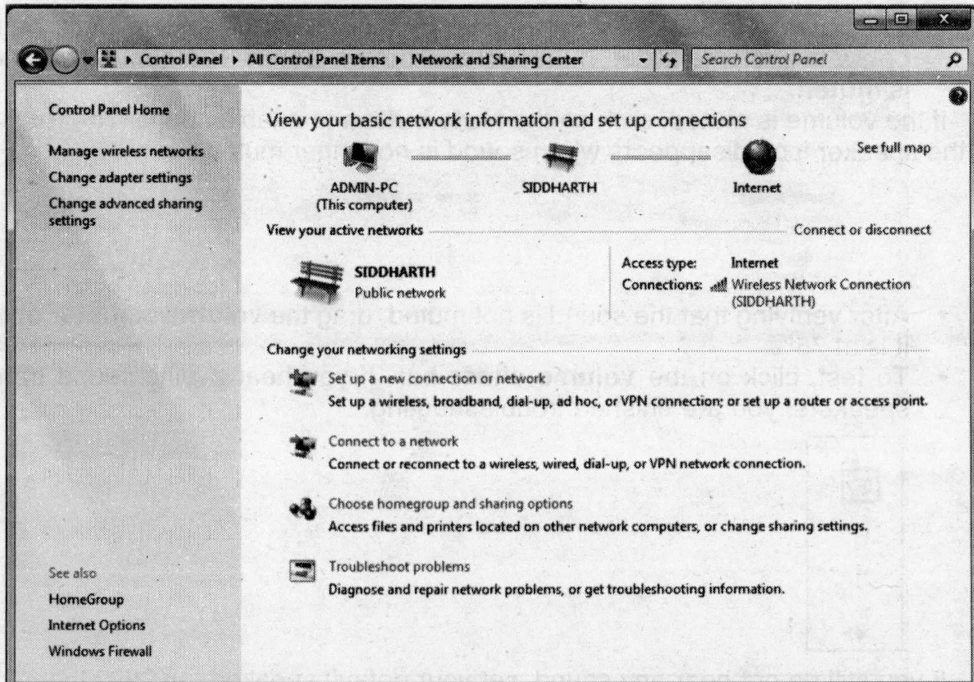

- Highlight **Set up a dial-up connection** and select **Next**.

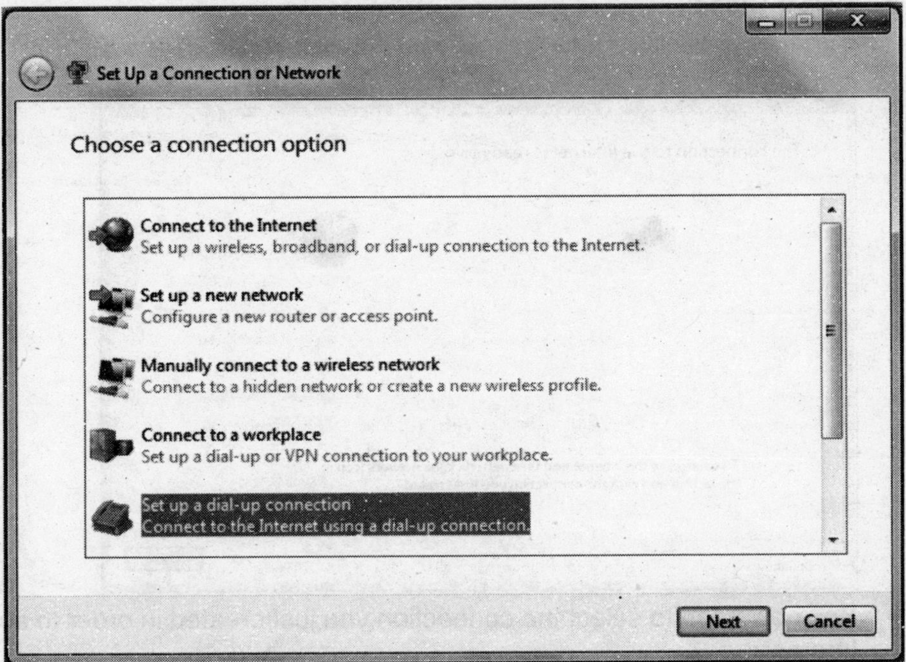

- Enter the **dialling number** ➢ Enter your **username** and **password** ➢ Check **Show characters and Remember password** ➢ Enter a **name for the connection.**
- Then click on Connect.

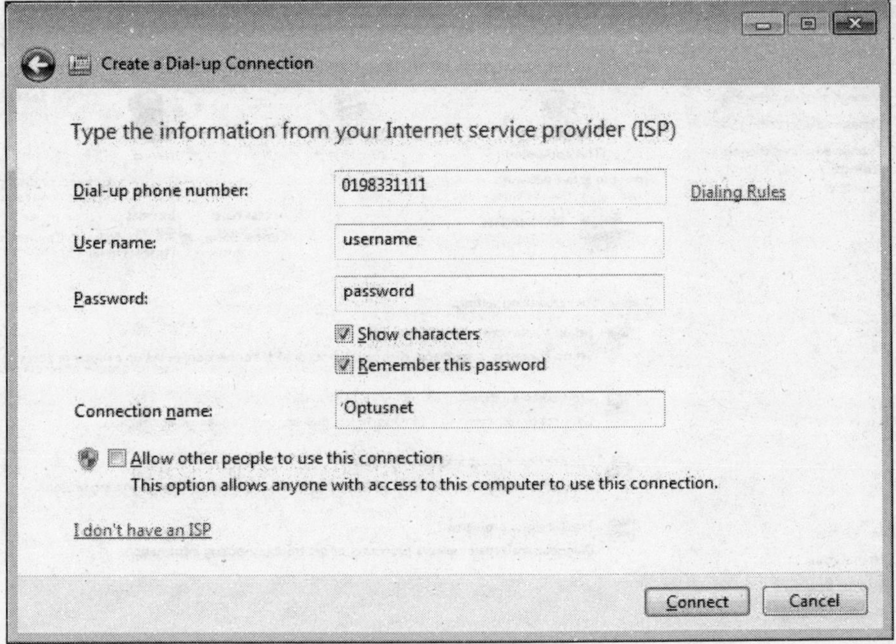

- The connection to the Internet is ready to use.
- Select **Close**.

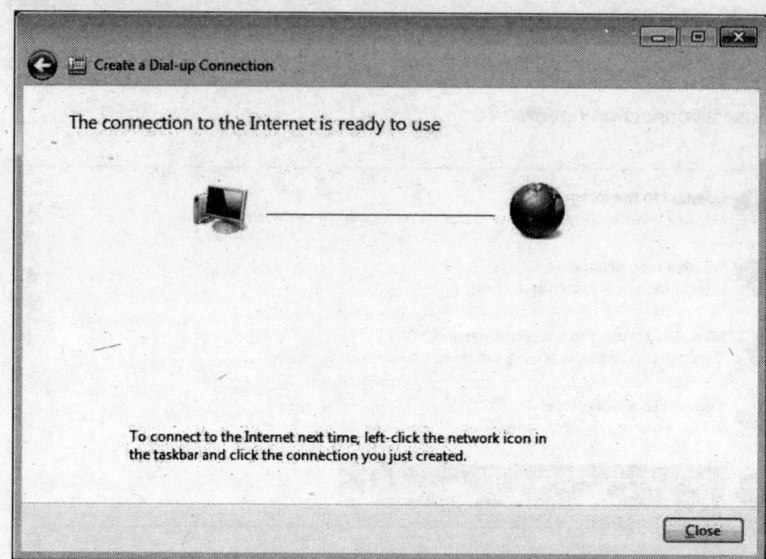

- You now need to select the connection you just created in order to access the Internet.
- Click on **Start Menu** ➢ Select **Control Panel**.
- In the Control Panel window, select **Network and Sharing Center Panel**.
- Select **Connect to a network**.

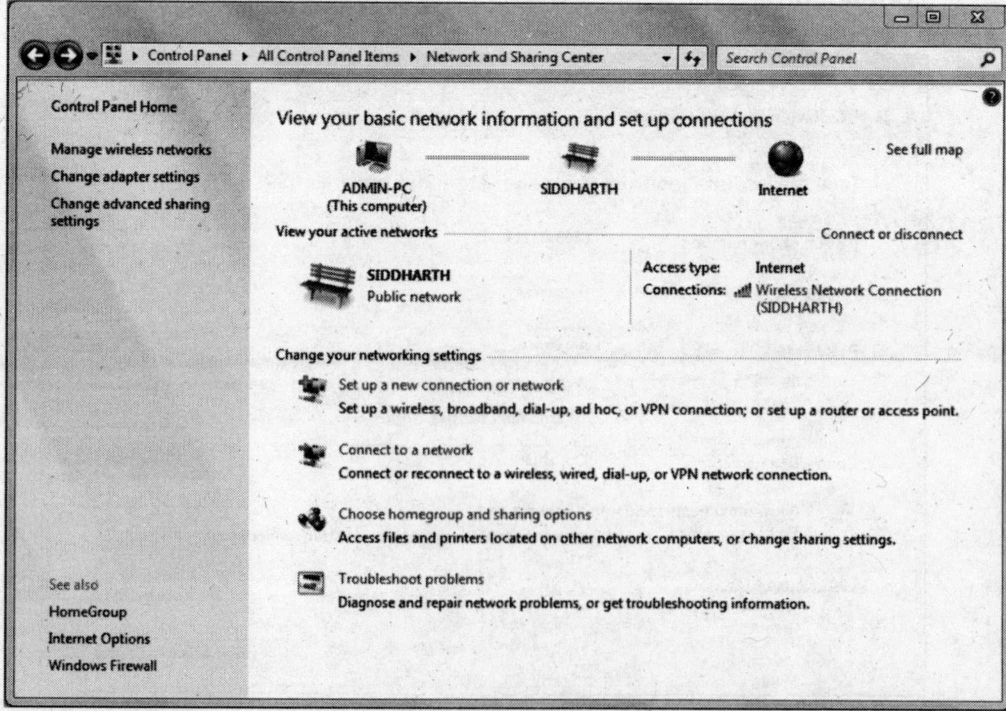

- The **Connect to a network item** will display all connection types ➢ Highlight the **Airtel Internet** option ➢ Click on the **Connect** button.

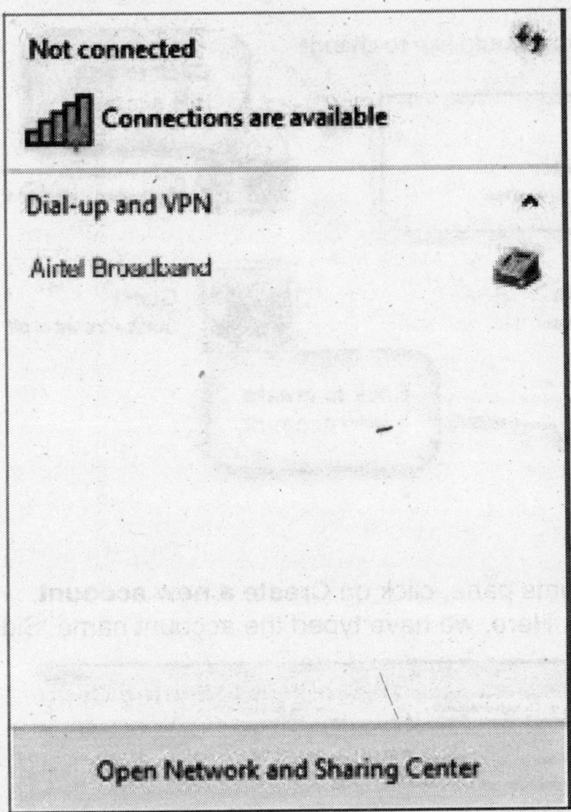

Your connection is complete. You should now configure your modem and connect to the Airtel Broadband service.

Controlling User Accounts

- Go to the **Control Panel** from the **Start** menu.
- Click on **Add or remove user accounts.**

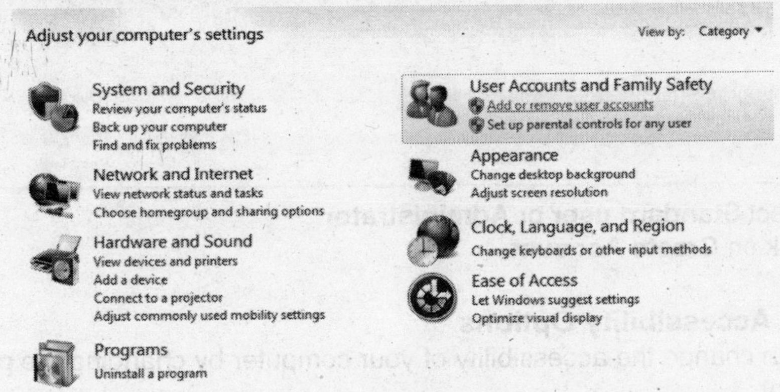

- The **Manage Accounts** pane will appear. You will see all the user accounts here, and you can add more accounts or manage existing ones.

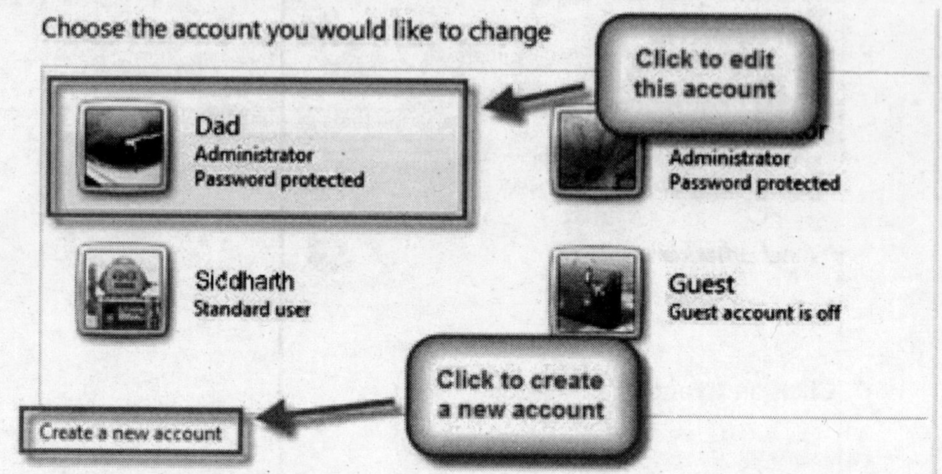

To Create a New Account

- From the Manage Accounts pane, click on **Create a new account.**
- Type an **account name**. Here, we have typed the account name 'Siddharth'.

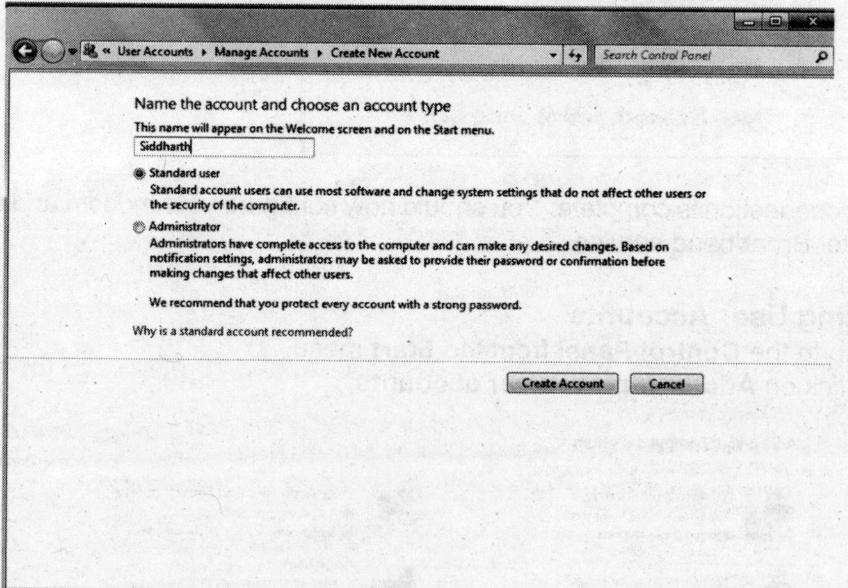

- Select **Standard user** or **Administrator**.
- Click on **Create Account**.

Changing Accessibility Options

You can change the accessibility of your computer by changing the password of your account.

To Create a Password

- From the Manage Accounts pane, click on the **account name** or **picture**.

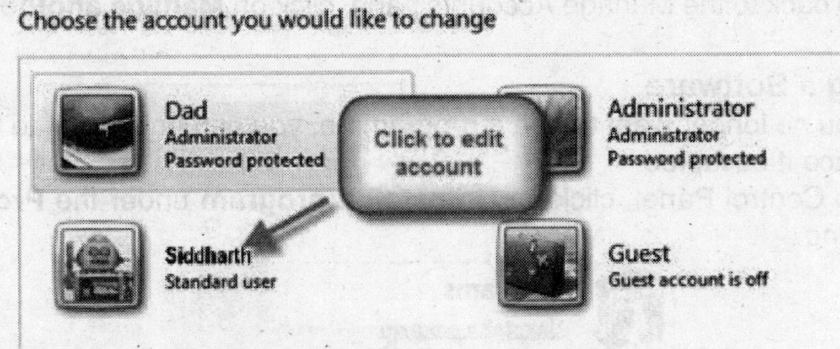

- Click on **Create a password.**

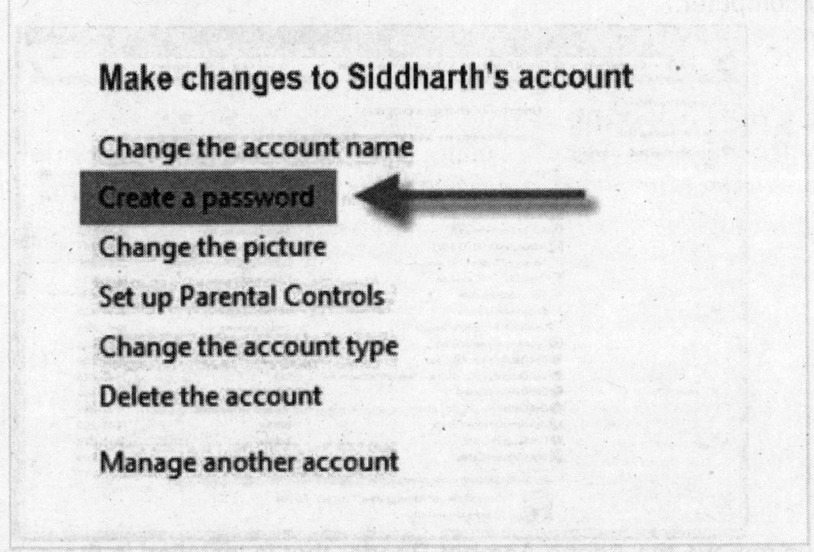

- Type a **password** in the **New password field**, and retype it in the **Confirm new password** field.

You are creating a password for Will Jr.

If you do this, Siddharth will lose all EFS-encrypted files, personal certificates and stored passwords for Web sites or network resources.

To avoid losing data in the future, ask Will Jr to make a password reset floppy disk.

New password

Confirm new password

If the password contains capital letters, they must be typed the same way every time.

How to create a strong password

Type a password hint

The password hint will be visible to everyone who uses this computer.

What is a password hint?

Create password | Cancel

- If you want, you can type a **password hint** to help you remember your password.
- Click on **Create password.**
- To go back to the Manage Accounts pane, click on **Manage another account**.

Uninstalling a Software

When you no longer want to use a programme, you can uninstall it to free up the hard disk space it occupied.

- In the Control Panel, click on **Uninstall a program** under the **Programmes** heading.

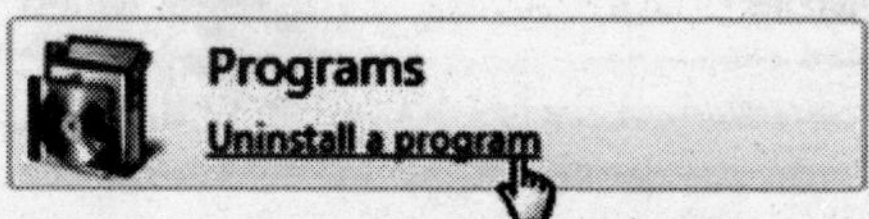

- This will open a new window that lists all programmes installed on your computer.

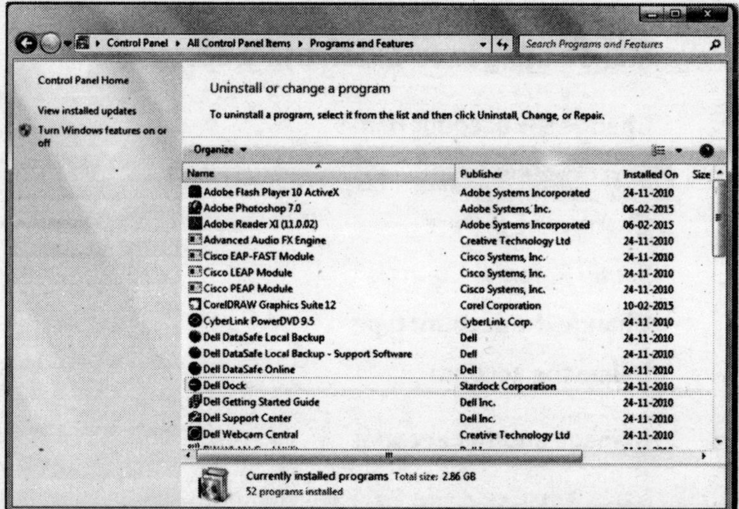

Let us remove the Adobe Acrobat Reader that is installed in the computer.

- Click on the **programme name** and then click on the **Uninstall** command.

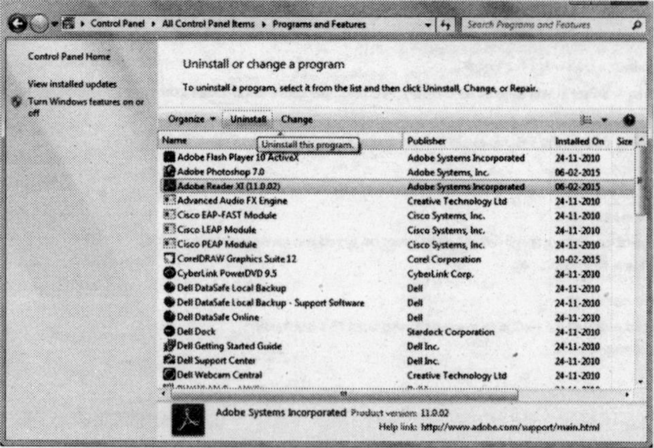

- You will be prompted to confirm your choice; click on **Yes** to continue.

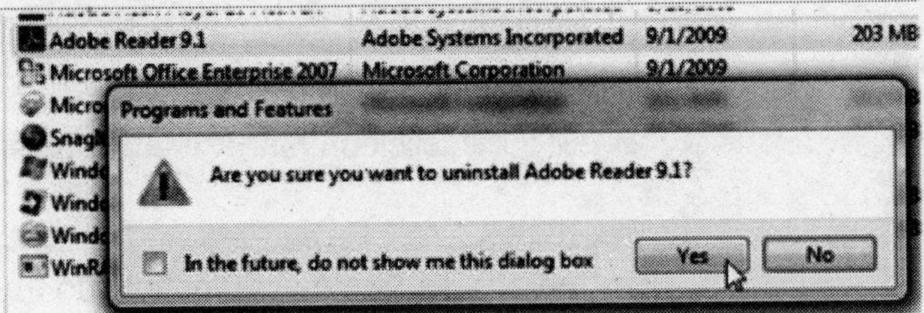

- Windows will compile a list of files and settings that will need to be removed and then uninstall the programme.

□

6

System Tools and Maintenance

Windows 7 comes with a bunch of built-in system computer maintenance tools that helps you to maintain your computer and keep it running smoothly.

The System and Maintenance area of the Control Panel in Windows 7 houses many programmes and utilities that you can use to configure Windows. Let us discuss some of them.

Disk Cleaner

The disk cleaner is a great Windows tool which performs disk clean-up operation. It basically finds and removes the temporary files, also empties the Recycle Bin and detects and removes the files that are no longer needed.

You can launch it from **Start** ➢ **All Programs** ➢ **Accessories** ➢ **System Tools** ➢ **Disk Clean-up**

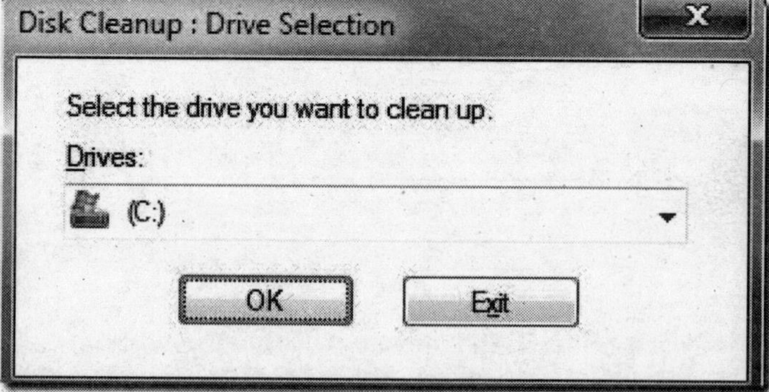

Choose the disk on which you wish to perform the clean-up operation from the Drives option and then click on the **OK** button to initiate the disk clean-up process.

Disk Defragmenter

Disk defragmenter lets you safely terminate the defrag process at any time and can also defrag multiple volumes at the same time.

Disk Defragmenter can be launched from **Start** ➢ **All Programs** ➢ **Accessories** ➢ **System Tools** ➢ **Disk Defragmenter**.

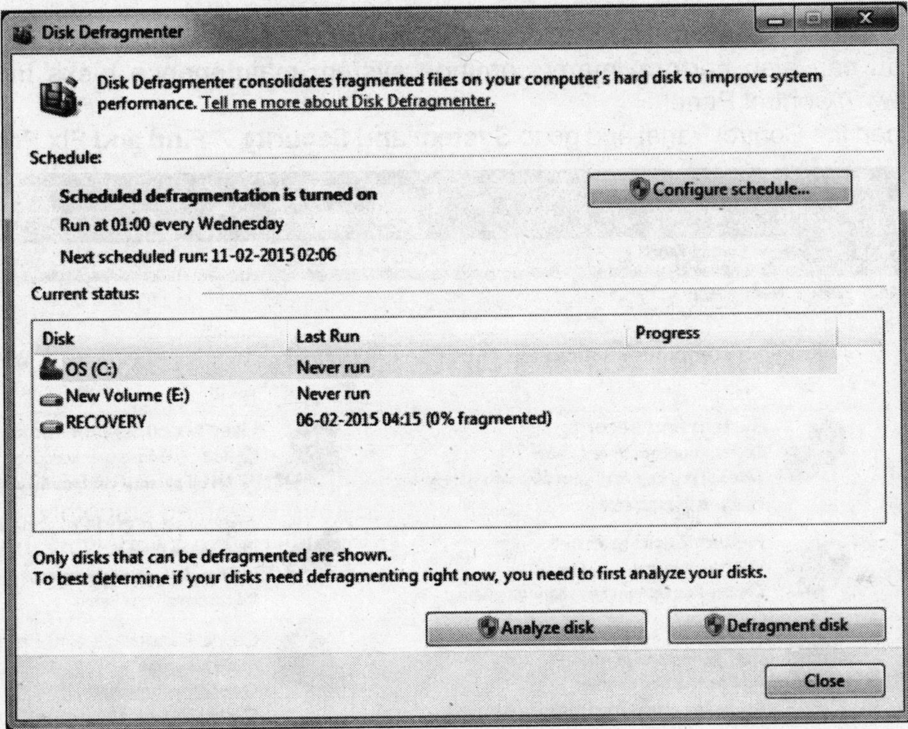

System Restore

System Restore allows you to restore system files, registry keys, installed programmes, etc. to a previous state in case of any disaster.

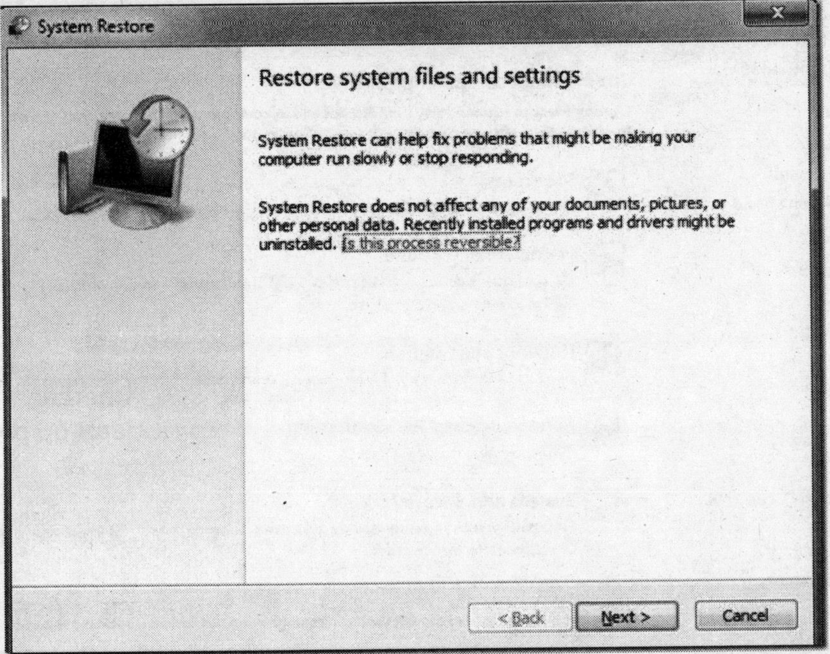

Control Panel System Maintenance Tool

You can also perform many common system maintenance tasks from the Windows 7 Control Panel.

Open the Control Panel and go to **System and Security ➢ Find and Fix Problem.**

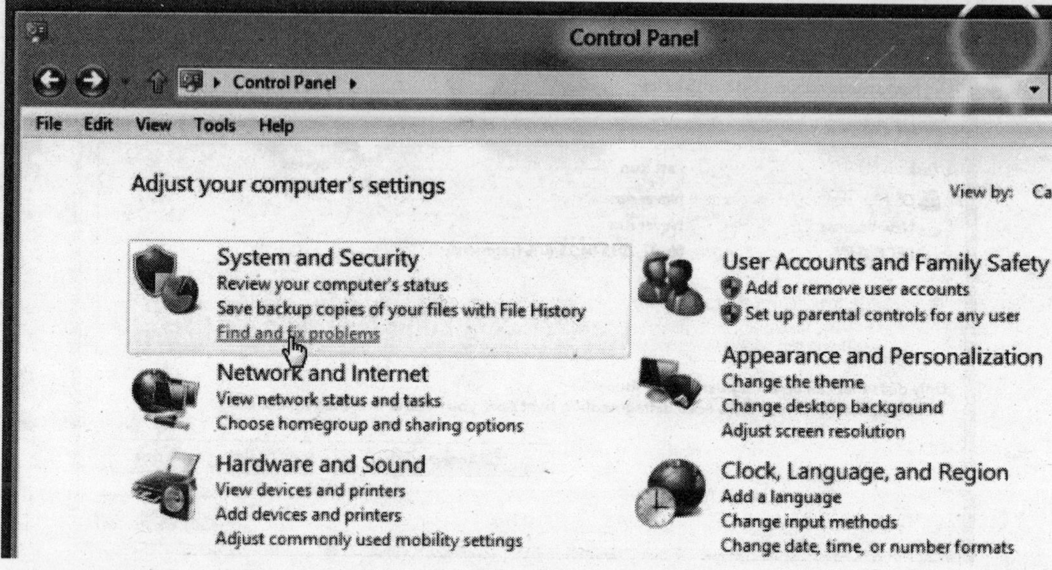

Now, the Troubleshooting option will be displayed and you can troubleshoot any problem relevant to the system, network, Internet, etc.

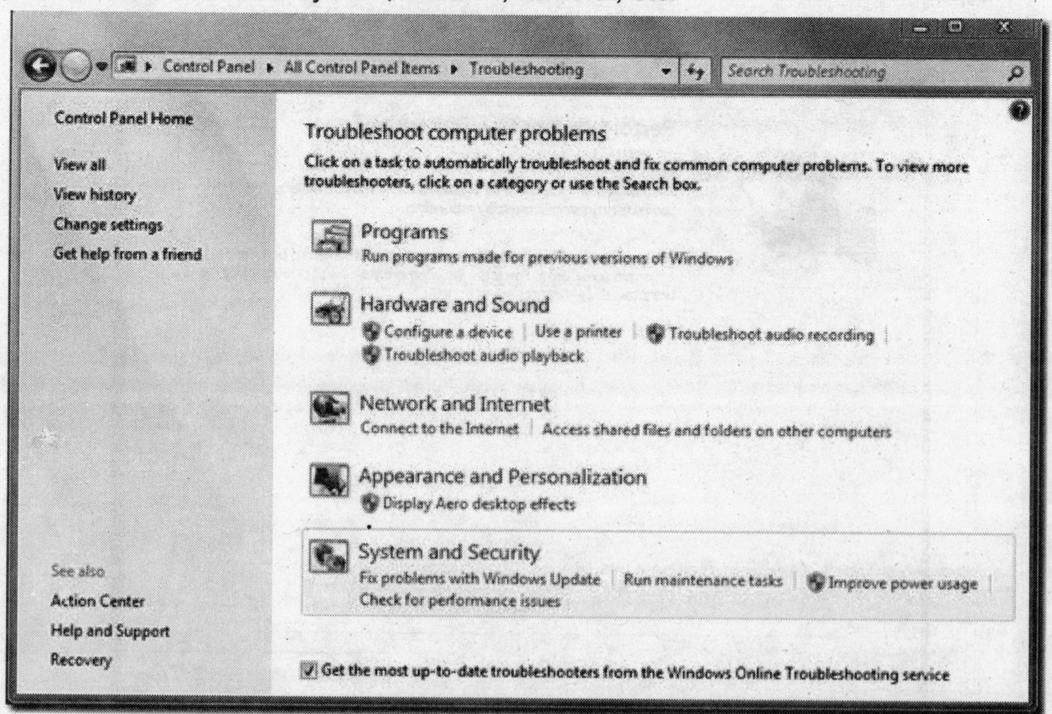

Back-up and Restore Files

To set up a back-up in Windows 7, open up **Computer** by **right-clicking** on your local drive and select **Properties**. Then click on the **Tools** tab and click on the **Back-up now...** button.

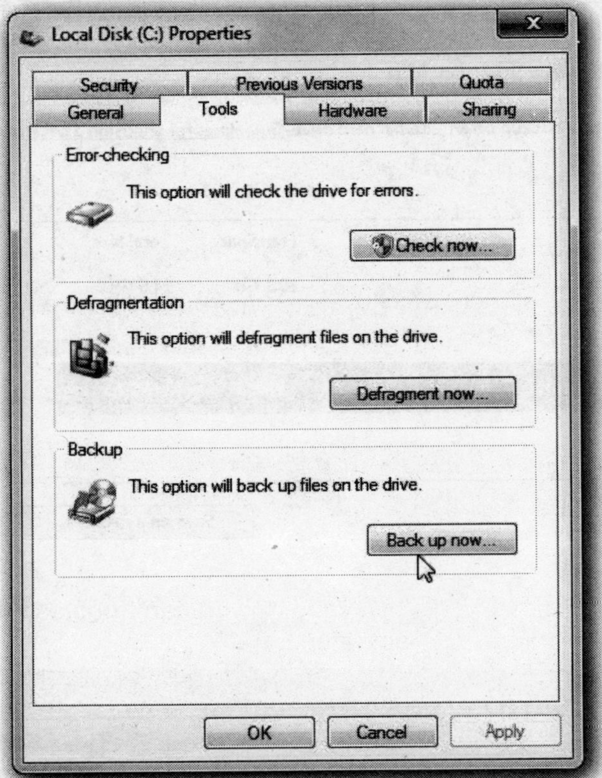

In the **Backup or restore your files** window, click on the link to set up backup.

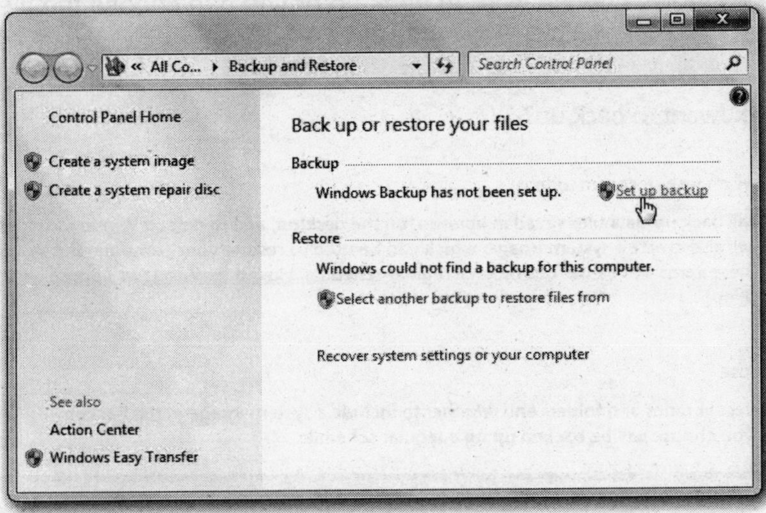

Windows will search for a suitable drive to store the back-up or you can also choose a location on your network. If you back-up to a network location, you might need the password to share.

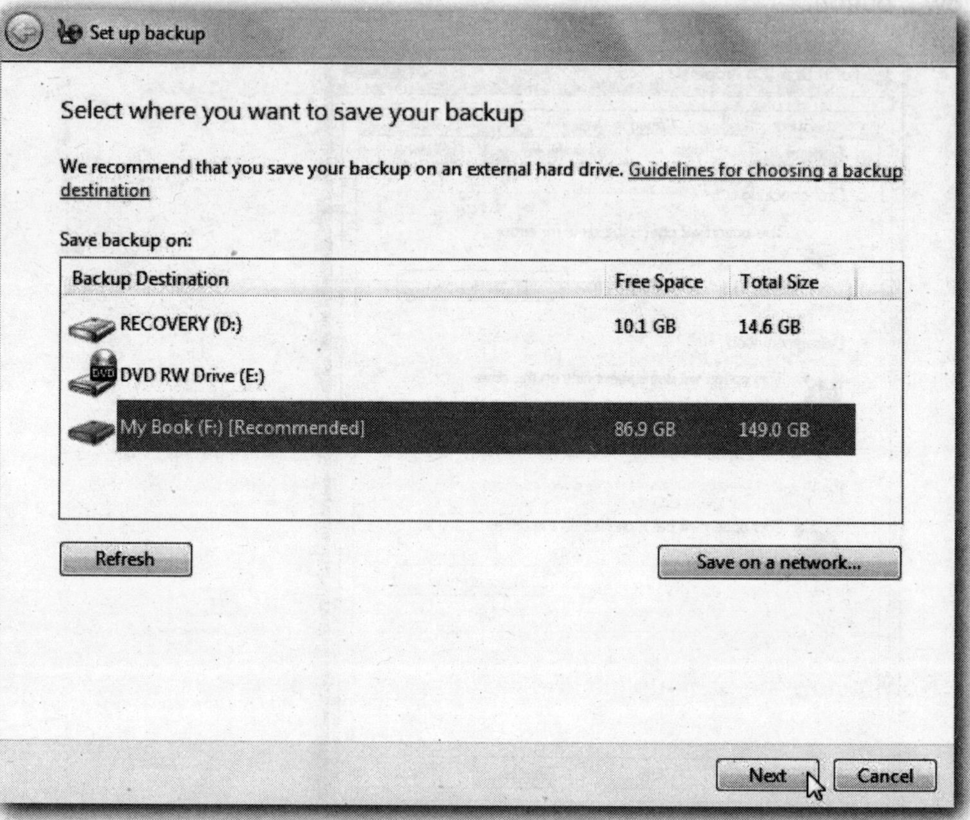

You can have Windows choose what to back-up or you can choose the files and directories.

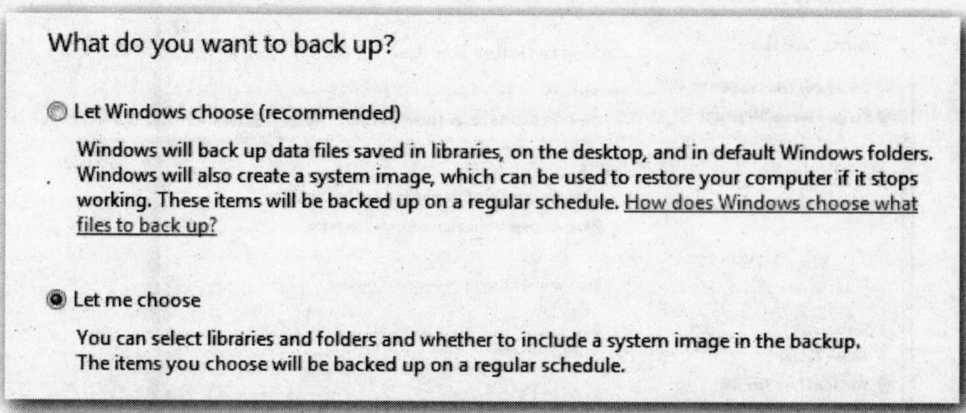

Select the files and folder to include in the back-up. Also notice you can select the option to create an image of your local drive.

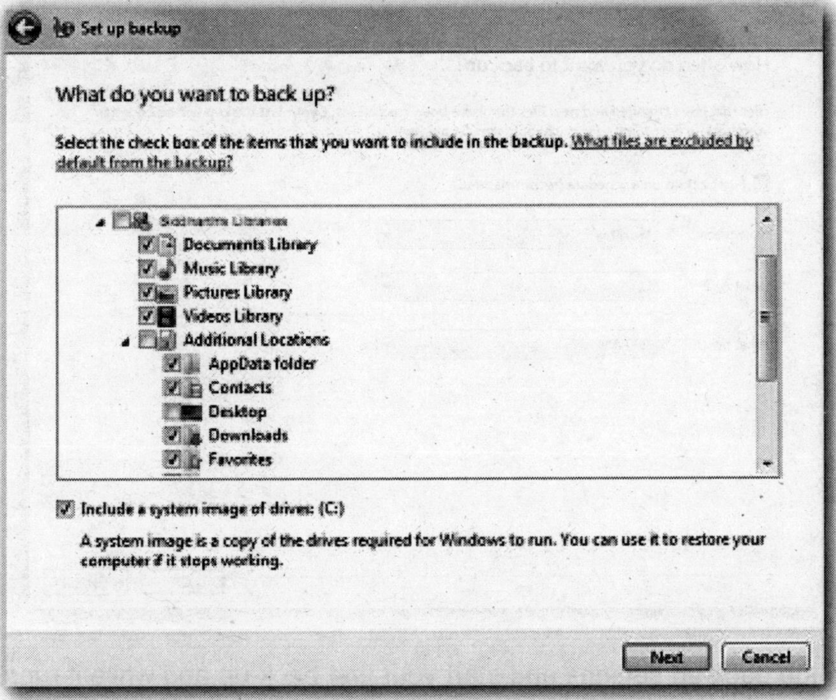

Now review the back-up job and make sure everything looks correct.

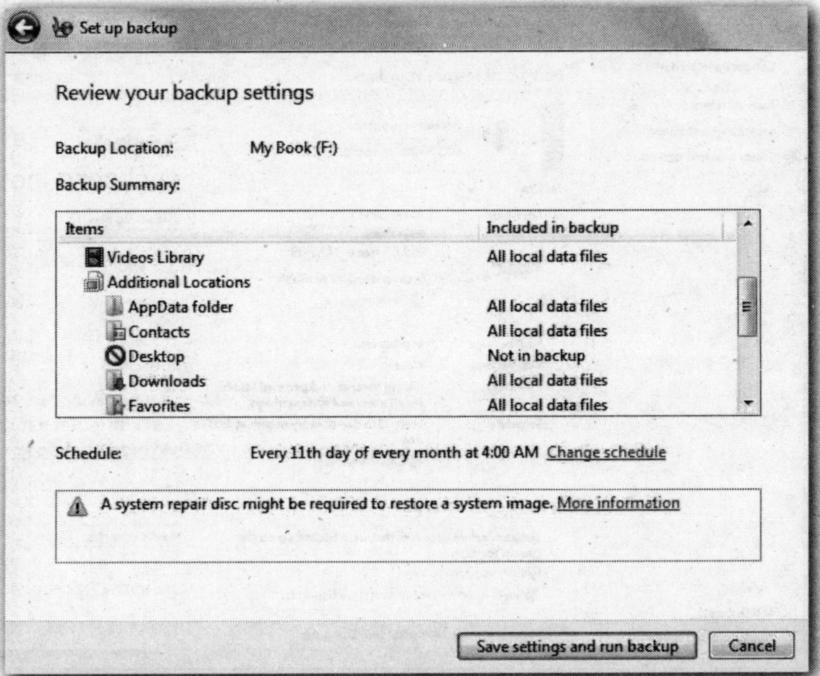

Here you can also schedule the days and times the back-up occurs.

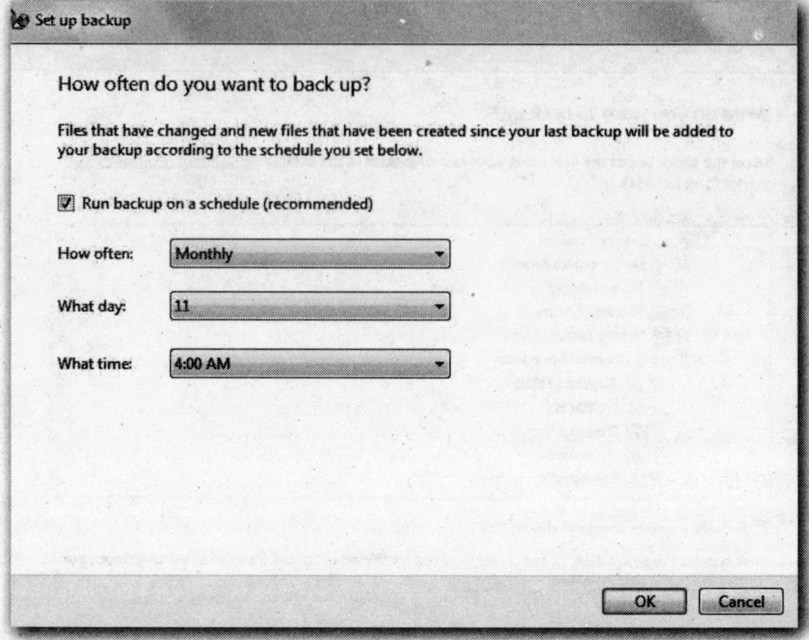

Save the back-up settings and start your first back-up and while it runs, you can monitor the progress.

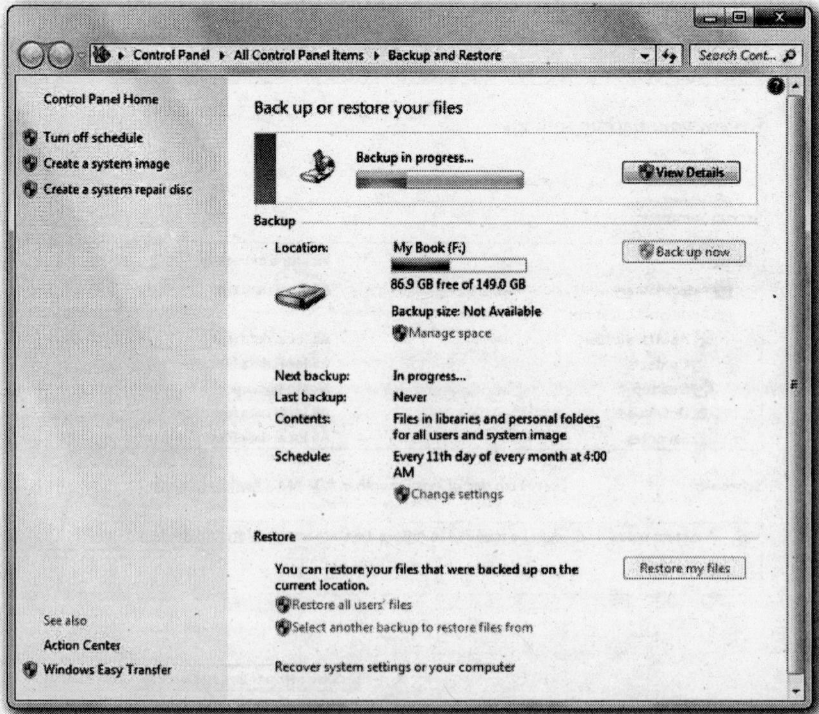

Click on the **View Details** button to see exactly what is being back-up during the process.

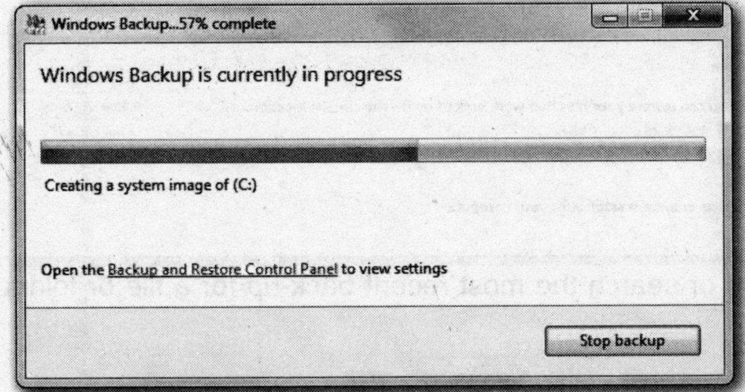

When the back-up is complete, you will see the two back-up files and image folder, if you created one.

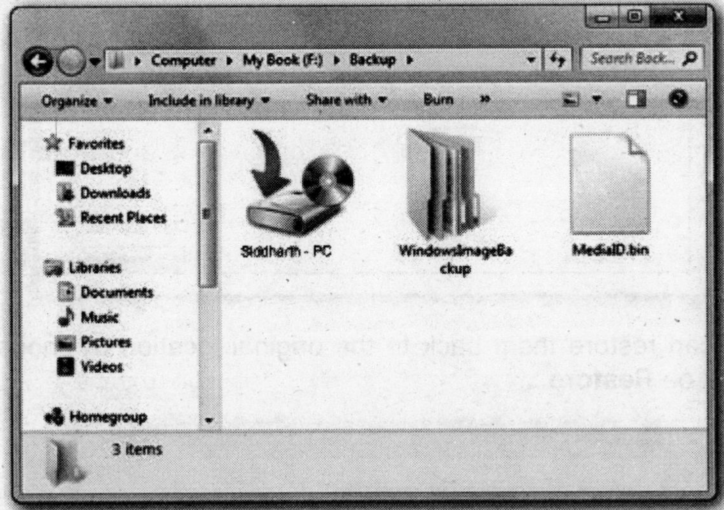

Double-click on the back-up file and restore files or manage the size of the back-up folder.

Restore Files from Back-up

If you need to go back and restore a file from a back-up, click on **Restore my files** in the **Back-up and Restore Center**.

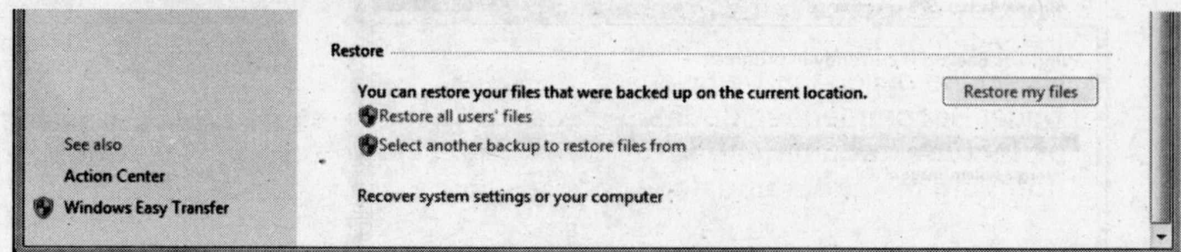

Now you can browse or search the most recent back-up for a file or folder you are missing.

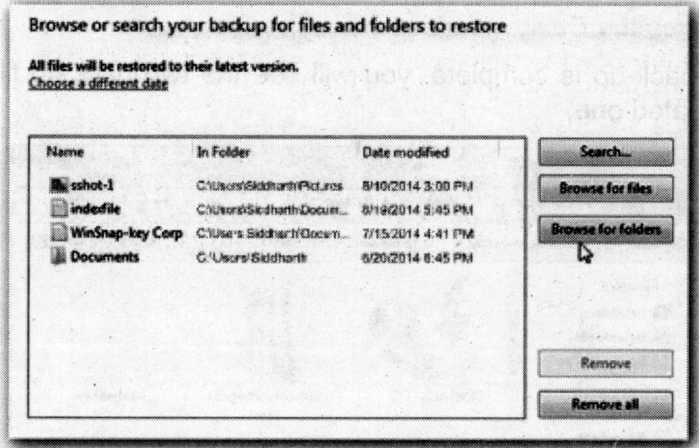

Next you can restore them back to the original location or choose a different spot. Then click on **Restore...**

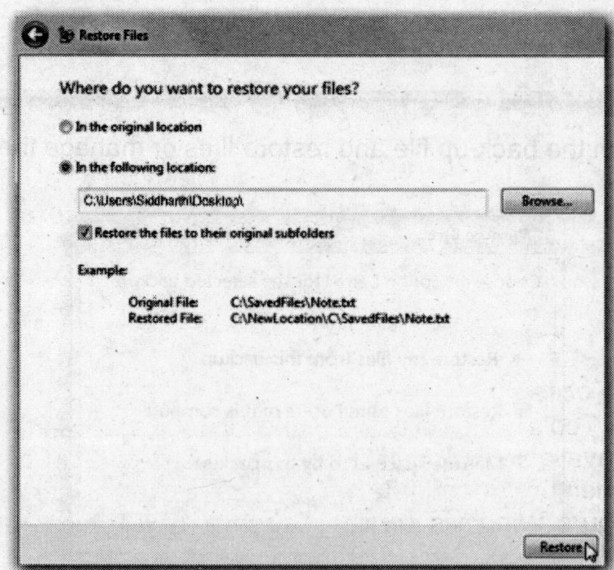

Windows Update

To turn on Automatic Updates, follow these steps:

- Click on **Start**. Then type **Windows update** in the search box. Next click on **Windows Update** in the Programmes list.
- In the left pane, click on **Change settings.**
- Select the option that you want.
- Under **Recommended updates**, select the **Give me recommended updates** or **Include recommended updates when downloading, installing or notifying me about updates** check box, and then click on **OK**.

Device Manager

Device Manager lets you check on your computer's hardware operating condition and modify or change a problem software driver.

You can open the Device Manager by the following steps:

- Click on the **Start** button.
- Then click on the **Control Panel**.
- Next click on **System and Security** ➢ under **System**, click on **Device Manager**.

If you are prompted for an administrator password or confirmation, type the password or provide confirmation.

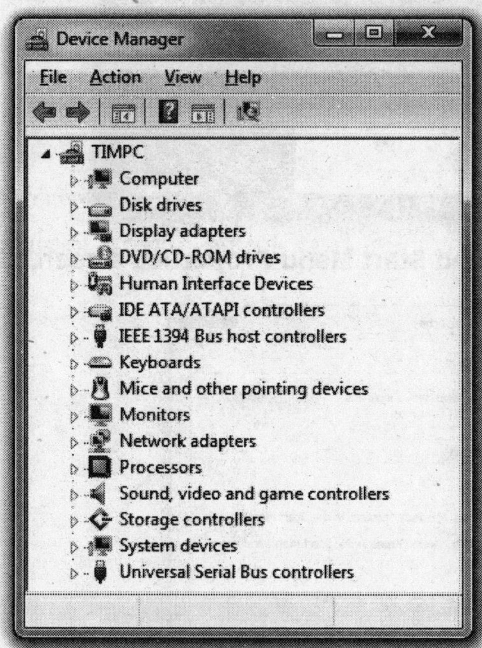

Administrative Tools

Administrative Tools is the collective name for several advanced tools in Windows. The programmes available in Administrative Tools can be used to schedule a test of your computer's memory, manage advanced aspects of users and groups, format hard drives, configure Windows services, change how the operating system starts and much more.

You need to navigate the Control Panel to access Administrative Tools.

Steps to Add Administrative Tools to the Start Menu

1. First **right-click** on the **Start Menu** and select **Properties**.

2. In the **Taskbar and Start Menu Properties** screen, click on **Customize...**

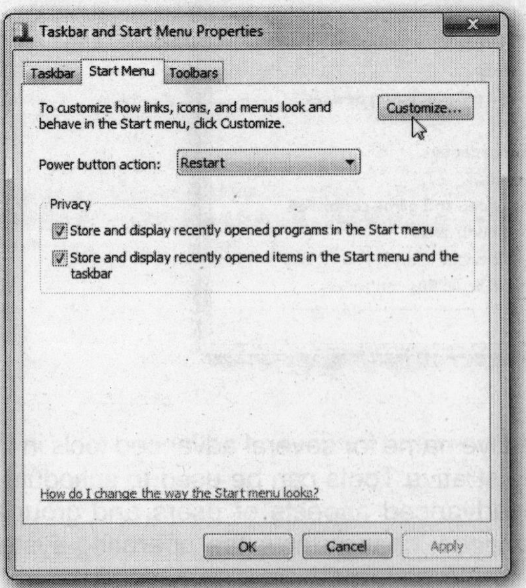

3. Scroll down System administrative tools and select **Display on the All Programs menu and the Start menu**.

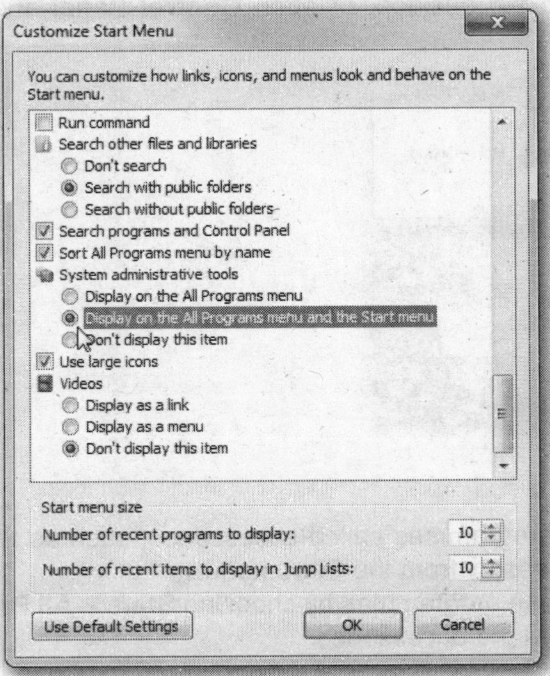

4. Click on **Ok** to accept the changes and close out of the remaining screens. Now when you click on the **Start Menu**, you will see **Administrative Tools** and can select the different settings and features contained there.

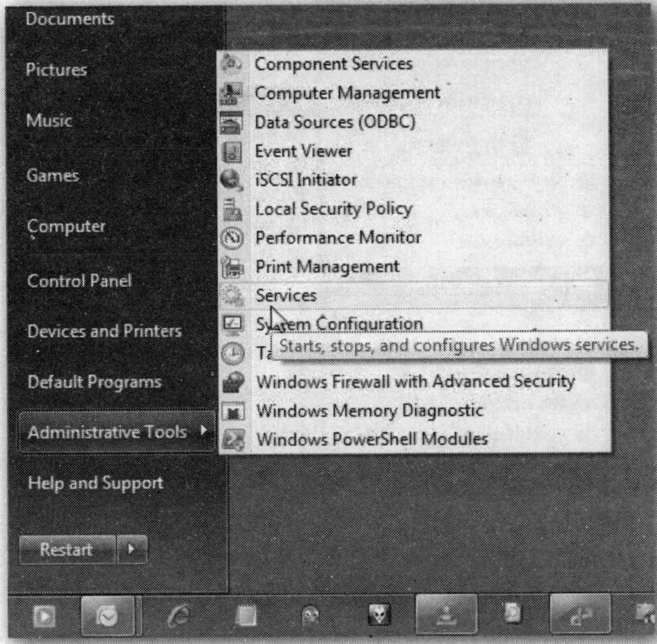

5. If you want to put a shortcut to Administrative Tools on the desktop, you can **right-click** on the **Administrative Tools** button that was just added to the **Start menu** and drag to the desktop, or open **Control Panel** and do the same thing.

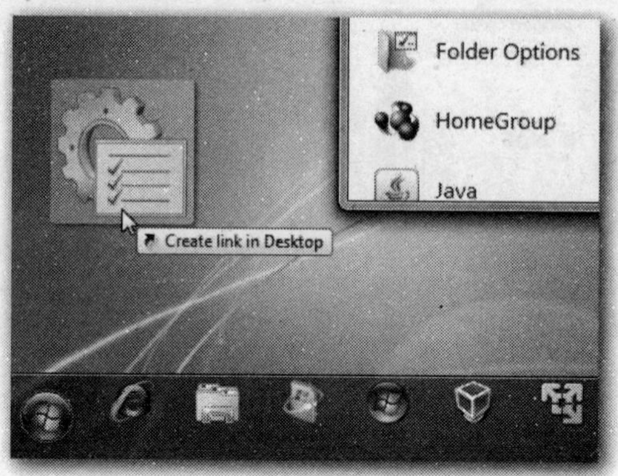

Accessories

Windows 7 includes a few programmes called accessories, such as the Clock and Paint. You can start any accessory from the Start menu.

You can also find most of these programmes by choosing **Start ➢ All Programs ➢ Accessories**, where you see all the accessories.

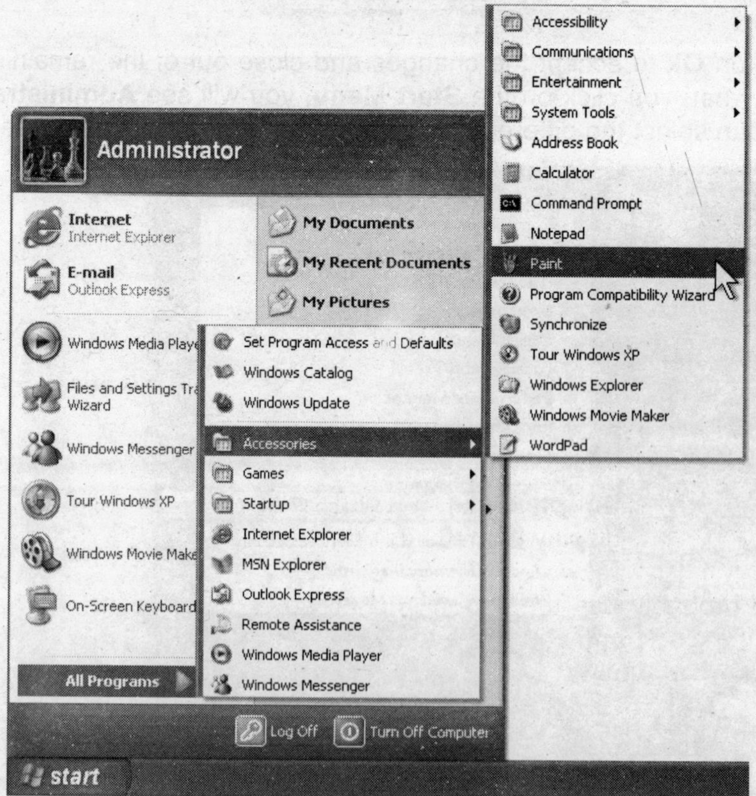

Get the time and weather with **desktop gadgets.**

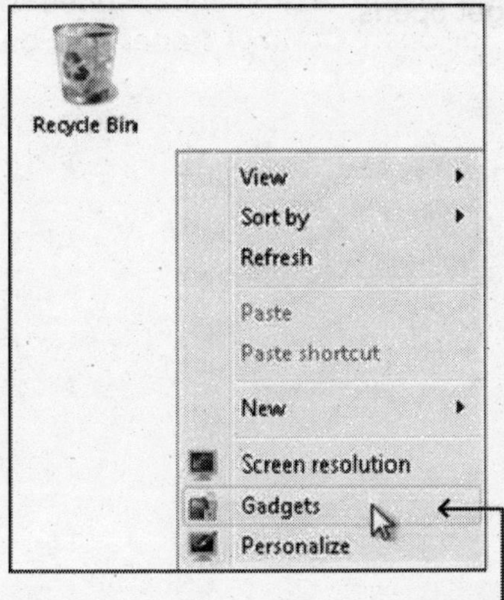

Right-click on the **desktop** and then click on **Gadgets**.

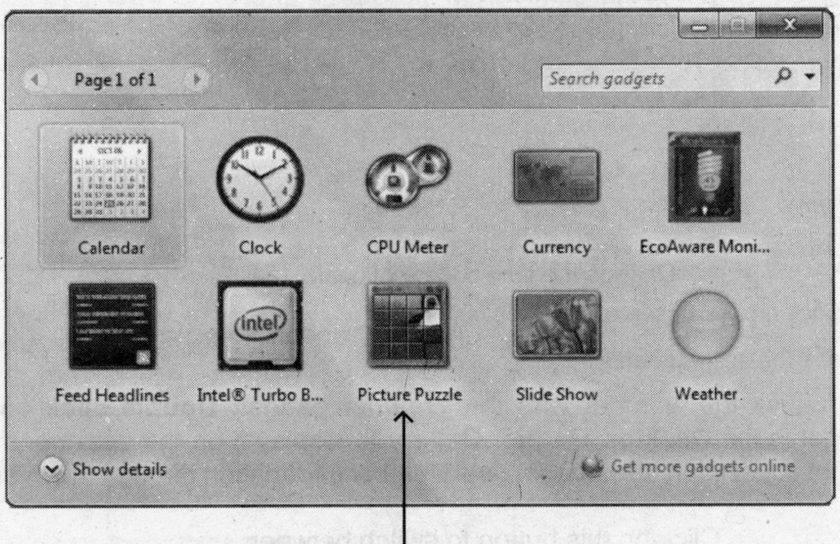

Double click on a **gadget** to display it on the desktop.

You will probably use the **Clock and Weather** gadgets the most. Hover your mouse over the clock, and you see a toolbar.

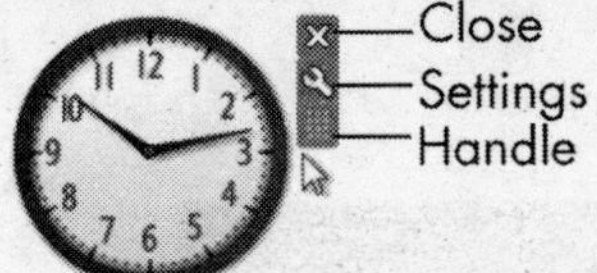

You can change the way the clock looks and works by clicking on the **Options** tool. The Options dialog box for the **Clock** gadget opens.

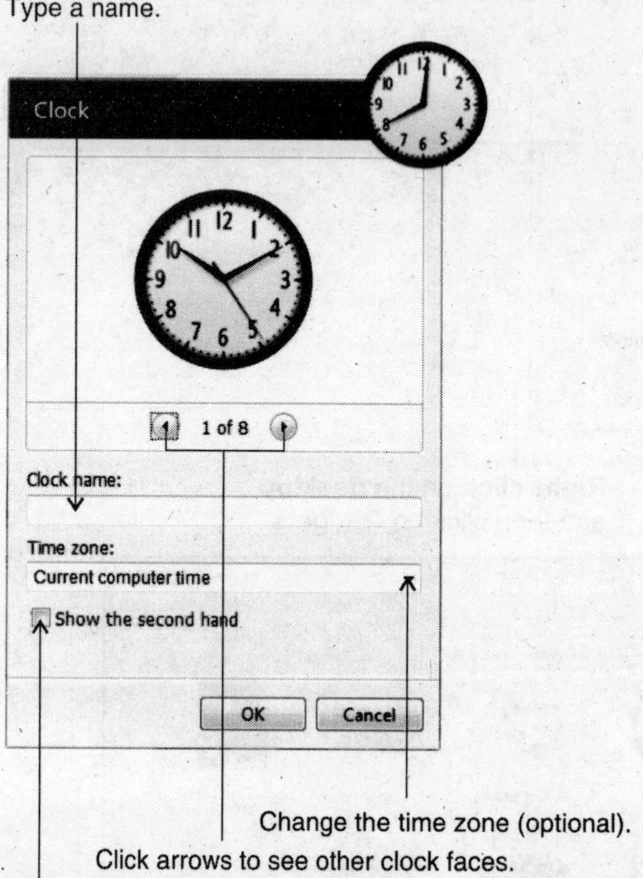

You can check the weather with the Weather gadget. **Double-click** on the **Weather** gadget in the **Desktop Gadget Gallery** to display it on the desktop. If you have an Internet connection, this gadget gets weather information through the Internet.

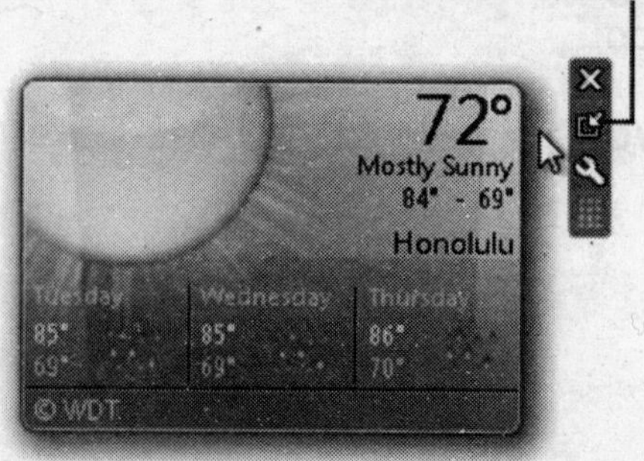

Using the Calculator

To use the **Calculator accessory**, click on the **Start** button, type **calc**, and click on **Calculator** in the search results. The Calculator appears on your desktop.

Entry or result appears here.

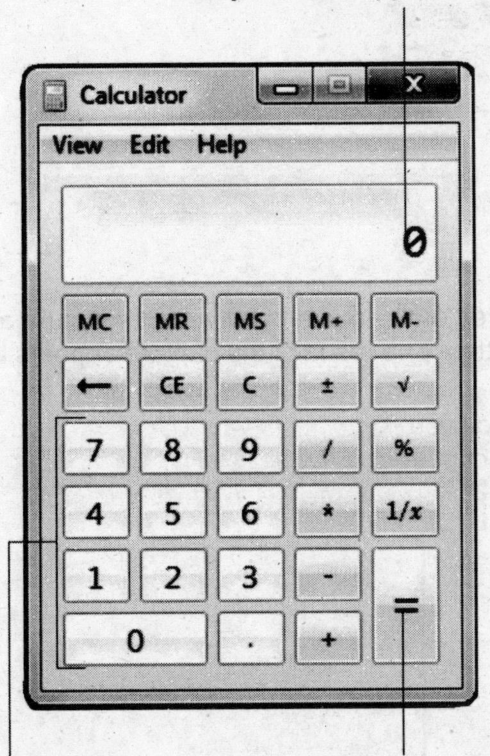

Click on the **buttons** or type numbers.

Click on the **equal sign** button or press **Enter** to see the result.

To Perform a Simple Calculation

- Use the **keyboard** to type the first number or click on the **number buttons** with the mouse.
- Type or click on the appropriate **math-symbol** button.
- Enter the second number.
- Then press the **Enter** key or click on the **equal-sign** button to see the results.

Capture the Computer Screen with the Windows Snipping Tool

The Snipping Tool captures all or part of the computer display screen as a picture.

Click on the **Start** button ➢ Type **snip** ➢ Click on the **Snipping Tool** from the search results.

The screen fades slightly, and the Snipping Tool toolbar appears.

Click and drag over the area you want to capture.

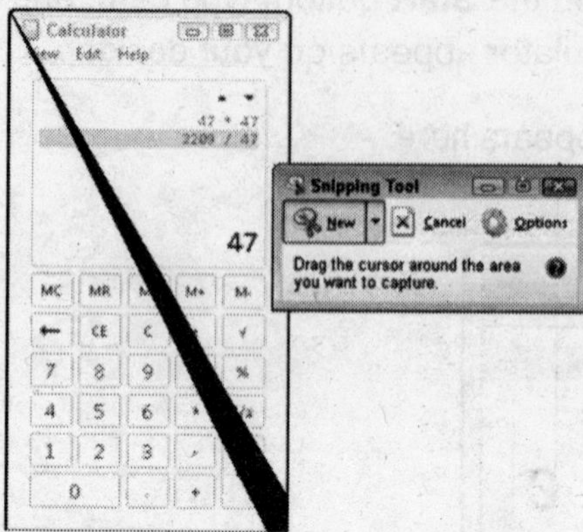

Click and drag over the area of the screen you want to capture as a picture and then release the left mouse button. The result of the capture appears in the **Snipping Tool editor**.

The area inside the box you create by dragging is captured.

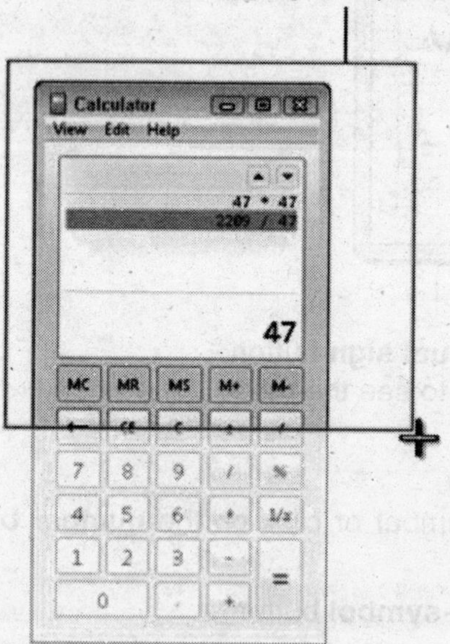

Draw with Paint in Windows 7

Microsoft Paint is an accessory that provides virtual pens and brushes to create art.

To use Paint

Click on the **Start** button ➤ Type **paint** ➤ Click on **Paint** in the search results. The Paint window opens.

You can draw on the canvas by simply clicking and dragging your mouse or using the brushes.

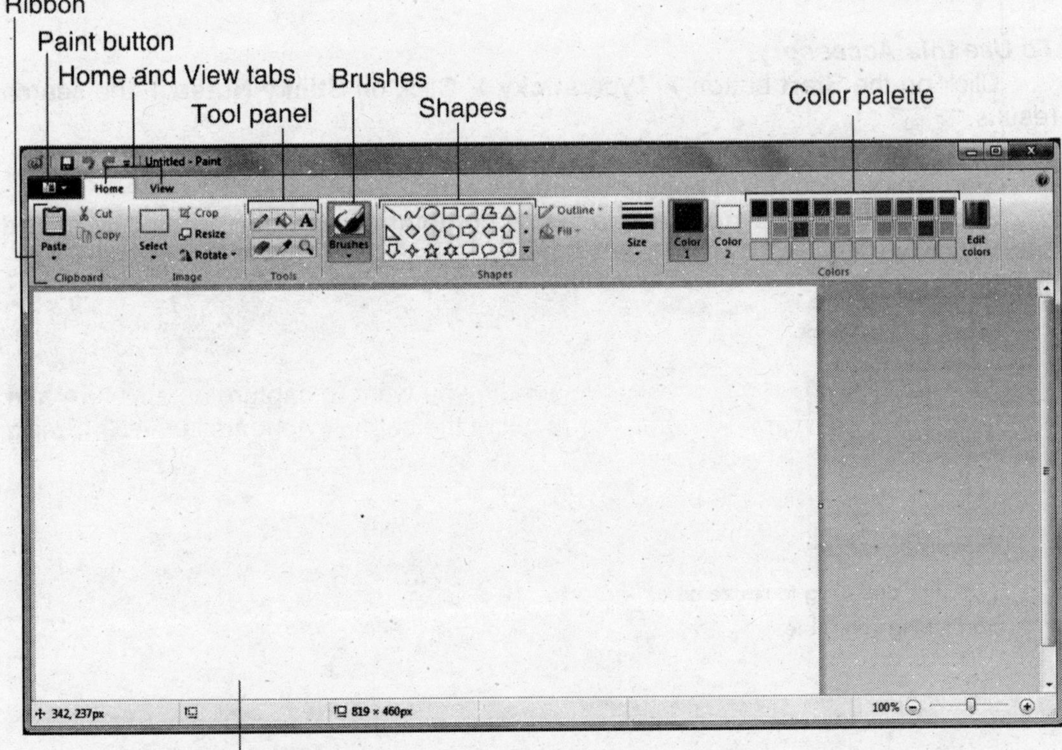

Talk to Sound Recorder

If your computer has a microphone, you can record audio notes or reminders to yourself with the **Sound Recorder** accessory.

To Open this Accessory

Click on the **Start** button ➢ Type **sound** ➢ Click on **Sound Recorder** in the search results

The Sound Recorder opens.

- To start recording, click on the **Start Recording** button, face the computer and talk.
- To stop recording, click on the **Stop Recording** button.

Take Sticky Notes

Sticky Notes is an accessory that puts yellow notes directly on your computer's desktop.

To Use this Accessory

Click on the **Start** button ➢ Type **sticky** ➢ Click on **Sticky Notes** in the search results.

Sticky Notes opens.

Start typing. Your text appears where the cursor is on the note.

Sticky Notes does not have a Save command, so your notes are saved automatically.

Add another note.

Delete

Click and drag to resize note.

Start typing your note.

□

7

Windows 7

Windows 7 is an operating system developed by Microsoft. It was released in 2009.

The features of Windows 7 are more or less same as Windows XP. However, there are some more interesting features in Windows 7.

Desktop

The Desktop is the main Windows 7 screen. It is the work area where dialog boxes, windows, icons and menus appear. From your desktop, you can perform file-management tasks and run software applications.

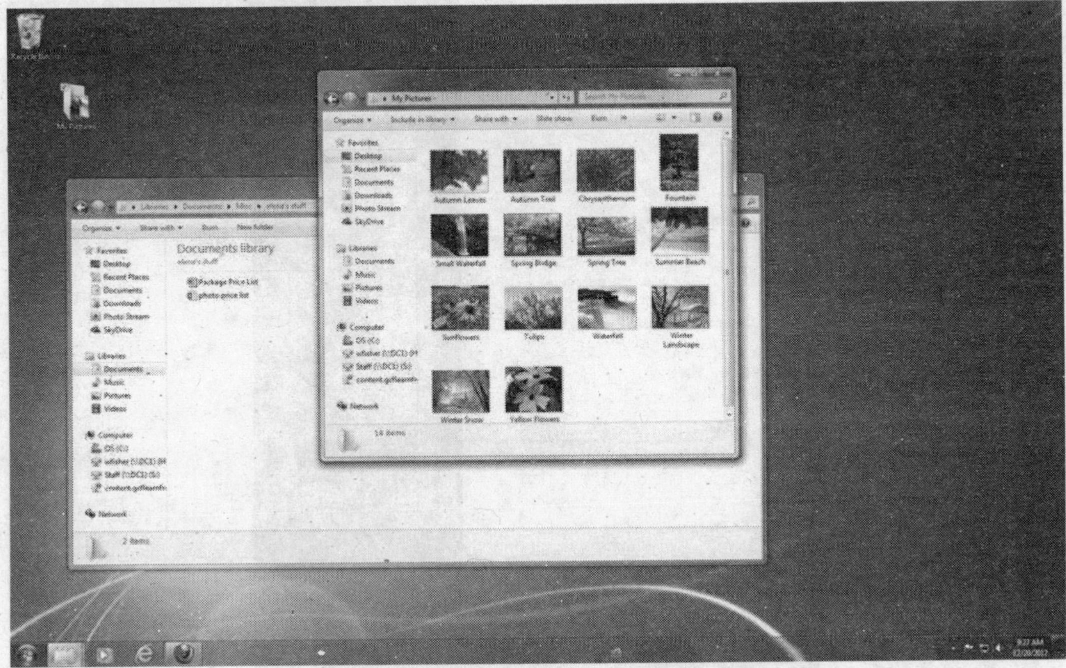

Desktop Icons

The Desktop is where you will find icons (small pictures) for many of your most frequently used programmes.

Recycle Bin

When you delete a file, it is moved to the **Recycle Bin**. To permanently delete the file, you will need to **empty** the Recycle Bin.

Computer

It allows you to see what drives are attached to your computer (for example, your local hard disk drive, your CD/DVD drives, any networked shared drives and external drives, such as a USB flash drive). You can also view the files that are located on these drives.

Windows Explorer

When you **double-click** on a folder, it will open in a specialised programme called **Windows Explorer**. This allows you to navigate to the specific folder or file that you want.

Start Button

Click on the Start button to access the **Start menu**. The Start menu lets you access applications, files and settings. You can also use the Start menu to shut down your computer.

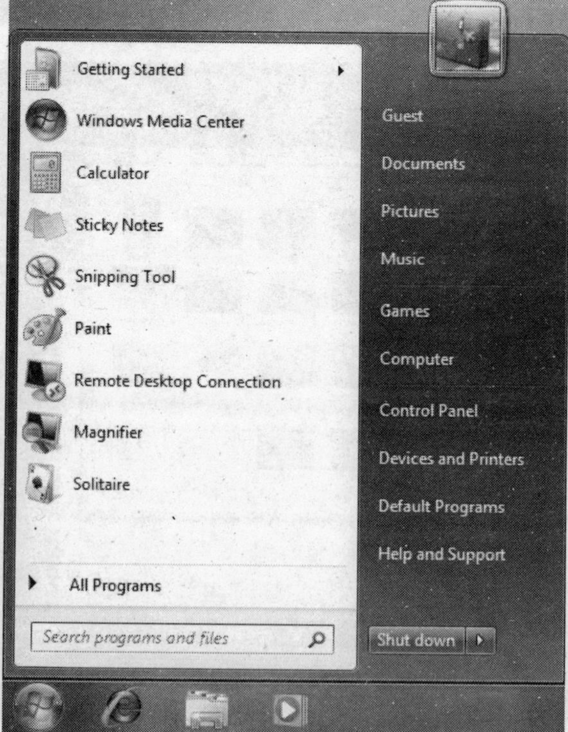

Shortcuts on Taskbar

Some programmes will have shortcuts on the taskbar for easy access. Here you see the shortcuts to Windows Explorer, Windows Media Player, Internet Explorer and Mozilla Firefox.

Taskbar

The taskbar contains the Start button, shortcuts to applications, date and time, and more.

When you open a programme or file, it will appear on the taskbar and you can easily switch between different programmes by selecting them on the taskbar.

Desktop Background

The Desktop Background (or wallpaper) allows you to personalise your computer. You can choose a built-in background, or use one of your own images.

Date and Time

On the right side of the taskbar, you will see the date and time. There will also be shortcuts to different settings, such as Internet settings and sound volume.

Changing Desktop Properties

You can change your wallpaper, screen saver and even your desktop theme in the Personalization (Display Properties). To access the window, **right-click** anywhere on an open space of your desktop and click on **Personalize**.

- **Change desktop icons** – Allows you to select which items will appear on your desktop.
- **Change mouse pointers** – Allows you to pick a different mouse pointer. You can also change how the mouse pointer looks during such activities as clicking and selecting.
- **Desktop** – Allows you to set the Desktop background picture.

- **Display** – Allows you to set your screen resolution and other advanced monitor and video settings.
- **Screen Saver** – Allows you to set a screen saver and its time interval. A screen saver is a picture or animation that covers your screen and appears when your computer is idle for a set period of time.
- **Sounds** – Changes which sounds are heard when you do everything from receiving e-mail to emptying your Recycle Bin.
- **Window Themes** – Allows you to set a theme for Windows which includes changing visual or auditory elements associated with menus, icons, backgrounds, screen savers, mouse pointers and some computer sounds.

Taskbar & Toolbars

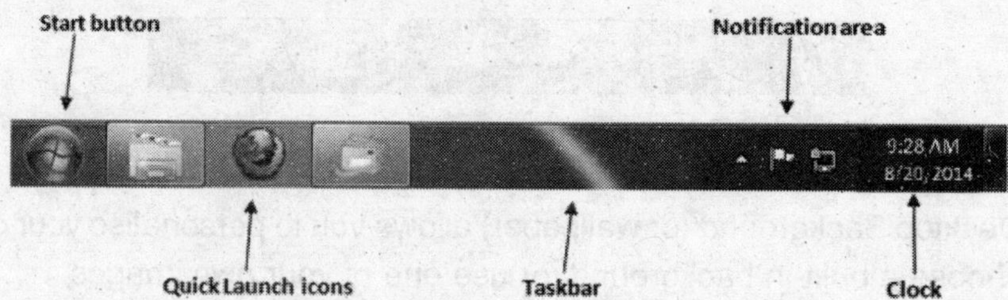

The bottom of your screen contains various toolbars and icons that allow you to see what programmes are running and what programmes you can access easily by clicking on its icon.

From the left to right, the areas are – the Start button, the Taskbar and the Notification Area (also called the system tray).

- **Display Desktop** – This feature will hide all open windows allowing the user to view their full Desktop. This feature is activated by clicking on the tall rectangular object to the right of the system date and time. Click on the object again to restore all of the hidden windows.
- **Notification Area** – Displays any programmes you have running in the background (such as a virus scanning programme) and displays the time and date.
- **Taskbar** – Shows any programmes or files you currently have open. You can click on the toolbar buttons to go back and forth between the open items.

Start Menu Basics

The Start Menu is the starting point in Windows 7. All of your programmes, settings, etc. can be accessed here.

To begin using it, click on the **Windows Icon** button in the bottom left corner or press the **Windows key** on your keyboard.

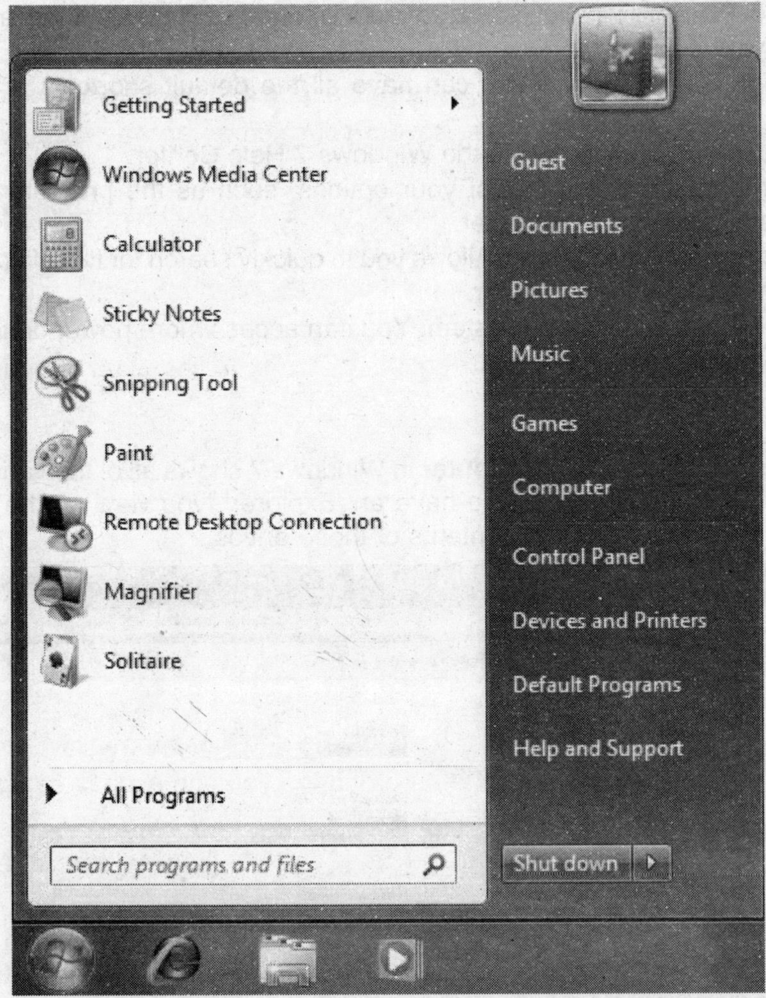

Here are some common items you will use on the Start Menu.

- **Account Name** – The account name for this computer is 'Guest'. The user will find access to all of his personal files and information stored in a single location.
- **Documents** – Many users will remember this item as 'My Documents'. From this menu item, users can access all of their files stored in the location.
- **Pictures** – From here, users can find all of their pictures stored in this location.
- **Music** – Users will find their music files stored in this location.
- **Games** – The Games folder offers game updates, statistics, news feeds and more.
- **Computer** – Formerly known as 'My Computer', this start menu item provides access to all storage drives (hard drives, flash drives, network drives, CDs, etc.) currently accessible through your computer.
- **Control Panel** – Allows you quick access to programmes that do everything from removing your programmes to adjusting your mouse settings.

- **Devices and Printers** – Allows you to view printers and devices currently installed on your system.
- **Default Programmes** – Here you can have all the default shortcuts in the Start Menu.
- **Help and Support** – Takes you to the Windows 7 Help Center.
- **All Programmes** – Stores most of your options, such as the programmes you have installed on your computer.
- **Search Programmes and Files** – Allows you to quickly search for files, folders and programmes on your computer.
- **Shut Down** – Powers down the system. You can access more power options by clicking on the arrow to the right.

Computer

Earlier known as 'My Computer', **Computer** in Windows 7 shows all of the various drives attached to your computer. You also have an 'Explorer' type view on the left side that allows you easy access to the contents of those drives.

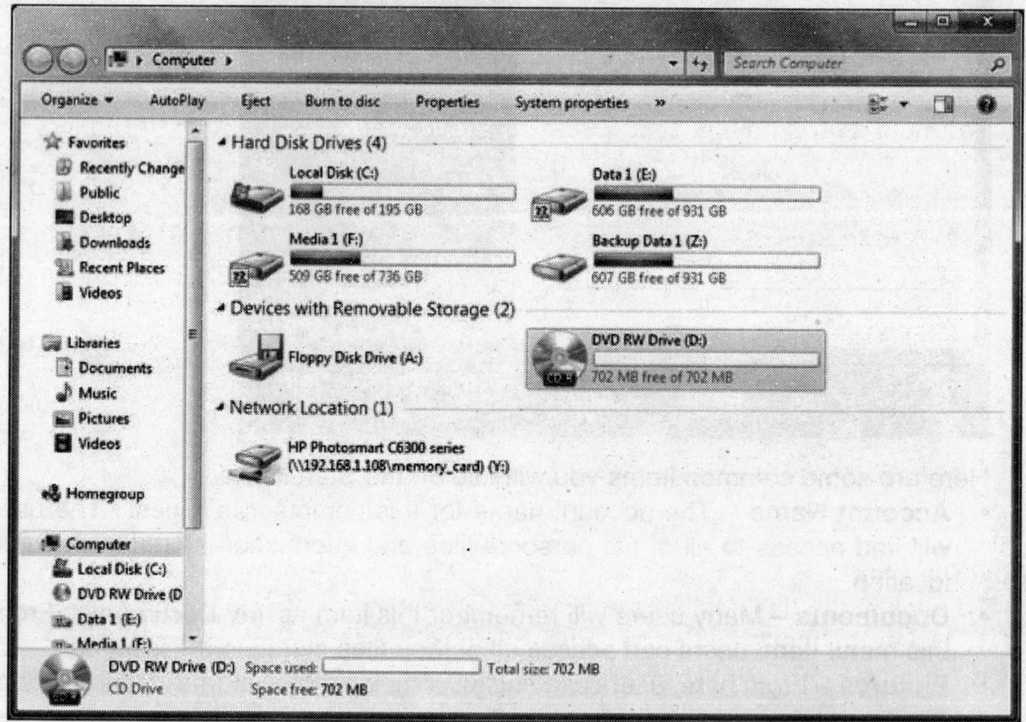

- **Hard Disk Drives** – This area lists all of the physical hard drives you have installed in your computer. This does not include any external hard drives or flash drives.
- **Devices with Removable Storage** – This area lists any external hard drives, flash drives, or CD/DVD drives.
- **Network Locations** – This area lists any network drives you may be connected to.

Quick Search

Windows 7 allows users to search individual windows through Quick Search.

Pin a Programme to the Taskbar

You can Pin programmes to the taskbar and access them with a single click of the mouse.

To Pin a programme, drag it to the taskbar and release.

To Unpin a programme, simply **right-click** on the icon and select **Unpin**.

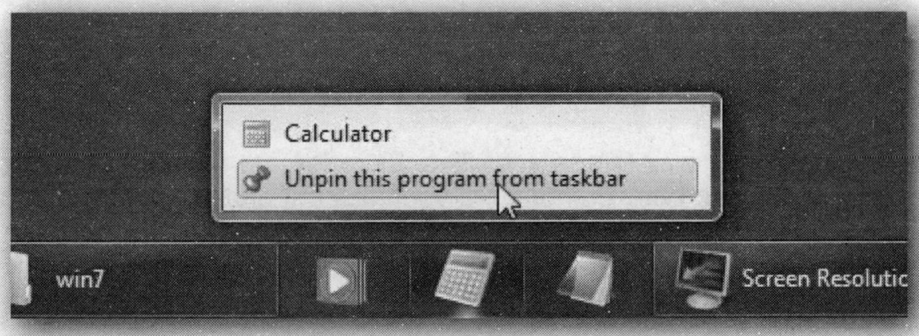

Show Desktop

To peek at the desktop without closing windows

1. Hover the mouse over the **Show desktop** button.

2. The windows will become transparent, allowing you to see the desktop.

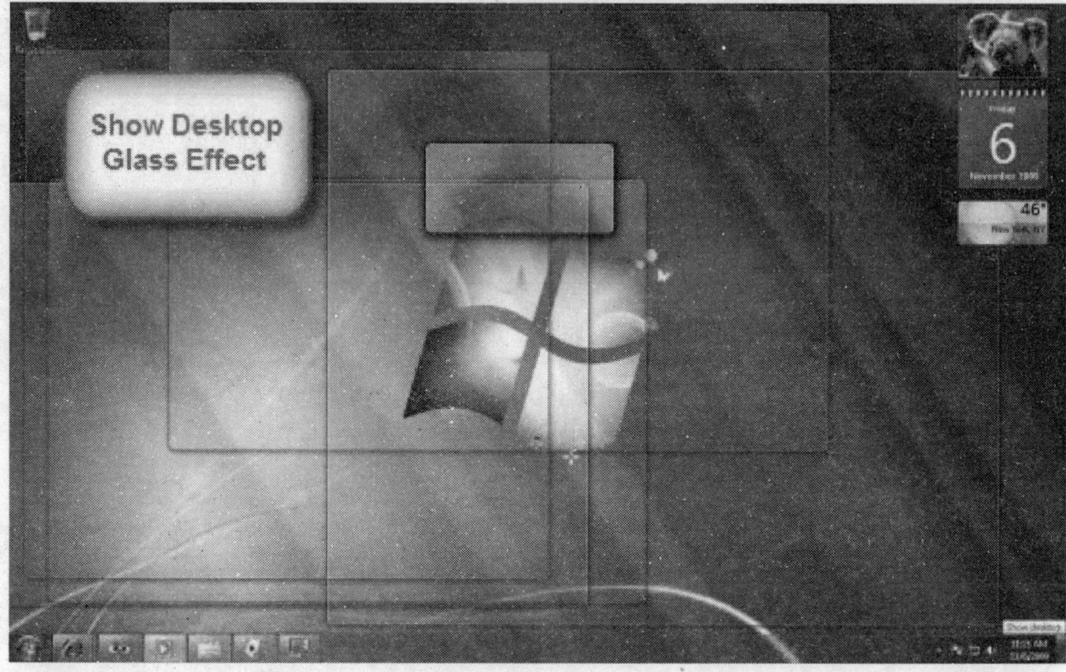

3. Click on the **Show desktop** button to close the windows.
4. Click again, and the windows will return.

Library

Libraries are a new way to see your files. Libraries are not folders but areas to locate and find your files. They do not store your files but gather the files in a way for you to easily locate them.

The four Libraries are **Documents, Music, Pictures** and **Videos**.

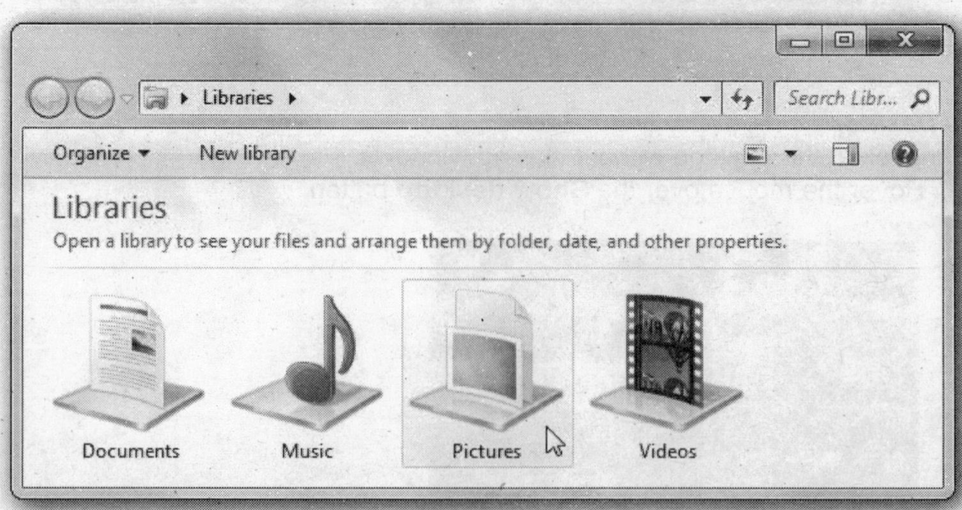

Aero Features

Windows 7 uses a group of features called **Windows Aero**. Aero is a visual desktop experience that combines transparent windows, appealing colour and graphics effects with convenient functionality.

Aero includes **Snap, Peek, Shake** and **Flip**.

Snap

Snap allows you to resize open windows to make reviewing and comparing easier. The images below show two windows before and after using the Snap feature.

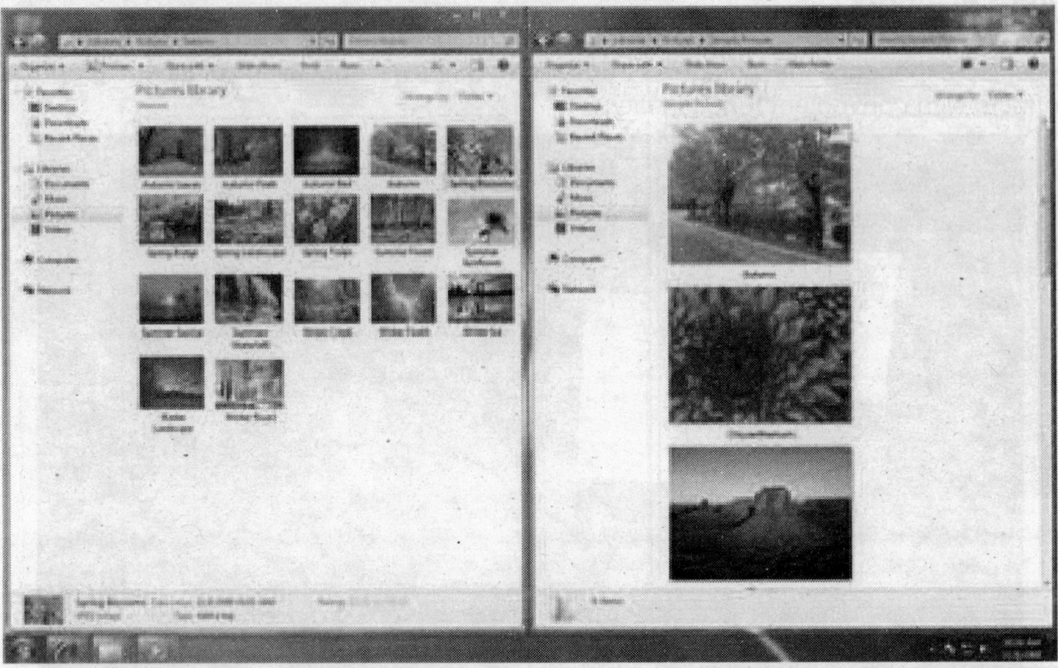

1. Place the mouse at the top of the window, drag to the left or right of the screen, wait for the transparent window to appear, and let go.
2. Your window should Snap into place.
3. To return to the full view, Snap the window to the top of the screen.

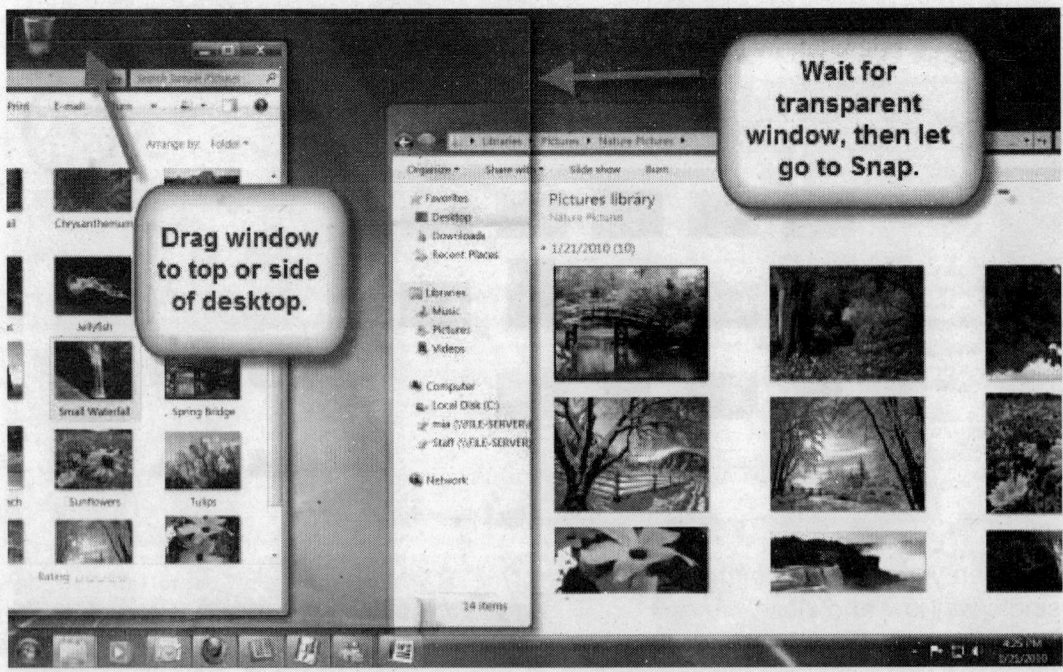

Peek

You can view your open windows on the taskbar by using Peek. Simply scroll the mouse over the taskbar icons, and a thumbnail preview of the open windows will appear.

1. Hover the mouse over the windows in Peek, and the full window will appear on your screen.
2. Click on the **Peek preview** to open the window, or click on the × to close the window from the Peek view.

Shake

When your desktop is messed with open windows, you can use Shake to select a single window and close the rest.

1. Click on the top of the window you want to focus on and shake your mouse and the rest of the windows will disappear.

2. Simply shake the window again and the closed windows will reappear.

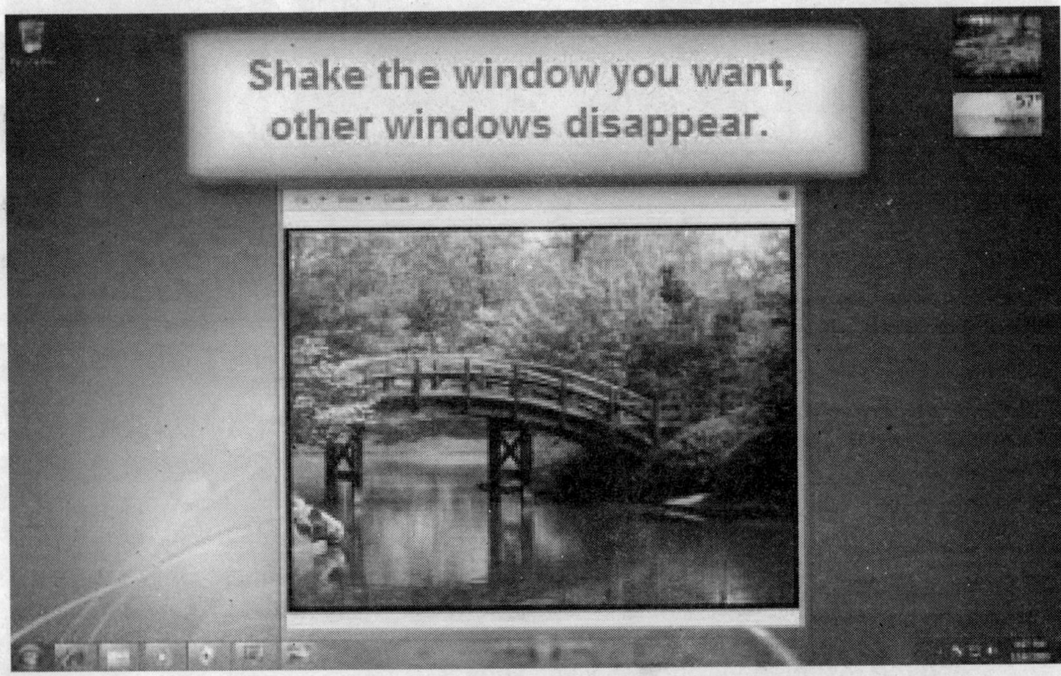

Flip

Flip and Flip 3D are two more ways you can preview your open windows.

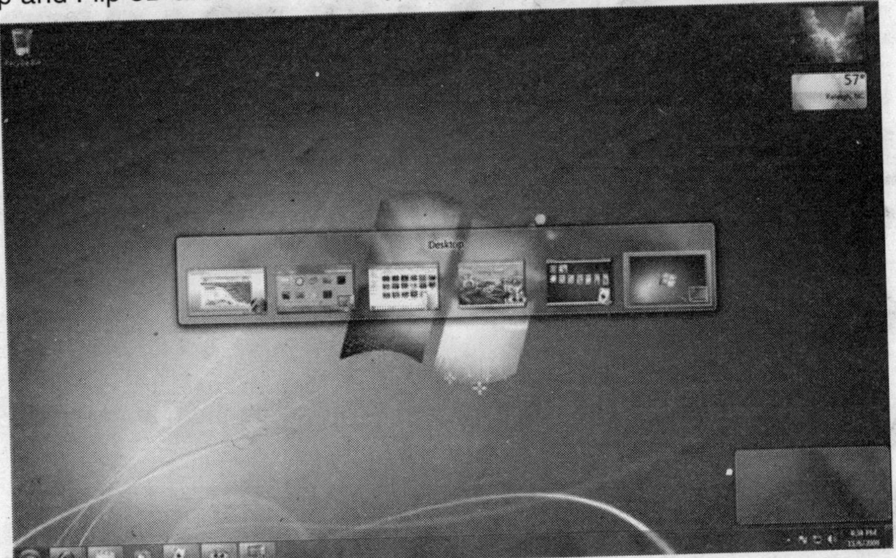

1. Press and hold the **Alt** key, then press **Tab** to open the **Flip view** of your open windows.
2. While still pressing the **Alt** key, you can flip through open windows by pressing the **Tab** key.
3. Stop on the window you want to open, and it will appear on the full screen.
4. Press and hold the **Windows** key, then press **Tab** for a **3D version** of Flip.
5. Use the **Tab** key or **Arrow** keys to flip through your open windows.

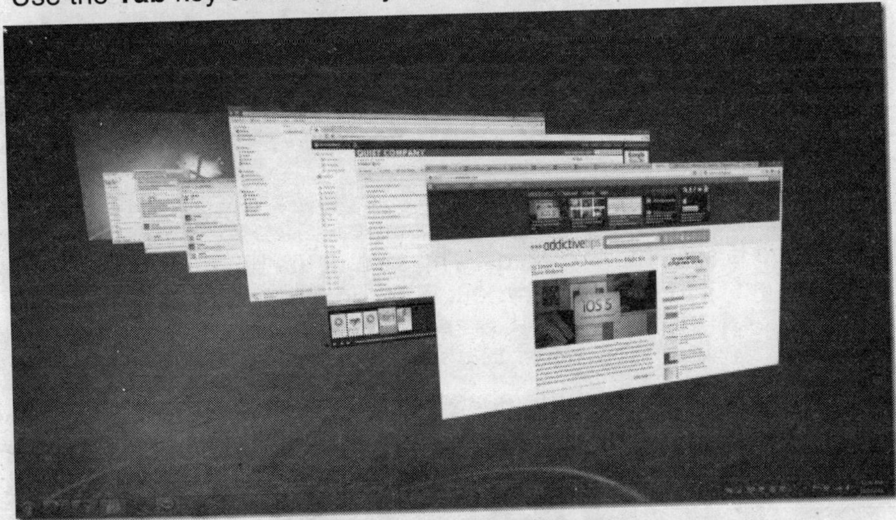

Gadgets

Desktop gadgets are customizable mini-programmes that can display information, such as continuously updated headlines or a picture slide show, without having to open a new window.

To Add Gadgets to Your Desktop

1. **Right-click** on your desktop and select **Gadgets**.

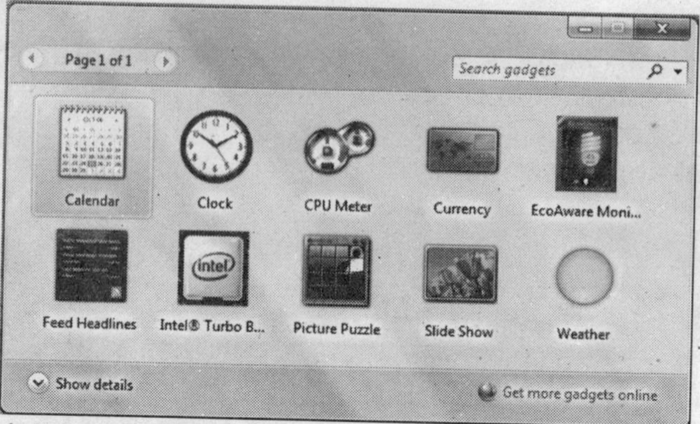

2. Select and drag the gadgets you desire, and place them anywhere you want on the desktop.

How to Start Windows 7

When you are through with the installation of Windows 7 and your computer starts for the first time, you will see this screen, called the Desktop.

The Desktop is split into two areas. The strip at the bottom, with the clock to the right and the round Start button to the left, is called the Taskbar.

The rest of the Desktop is the space where all your programmes will appear when you start them up. This space contains a default background wallpaper, but it can also contain shortcuts to programmes, documents and folder.

Getting Help from Windows 7

If you're connected to the Internet, make sure Windows Help and Support is set to Online Help. Online Help includes new Help topics and the latest versions of existing topics.

- Click on the **Start** button, and then click on **Help and Support**.
- On the toolbar in Windows Help and Support, click on **Options**, and then click on **Settings**.
- Under Search results, select the **Improve my search results** by **using online Help (recommended)** check box, and then click on **OK**. The words **Online Help** will be displayed in the lower-right corner of the Help and Support window when you are connected.

Search Help

The fastest way to get help is to type a word or two in the search box. For example, to get information about wireless networking, type wireless network, and then press **Enter**. A list of results appears, with the most useful results shown at the top. Click one of the results to read the topic.

(The search box in Windows Help and Support)

Browse Help

You can browse Help topics by subject. Click on the **Browse Help button**, and then click on an item in the list of subject headings that appears. Subject headings can contain Help topics or other subject headings. Click on a Help topic to open it, or click on another heading to visit the subject list.

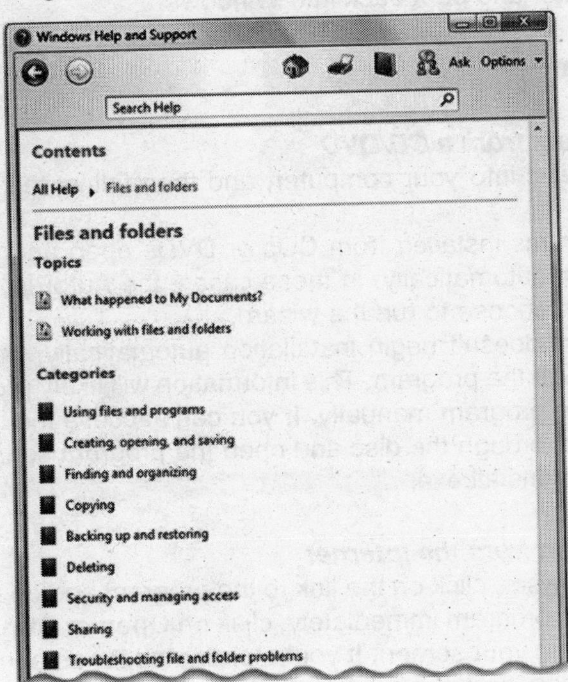

Restart a Window

To shut down or restart your computer in Windows 7, click on the Start button to open the Windows 7 Start Menu.

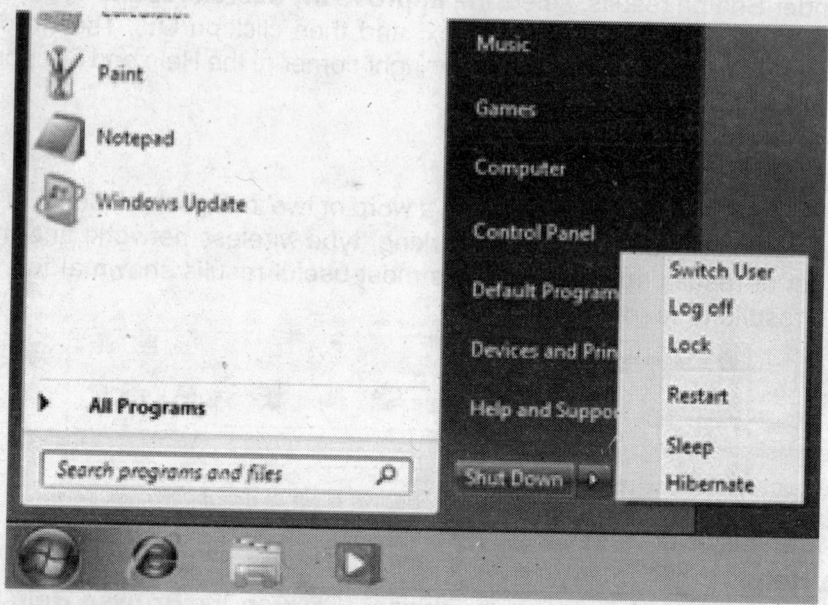

Once the Start Menu is open, click on Shut down button to shut down Windows and your computer. If you would like to restart your computer, click on the arrow next to the Shut down button. This will open another menu where you can click on Restart to restart your computer and boot back into Windows.

Install a Program

To Install a Program from a CD/DVD

- Insert the disc into your computer, and then follow the instructions on your screen.
- Many programs installed from CDs or DVDs open an installation wizard for the program automatically. In these cases, the AutoPlay dialog box appears and you can choose to run the wizard.
- If a program doesn't begin installation automatically, check the information that came with the program. This information will likely provide instructions for installing the program manually. If you can't access the information, you can also browse through the disc and open the program setup file, usually called Setup.exe or Install.exe.

To Install a Program from the Internet

In your web browser, click on the link to the program and do one of the following:

- To install the program immediately, click on **Open** or **Run**, and then follow the instructions on your screen. If you're prompted for an administrator password or confirmation, type the password or provide confirmation.

- To install the program later, click on **Save**, and then download the installation file to your computer. When you're ready to install the program, double-click on the file, and then follow the instructions on your screen.

Uninstall/Change/Repair a Program

- Open **Programs and Features** by clicking the **Start** button. Then click on **Control Panel** → **Programs**, and then click on **Programs and Features**.
- Select a program, and then click on **Uninstall**. Some programs include the option to change or repair the program in addition to uninstalling it, but many simply offer the option to uninstall.
- To change a program, click on **Change** or **Repair**.

Apply Themes

Using Themes

A theme is a combination of pictures, colors, and sounds. In Windows 7, you can change the desktop background, window border color, sounds and screen saver on your computer all at once and as often as you like by using themes.

Themes include:

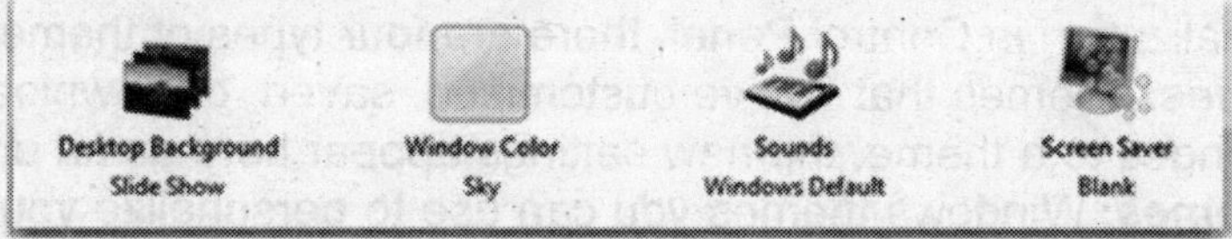

Parts of a Theme

A desktop background: A picture, color, or design that provides a backdrop to your open windows. The desktop background can be a single picture or a slide show. You can choose from the desktop background pictures that come with Windows, or you can use your own pictures.

(Some of the desktop background choices in Windows 7)

A window border color: The color of your window borders, taskbar and Start menu.

(Window border colors that are available with Aero in Windows 7)

Sounds: A collection of related sounds that you hear when events occur on your computer. An event can be an action that you perform, such as logging on to your computer, or an action that your computer performs, such as alerting you when you receive new email.

A screen saver: A moving picture or pattern that appears on your computer screen when you haven't used the mouse or keyboard for a specified period of time.

You can find all of your themes in **Personalization** in **Control Panel**. Click on any theme to apply it to your desktop.

Open **Personalization** by clicking on the **Start** button, and then click on **Control Panel**. In the search box, type **personalization**, and then click on **Personalization**.

In Personalization in Control Panel, there are four types of themes:

My Themes: Themes that you've customized, saved, or downloaded. Any time you make changes to a theme, the new settings appear here as an unsaved theme.

Aero Themes: Windows themes you can use to personalize your computer. All of the Aero themes include Aero glass effects, and many of them include a desktop background slide show.

Installed Themes: Themes that were created by your computer manufacturer or other non-Microsoft providers.

Basic and High Contrast Themes: Themes that are designed to help improve your computer's performance or make items on your screen easier to see. The Basic and High Contrast themes don't include Aero glass effects.

Creating Themes

Click on any theme to apply it to your desktop. Then change each part of the theme until the desktop background, window border color, sounds and screen saver are just how you want them to be. All of your changes will be saved under **My Themes** as an unsaved theme.

If you're content with the way your new theme looks and sounds, you can save it so you can use it whenever you like.

Saving a Theme

- Open **Personalization** by clicking on the **Start** button, and then click on **Control Panel**. In the search box, type **personalization**, and then click on **Personalization**.
- Click on your customized theme to apply it to the desktop.

- Click on **Save theme**.
- Type a name for your theme, and then click on **Save**.
- The theme will appear under **My Themes**.

Maximize and Minimize a Window

To Maximize a Window

In Windows 7, you can use Snap to maximize a window, which makes it easier to focus on that window because of less distraction from other open windows.

- Drag the title bar of the window to the top of the screen. The window's outline expands to fill the screen.
- Release the window to expand it to fill the entire desktop.
- To return the window to its original size, drag the title bar of the window away from the top of the screen.

Other Ways to Maximize an Open Window

- Double-click on the top of an open window just below the top edge.
- To restore a maximized window to its original size, double click on the top of the window again.
- On the taskbar, press Shift and right click on a taskbar button or a preview of an open window, and then click on Maximize.

Maximize an Open Window Using the Keyboard

- Press the Windows logo key + Up-arrow.

To Minimize a Open Window

There are different ways to minimize open windows in Windows 7.

(Show desktop button on the taskbar)

Minimize Open Windows Using the Mouse

- Click on the Show desktop button at the end of the notification area on the taskbar.
- To restore minimized windows, click on the **Show desktop** button again.

Minimize Open Windows Using the Keyboard

- Press the Windows logo key + D.
- To restore minimized windows, press the Windows logo key + D again.

Move or Resize a window

Windows 7 has a feature that lets you snap windows to the left-hand or right-hand side of the screen. Snap is a quick way to resize open windows, simply by dragging them to the edges of your screen. Depending on where you drag a window, you can make it expand vertically, take up the entire screen, or appear side-by-side with another window.

If you drag a window to the right or left, it will automatically resize and snap to the side.

- To do this using the keyboard, press the Windows logo key + the right or left arrow. Make sure to hold down the Windows logo key while pressing the left and right arrow keys.

Besides this method of using Snap, you can also follow these steps to move a window:

- Either click on the window or if you want to use the keyboard, press **ALT + TAB** and make the window you want to move active.
- Now press **ALT + SPACEBAR** and you'll see a small menu appear in the window.

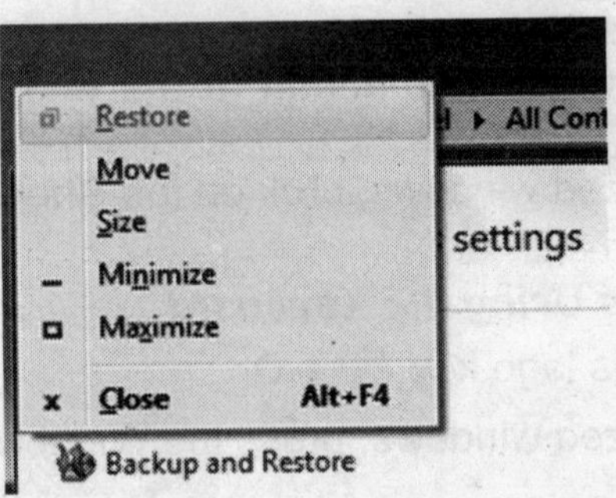

- Now press **M**, which will basically choose the **Move** option in the menu.
- Now use the arrow keys on your keyboard to move the window to the new position that you desire.
- Press the **Enter** key to get out of the move mode. Also, if you want to have the window go back to the original position before you started the move, press the **Esc** key instead.

To Add (pin), Remove (unpin) and Move a Program in Start Menu

Pin a Program Icon to the Start Menu

If you use a program regularly, you can create a shortcut to it by pinning the program icon to the Start menu. Pinned program icons appear on the left side of the Start menu.

- Right-click on the program icon you want to pin to the Start menu, and then click on **Pin to Start Menu**.

Remove a Program Icon from the Start Menu

Removing a program icon from the Start menu doesn't remove it from the All Programs list or uninstall the program.

- Click on the Start button.
- Right-click on the program icon you want to remove from the Start menu, and then click on **Remove from this list**.

Move the Start Button

The Start button is located on the taskbar. Although you can't remove the Start button from the taskbar, you can move the taskbar and the Start button along with it.

- Right-click on an empty space on the taskbar. If Lock the taskbar has a check mark beside it, click on it to remove the check mark.
- Click on an empty space on the taskbar, and then hold down the mouse button as you drag the taskbar to one of the four edges of the desktop. When the taskbar is where you want it, release the mouse button.

Shut Down

To Shut Down or Turn Off Your Computer

1. Go to the **Start menu**.

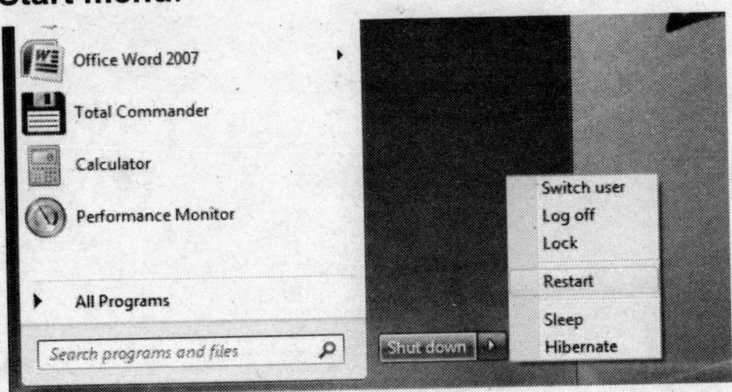

2. Click on the **Start** button and then on the lower-right corner of the Start menu, click on **Shut down**.

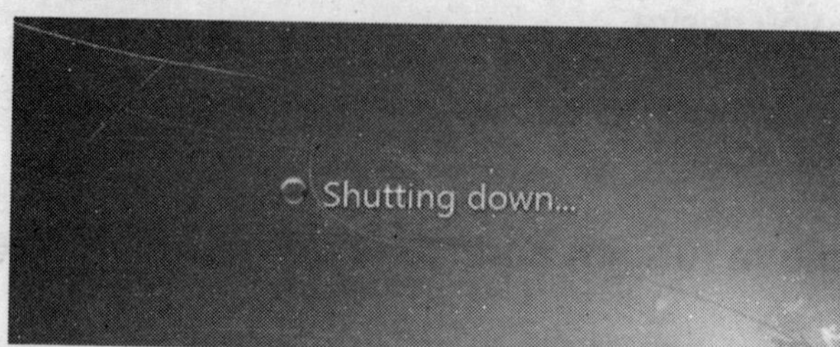

When you click on **Shut down**, your computer closes all open programmes alongwith Windows itself.

□

8

Some Useful Software in General Use

NOTEPAD

Notepad is a very basic text editor which is a part of the MS Windows. It is found in the Accessories folder. It's great for writing relatively short documents that you want to save as plain text. Notepad is just a text editor and if you try to paste graphics into it, it won't work.

Notepad is essentially the same in Windows 7 and Windows 8. Here, you will know about Notepad by using the Windows 7 version. The only difference is in how you open the application in each operating system.

How to Open Notepad

In Windows 7, Notepad is found in the Accessories folder in the Start Menu.

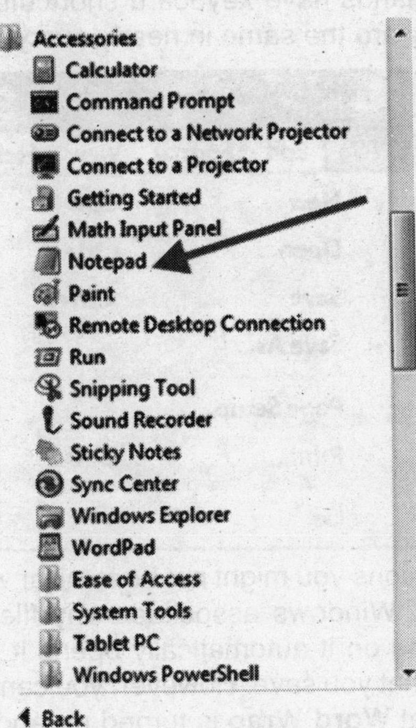

To find Notepad in Windows 8, either type notepad on the Start screen, or bring up the charms and type into the search box.

When Notepad opens, either in Widows 7 or Windows 8, you'll see this no-frills screen. At the top of the window you'll see menus for File, Edit, Format, View and Help.

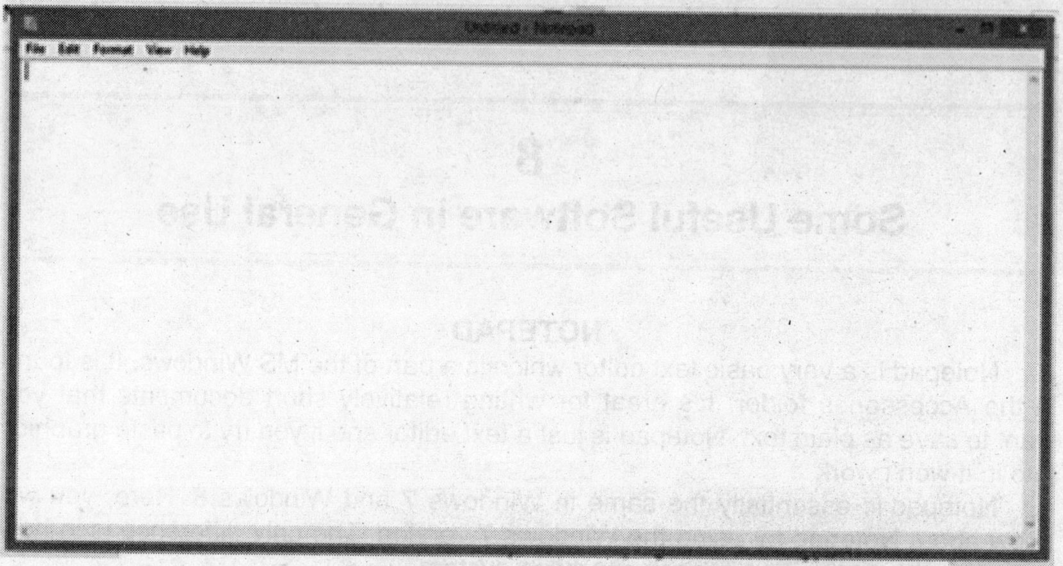

Using the File Menu in Notepad

Your choices are New, Open, Save, Save As, Page Setup and Print. As you can see, many of these commands have keyboard shortcuts as well, which you should be familiar with, since they are the same in nearly every Windows application.

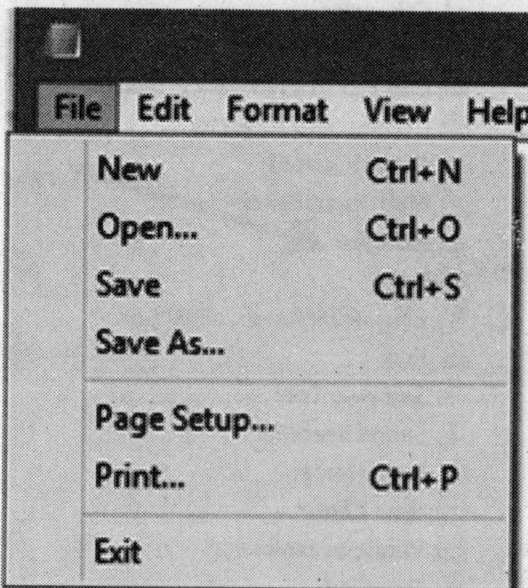

You do have some options you might not be familiar with when you use the **Save As** command. By default, Windows associates any file with a **.txt** extension with Notepad, so double clicking on it automatically opens it in Notepad, and that is the default format for the files that you save. However, you can also use Notepad to create HTML files. Make sure that **Word Wrap** is turned on and type your HTML code the way you would type plain text. When it's time to save your work, choose **Save As**, and select **All Files** from the list of choices. Then save your file with the **.htm** or **.html** extension. The default folder is the My Documents folder attached to your username in Windows 7, and the OneDrive folder in Windows 8.

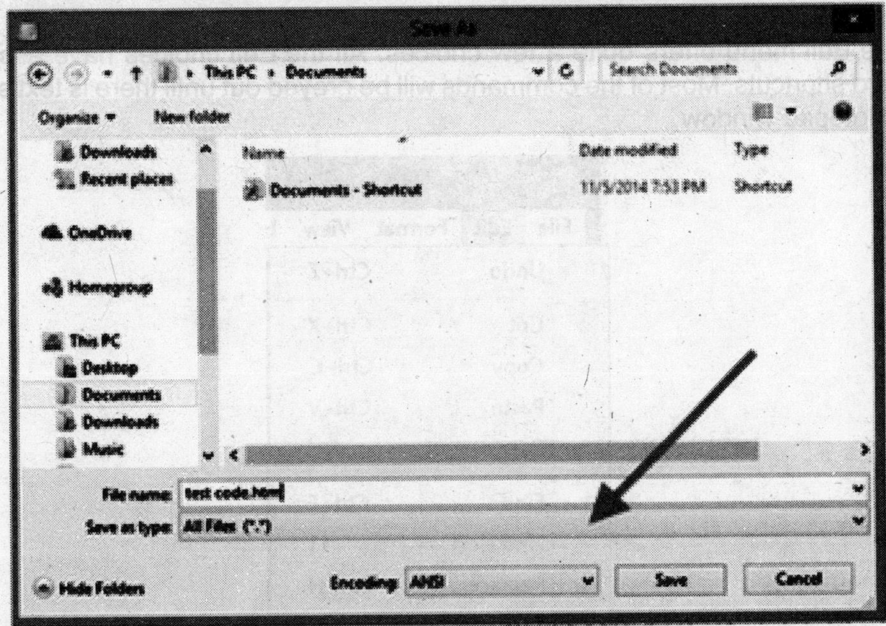

Once you're finished, use the **Save As** command to save your work.

The only item on the File menu that you might be less familiar with is **Page Setup**. In Notepad, your choices are simple. You can choose the paper size and where your printer keeps the paper, the page orientation and whether to have a header and/ or footer.

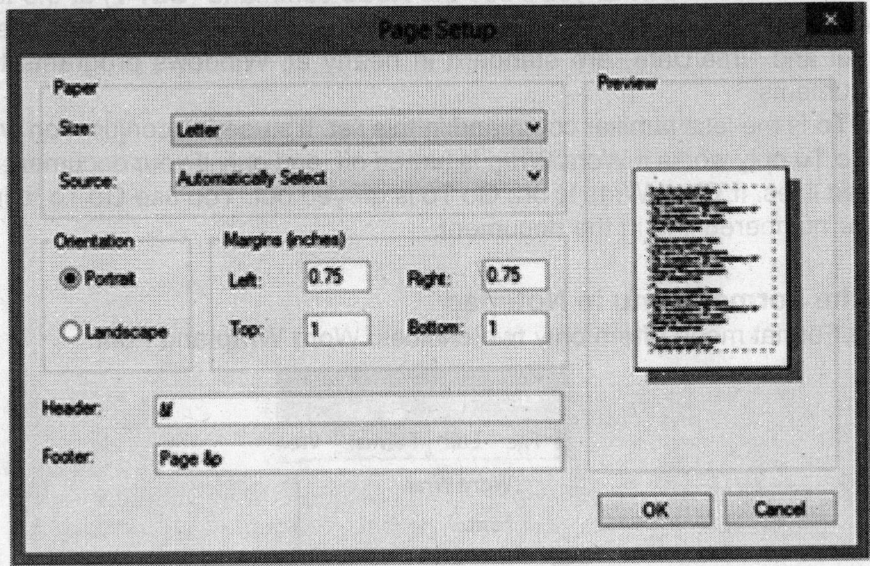

By default, the text in the header is the name of the document and the date it was printed, and the text in the footer is the page number. If you don't want this information printed, just delete the codes.

Using the Edit Menu in Notepad

The Edit menu offers quite a few choices. All the Edit choices have associated keyboard shortcuts. Most of the commands will be greyed out until there is text selected in the Notepad window.

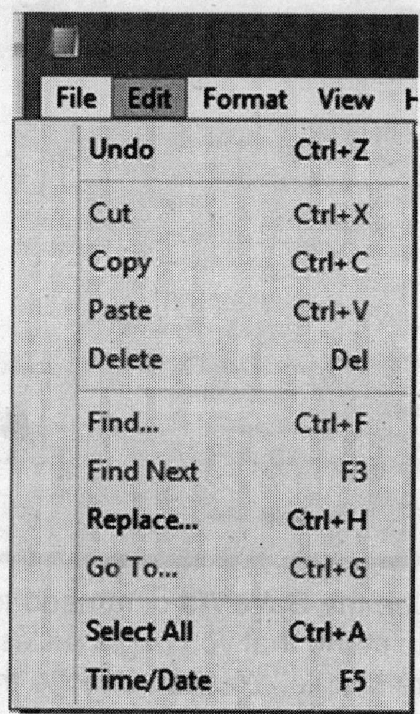

The first item on the Edit menu is Undo/Redo. If you have just used the **Undo** command or pressed **Ctrl-Z**, you'll see the **Redo** command (**Ctrl-Y**) at the top of the list. The rest of the menu, Cut, Copy, Paste, Delete, Find, Find Next, Replace, Go To, Select All and Time/Date, are standard in nearly all Windows programs that deal with documents.

Go To is the less familiar command in this list. It's used in conjunction with Word Wrap. **Go To** only works if Word Wrap is turned off, and only if your document contains numbered lines. If Word Wrap is on, Go To is greyed out. You use Go To to jump to a particular numbered line in the document.

Using the Format Menu in Notepad

The Format menu offers only two choices: Word Wrap and Font.

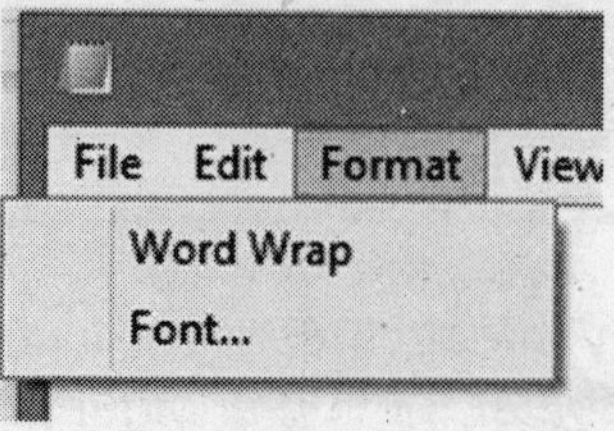

Notepad has always come with Word Wrap turned off. This means everything you type ends up on one long line, until you press **Enter**, which will start another long line.

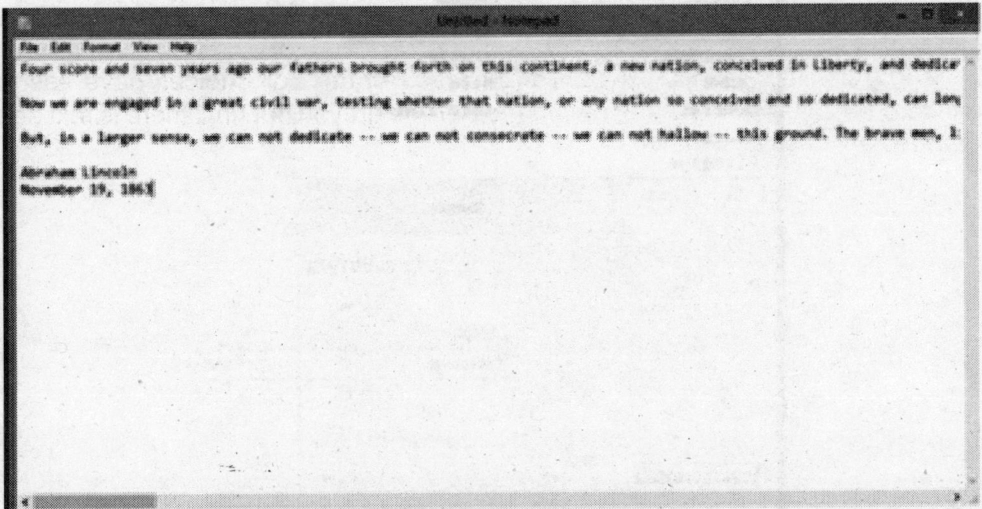

You have the option of pressing Enter when your typing approaches the right margin of the Notepad window, but that makes the lines some arbitrary length depending on the size of your window. If you'd like to see what you're typing without having to scroll all the way to the right, turn Word Wrap on. Then Notepad will behave just like any other word processing program and automatically wrap the text to the next line as you approach the right margin of your window.

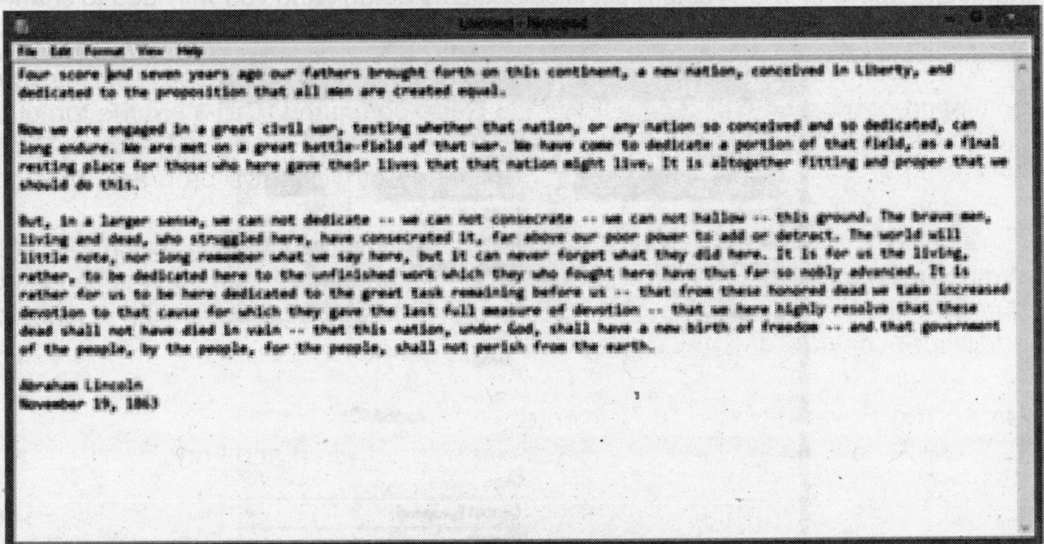

The Font offers you a list of all your installed fonts, and the option to use bold, italic and the like. However, unlike the way it works in programs like Microsoft Word, a change of font immediately affects the entire document. You can't use one font on part of the document and another font on another part of it.

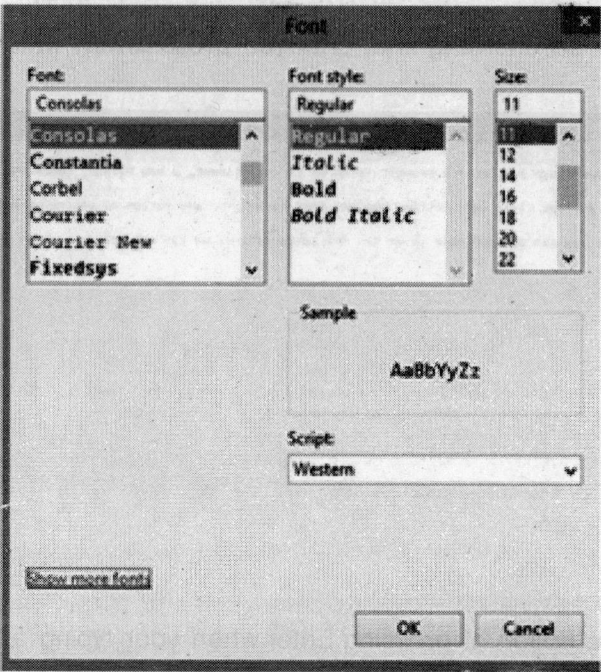

In the Font menu, there is a less familiar option available, the drop down menu labeled Script. This lets you choose characters that are not available in the standard "Western" style fonts. The choices are Western, Greek, Turkish, Baltic, Central European, Cyrillic and Vietnamese. Choose a set and you'll see some representative characters above it. The Western set is selected by default and you will need to change it to another one, if necessary.

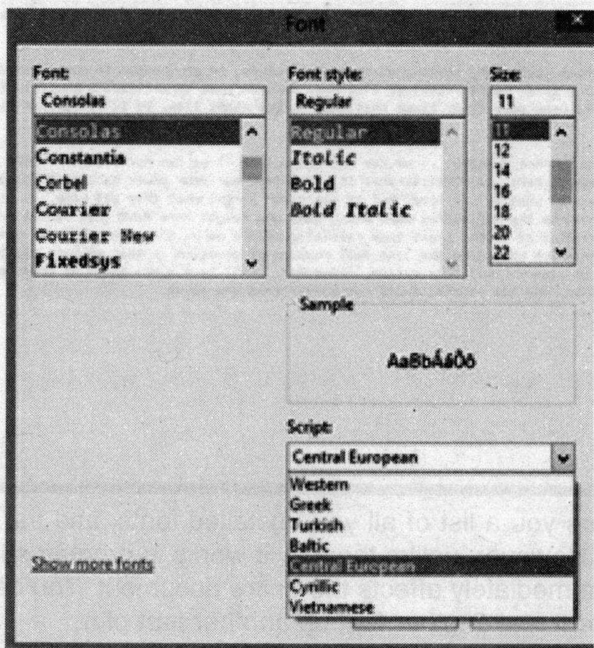

Using the View Menu in Notepad

The View menu offers only one option, Status Bar. And that, like the Go To command in the Edit menu, is linked with Word Wrap. If Word Wrap is off, you will see a notification in the lower border of your window, showing you where the cursor is currently located in a document that is not word-wrapped. If Word Wrap is on, the lower border is blank.

Open a Notepad Document

To open an existing notepad document click on **File →Open...**

If you have not saved a document you are working on, Notepad will ask you if you want to save it or discard it. The Open window appears which allows you to browse to your existing document.

Print a Notepad Document

To print a Notepad document go to **File →Print...** The three dots after the word Print means there will be another screen that pops up. This is a Windows standard.

Select the printer you wish to print to then click the **Print** button.

PAINT

Paint is a feature in Windows 7 that you can use to create drawings on a blank drawing area or in existing pictures. Many of the tools you use in Paint are found in the ribbon, which is near the top of the Paint window. In both Windows 7 and Windows 8, the application is the same.

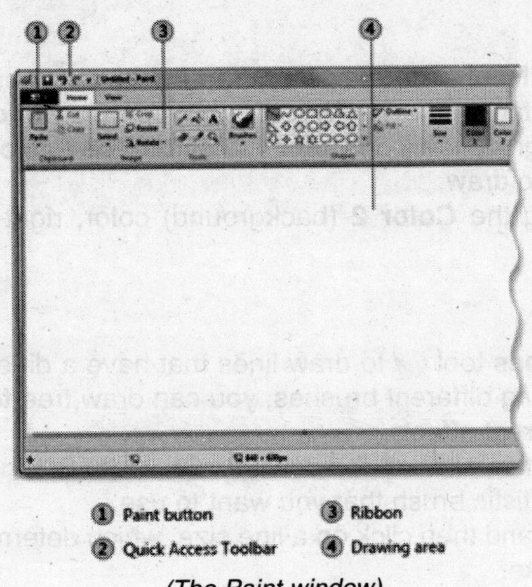

(The Paint window)

How to Open Paint

In Windows 7, Paint is found in the Accessories folder in the Start Menu. You can open Paint by clicking on the **Start** button, then clicking on **All Programs → Accessories → Paint**.

You can also find Paint by typing the word 'paint' in the search box of the Start Menu, in Windows 7, and directly on the Start screen, in Windows 8. Here, you will know about Paint by using the Windows 7 version.

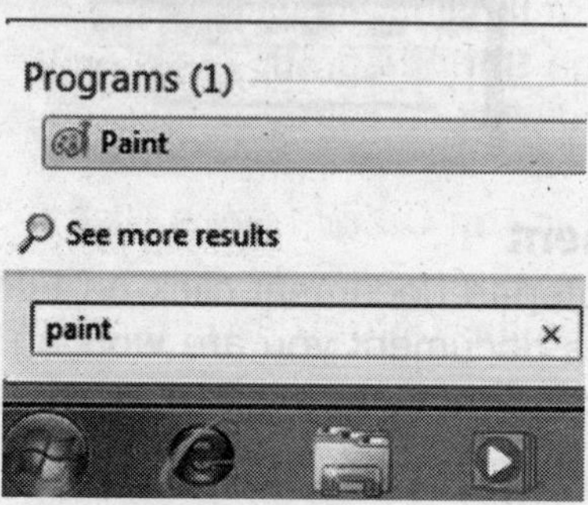

The Ribbon in Paint

The version of Paint in Windows 7 is almost identical to the version in Windows 8. The only difference is the fact that the interface looks flat and doesn't have any transparency. Rest, all the options, features and menus are the same.

Drawing Lines

Here, you can use several different tools to draw in Paint. The tool you use and the options you select determine how the line appears in your drawing. These are the tools you can use to draw lines in Paint.

Pencil Tool

- Use the **Pencil** tool to draw thin, free-form lines or curves.
- On the **Home** tab, in the **Tools** group, click on the **Pencil** tool.
- In the **Colors** group, click on **Color 1**, then click on a color, and drag the pointer in the picture to draw.
- To draw using the **Color 2** (background) color, right-click while you drag the pointer.

Brushes

- Use the **Brushes** tool to draw lines that have a different appearance and texture. By using different brushes, you can draw free-form and curving lines that have different effects.
- On the **Home** tab, click on the down arrow under Brushes.
- Click on the artistic brush that you want to use.
- Click on **Size**, and then click on a line size, which determines the thickness of the brush stroke.

- In the **Colors** group, click on **Color 1**, then click on a color, and drag the pointer to paint.
- To paint using the **Color 2** (background) color, right-click while you drag the pointer.

Line Tool

- Use the **Line** tool to draw a straight line. When using this tool, you can choose the thickness of the line, as well as the appearance of it.
- On the **Home** tab in the **Shapes** group, click on the **Line** tool .
- Click on **Size**, and then click on a line size, which determines the thickness of the line.
- In the **Colors** group, click on **Color 1**, then click on a color, and then drag the pointer to draw the line.
- To draw a line that uses the **Color 2** (background) color, right-click while you drag the pointer.

Curve Tool

- Use the **Curve** tool to draw a smooth, curved line.
- On the **Home** tab, in the **Shapes** group, click on the **Curve** tool .
- Click on **Size**, and then click on a line size, which determine the thickness of the line.
- In the **Colors** group, click on **Color 1**, then click on a color, and drag the pointer to draw the line.
- To draw a line that uses the **Color 2** (background) color, right-click while you drag the pointer.
- After you have created the line, click on the area in the picture where you want the arc of the curve to be, and then drag the pointer to adjust the curve.

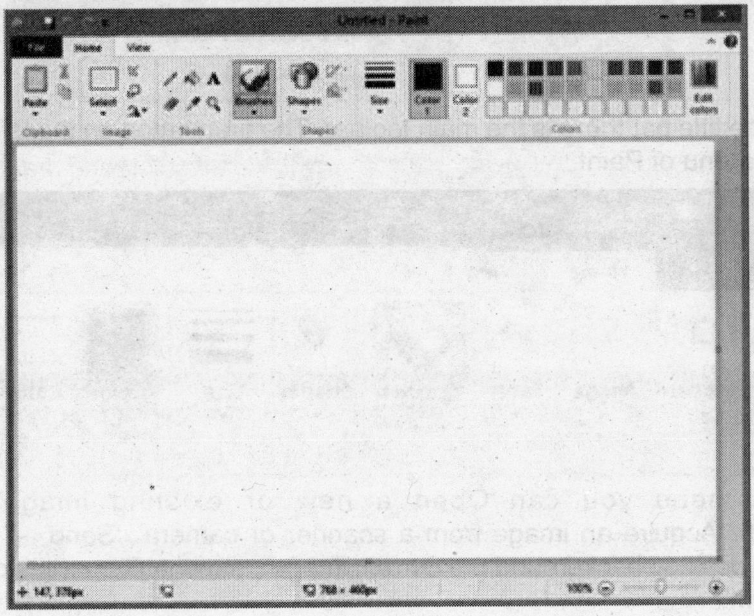

At the top of the window, on the title bar, there is a **Quick Access Toolbar** with some of the most important buttons: Save, Undo and Redo.

If you click on the small arrow right next to the Redo button, a menu will open up which will allow you to customize the Quick Access Toolbar. You can add buttons, like New (image), Open, Print or remove any of the existing ones. All you have to do is to click on the buttons you want to add or remove.

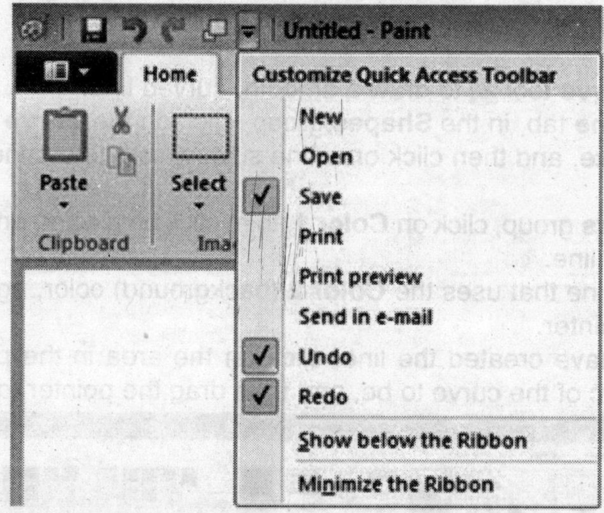

Under the title bar there is the main toolbar. The first button on the left side opens up the main menu of Paint.

In this menu you can 'Open a new or existing image', 'Save an image', 'Print', 'Acquire an image from a scanner or camera', 'Send an image in e-mail', 'Set as desktop background the current image', 'see the Properties of the image' and 'Exit Paint'.

Working with Color

There are a number of tools to help you work specifically with color in Paint. They let you use the colors you want when you're drawing and editing in Paint.

Color Boxes

The Color boxes indicate the current **Color 1** (foreground color) and **Color 2** (background color) colors. How they're used depends on what you're doing in Paint.

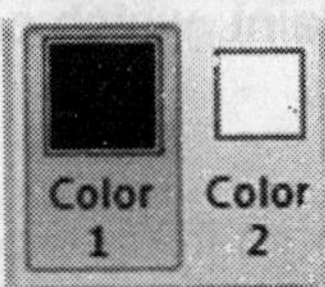

When using the color boxes, you can do one or more of the following:

- To change the selected foreground color, on the **Home** tab, in the **Colors** group, click on **Color 1**, and then click on a color square.
- To change the selected background color, on the **Home** tab, in the **Colors** group, click on **Color 2**, and then click on a color square.
- To paint with the selected foreground color, drag the pointer.
- To paint with the selected background color, right-click while you drag the pointer.

Color Picker

Use the **Color picker** tool to set the current foreground or background color. By picking a color from the picture, you can make sure that you're using the color you want when drawing in Paint, so your colors match.

- On the **Home** tab, in the **Tools** group, click on **Color picker** .
- Click on the color in your picture that you want to set as the foreground color, or right-click on the color in your picture that you want to set as the background color.

Fill with Color

Use the **Fill with color** tool to fill the entire picture or an enclosed shape with color.

- On the **Home** tab, in the **Tools** group, click on **Fill with color** .
- In the **Colors** group, click on **Color 1**, then click on a color, and then click inside the area to fill it.
- To remove the color and replace it with the background color instead, click on **Color 2**, then click on a color, and then right-click the area to fill it.

Editing Colors

Use **Edit** colors to pick a new color. Mixing colors in Paint lets you choose the exact color that you want to use.

- On the **Home** tab, in the **Colors** group, click on **Edit** colors.
- In the **Edit Colors** dialog box, click on a color in the color palette, and then click on **OK**.

- The color will appear in one of the color boxes, so you can use that color in Paint.

Viewing Your Picture

Changing the view in Paint lets you choose how you want to work with the picture. You can zoom in on a certain part of the picture or the whole picture, if you want. Conversely, you can zoom out if the picture is too large. In addition, you can show rulers and gridlines as you work in Paint, which can help you work better in Paint.

Magnifier

Use the **Magnifier** tool to zoom in on a part of your picture.

- On the **Home** tab, in the **Tools** group, click on the **Magnifier**, move the magnifier, and then click to zoom in on the part of the image shown in the square.
- Drag the horizontal and vertical scroll bars on the bottom and right side of the window to move around the picture.
- To reduce the zoom level, right-click on the **Magnifier** again.

Zoom In and Out

Use **Zoom in** and **Zoom out** to see a larger or smaller view of your image. In Paint, there are few different ways to zoom in or out, depending on what you want to do.

- To increase the zoom level, on the **View** tab, in the **Zoom** group, click on **Zoom in**.
- To reduce the zoom level, on the **View** tab, in the **Zoom** group, click on **Zoom out**.
- To view the picture in the Paint window at its actual size, on the **View** tab, in the **Zoom** group, click on **100%**.

Saving and Using Your Picture

When editing in Paint, you should save your work frequently so you don't accidentally lose it.

Save a Picture

When you save a new picture for the first time, you'll need to give it a file name.

- Click on the **Paint** button, and then click on **Save**.
- In the **Save as type** box, select the file format you want.
- In the **File name** box, type a name, and then click on **Save**.

Open a Picture

Instead of starting with a new picture, you might want to open an existing picture and edit in Paint.

- Click on the **Paint** button, and then click on **Open**.
- Find the picture you want to open in Paint, click on it, and then click on **Open**.

Set Your Picture as Your Desktop Background

You can also set the picture as the desktop background on your computer.

- Click on the **Paint** button, and then click on **Save**.
- Click on the **Paint** button, point to **Set as desktop background**, and then click on one of the desktop background settings.

In Paint, the **Home** tab has all the main image editing items.

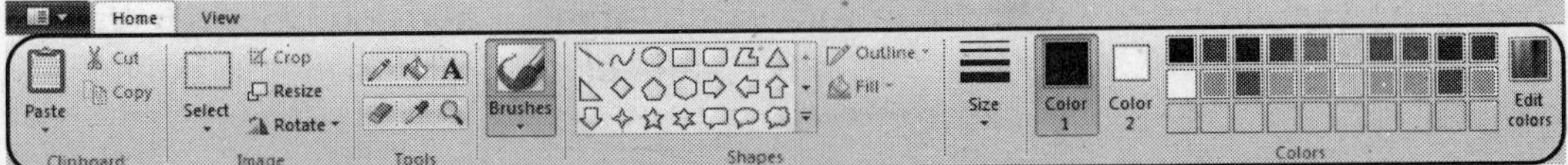

One of the things you can do is to add any of the tools from the Home tab to the **Quick Access Toolbar**. Just right-click on the tool that you want to add and select **Add to Quick Access Toolbar** from the right-click menu.

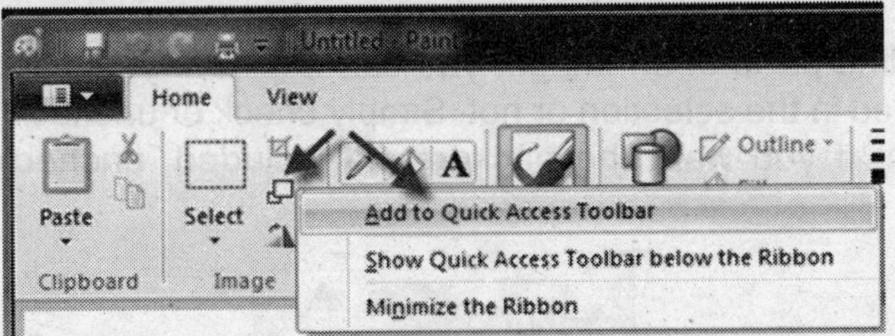

Next to the **Home** tab there is the **View** tab. Here you can **Zoom In** or **Zoom Out** or see an image in **Full Screen** mode. Also you can select to show **Rulers and Gridlines** on an image which can help you align elements in an image.

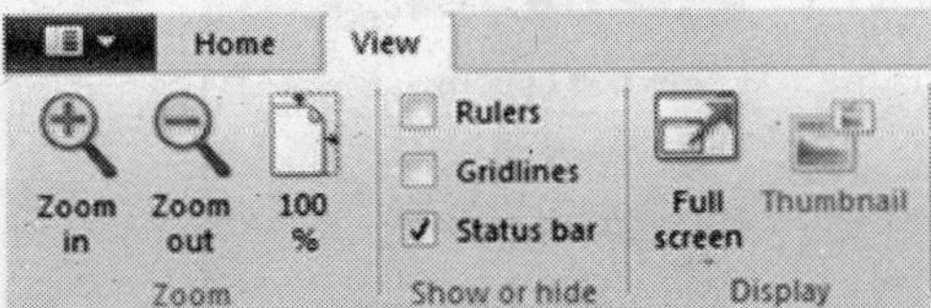

Finally, under the tabbed menu, there is the Drawing area and below it the **Status** bar where you can see general information about the current image.

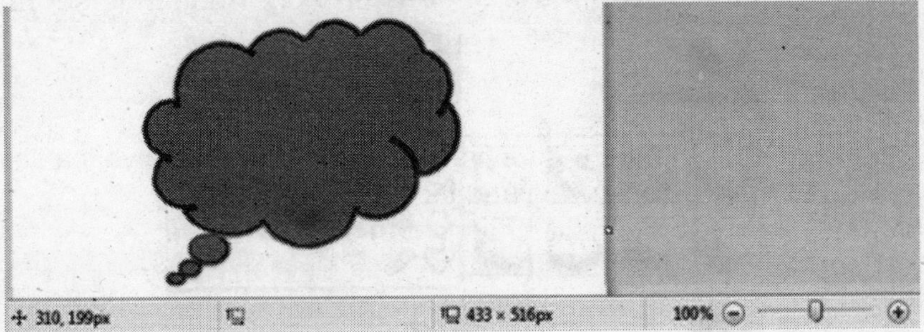

The Home Tab

The first section of the **Home** tab contains the **Clipboard tools**: Paste from, Copy and Cut. Then you have the **Image** section, with the Crop, Resize, Rotate and Select tools.

You can also resize a picture by percentage or by pixels.

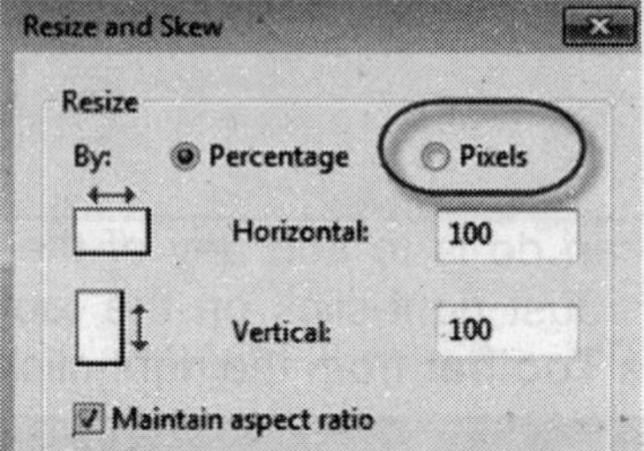

When selecting parts of an image, you can decide if you want the background color to be included in the selection or not. Simply check or uncheck the **Transparent selection** option. If you want the background included, uncheck the option and vice-versa.

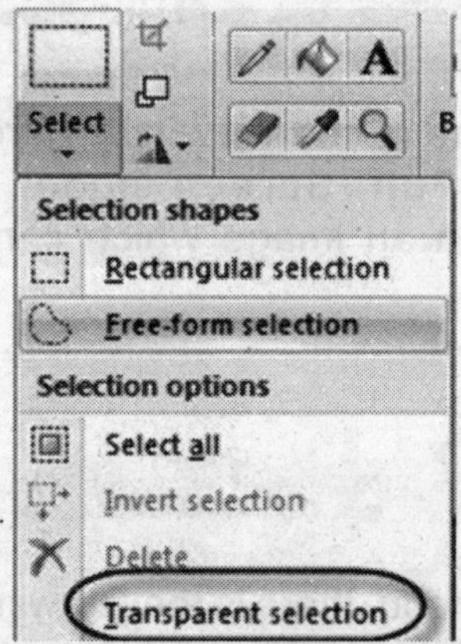

Finally, there are the **Brushes** and **Shapes** tools.

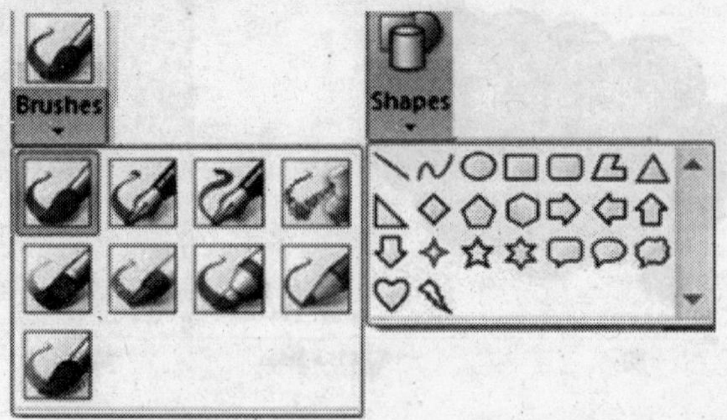

Drawing Different Shapes

You can use Paint to add different shapes in a picture. If you want to make your own custom shape, you can use to the **Polygon** tool to do this.

You can use Paint to draw different types of ready-made shapes. Here's a list of them:

- Line
- Curve
- Oval
- Rectangle and Rounded rectangle
- Triangle and Right triangle
- Diamond
- Pentagon
- Hexagon
- Arrows (Right arrow, Left arrow, Up arrow, Down arrow)
- Stars (Four-point star, Five-point star, Six-point star)
- Callouts (Rounded rectangular callout, Oval callout, Cloud callout)
- Heart
- Lightning bolt

Adding Text

In Paint, you can also add your own text or message in your picture.

Text Tool

Use the **Text** tool **A** to enter text in the picture.

- On the **Home** tab, in the **Tools** group, click on the **Text** tool **A**.
- Drag the pointer in the drawing area where you want to add text.
- Under **Text** tools, on the **Text** tab, in the **Font** group, click on the font face, size and style.

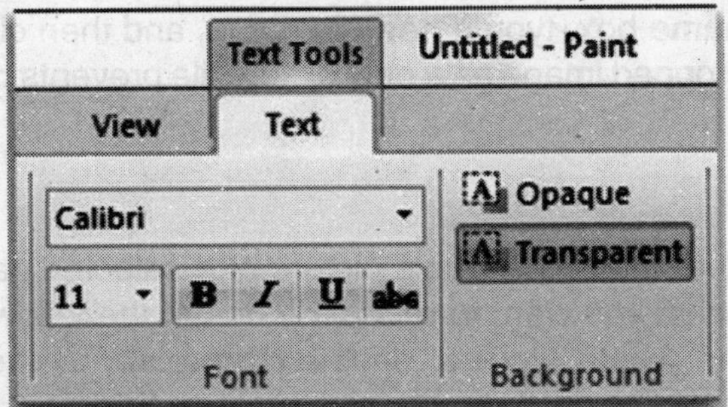

The Font Group

- In the **Colors** group, click on **Color 1**, and then click on a color for the text.
- Type the text that you want to add.

Selecting and Editing Objects

In Paint, if you want to make a change to a part of a picture or an object, you need to select the part of the picture that you want to change, and then make the edit. Some changes you can make include the following: resizing an object, moving or copying an object, rotating it, or cropping the picture to only show the selected item.

Select Tool

Use the **Select** tool to select part of the picture that you want to change.

- On the **Home** tab, in the **Image** group, click on the down arrow under **Select**.

Do one of the following, depending on what you want to select.

- To select any square or rectangular part of the picture, click on **Rectangular** selection, and then drag the pointer to select the part of the picture you want to work with.
- To select any irregularly shaped part of the picture, click on **Free-form selection**, and then drag the pointer to select the part of the picture you want to work with.
- To select the whole picture, click on **Select all**.
- To select everything in the picture except for the currently selected area, click on **Invert selection**.
- To delete the selected object, click on **Delete**.

Crop

Use **Crop** to crop a picture so only the part you selected appears in your picture. Cropping lets you change the picture so only the selected object or person is visible.

- On the **Home** tab, in the **Image** group, click on the arrow under **Select**, and then click on the kind of selection you want to make.
- Drag the pointer to select the part of the picture you want to show.
- In the **Image** group, click on **Crop**.
- To save the cropped picture as a new file, click on the **Paint** button, point to **Save as**, and then click on the file type for the current picture.
- In the **File name** box, type a new file name, and then click on **Save.**
- Saving the cropped image as a new picture file prevents overwriting the original picture file.

Rotate

Use **Rotate** to rotate the whole picture or a selected part of it.

Depending on what you want to rotate, do one of the following:

- To rotate the whole picture, on the **Home** tab, in the **Image** group, click on **Rotate**, and then click on the rotation direction.
- To rotate an object or part of a picture, on the **Home** tab, in the **Image** group, click on **Select**. Drag the pointer to select the area or object, click on **Rotate**, and then click the rotation direction.

Erasing Part of a Picture

Use the **Eraser** tool to erase areas of your picture.

- On the **Home** tab, in the **Tools** group, click on the **Eraser** .
- Click on **Size**, click on an **eraser size**, and then drag the eraser over the area of the picture that you want to erase. Any areas that you erase will reveal the background color (Color 2).

WORDPAD

WordPad is a text-editing program. This tool enables you to create, edit, view and print text documents. It can be used to type memos, create quick reports or other simple documents. Unlike Notepad, WordPad documents can include rich formatting and graphics.

How to Find WordPad

In Windows 7, you can go to the **Start** menu and in the **Accessories** folder, you can find **WordPad**.

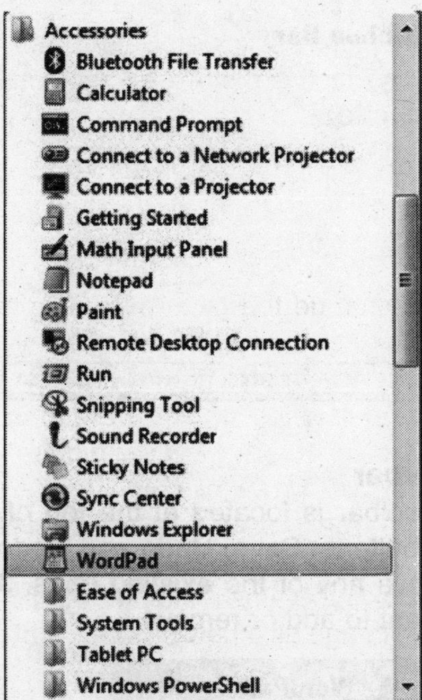

This opens the WordPad application.

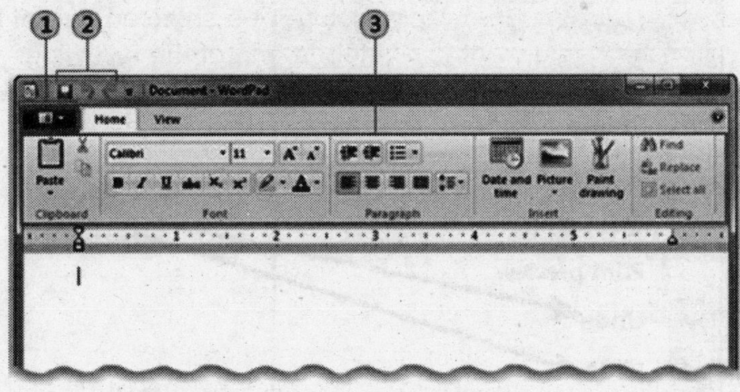

① The WordPad button ② Quick Access toolbar

③ The Ribbon

In Windows 7, there is a new ribbon, which shows the choices in the open rather than in menus.

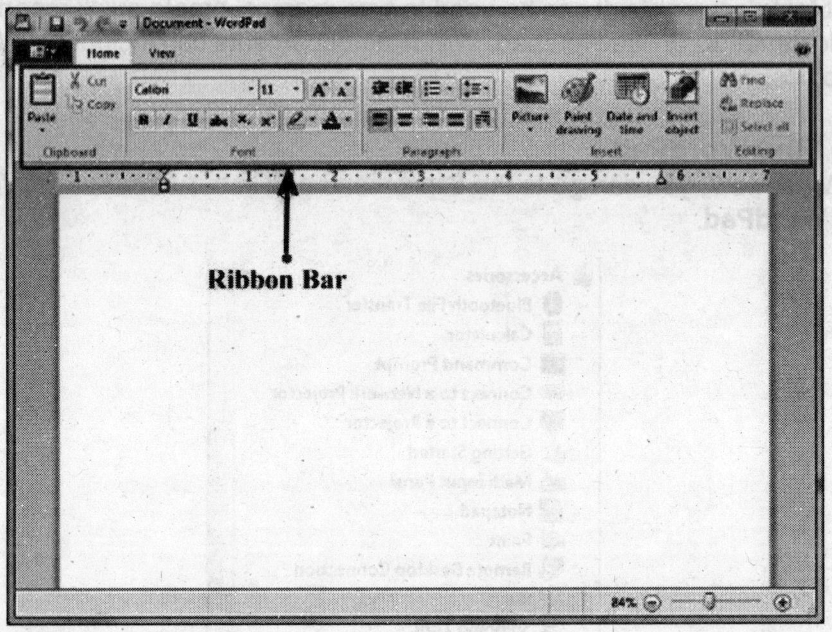

The Quick Access Toolbar

The Quick Access Toolbar is located at the top of the WordPad window and contains a few important buttons: Save, Undo and Redo. You can add buttons like New, Open, Print or remove any of the existing ones. Just click on the arrow and choose the buttons you want to add or remove.

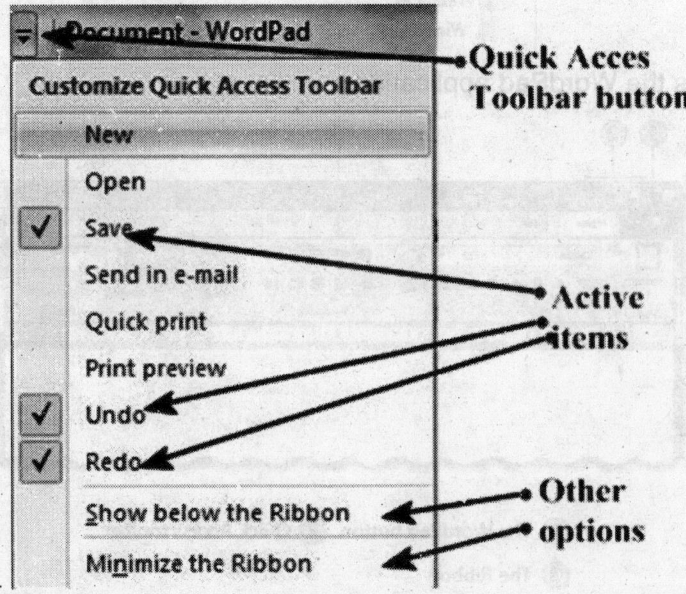

Another way to add items to Quick Access Toolbar is to right-click on the option that you want to add from the ribbon and choose **Add to Quick Access Toolbar**.

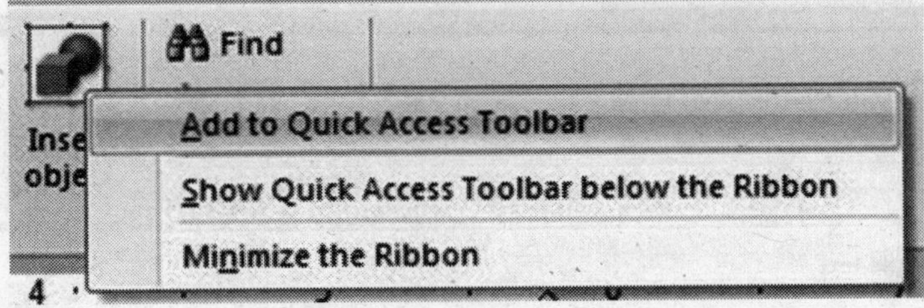

Home Tab

The first tab in the WordPad window is the Home tab. It offers a number of customizing options, grouped by functionality. From here you can change things like the spacing used, the alignment, the font, size or color.

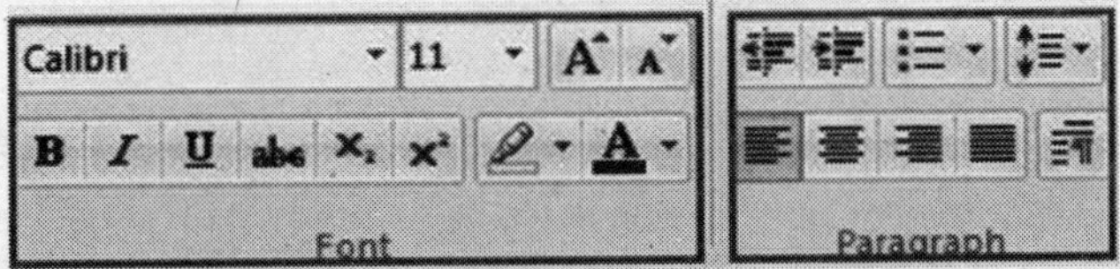

Next, there is the Insert section, where you can find options for inserting pictures, custom drawings, date and time or others objects, like charts or different documents.

There are also options like Find, Replace or Select all.

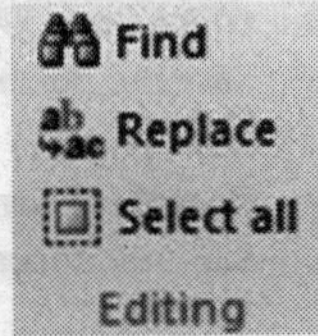

View Tab

The View tab has a few display options, including zoom or the ability to show or hide the ruler and the status bar.

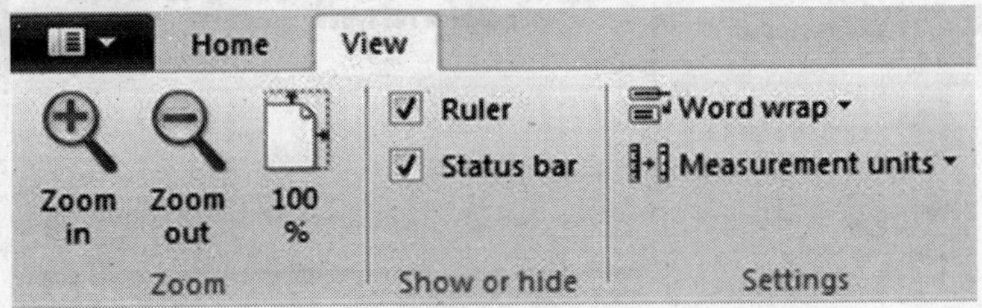

How to Create a WordPad Document

To create a new document, open WordPad and write the text you wish to enter.

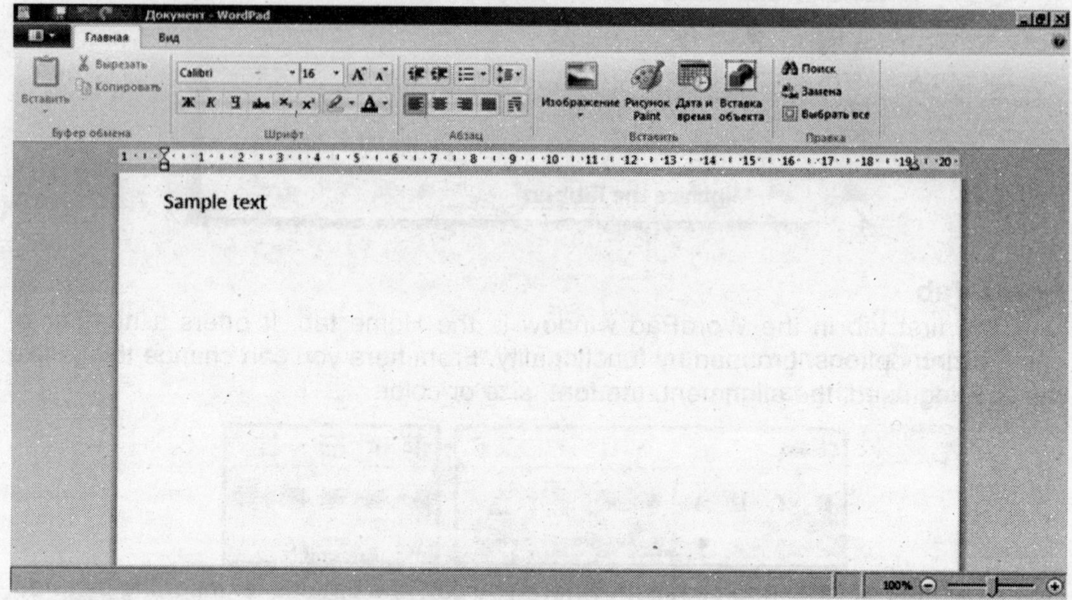

When done, save your document by going to the **File** menu and choose **Save As**. There are five options available for saving documents.

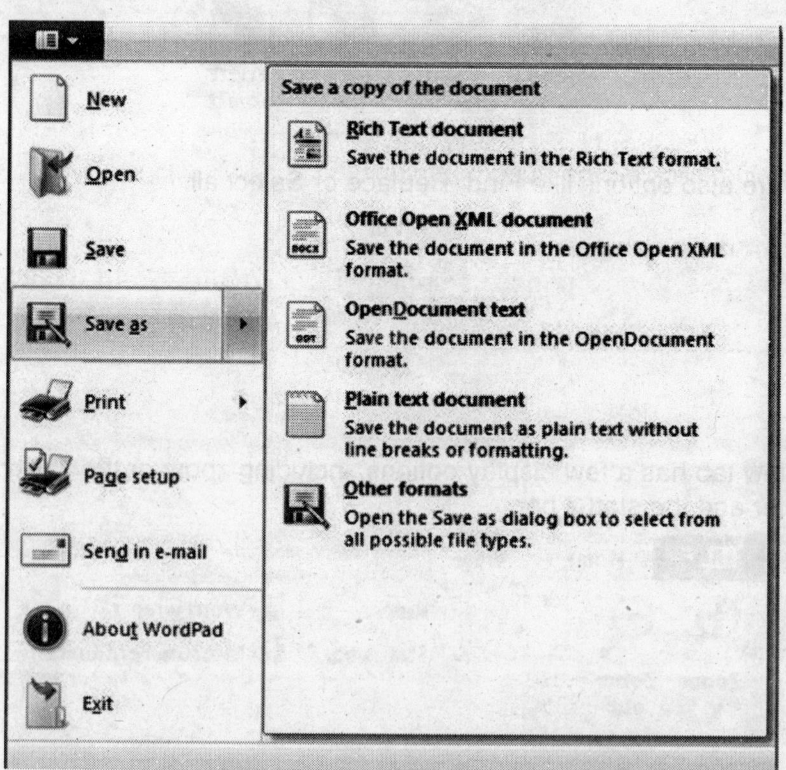

Select the format you prefer, provide the location of the file and type its name. When done, press the **Save** button.

How to Open a WordPad Document

To open a WordPad document, click on the **File** menu and then click on **Open**.

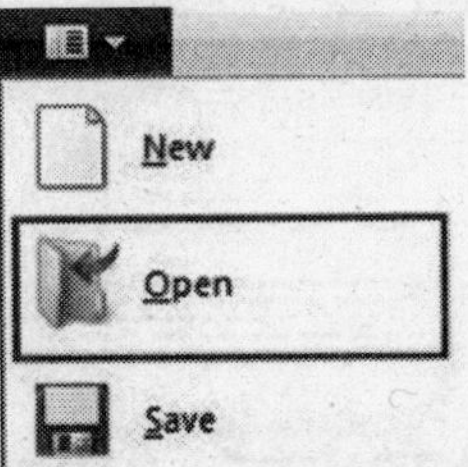

To open a recent document that you have worked with, go to the **Open** menu and you can find the recent documents list being displayed.

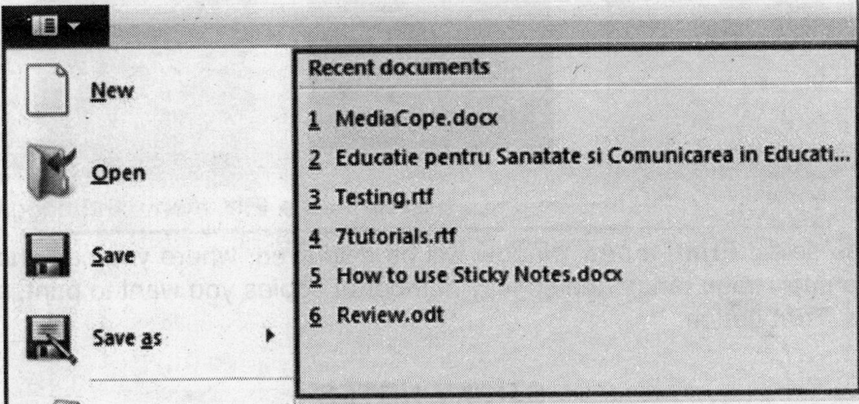

You can just click on the document you wish to open and it will open for you.

How to Print a Document

WordPad has three options for printing documents: Print, Quick print and Print preview.

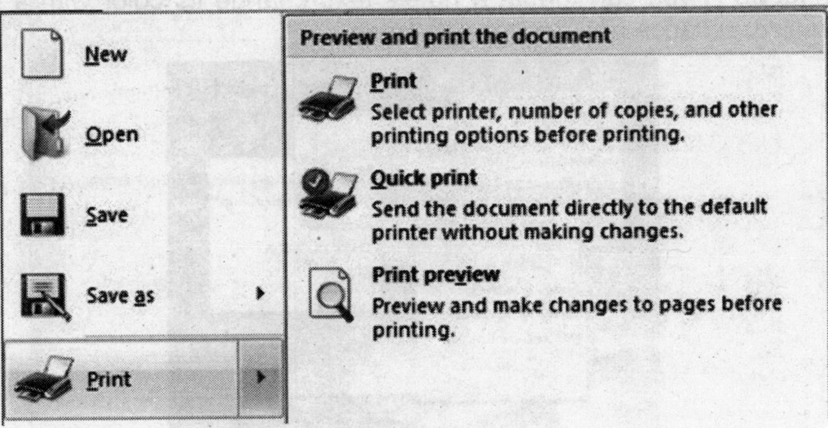

Print preview allows you to see how the document will look before you print it. To use this option, use the **File** menu, choose **Print** and then click on **Print preview**. When you are done with the preview of the document, click on **Close print preview**.

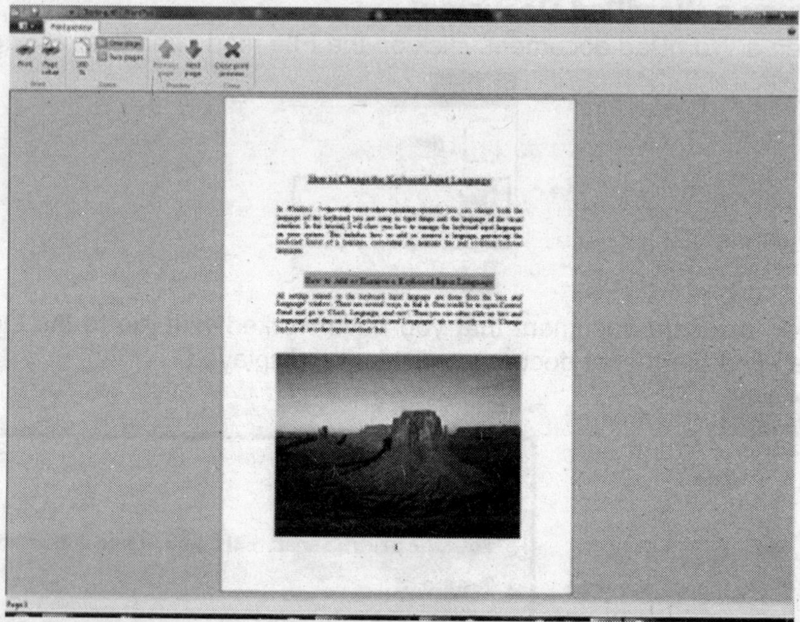

If you select **Print**, a new window will be displayed, where you can choose the desired printer, page range and specify number of copies you want to print, and then press the **Print** button.

STICKY NOTES

Sticky Notes is a small utility application that allows you to create all kinds of notes. You can place them anywhere you want on your Desktop, you can format their text, resize and paint them in a variety of colors easily. They will remain there as long as the application is running and each time you open it, your latest written notes are restored.

In Windows 7, you can format a note's text, change its color with a click, and speedily resize, collapse and flip through notes.

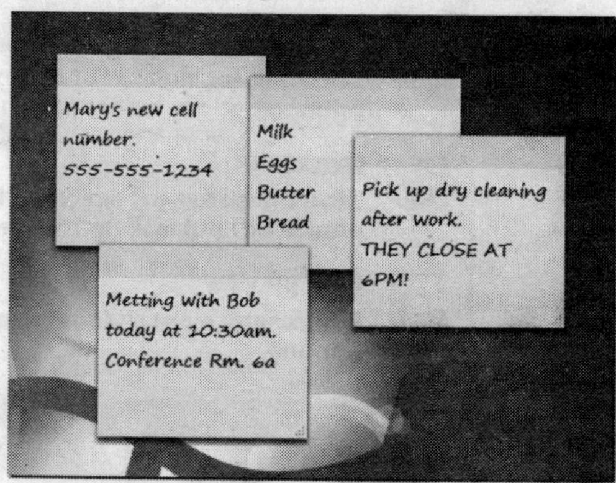

How to Start the Sticky Notes Application

The Sticky Notes application is located in the Accessories section of Windows 7 Start Menu.

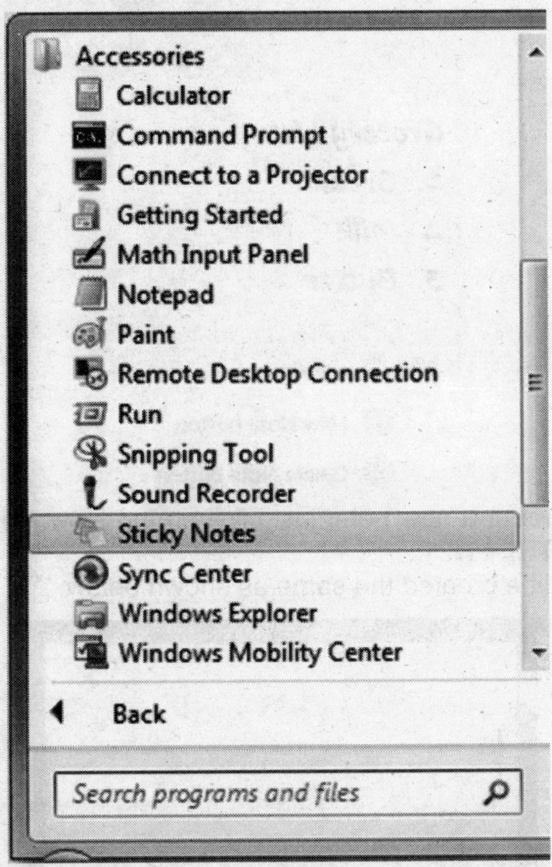

The first note will be displayed and it should look similar to the one below. You can start typing if you want to create your first note.

Using Sticky Notes

You can use Sticky Notes to write a to-do list, jot down a phone number, or do anything else that you'd use a pad of paper for. To type a note, click where you want the text to appear, and then start typing.

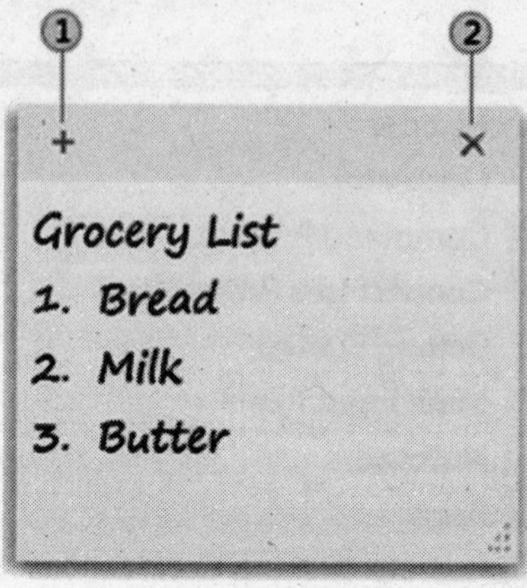

① New Note button

② Delete Note button

If you want to create a new note, just click on the **New Note** button or use the keyboard shortcut **CTRL+ N**.

A blank note will be created the same as shown below.

How to Delete a Note in Sticky Notes

If you want to delete a note, click on the **Delete Note** button or use the keyboard shortcut **CTRL + D**.

You'll be prompted to confirm your choice. Click on **Yes** to delete the note.

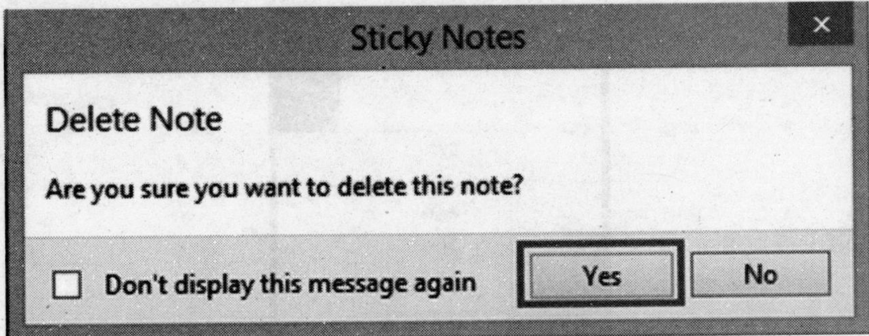

If you no longer want to be asked to confirm your choice each time you remove a note, check the box that says **Don't display this message again**, before clicking on **Yes**.

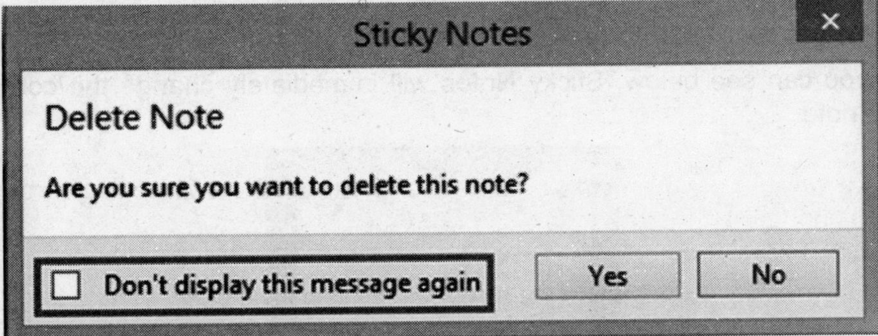

When you close Sticky Notes from the taskbar, the notes you have created will be displayed the next time you open the application, exactly in the same place and form as they were when you closed it.

How to customize a note in Sticky Notes

The application offers some customization options, like resizing, changing the background color or formatting the text. To change its size, drag it from its bottom right corner.

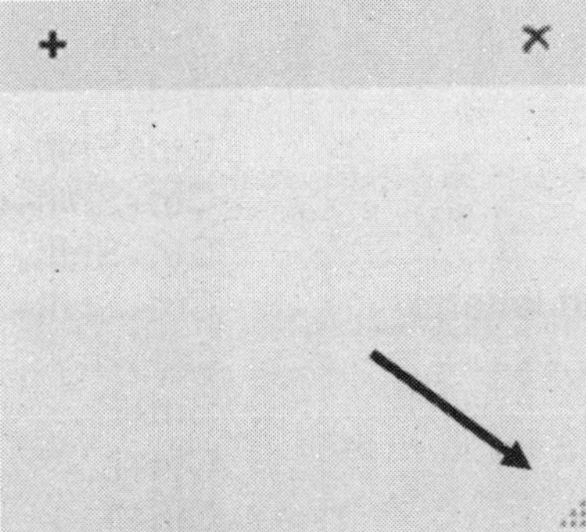

You can also change the color of the notes to help you organize them. The choices available are: Blue, Green, Pink, Purple, White, or Yellow. To do this, right-click and hold the note to bring up the color options menu and select the color you desire.

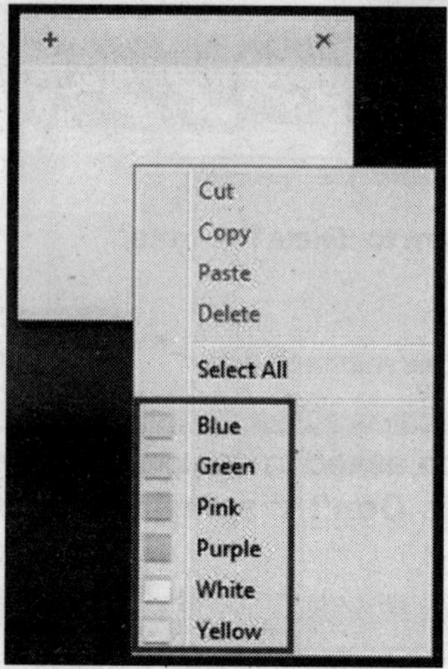

As you can see below, Sticky Notes will immediately change the color of the selected note.

Sticky Notes offers the possibility to format the text with the help of the keyboard keys. You just need to select the text and press one of the following keyboard shortcuts to get the desired formatting:

Bold:	Ctrl+B
Italics:	Ctrl+I
Underline:	Ctrl+U
Strikethrough:	Ctrl+T
Bullet list:	Ctrl+Shift+L
Bigger font:	Ctrl+Shift+>
Smaller font:	Ctrl+Shift+
Capitalize or highlighted letters:	Ctrl+Shift+A
Right Align:	Ctrl+R
Center align:	Ctrl+E
Left Align:	Ctrl+L
Single line space:	Ctrl+1
Double line space:	Ctrl+2
1.5 line space:	Ctrl+5

□

9
An Introduction to Microsoft Word 2010

Microsoft Office Word 2010 is a word-processing programme that allows you to create and edit documents, such as letters, reports, invoices, e-mails and books. By default, documents saved in Word 2010 are saved with the **.docx** extension.

Getting Started with MS Word 2010

1. Click on the **Start** button.
2. Click on **All Programs** option from the menu.
3. Search for **Microsoft Office** from the submenu and click on it.
4. Search for **Microsoft Word 2010** from the submenu and click on it.

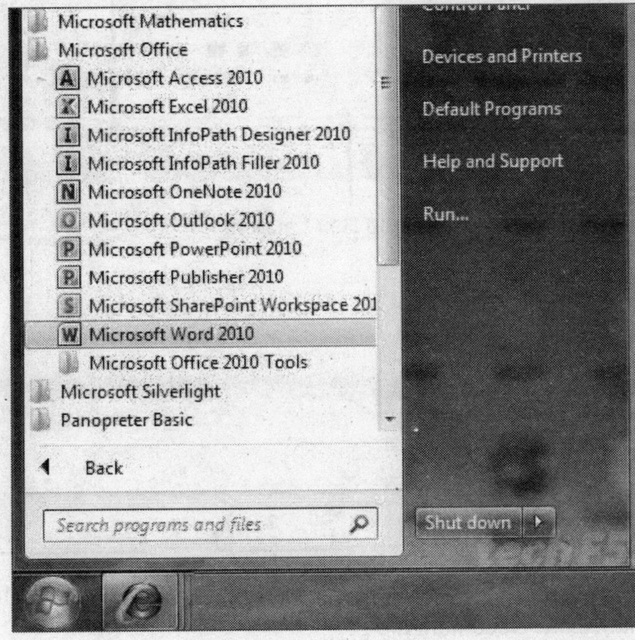

This will launch Microsoft Word 2010 application and you will see the following word window.

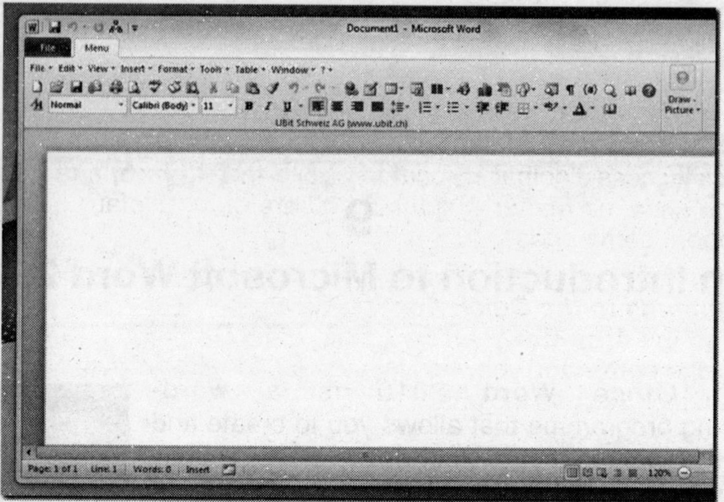

Explore Window

Following is the basic window which you get when you start word application. Let us understand various important parts of this window.

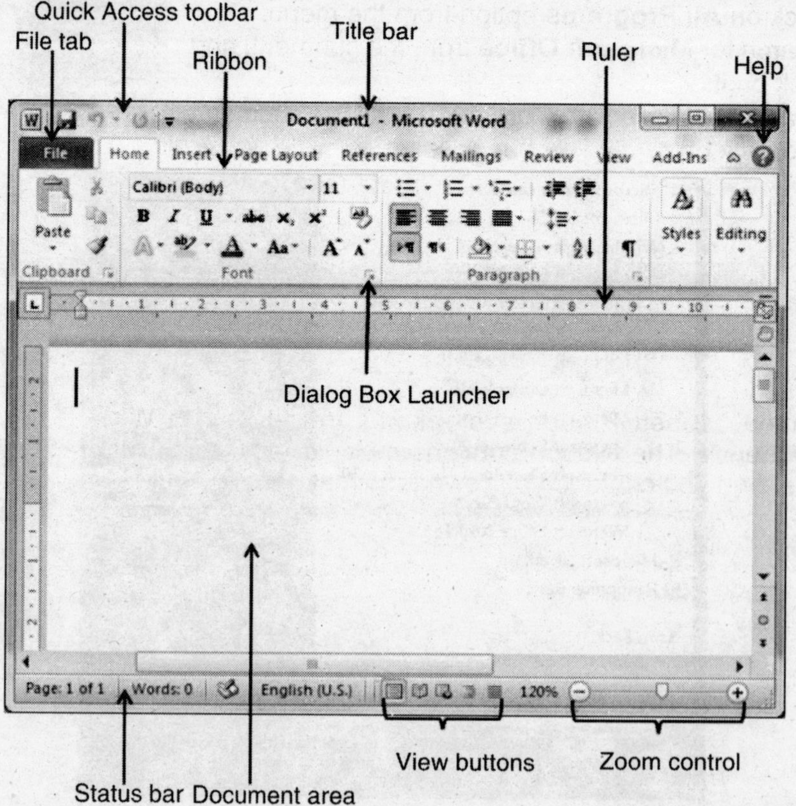

File Tab

The File tab replaces the **Office** button from Word 2007. You can click on the **File tab** to check **Backstage view**, which is the place to come when you need to open or save files, create new documents, print a document and do other file-related operations.

Quick Access Toolbar

The Quick Access Toolbar is located above the **Ribbon**, and it lets you access common commands, no matter which tab you are on. By default, it shows the Save, Undo and Repeat commands.

To Add Commands to the Quick Access Toolbar

1. Click on the **drop-down arrow** to the right of the **Quick Access Toolbar**.
2. Select the **command** you wish to add from the **drop-down menu**. It will appear in the Quick Access toolbar.

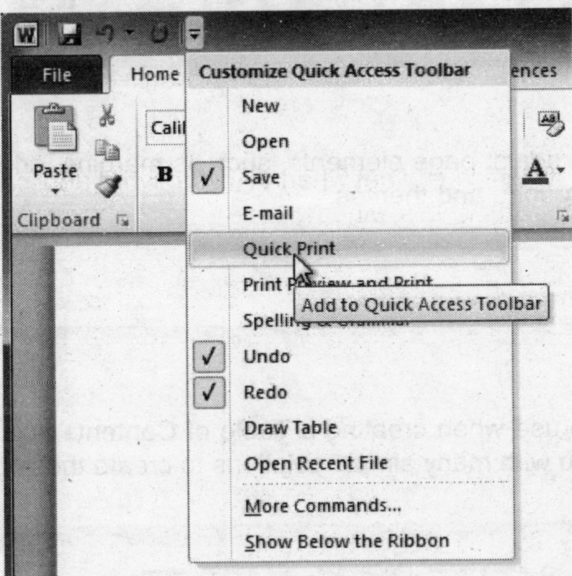

The Ribbon

The new, tabbed Ribbon system was introduced in Word 2007 to replace traditional menus. The Ribbon contains multiple tabs, each with several groups of commands, and you can add your own tabs that contain your favourite commands.

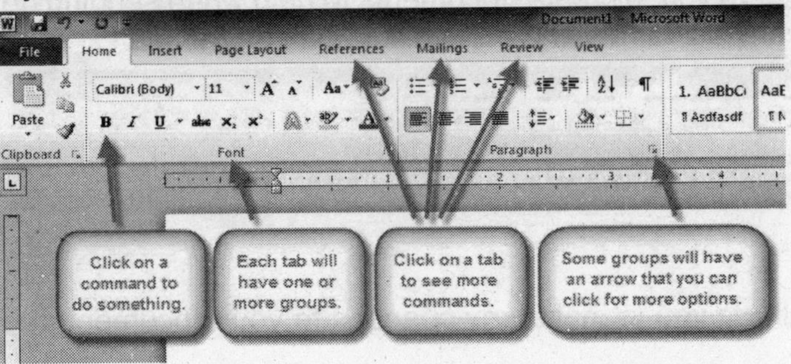

Home Tab

This is the most used tab. It incorporates all text formatting features, such as font and paragraph changes.

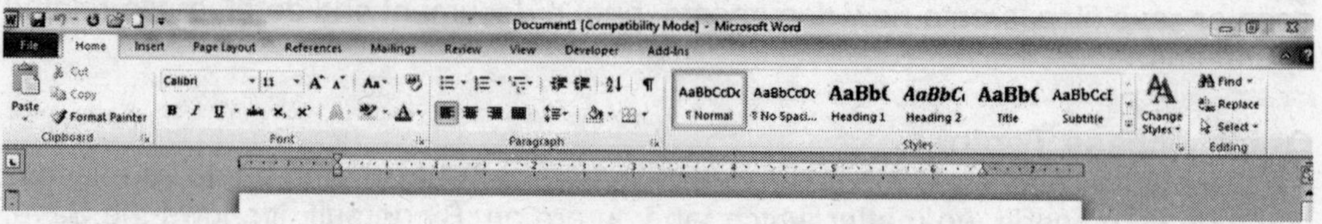

Insert Tab

This tab allows you to insert a variety of items into a document from pictures, clip art, tables and headers and footers.

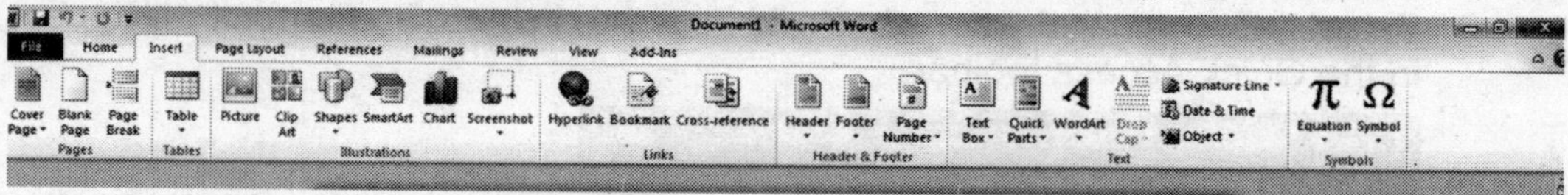

Page Layout Tab

This tab has commands to adjust page elements, such as margins, orientation, inserting columns, page backgrounds and themes.

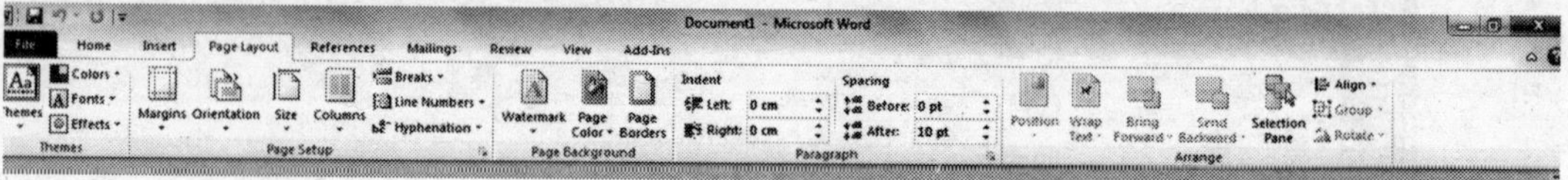

References Tab

This tab has commands to use when creating a Table of Contents and citation page for a paper. It provides you with many simple solutions to create these typically difficult to produce documents.

Mailings Tab

This tab allows you to create documents to help when sending out mailings, such as printing envelopes, labels and processing mail merges.

Review Tab

This tab allows you to make any changes to your document due to spelling and grammar issues. It also holds the track changes feature which provides the ability to make notes and changes to a document of another person.

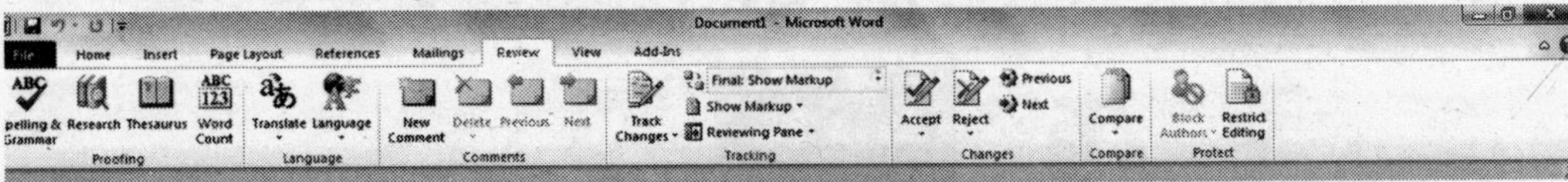

View Tab

This tab allows you to change the view of your document to a different two-page document or zoom.

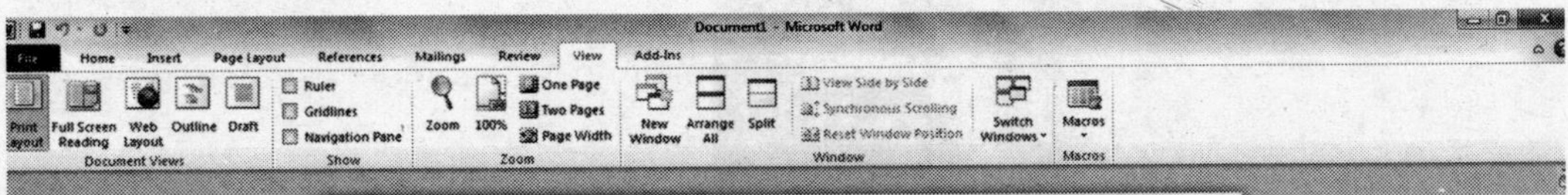

Title Bar

This tab lies in the middle and at the top of the window. Title bar shows the programme and document titles.

Rulers

The Ruler is located at the top and to the left of your document. It makes easier to adjust your document with precision. Word has two rulers—a horizontal ruler and a vertical ruler.

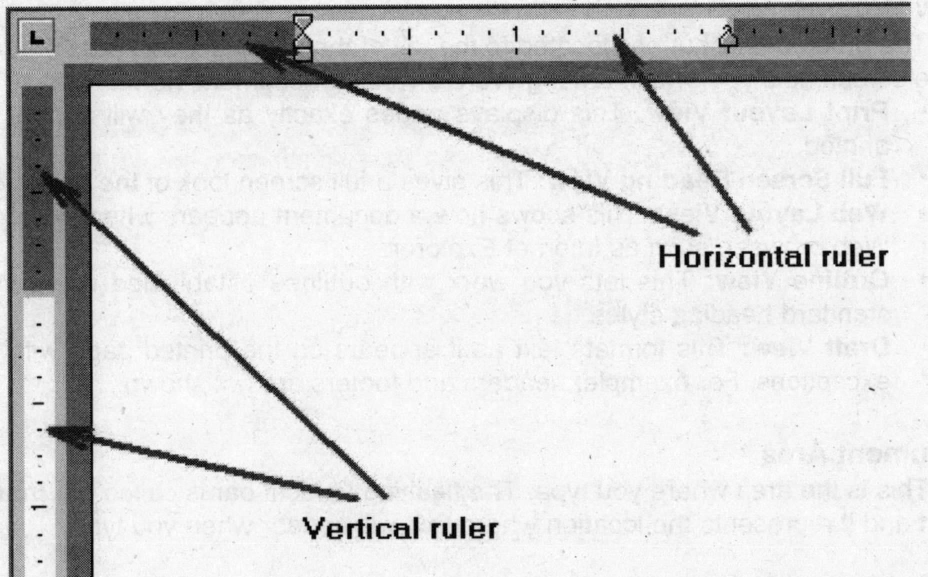

The horizontal ruler appears just beneath the Ribbon and is used to set margins and tab stops.

The vertical ruler appears on the left edge of the Word window and is used to gauge the vertical position of elements on the page.

To Hide or View the Ruler

Click on the **View Ruler icon** over the scrollbar to hide the ruler.

To show the ruler, click on the **View Ruler icon** again.

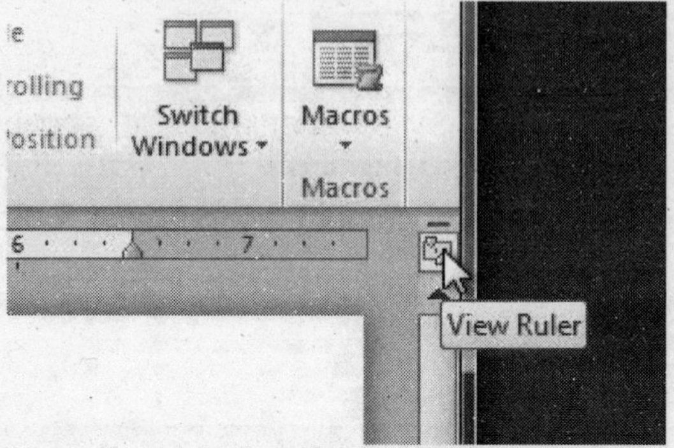

Help

The Help icon can be used to get word-related help any time you like.

Zoom Control

Zoom control lets you zoom in for a closer look at your text. The zoom control consists of a slider that you can slide left or right to **zoom in** or **zoom out**, like + and – buttons which you can click to **increase** or **decrease** the zoom, respectively.

View Buttons

The group of five buttons located to the left of the Zoom control, near the bottom of the screen, lets you switch among Word's various document views.

- **Print Layout View:** This displays pages exactly as they will appear when printed.
- **Full Screen Reading View:** This gives a full screen look of the document.
- **Web Layout View:** This shows how a document appears when viewed by a Web browser, such as Internet Explorer.
- **Outline View:** This lets you work with outlines established using Word's standard heading styles.
- **Draft View:** This formats text as it appears on the printed page with a few exceptions. For example, headers and footers are not shown.

Document Area

This is the area where you type. The flashing vertical bar is called the **insertion point** and it represents the location where text will appear when you type.

Status Bar

This displays document information as well as the insertion point location. From left to right, this bar contains the total number of pages and words in the document, language, etc.

Dialog Box Launcher

This appears as a very small arrow in the lower-right corner of many groups on the Ribbon. Clicking on this button opens a dialog box or task pane that provides more options about the group.

Backstage View

Backstage view gives you various options for saving, opening a file, printing or sharing your document. It is similar to the **Office Button Menu** from Word 2007 or the **File Menu** from earlier versions of Word.

1. Click on the **File tab**.

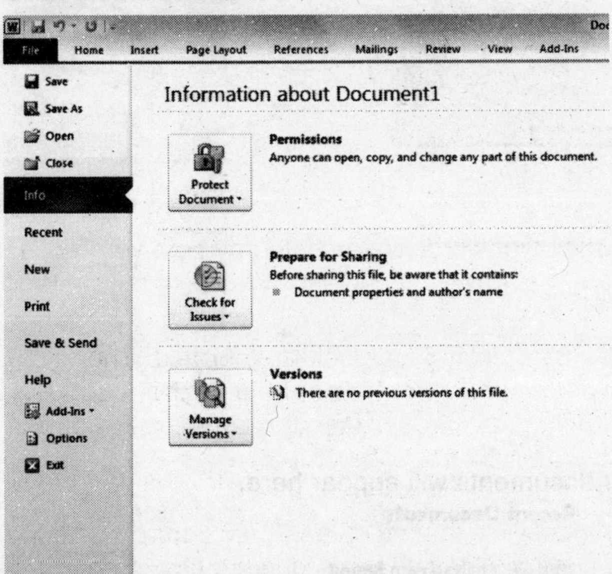

2. You can choose an option on the left side of the page.
3. To get back to your document, just click on **any tab** on the **Ribbon**.

The different things that you can do in Backstage view are as follows:

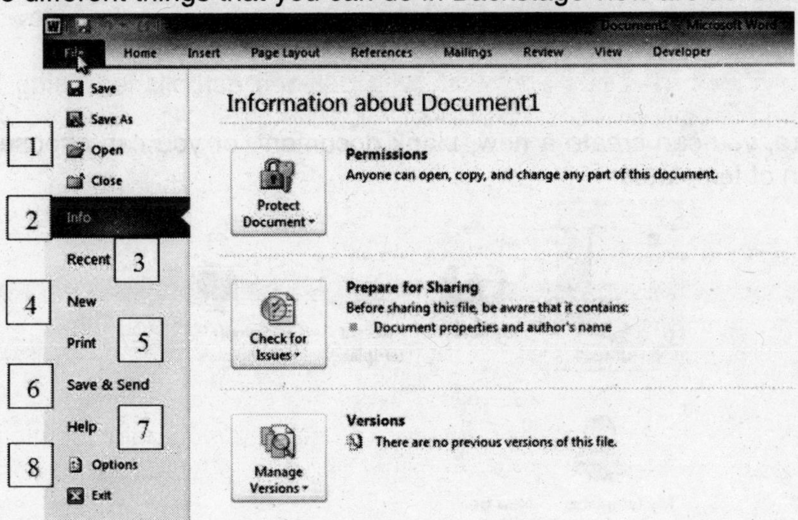

1. Save, Save As, Open and Close

Familiar tasks, such as Save, Save As, Open and Close are now found in Backstage view.

2. Info

Info contains information about the current document. You can also inspect the document and edit the document permissions.

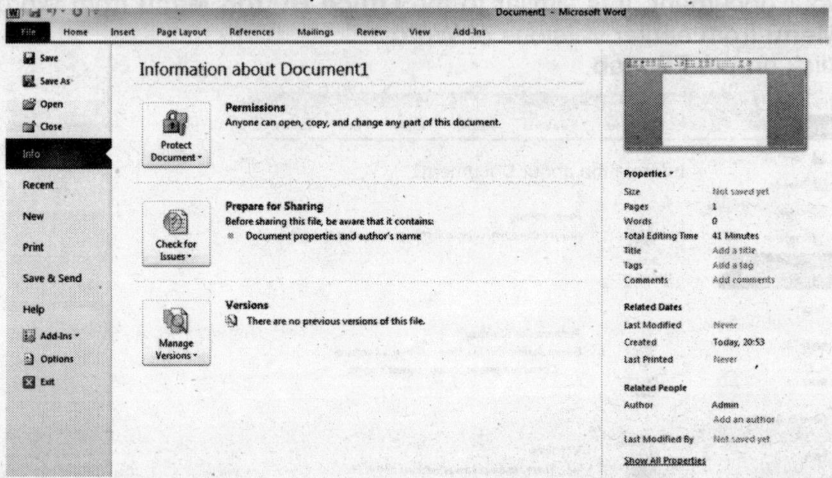

3. Recent

For convenience, recent documents will appear here.

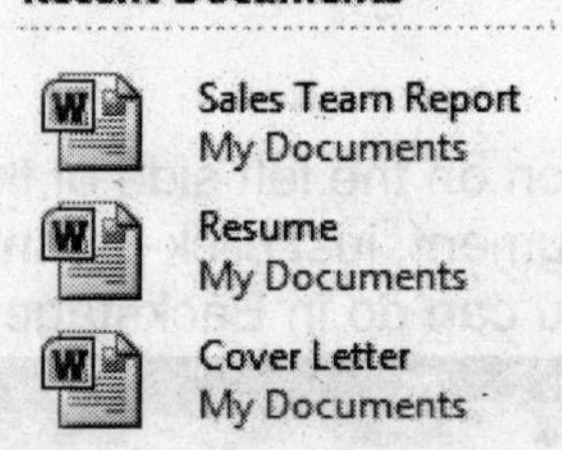

4. New

From here, you can create a new, blank document, or you can choose from a large selection of templates.

5. Print

From the Print pane, you can change the print settings and print your document. You can also see a preview of your document.

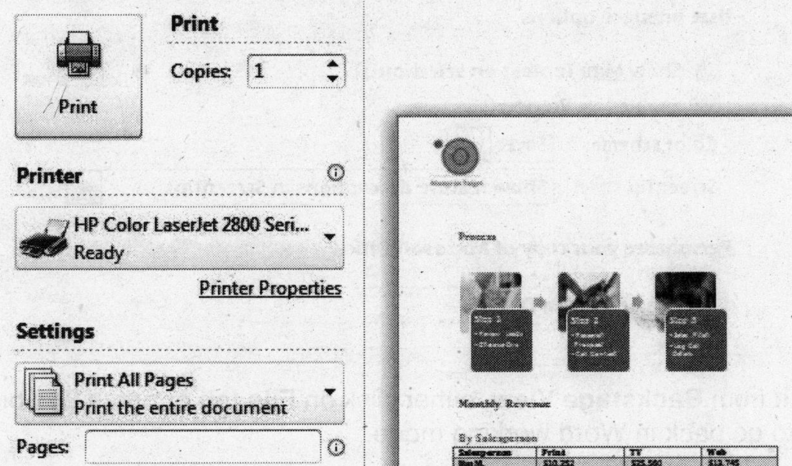

6. Save & Send

Save & Send makes it easy to e-mail your document, post it on the web, or change the file format.

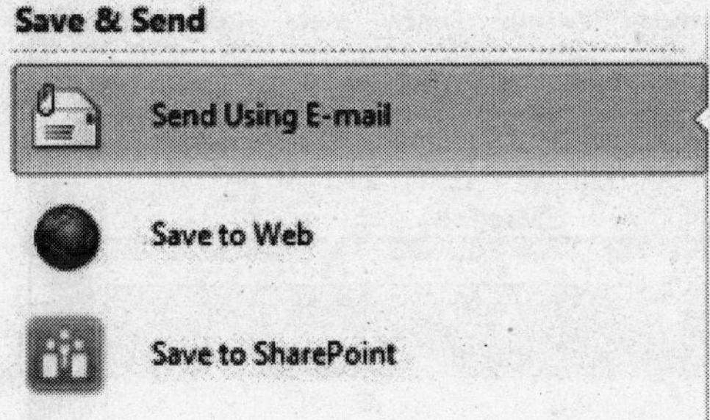

7. Help

From here, you can access Microsoft Office Help or check for updates.

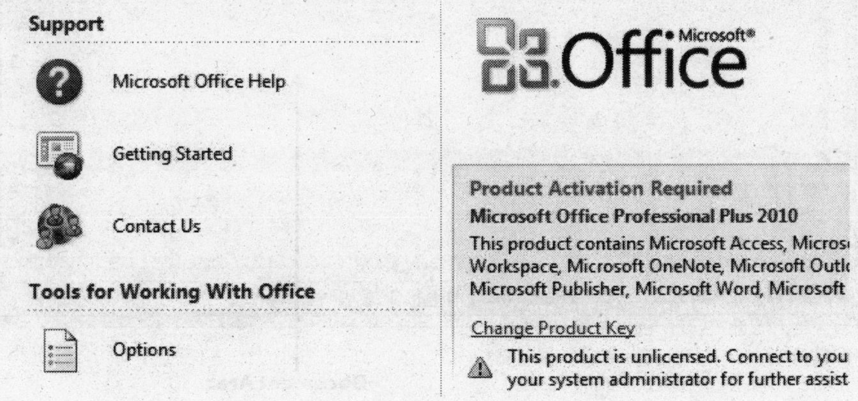

8. Options

Here you can change various Word options. For example, you can control the spelling and grammar check settings, AutoRecover settings, or Language preferences.

User Interface options

- [x] Show Mini Toolbar on selection
- [x] Enable Live Preview

Color scheme: Silver

ScreenTip style: Show feature descriptions in ScreenTips

Personalize your copy of Microsoft Office

User name: John Doe

Initials: JD

To **exit** from **Backstage View**, either click on **File tab** or press **Esc** button on the keyboard to go back in Word working mode.

Entering Text

When you start Word, it displays a new document by default as shown below.

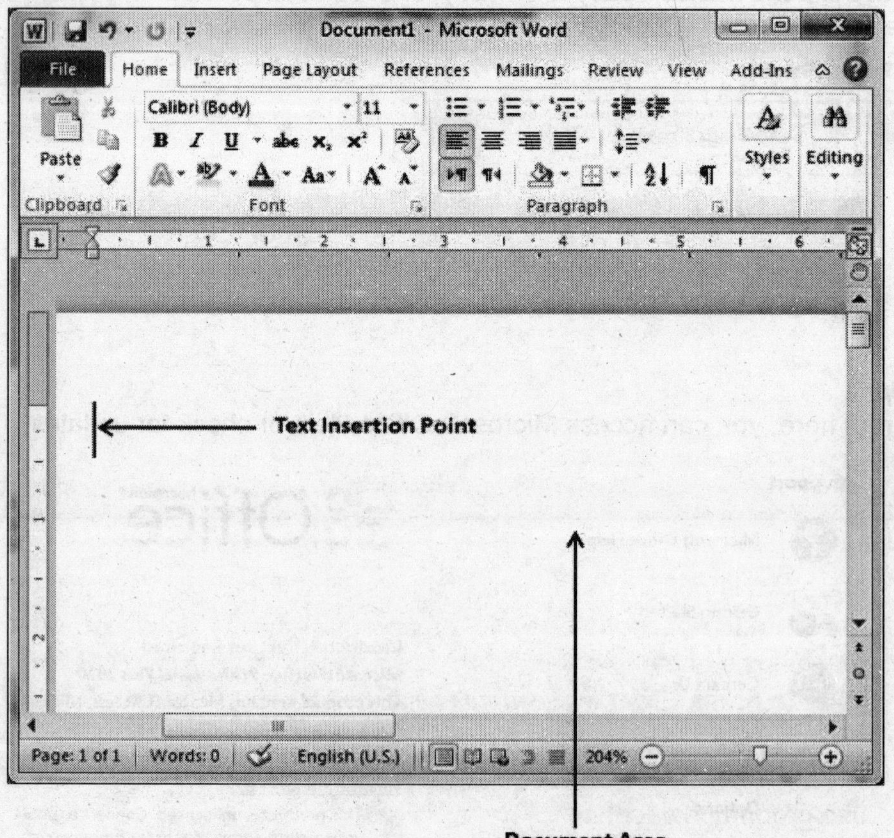

Document area is the area where you type your text. The flashing vertical bar is called the **insertion point**. It represents the location where text will appear when you type.

Keep your mouse cursor at the text insertion point and start typing whatever text you would like to type.

Let us type two words – 'Hello Word'. The text appears to the left of the insertion point as you type.

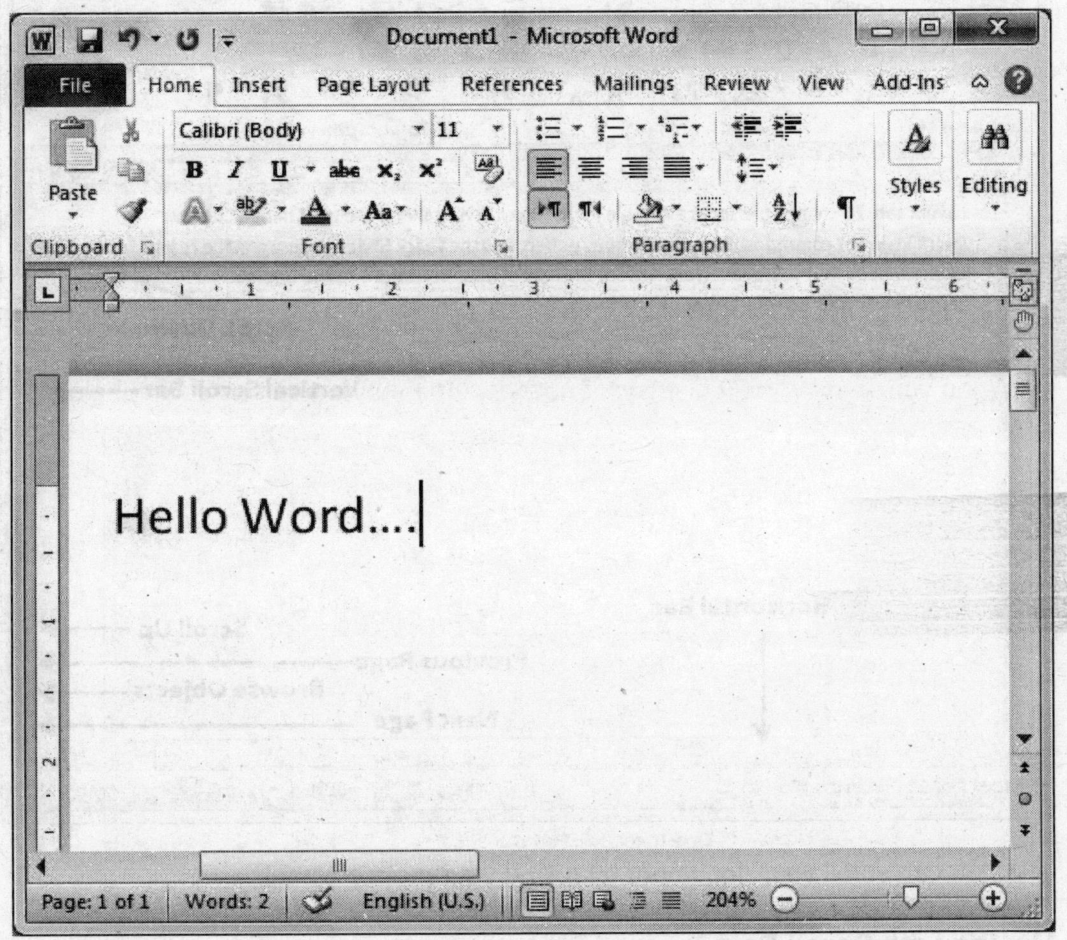

There are two important points which you need to remember while typing:

(i) You **should not press Enter** to start a **new line**, as when the insertion point reaches the end of the line, Word automatically starts a new one. You would need to **press Enter** if you want to have a **new paragraph**.

(ii) When you want to add more than one space between words, use the **Tab** key instead of the spacebar. This way you can properly align text when you use proportional fonts.

Moving with Mouse

You can easily move the insertion point by clicking on your text anywhere on the screen. But if the document is big, then you would have to use the scroll bars.

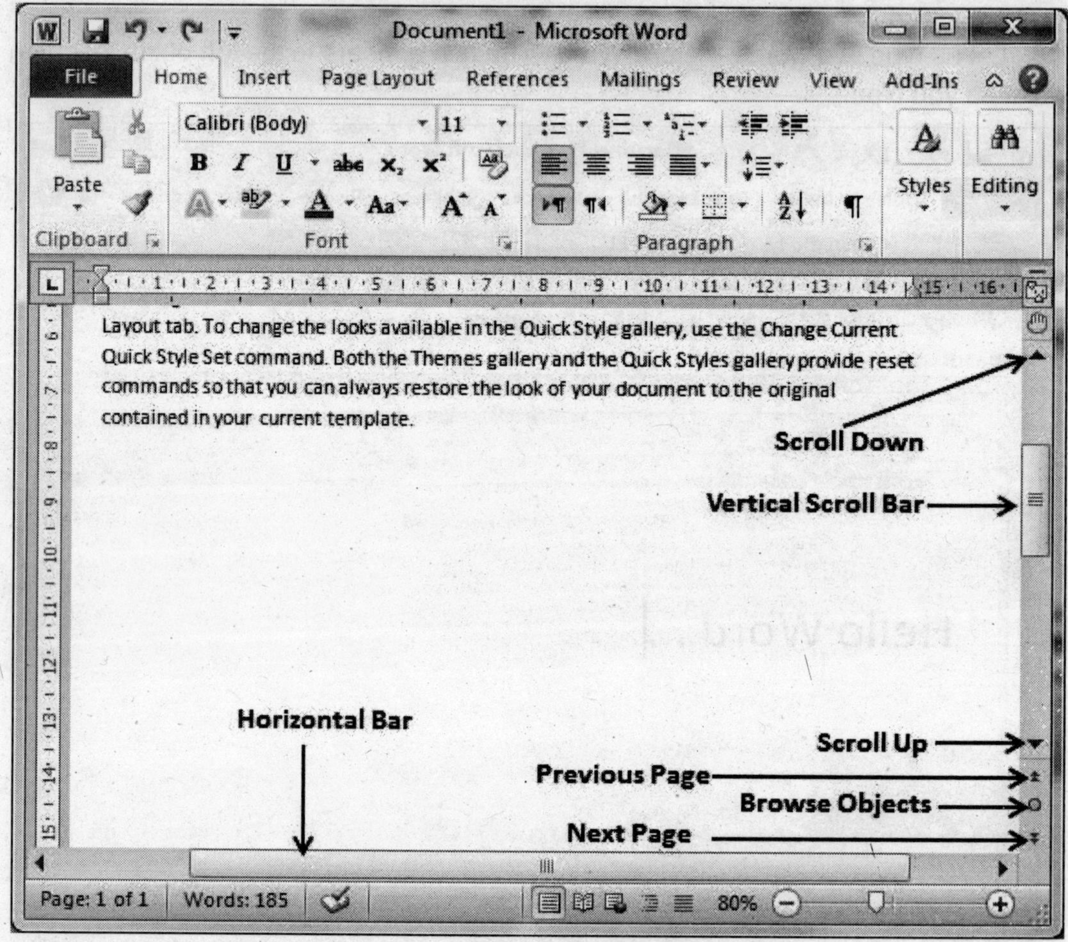

You can scroll your document by rolling your mouse wheel.

Moving with Scroll Bars

As you can see above, there are two scroll bars—one for moving vertically within the document, and other for moving horizontally.

Using the vertical scroll bar, you may:

- Move upward by one line by clicking on the upward-pointing scroll arrow.
- Move downward by one line by clicking on the downward-pointing scroll arrow.
- Move one next page using next page button (footnote).
- Move one previous page, using previous page button (footnote).
- Use Browse Object button to move through the document, going from one chosen object to the next.

Moving with Go To Command

Press **F5** key to use **Go To** command, which will display a dialog box where you will have various options to reach to a particular page.

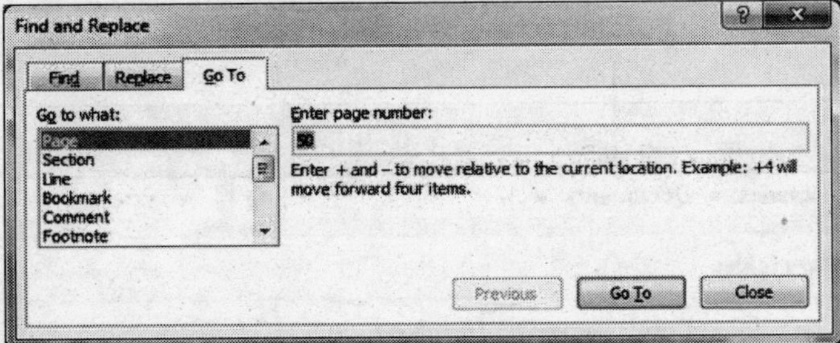

Saving New Document

Once you are done with typing in your new word document, it is time to save your document to avoid losing work you have done on a Word document.

Following are the steps to save an edited Word document:

1. Click on the **File tab** and select **Save As** option.

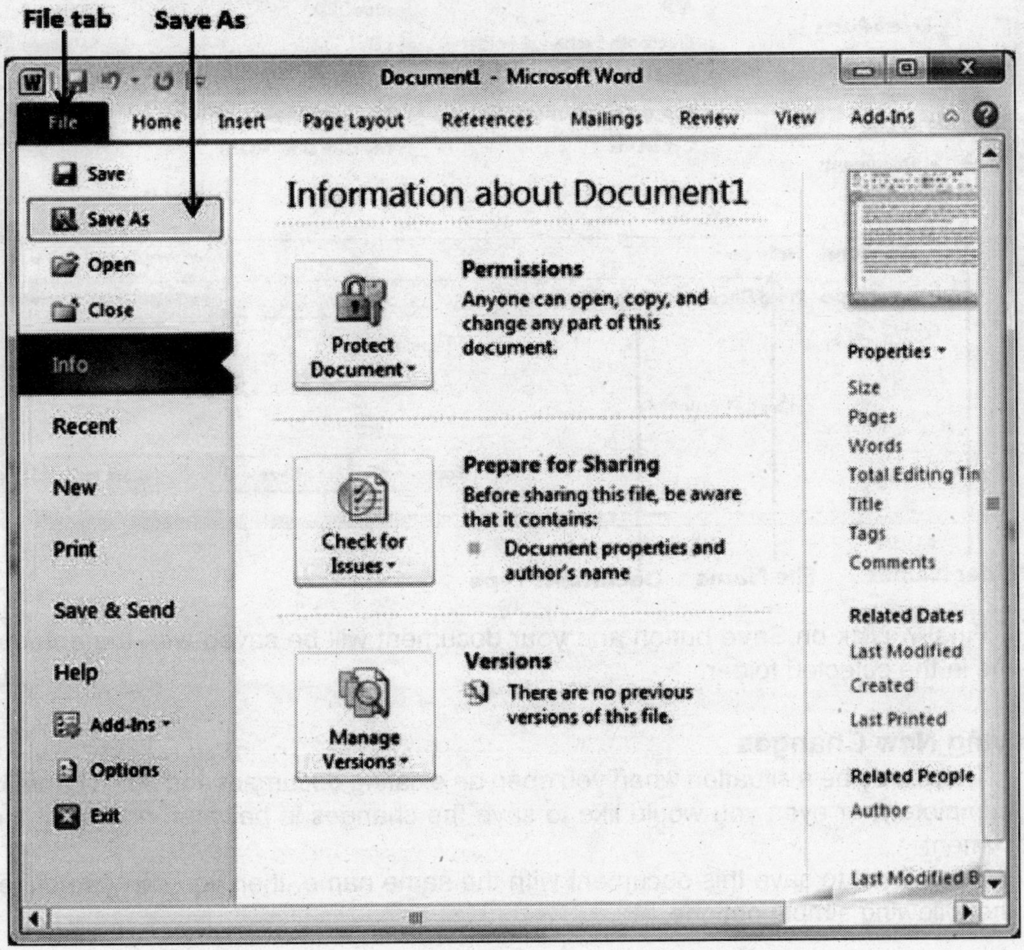

File tab **Save As**

Select a folder where you would like to save the document, Enter file name which you want to give to your document and select a **Save as** type; by default it is **.docx** format.

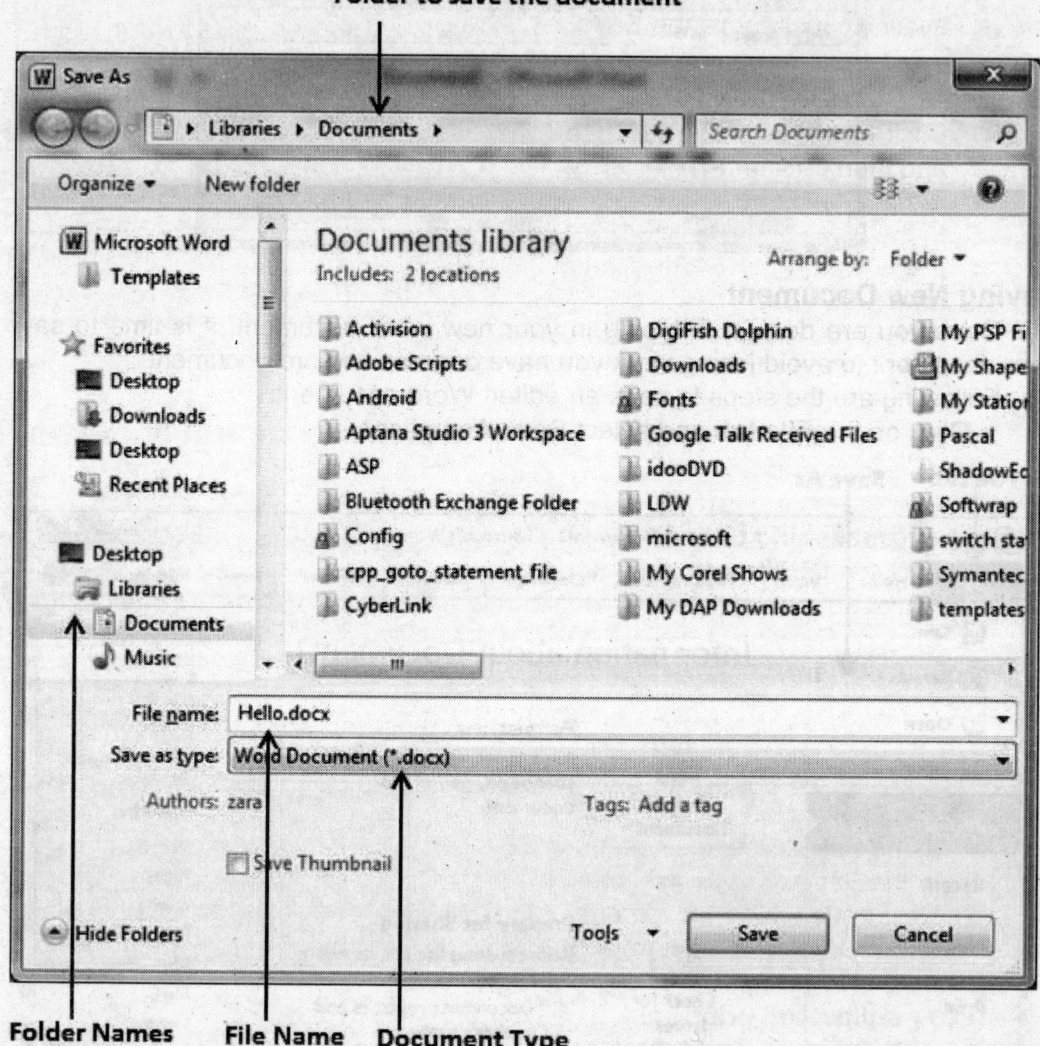

Finally, click on **Save** button and your document will be saved with the entered name in the selected folder.

Saving New Changes

There may be a situation when you open an existing document and edit it partially or completely, or even you would like to save the changes in between editing of the document.

If you want to save this document with the same name, then you can use either of the following simple options.

1. Just press **Ctrl + S** keys to save the changes.
2. Optionally you can click on the **floppy icon** available at the top left corner and just above the File tab. This option will also save the changes.
3. You can also use third method to save the changes, which is **Save** option available just above the **Save As** option.

Saving a Document as PDF

1. Click on the **Microsoft Office Button**, point to the arrow next to **Save As**, and then click on **PDF** or **XPS**.
2. In the **File Name** list, type or select a name for the document.
3. In the **Save as type** list, click on **PDF**.
4. If you want to open the file immediately after saving it, select the **Open file after publishing** check box. (This check box is available only if you have a PDF reader installed on your computer.)
5. Next to **Optimize for**, do one of the following, depending on whether file size or print quality is more important to you:
   - If the document requires high print quality, click on **Standard (publishing online and printing)**.
   - If the print quality is less important than file size, click on **Minimum size (publishing online)**.
6. Click on **Options** to set the page range to be printed, to choose whether markup should be printed, and to select the output options. Click on **OK**.
7. Click on **Publish**.

Your document has now changed into a PDF.

Saving a Document as XPS

1. Click on the **Microsoft Office Button**, point to the arrow next to **Save As**, and then click on **PDF** or **XPS**.
2. In the **File Name** list, type or select a name for the document.
3. In the **Save as type** list, click on **XPS**.
4. Next to **Optimize for**, do one of the following, depending on whether file size or print quality is more important to you:
   - If the document requires high print quality, click **Standard (publishing online and printing)**.
   - If the print quality is less important than file size, click **Minimum size (publishing online)**.
5. Click on **Options** to set the page range to be printed, to choose whether markup should be printed, and to select the output options. Click on **OK**.
6. Click on **Publish**.

Opening New Document

A new, blank document always opens when you start Microsoft Word. But suppose that you want to start another new document while you are working on another document, or you closed an already opened document and want to start a new document.

Opening New Document

1. Click on the **File tab** and select **New** option.

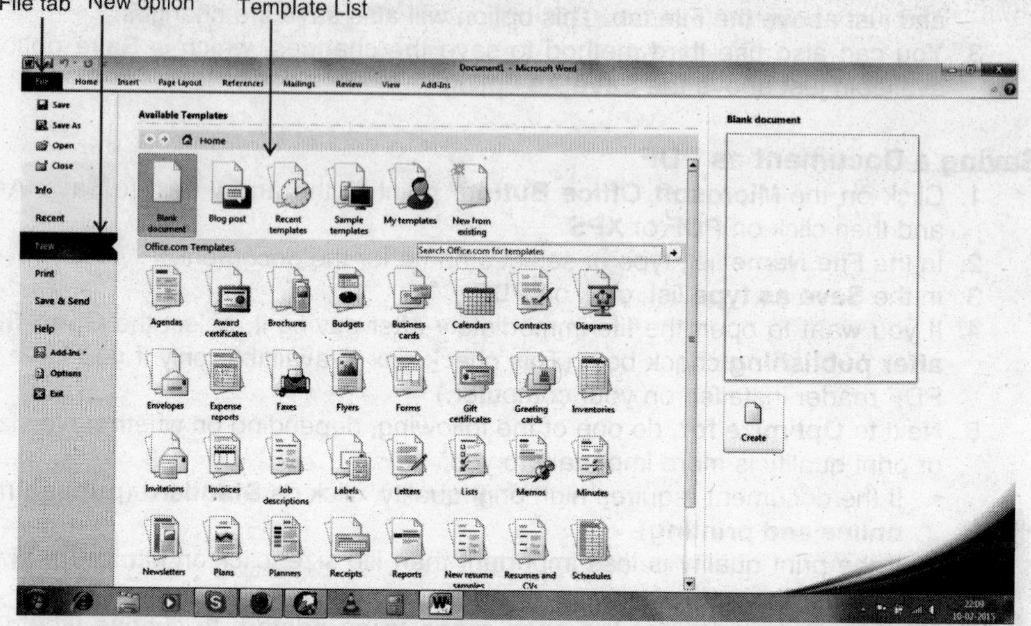

2. When you select **New** option from the first column, it will display a list of templates in the second column. Just **double-click** on **Blank document**, which is the very first option in the template list.

Now you should have your blank document as shown below and get ready to start typing your text.

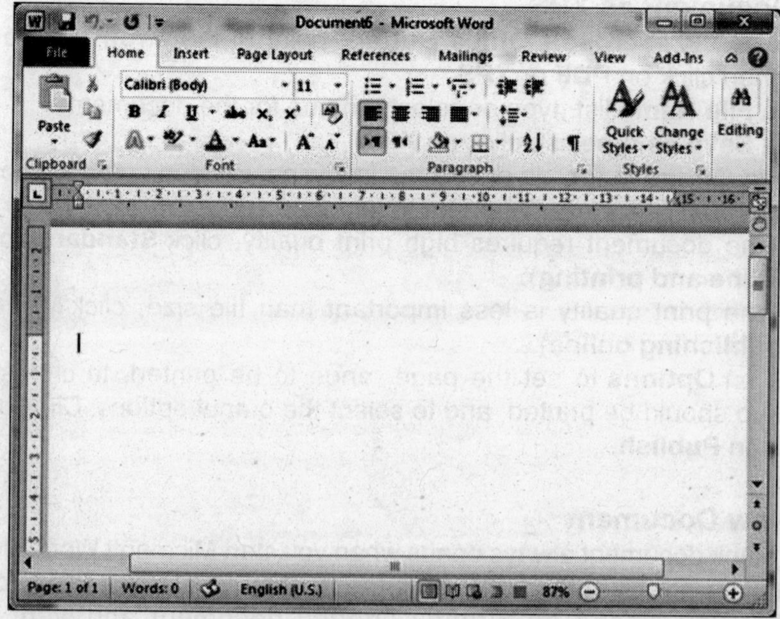

You can use a shortcut **Ctrl + N** to open a **new blank document** any time.

Opening Existing Document

If you want to open an existing document, then follow these options:

1. Click on the **File tab** and select **Open** option.

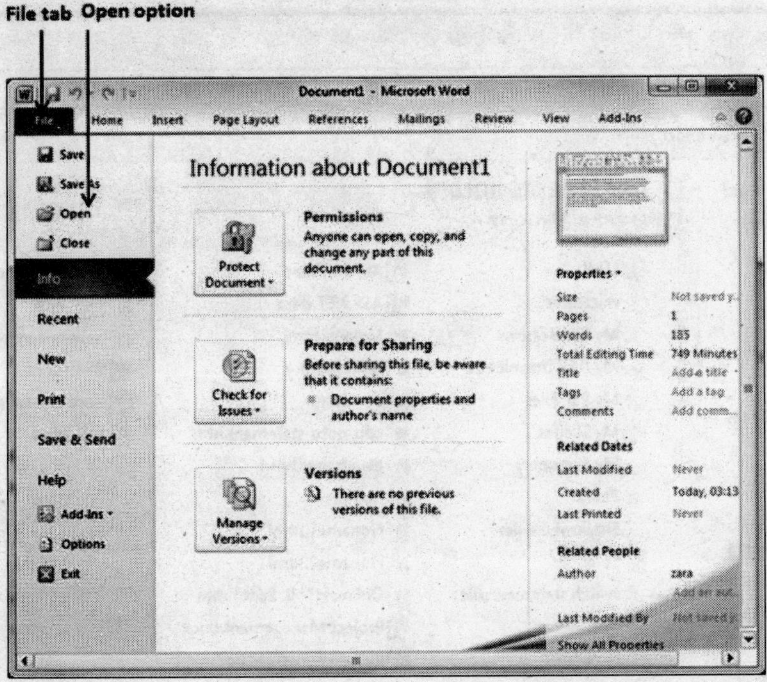

2. This will display the following file **Open dialog box**, which lets you navigate through different file folders and also lets you select a file which you want to open.

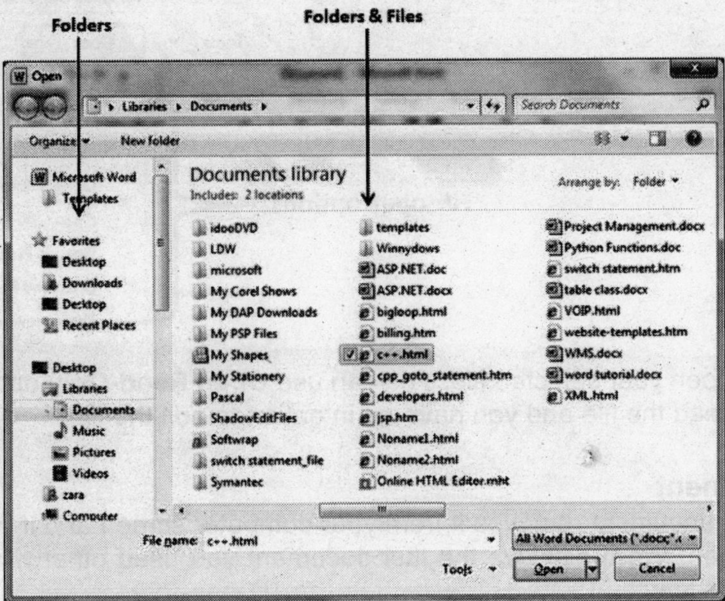

3. Finally, locate and select a file which you want to open and click on the **small triangle** available on **Open** button to open the file. You will have different options to open the file, but simply use **Open** option.

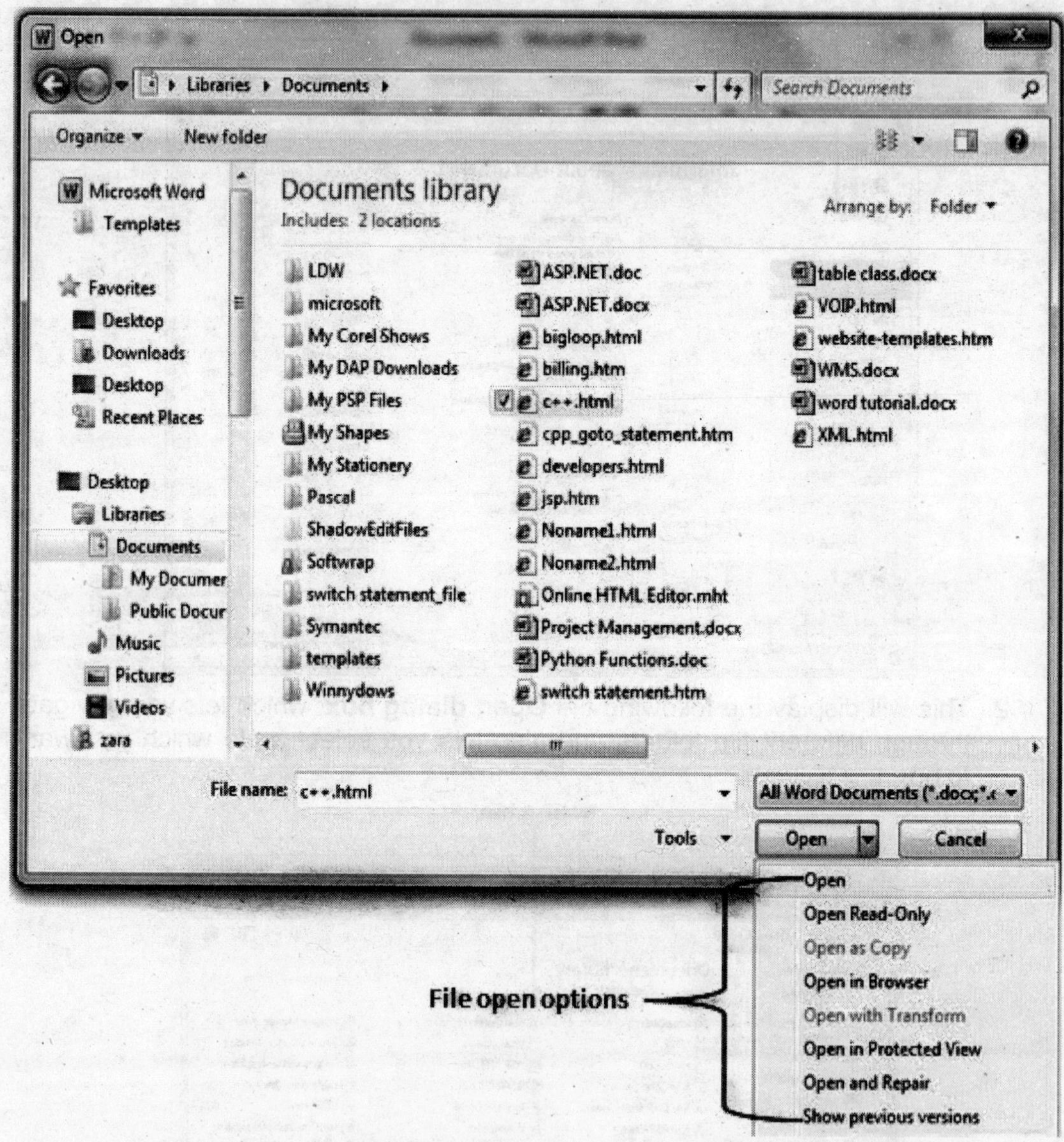

This will open your selected file. You can use **Open Read-Only** option if you are willing just to read the file and you have no intention to edit the file.

Close Document

Closing a document removes it from your computer screen and if you had other documents open, Word displays the last document you used otherwise, you see a blank Word window.

Closing an Opened Document

1. Click on the **File tab** and select **Close** option.

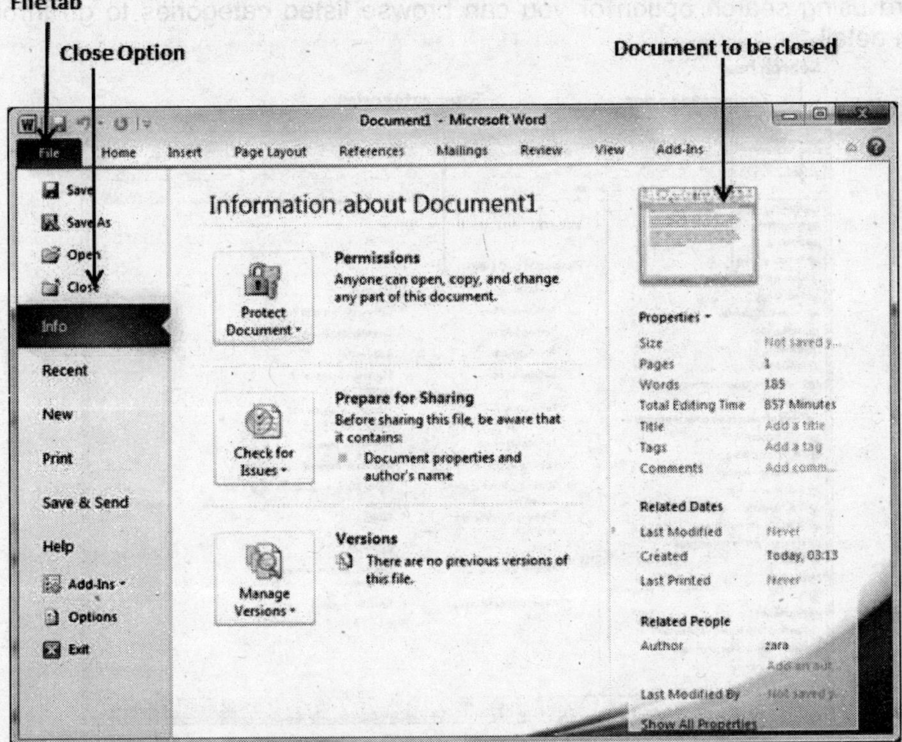

2. When you select the **Close** option and if the document is not saved before closing, it will display the following **Warning** box asking whether the document should be saved or not.

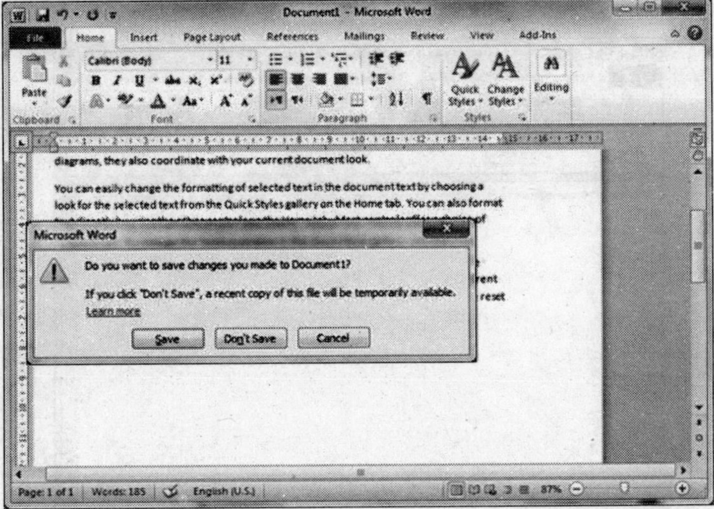

3. If you want to save the changes, then click on **Save**, otherwise click on the **Don't Save** button. To go back to the document, click on the **Cancel** button.

Using F1 Button

You can press **F1** when you are in the midst of doing something and Office will display you various categories of help as shown below. You can either search a keyword using search option or you can browse listed categories to go through a topic in detail.

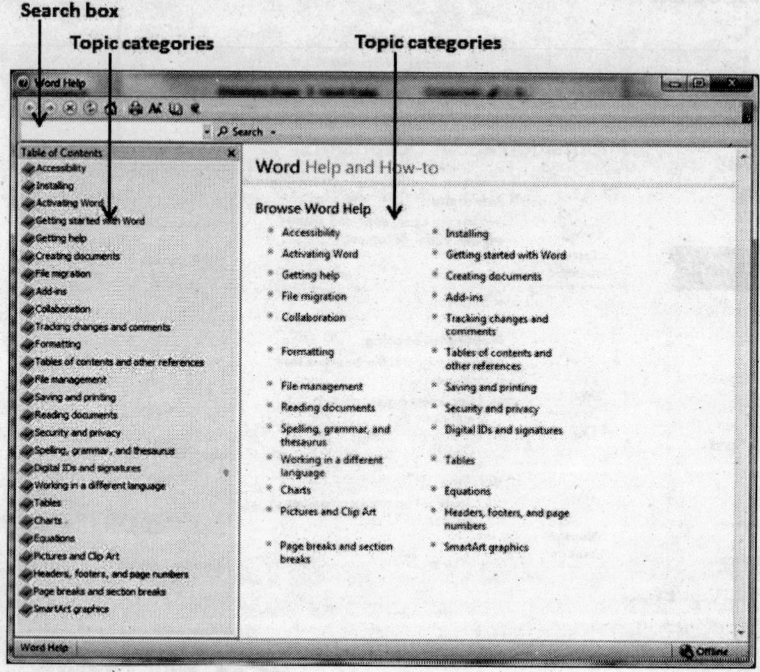

Using Help Icon

You can also have similar help window as shown above, by clicking on the **Help icon** located just above the right edge of the ribbon.

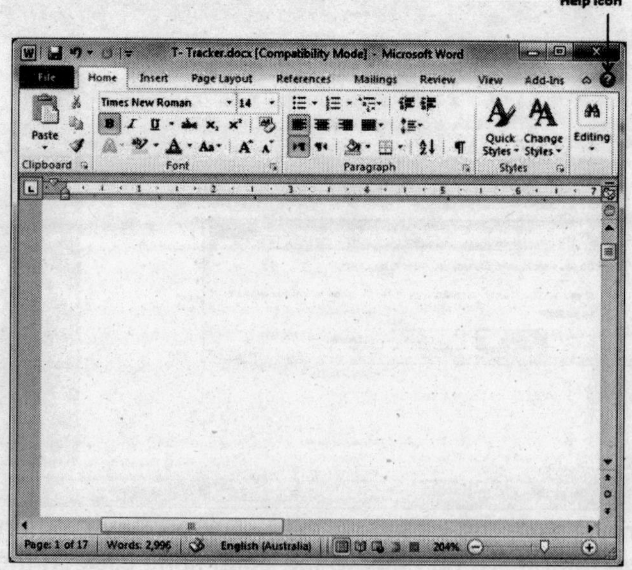

Using Help Option

You can communicate with Microsoft using **Help** option available under the **File tab**.

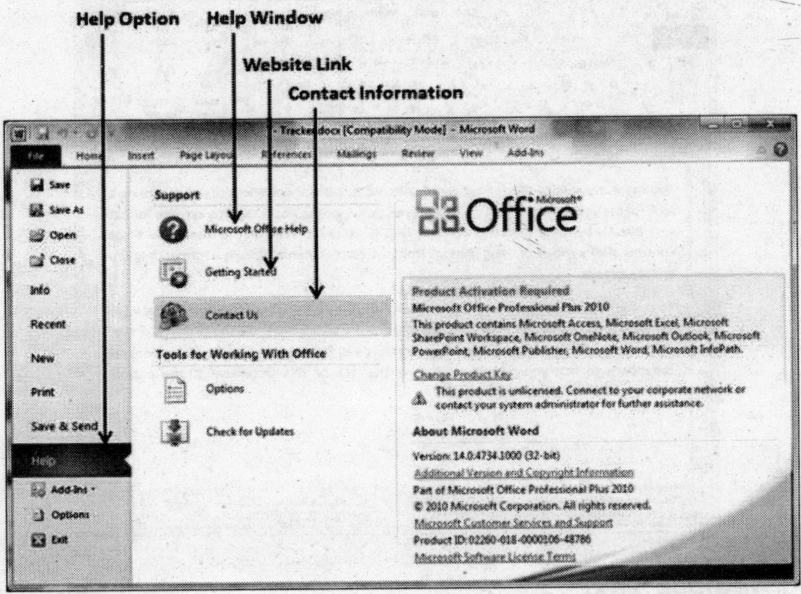

Insert and Add Text

Microsoft Word provides two ways to insert text in existing text without replacing any existing content.

1. Click on the **location** where you want to insert text or you can use keyboard arrows to locate the place where you would like to insert the text.

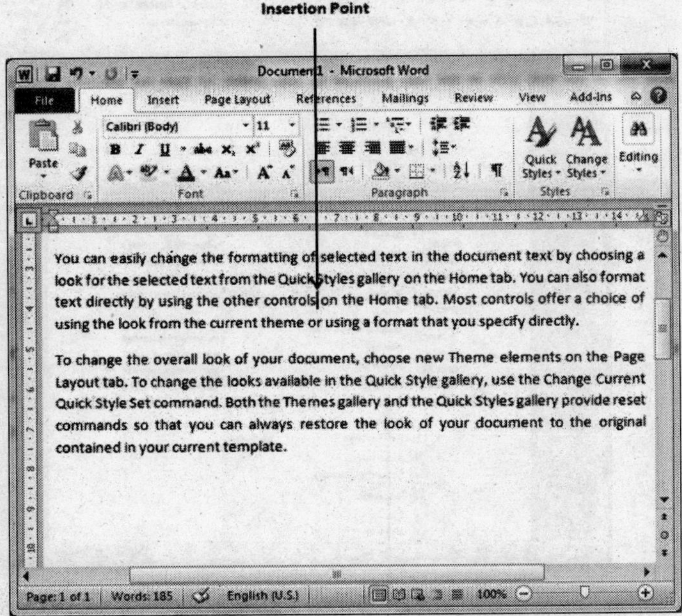

2. Start typing your text you want to insert. Word inserts the text to the left of the insertion point, moving existing text to the right.

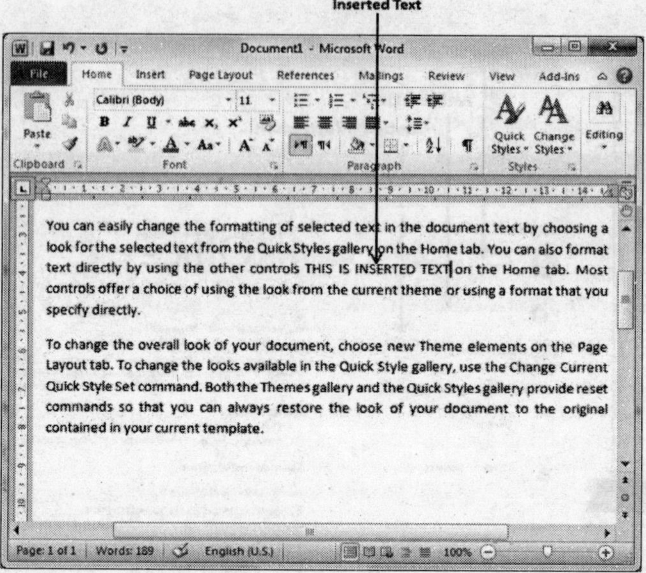

Insert and Replace Text

Here, the text will be added into the existing content, but at the same time, it will overwrite all the content which comes in its way.

1. **Right-click** on the **status bar** and select **Overtype** option from the displayed menu.

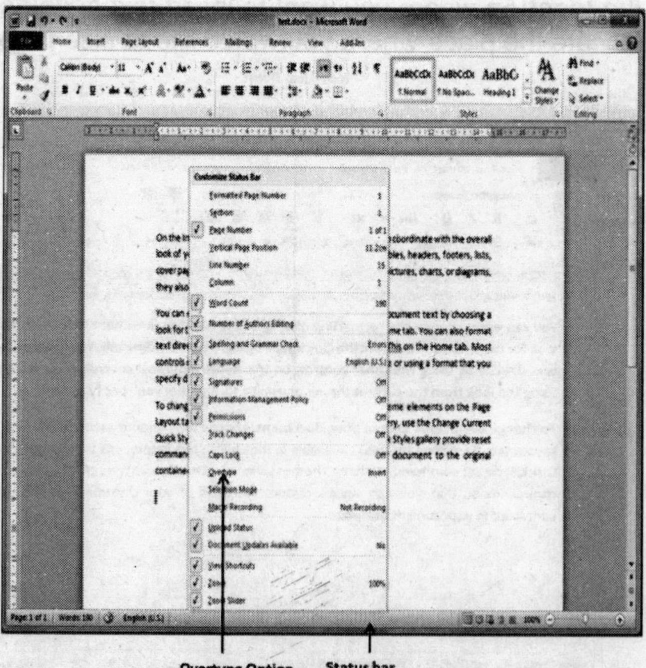

When you select the **Overtype** option, the status bar will show insert mode as shown below.

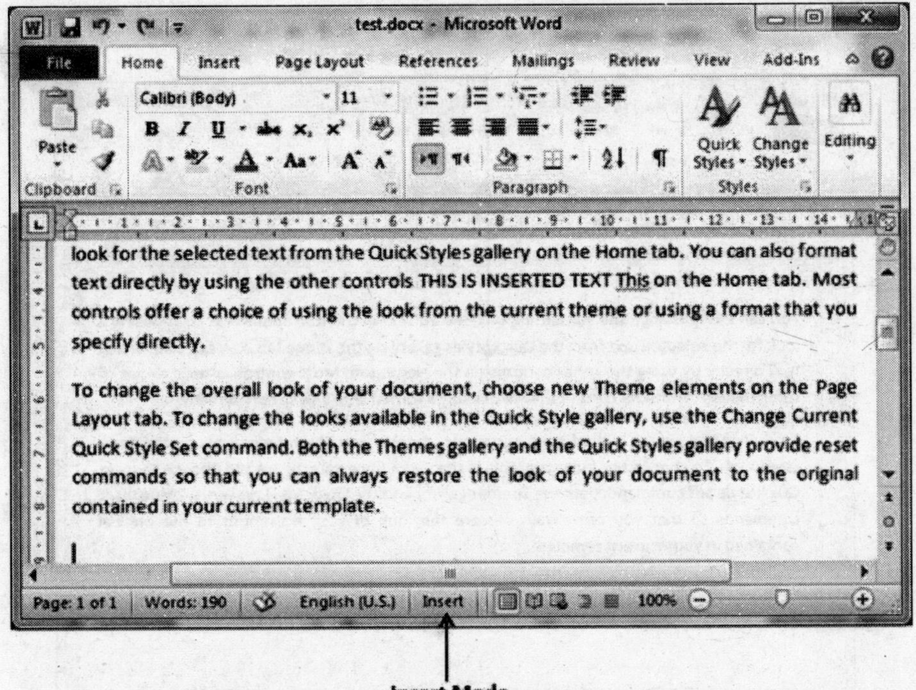

Insert Mode

2. Click on the **Insert text** available at the status bar and it will switch to **Overtype** mode as shown below.

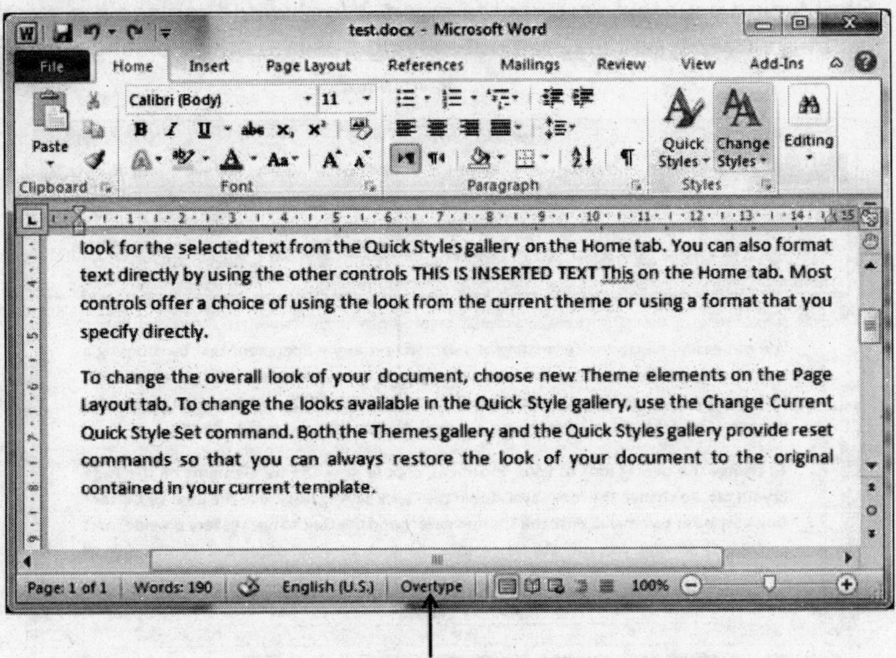

Overtype Mode

3. Now click on the location where you want to insert text or you can use keyboard arrows to locate the place where you would like to insert the text.

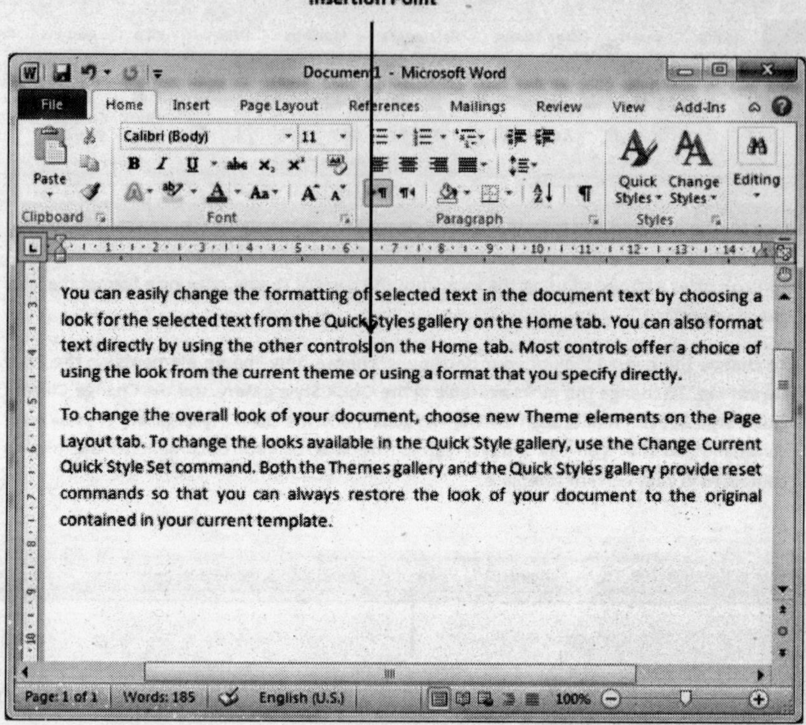

4. Start typing your text you want to insert. Word would replace the existing text with the newly-typed text without moving position of the exiting text.

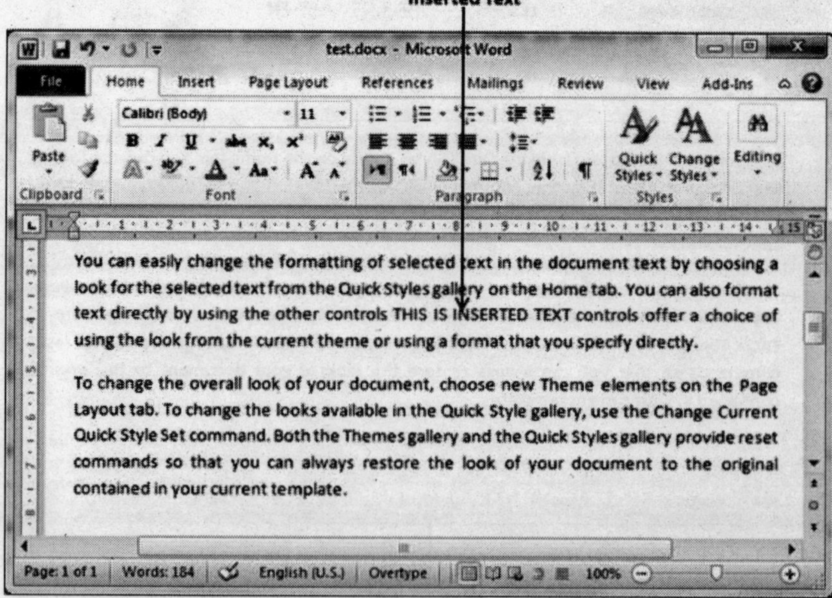

Move within the Same Document

1. Select a portion of the text using any of the text selection methods.

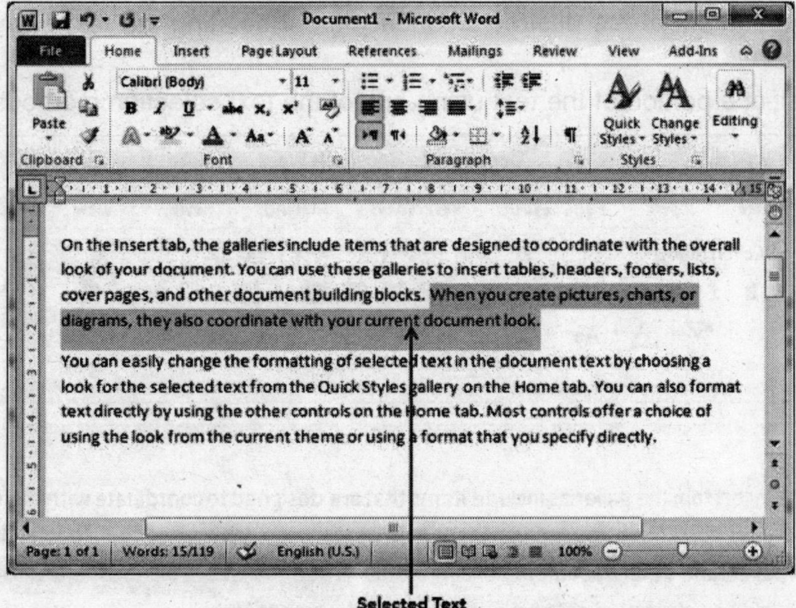

2. Now take your mouse pointer over the selected text and hold the mouse left button, and keep holding it while moving around the document.
3. Take your mouse pointer at the place where you want to move the selected text and release the mouse button. You will see that the selected text is moved to the desired location.

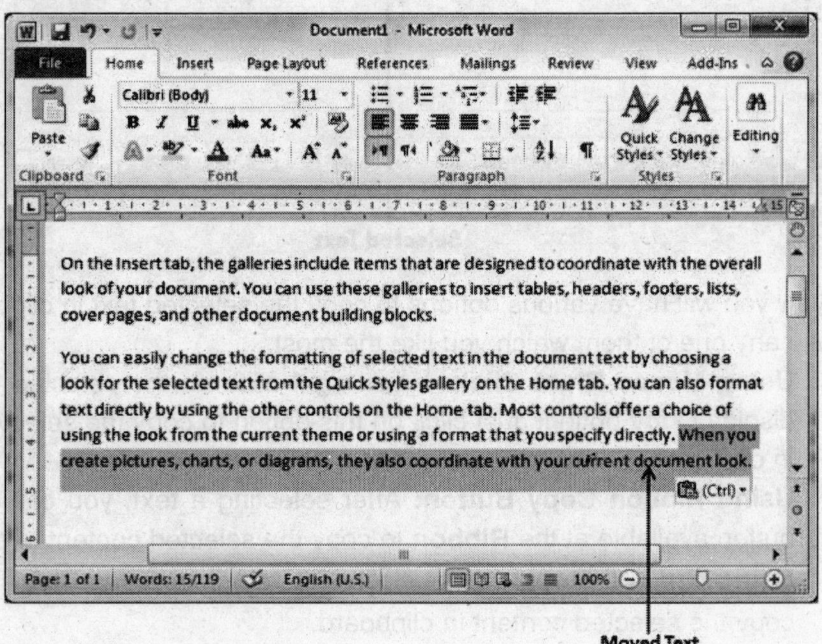

Copy & Paste Option

Copy option will just copy the content from its original place and create a duplicate copy of the content at the desired location without deleting the text from its original location.

1. Select a portion of the text using any of the text selection methods.

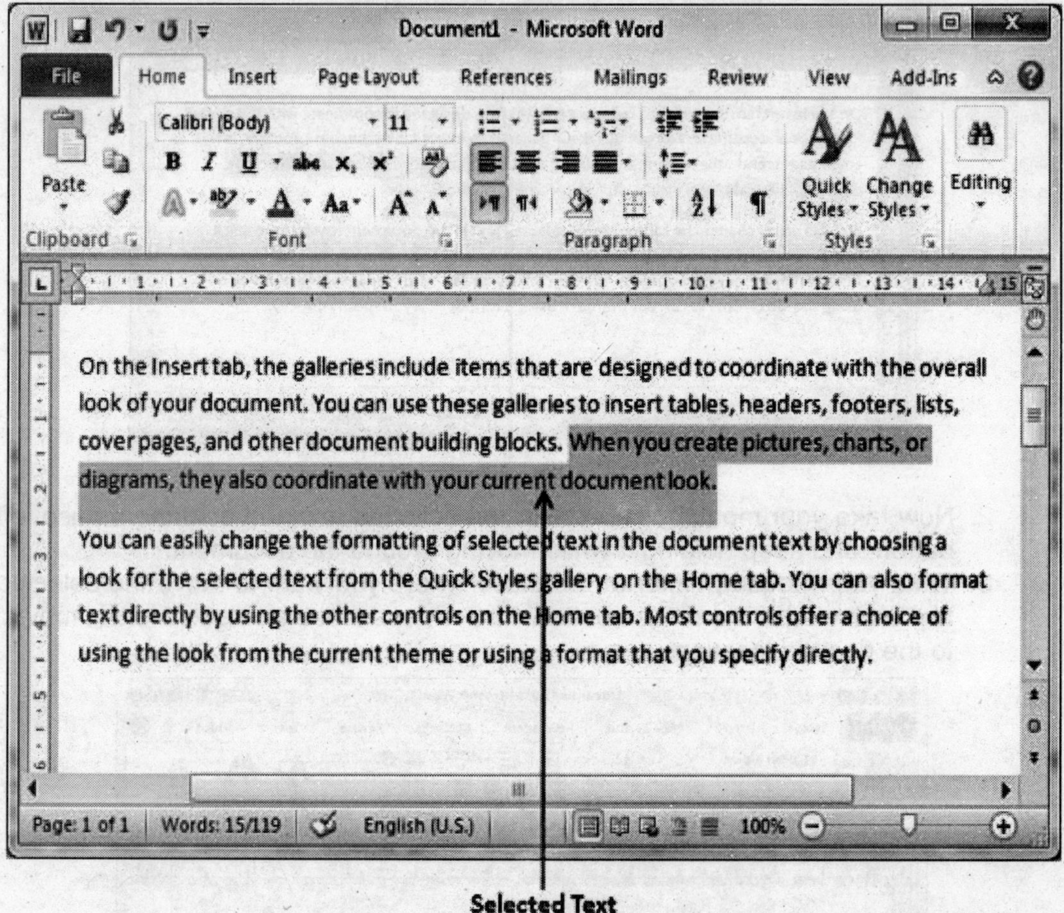

Selected Text

2. Now you will have various options to copy the selected text in clipboard. Just use any one of them which you like the most.
   - **Using Mouse Right Click:** If you right click on the selected text, it will display **Copy** option. Just click on this option to copy the selected content in clipboard.
   - **Using Ribbon Copy Button:** After selecting a text, you can use **Copy** button available at the **Ribbon** to copy the selected content in clipboard.
   - **Using Ctrl + C Keys:** After selecting a text, just press **Ctrl + C** keys to copy the selected content in clipboard.

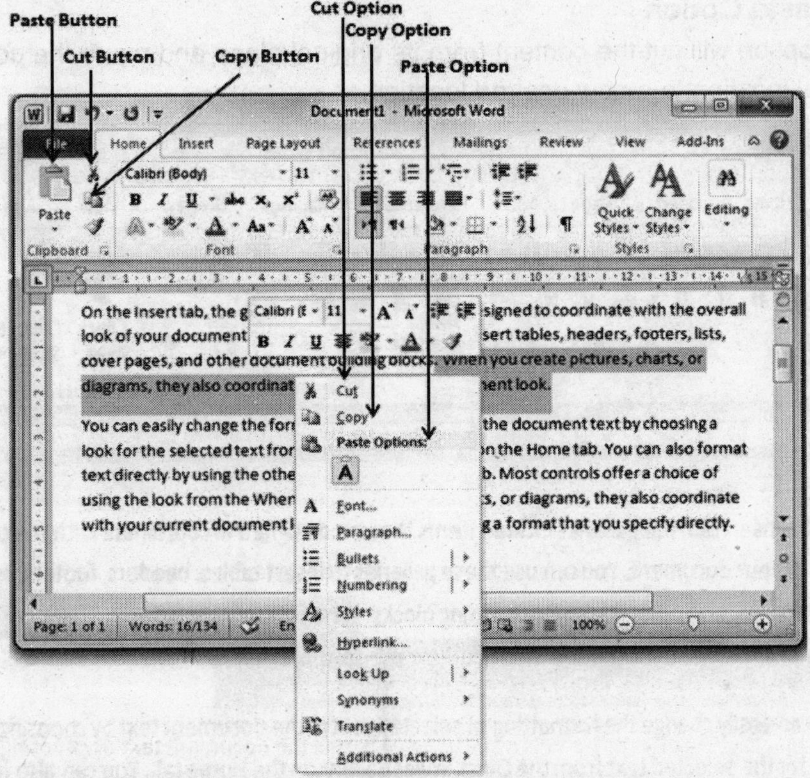

3. Finally, click on the place where you want to copy the selected text and use either of these two simple options:
   - **Using Ribbon Paste Button:** Just click on **Paste** button available at the **Ribbon** to paste the copied content at the desired location.
   - **Using Ctrl + V Keys:** This is the simplest way of pasting the content. Just press **Ctrl + V** keys to paste the content at the new location.

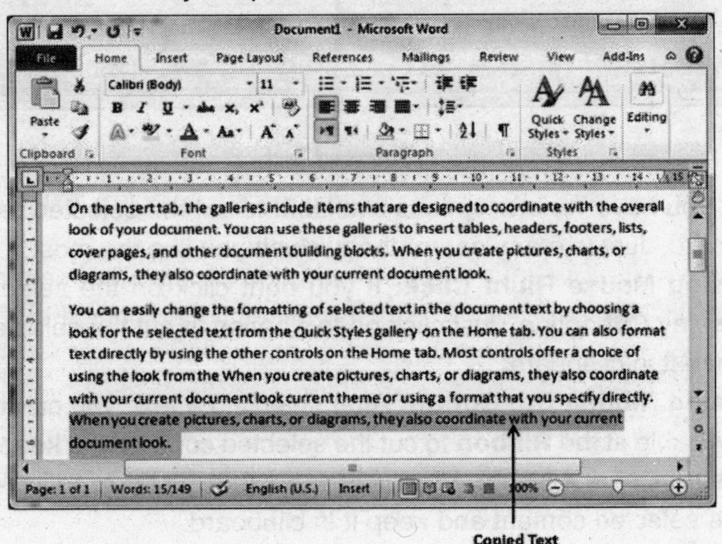

Cut & Paste Option

Cut option will cut the content from its original place and move the content from its original location to a new desired location.

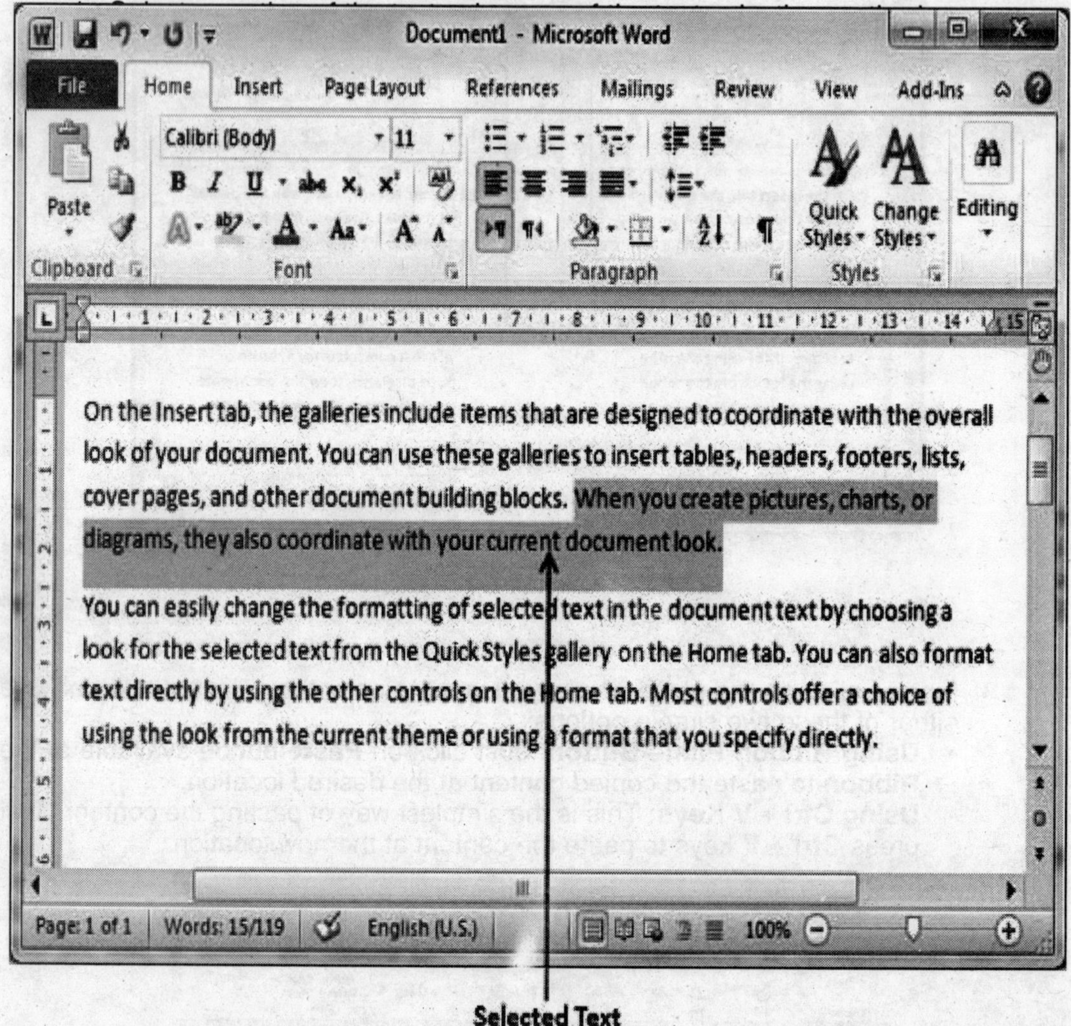

2. Now, you have various options available to cut the selected text and put it in clipboard. Just use any one of them which you like the most:
   - **Using Mouse Right Click:** If you right click on the selected text, it will display **Cut** option. Just click on this option to cut the selected content and keep it in clipboard.
   - **Using Ribbon Cut Button:** After selecting a text, you can use **Cut** button available at the **Ribbon** to cut the selected content and keep it in clipboard.
   - **Using Ctrl + X Keys:** After selecting a text, just press **Ctrl + X** keys to cut the selected content and keep it in clipboard.

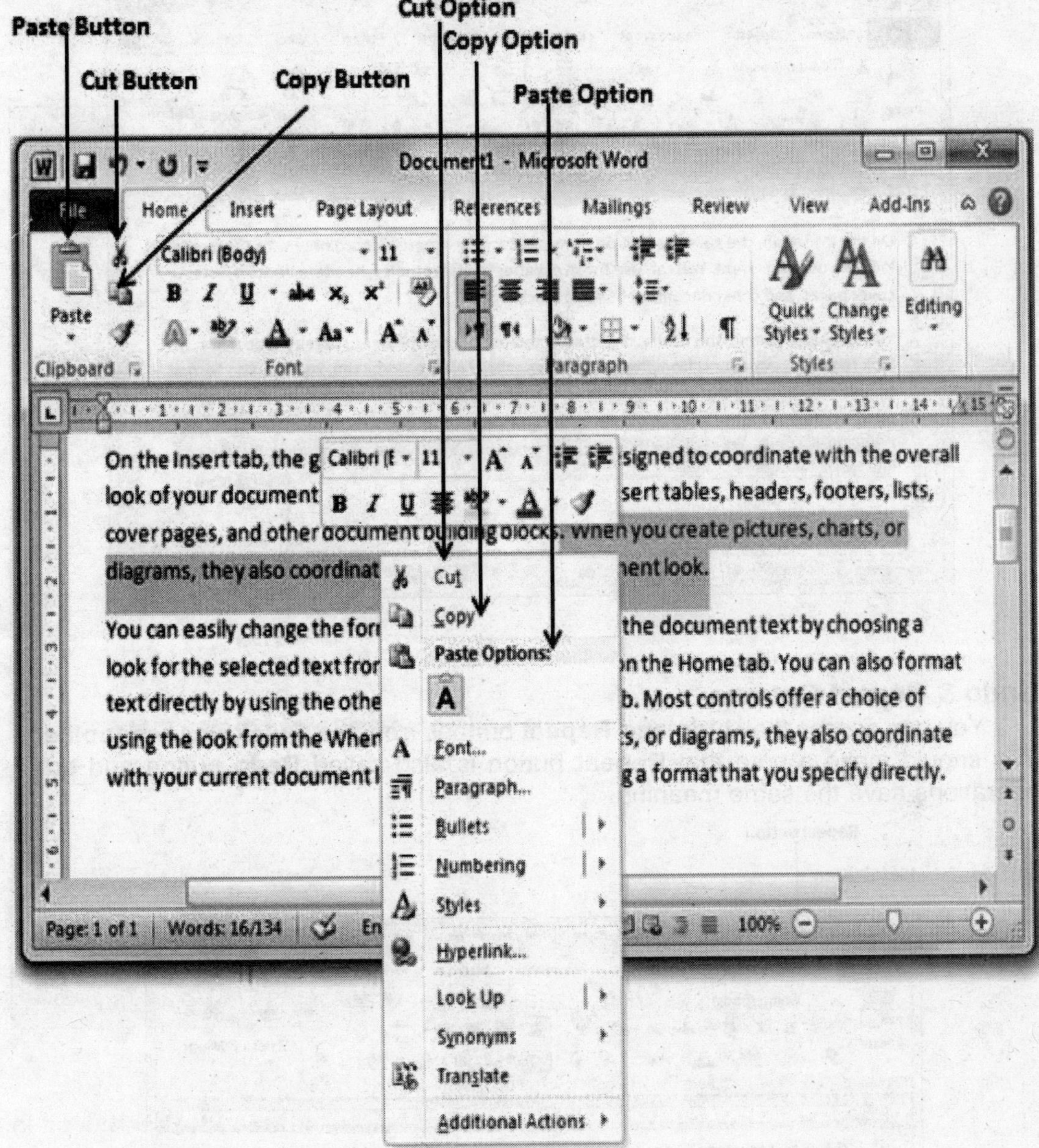

3. Finally, click on the place where you want to move the selected text and use either of these two simple options:
   - **Using Ribbon Paste Button:** Just click on **Paste** button available at the **Ribbon** to paste the content at the new location.
   - **Using Ctrl + V Keys:** This is the simplest way of pasting the content. Just press **Ctrl + V** keys to paste the content at the new location.

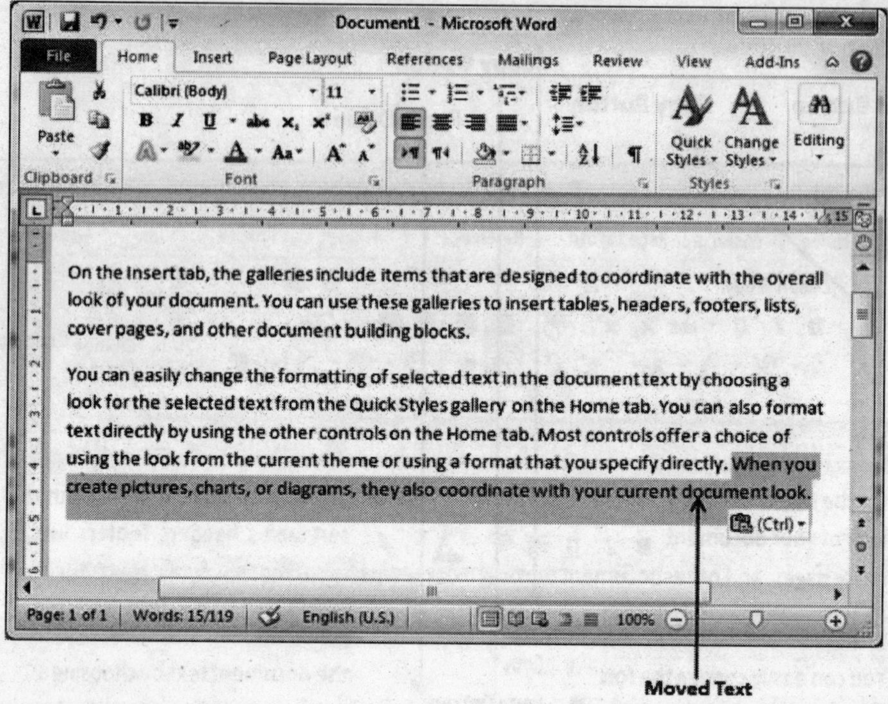

Undo & Repeat Options

You can access the **Undo and Repeat** buttons from the **Quick Access toolbar**. You should make a note that **Repeat** button is also called **Redo** button and both operations have the same meaning.

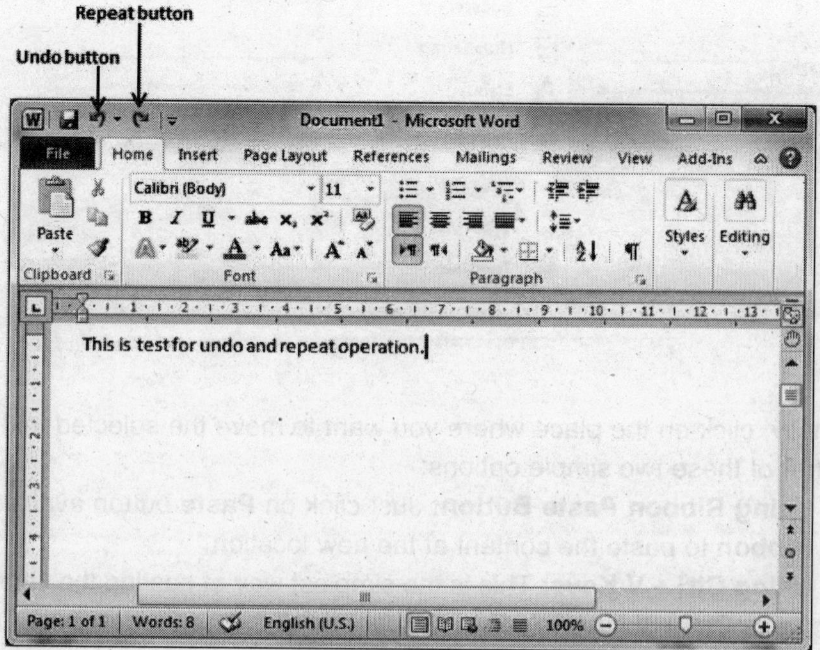

The simple procedure to apply undo or repeat (redo) operations:

1. Let us type some text in a blank document. Now click on **Repeat (Redo)** button and you will see that Word would repeat the same operation for you.

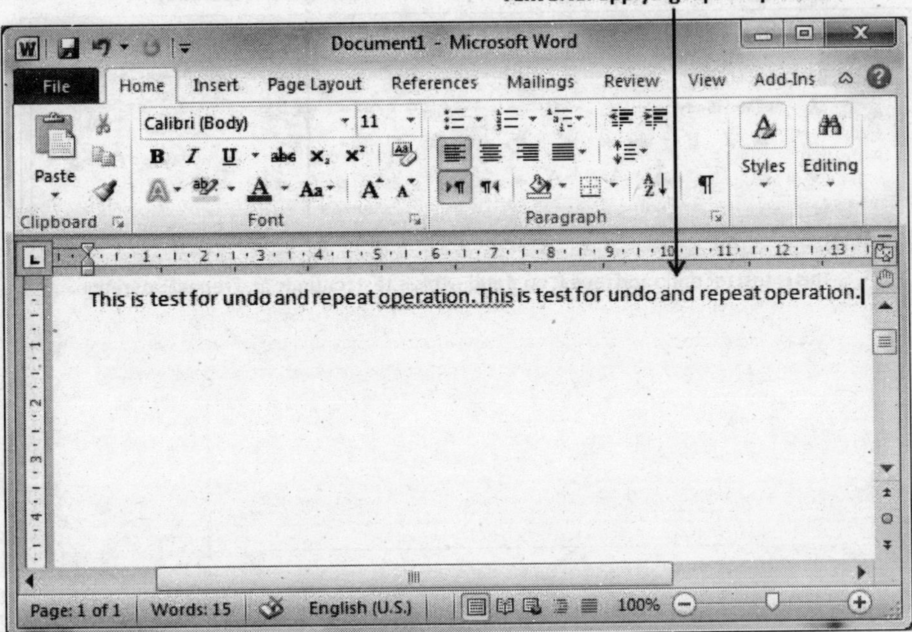

2. Now to examine undo operation, let us delete the last word **operation** character by character so that you have the following text remaining in the line.

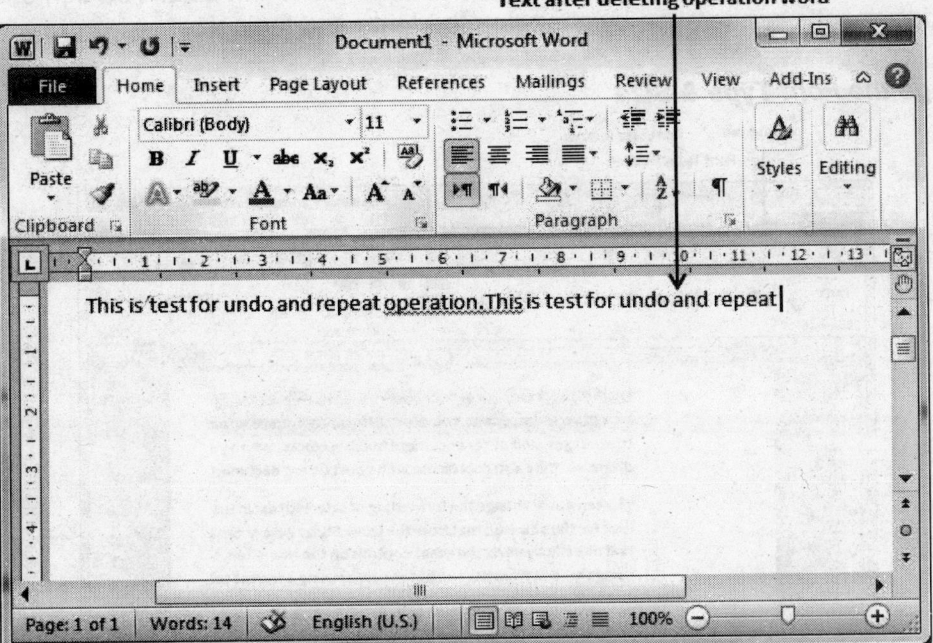

3. Let us try to click on **Undo** button one by one. You will see that Word would recover all the deleted characters one by one after performing few undo operations.

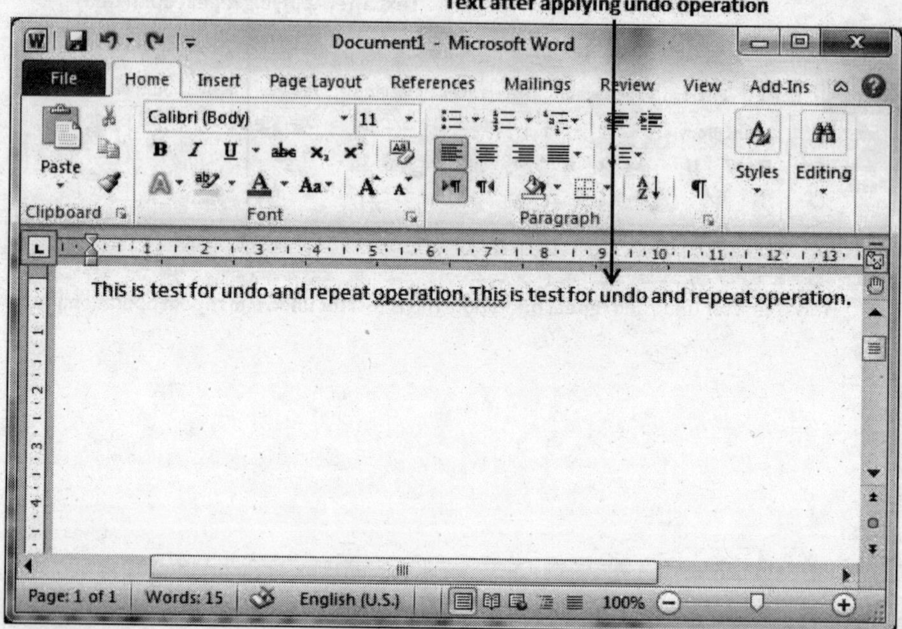

Formatting Text

Formatting a document can range from modifying text size to adding graphics. Microsoft Word allows you to use different fonts with different size. You can change your document's appearance by changing the fonts and their size.

Change the Font Type & Size

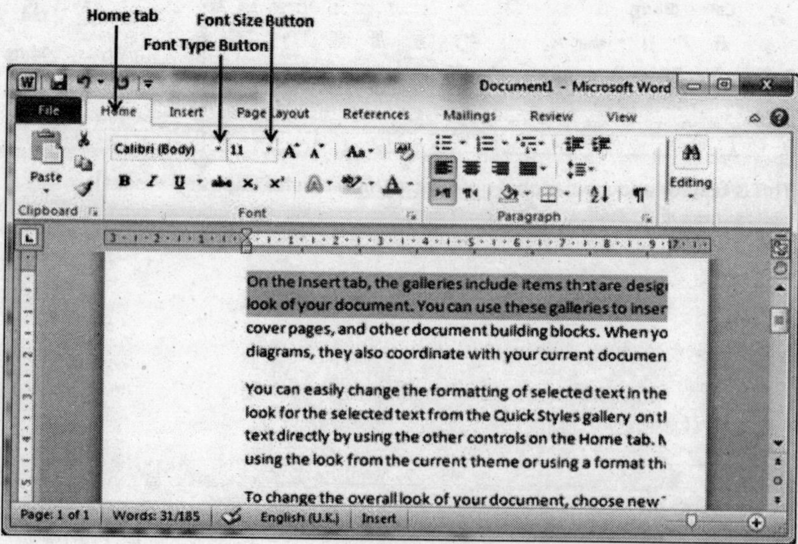

1. Select the text that you want to change to a different font and click on **Home tab**. Now click on **Font Type** button to list down all the fonts available as shown below.

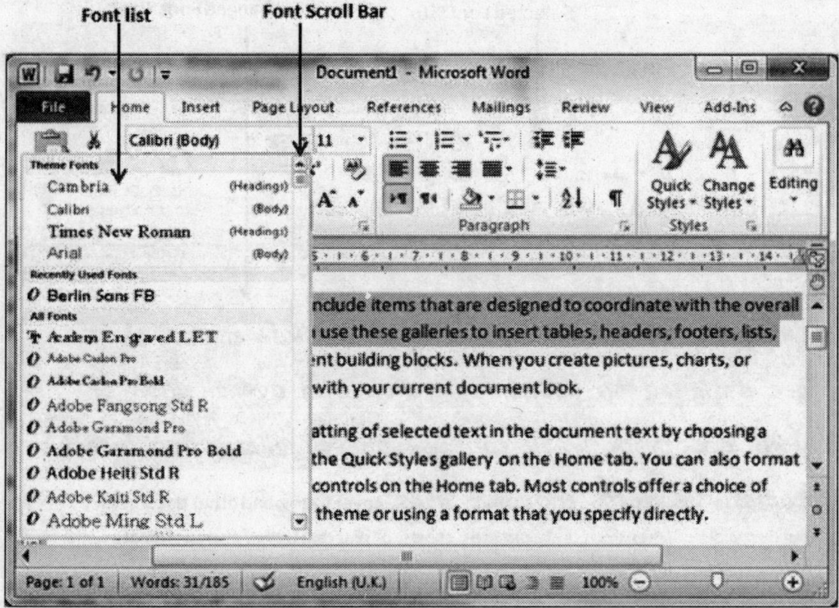

2. Try to move the mouse pointer over different fonts listed. You will see that text font changes when you move the mouse pointer over different fonts. You can use **Font Scroll Bar** to display more fonts available. Finally, select a desired font by clicking on the font in the list. Here, font selected for the text is **MV Boli**.

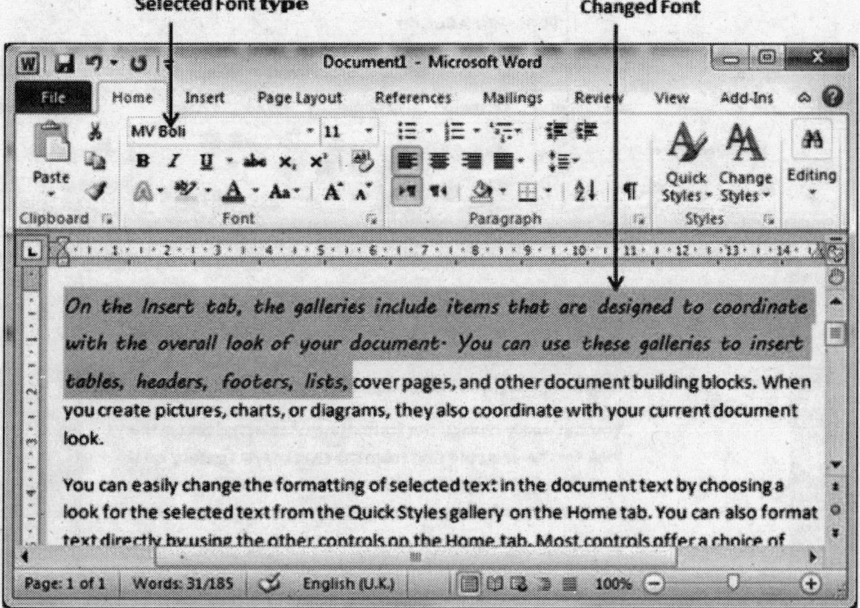

3. Similarly, to change the font size, click on the **Font Size** button which will display a font size list. You will use same procedure to select a desired font size what you have used while selecting a font type.

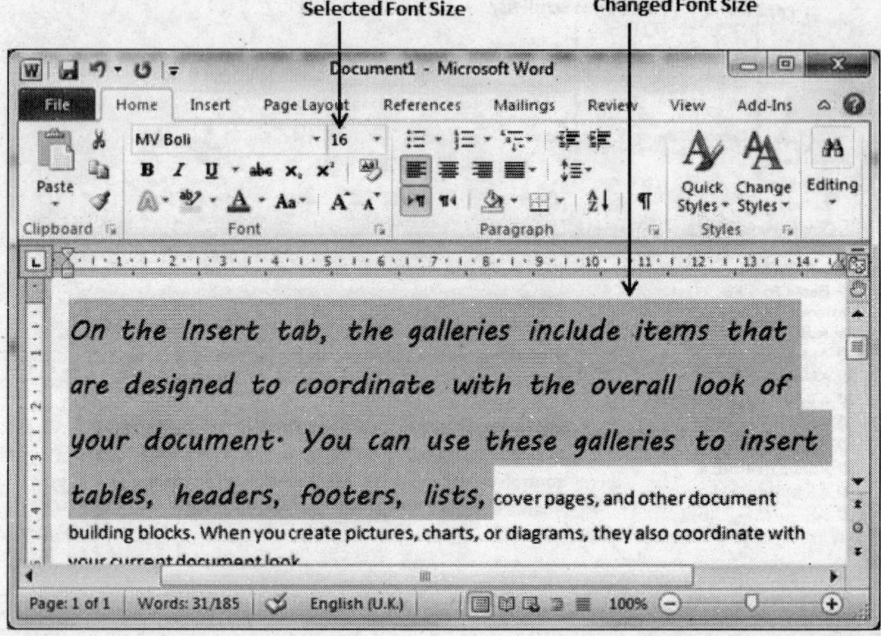

Use Shrink and Grow Buttons

You can use **Shrink Font** button to **reduce** the font size whereas, **Grow Font** button to **enlarge** font size.

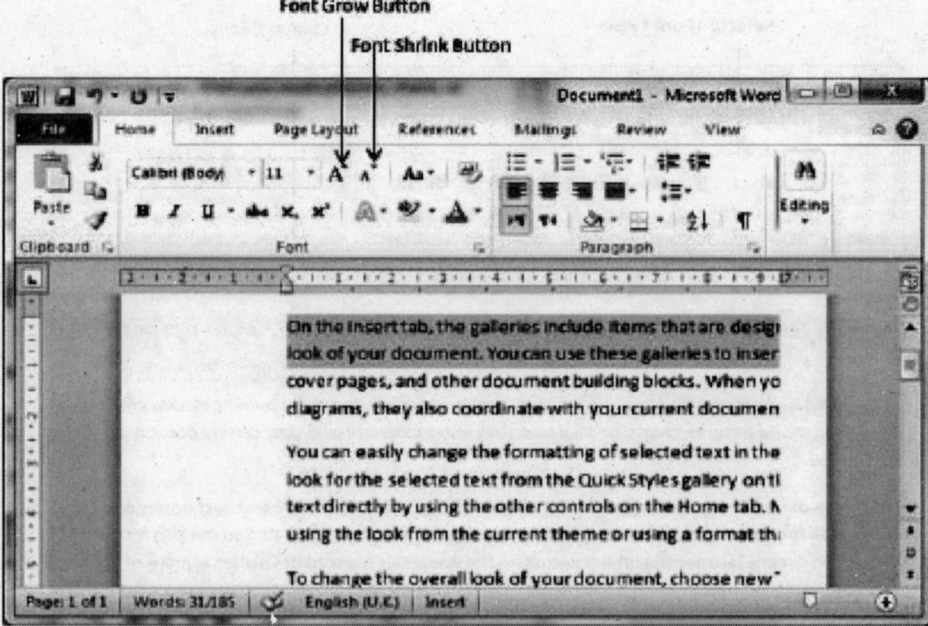

You can click on a single button multiple times to apply the effect. Each time you click on either of the buttons, it will enlarge or reduce the font size by 1 point.

Clear Formatting Options

All of the settings can be reset to the plain text, or the default formatting.

To Reset Text to Default Settings

1. Select the text that you want to reset.
2. Click on **Clear Formatting** button in the **Home tab Font group**, or simply use **Ctrl + SPACEBAR**.

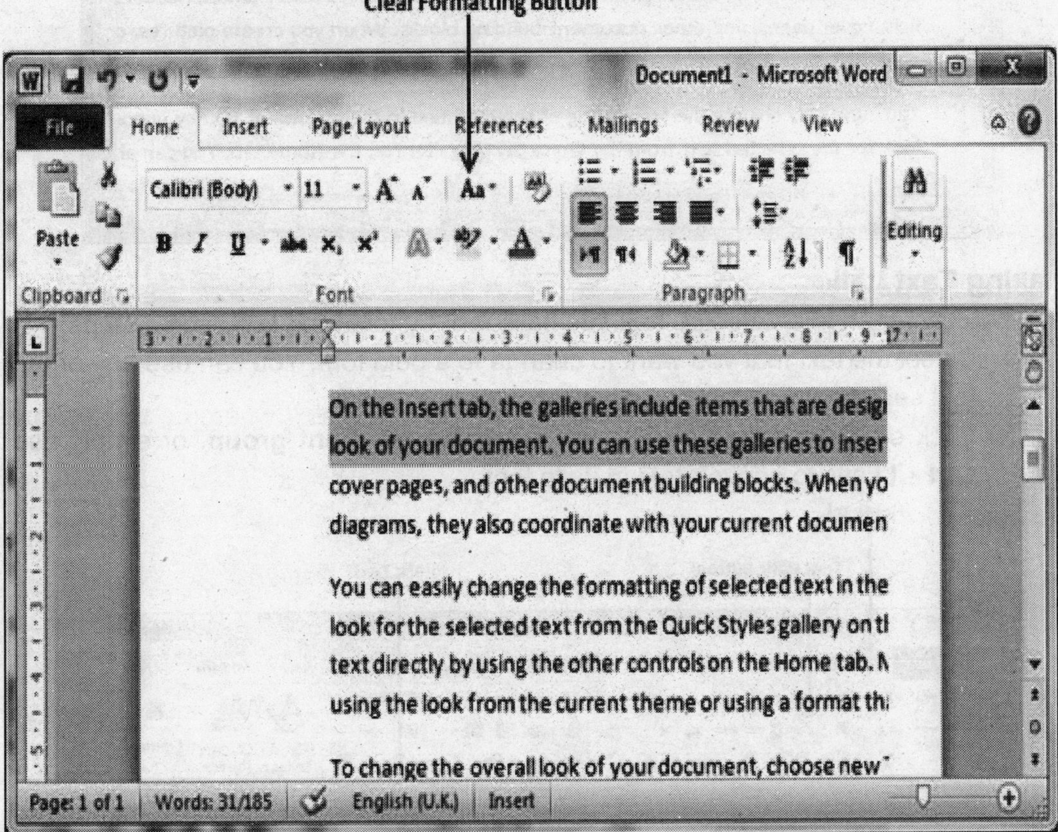

Making Text Bold

You can change a selected text into bold font by following two simple steps:

1. Select the text that you want to change to a bold font. You can use any of the text selection methods to select the text.
2. Click on **Font Bold** [**B**] button in the **Home tab Font group**, or simply use **Ctrl + B** keys to make selected text bold.

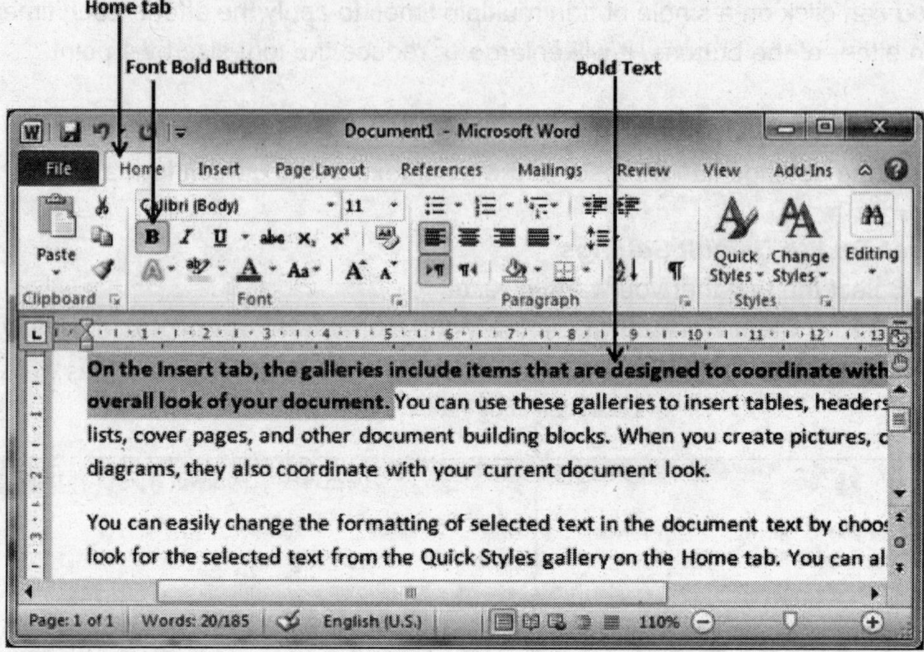

Making Text Italic

You can change a selected text into italic font by following two simple steps:

1. Select the text that you want to change to a bold font. You can use any of the text selection methods to select the text.
2. Click on **Font Italic [I]** button in the **Home tab Font group**, or simply use **Ctrl + I** keys to convert text in italic font.

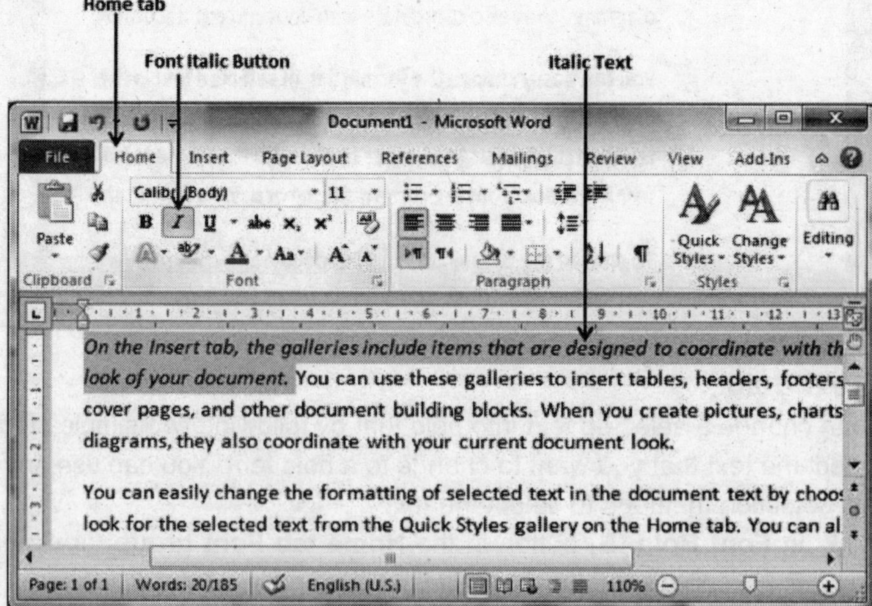

Underline the Text

You can underline a selected text by following two simple steps:

1. Select the text that you want to change to a bold font. You can use any of the text selection method to select the text.
2. Click on **Font Underline** [U] button in the **Home tab Font group**, or simply use **Ctrl + U** keys to put an underline under the text.

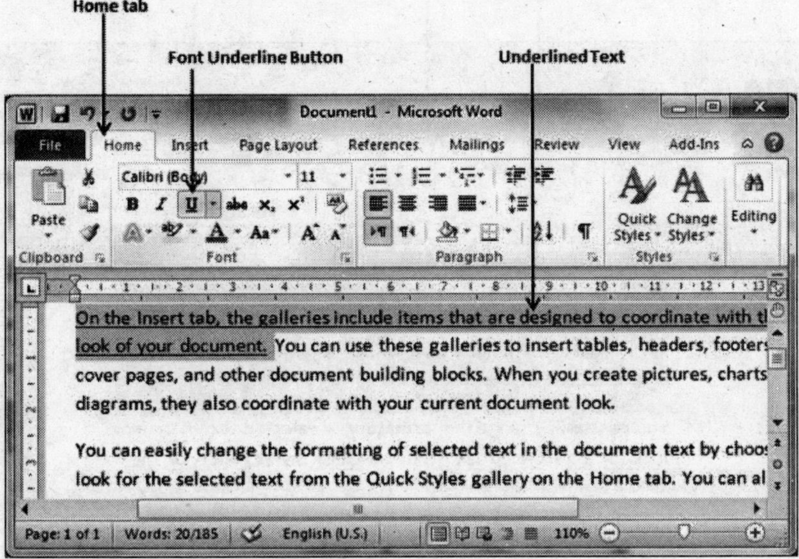

Strikethrough Text

A strikethrough text indicates that it has been deleted and not any more required.

Select the text that you want to strikethrough. Click on **Font Strikethrough** [**abc**] button in the **Home tab Font group** to put a line in the middle of the text.

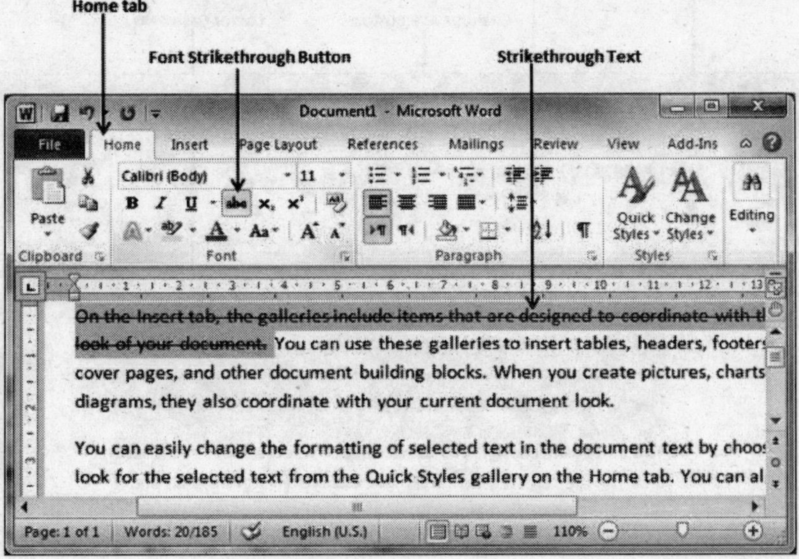

Change Text to Sentence Case

A sentence case is the case where first character of every sentence is capitalised.

Select the text that you want to change. Click on the **Change Case** button and then select **Sentence case** option to capitalise the first character of every selected sentence.

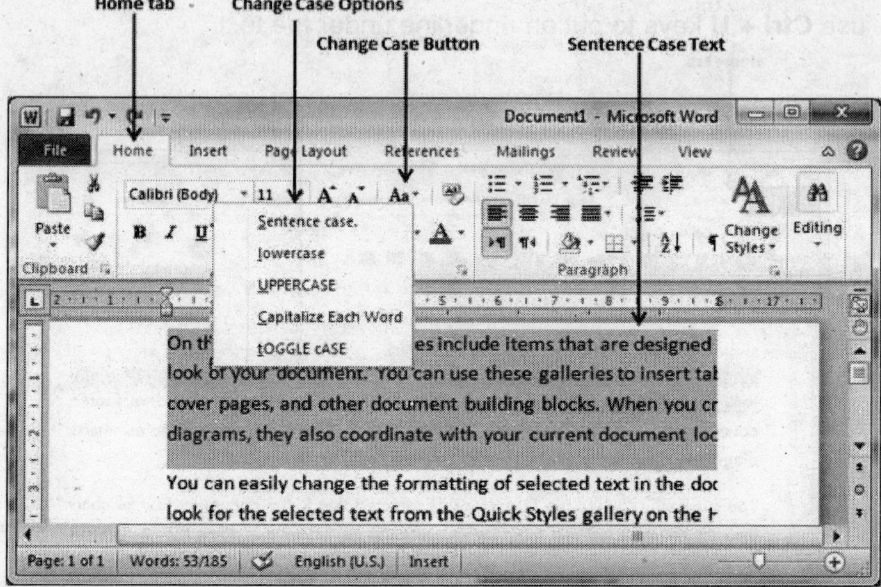

Change Text to Lowercase

A lowercase is the case where every word of a sentence is in lowercase.

Select the text that you want to change. Click on the **Change Case** button and then select **Lowercase** option to display all selected words in lowercase.

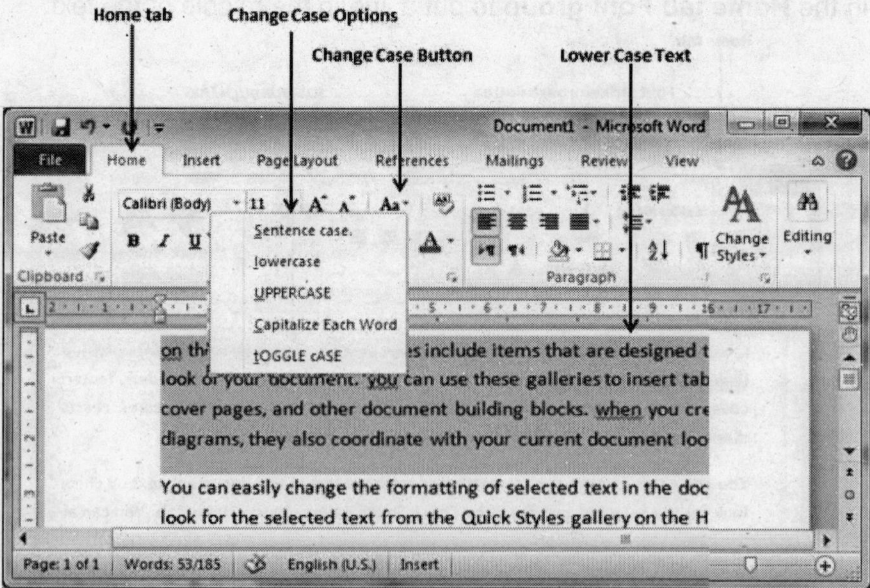

Change Text to Uppercase

An uppercase is the case where every word of a sentence is in capital.

Select the text that you want to change. Click on the **Change Case** button and then select **UPPERCASE** option to display all selected words in all caps. All characters of every selected word will be capitalised.

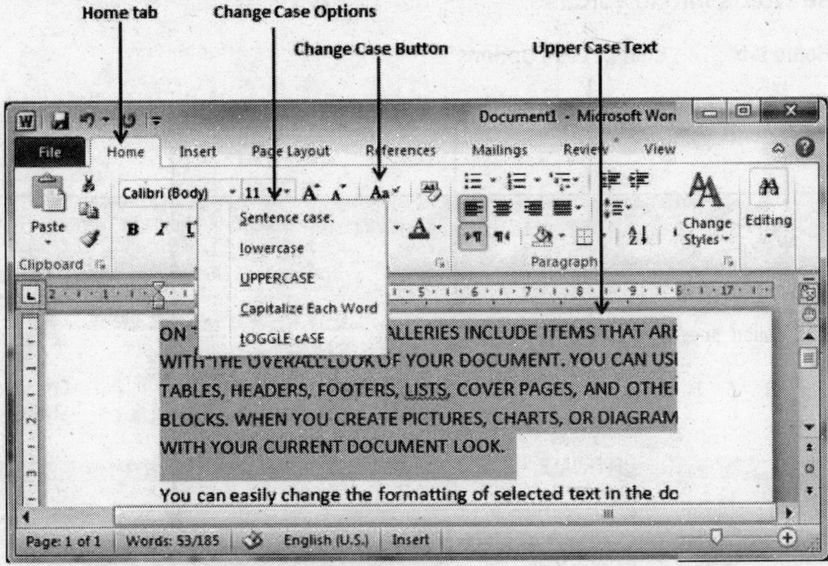

Change Text to Capitalise

A capitalise case is the case where every first character of every selected word is in capital.

Select the text that you want to change. Click on the **Change Case** button and then select **Capitalise Each Word** option to put a leading cap on each selected word.

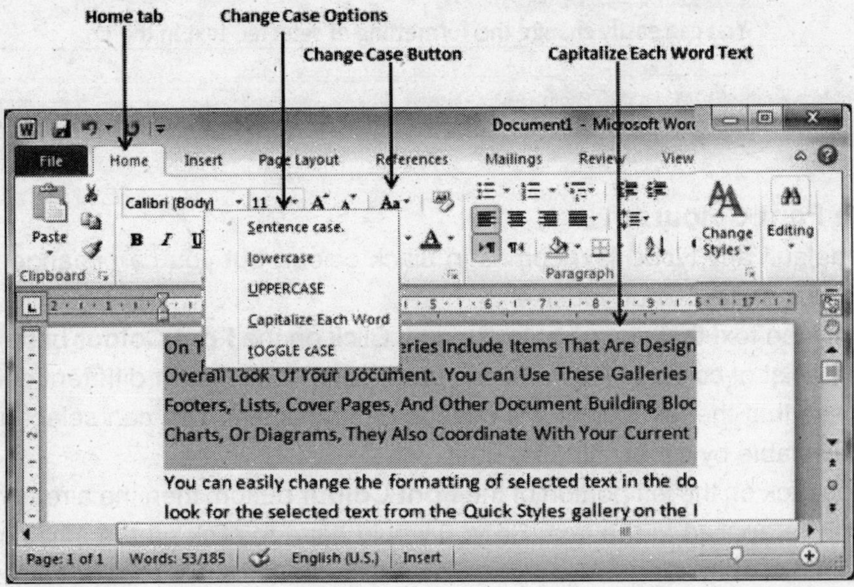

Toggle the Text

Toggle operation will change the case of every character in reverse way.

Select the text that you want to change. Click on the **Change Case** button and then select **tOGGLE cASE** option to change all lowercase words into uppercase and uppercase words into lowercase.

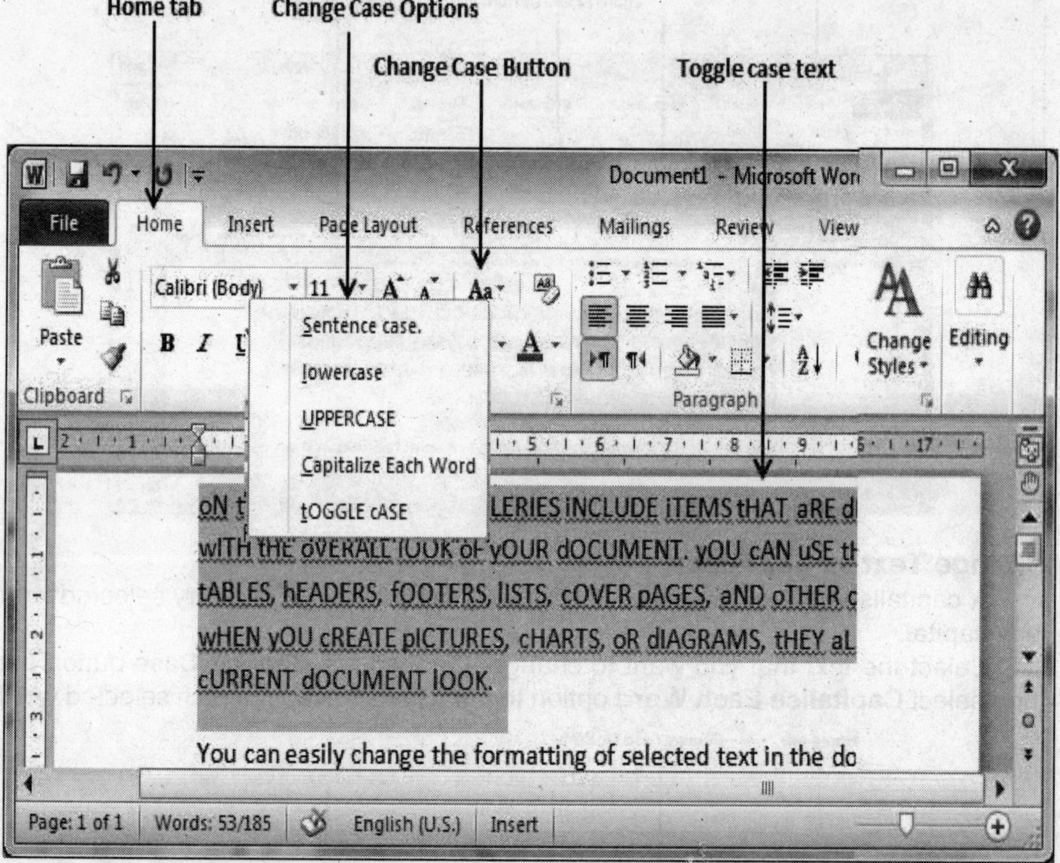

Change Font Colours

By default any typed text comes in black colour, but you can change your font colour to any of the colour you like.

Select the text that you want to change. Click on the **Font Colour** button triangle to display a list of colours. Try to move your mouse pointer over different colours and you will see that the text colour will change automatically. You can select any of the colours available by simply clicking on it.

If you click on the left portion of the **Font Colour** button, then the already selected colour will be applied to the text. So you would have to click on the small triangle to display a list of colours.

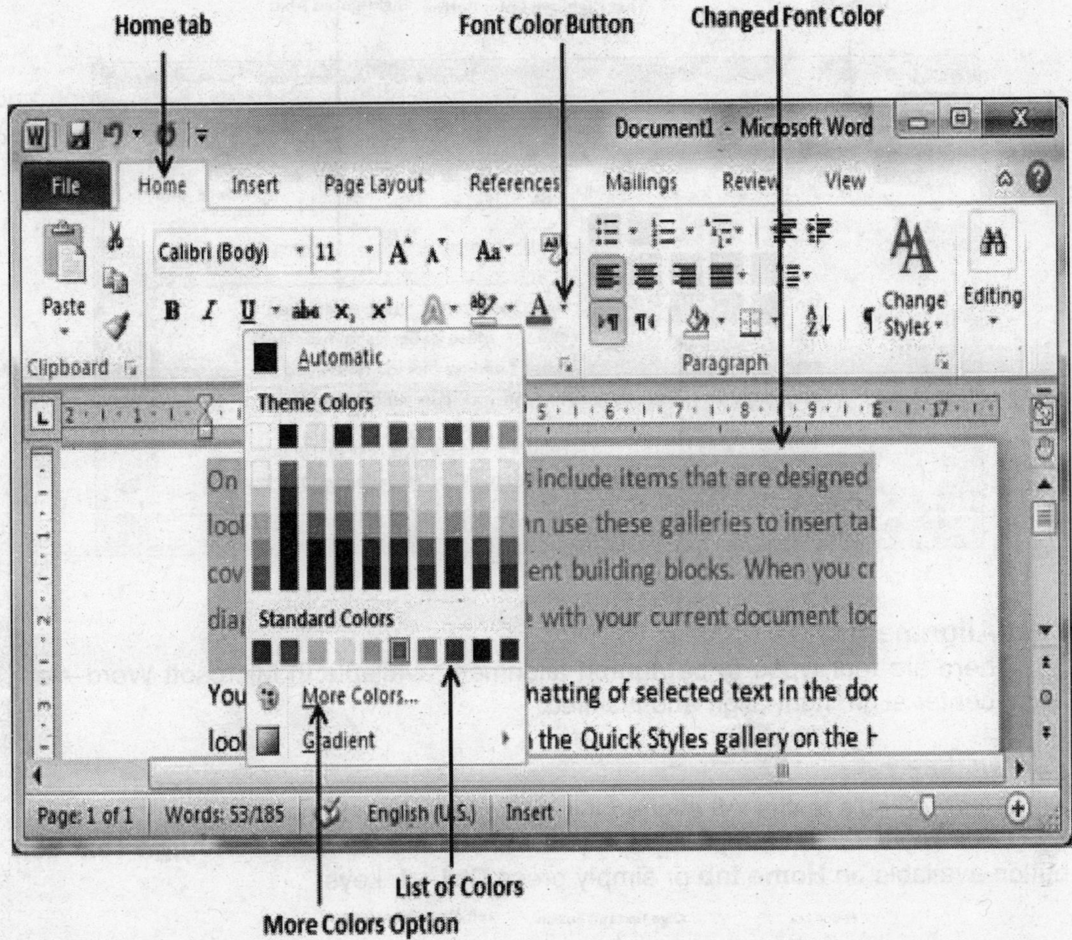

If you do not find a colour of your choice, you can use **More Colours...** option to display the colour pallet box which allows you to select a colour from range of millions of colours.

Highlight Text with Colours

You can highlight a selected text by using any colour and it will look like it was marked with a highlighter pen.

Select the text that you want to change. Click on the **Text Highlight Colour** button triangle to display a list of colours. Try to move your mouse pointer over different colours and you will see that the text colour will change automatically. You can select any of the colours available by simply clicking on it.

If you click on the left portion of the **Text Highlight Colour** button, then the already selected colour will be applied to the text. So you would have to click on the small triangle to display a list of colours.

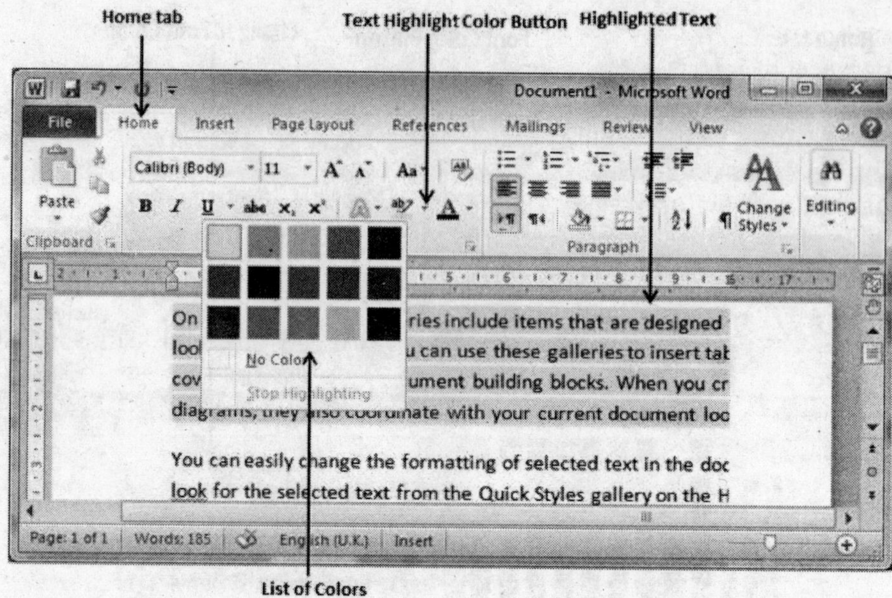

Text Alignments

There are four types of paragraph alignment available in Microsoft Word—left-align, center-align, right-align and justified.

Left Aligned Text

A paragraph's text is left aligned if it is aligned with left margin.

Click anywhere on the paragraph you want to align and click on **Align Text Left** button available on **Home tab** or simply press **Ctrl + L** keys.

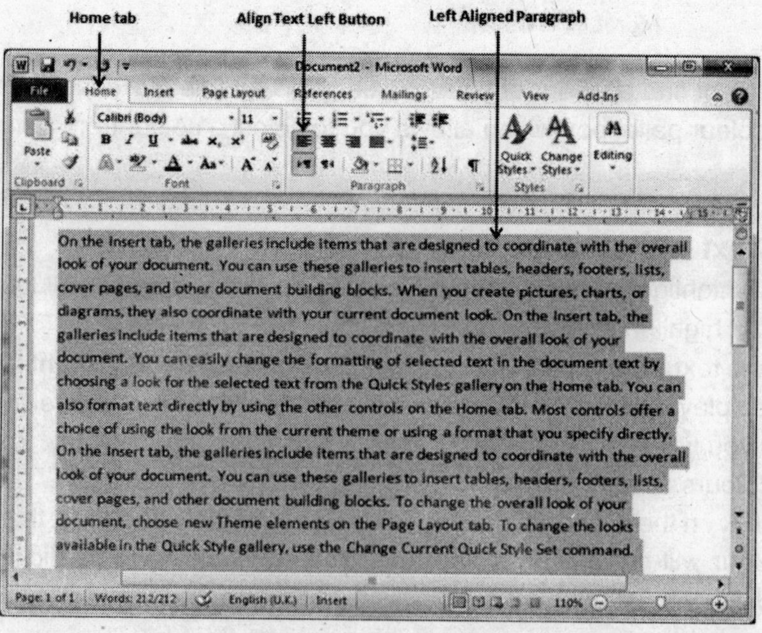

Center Aligned Text

A paragraph's text is center aligned if it is in the center of the left and right margins.

Click anywhere on the paragraph you want to align and click on the **Center** button available on **Home tab** or simply press **Ctrl + E** keys.

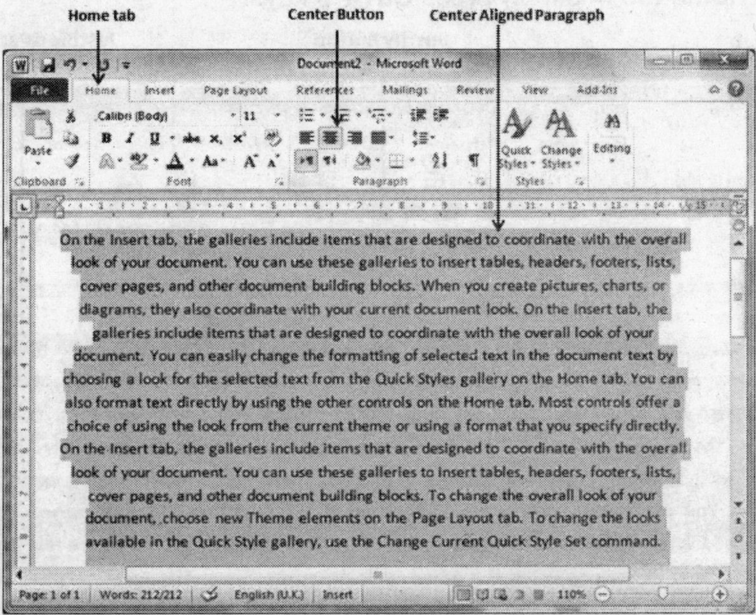

Right Aligned Text

A paragraph's text is right aligned if it is aligned with right margin.

Click anywhere on the paragraph you want to align and click on **Align Text Right** button available on **Home tab** or simply press **Ctrl + R** keys.

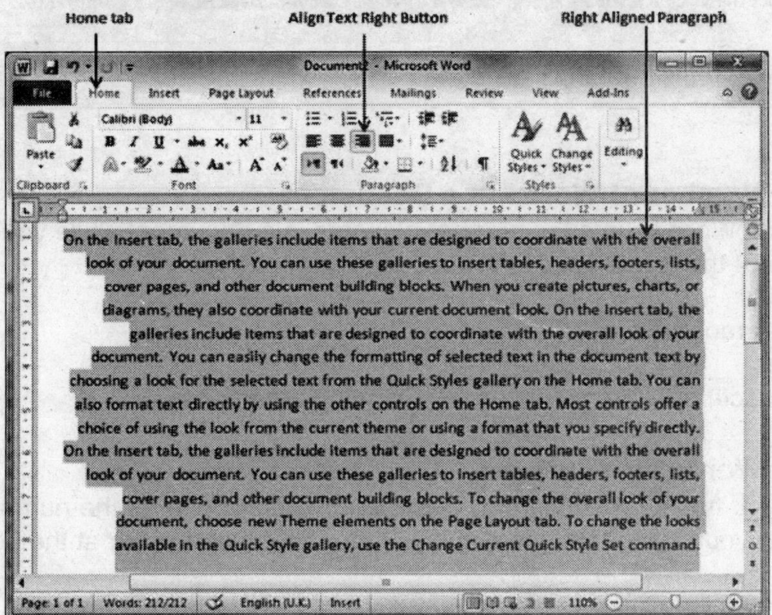

Justify Aligned Text

A paragraph's text is aligned justified if it is aligned with both left and right margins.

Click anywhere on the paragraph you want to align and click on **Justify** button available on **Home tab** or simply press **Ctrl + J** keys.

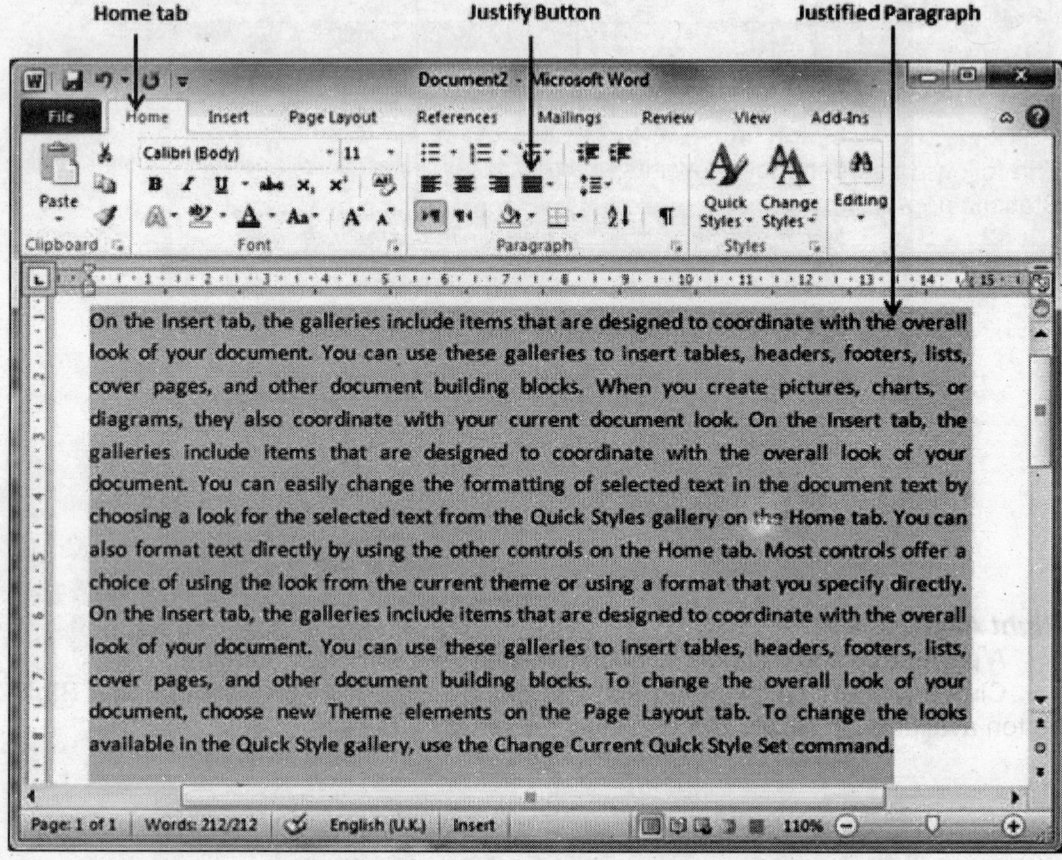

Count the Number of Words in a Document

Microsoft Word counts the number of words in a document while you type. Word can also count the following:

- Pages
- Paragraphs
- Lines
- Characters, either including or excluding the spaces

Count the Words as You Type

When you type in a document, Word automatically counts the number of pages and words in your document and displays them on the status bar at the bottom of the workspace.

1. Click on **Review** tab

2. Move to **Proofing** group
3. Click on **Word Count** icon to get the Statistics window.

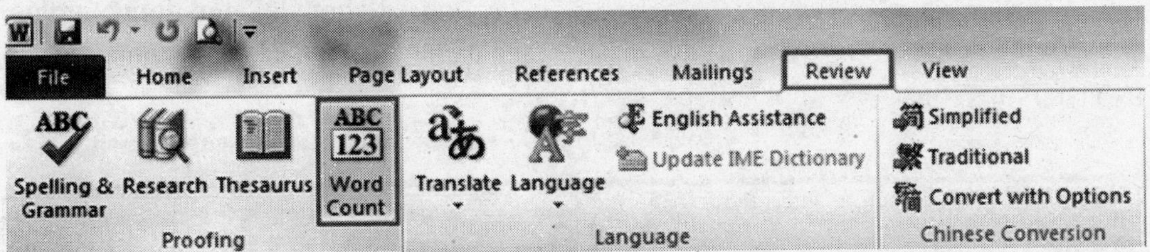

Or, you can simply move to the Status Bar and find out the Word Count there. The following screenshot shows its position. Just click on it and you can also see the Statistic pop-up window.

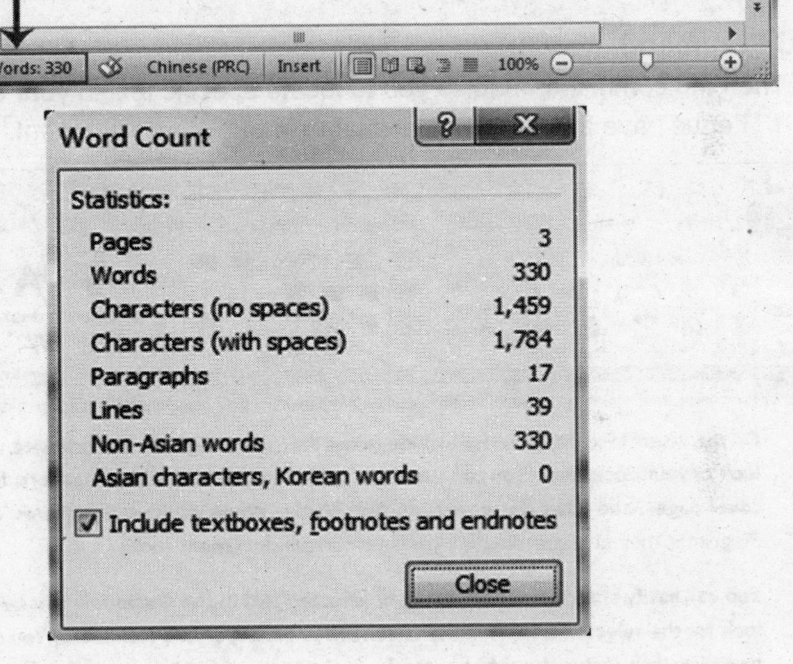

□

10
Advanced Functions in MS Word

Find Command

The Find command enables you to locate specific text in your document.

1. Let us have a sample text available in our Word document.

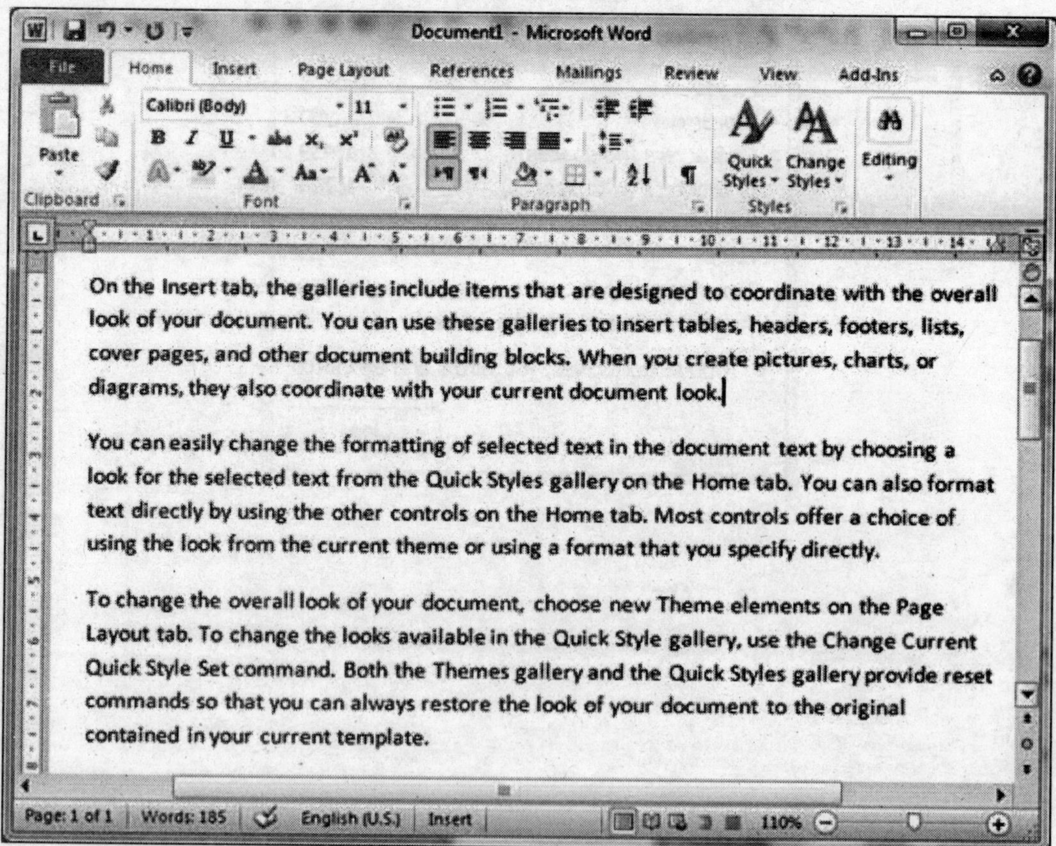

2. Click on **Find** option in the **Editing group** on the **Home tab** or press **Ctrl + F** to launch the **Navigation pane** shown below.

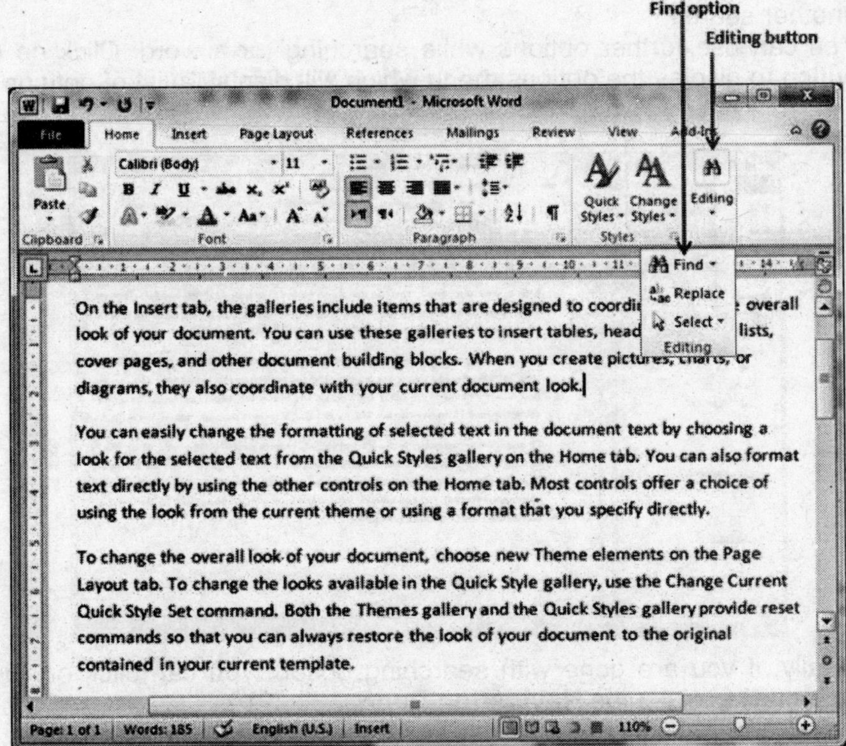

3. Enter a word that you want to search in the search box. As soon as you have finished typing, Word searches for the text you have entered and displays the results in the navigation pane and highlights the Word in the document as well.

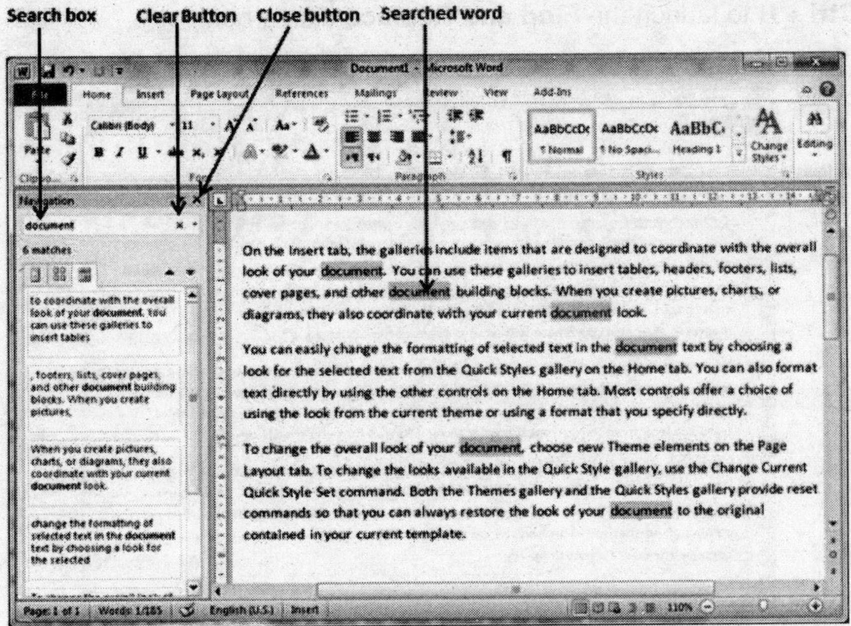

4. You can click on the **Clear** button [**X**] to clear the search results and perform another search.
5. You can use further options while searching for a word. Click on **Options** button to display the options menu which will display a list of options.

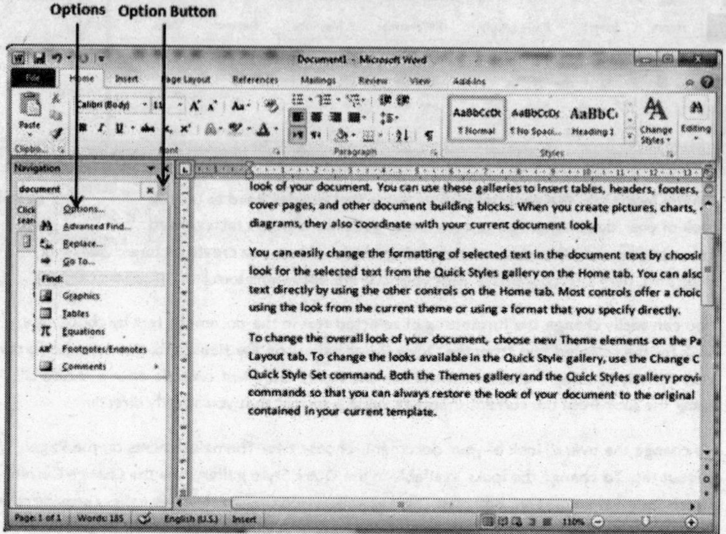

6. Finally, if you are done with searching option, you can click on the **Close** button [**X**] to close the **Navigation Pane**.

Find & Replace Option

You can replace an existing word in your document with the help of the following steps:

1. Click on the **Replace** option in the **Editing group** on the **Home tab** or press **Ctrl + H** to launch the **Find and Replace** dialog box.

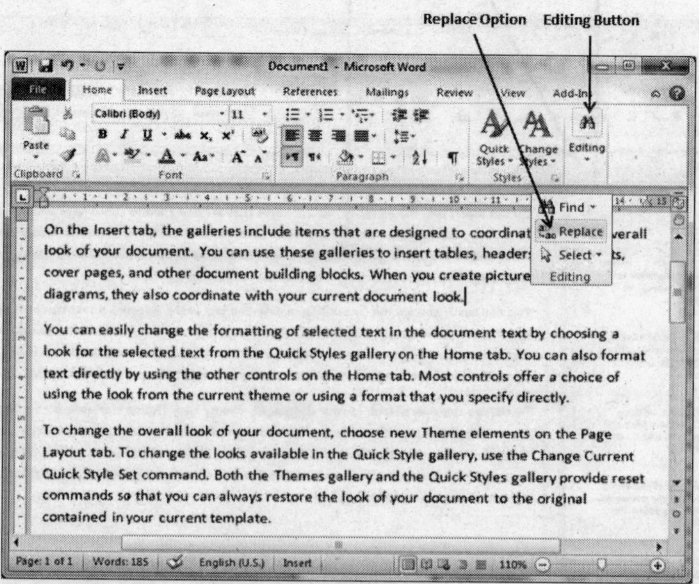

2. Type a word which you want to search and a word which you would like to replace with in the **Find and Replace** dialog box.

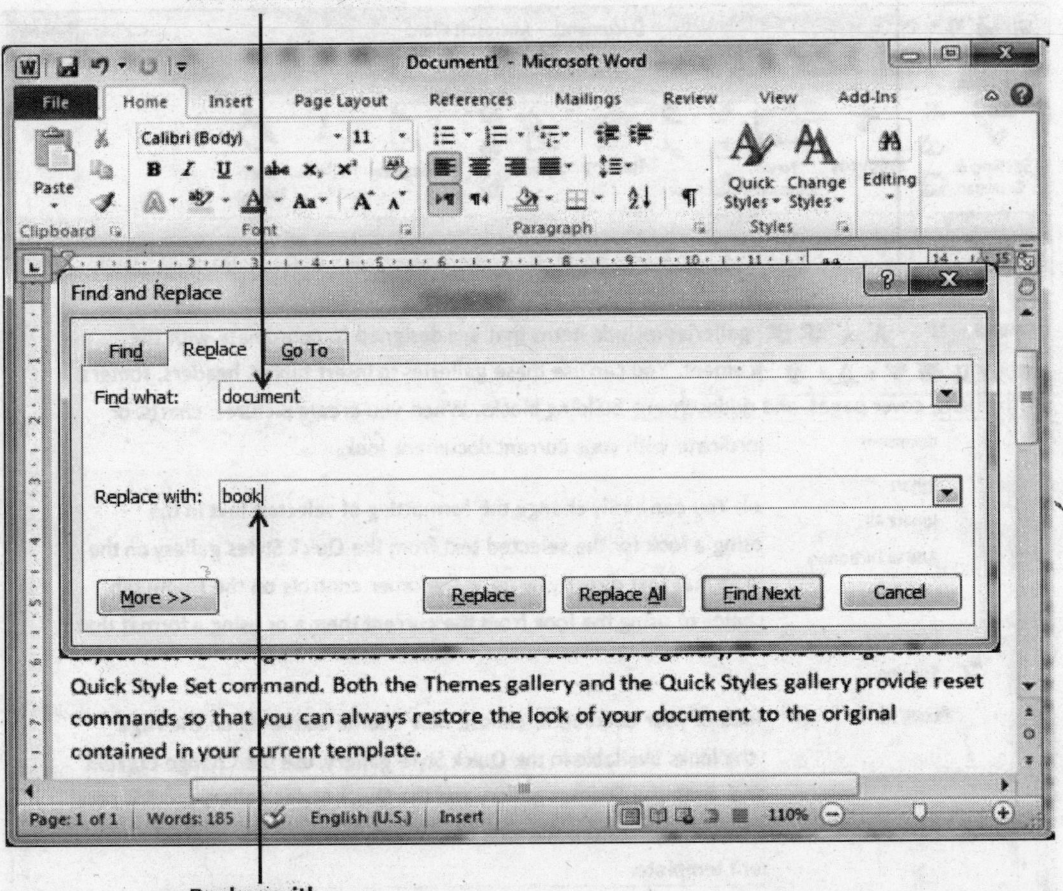

3. Click on **Replace** button available on **Find and Replace** dialog box and you will see the first occurrence of the searched word would be replaced with the **Replace with** word. Clicking again on **Replace** button would replace next occurrence of the searched word. If you will click on **Replace All** button, then it would replace all the found words in one go. You can also use **Find Next** button just to search the next occurrence and later you can use **Replace** button to replace the found word.
4. You can use **More >>** button available on the dialog box to use more options and to make your search more specific, like case sensitive search or searching for whole word only.
5. Finally, if you are done with finding and replacing option, you can click on **Close** [X] or **Cancel** button of the dialog box to close the box.

Spell Check and Grammar

Spelling Fix Menu

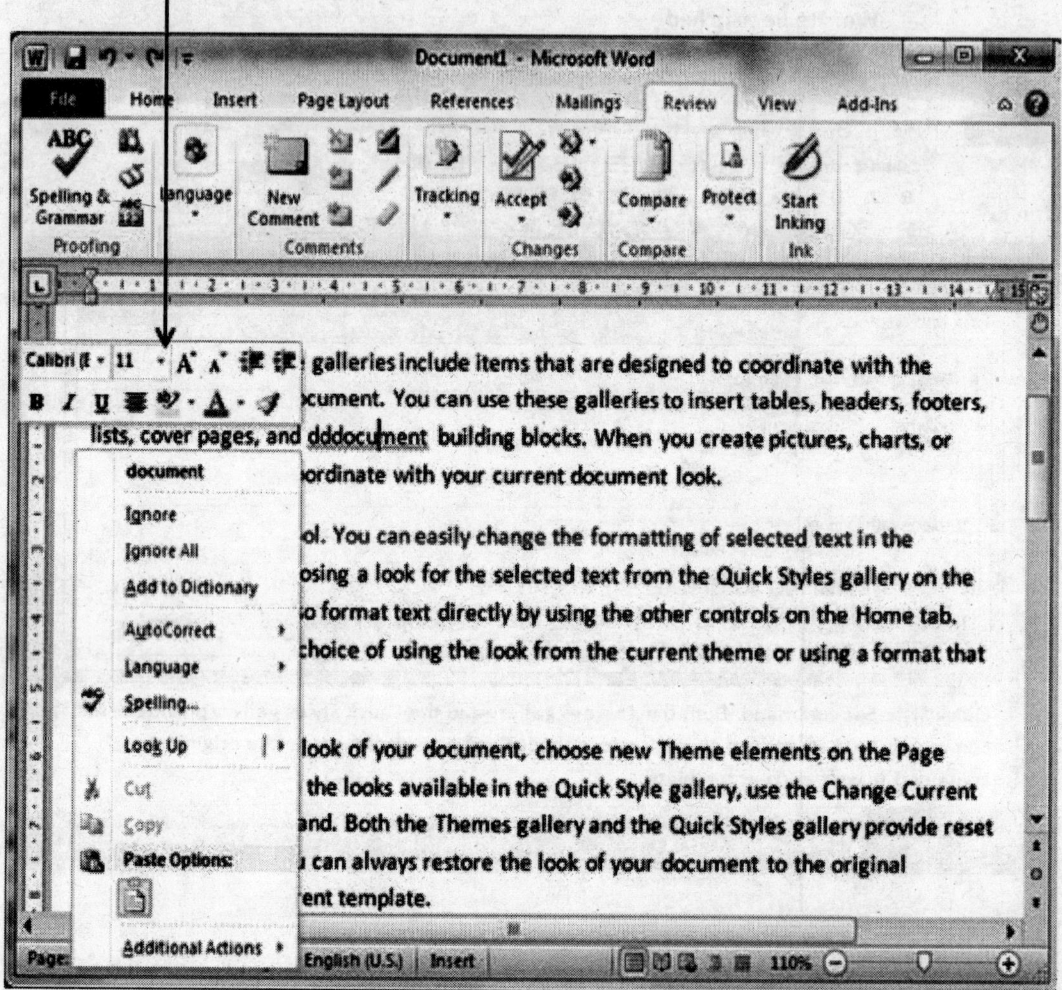

Create Bullets

Microsoft Word provides bullets and numbers to put a list of items in a nice order.

Create a List from Existing Text

It is very simple to convert a list of lines into a bulleted or numbered list.

1. Select a list of text to which you want to assign bullets or numbers. You can use any of the text selection methods to select the text.
2. Click on the **Bullet** button triangle to display a list of bullets you want to assign to the list. You can select any of the bullet styles available by simply clicking over it.

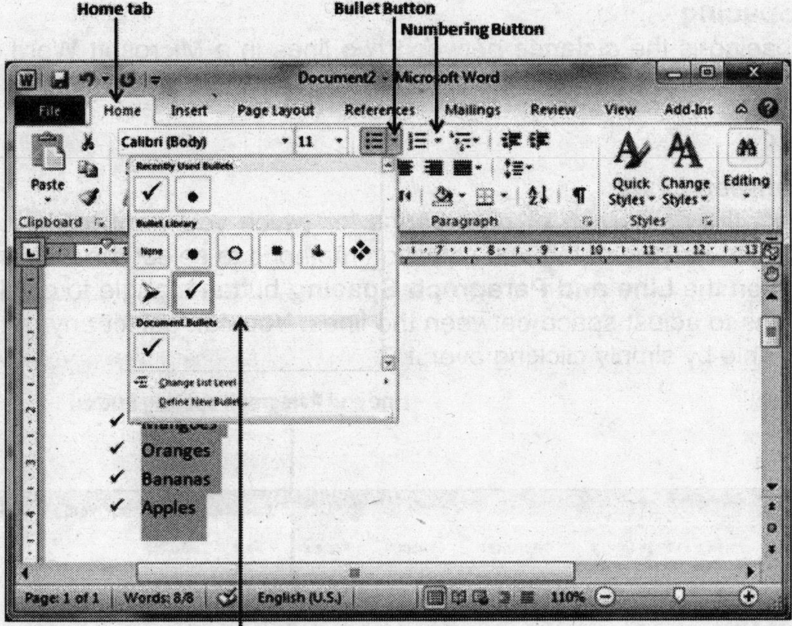

3. If you are willing to create a list with numbers, then click on the **Numbering** button triangle instead of **Bullet** button to display a list of numbers you want to assign to the list. You can select any of the numbering styles available by simply clicking over it.

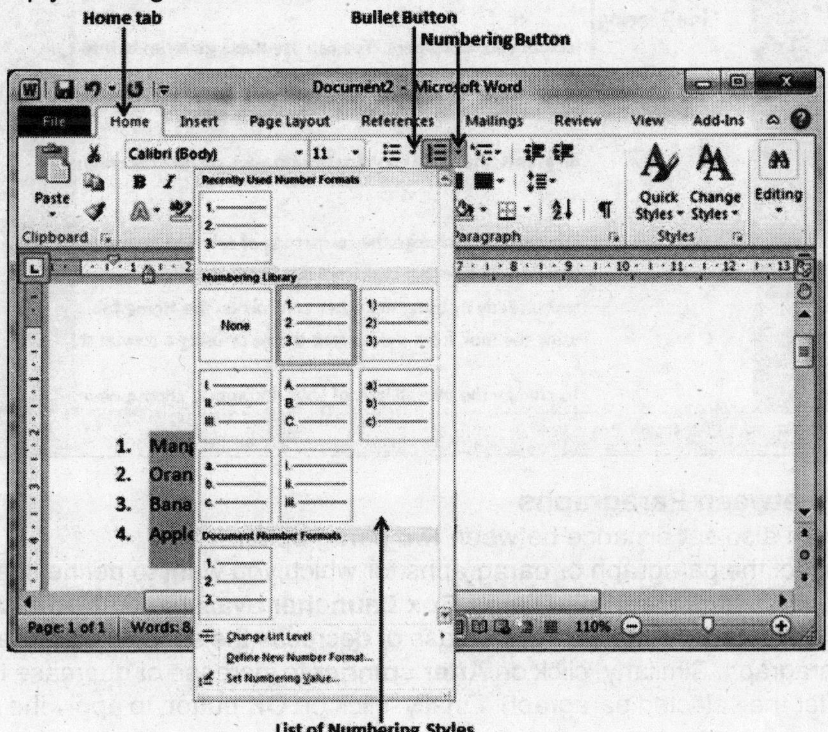

Set Line Spacing

Line spacing is the distance between two lines in a Microsoft Word document. You can increase or decrease this distance as per your requirement by following few simple steps.

Spacing between Lines

1. Select the paragraph or paragraphs for which you want to define spacing. You can use any of the text selection methods to select the paragraph(s).
2. Click on the **Line and Paragraph Spacing** button triangle to display a list of options to adjust space between the lines. You can select any of the options available by simply clicking over it.

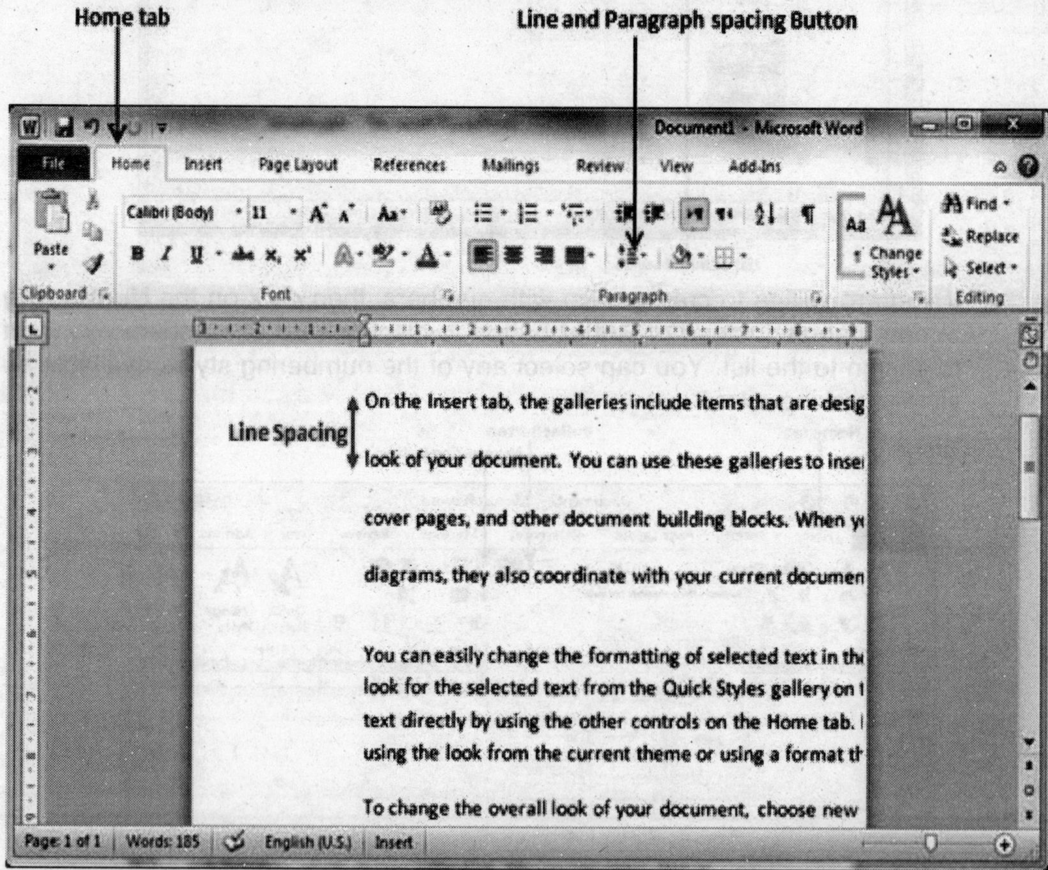

Spacing between Paragraphs

You can also set distance between two paragraphs.

1. Select the paragraph or paragraphs for which you want to define spacing and click on the **Paragraph Dialog Box Launcher** available on **Home tab.**
2. Click on **Before spinner** to increase or decrease the space before the selected paragraph. Similarly, click on **After spinner** to increase or decrease the space after the selected paragraph. Finally, click on **OK** button to apply the changes.

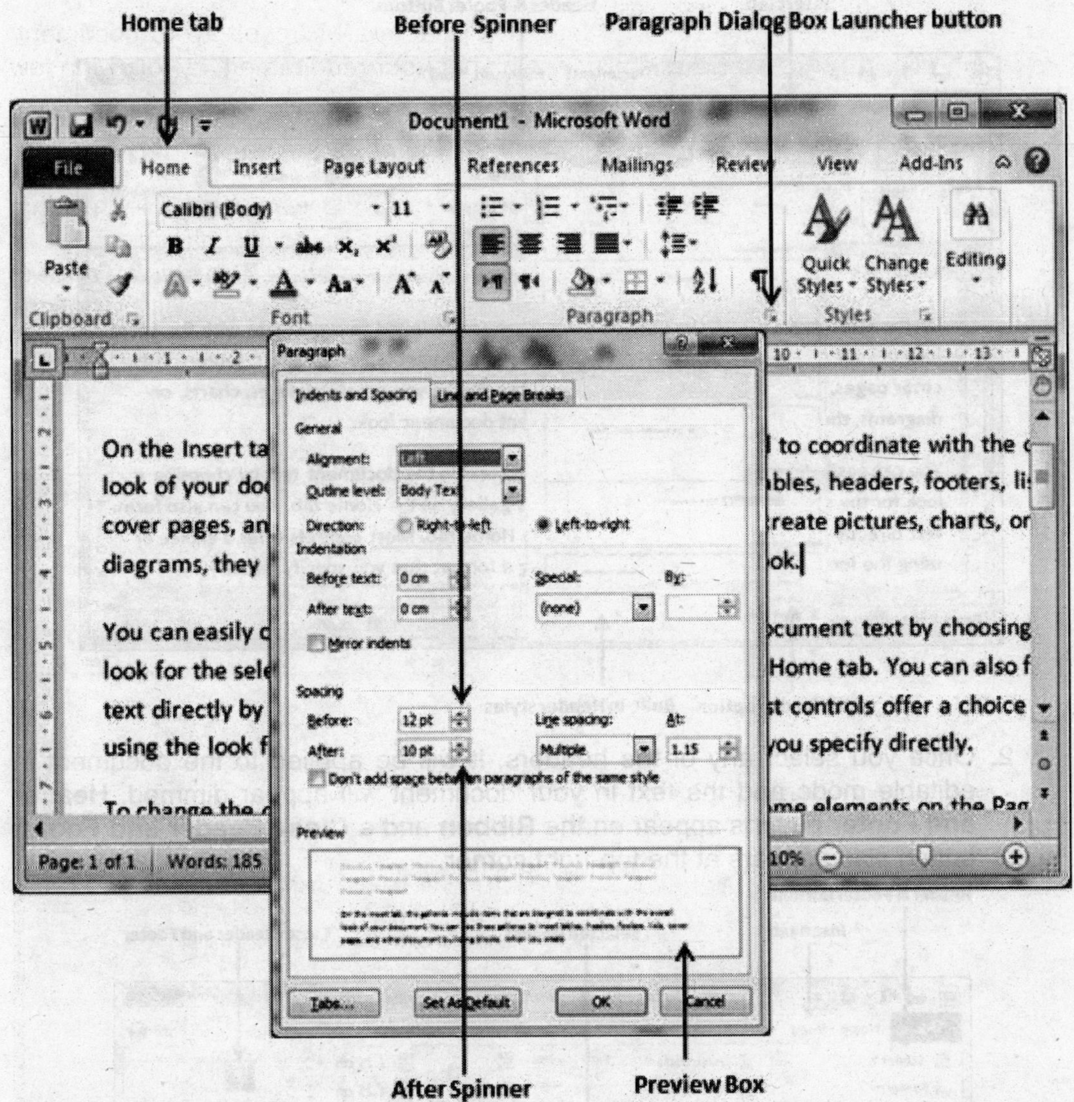

Header and Footer

Headers and footers are parts of a document that contain special information, such as page numbers and the total number of pages, the document title, company logo or any photo. The header appears at the top of every page, and the footer appears at the bottom of every page.

Add Header and Footer

1. Click on the **Insert tab**, and click on either **Header** button or **Footer** button whatever you want to add first. Assume you are going to add Header. So when you click on **Header** button, it will display a list of **built-in Headers** from where you can choose any of the headers by simply clicking on it.

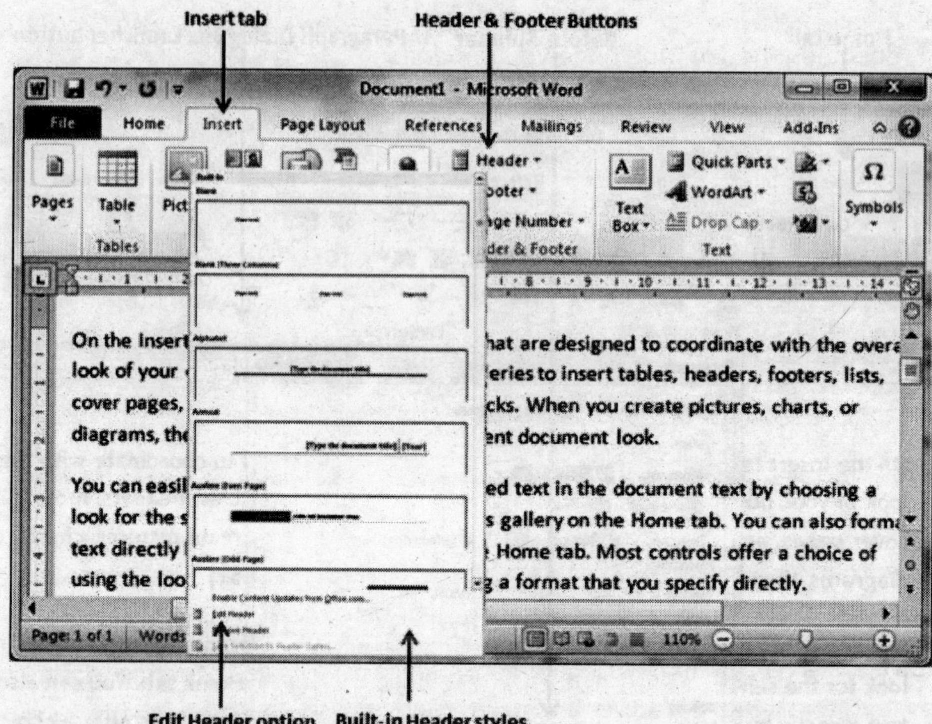

2. Once you select any of the headers, it will be applied to the document in editable mode and the text in your document will appear dimmed. **Header and Footer** buttons appear on the **Ribbon** and a **Close Header and Footer** button also appears at the top-right corner.

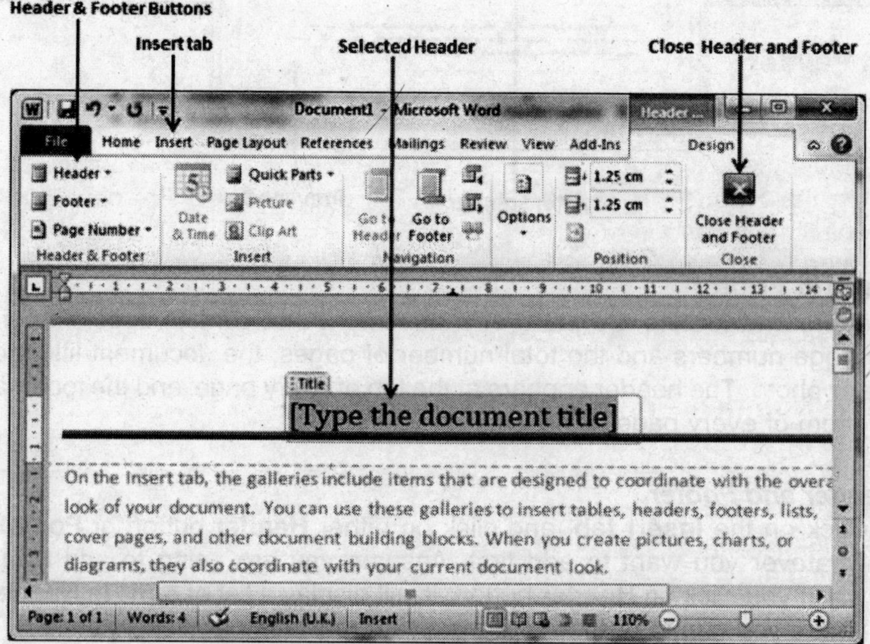

3. Finally, you can type your information whatever you want to have in your document header and once you are done, click on **Close Header and Footer** to come out of header insertion mode. You will see final result as follows:

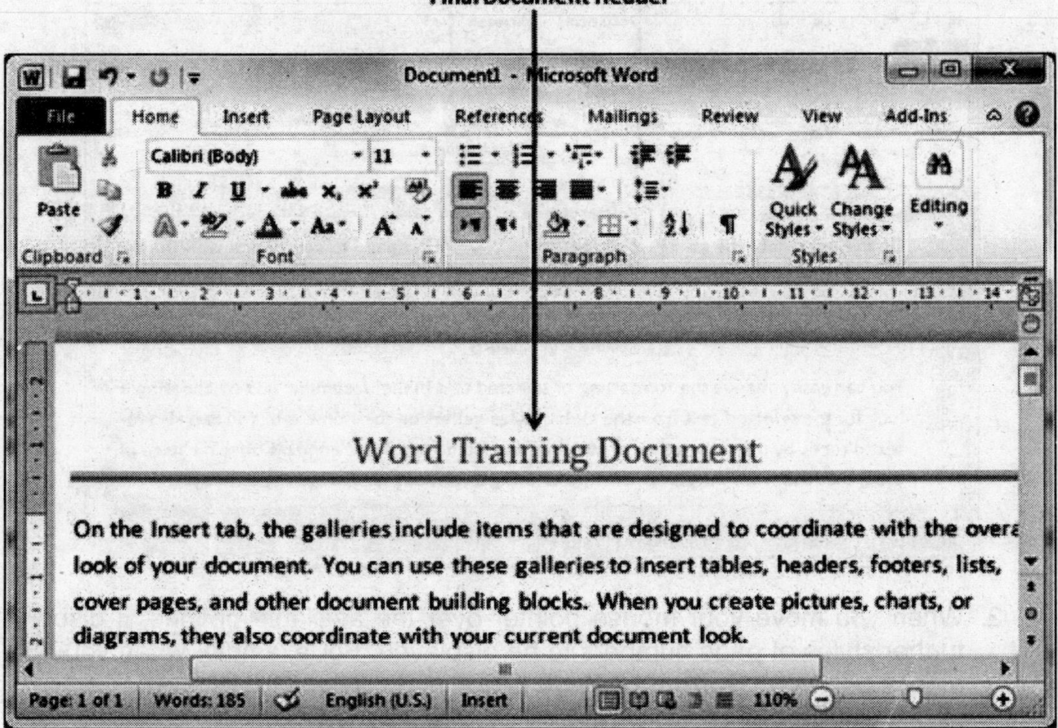

Format Painter

The Format Painter feature allows you to quickly copy a format that you have applied to text already in your document.

1. Select the text or graphic that has the formatting that you want to copy.
2. On the **Home tab**, in the **Clipboard group**, click on **Format Painter**. The pointer will change to a **paintbrush icon**.
3. Bring your cursor to the text or graphic that you want to format and click on the text.
4. To stop formatting, press **ESC** or click on the **Format Painter** command again.

Add Page Numbers

Microsoft Word automatically assigns page numbers on the pages of your document. Typically, page numbers are printed either in header or footer; but there are also options through which you can display the page numbers in the left or right margins or at the top or the bottom of a page.

Following are the steps to add page numbers in a Word document:

1. Click on the **Insert tab**, and then click on **Page Number** button available in

header and footer section. This will display a list of options to display page number at the top, bottom, current position, etc.

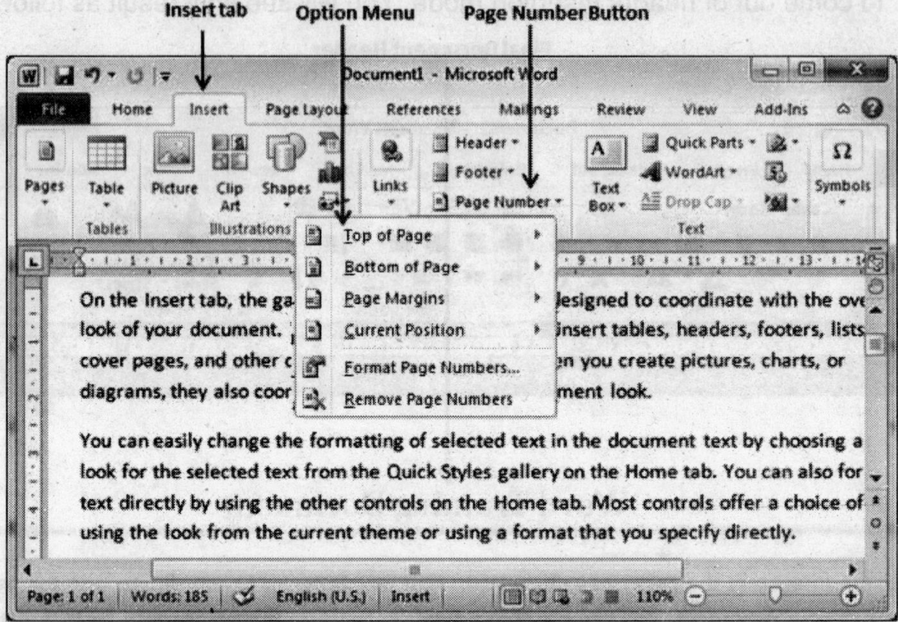

2. When you move your mouse pointer over the available options, it displays further styles of page numbers to be displayed. For example, when you take mouse pointer at **Bottom of Page** option, it displays a list of styles.

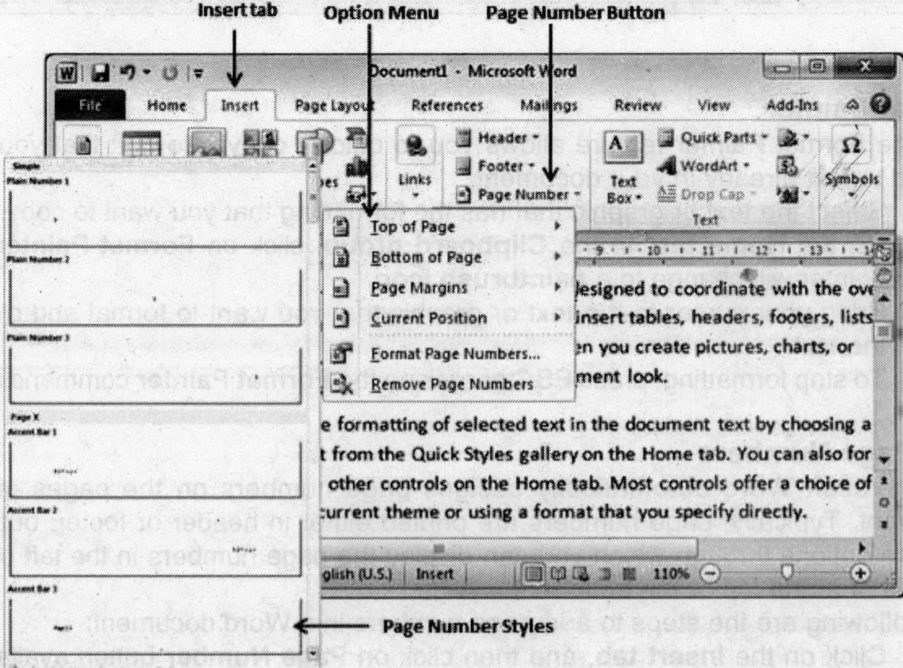

3. Finally, select the page number styles that you like. Here, **Accent Bar 1** style has been selected by clicking on it. After this step, you will enter in **Page Footer modification mode**, and then click on **Close Header and Footer** button to come out of footer edit mode.

You can format your page numbers using **Format Page Numbers** option available under the listed options.

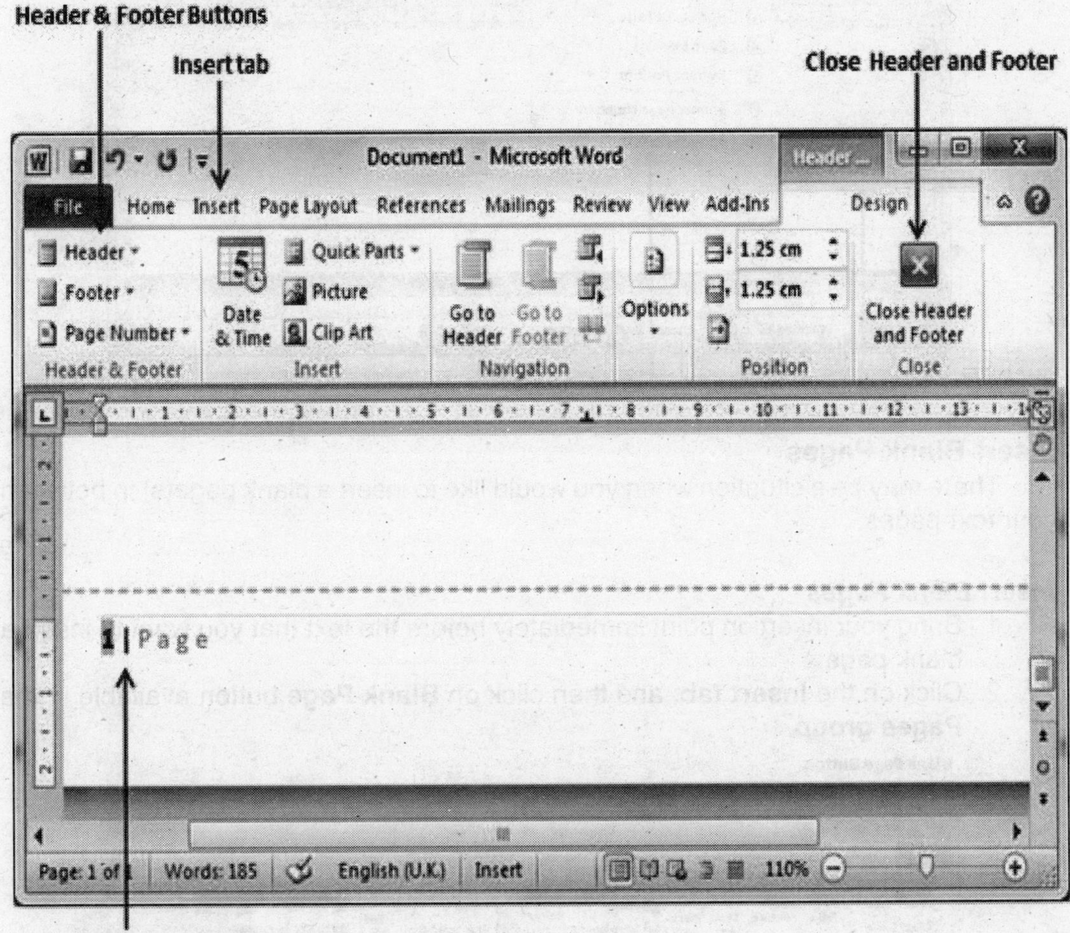

Remove Page Numbers

Following is the method of removing page numbers from a Word document:

Click on the **Insert tab**, and then click on **Page Number** button available in header and footer section. This will display a list of options to display page number at the top, bottom, current position, etc.; and at the bottom, you will have **Remove Page Numbers** option. Just click on this option and it will delete all the page numbers set in your document.

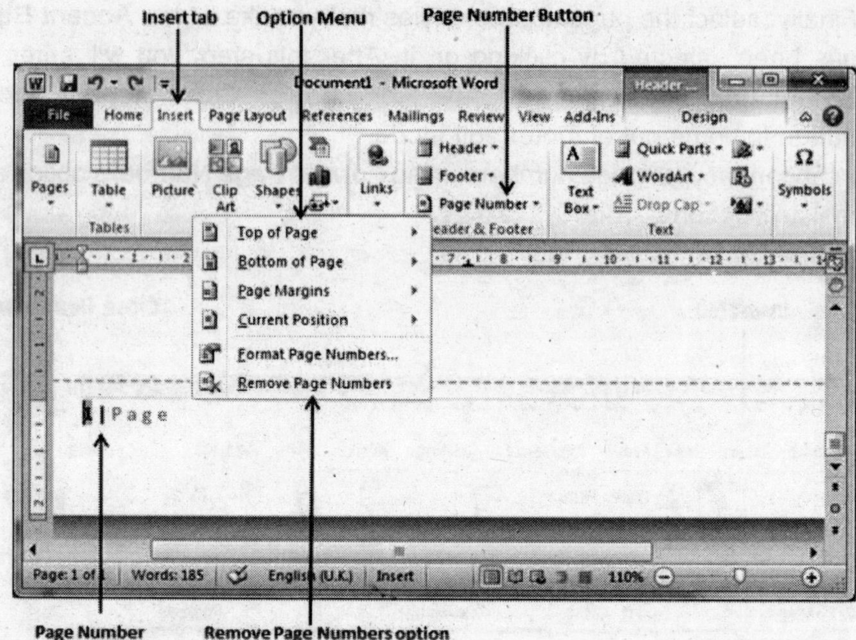

Insert Blank Pages

There may be a situation when you would like to insert a blank page(s) in between your text pages.

Insert Blank Pages

1. Bring your insertion point immediately before the text that you want to insert a blank page.
2. Click on the **Insert tab**, and then click on **Blank Page** button available in the **Pages group**.

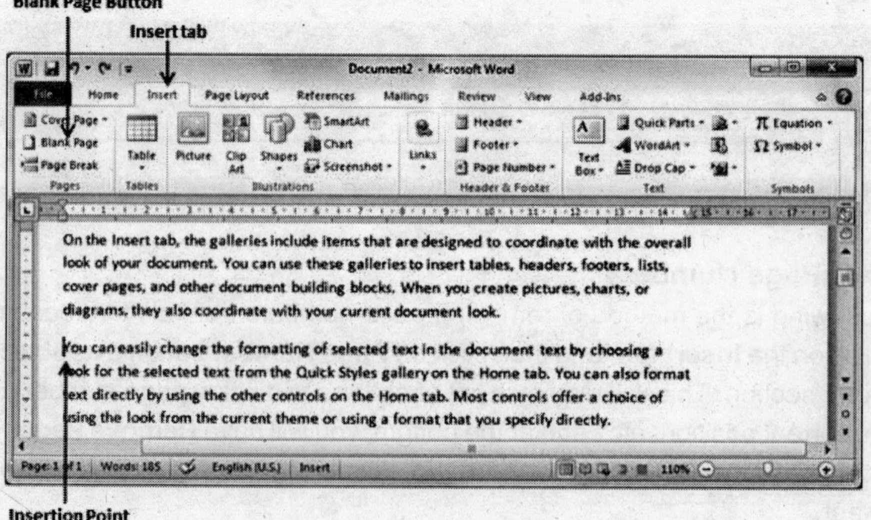

Word inserts a new blank page and moves all text after the page break onto a new page.

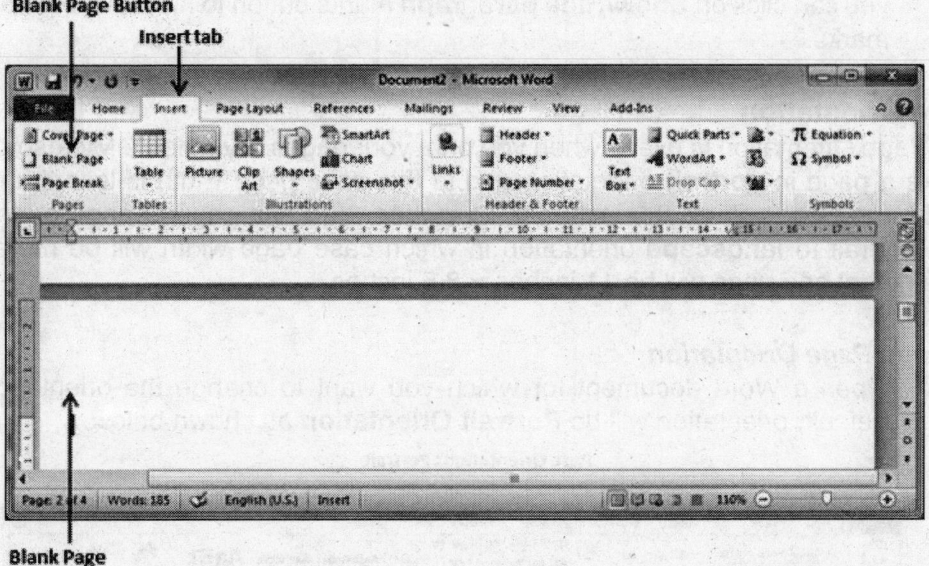

Delete Blank Pages

Following are the steps to delete a blank page from a word document:

1. Click on the **Home tab**, and then click on **Show/Hide ¶ paragraph marks** button available in the **Paragraph group** or simply press **Ctrl + Shift + *** keys. This will display all the page breaks.

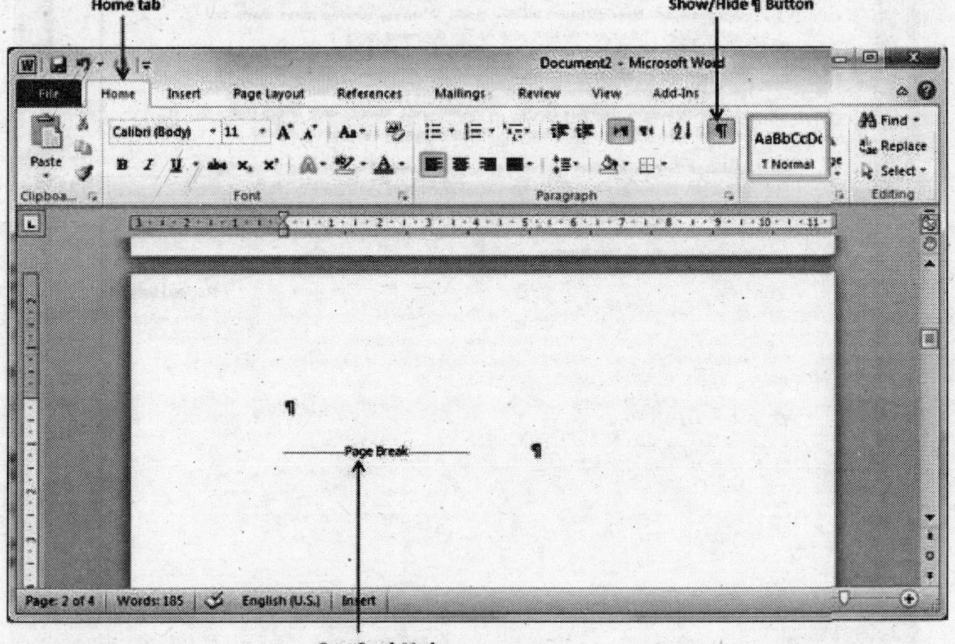

2. Bring your cursor immediately before the **Page Break** mark available on the blank page and press **Delete** key. This will delete the blank page and again you can click on **Show/Hide paragraph** marks button to hide all the paragraph marks.

Page Orientation

Page Orientation is useful when you print your pages. By default, Microsoft Word shows a page in **portrait** orientation and in this case page width is less than page height and page will be 8.5 inches × 11 inches. You can change page orientation from portrait to **landscape** orientation in which case page width will be more than page height and page will be 11 inches × 8.5 inches.

Change Page Orientation

1. Open a Word document for which you want to change the orientation. By default, orientation will be **Portrait Orientation** as shown below.

Page Orientation : Portrait

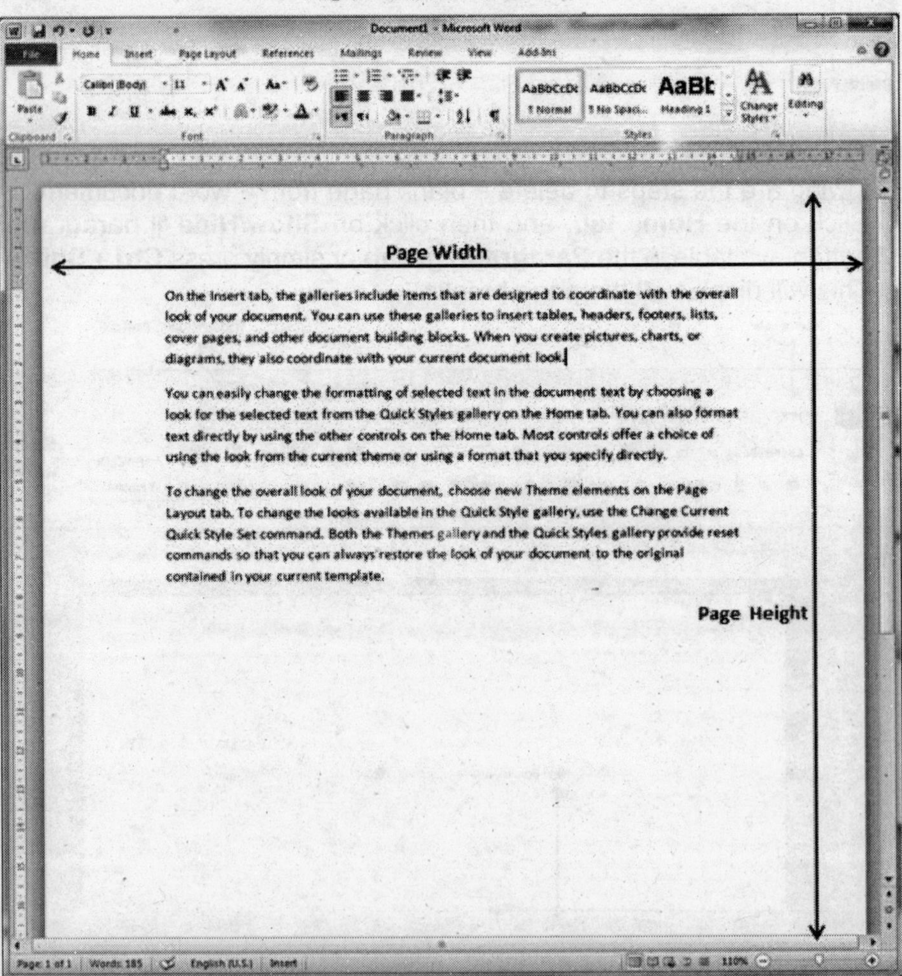

2. Click on the **Page Layout tab**, and then click on **Orientation** button available in the **Page Setup group**. This will display an **Option Menu** having both the options (Portrait and Landscape) to be selected.

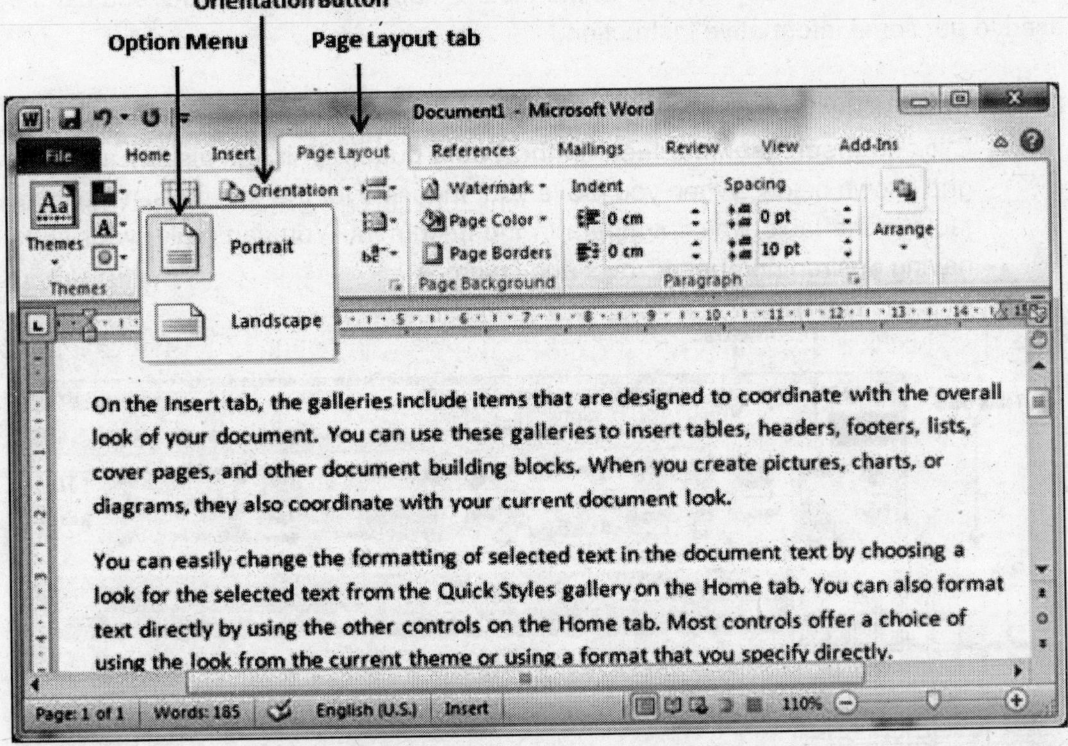

3. Click on any of the options you want to set to orientation. If your page is already in portrait orientation, you will have to click on **Landscape** option to change the orientation to landscape orientation.

Page Orientation : Landscape

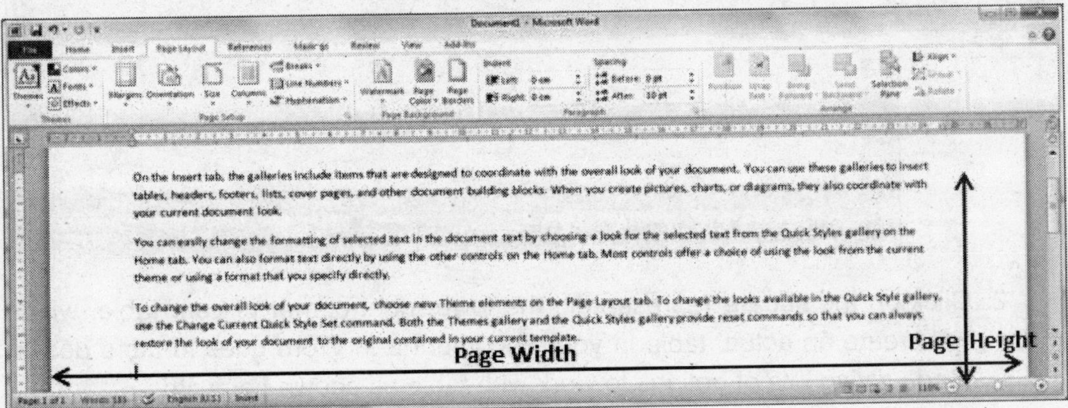

Create a Table

A table is a structure of vertical columns and horizontal rows with a cell at every intersection. Each cell can contain text or graphics, and you can format the table in any way you want. Usually, top row in the table is kept as a table header and can be used to put some informative instruction.

Creating a Table

1. Click on **Insert tab**, and then on the **Table** button. This will display a simple grid shown below. When you move your mouse over the grid cells, it makes a table in the table which appears in the document. You can make your table having desired number of rows and columns.

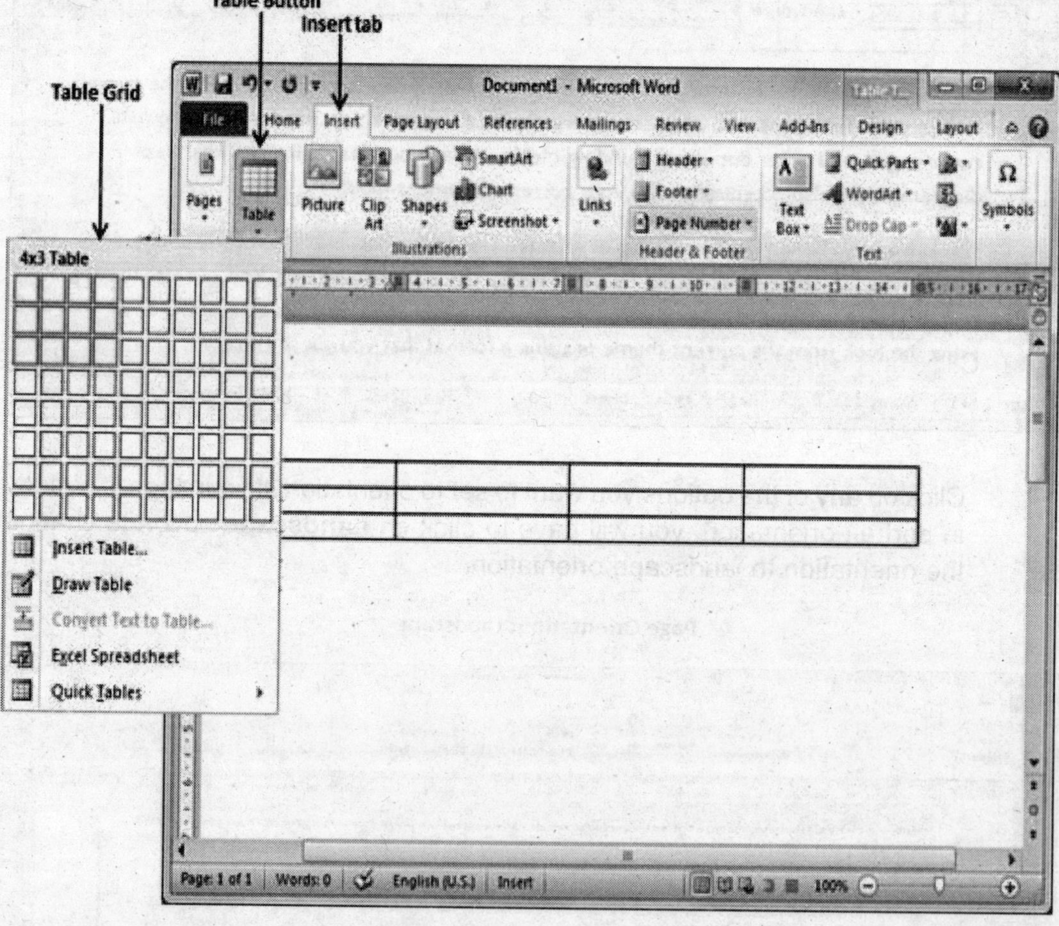

2. Click on the square representing the lower-right corner of your table, which will create an actual table in your document and Word goes in table design mode giving lots of options to work with table as shown herewith.

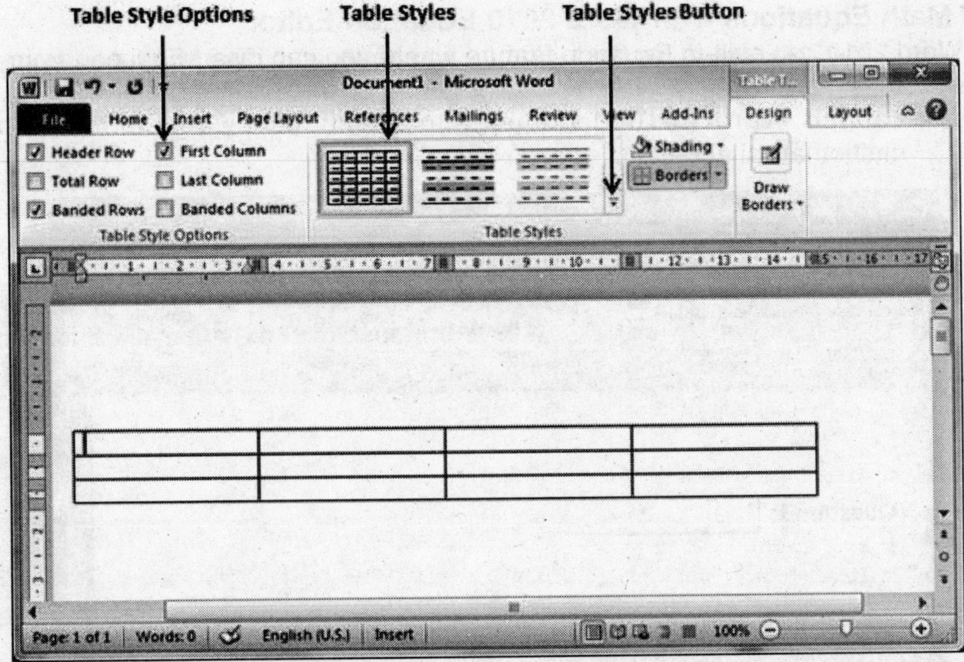

Delete a Table

Following are the steps to delete an existing table from a Word document:

1. Click anywhere on the table you want to delete.
2. Click on the **Layout tab**, and then click on **Delete Table** option under the **Delete Table** button to delete complete table from the document along with its content.

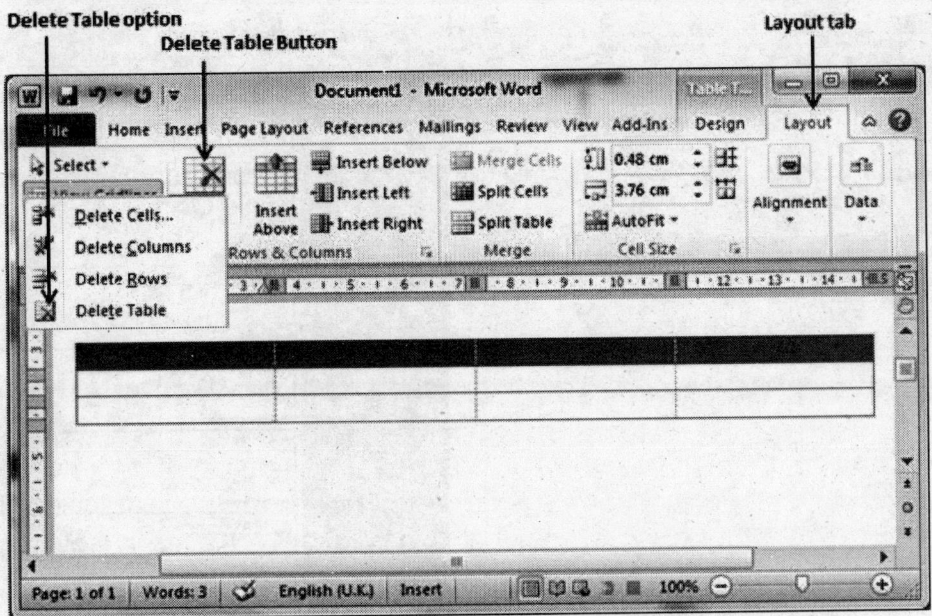

Add Math Equations with Word 2010 Equation Editor

Word 2010 has built-in Equation feature where you can insert Equation from the built-in list instantly.

1. Launch Word 2010 document, in which you want to insert any mathematical equation.

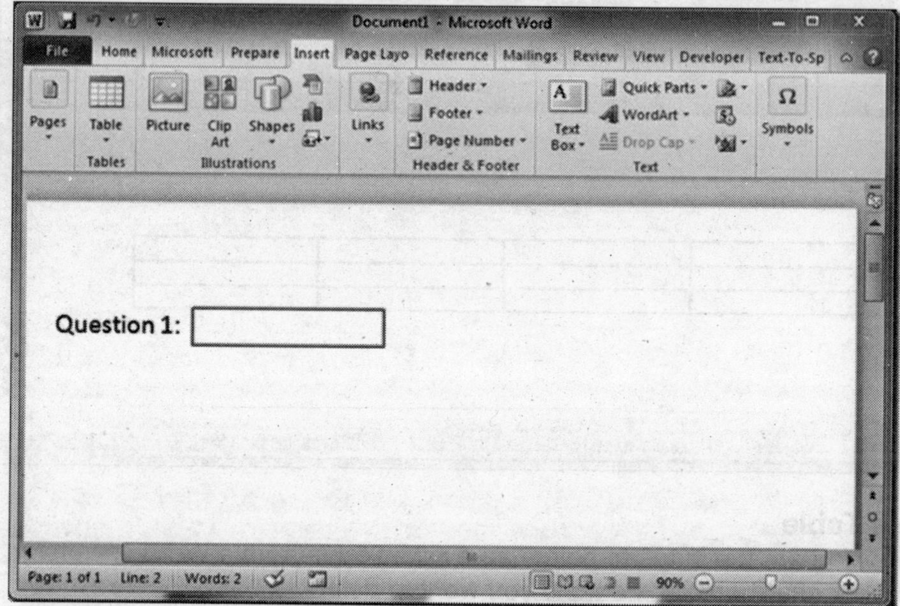

2. Now navigate to **Insert** tab, and click on **Equation** drop-down button to view built-in list, containing different equations.

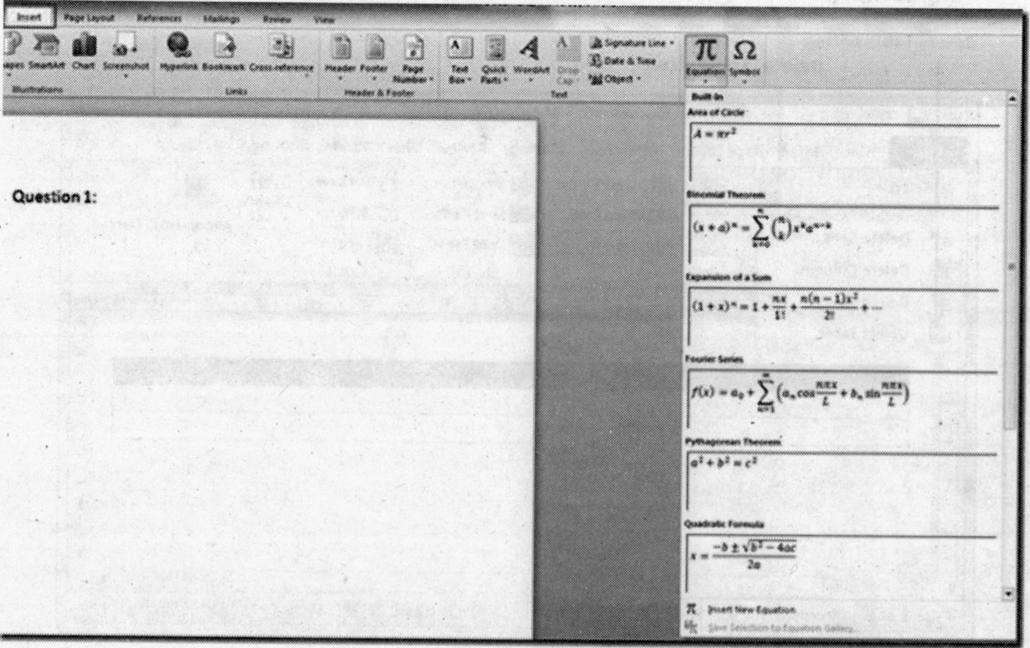

3. Upon click desired equation from list, it will be automatically added into the document. Now click on the drop-down button being present in the equation box for more options, then click on **Change to Inline** to place it in the line you were editing.

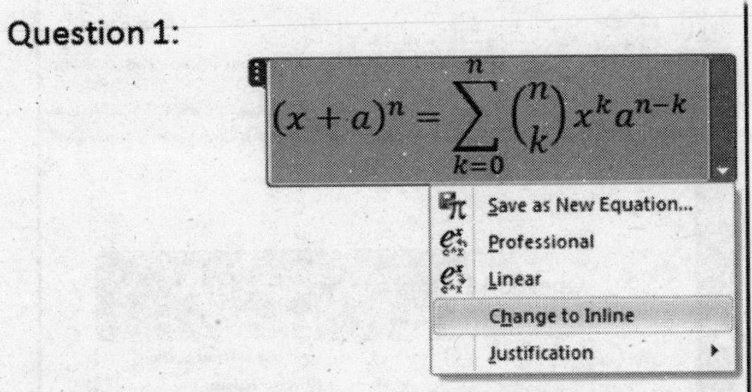

4. Upon click, it will be adjusted properly in the line, as shown in the screenshot below.

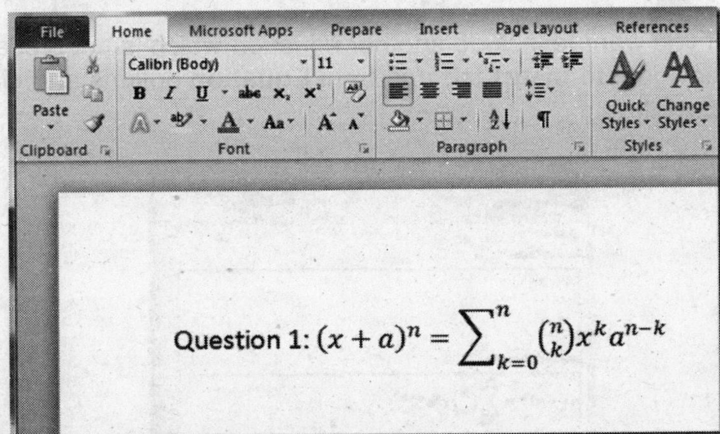

5. For editing equation values, you need to click inside the equation box to change values manually.

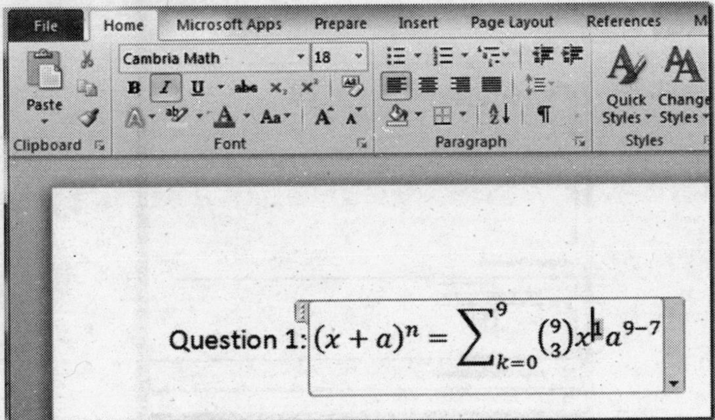

6. For viewing it or checking equivalent linear equation, click on drop-down button in equation box and click on **Linear**. You can also save the newly created equation through single click on **Save as New Equation**.

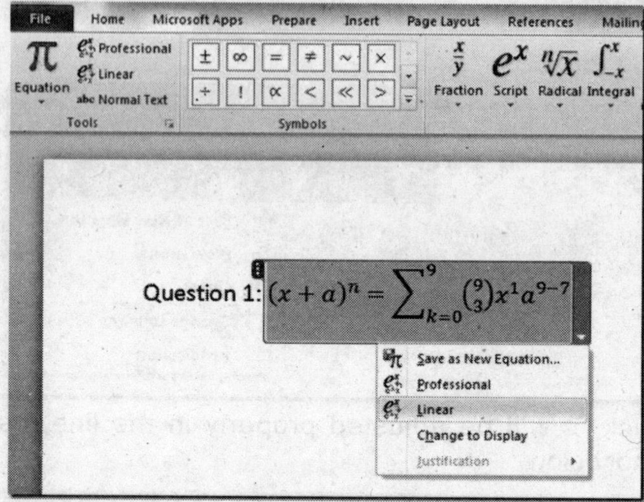

7. Now if you want to include another equation which is not present in the list, then navigate to **Insert** tab and from **Equation** options and click on **Insert New Equation**.

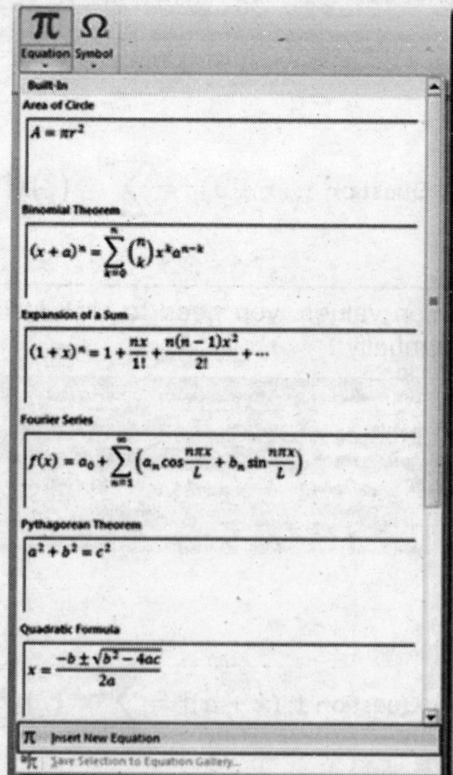

8. You will notice a **Equation Tools Design** tab will appear from **Structures** Group, you can select new equation from a given extended list. From **Symbols** group you can choose different symbols to use with equations.

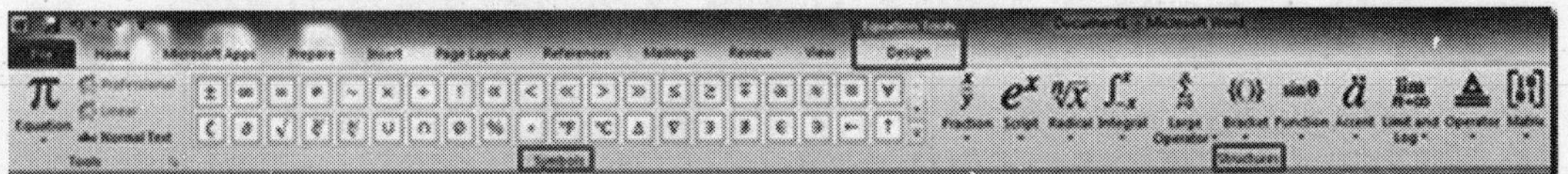

9. Now for inserting another equation, choose the equation you want to insert in the document from **Structures** group.

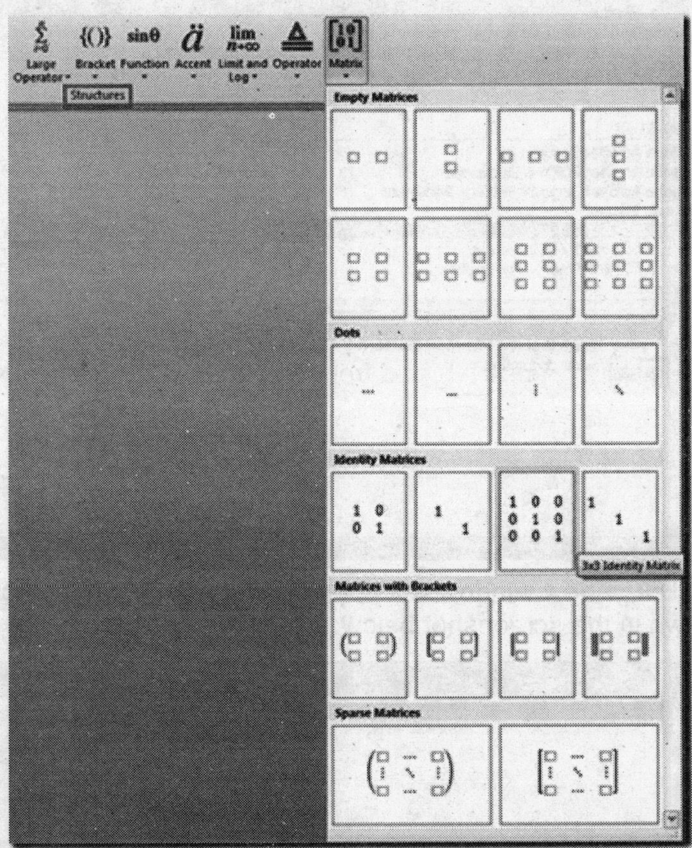

10. Upon click, it will automatically insert equation in to the document.

Question 1: $(x+a)^n = \sum_{k=0}^{9} \binom{9}{3} x^1 a^{9-7}$

Question 2: $\begin{matrix} 1 & 2 & a \\ 0 & 14 & b \\ 2 & c & 11 \end{matrix}$

11. You can also include equation from Microsoft Equation 3.0, as an object. For this, navigate to **Insert** tab, click on **Object**, that will open Object dialog to insert any object, select **Microsoft Equation 3.0** from Object type, and click on **OK**.

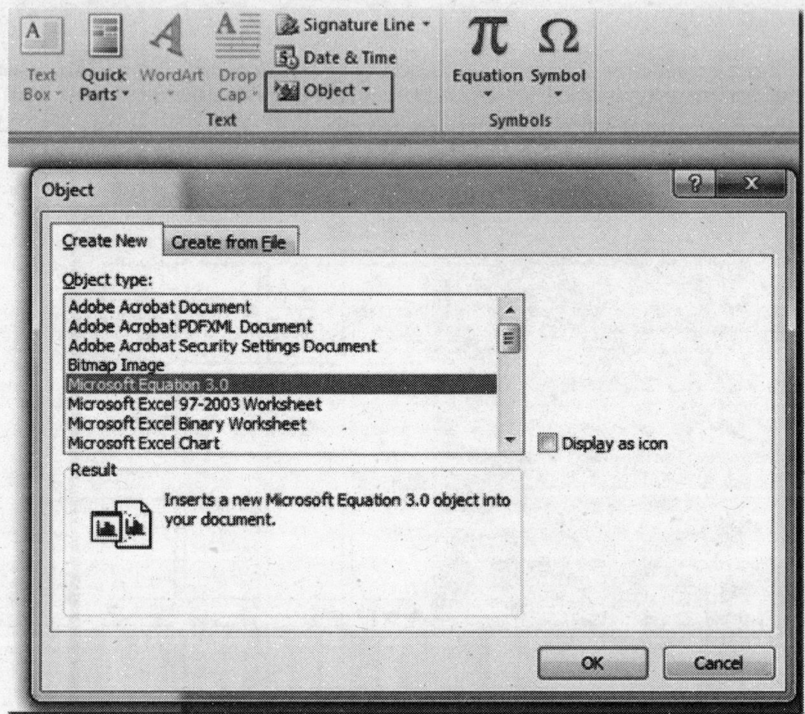

12. Upon click, a new window will open up where you can customize equation as shown in the screenshot below.

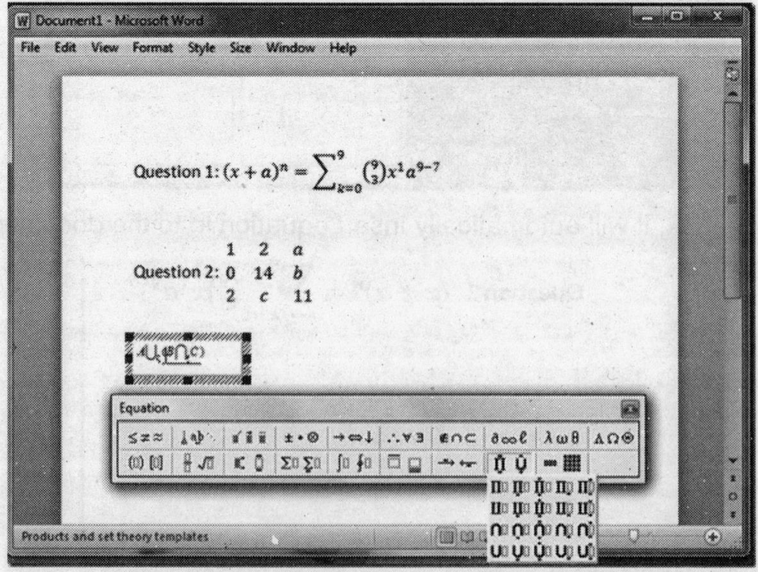

Translate Document in Word 2010

Word 2010 has a feature that can translate text in many languages. The integrated Mini Translator allows text to be translated flawlessly. The Mini Translator shows the translated text over the highlighted text. You can easily change the translation language from Language Translation Options and configure Mini Translator as per your liking.

1. In order to use the Microsoft Translator in Word, open the Word document in which you need to translate document content.

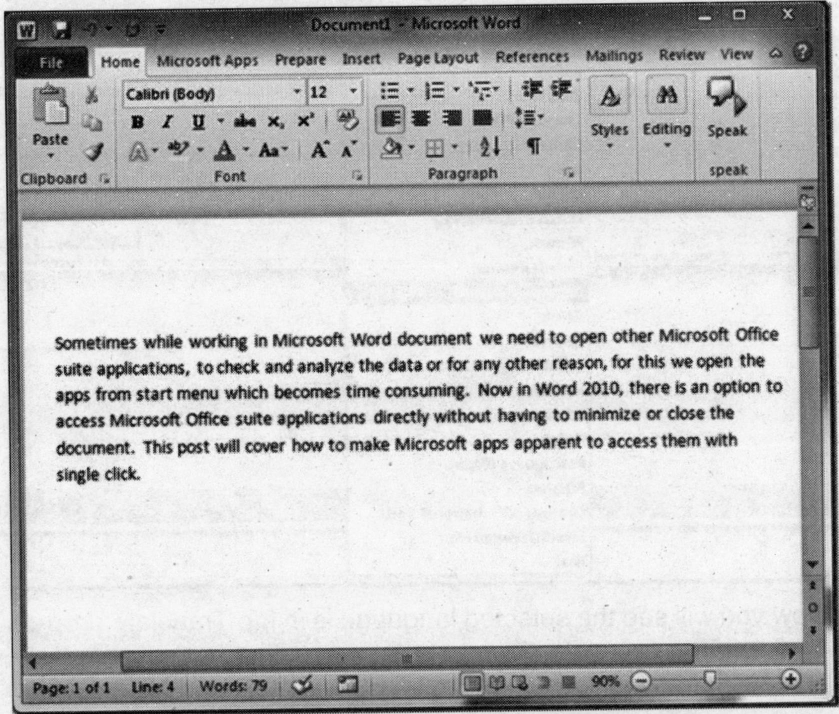

2. Now head over to **Review** tab and from **Translate** options, click on **Choose Translation Language**.

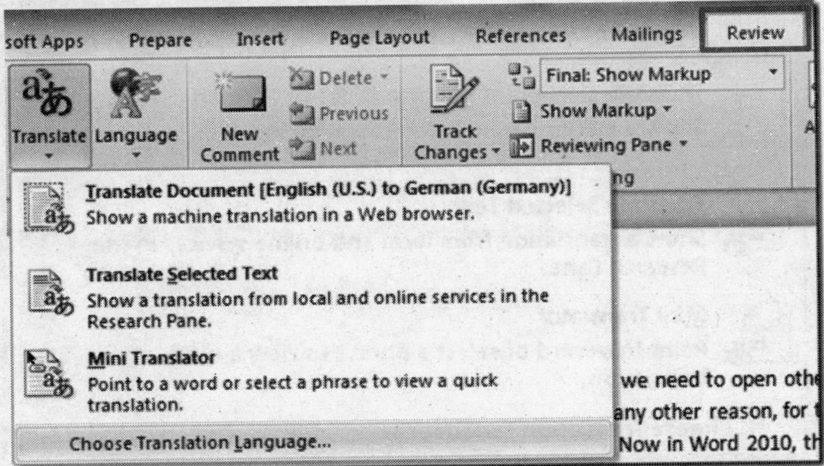

3. Upon click, it opens **Translation language Options** dialog. From the right pane, choose the desired languages as shown in the screenshot below.

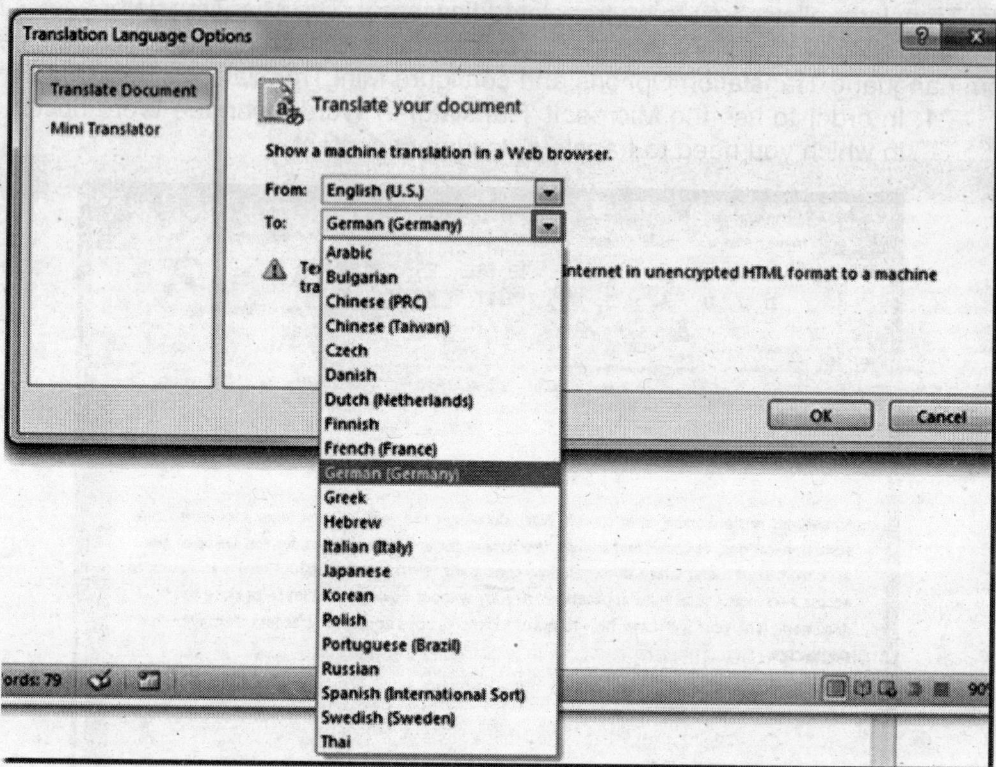

4. Now you will see the selected language is in the Translate drop-down menu. Click on it to translate document into specified language, as shown in the screenshot below.

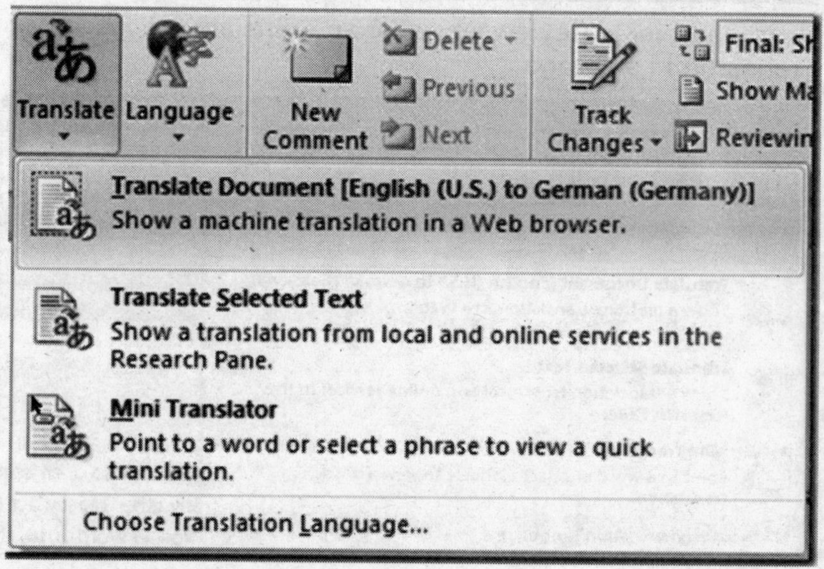

5. Upon click, it will lead you to the Microsoft Translator webpage, showing document content in both languages.

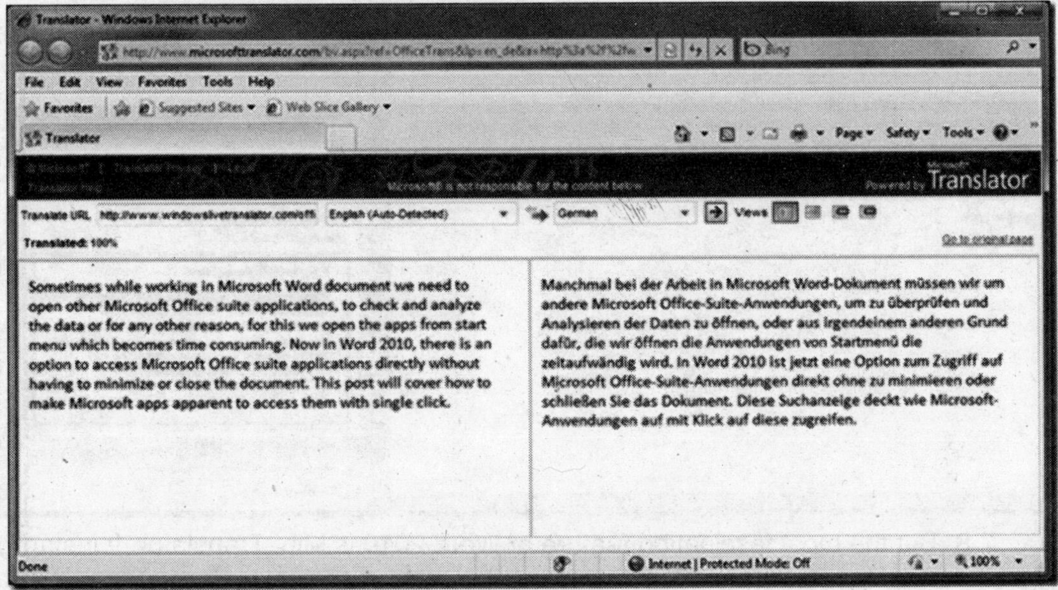

6. If you want to translate a selected portion of the document content, right-click on it and then click on **Translate**.

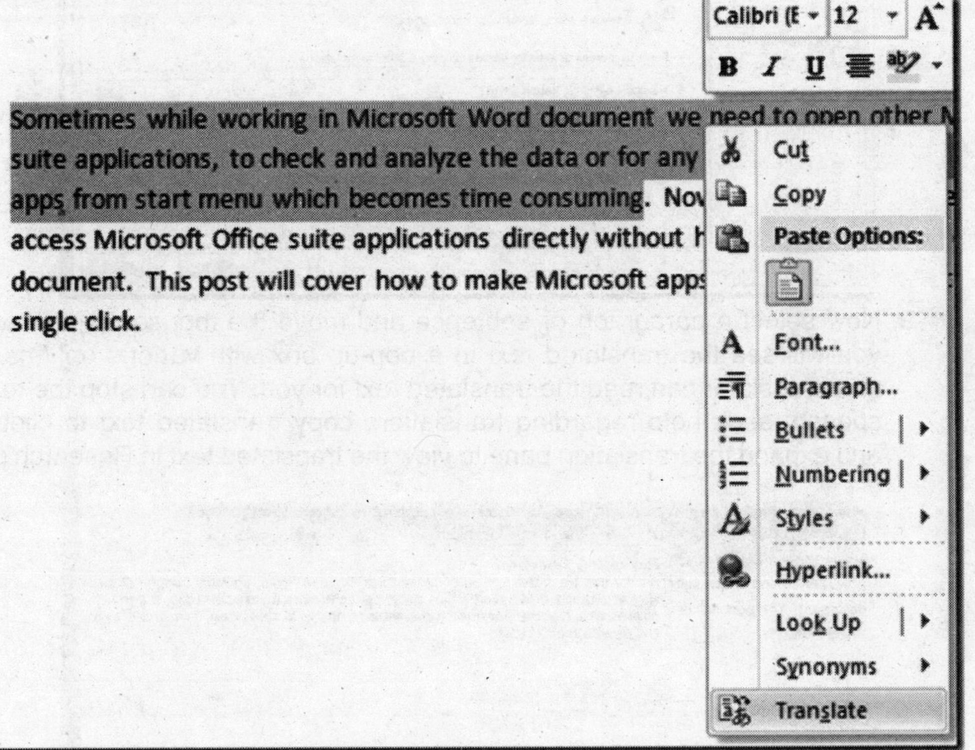

7. Immediately a right side-bar will appear showing you the translated text.

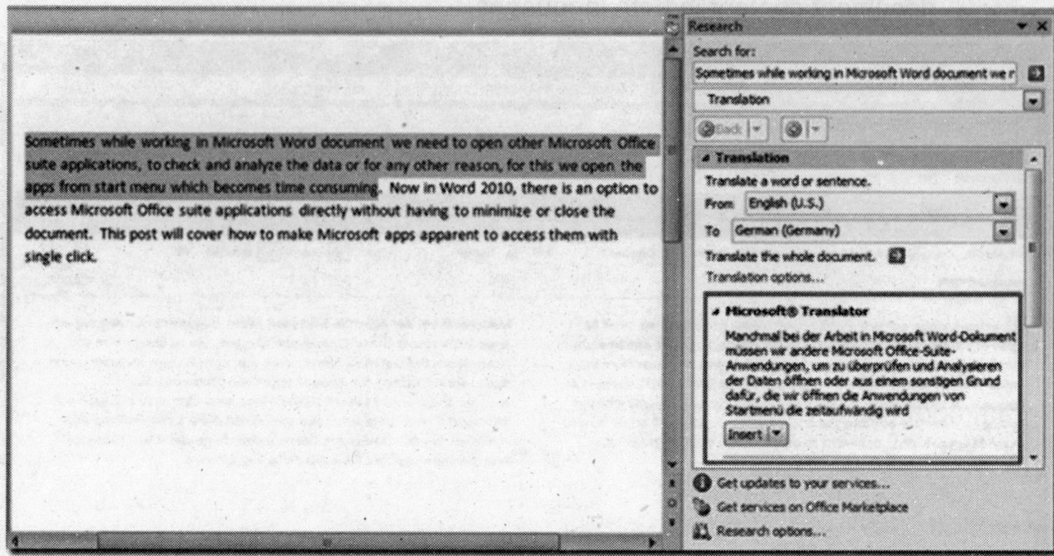

8. But the most fascinating feature of Word 2010 is Mini-Translator. It instantly displays the translated text over the highlighted text. From **Translation** options, click on **Mini Translator**, choose the language, and click on **OK**.

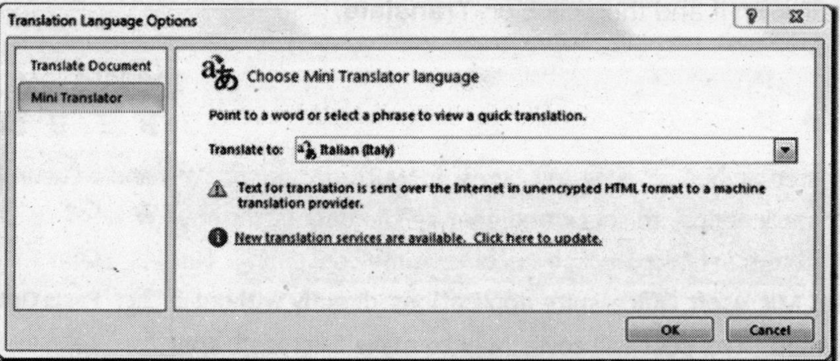

9. Now select a paragraph or sentence and move the mouse pointer over it, you will see the translated text in a pop-up box with various options. The mini-translator can read the translated text for you. You can stop the text-to-speech, seek help regarding translation, copy translated text to clipboard and expand the translation pane to view the translated text in Research pane.

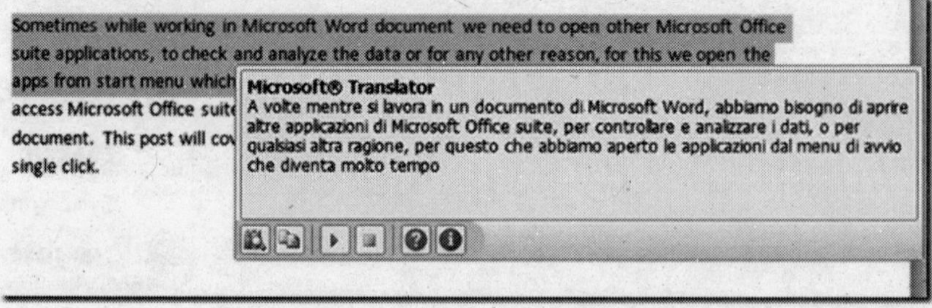

10. Hover the mouse over a word and you will see the translated version in the language you specified.

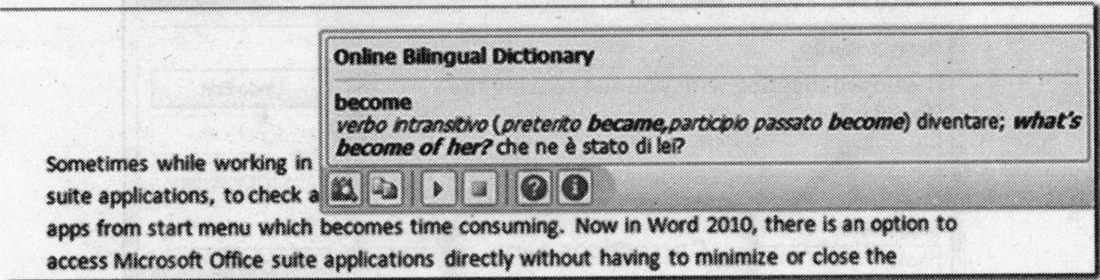

Checking Spelling and Grammar

Word has several options for checking your spelling. You can run a spelling and grammar check, or you can allow Word to check your spelling automatically as you type.

To Run a Spelling and Grammar Check

1. Go to the **Review** tab.
2. Click on the **Spelling & Grammar** command.

3. The **Spelling and Grammar** dialog box will open. For each error in your document, Word will try to offer one or more suggestions. You can select a suggestion and click on **Change** to correct the error.

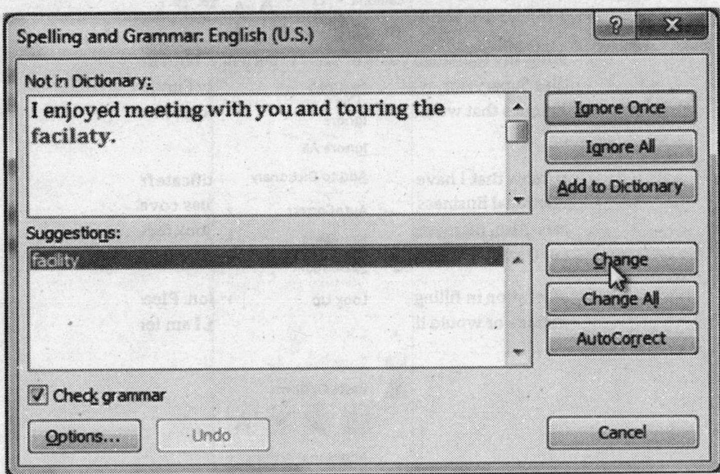

4. If no suggestions are given, you can manually type the correct spelling.

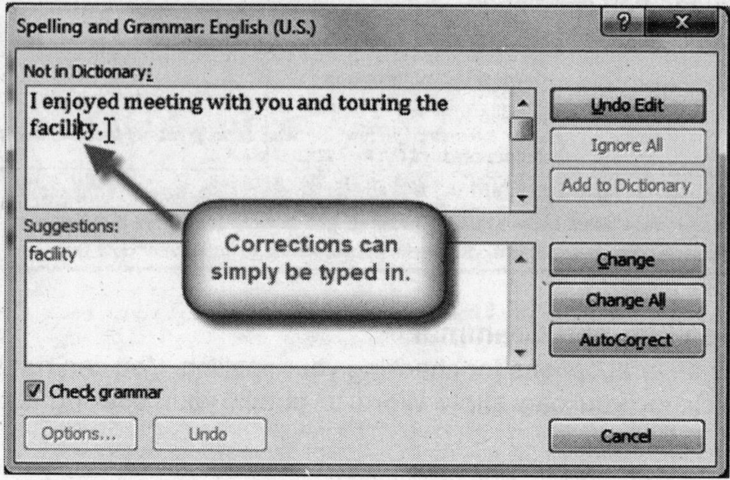

Automatic Spelling and Grammar Checking

By default, Word automatically checks your document for spelling and grammar errors, so you may not even need to run a separate spelling and grammar check. These errors are indicated by colored wavy lines.

- The **red line** indicates a misspelled word.
- The **green line** indicates a grammatical error.
- The **blue line** indicates a contextual spelling error. This feature is turned off by default.

To Use the Spelling Check Feature

1. Right-click on the underlined word. A menu will appear.
2. Click on the correct spelling of the word from the listed suggestions.
3. The corrected word will appear in the document.

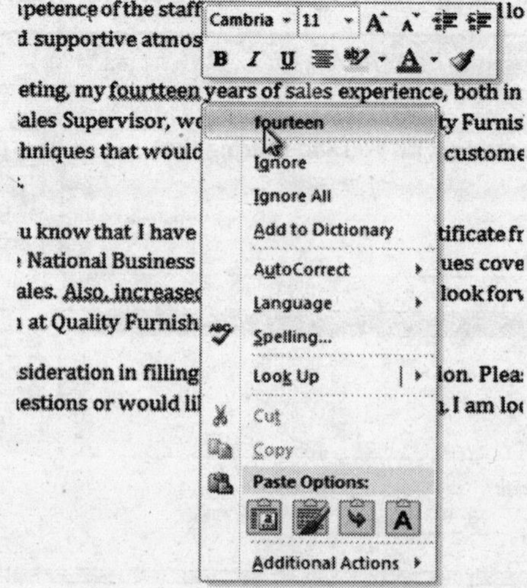

To Use the Grammar Check Feature

1. Right-click on the underlined word or phrase. A menu will appear.
2. Click on the correct phrase from the listed suggestions.
3. The corrected phrase will appear in the document.

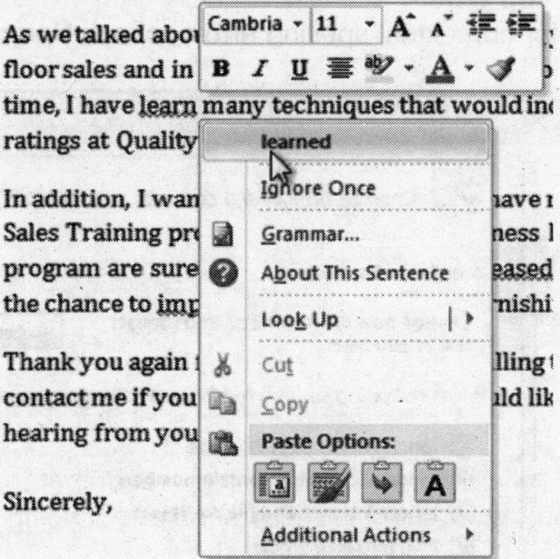

To Change the Automatic Spelling and Grammar Check Settings

1. From **Backstage** view, click on **Options**.

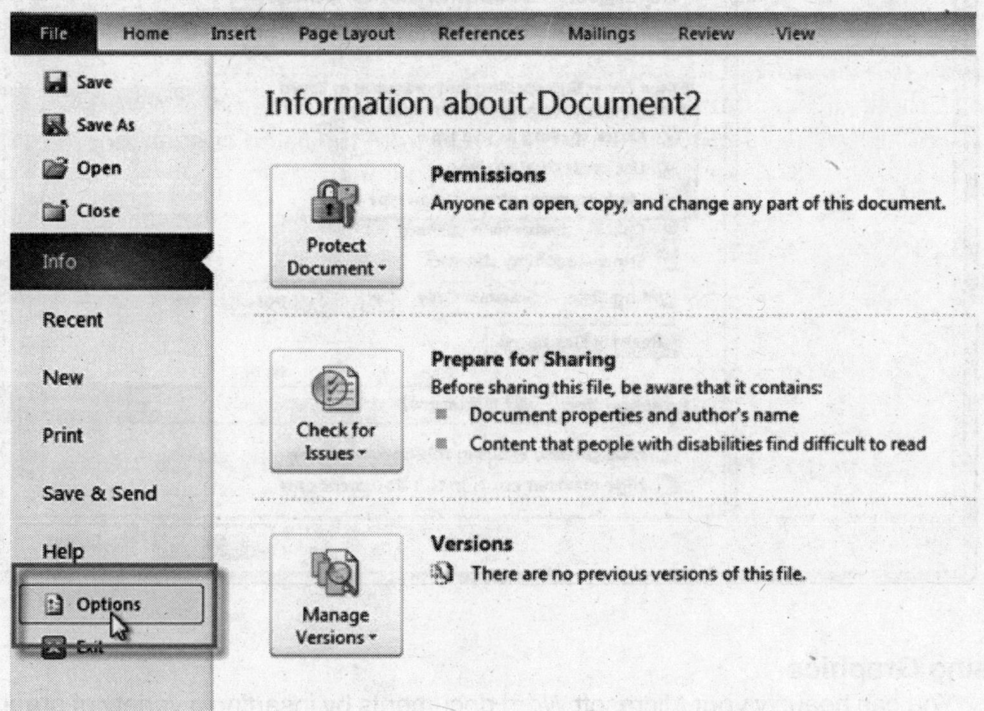

2. Select **Proofing**. The dialog box gives you several options to choose from.
   - If you don't want Word to automatically check spelling, uncheck **Check spelling as you type.**
   - If you don't want grammar errors to be marked, uncheck M**ark grammar errors as you type.**
   - To check for contextual spelling errors, check **Use contextual spelling.**

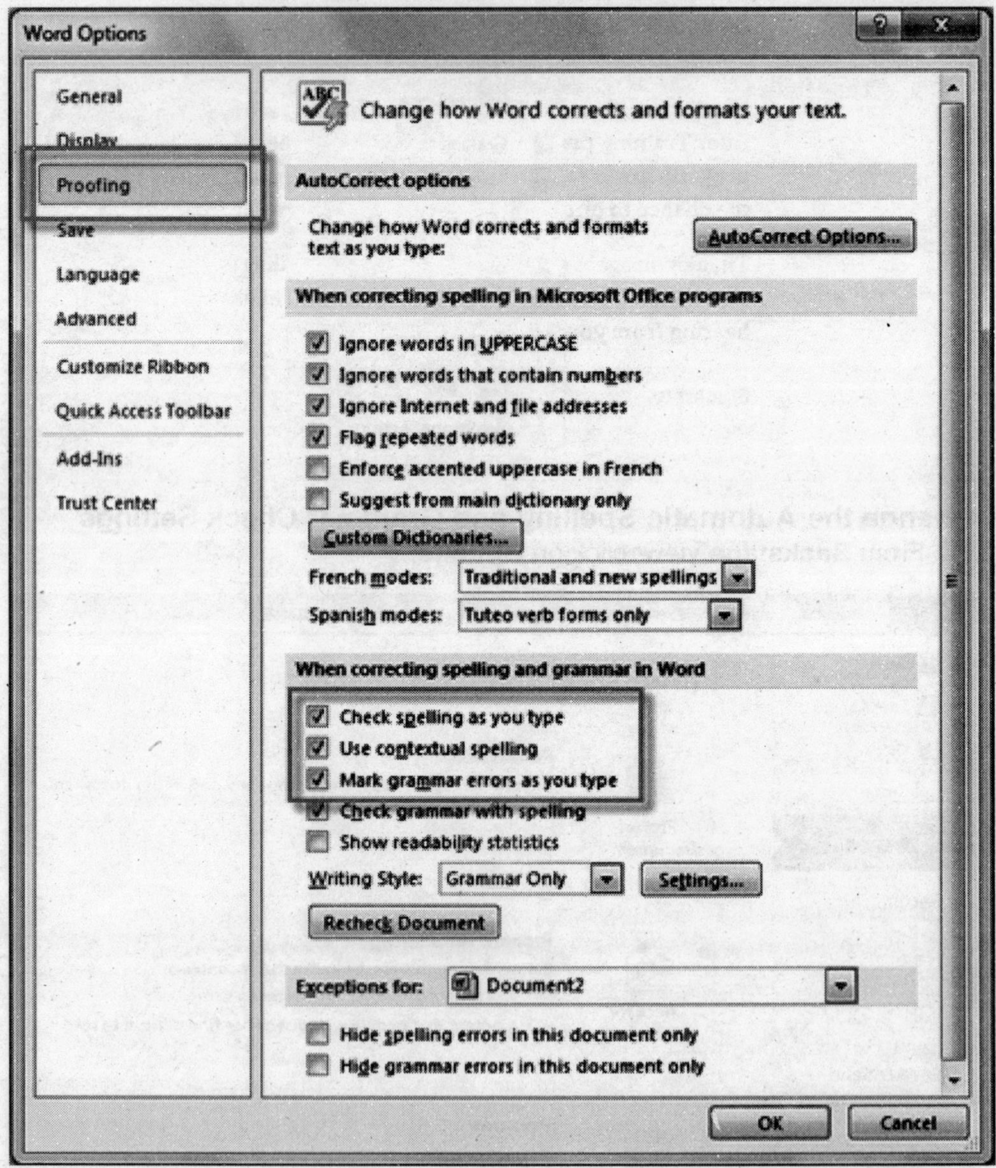

Using Graphics

You can beautify your Microsoft Word documents by inserting a variety of graphics.

Adding Picture in Document

Pictures and clip art can be inserted or copied into a document from many different sources, including downloaded from a clip art website provider, copied from a Web page, or inserted from a folder where you save pictures.

Following are the steps to add an existing picture in your Word document:

1. Click on your document where you want to add a picture.
2. Click on the **Insert tab** and then click on **Picture** option available in **Illustrations group**, which will display **Insert Picture dialog box**.

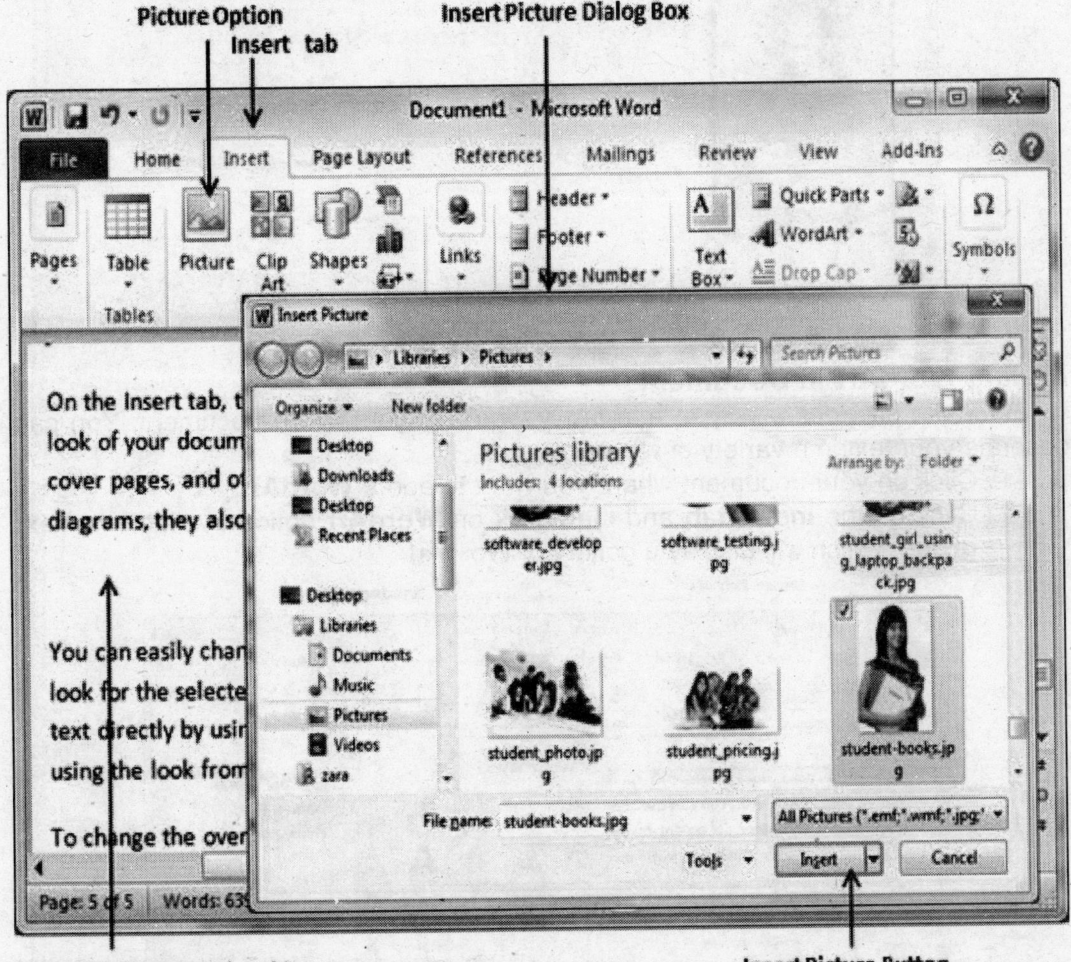

3. You can select a required picture using **Insert Picture dialog box**. When you click on **Insert** button, the selected picture will be inserted in your document.

You can apply quick styles to your picture, you can resize it, or you can change its colour. To try it, just **double-click** on your inserted image and Word will give you numerous options available under **Format tab** to format your inserted graphics.

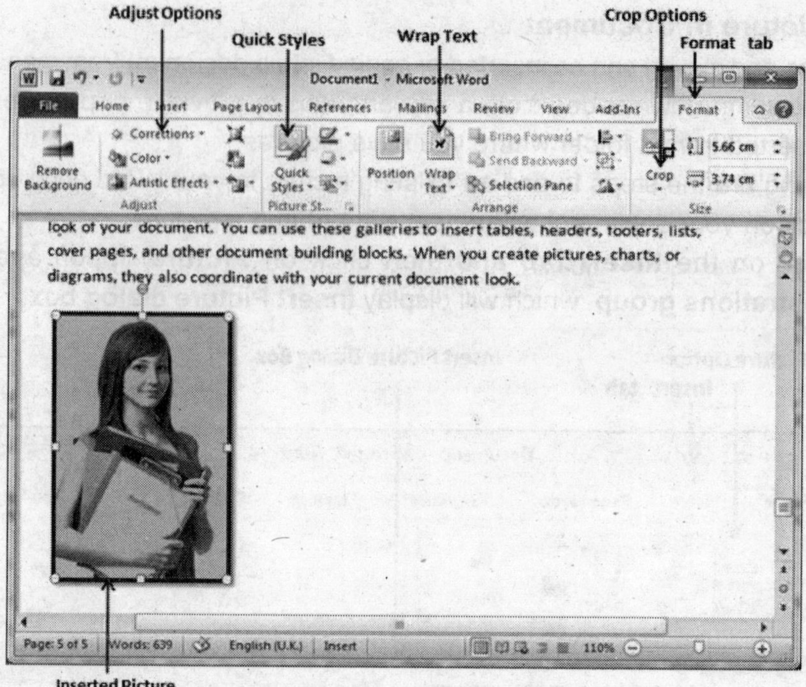

Adding WordArt in Document

WordArt provides a way to add fancy words in your Word document. You can decorate your text in a variety of ways:

1. Click on your document where you want to add a **WordArt**.
2. Click on the **Insert tab** and then click on **WordArt** option available in **Text group**, which will display a gallery of WordArt.

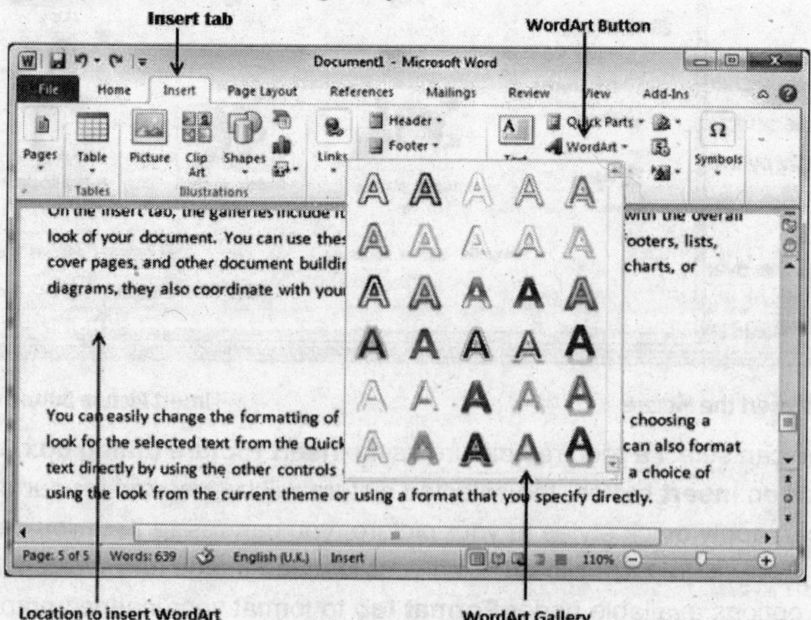

3. You can select any of the WordArt styles from the displayed gallery by clicking on it. Now you can modify the inserted text as per your requirement and you can make it further beautiful by using different options available.

To try it, just **double-click** on your inserted WordArt and Word will give you numerous options available from **Format tab** to format your image. Most frequently used options are **Shape Styles** and **WordArt Styles**.

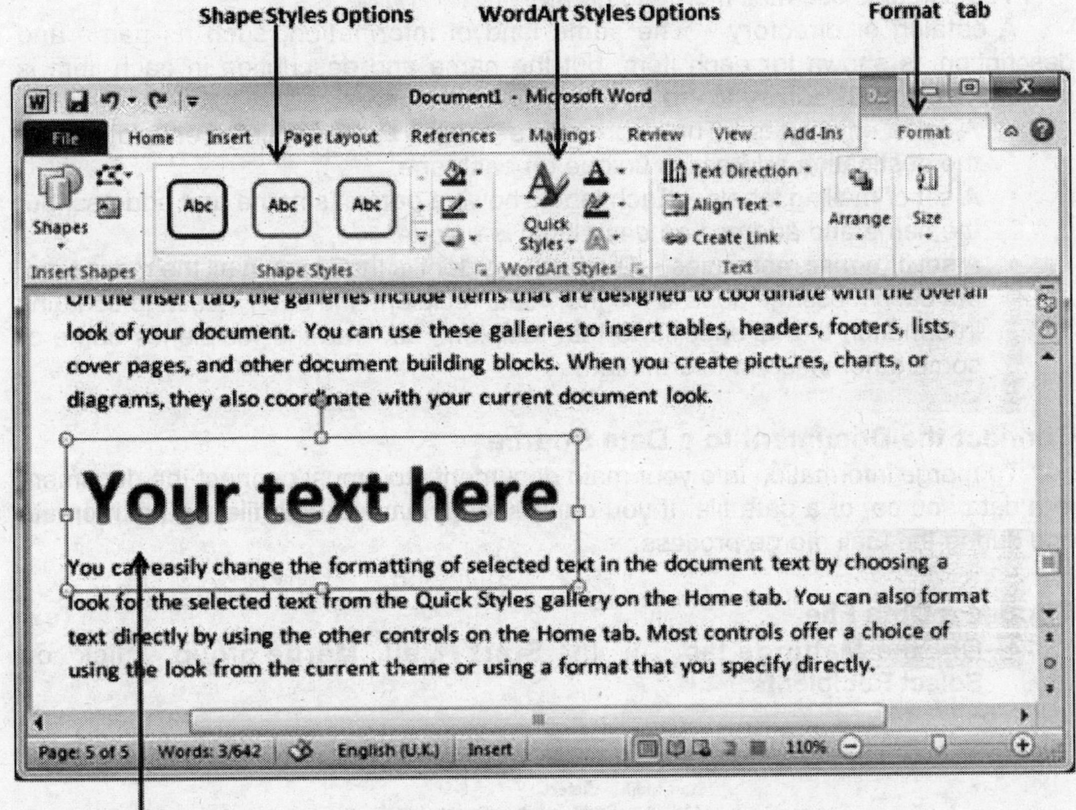

Use Mail Merge

Mail merge is used when you want to create a set of documents, such as a letter that is sent to many customers. Each document has the same kind of information, yet some of the content is unique. For example, in letters to your customers, you can personalize each letter to address each customer by name. The unique information in each letter comes from entries in a data source.

The mail merge process involves the following steps:

Set Up the Main Document

1. Start Word. A blank document opens by default. Leave it open. If you close it, the commands in the next step are not available.

2. On the **Mailings** tab, in the **Start Mail Merge** group, click on **Start Mail Merge**.

3. Click on **Letters**.

You can also use mail merge to create:

A catalog or directory – The same kind of information, such as name and description, is shown for each item, but the name and description in each item is unique. Click on **Directory** to create this type of document.

- A set of envelopes – The return address is the same on all the envelopes, but the destination address is unique on each one.
- A set of mailing labels – Each label shows a person's name and address, but the name and address on each label is unique.
- A set of e-mail messages – The basic content is the same in all the messages, but each message goes to the individual recipient and each message contains information that is specific to that recipient, such as the recipient's name or some other piece of information.

Connect the Document to a Data Source

To merge information into your main document, you must connect the document to a data source, or a data file. If you don't already have a data file, you can create one during the mail merge process.

Choose a Data File

1. On the **Mailings** tab, in the **Start Mail Merge** group, click on **Select Recipients**.

2. Do one of the following:
   - Use Outlook Contacts – If you want to use your Contacts list in Microsoft Outlook, click on **Select from Outlook Contacts**.

Use an existing data source file – If you have a Microsoft Excel worksheet, a Microsoft Access database, or another type of data file, click on **Use Existing List**, and then locate the file in the **Select Data Source** dialog box.

For Excel, you can select data from any worksheet or named range within a workbook. For Access, you can select data from any table or query that is defined in the database. For another type of data file, select the file in the **Select Data Source** dialog box.

- Create a new data file in Word – If you don't have a data file yet, click on **Type New List**, and then use the form that opens to create your list. The list is saved as a database (.mdb) file that you can reuse.

Type a New List

1. In the **New Address List** dialog box, type the information for the first address, or record, that you want to include in your mail merge.
   - If you want to add or remove columns, click on **Customize Columns**, and then make the changes that you want.
2. After you type all the information for your first record, click on **New Entry**, and then type the information for the next record. Continue until you have typed information for all the records that you want to include.
3. When your new list is complete, click on **OK**.
4. In the **Save Address List** dialog box, type a name for your new list, and then click on **Save**.

Refine the List of Recipients or Items

When you connect to a certain data file, you might not want to merge information from all the records (or rows) in that data file into your main document.

To narrow the list of recipients or use a subset of the items in your data file, do the following:

1. On the **Mailings** tab, in the **Start Mail Merge** group, click on **Edit Recipient List**.

2. In the **Mail Merge Recipients** dialog box, do any of the following:
   - Select individual records – This method is most useful if your list is short. Select the check boxes next to the recipients you want to include, and clear the check boxes next to the recipients you want to exclude.
     If you know that you want to include only a few records in your merge, you can clear the check box in the header row and then select only those records that you want. Similarly, if you want to include most of the list, select the check box in the header row, and then clear the check boxes for the records that you don't want to include.
   - Sort records – Click on the column heading of the item that you want to sort by. The list sorts in ascending alphabetical order (from A to Z). Click on the column heading again to sort the list in descending alphabetical order (Z to A).
     If you want more complex sorting, click **Sort** under **Refine recipient** list and choose your sorting preferences on the **Sort Records** tab in the **Filter and Sort** dialog box.
   - Filter records – This is useful if the list contains records that you know you don't want to see or include in the merge. After you filter the list, you can select or clear the check boxes to include or exclude records.

To filter records, do the following:

1. Under **Refine recipient** list, click on Filter.

2. On the **Filter Records** tab in the **Filter and Sort dialog** box, choose the criteria that you want to use for the filter.
3. To refine the filter further, click **And** or **Or** and choose more criteria.

To add recipients to the list, do the following:

Under **Data source**, click on the name of your data file.

Click on Edit.

In the **Edit Data Source** dialog box, click on **New Entry**, and then type the information for that recipient.

Add Placeholders to the Document

After you connect your main document to a data file, you are ready to type the text of the document and add placeholders that indicate where the unique information will appear in each copy of the document.

The placeholders, such as address and greeting, are called mail merge fields. Fields in Word correspond to the column headings in the data file that you select.

	A	B	C
1	Name (1)	Last Name	Street Address
2	Nancy	Anderson	123 Main St.
3	Ann	Beebe	567 Country Rd. (2)
4			
5			
6			
7			
8			
9			

1. Columns in a data file represent categories of information. Fields that you add to the main document are placeholders for these categories.
2. Rows in a data file represent records of information. Word generates a copy of the main document for each record when you perform a mail merge.

By putting a field in your main document, you indicate that you want a certain category of information, such as name or address, to appear in that location.

When you merge, information from the first row in the data file replaces the fields in your main document to create the first merged document. Information from the second row in the data file replaces the fields to create the second merged document, and so on.

You can add any column heading from your data file to the main document as a field. This gives you flexibility when you design form letters and other merged documents.

Type the Content and Add the Placeholders, or Fields

1. In the main document, type any content that you want to appear on every copy of the document.
    - To add a picture, such as a logo, click on **Picture** in the **Illustrations** group on the **Insert** tab.
2. Click where you want to insert the field.
3. Use the **Write & Insert Fields** group on the **Mailings** tab.

4. Add any of the following:

Address Block with Name, Address and Other Information

1. Click on **Address block**.
2. In the **Insert Address Block** dialog box, select the address elements that you want to include and the formats that you want, and then click on **OK**.
3. If the **Match Fields** dialog box appears, Word may have been unable to find some of the information that it needs for the address block. Click on the arrow next to (not matched), and then select the field from your data source that corresponds to the field that is required for the mail merge.

Greeting Line

1. Click on **Greeting** line.
2. Select the greeting line format, which includes the salutation, name format and following punctuation.
3. Select the text that you want to appear in cases where Microsoft Word can't interpret the recipient's name, for example, when the data source contains no first or last name for a recipient, but only a company name.
4. Click on **OK**.
5. If the **Match Fields** dialog box appears, Word may have been unable to find some of the information that it needs for the greeting line. Click on the arrow next to (not matched), and then select the field from your data source that corresponds to the field that is required for the mail merge.

Individual Fields

You can insert information from individual fields, such as first name, telephone number, or the amount of a contribution from a list of donors. To quickly add a field from your data file to the main document, click on the arrow next to **Insert Merge Field**, and then click the field name.

For more options with inserting individual fields in the document, do the following:

1. On the **Mailings** tab, in the **Write & Insert Fields** group, click on **Insert Merge Field**.
2. In the **Insert Merge Field** dialog box, do one of the following:
   - To select address fields that will automatically correspond to fields in your data source, even if the data source's fields don't have the same name as your fields, click on **Address Fields**.
   - To select fields that always take data directly from a column in your data file, click on **Database Fields**.
3. In the **Fields** box, click on the field you want.
4. Click on **Insert**, and then click on **Close**.
5. If the **Match Fields** dialog box appears, Microsoft Word may have been unable to find some of the information it needs to insert the field. Click on the arrow next to (not matched), and then select the field from your data source that corresponds to the field that is required for the mail merge.

Custom Fields from Outlook Contacts

The only way to include custom contact fields in your main document is to start the mail merge from within Outlook. First, set up a view of your contacts with the fields that you want to use in the merge. Then, start the mail merge. After you choose the settings that you want, Word will automatically open, and you can complete the merge.

Set up a view of your contacts that includes custom fields

1. In Outlook Contacts, on the **View** tab, click **Change View**, and then click **List**.
2. Right-click on a column heading, and then click on **Field Chooser** on the shortcut menu.
3. In the drop-down list at the top of the **Field Chooser** dialog box, select **User-defined fields in folder**.
4. Drag the field that you to add from the dialog box to the column headings. A little red arrow helps you place the field in the location that you want.

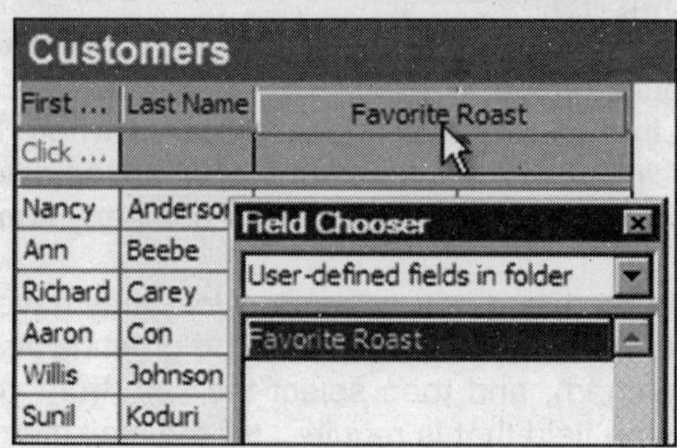

5. After you add all of your custom fields to the view, close the **Field Chooser** dialog box.
6. To remove a field that you do not want included in the mail merge, click on the field name in the column heading in List view, and drag it off the column heading.

Run Mail Merge from Outlook

In Outlook Contacts, select individual contacts by pressing **Shift** and clicking to select a range or by pressing **Ctrl** and clicking to select individuals. If you want to include all the contacts currently visible in the view, do not click on any contacts.

1. On the **Home** tab, click on **Mail Merge**.
2. If you selected individual contacts to include in the mail merge, click on **Only selected contacts**. If you want to include all the contacts that are currently visible in the view, click on **All contacts in current view**.
3. If you configured the List view so that it displays exactly the fields that you want to use in the mail merge, click on **Contact fields in current view**. Otherwise, click on **All contact fields** to make all of the contact fields available in the mail merge.
4. If you want to generate a new main document for the merge, click on **New document**. Otherwise, click on **Existing document**, and click on **Browse** to locate the document to use as the main document.
5. If you want to save the contacts and fields that you have selected, so that they can be reused, select the **Permanent file** check box, and then click on **Browse** to save the file.
6. Select any merge options you want:
   - **Form Letters** – Prepare a batch of letters for a mass mailing.
   - **Mailing Labels** – Set up address labels for a mass mailing.
   - **Envelopes** – Set up envelopes for a mass mailing.
   - **Catalog** – Create a single document that contains a catalog or address list.
   - **New Document** – Generate merged documents, which you can edit individually in Word.
   - **Printer** – Send merged documents directly to the default printer.
   - **E-mail** – Generate merged documents designed to be e-mail messages. When you are ready to complete the merge in Word, on the **Mailings** tab in the **Finish** group, click on **Finish & Merge**, and then click on **Send E-mail Messages**. The **Subject** line is filled with the text you typed in the **Mail Merge Contacts** dialog box in Outlook.
7. Click on **OK**. When the document opens in Word, on the **Mailings** tab, in the **Write & Insert Fields** group, click on the arrow next to **Insert Merge Field**, and then click on the fields that you want to add the document.

Add Formatting

1. Select the mail merge field. Make sure that the selection includes the chevrons (« ») that surround the field.

2. On the **Home** tab, in the **Font** group, apply the formatting that you want; or click on the **Font Dialog Box** launcher for more options.

Preview, Complete the Merge, and Print the Documents

After you add fields to your main document, you are ready to preview the merge results. When you are satisfied with the preview, you can complete the merge.

Preview the Merge

You can preview your merged documents and make changes before you actually complete the merge.

1. To preview, do any of the following in the **Preview Results** group of the **Mailings** tab:

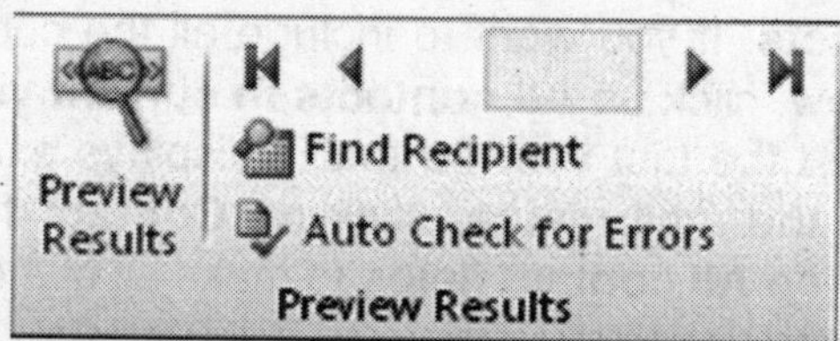

2. Click on **Preview Results.**
3. Page through each merged document by using the **Next Record** and **Previous Record** buttons in the **Preview Results** group.
4. Preview a specific document by clicking on **Find Recipient**.

Complete the Merge

- You can print the merged documents or modify them individually. You can print or change all or just a subset of the documents.
- If you want to print a subset of the documents, you can specify the set by a range of record numbers.

Print the Merged Documents

1. On the **Mailings** tab, in the **Finish** group, click on **Finish & Merge**, and then click on **Print Documents**.

2. Choose whether to print the whole set of documents, only the copy that's currently visible, or a subset of the set, which you specify by record number. Word compiles the copies that you want to edit into a single file, with a page break between each copy of the document.

After you finish editing the new file of documents, you can print the documents by clicking on the **File** tab, clicking on **Print**, and then clicking on the **Print** button.

Save the Main Document

Remember that merged documents that you save are separate from the main document. It's a good idea to save the main document itself if you plan to use it for another mail merge.

When you save the main document, you also save its connection to the data file. The next time that you open the main document, you are prompted to choose whether you want the information from the data file to be merged again into the main document.

- If you click on **Yes**, the document opens with information from the first record merged in.
- If you click on **No**, the connection between the main document and the data file is broken. The main document becomes a standard Word document. Fields are replaced with the unique information from the first record.

Preview Documents

When you are ready for printing your Word document, it is always recommended to preview the document before you send document for final printing. During preview of the document, you might discover that set margin is not appropriate or many items may not look good after printing. So it is better to fix them after having a preview of the document. You can also have the option to specify which pages to print, select a printer, specify the paper size on which you want to print, and set other printing options.

Following are the steps to preview your Microsoft Word Document:

1. Open the document for which you want to see the preview.

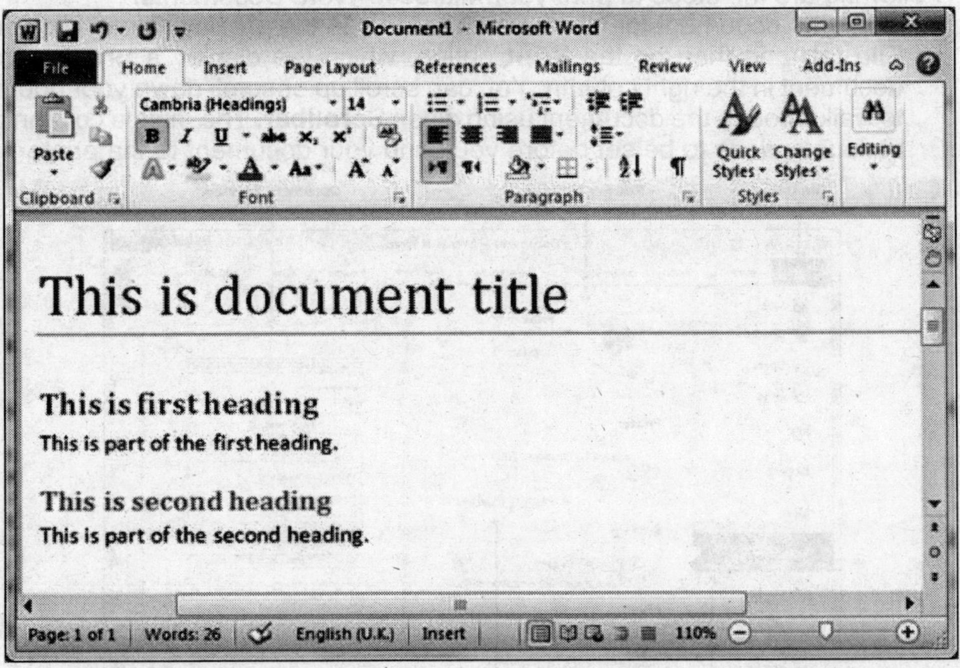

2. Click on the **File tab** and then on the **Print** option which will display a **preview** of the document in the right column. You can scroll up or scroll down your document to walk through the document using given **Scrollbar**.

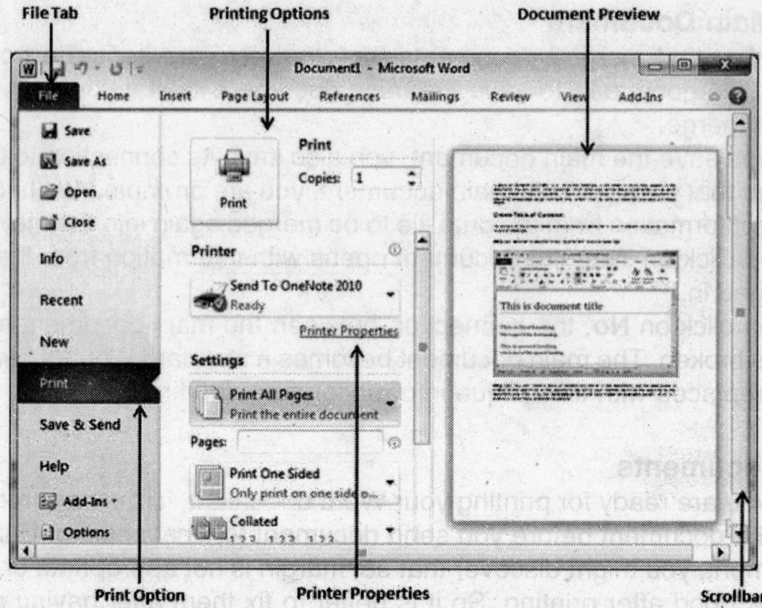

3. Once you are done with your preview, you can click on **Home tab** to go to the actual content of the document.

Printing Documents

Following are the steps to print your Microsoft Word Documents:

1. Open the document for which you want to see the preview. Next, click on the **File tab** and then on the **Print** option, which will display a **preview** of the document in the right column. You can scroll up or scroll down your document to walk through the document using given **Scrollbar**. The middle column gives various options to be set before you send your document to the printer.

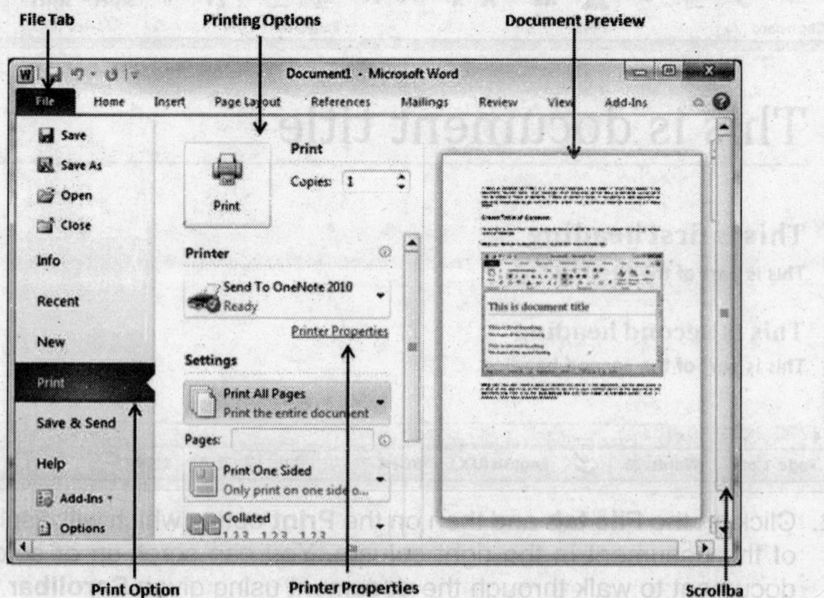

2. You can set various other printing options available. Select from among the following options, depending on your preferences.

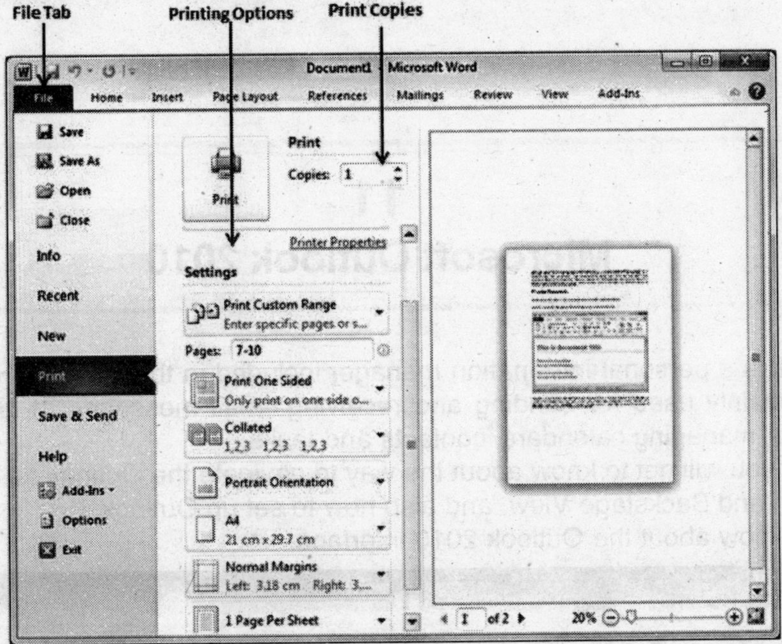

3. Once you are done with your setting, click on **Print** button, which will send your document to the printer for final printing.

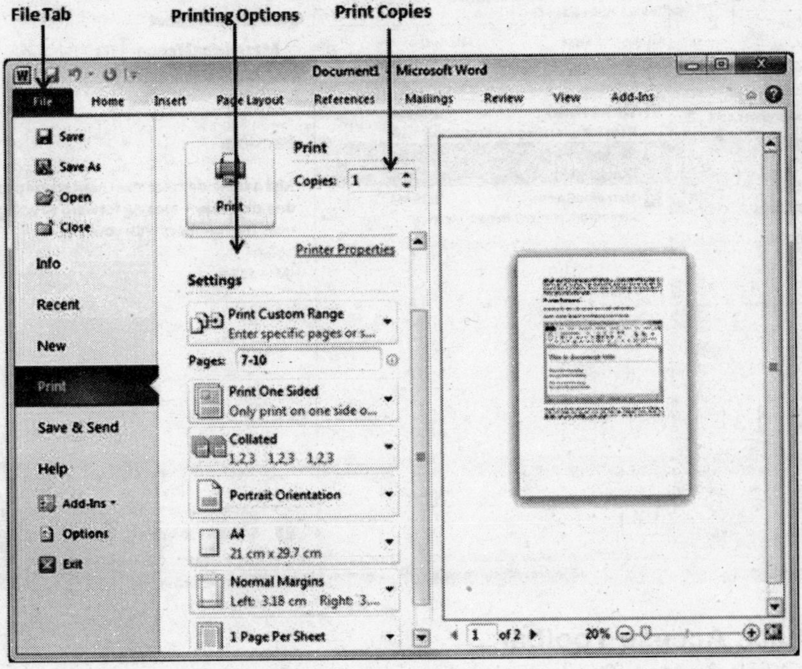

□

11
Microsoft Outlook 2010

Outlook is a personal information manager included in the Microsoft Office suite. It is mainly used for sending and receiving email messages. It also includes features for managing calendars, contacts and tasks.

Here, you will get to know about the way to navigate the Outlook 2010 interface, the Ribbon and Backstage View, and also how to set up Outlook.

Let's know about the Outlook 2010 interface.

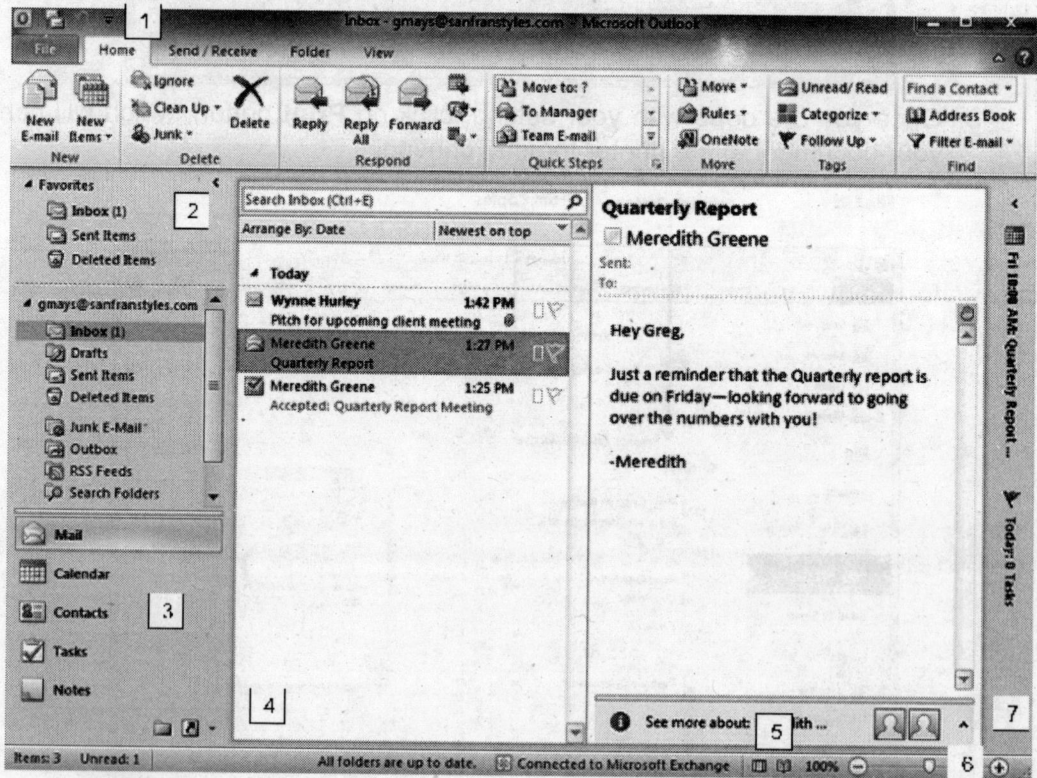

1. The Quick Access Toolbar

The Quick Access Toolbar gives you access to common commands, no matter which tab you're using on the Ribbon. By default, it shows the **Check Inbox** and **Undo** commands.

To add more commands, click on the drop-down arrow and then select the desired command(s) from the menu.

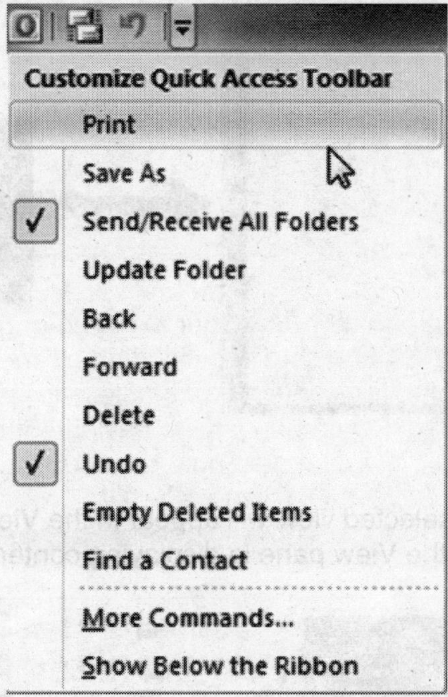

2. Navigation Pane

Every view uses the Navigation pane to display navigational options. In the screenshot below, you can see the navigation pane is displaying options for the Mail view.

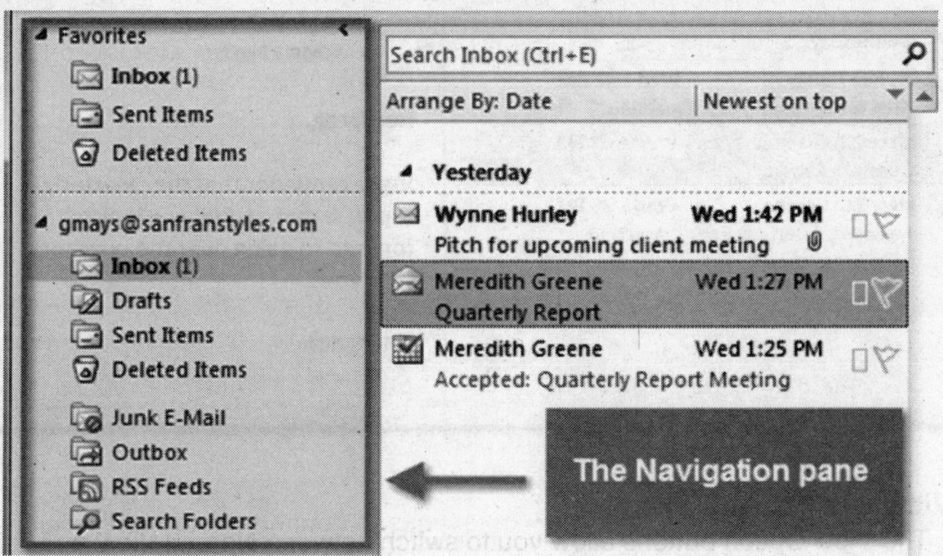

3. View Tabs

You will use the View tabs to switch between different views in Outlook, including Mail, Calendar, Contacts, Tasks and Notes. The Mail view is selected by default whenever you open Outlook.

4. View Pane

The content for the selected view will appear in the View pane. In the screenshot below, you can see that the View pane is displaying content from the Mail view.

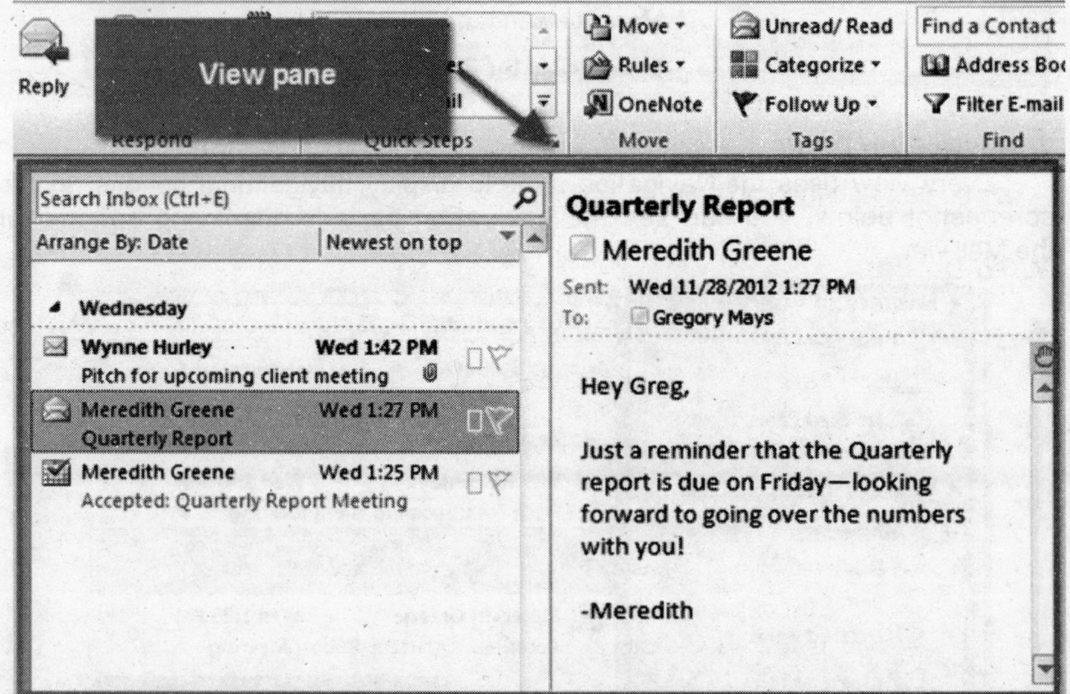

5. View Options

The View Option buttons allow you to switch between Normal View and Reading

View. Reading View will minimize the Navigation pane, the Ribbon and the To-Do Bar, making it easier to see the content in the View pane.

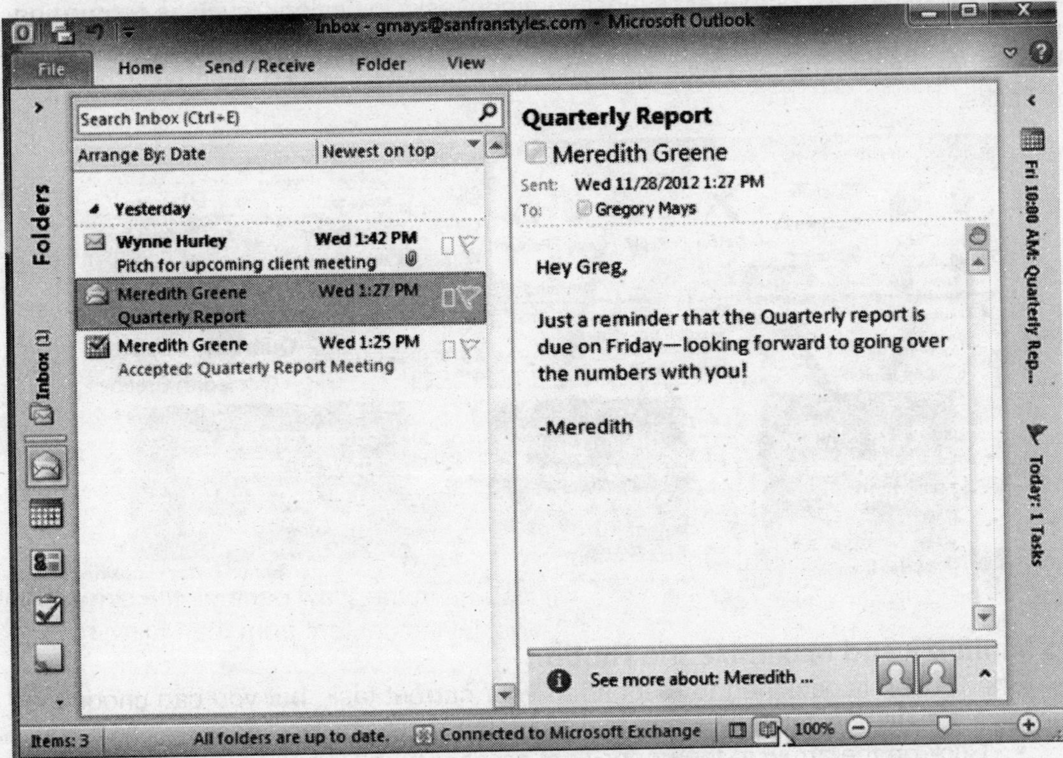

6. Zoom Slider

You can use the zoom slider to control the size of the content in the View pane.

7. To-Do Bar

A summary of your daily calendar appointments and tasks will appear in the To-Do Bar. You can click on the arrow to expand the To-Do Bar.

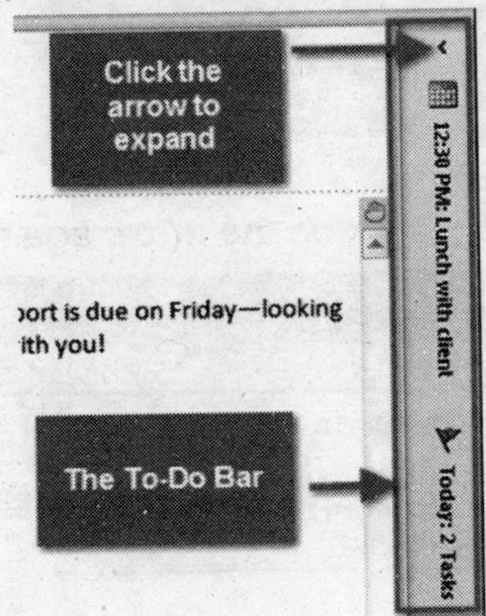

The Ribbon

The Ribbon contains multiple tabs, each with several groups of commands. You will use these tabs to complete the most common tasks in Outlook, such as composing an email, scheduling a meeting, or adding a contact. The commands on the Ribbon will change depending on which view you have selected: Mail, Calendar, Contacts, or Tasks.

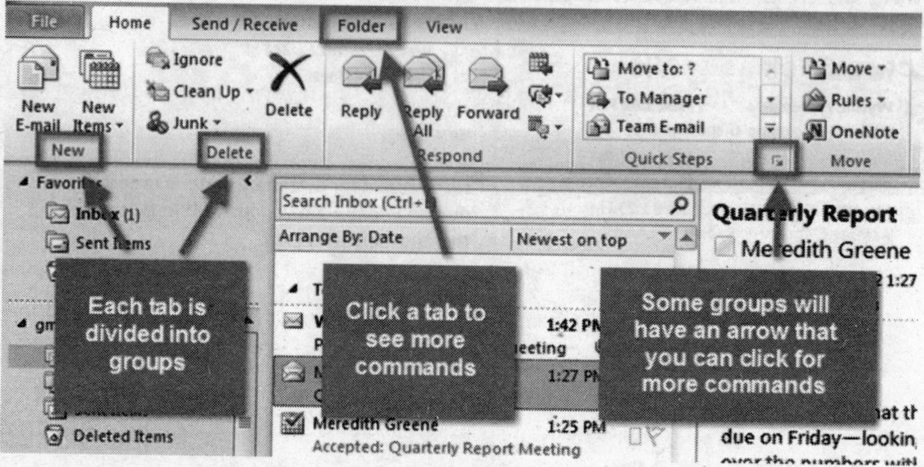

To Minimize and Maximize the Ribbon

The Ribbon is designed to respond to your current task, but you can choose to minimize the Ribbon if you find that it takes up too much screen space.

- Click on the arrow in the upper-right corner of the Ribbon.

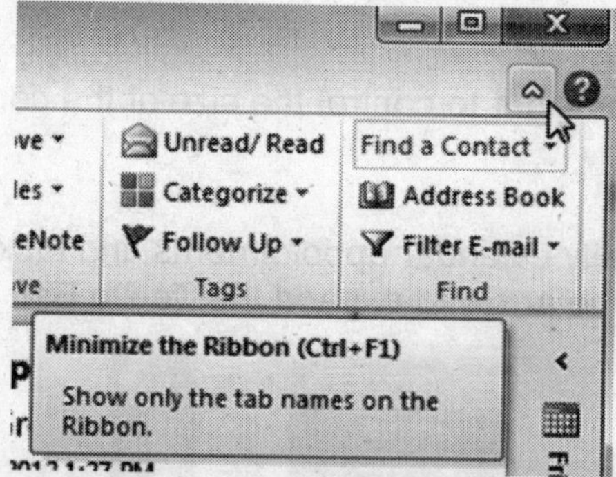

The Ribbon will be minimized.

- To maximize the Ribbon, click on the arrow again.

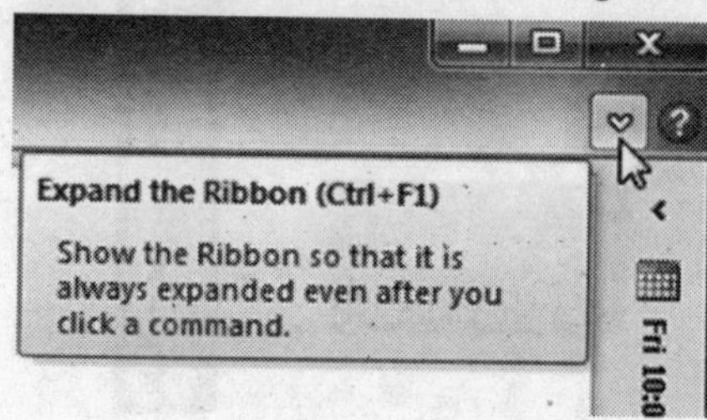

Backstage View

The Backstage view gives you various options for managing accounts, saving and printing items, like an email message or calendar, and more. Although it is similar to the File Menu from earlier versions of Outlook, Backstage view will expand to fill the entire screen, unlike a traditional menu. The options in Backstage view will change depending on which view you have selected.

To Access Backstage View

- Click on the **File** tab on the Ribbon. Backstage view will appear.

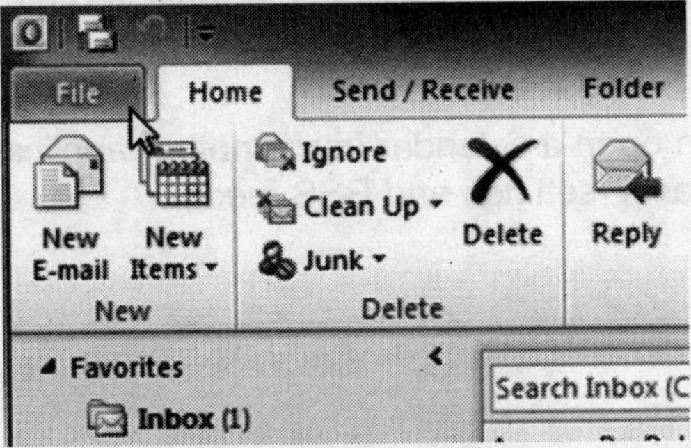

Let's learn about using the Backstage view.

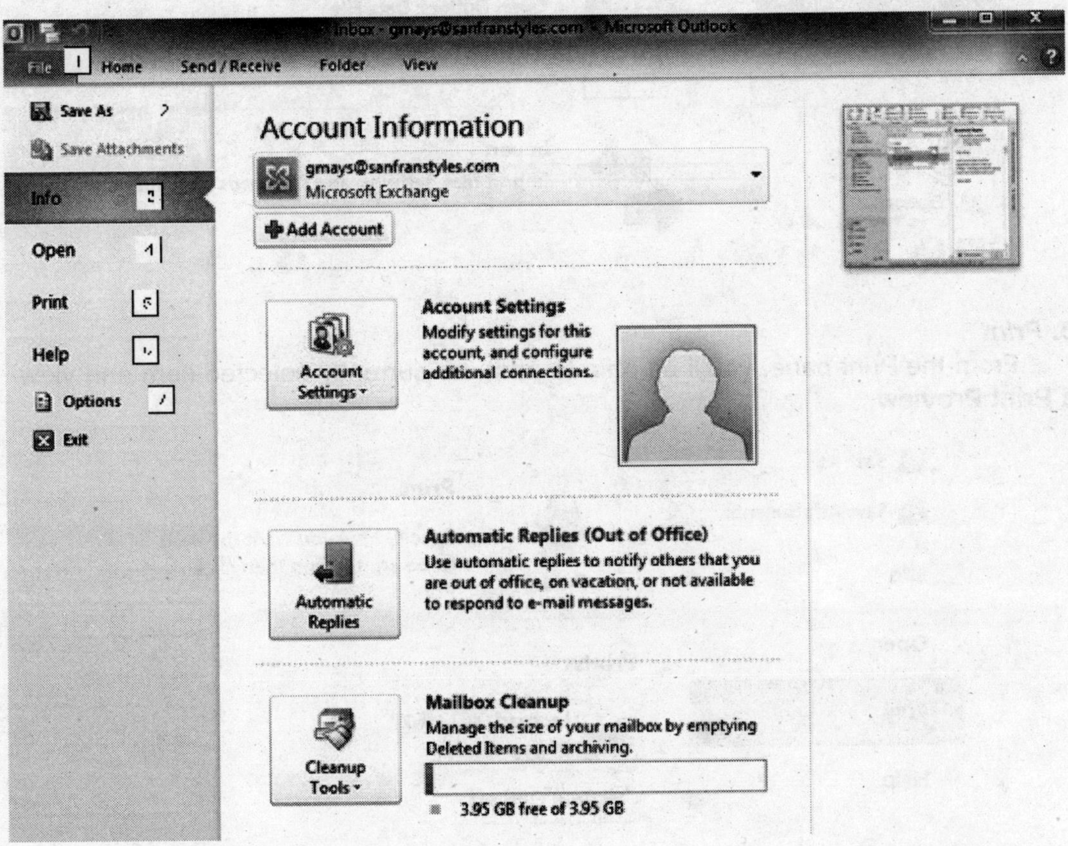

1. Return to Outlook

Click any tab on the Ribbon to close the Backstage view.

2. Save As

Click on **Save As** to save the currently selected item, such as an email message or a calendar, to another location on your computer.

3. Info

Info displays basic information about your email account. From here, you can also modify your account settings, set a vacation reply and more.

4. Open

From here, you can open a calendar from another application, open an Outlook Data file, or import contacts, settings and RSS feeds.

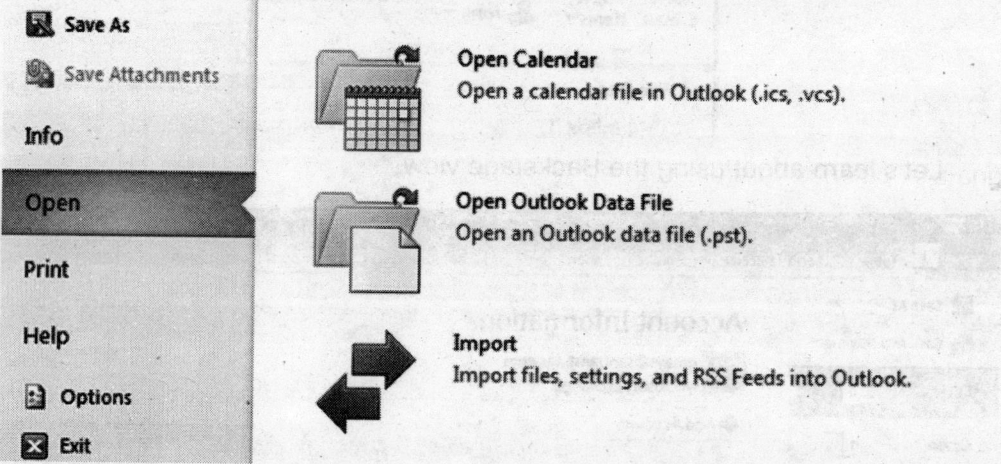

5. Print

From the Print pane, you'll be able to print the currently selected item and view a **Print Preview**.

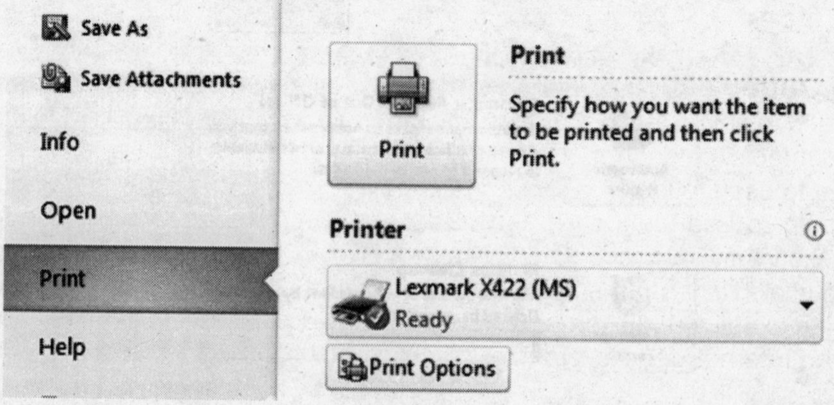

6. Help

From here, you can access Microsoft support and check for updates.

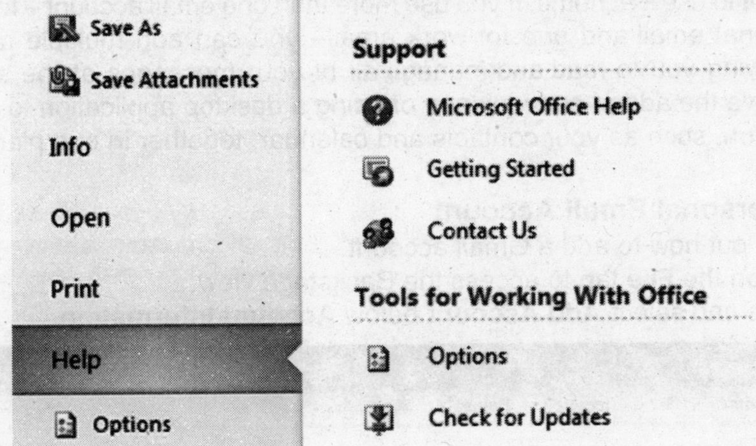

7. Options

Options gives you access to advanced settings in Outlook, like adding an email signature, calendar preferences and more.

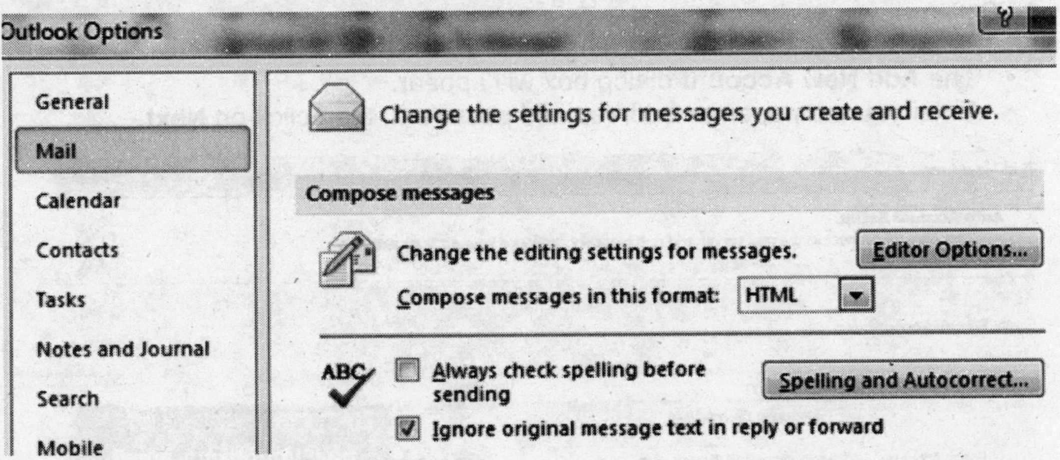

Setting up Outlook 2010

You'll need to set up Outlook before you can start using the application to manage your email, contacts, calendars, and tasks. The setup process will vary depending on how you plan to use Outlook:

If you plan to use Outlook in the workplace with an employer-provided email account, it's likely that your account will already be set up when you start using Outlook. If not, your office's IT department or supervisor will help you with the setup process.

If you plan to use Outlook on your home computer with a personal email account, either from an Internet service provider or a webmail service like Gmail, it's easy to get started.

Using Outlook with a Personal Email Account

While Outlook is most commonly used in the workplace, there are several reasons you might want to use it at home. If you use more than one email account – for example, one for personal email and one for work email– you can add multiple accounts to Outlook, allowing you to read and manage all of your messages at the same time. You'll also have the added convenience of using a desktop application to keep all of your information, such as your contacts and calendar, together in one place.

To Add a Personal Email Account

Let's find out how to add a Gmail account.

- Click on the **File** tab to access the Backstage view.
- Locate and select **Add Account** below **Account Information**.

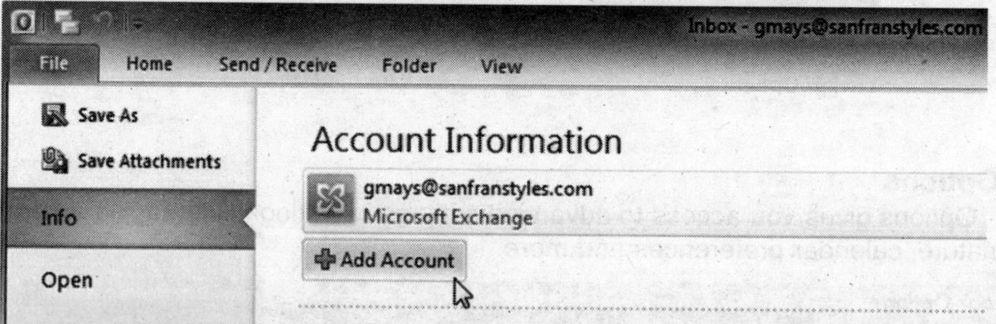

- The **Add New Account** dialog box will appear.
- Enter your name, email address and password, then click on **Next**.

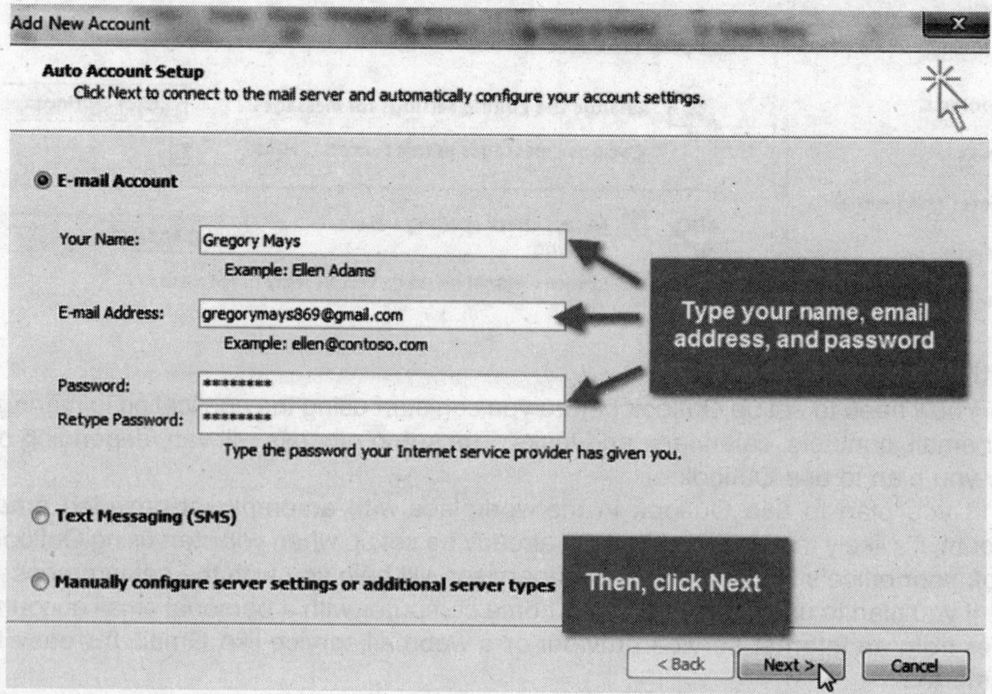

Outlook will configure the account. This process can take several minutes.

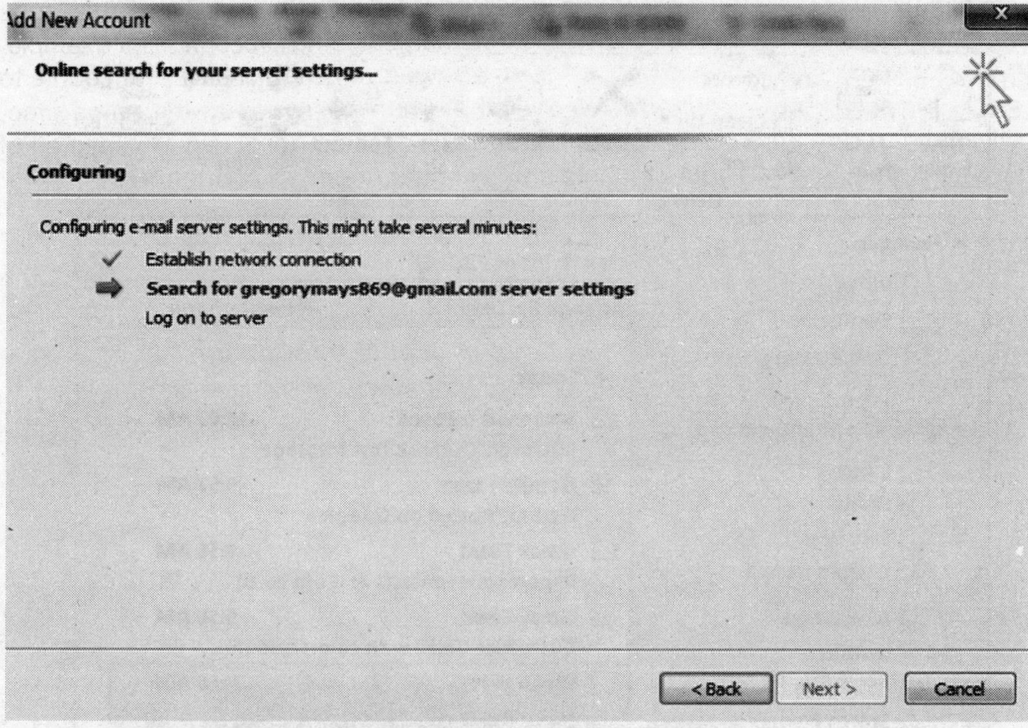

- Once the configuration is complete, click on **Finish**.

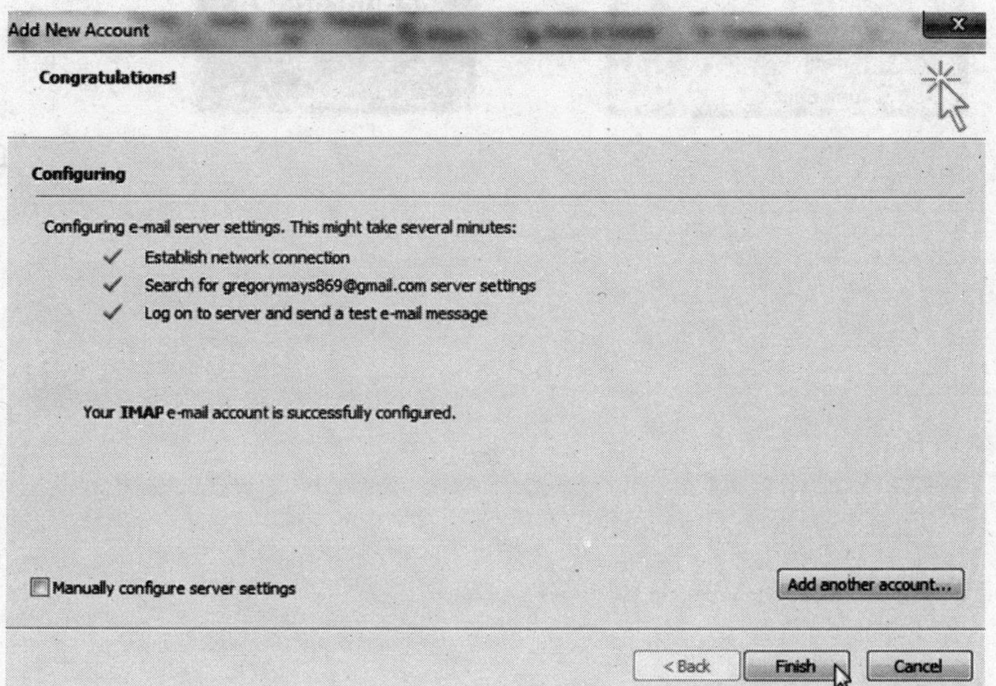

The email account will be added to Outlook.

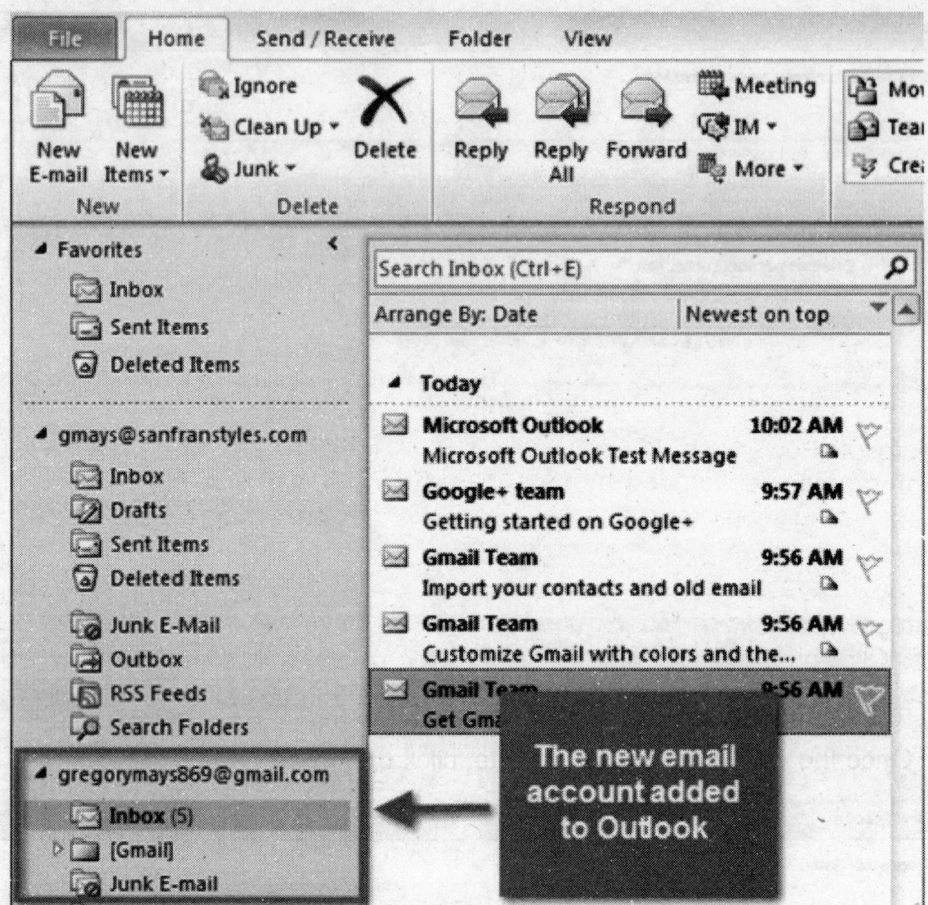

12
Microsoft PowerPoint 2010

Microsoft PowerPoint 2010 is a slide show presentation programme developed by Microsoft. It allows you to create amazing slide presentation.

Getting Started with MS PowerPoint 2010

1. Click on the **Start** button.
2. Click on **All Programs** option from the menu.
3. Search for **Microsoft Office** from the submenu and click on it.
4. Search for **Microsoft PowerPoint 2010** from the submenu and click on it.

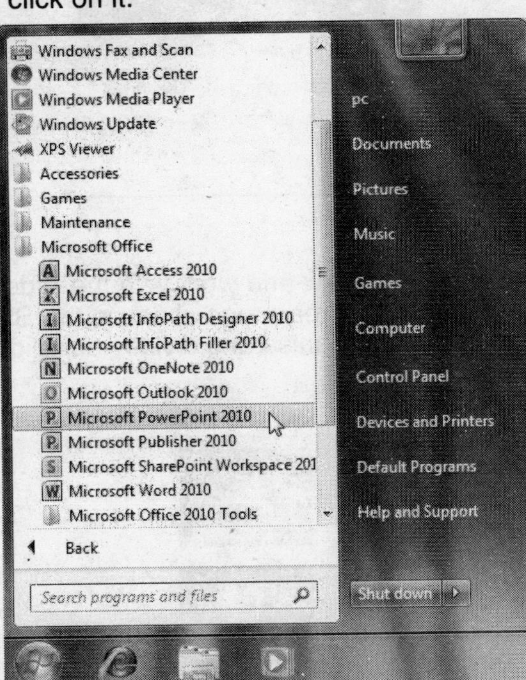

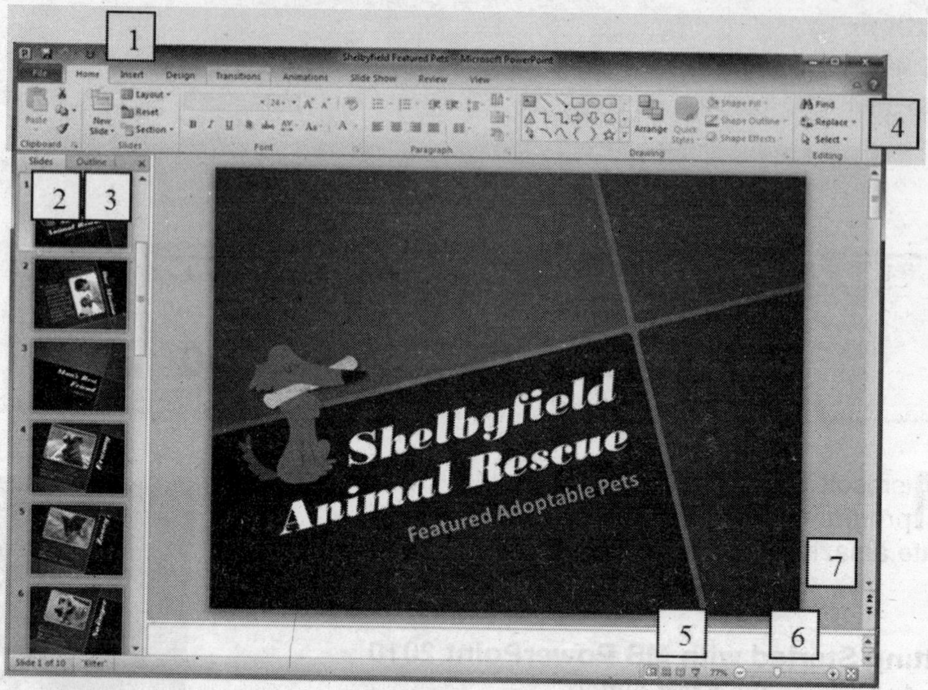

1. Quick Access Toolbar

The Quick Access Toolbar lets you access common commands, no matter which tab you are on in the Ribbon. By default, it shows the Save, Undo and Repeat commands. You can add other commands to make it more convenient for you.

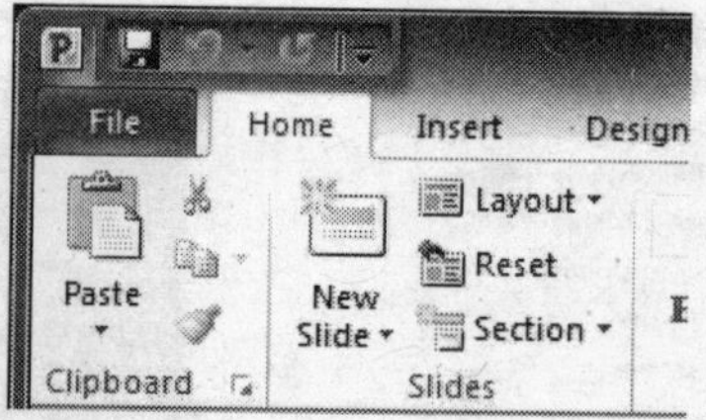

2. Slides Tab

The Slides tab allows you to view and work with the slides in your presentation. You can add, delete, duplicate and rearrange slides in the Slides tab. You can also add sections to the Slides tab to organise and divide your slides.

3. Outline Tab

The Outline tab conveniently displays the text content of each slide. You can edit your text directly from the outline view.

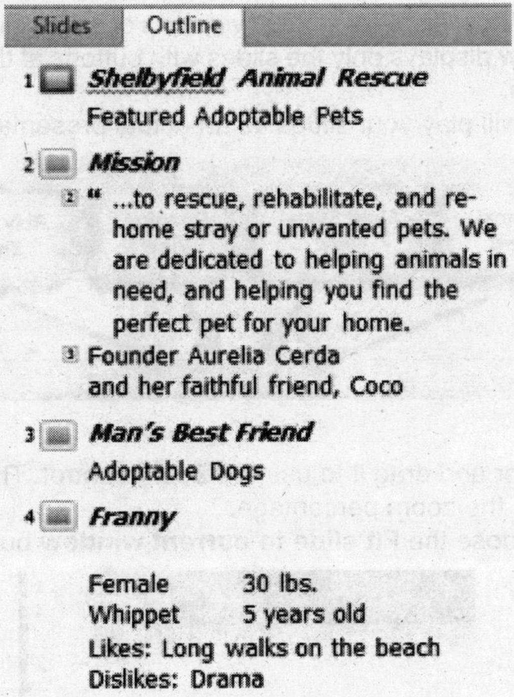

4. Ribbon

The Ribbon contains all the commands you will need in order to do common tasks. It has multiple tabs, each with several groups of commands, and you can add your own tabs to customize your favourites.

In addition, special 'tools' tabs will appear when you are formatting certain items like images or tables.

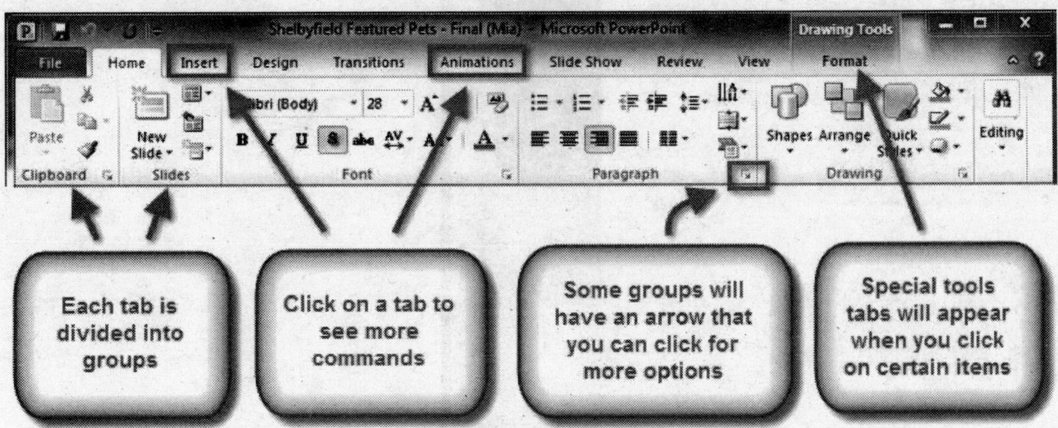

5. Slide Views

Adjust your slide view by choosing any one of the following:

- **Normal View** is selected by default, and shows the **Slide and Outline tabs** along with displaying the current slide.
- **Slide Sorter View** displays smaller versions of all the slides in the presentation.
- **Reading View** displays only the slides with buttons at the bottom of the screen for navigation.
- **Slide Show** will play your slides as an actual presentation.

6. Zoom Control

Click on the slider and drag it to use the Zoom control. The number to the left of the slider bar reflects the zoom percentage.

You can also choose the **Fit slide to current window** button.

7. Scroll Bar

You can also navigate through your slide show by clicking and dragging the scroll bar or by selecting the **Previous Slide** and **Next Slide** arrows.

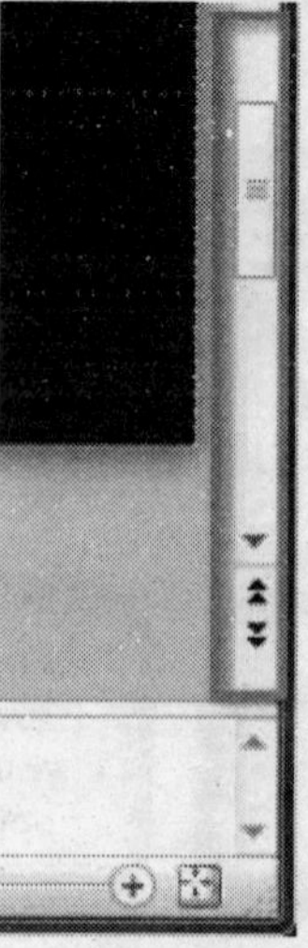

The Ribbon

The Ribbon contains multiple tabs, each with several groups of commands. Some tabs, like Drawing Tools or Table Tools, may appear only when you are working with certain items like images or tables. In addition, you can add your own customized tabs that contain your favourite commands.

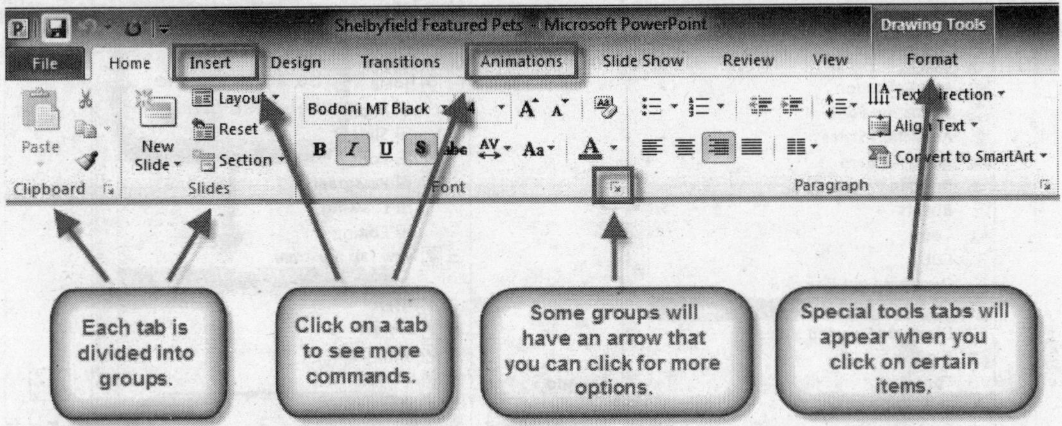

To Customize the Ribbon

You can customize the Ribbon by creating your own tabs that house your desired commands. Commands are always housed within a group, and you can create as many groups as you need to keep your tabs organised. In addition, you can even add commands to any of the default tabs, as long as you create a custom group within the tab.

1. **Right-click** on the **Ribbon**, and select **Customize the Ribbon....** A dialog box will appear.

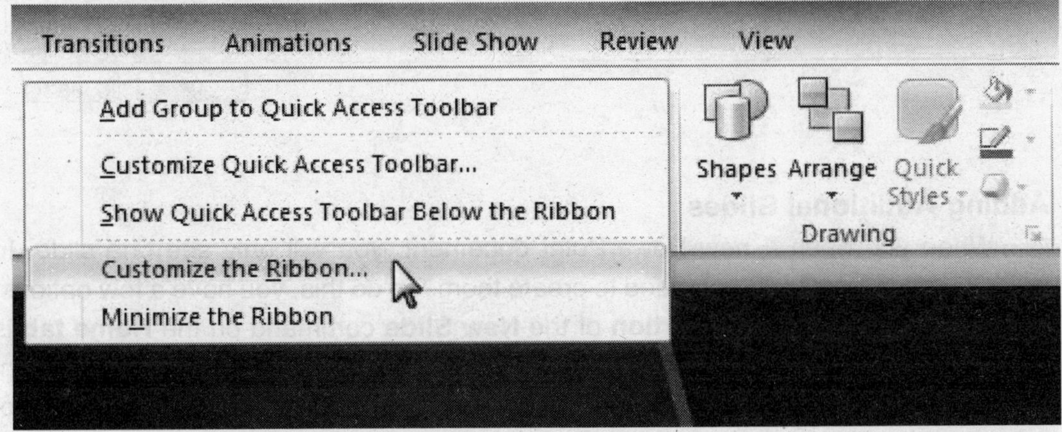

2. Click on **New Tab**. A new tab will be created with a new group inside it.
3. Make sure the new group is selected.
4. Select a command from the list on the left, then click on **Add**. You can also drag commands directly into a group.

5. When you are done adding commands, click on **OK**.

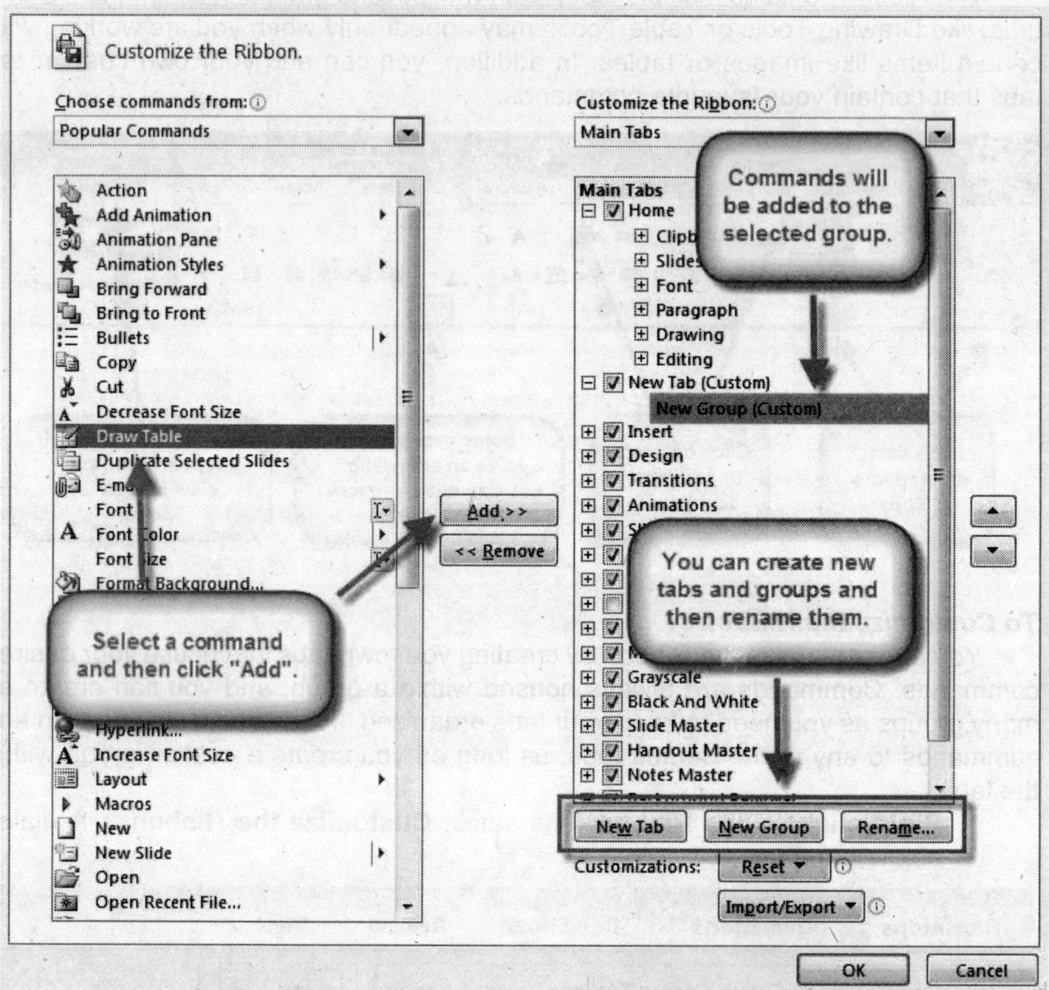

Adding Additional Slides

When you open a new PowerPoint document, you will only see one slide. In order to add more slides, you need to create them. To do this, you have a few options.

1. Clicking on the **top portion** of the **New Slide** command on the **Home tab** is the easiest method because a new slide will be added immediately. PowerPoint will automatically insert a **Title and Content slide** when using this method of adding slides.
2. If you click on the **bottom part** of the **New Slide** command, a box will appear and you will see a gallery of layouts for you to choose from, which will be inserted after your previous slide, once you click on your preferred slide option.

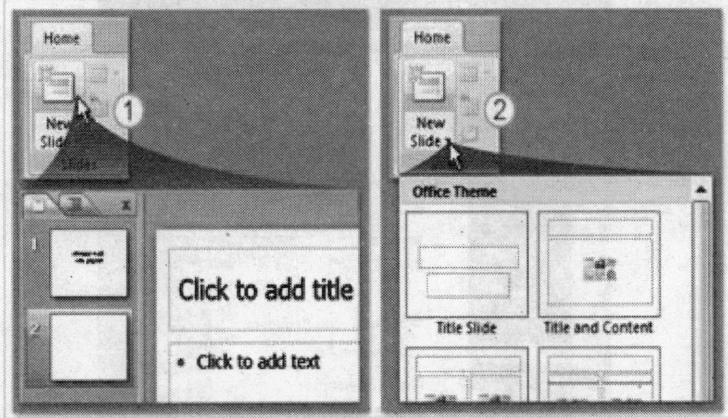

To Minimize and Maximize the Ribbon

The Ribbon is designed to be easy to use and responsive to your current task, but if you find it is taking up too much of your screen space, you can minimize it.

1. Click on the arrow in the upper-right corner of the Ribbon to minimize it.

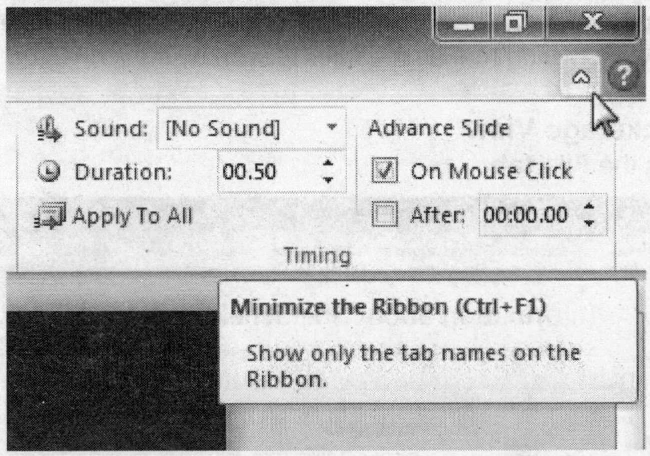

2. To maximize the Ribbon, click on the arrow again.

The Quick Access Toolbar

The Quick Access Toolbar is located above the Ribbon, and it lets you access common commands, no matter which tab you are on. By default, it shows the Save, Undo and Repeat commands. You can add other commands to make it more convenient for you.

To Add Commands to the Quick Access Toolbar

Click on the **drop-down arrow** to the right of the **Quick Access toolbar**. Select the command you wish to add from the drop-down menu. To choose from more commands, select **More Commands**.

Backstage View

Backstage view gives you various options for saving, opening a file, printing, or sharing your document. It is similar to the **Office button menu** from PowerPoint 2007 or the **File menu** from earlier versions of PowerPoint. However, instead of just a menu, it is a full-page view, which makes it easier to work with.

To Get to Backstage View

1. Click on the **File tab.**

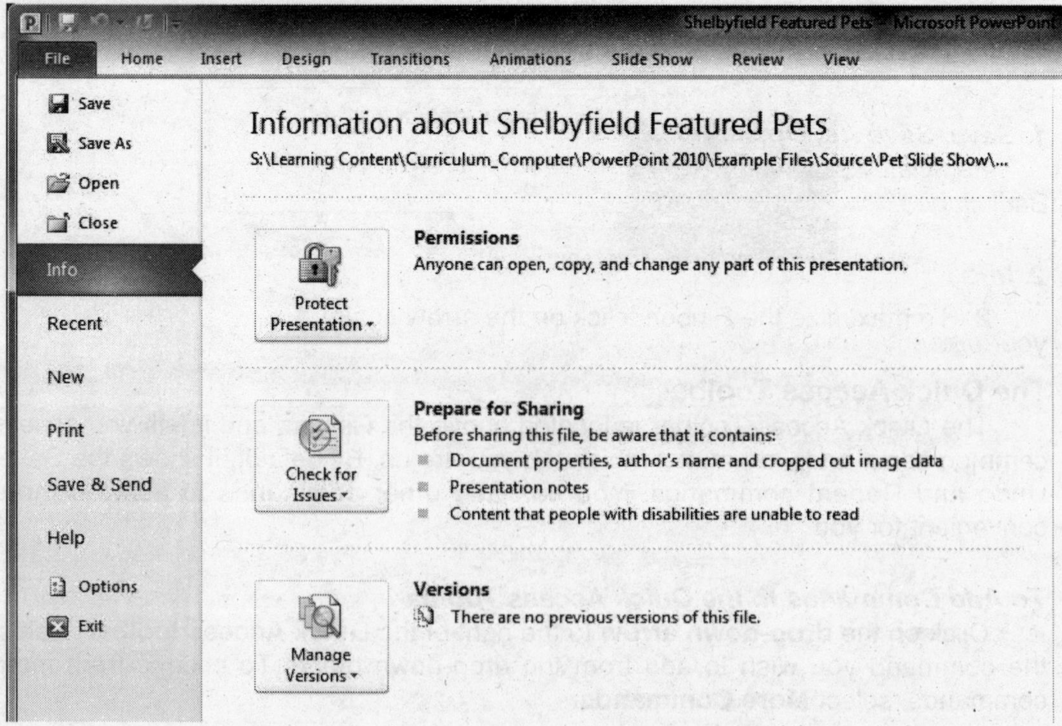

2. You can choose an option on the left side of the page.
3. To get back to your document, just click on **any tab** on the **Ribbon**.

The different things that you can do in Backstage view are as follows:

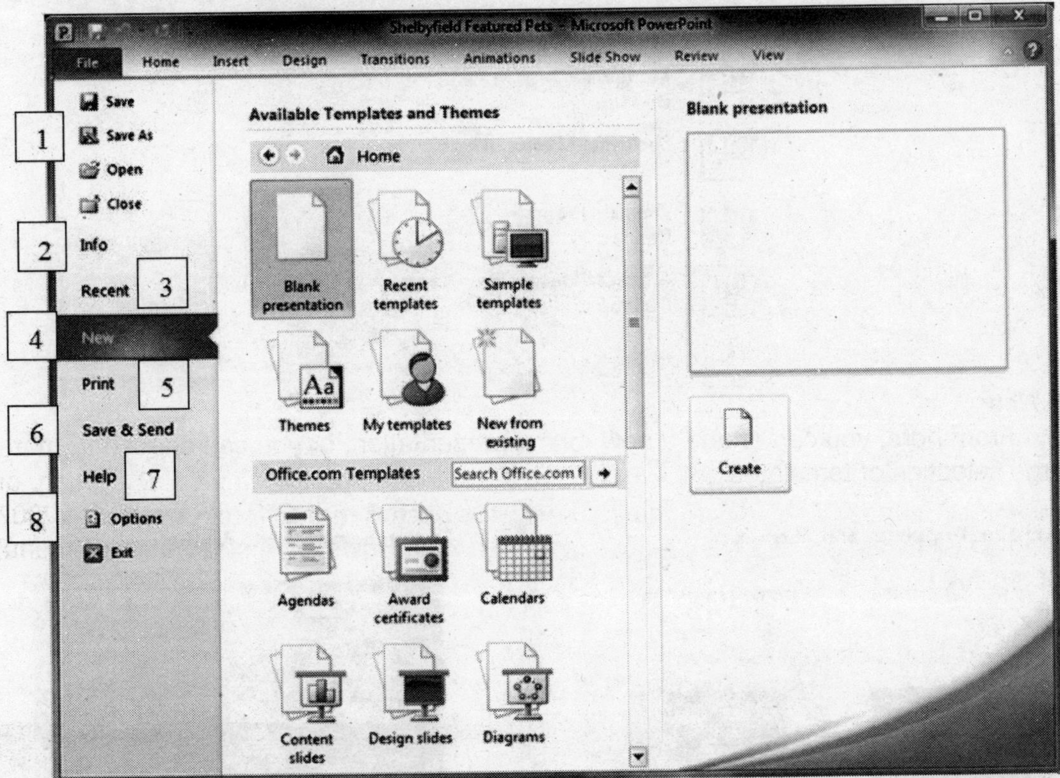

1. Save, Save As, Open and Close

Familiar tasks, such as Save, Save As, Open and Close are now found in Backstage View.

2. Info

Info contains information about the current presentation. You can also inspect your presentation and edit its permissions from this pane.

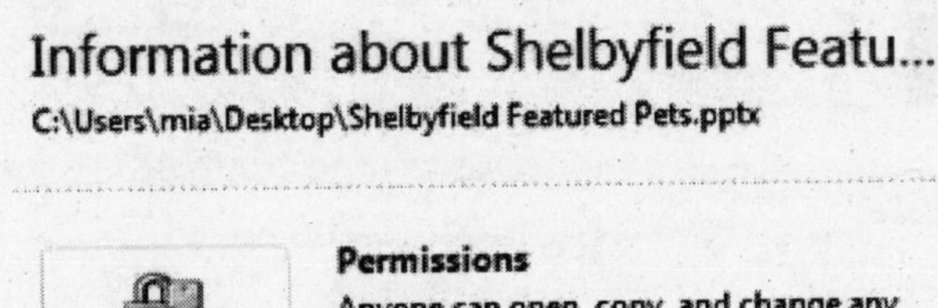

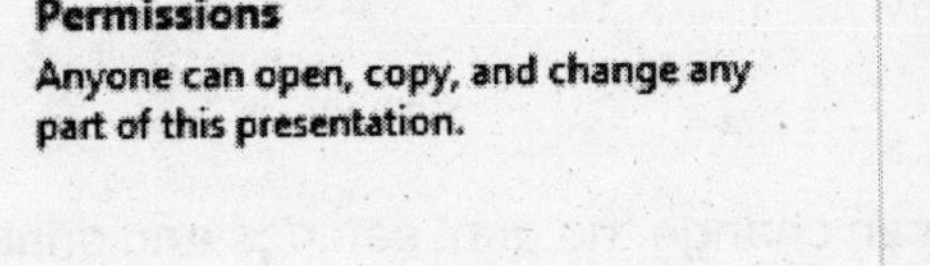

3. Recent

The Recent pane allows you to conveniently access recent presentations and file folders.

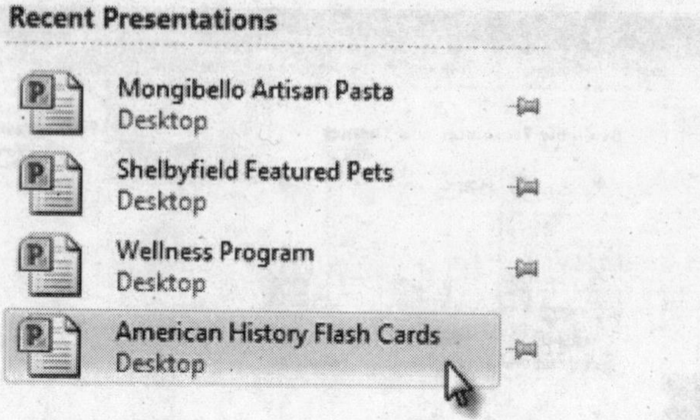

4. New

From here, you can create a new, blank presentation, or you can choose from a large selection of templates.

5. Print

From the Print pane, you can change the print settings and print your presentation. You can also see a preview of how your presentation will look on the page.

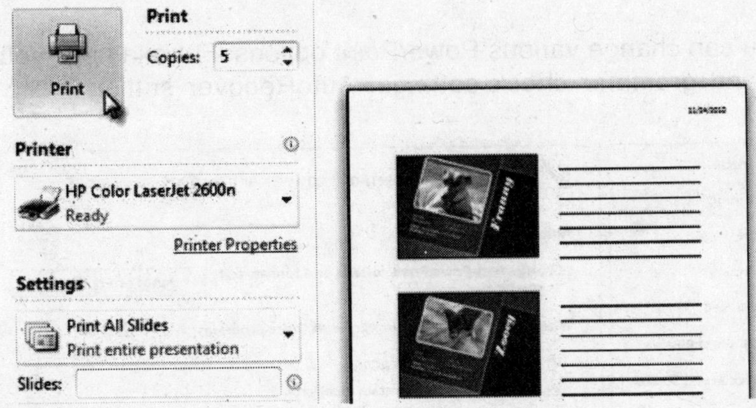

6. Save & Send

Save & Send provides options for you to share your presentation and change its file formats. In addition, you can create a video, CD, or handouts of your presentation from here.

7. Help

From the Help pane, you can access Microsoft Office Help or check for updates for your software.

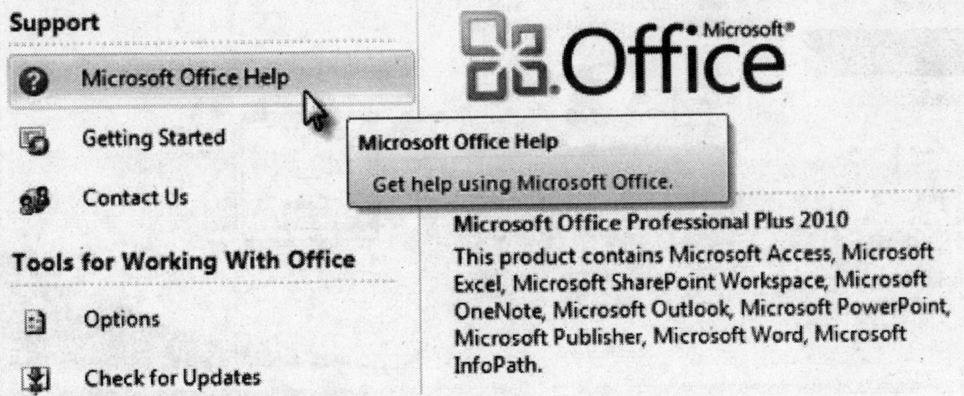

8. Options

Here, you can change various PowerPoint options. For example, you can adjust the spelling and grammar check settings, AutoRecover settings, and Language preferences.

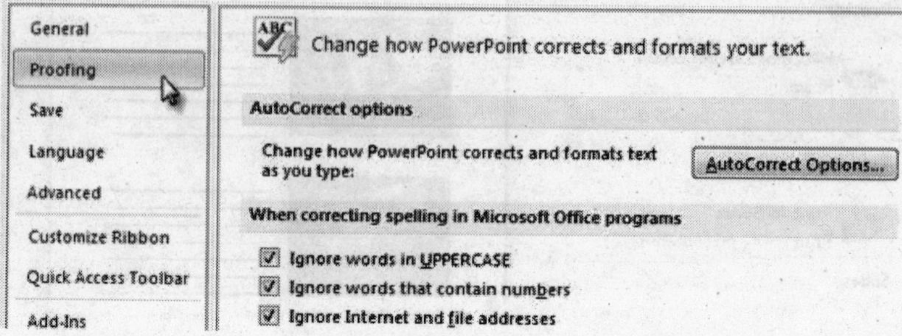

Creating and Opening Presentations

PowerPoint files are called **presentations**. Whenever you start a new project in PowerPoint, you will need to create a new presentation. You will also need to know how to open an existing presentation.

To Create a New, Blank Presentation

1. Click on the **File tab**. This takes you to **Backstage view**.
2. Select **New**.
3. Select **Blank presentation** under **Available Templates and Themes**. It will be highlighted by default.
4. Click on **Create**. A new, blank presentation appears in the PowerPoint window.

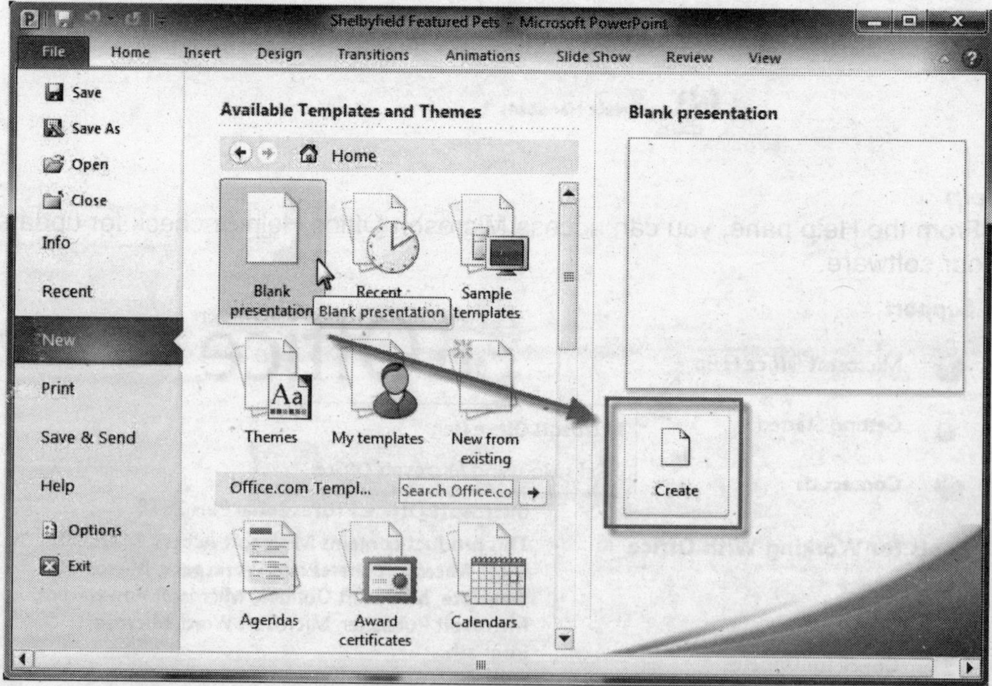

To Open an Existing Presentation

1. Click on the **File tab**. This takes you to **Backstage view**.
2. Select **Open**. The **Open dialog box** appears.

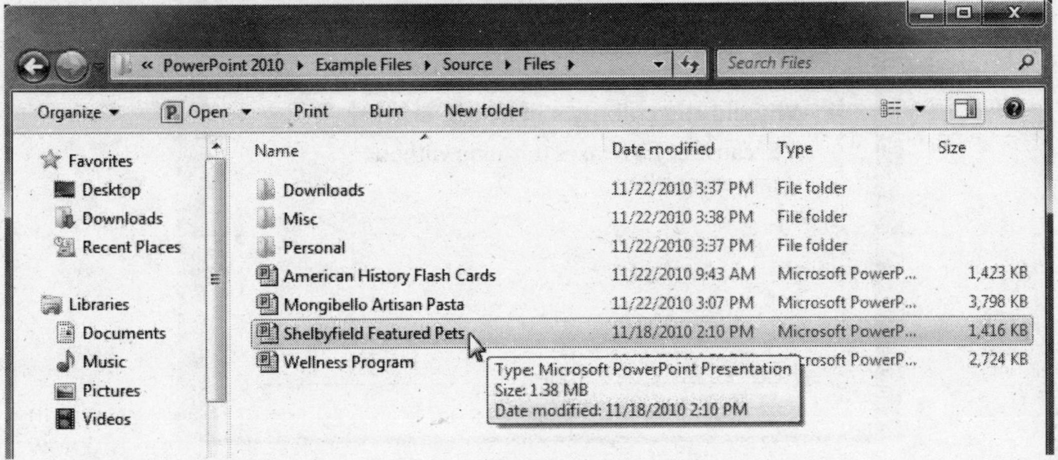

3. Select your desired presentation, then click on **Open**.

Formatting Text

In order to add and arrange text on your slides, you need to follow some basic steps.

To Insert Text

1. Click the **placeholder** or **text box** where you want to insert text.
2. The **insertion point** appears.

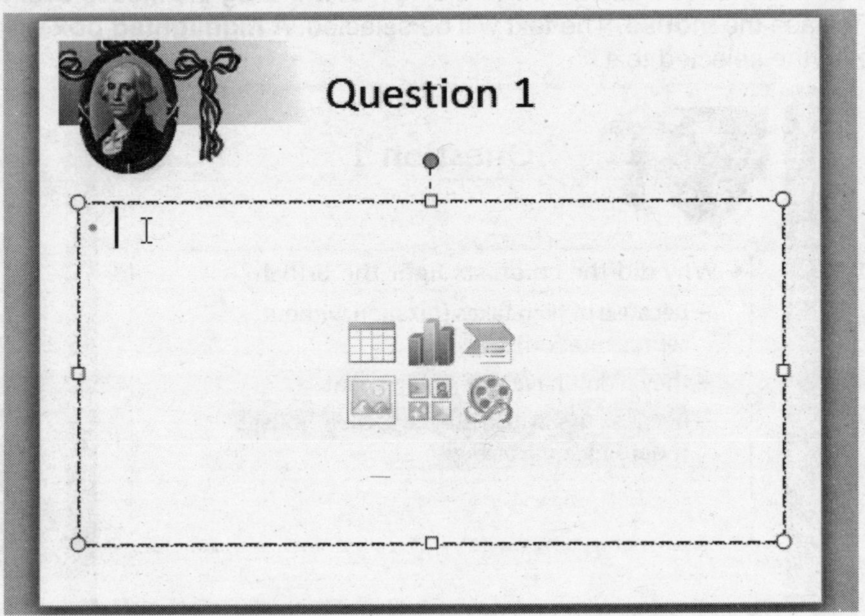

3. Type directly into the **placeholder** or **text box**.

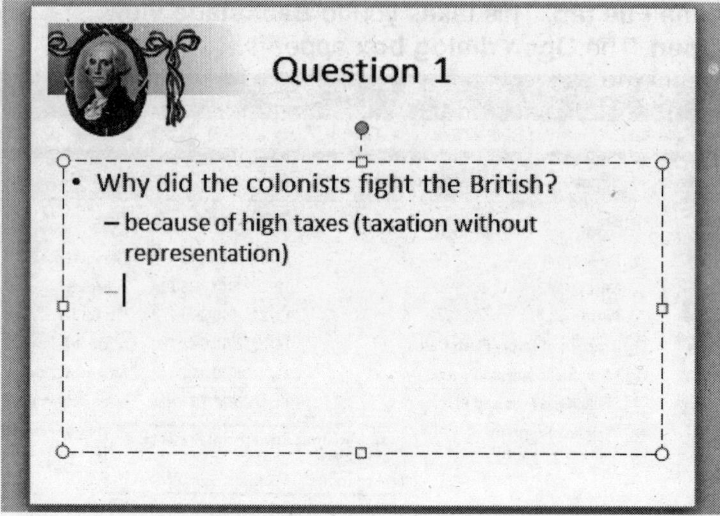

To Delete Text

1. Place the **insertion point** next to the text you want to delete.
2. Press the **Backspace** key on your keyboard to delete text to the left of the insertion point.
3. Press the **Delete** key on your keyboard to delete text to the right of the insertion point.

To Select Text

1. Place the **insertion point** next to the text you want to select.
2. Click the **mouse** button. While holding it down, **drag** the mouse over the text.
3. Release the **mouse**. The text will be selected. A **highlighted box** will appear over the selected text.

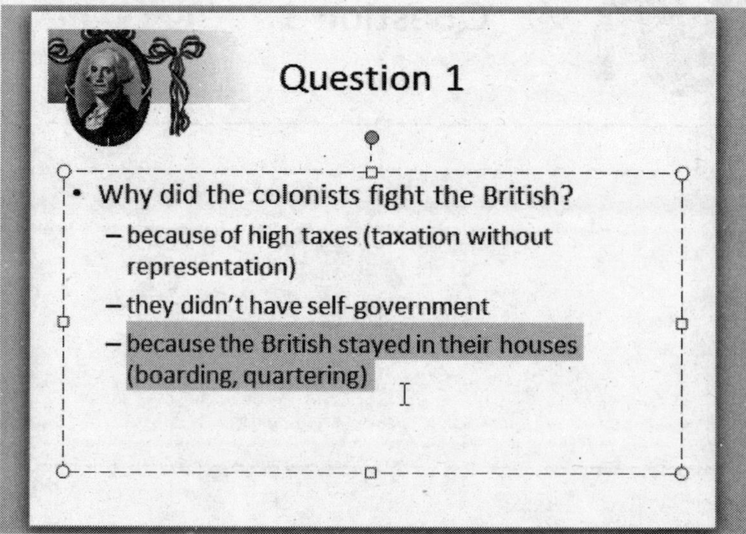

To Add A Text Box

Text can be inserted into both placeholders and text boxes. A placeholder is a kind of text box, but it's unique because it is part of the slide layout and often contains formatting specific to the slide.

1. From the **Insert** tab, click on the **Text Box** command.

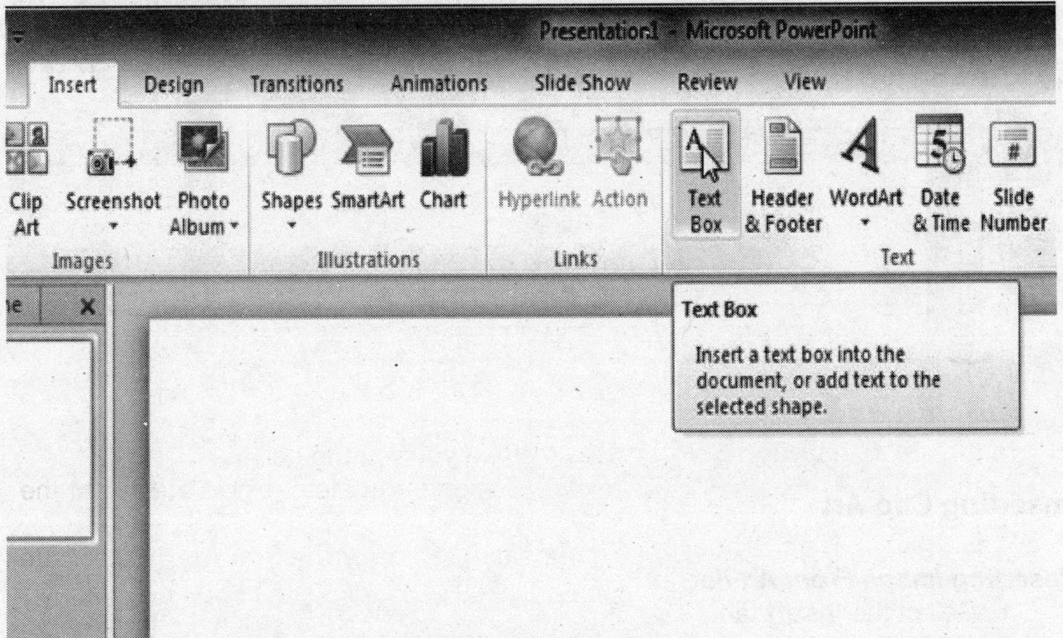

2. The cursor will turn into an **upside-down** cross.

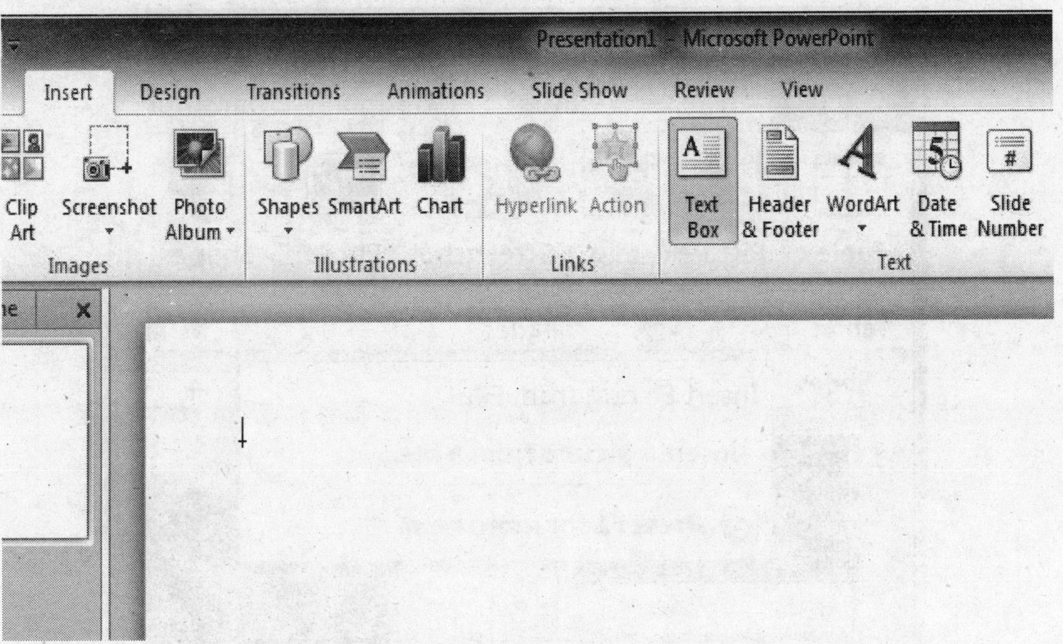

3. Click on the area on the slide where you want to add a text box. A text box will appear with an **insertion point** inside.

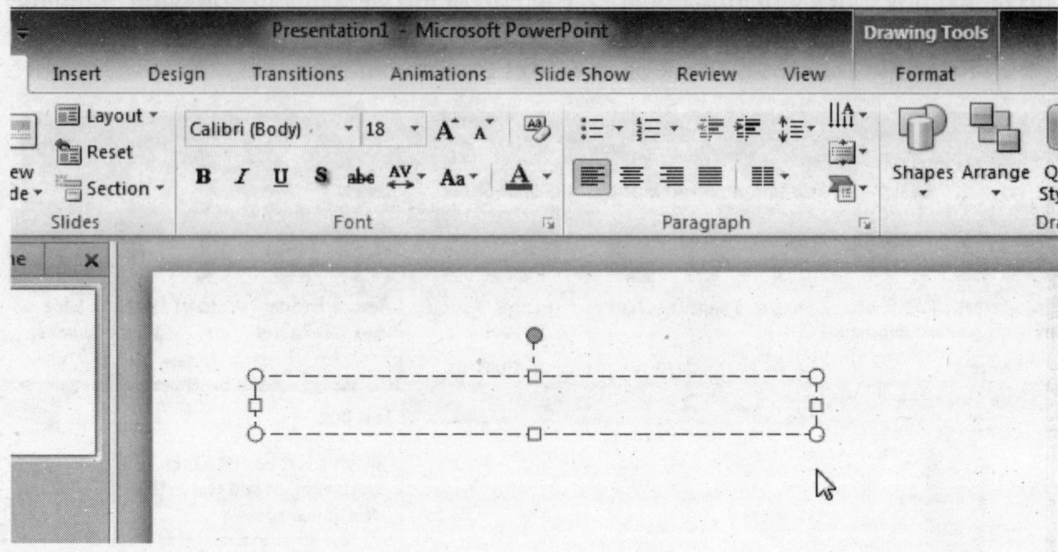

Inserting Clip Art

Inserting Image From A File

1. Select the **Insert** tab.
2. Click the **Picture** command in the **Images** group. The **Insert Picture** dialog box appears.

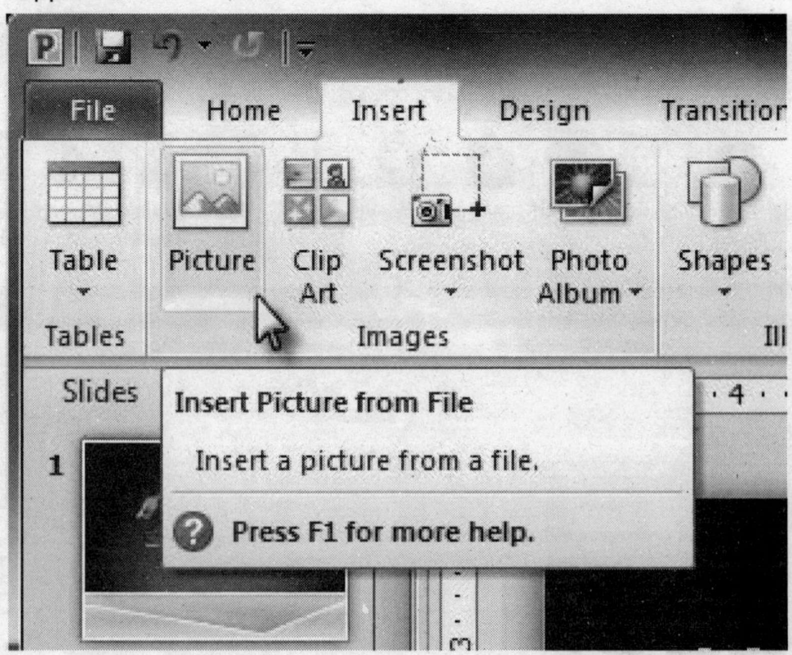

3. Select the desired image file, then click on **Insert**.

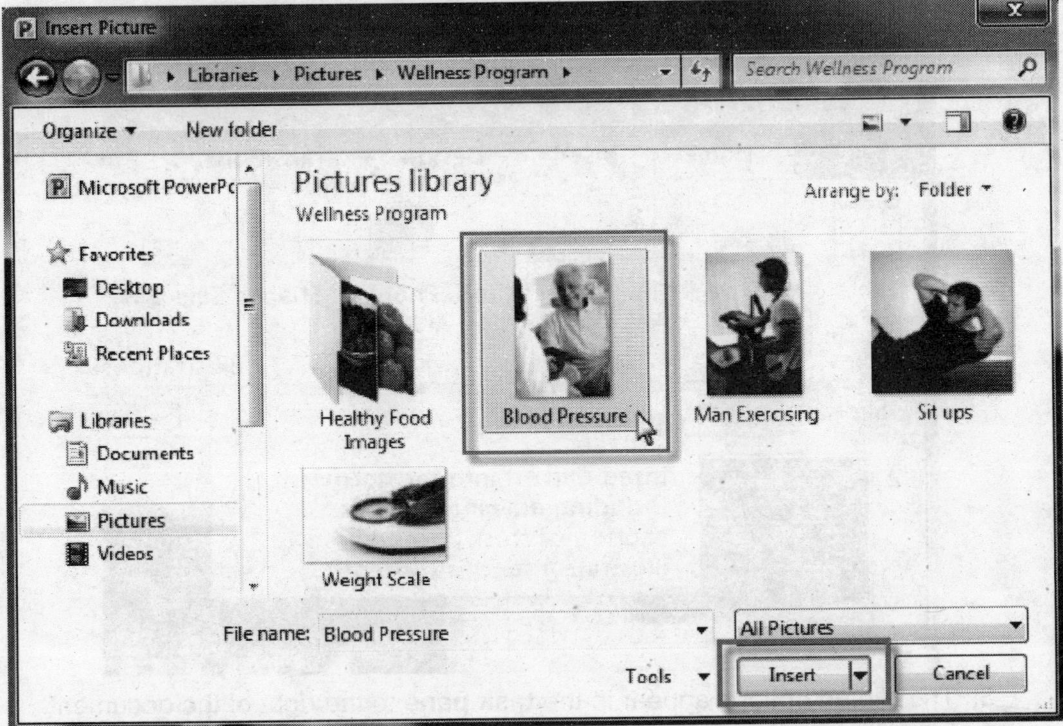

4. The picture will appear in your slide.

Finding Clip Art

1. Select the **Insert** tab.
2. Click on the **Clip Art** command in the **Images** group.

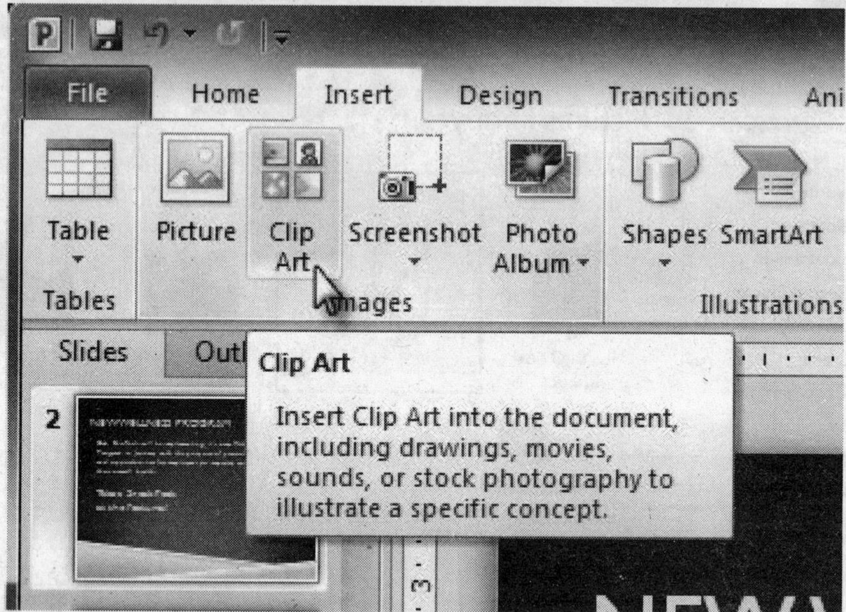

3. The clip art options appear in the **task pane** to the right of the document.
4. Enter keywords in the **Search for:** field that are related to the image you want to insert.
5. Click the drop-down arrow in the **Results should be:** field.
6. Deselect any types of media you do not want to see.

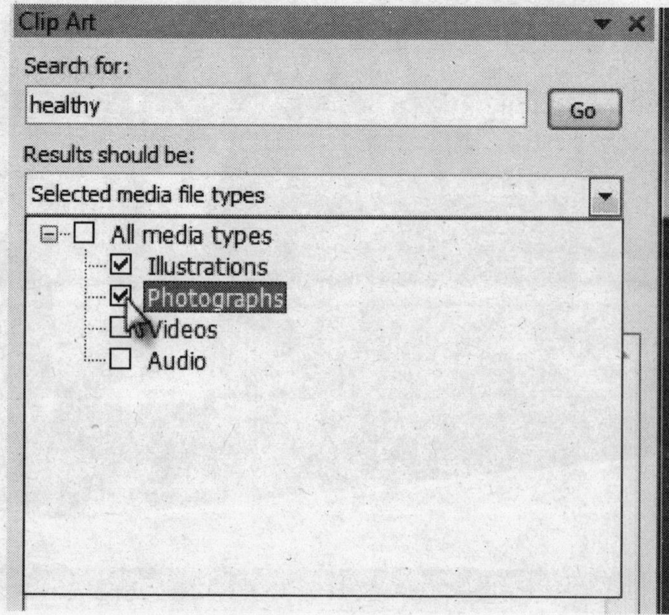

Inserting Clip Art

1. Review the results from a clip art search in the **Clip Art** pane.
2. Select the desired image.

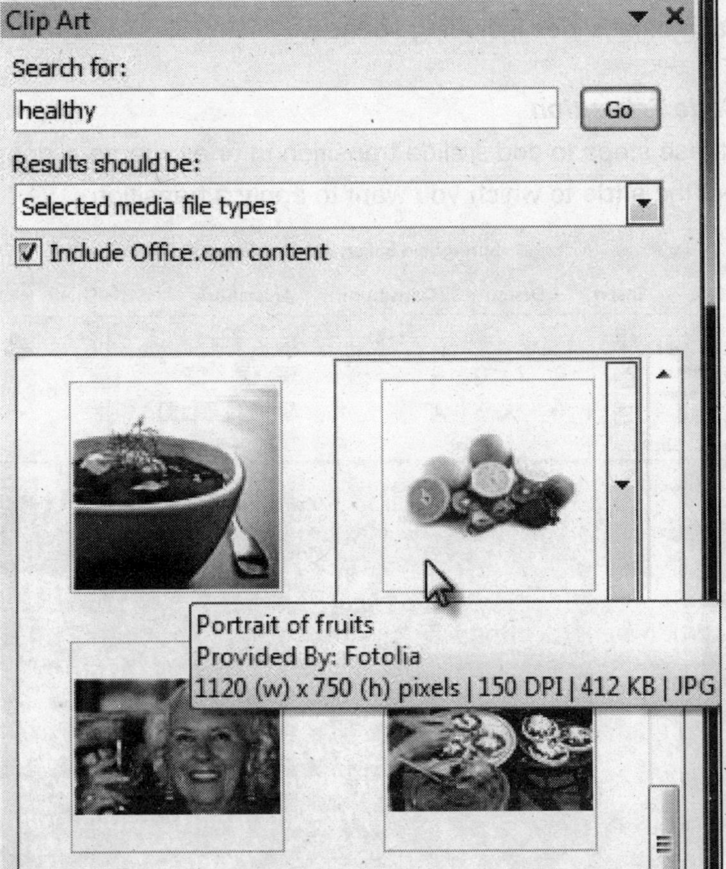

3. The clip art will appear in your slide.

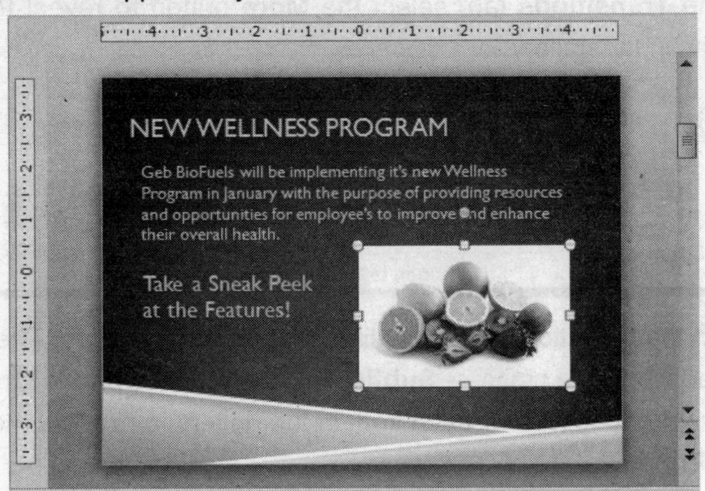

Slide Transitions

Slide transitions provide an animated effect to each slide when moving from one slide to the next during a slide show. There are a variety of transitions that can be applied to each or all slides including sounds.

Adding A Slide Transition

Follow these steps to add a slide transition to one or more slides:

1. Select the **slide** to which you want to apply a transition.

2. On the **Transitions** tab, select the **More** button to reveal the all transition options in the gallery.

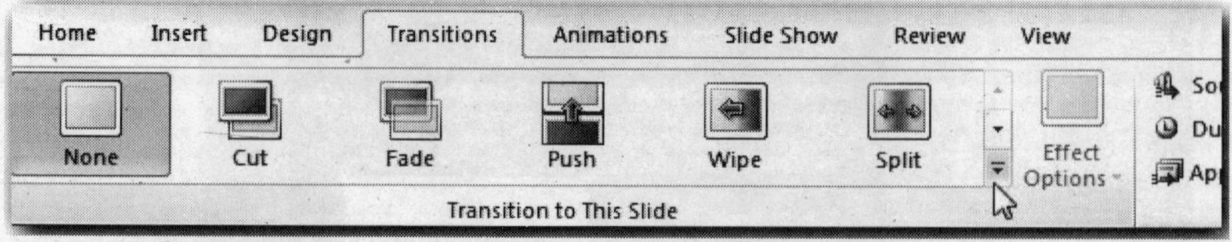

3. Select the transition you would like to apply to your slide. The transitions are divided into three types — **Subtle**, **Exciting** and **Dynamic Content**. You can hover your mouse over each item in the gallery to preview the transition with **Live Preview**.

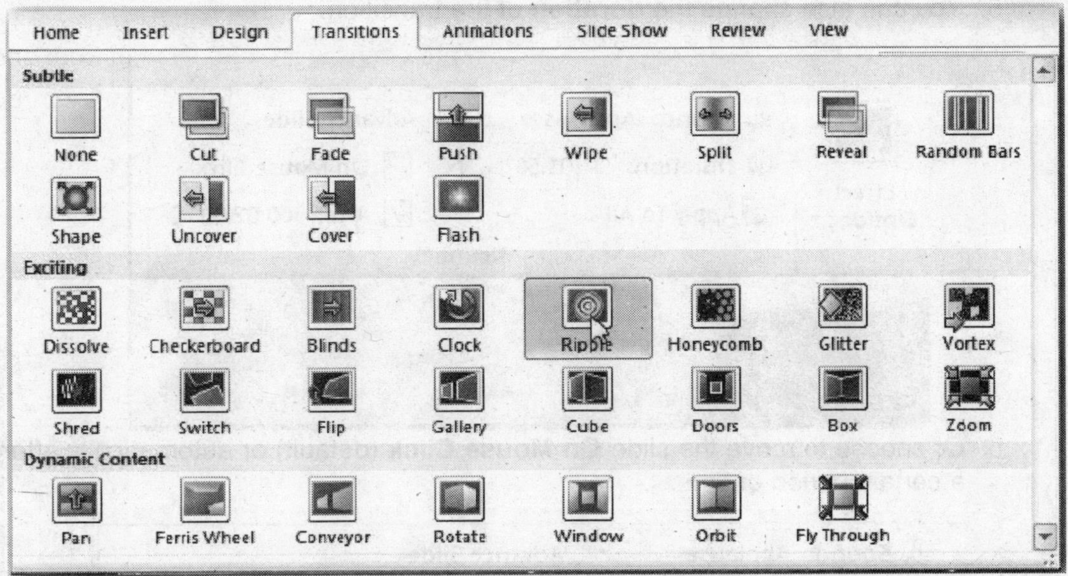

4. You can adjust many of the transitions using **Effect Options**. The options will vary depending on which transition you have selected.

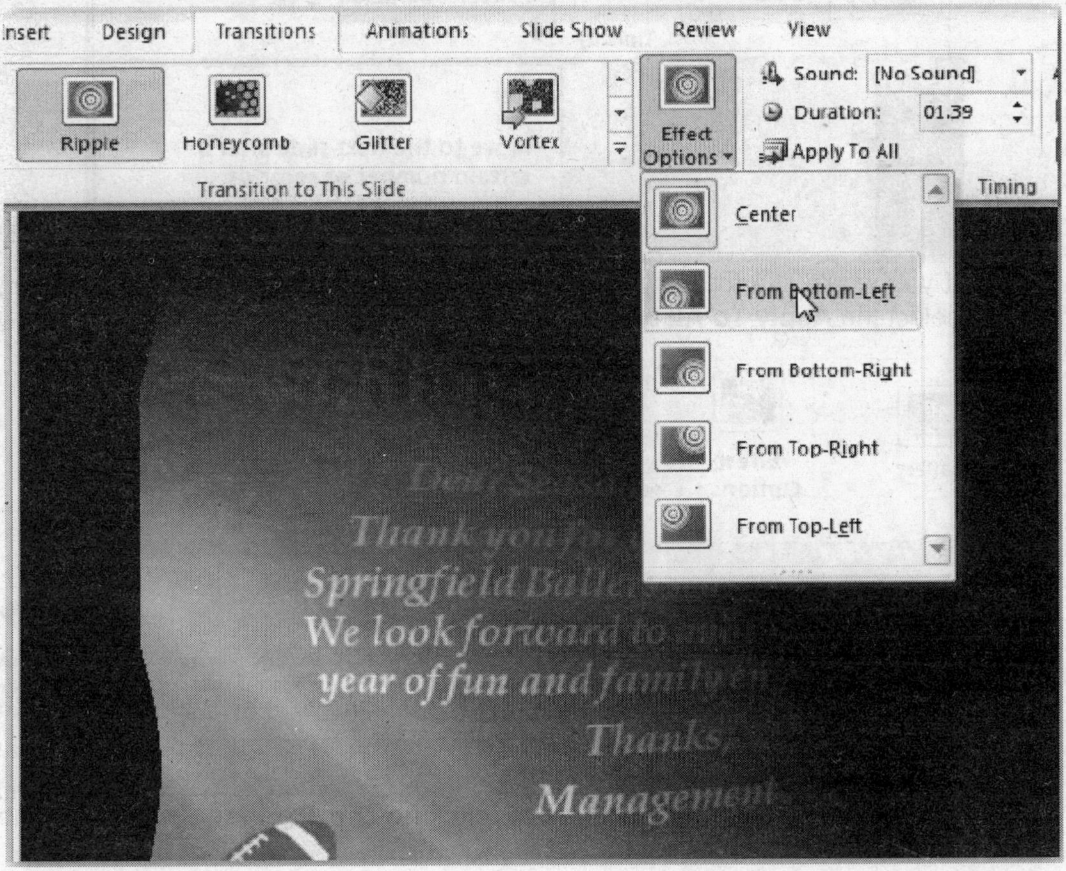

5. You can also change the **duration** of the transition.

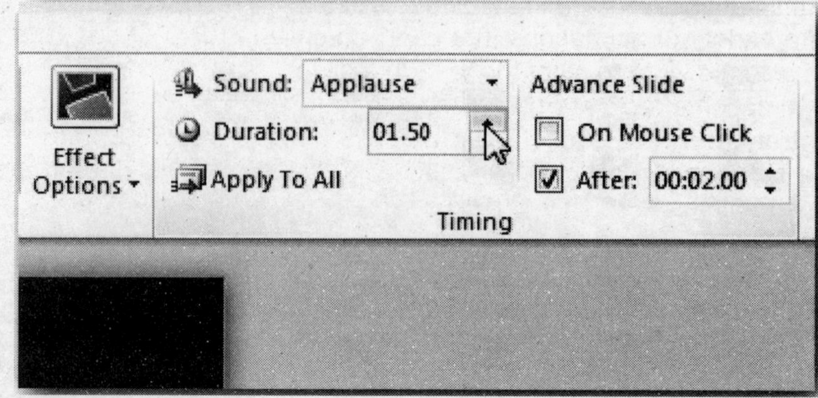

6. Or choose to move the slide **On Mouse Click** (default) or automatically after a certain period of time.

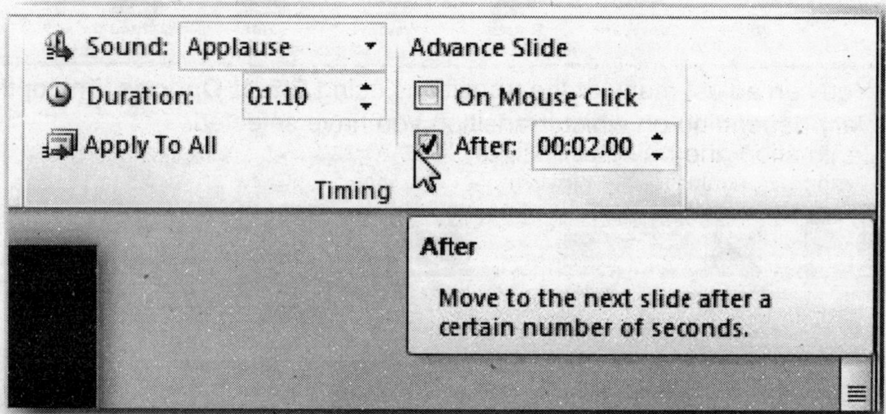

7. If you would like to apply one transition to every slide in your presentation, select the **Apply To All** button.

You can preview your transition by clicking the **Preview** button on the **Transitions** tab.

Slide Animations

Slide animations create animated effects to text and graphics during a slide show. There are a variety of animations that can be applied to text or graphics in multiple ways from a single word to all of the text on a slide.

The animation effects are organized into four types:

- **Entrance:** These control how the object enters the slide. For example, with the **Bounce** animation, the object will drop onto the slide and then bounce several times.

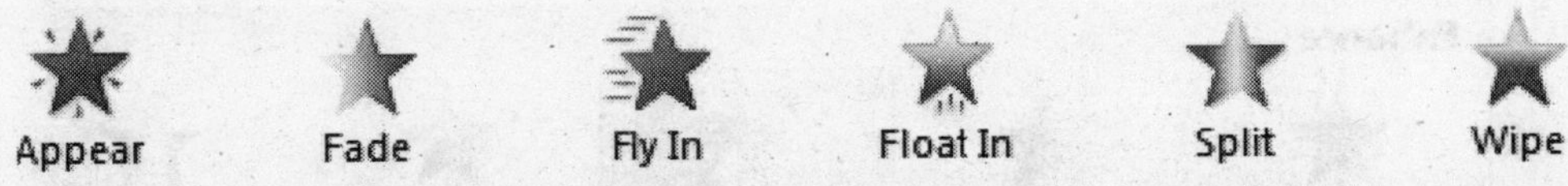

- **Emphasis:** These animations occur while the object is on the slide and are often triggered by a **mouse click**. For example, you can set an object to **Spin** when you click the mouse.

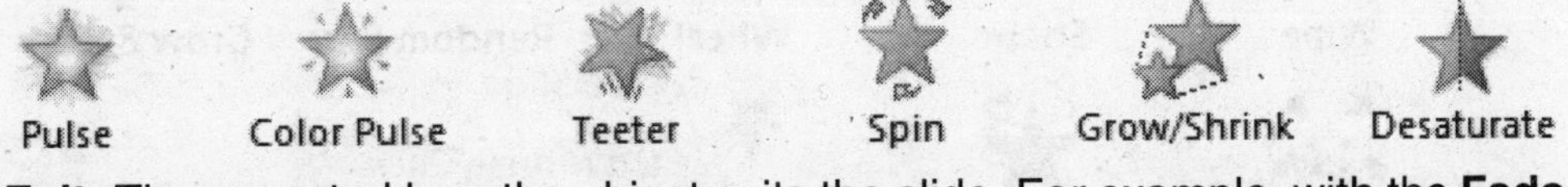

- **Exit:** These control how the object exits the slide. For example, with the **Fade** animation, the object will simply fade away.

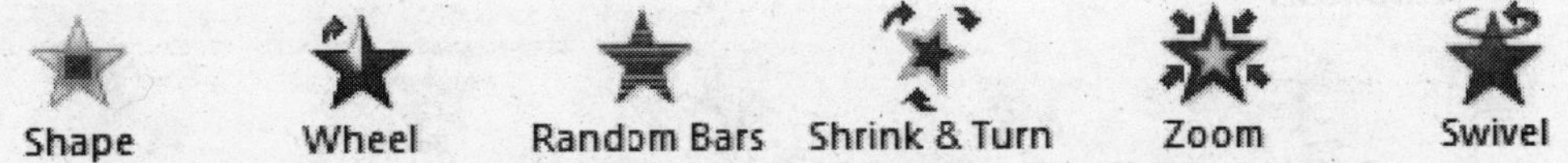

- **Motion Paths:** These are similar to **Emphasis** effects, except the object moves within the slide along a predetermined path, like a **circle**.

To Apply An Animation To An Object

1. Select an object.
2. Click the **Animations** tab.
3. In the **Animation** group, click the **More** drop-down arrow to view the available animations.

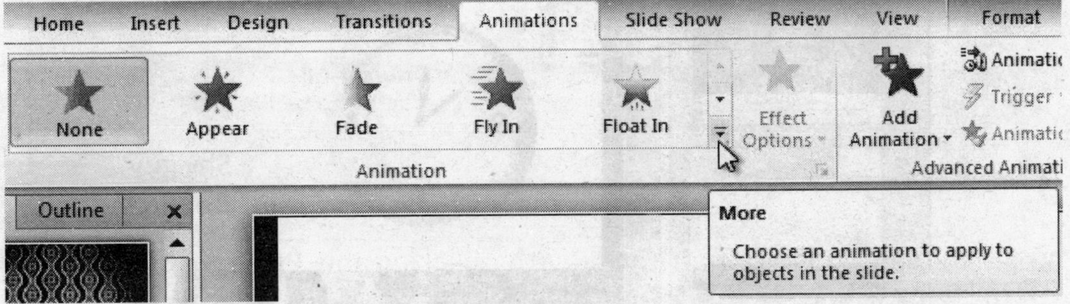

4. Select the desired animation effect.

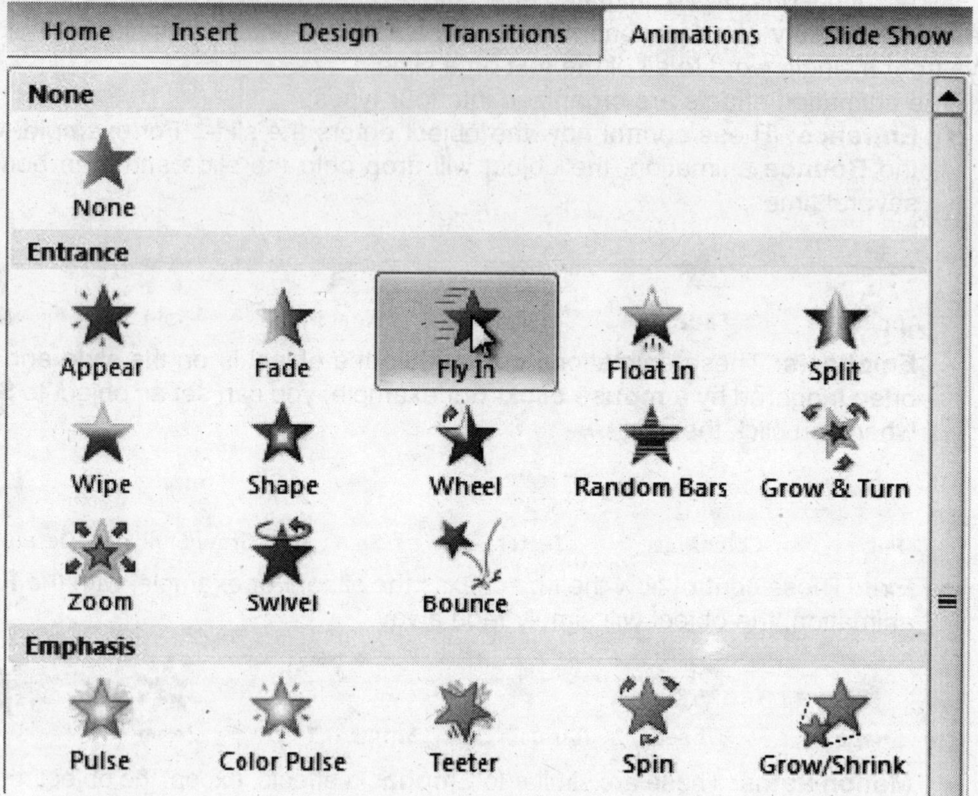

5. The object will now have a small number next to it to show that it has an animation. Also, in the **Slide** pane, the slide will now have a **star** symbol next to it.

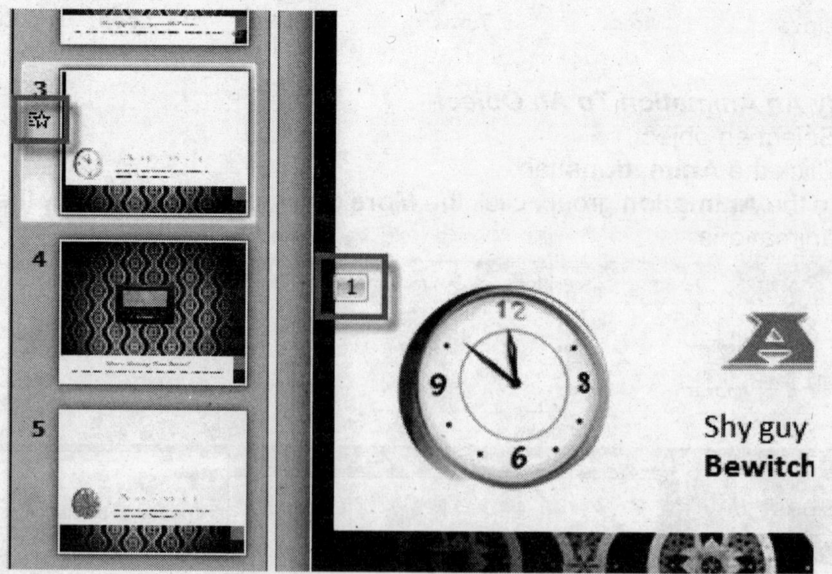

Previewing Your Show

The Slideshow tab will let you set up how your show will progress. First, you may want to preview your raw show to see if the slides seem in the proper order and if you like the transitions.

To preview, click on the **Slideshow tab** and select either **From Beginning** (to see show from the first slide on) or **From Current Slide** (to see show from a slide selected in the Slide Pane onwards).

Use the **Set Up Show** feature to create the delivery of your show.

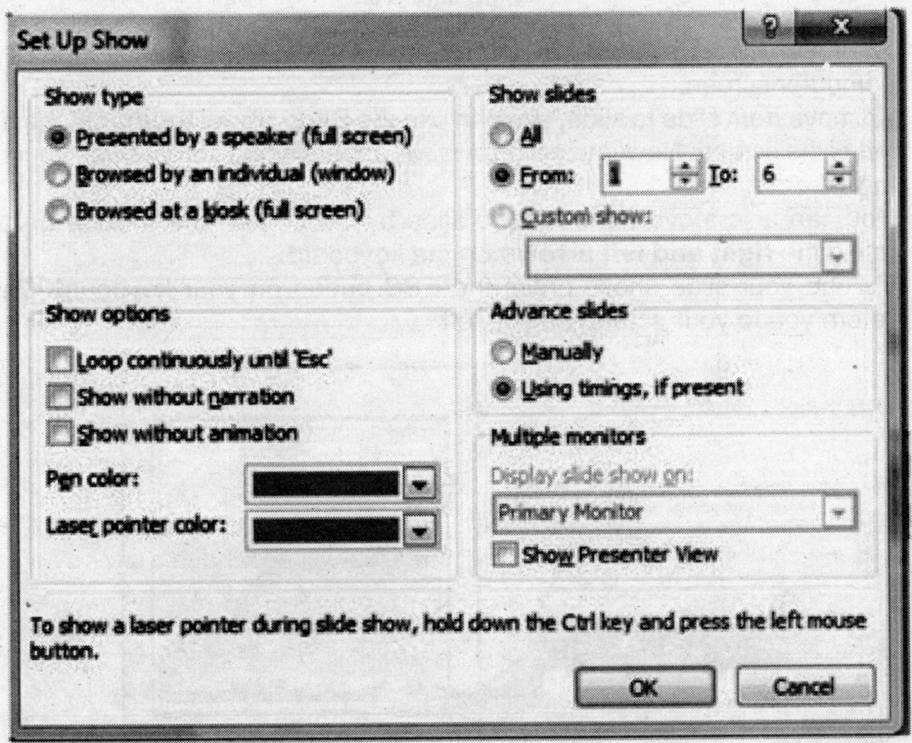

Note that timings for your slides were supposed to be set up in the **Slide Transitions** step. You can always go back and adjust them.

The easiest way to set the slide timings is to rehearse and time your PowerPoint presentation by progressing through the slides as if you were seeing them for the first time. As you click on the mouse to advance the slides, PowerPoint can record the timings on the slides for you.

Starting a Slide Show

The best way to view your slides as a show, whether you are previewing your documents or presenting to an audience, go to the **Slide Show tab** on the **Ribbon**.

1. To view your slide show, go to the **Start Slide Show group**. To start on the first slide, click on the **From Beginning** command. To start on the current slide, click on the **From Current Slide** command.

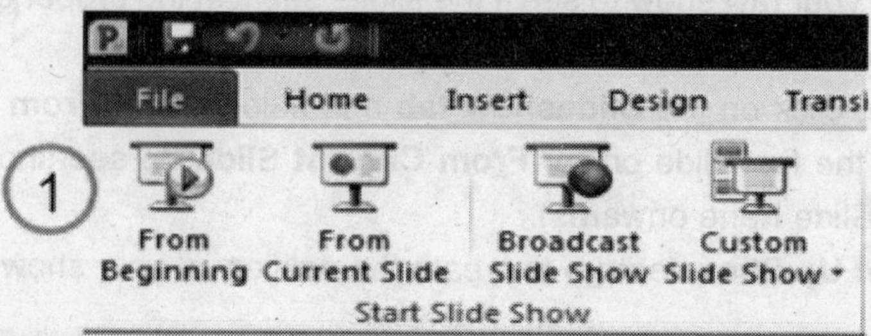

2. Your computer screen will disappear and a **slide show** will fill your computer screen.
3. To move from slide to slide, you can use the **Slide Show toolbar** at the bottom left of the screen. Navigational arrows will appear when you position your cursor in that area.
   You can also move from slide to slide by clicking on the **mouse button** or using the **right and left arrows** on the keyboard.
4. To end your slide show, press the **ESC** button on your keyboard. This will return you to your screen as you left.

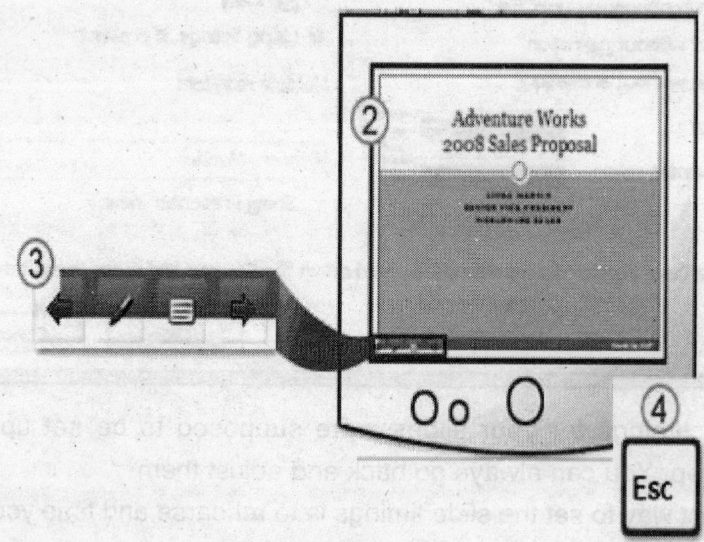

Printing Slides

One new feature in PowerPoint 2010 is the **File tab**. This tab incorporates many of the features in the 2003 and 2007 versions of PowerPoint but makes them much more user-friendly.

- To print your slides, click on the **File tab**, then on the **Print** command. When you select the Print command, you will notice all your printing options including a preview of your document are right at your fingertips.

- Select your Print options and click on the **Print** command.

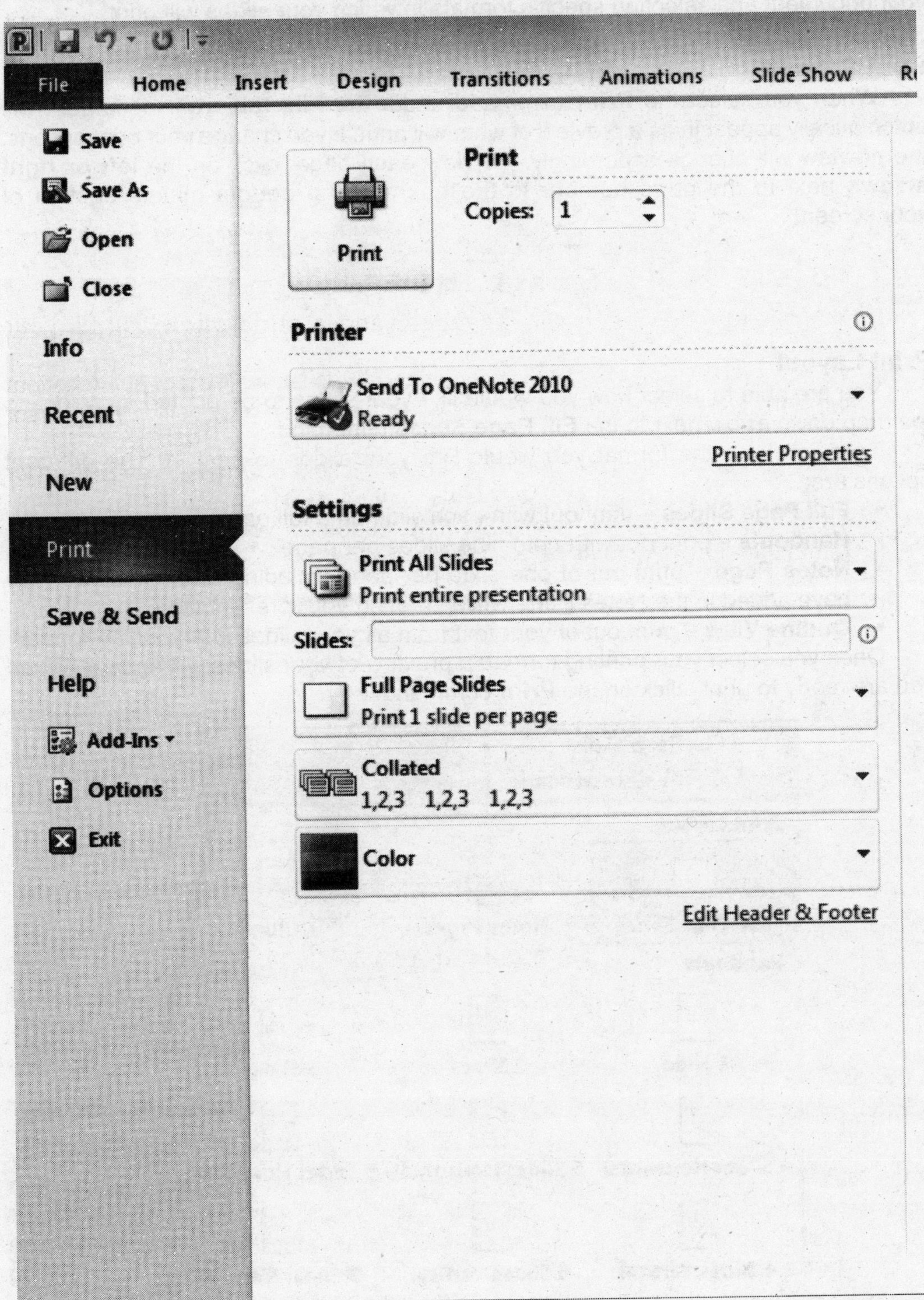

PowerPoint provides a variety of Print options, such as automatically previewing your document and selecting specific formats in which your slides will print.

Print Preview

When you select the **Print** command under the **File tab**, your document will automatically appear in as a preview of what will print. If you change your print options, the preview will change accordingly. To view each page, click on the **left or right arrows** next to the page number in the box and the bottom middle section of your screen.

Print Layout

You are able to select how you would like your slides to be printed by selecting the drop down arrow next to the **Fill Page Slides** command.

Then, click on the format you would like your slides to print in. The different options are:

- **Full Page Slides** – print out with each slide on a full page
- **Handouts** – print out with upto nine slides per page
- **Notes Page** – print out of one slide per page including any notes you may have added in the Notes Pane while creating your presentation
- **Outline View** – print out of your text from all your slides in an outline format

Once you select your printing format, a preview of your slides will appear. When you are ready to print, click on the **Print** command.

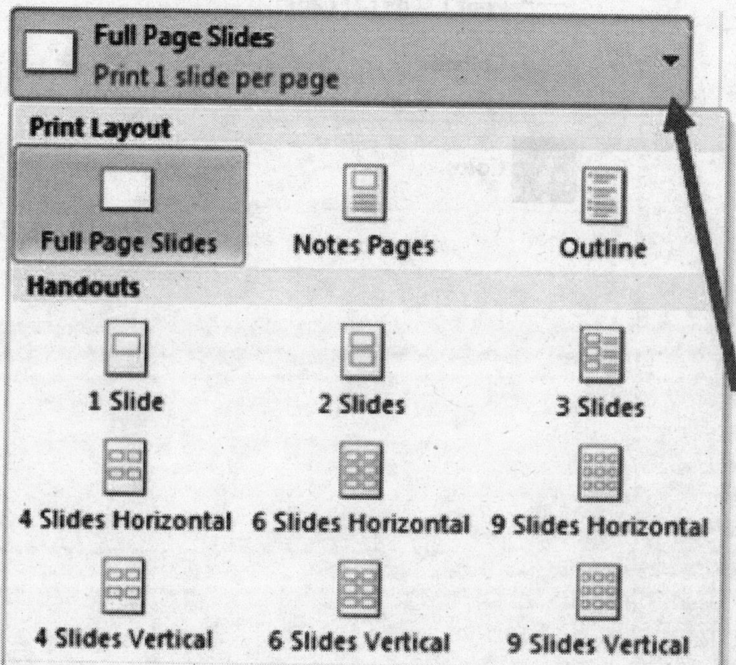

Slide Colour

Another helpful printing option allows you to print your slides in different colours. This can reduce the amount of expensive colour ink when printing PowerPoint slides.

- Click on the **Colour** command.
- Select the **colour** you would like your slides to appear in.
- Preview the slides and then click on the **Print** command.

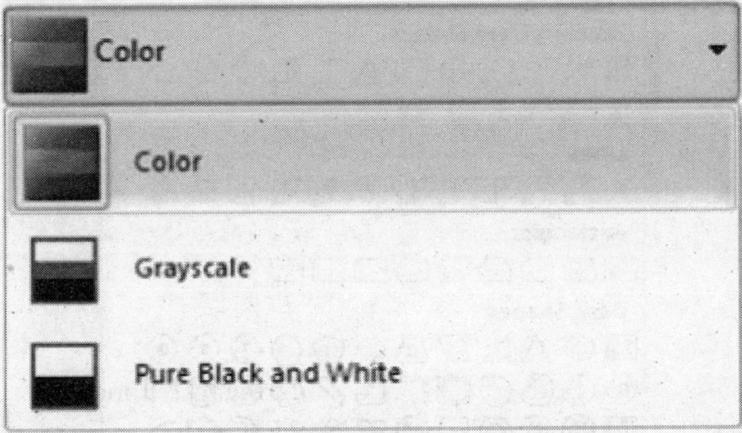

Saving Slides

To Save your slides, go to the **File tab** and select **Save** or **Save As**.

Save As—use when you save any document for the first time, it will automatically ask you where to save the document on your computer and to change the name of the document.

Save—automatically saves the document to a default location and name or the location and name you selected when first using the **Save As** feature.

Insert Shapes

Shapes can be used in PowerPoint as a graphic to enhance the presentation or to insert text into to add visual appeal to a slide.

1. Go to the **Insert Tab**.
2. Click on the **Shapes** command.
3. A large selection of shapes will appear in a drop-down menu.
4. **Double-click** on the shape you want to insert.
5. The shape will appear on the slide.
6. Move the shape to any area of the slide by **clicking on the edge** of the shape and **dragging** it. Expand or shrink the shape by clicking on the circles surrounding the shape and drag.

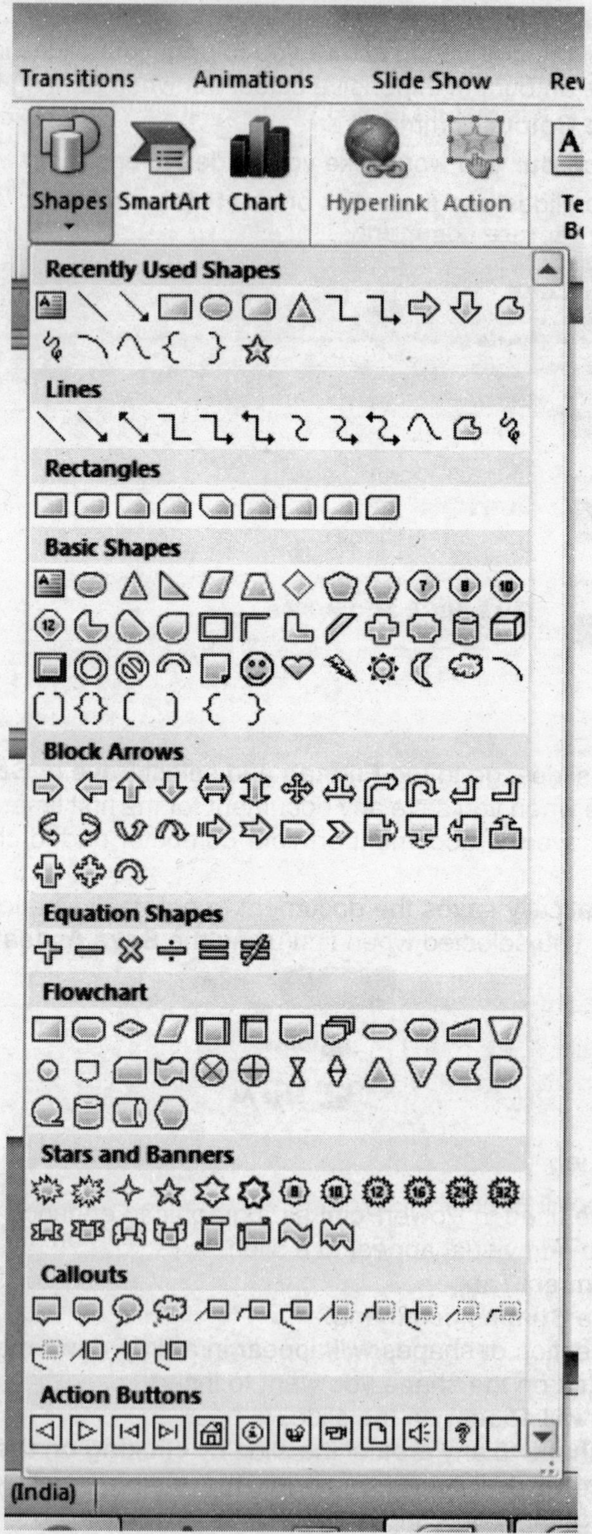
Transitions
Animations
Slide Show
Shapes
SmartArt
Chart
Hyperlink
Action
Recently Used Shapes
Lines
Rectangles
Basic Shapes
Block Arrows
Equation Shapes
Flowchart
Stars and Banners
Callouts
Action Buttons
(India)

Inserting Pictures

Pictures are another way to include graphics into a PowerPoint presentation. Many people like using this feature to incorporate pictures from their personal collection to distinguish their presentation.

1. Go to the **Insert Tab**.
2. Click on the **Picture** command.

3. An **Insert Picture box** will appear.
4. Select the picture to insert using the folders on the left of the Insert Picture box.
5. Click on **Open**.
6. The picture will appear on the slide.
7. Move the picture to any area of the slide by clicking on the edge of the picture and dragging it. Expand or shrink the picture by clicking on the circles surrounding the picture and drag.

Inserting WordArt

WordArt can be used to accentuate important words in a presentation, such as the title.

1. Go to the **Insert tab**.

2. Click on the **WordArt** command.

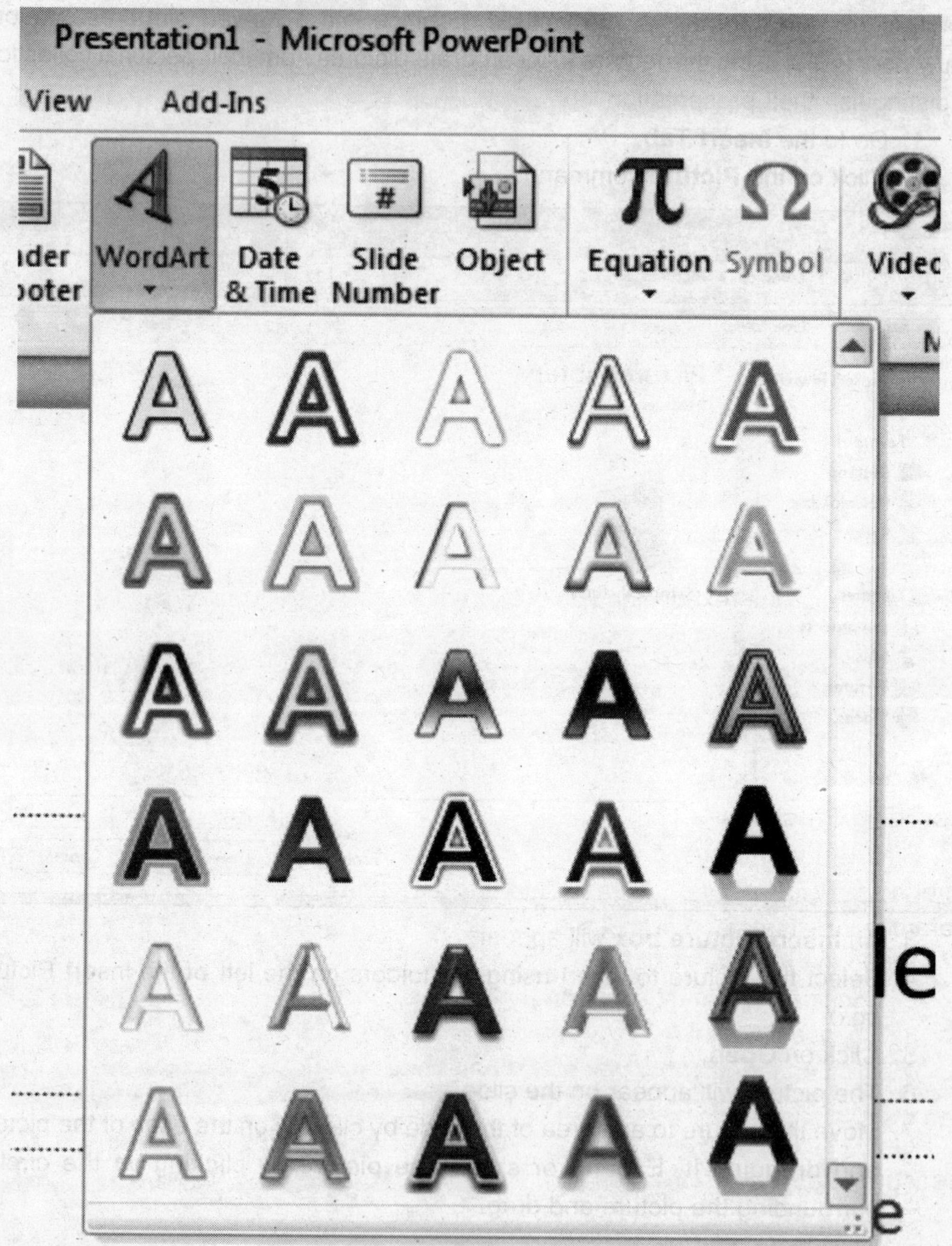

Inserting SmartArt

To insert SmartArt—

1. Go to the **Insert tab**.

2. Click on the **SmartArt** command.

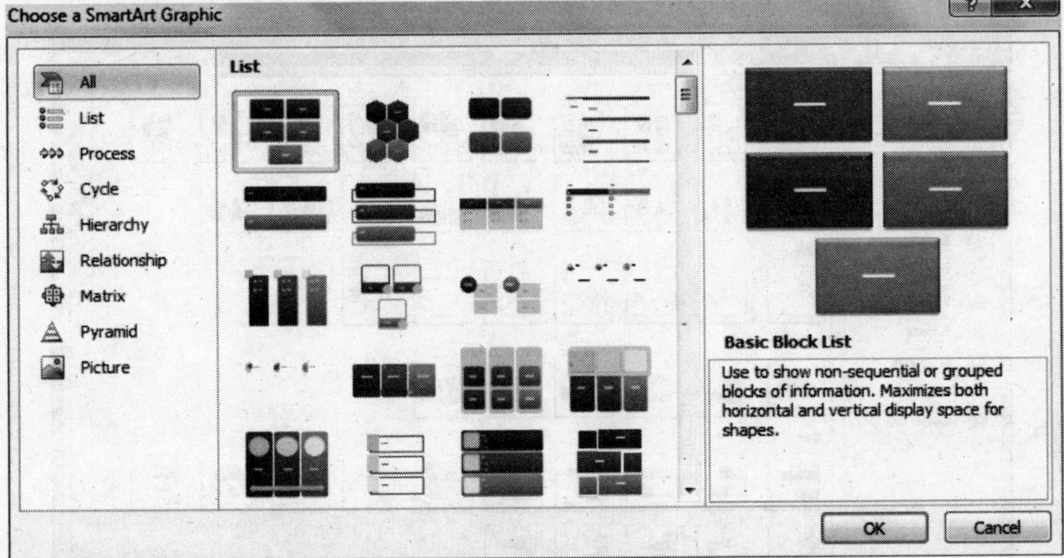

3. A drop-down menu of text options will appear.
4. Click on the text design you prefer and a text box will appear on your slide.
5. Click on the text box to modify the text.
6. Move the WordArt to any area of the slide by clicking on the edge of the text and dragging it. Expand or shrink the WordArt by clicking on the circles surrounding the text and drag.

Inserting SmartArt

SmartArt can be used similar to a graphic by inserting a SmartArt design and entering text in specified areas. This can be especially helpful when illustrating hierarchy structures and processes.

1. Go to the **Insert Tab**.
2. Click on the **SmartArt** command.
3. Choose a **SmartArt Graphic box** that will appear.
4. Click on the **graphic** you prefer and it will appear on your slide.
5. Click on the **areas** of the SmartArt graphic to enter text in the graphic.

Inserting Tables or Charts

Tables and Charts can be used to express data in a presentation.

First, go to the **Insert Tab**.

To insert a Chart:

1. Click on the **Chart** command.
2. An **Insert Chart box** will appear.
3. Click on the **chart** you prefer.

4. An **Excel worksheet** will open. Enter the data in the Excel Document that you want to be displayed on the chart.

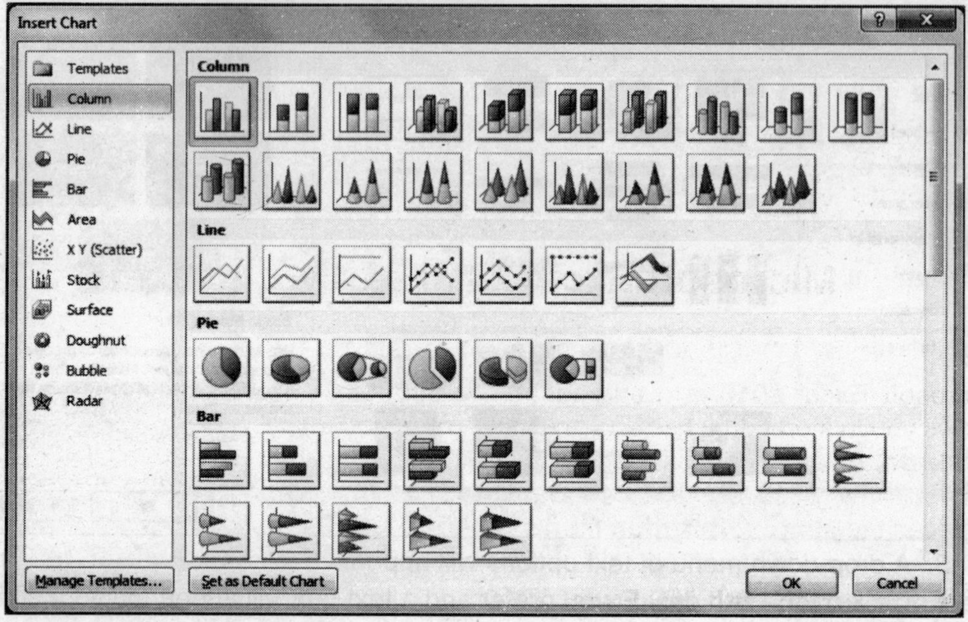

To Insert a Table

1. Click on the **Table** command.
2. Highlight the **number of cells** you want in your table.
3. Click on the **table** to appear on your slide.
4. Click on **each cell** to enter the data you want to be displayed.

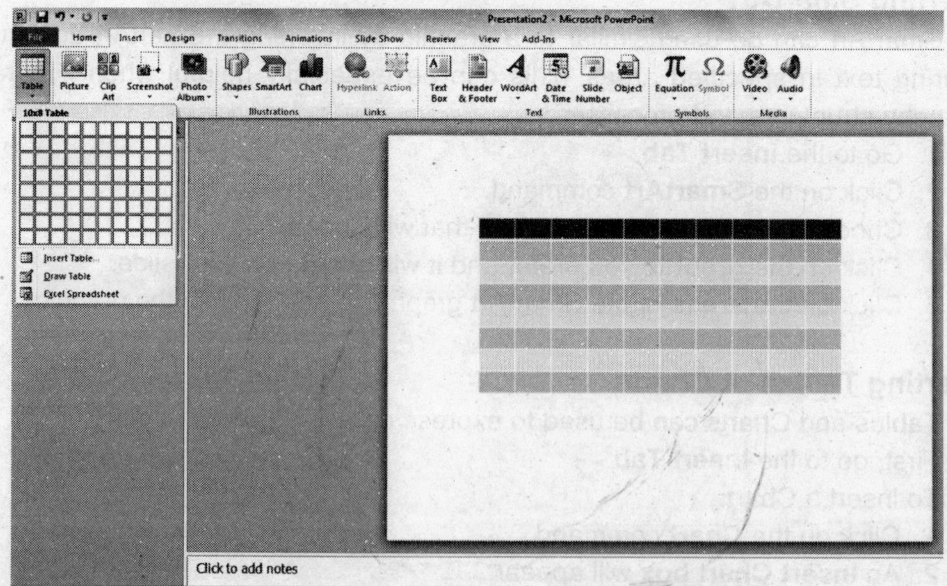

13
Microsoft Excel 2010 and Worksheet

Microsoft Excel 2010 is a spreadsheet programme that allows you to store, organise and analyse information. Excel 2010 has advanced options and features than its previous version, which includes the new **Backstage view**, which replaces the **Microsoft Button menu** from Excel 2007.

Getting Started with MS Excel 2010

1. Click on the **Start** button.
2. Click on **All Programs** option from the menu.
3. Search for **Microsoft Office** from the submenu and click on it.
4. Search for **Microsoft Excel 2010** from the submenu and click on it.

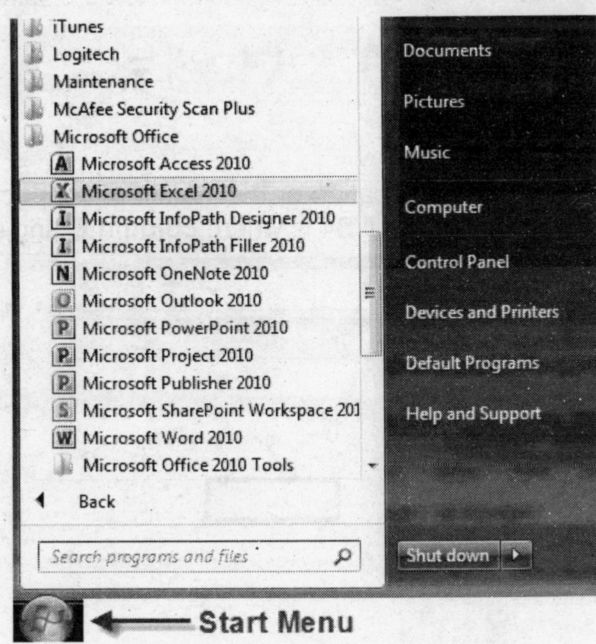

This will launch Microsoft Excel 2010 application and you will see the following Excel window.

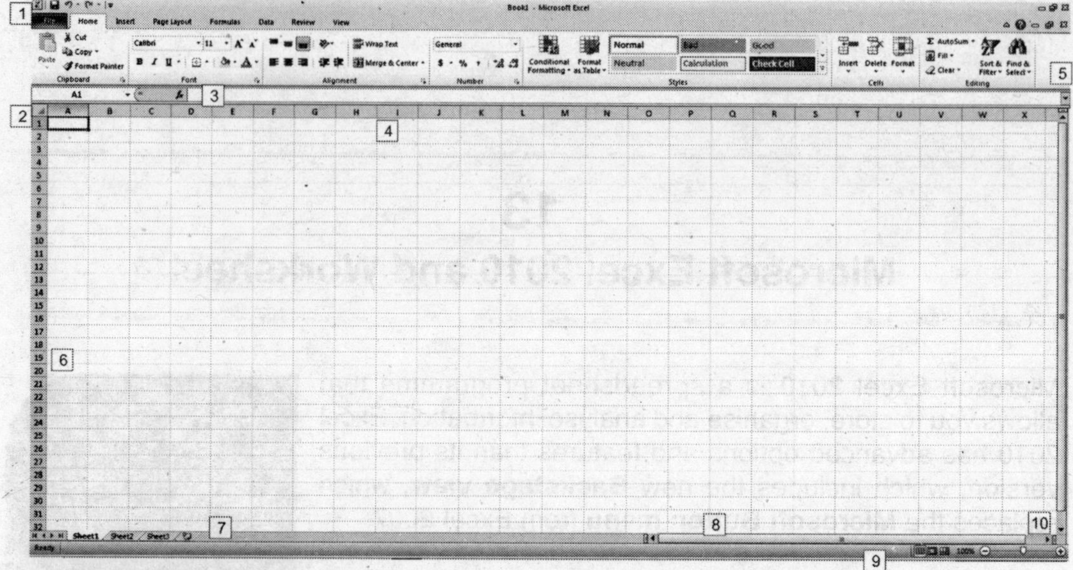

Following is the basic window which you get when you start Excel. Let us understand various important parts of this window.

1. Quick Access Toolbar

The Quick Access Toolbar lets you access common commands, no matter which tab you are on. By default, it shows the Save, Undo and Repeat commands. You can add other commands to make it more convenient for you.

2. Name Box

The Name box tells you the location or the 'name' of a selected cell. Here, **cell B4** is in the Name box. Note how cell B4 is where **column B** and **row 4** intersect.

3. Formula Bar

In the formula bar, you can enter or edit data, a formula, or a function that will appear in a specific cell. Here, **cell C1** is selected and 1984 is entered into the formula bar. Note how the data appears in both the formula bar and in cell C1.

C1					
	A	**B**	**C**	**D**	**E**	**F**
1			1984			
2						
3						

4. Column

A column is a group of cells that runs from the top of the page to the bottom. In Excel, columns are identified by letters. Here, **column L** is being selected.

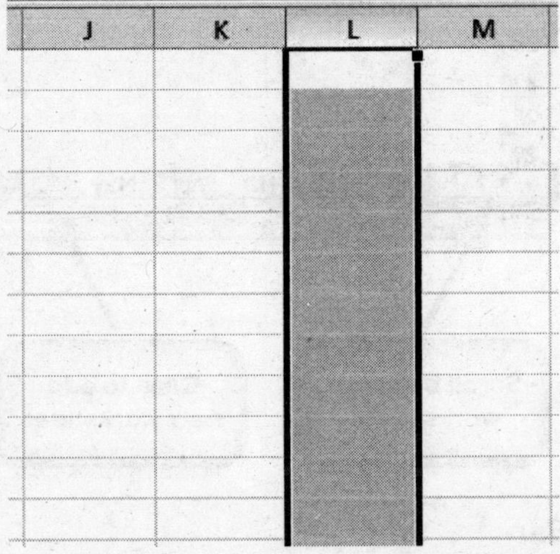

5. Ribbon

The ribbon contains all the commands you will need in order to do common tasks. It has multiple tabs, each with several groups of commands, and you can add your own tabs that contain your favourite commands. Some groups have an arrow in the bottom-right corner that you can click to see even more options.

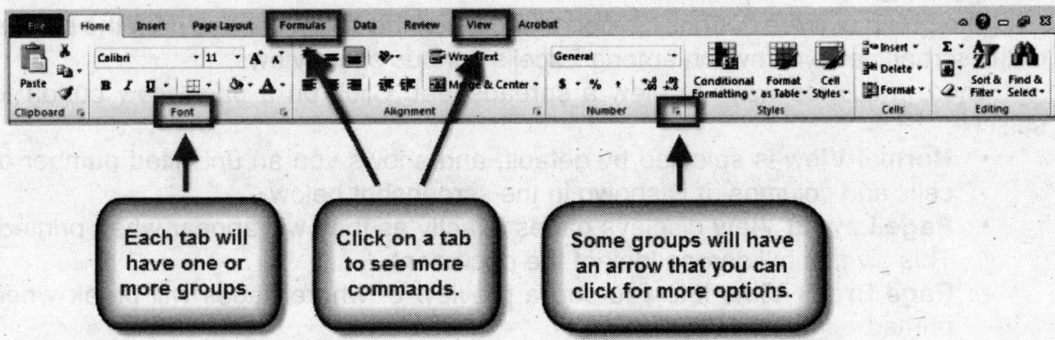

6. Row

A row is a group of cells that runs from the left of the page to the right. In Excel, rows are identified by numbers. Here, **row 15** is being selected.

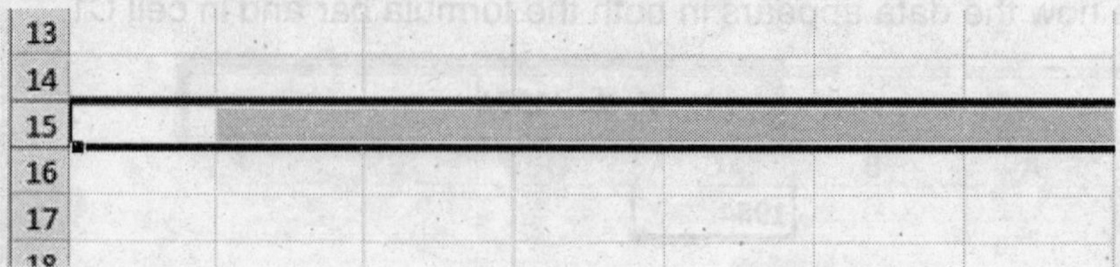

7. Worksheets

Excel files are called **workbooks**. Each workbook holds one or more worksheets (also known as **'spreadsheets'**).

Three worksheets appear by default when you open an Excel workbook. You can rename, add and delete worksheets.

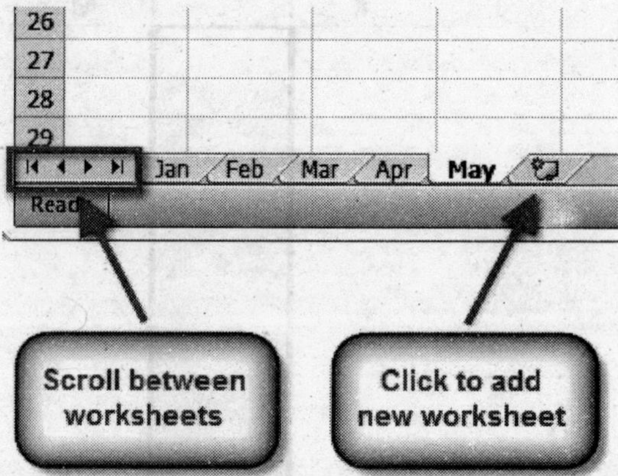

8. Horizontal Scroll Bar

You may have more data than you can see on the screen all at once. Click and hold the horizontal scroll bar and slide it to the left or right depending on what part of the page you want to see.

9. Page View

The group of three buttons located to the left of the Zoom control, near the bottom of the screen, lets you switch among Excel's various sheet views.

There are three ways to view a spreadsheet. Click on a page view button to select it.

- **Normal View** is selected by default, and shows you an unlimited number of cells and columns. It is shown in the screenshot below.
- **Page Layout View** displays pages exactly as they will appear when printed. This gives a full screen look of the document.
- **Page Break View** lets you see a preview of where pages will break when printed.

10. Zoom Control

Click on the slider and drag it to use the Zoom control. The number to the left of the slider bar reflects the zoom percentage.

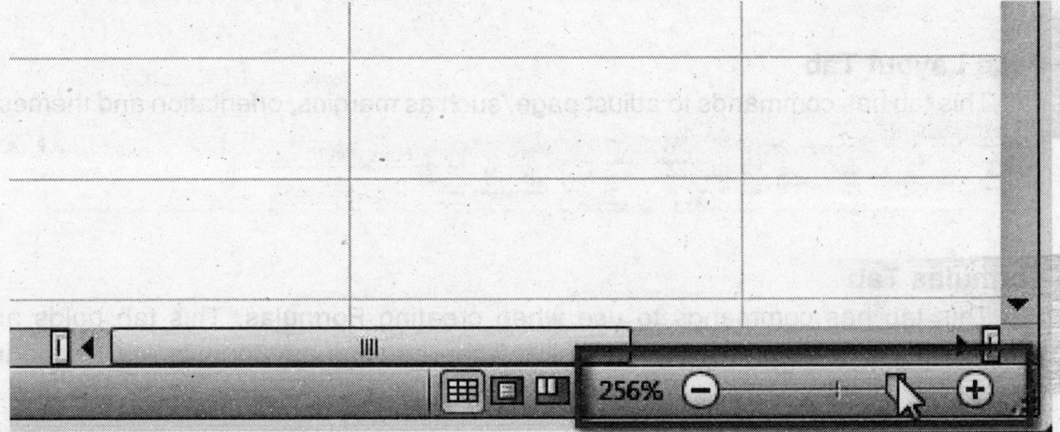

The Ribbon

The ribbon holds all the information in a more visual streamline manner through a series of tabs that include an immense variety of programme features.

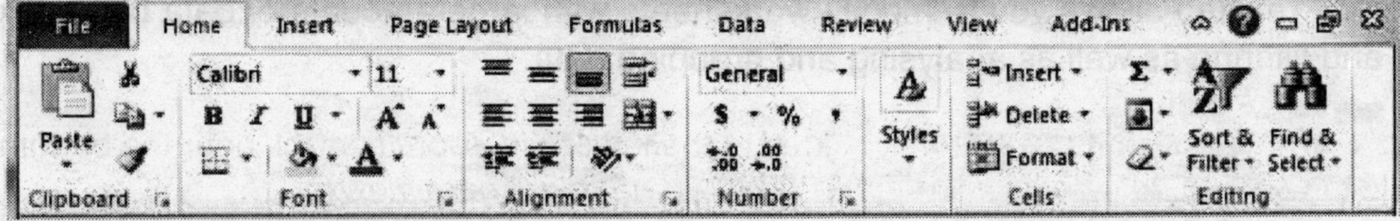

Ribbon contains commands organised in three components:

(i) Tabs: They appear across the top of the Ribbon and contain groups of related commands. Home, Insert and Page Layout are examples of ribbon tabs.

(ii) Groups: They organise related commands; each group name appears below the group on the Ribbon. For example, group of commands related to fonts or group of commands related to alignment, etc.

(iii) Commands: Commands appear within each group as mentioned above.

Home Tab

This is the most used tab. It incorporates all text and cell formatting features, such as font and paragraph changes. The Home Tab also includes basic spreadsheet formatting elements, such as text wrap, merging cells and cell style.

Insert Tab

This tab allows you to insert a variety of items into a document from pictures, clip art, and headers and footers.

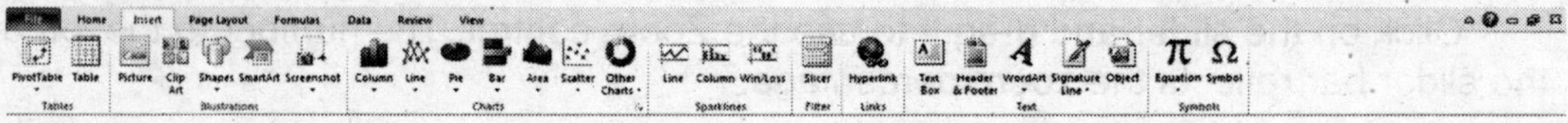

Page Layout Tab

This tab has commands to adjust page, such as margins, orientation and themes.

Formulas Tab

This tab has commands to use when creating Formulas. This tab holds an immense function library which can assist when creating any formula or function in your Spreadsheet.

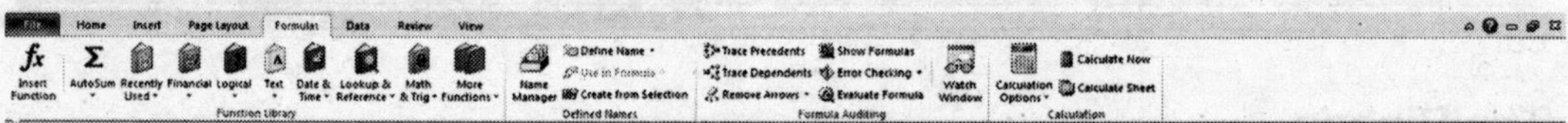

Data Tab

This tab allows you to modify worksheets with large amounts of data by sorting and filtering as well as analysing and grouping data.

Review Tab

This tab allows you to correct spelling and grammar issues as well as set up security protections. It also provides the track changes and notes feature providing the ability to make notes and changes in other's document.

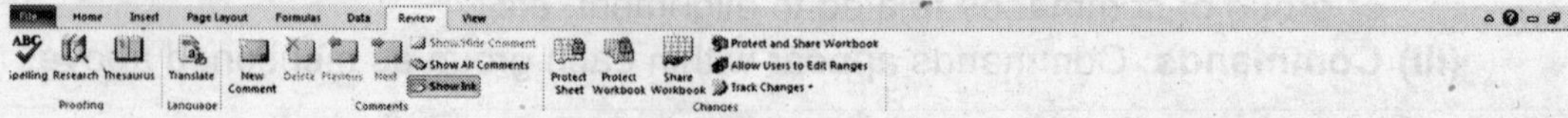

View Tab

This tab allows you to change the view of your document, including freezing or splitting panes, viewing gridlines and hide cells.

File Tab

The File tab replaces the Office button from Excel 2007. You can click on it to check Backstage view, which is the place to come when you need to open or save files, create new sheets, print a sheet, and do other file-related operations.

Title Bar

The Title bar lies in the middle and at the top of the window. Title bar shows the programme and sheet titles.

Help

The Help Icon can be used to get Excel-related help any time you like. This provides nice tutorial on various subjects related to Excel.

Zoom Control

Zoom control lets you zoom in for a closer look at your text. The zoom control consists of a slider that you can slide left or right to zoom in or out, and + buttons you can click to increase or decrease the zoom factor.

Sheet Area

This is the area where you enter data. The flashing vertical bar is called the insertion point and it represents the location where text will appear when you type.

Row Bar

Rows are numbered from 1 onwards and keep on increasing as you keep entering data. The maximum limit is 1,048,576 rows.

Column Bar

Columns are numbered from A onwards and keep on increasing as you keep entering data. After Z, it will start series of AA, AB and so on. The maximum limit is 16,384 columns.

Status Bar

This displays sheet information as well as the insertion point location. From left to right, this bar contains the total number of pages and words in the document, language, etc.

Backstage View

The Backstage View has been introduced in Excel 2010 and acts as the central place for managing your sheets. The Backstage View helps in creating new sheet, saving and opening sheets, printing and sharing sheets, and so on.

Getting to the Backstage View is easy. Just click on the **File tab**, located in the upper-left corner of the Excel Ribbon. If you already do not have any opened sheet, then you will see a window listing down all the recently opened sheets as follows.

File Tab

If you already have an opened sheet, then it will display a window showing detail about the opened sheet as shown in the screenshot below. Backstage View shows three columns when you select most of the available options in the first column.

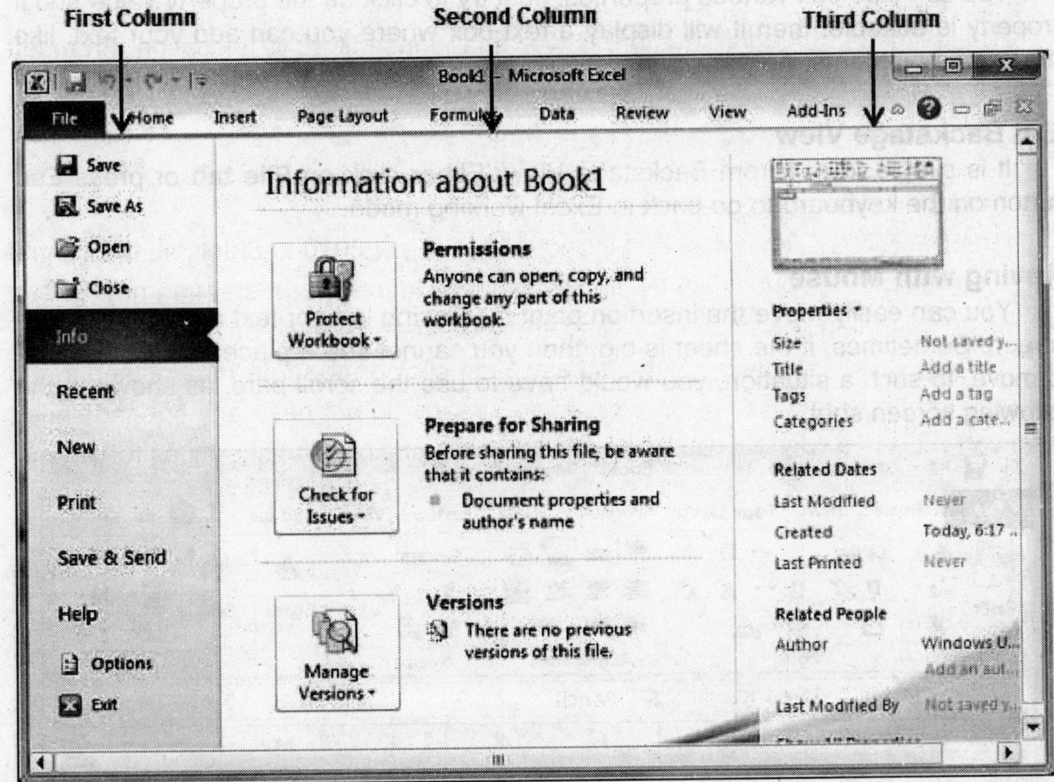

Info: This option will display information about the opened sheet.

Sheet Information

When you click on Info option available in the first column, it displays the following information in the second column of the Backstage View.

Compatibility Mode: If the sheet is not a native Excel 2007/2010 sheet, a Convert button appears here, enabling you to easily update its format. Otherwise, this category does not appear.

Permissions: You can use this option to protect your excel sheet. You can set a password so that nobody can open your sheet, or you can lock the sheet so that nobody can edit your sheet.

Prepare for Sharing: This section highlights important information that you should know about your sheet before you send it to others, such as a record of the edits you made as you developed the sheet.

Versions: If the sheet has been saved several times, you may be able to access previous versions of it from this section.

Sheet Properties

When you click on **Info** option available in the first column, it displays various properties in the third column of the Backstage view. These properties include sheet size, title, tags, categories, etc.

You can also edit various properties. Just try to click on the property value and if property is editable, then it will display a text box where you can add your text, like title, tags, comments, Author.

Exit Backstage View

It is simple to exit from Backstage View. Either click on **File tab** or press **Esc** button on the keyboard to go back in Excel working mode.

Moving with Mouse

You can easily move the insertion point by clicking in your text anywhere on the screen. Sometimes, if the sheet is big, then you cannot see a place where you want to move. In such a situation, you would have to use the scroll bars, as shown in the following screen shot.

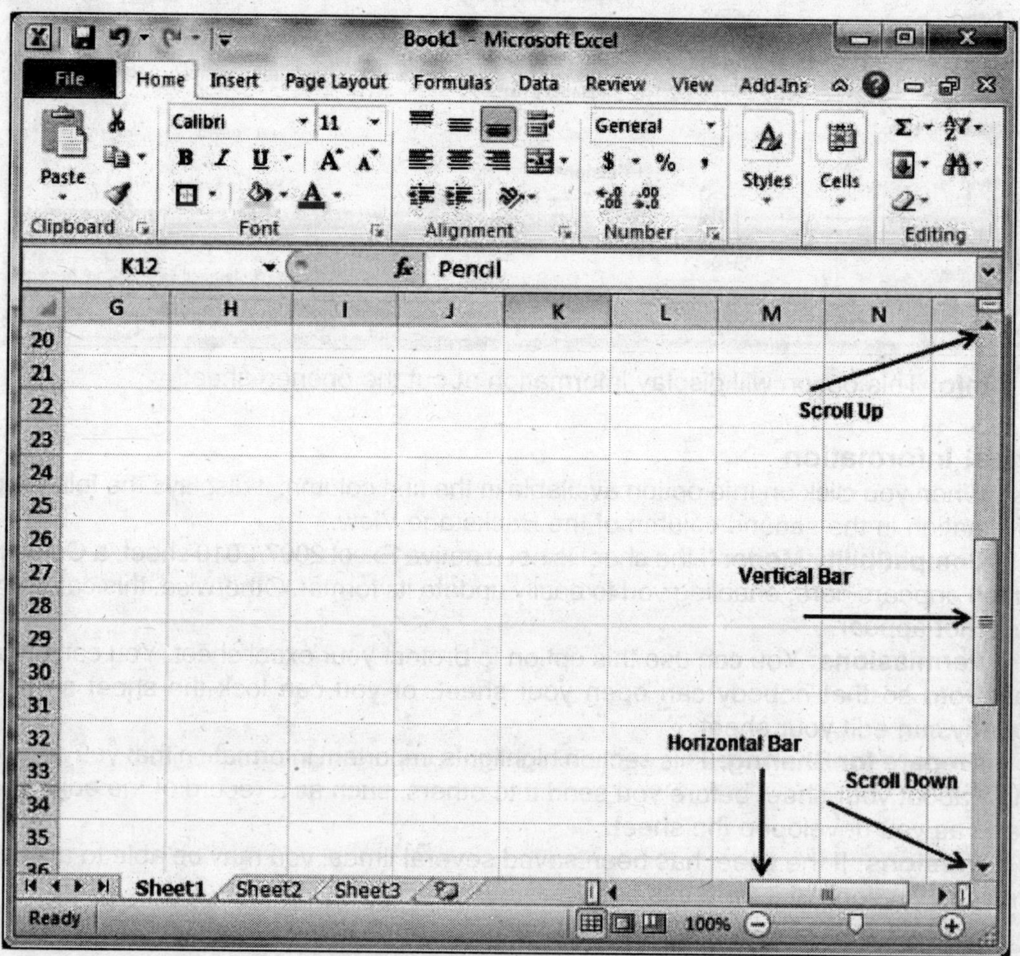

You can scroll your sheet by rolling your mouse wheel, which is the same as clicking the up-arrow or down-arrow buttons in the scroll bar.

□

14
Functions of Spreadsheet and Formatting

Entering Text

Let us see how easy it is to enter text in an Excel sheet. Hope you are aware that when you start a sheet, it displays a new sheet by default as shown below.

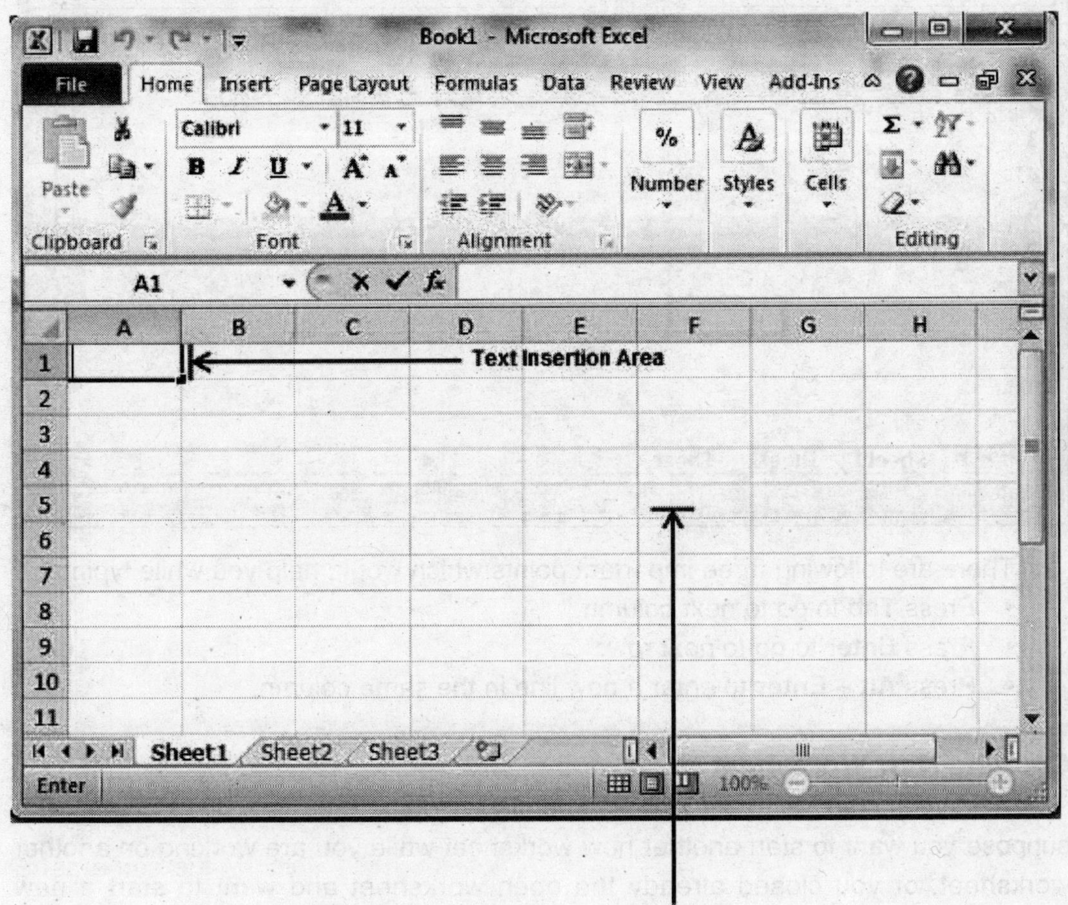

Sheet area is the area where you type your text. The flashing vertical bar is called the **insertion point** and it represents the location where text will appear when you type. When you click on a box, the box gets highlighted. When you double click on the box, flashing vertical bar will come and you can start entering data then.

So, just keep your mouse cursor at the text insertion point and start typing whatever text you would like to type. Here, two words "Hello Excel" have been typed. The text appears to the left of the insertion point.

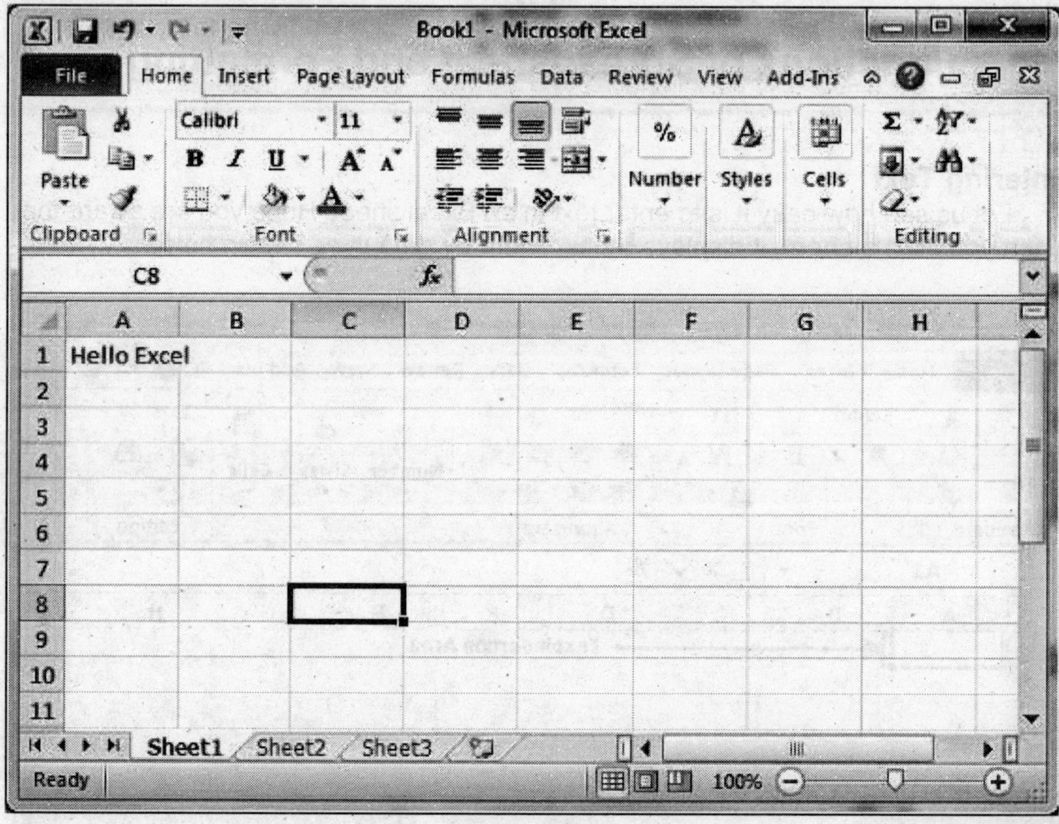

There are following three important points which would help you while typing.

- Press **Tab** to go to next column.
- Press **Enter** to go to next row.
- Press **Alt + Enter** to enter a new line in the same column.

Creating New Worksheet

When you start Microsoft Excel, there always open three new blank sheets. But suppose you want to start another new worksheet while you are working on another worksheet, or you closed already the open worksheet and want to start a new worksheet, here are the steps to create a new worksheet:

1. **Right click** on the **Sheet Name** and select **Insert** option.

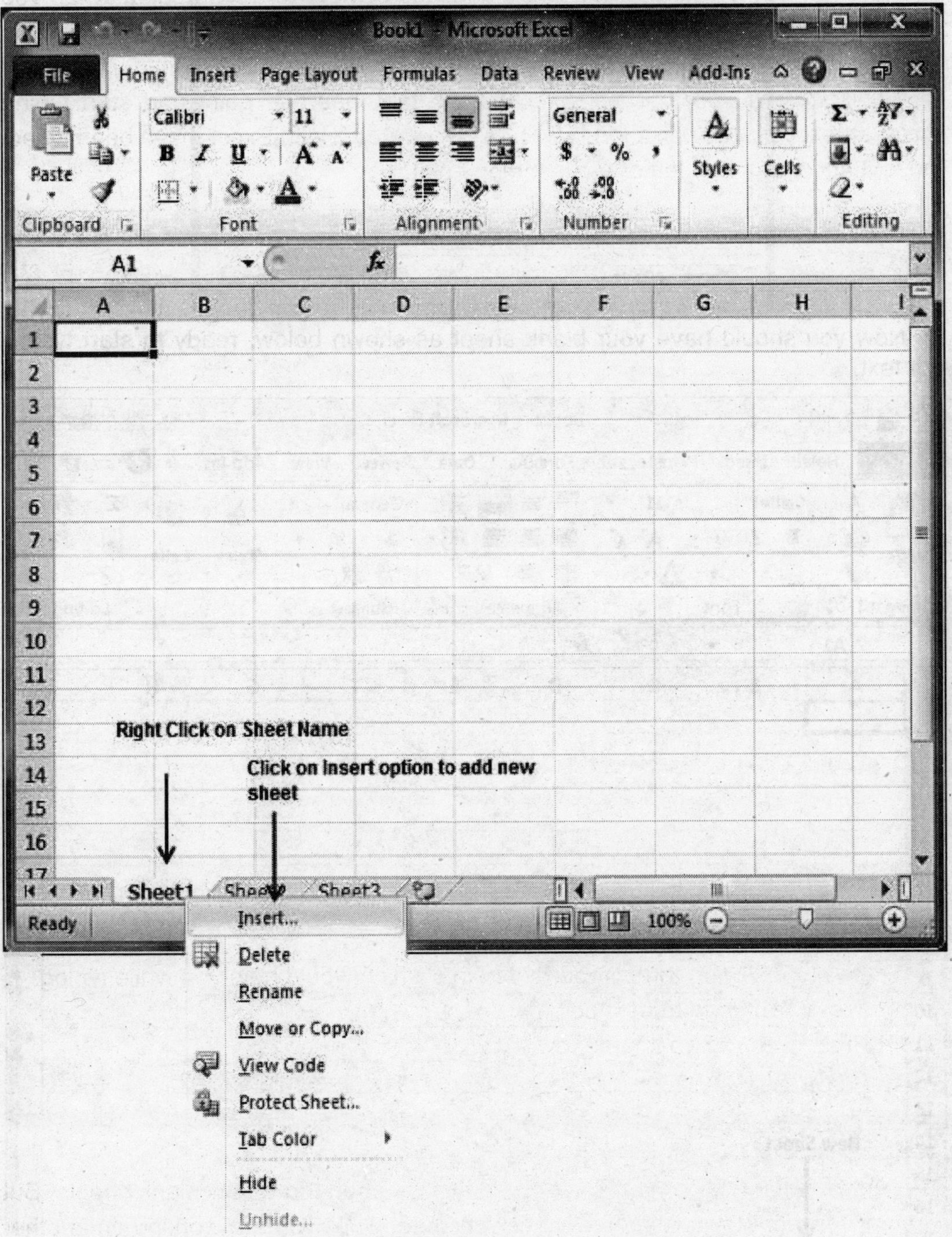

2. Now you will see the **Insert dialog with select Worksheet** option as selected from the general tab. Click on **OK** button.

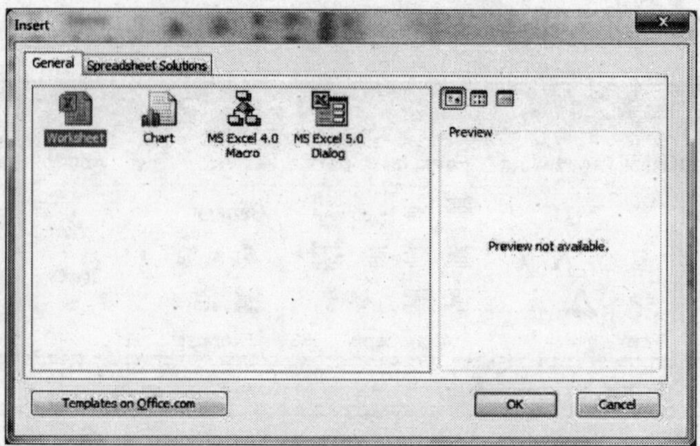

Now you should have your blank sheet as shown below, ready to start typing your text.

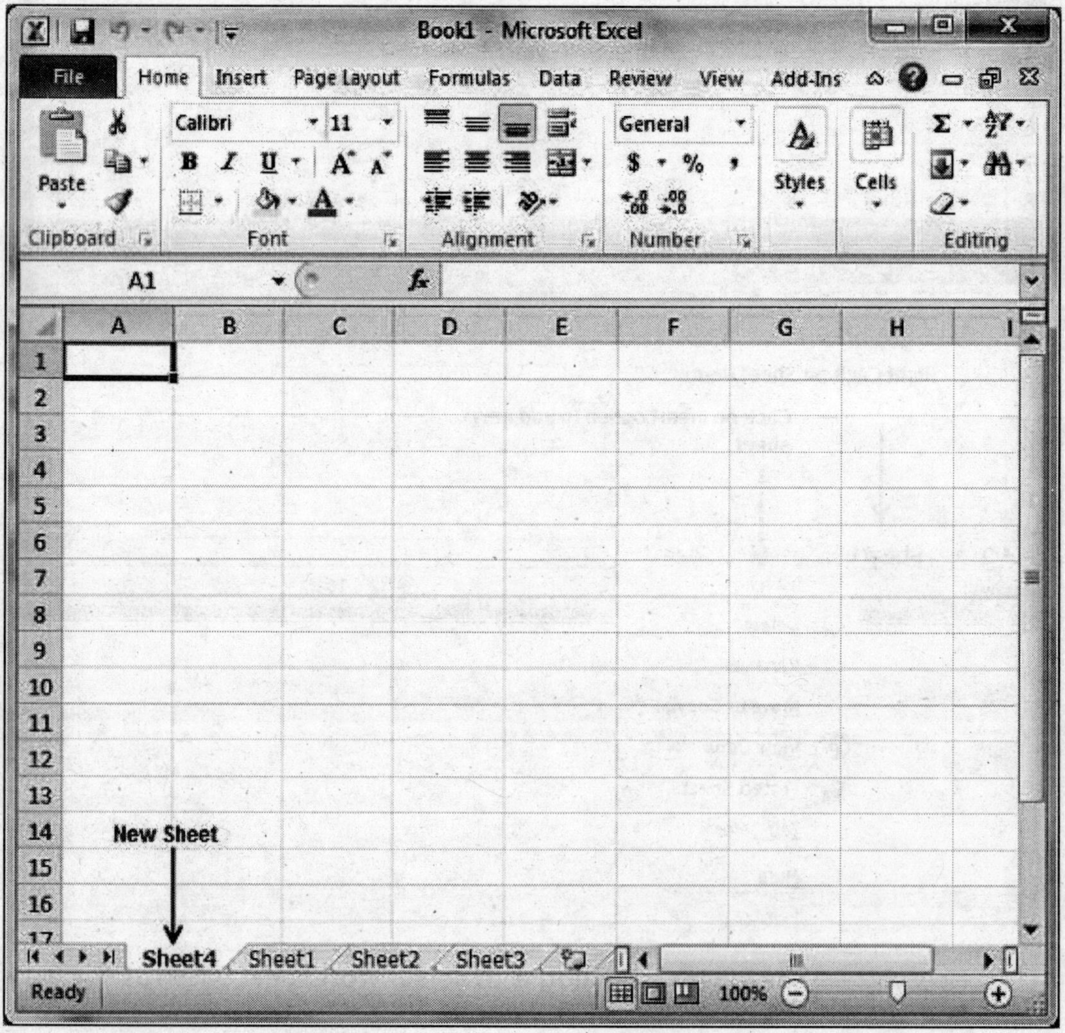

You can use a shortcut to create a blank sheet any time. Try using **Shift + F11** keys and you will see a new blank sheet similar to above sheet is opened.

Saving New Sheet

Once you are done with typing in your new Excel sheet, it is time to save your sheet/workbook to avoid losing work you have done on an Excel sheet.

Following are the steps to save an edited excel sheet:

1. Click on the **File tab** and select **Save As** option.

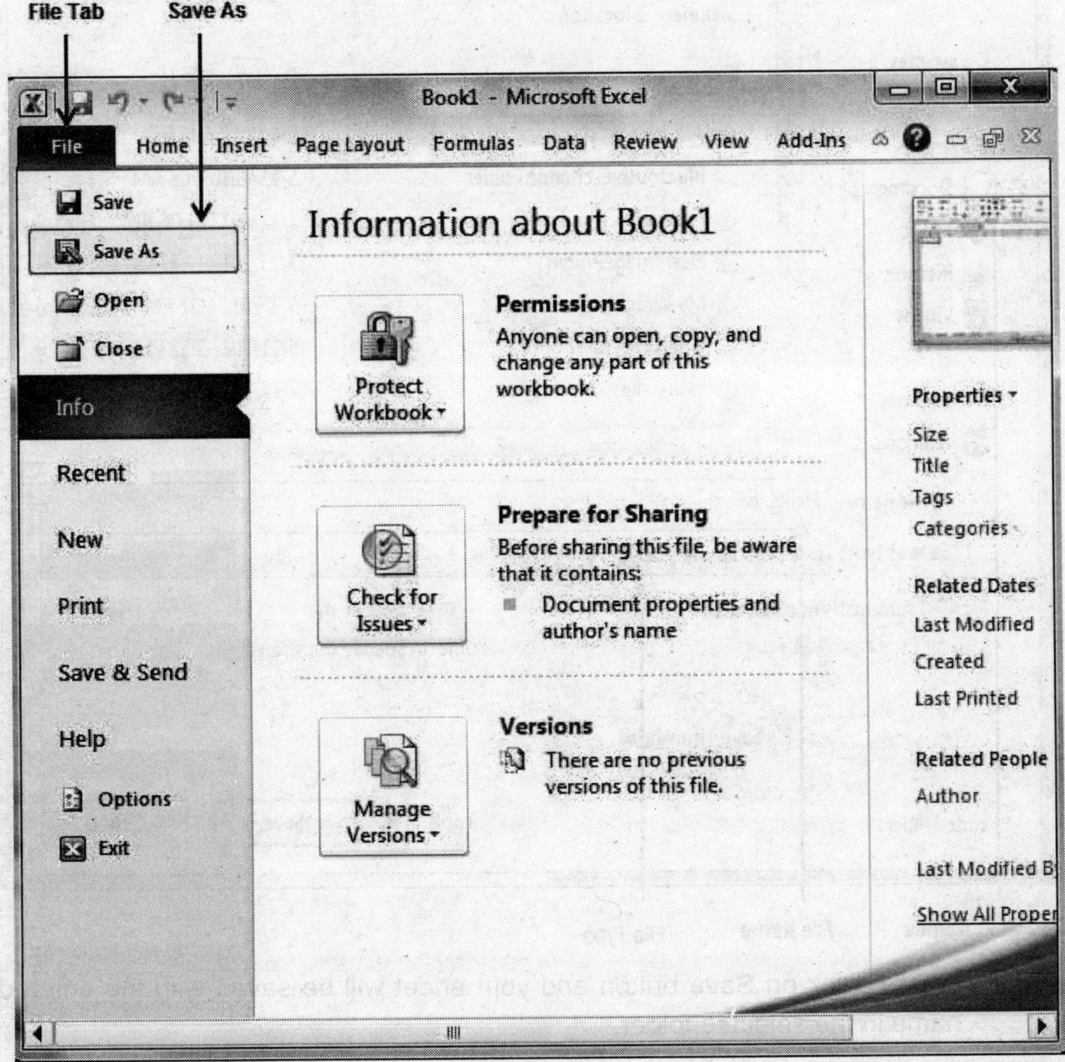

2. Select a folder where you would like to save the sheet, enter file name which you want to give to your sheet and select a **Save As** type. By default it is **.xlsx** format.

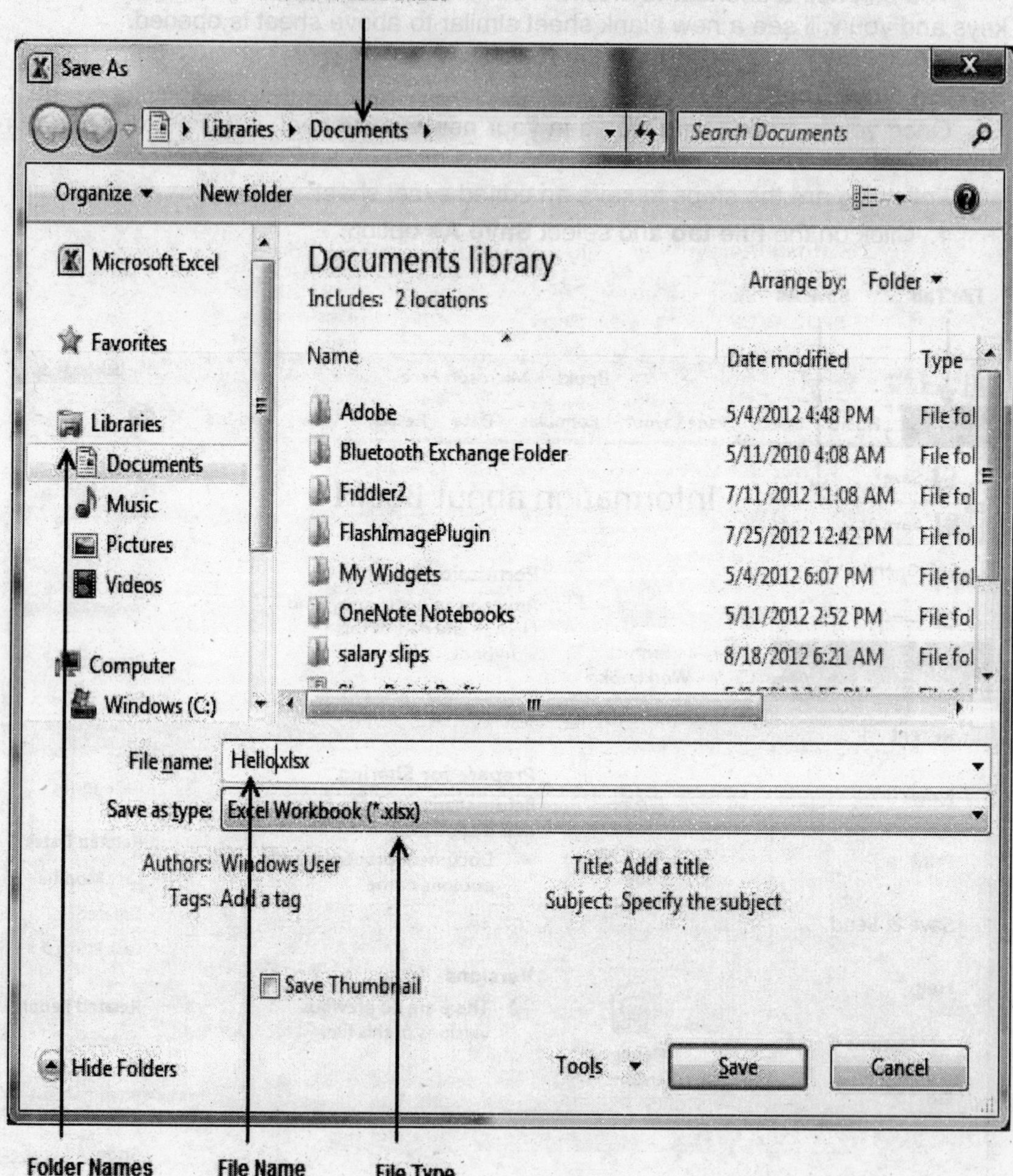

3. Finally, click on **Save** button and your sheet will be saved with the entered name in the selected folder.

Copying a Worksheet

Here are the following steps:

1. **Right click** on the **Sheet Name** and select **Move or Copy** option.

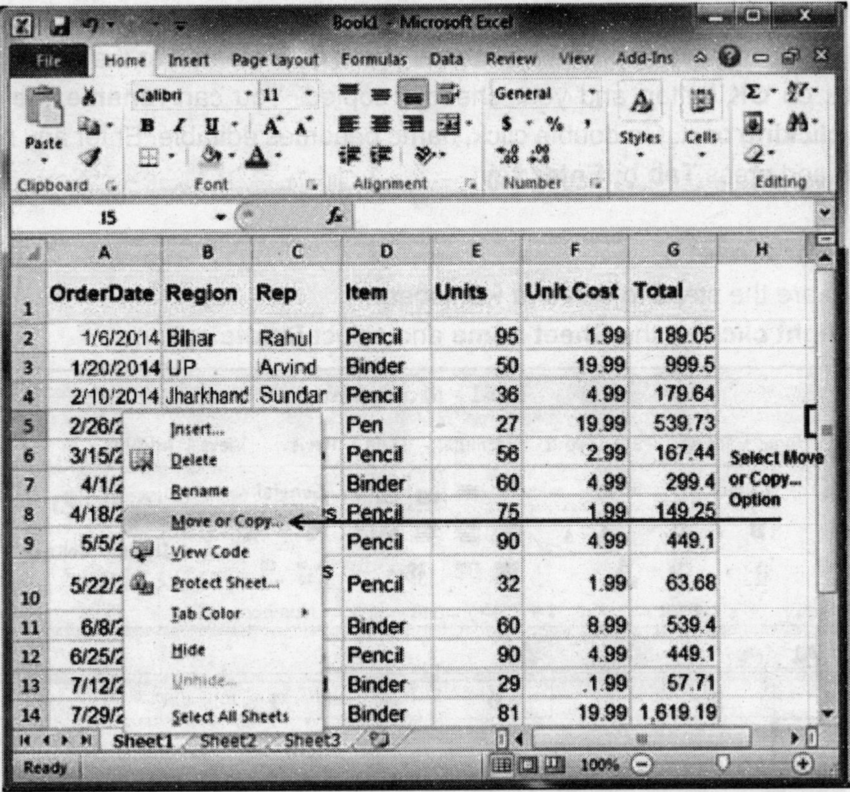

2. Now you will see the **Move or Copy dialog with select Worksheet** option as selected from the general tab. Click on **OK** button.

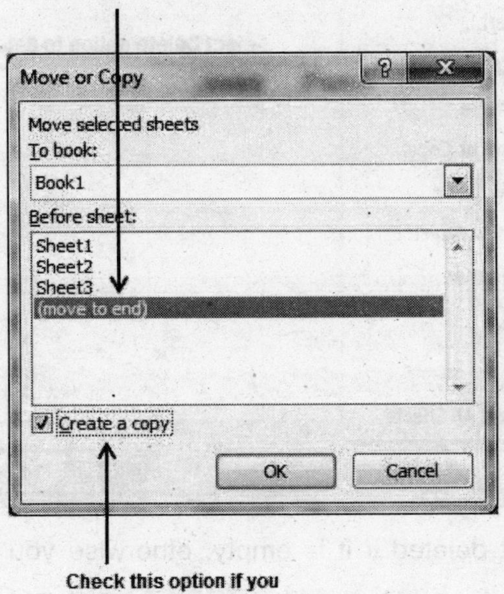

Select **Create a copy** checkbox to create a copy of current sheet and before sheet option as (move to end) so that new sheet gets created at the end.

Click on **OK** button and your sheet is copied. You can **rename the sheet** by **double clicking** on it. On double click, name becomes editable. Enter any name (say Sheet 5) and press **Tab** or **Enter** key.

Delete Worksheet

Here are the steps to delete a worksheet:

1. **Right click** on the **Sheet name** and select **Delete** option.

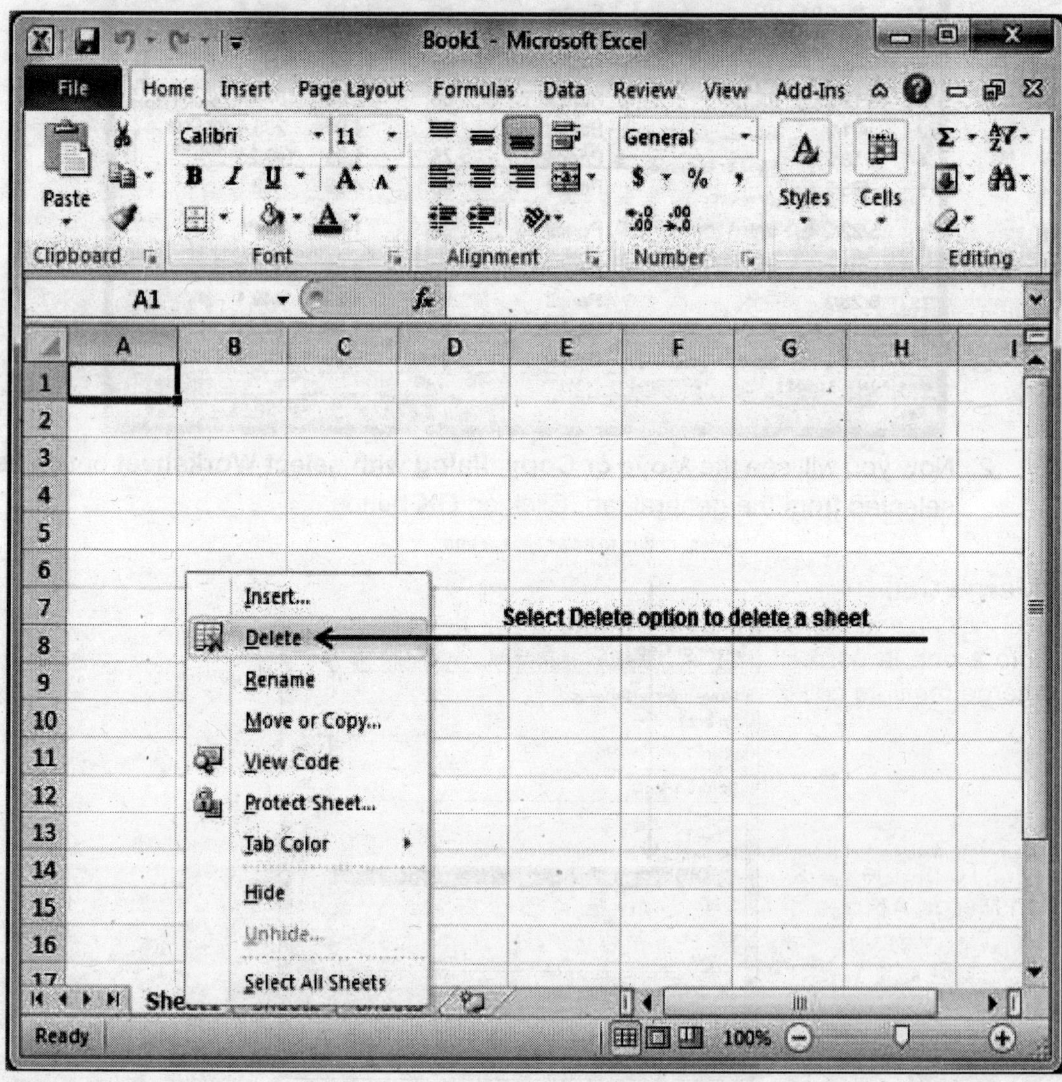

Sheet will get deleted if it is empty, otherwise you will see a confirmation message.

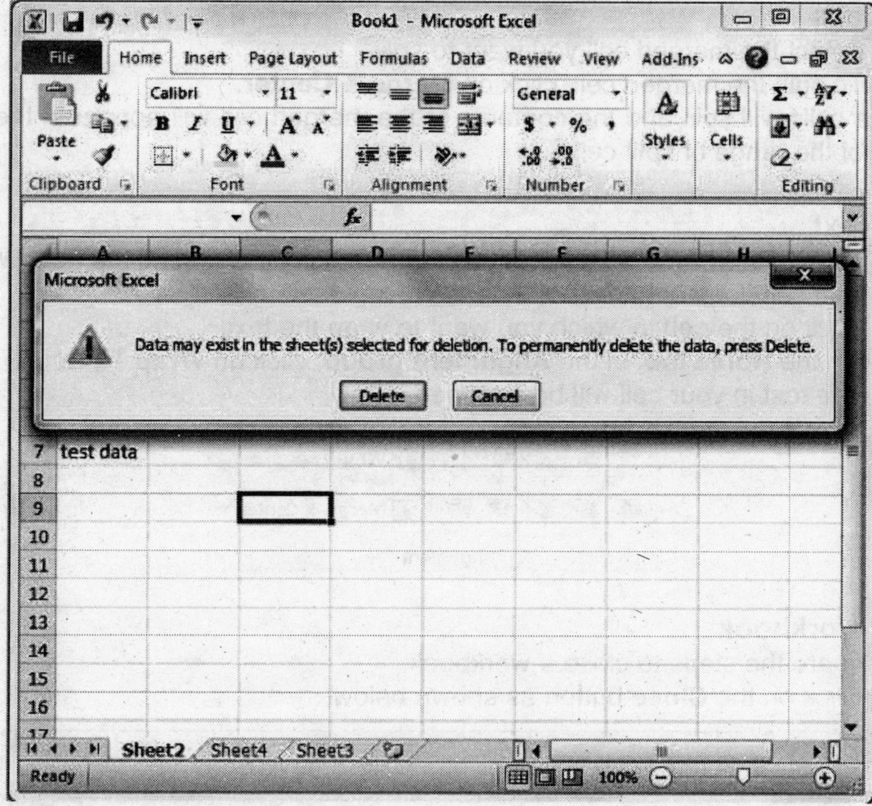

2. Press the **Delete** button.
   Your worksheet will get deleted.

Merge Cells

When you merge two or more adjacent horizontal or vertical cells, the cells convert into a one larger cell that is displayed across multiple columns or rows. When you merge multiple cells, the contents of only one cell appear in the merged cell.

To merge cells only, click on the arrow next to **Merge & Center**, and then click on **Merge Across** or **Merge Cells**.

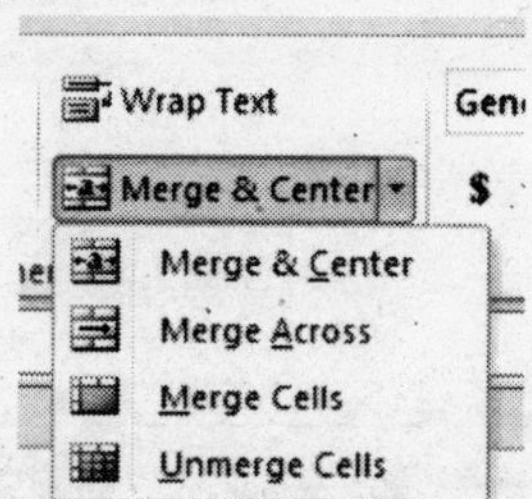

Split Cells

1. Select the merged cell you want to split.
2. To split the merged cell, click on **Merge & Center**.

The cells will split and the contents of the merged cell will appear in the upper-left cell of the range of split cells.

Wrap Text

You can display multiple lines of text inside a cell by wrapping the text. Wrapping the text in a cell does not affect other cells.

1. Click on the **cell** in which you want to wrap the text.
2. On the **Home tab**, in the **Alignment group**, click on **Wrap Text**.
3. The text in your cell will be wrapped.

Close Workbook

Here are the steps to close a workbook:

1. Click on the **Close** button as shown below.

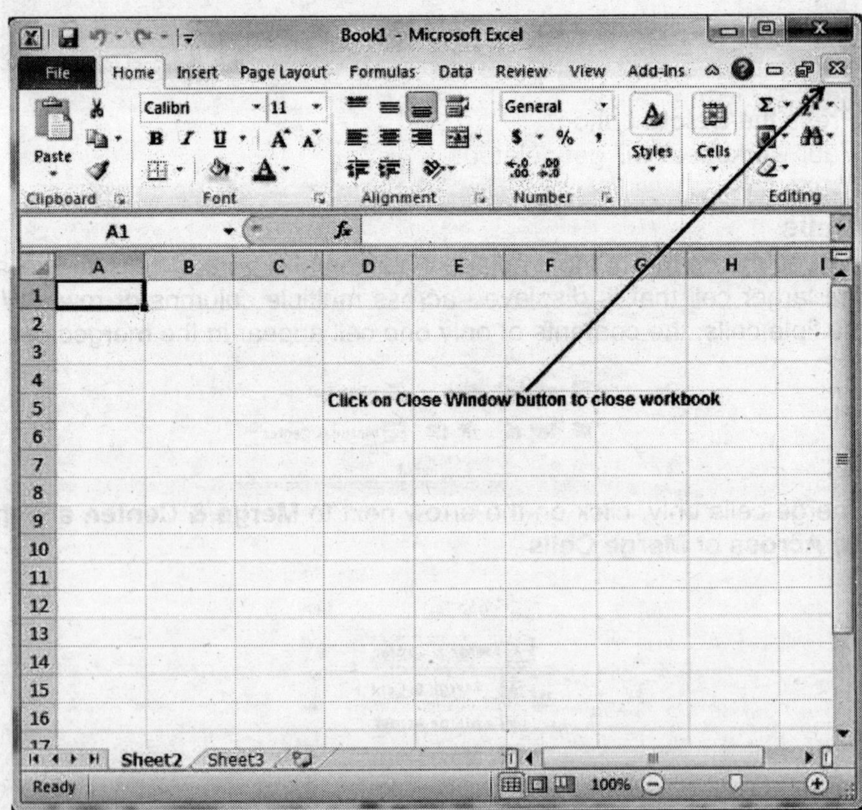

You will see a confirmation message to save the workbook.

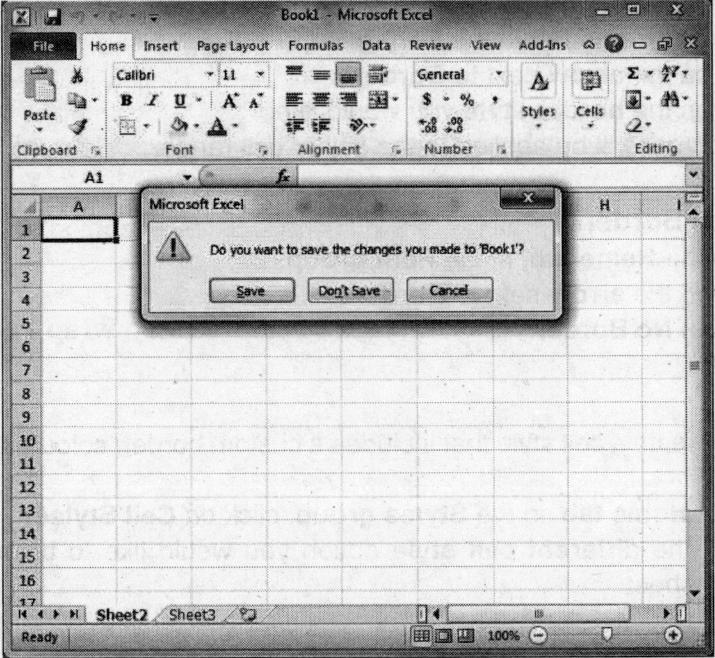

2. Press the **Save** button to save the workbook.
   Now your worksheet will get closed.

Apply Cell Borders

You can quickly add a border around cells or range of cells.

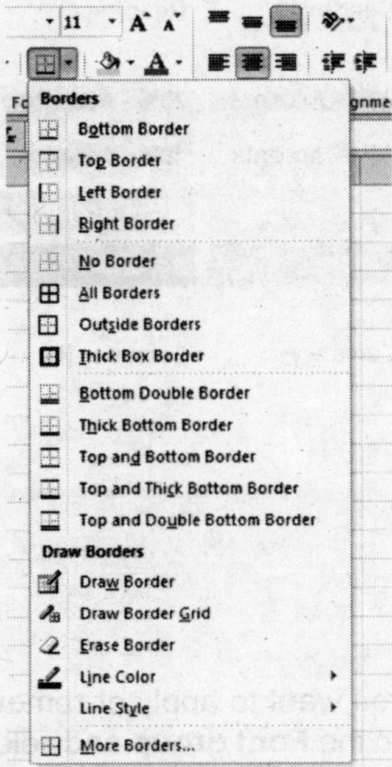

1. On a worksheet, select the cell or range of cells that you want to add a border to, change the border style on, or remove a border from.
2. Go to the **Home tab** in the **Font group**.
3. Click on the **arrow** next to **Borders**.
4. Click on the **border style** you would like.
5. The border will be applied to the cell or cell range.

Remove Cell Borders

1. Go to the **Home tab**, in the **Font group**.
2. Click on the **arrow** next to **Borders**.
3. Click on **No Border**.

Cell Styles

You can create a cell style that includes a custom border, colours and accounting formatting.

1. On the **Home tab**, in the **Styles group**, click on **Cell Styles**.
2. Select the **different cell style** option you would like to be applied to your spreadsheet.

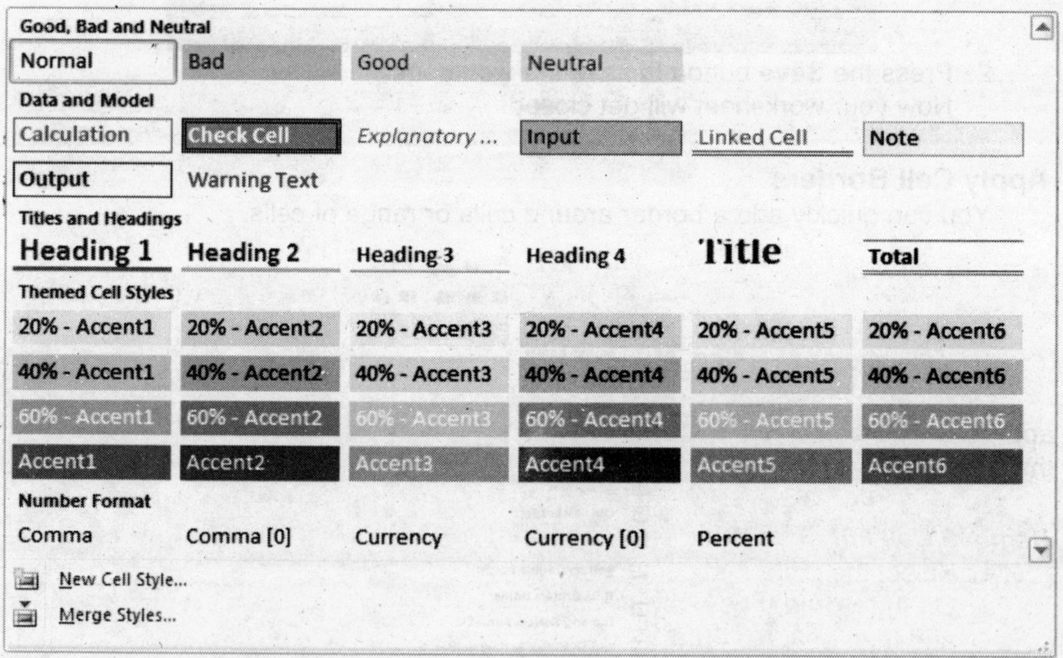

Cell and Text Colouring

Cell Fill

1. Select the cells that you want to apply or remove a fill colour from.
2. Go to the **Home tab**, in the **Font group** and select one of the following options:

- To fill cells with a solid colour, click on the **arrow** next to **Fill Colour**, and then under **Theme Colours** or **Standard Colours**, click on the **colour** that you want.
- To fill cells with a custom colour, click on the **arrow** next to **Fill Colour**, then click on **More Colours**, and then in the **Colours dialog box**, select the colour that you want.
- To apply the most recently selected colour, click on **Fill Colour**.

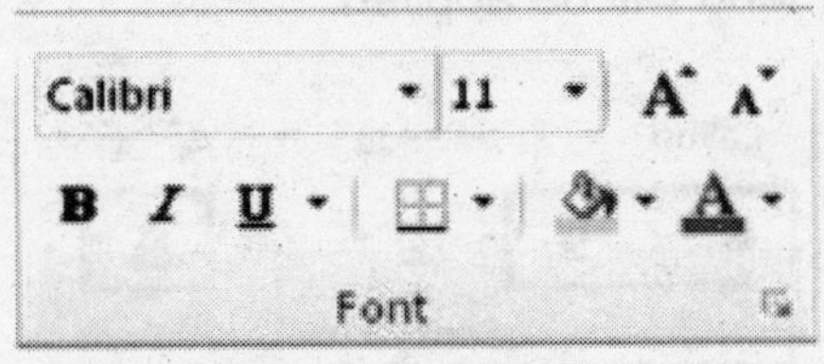

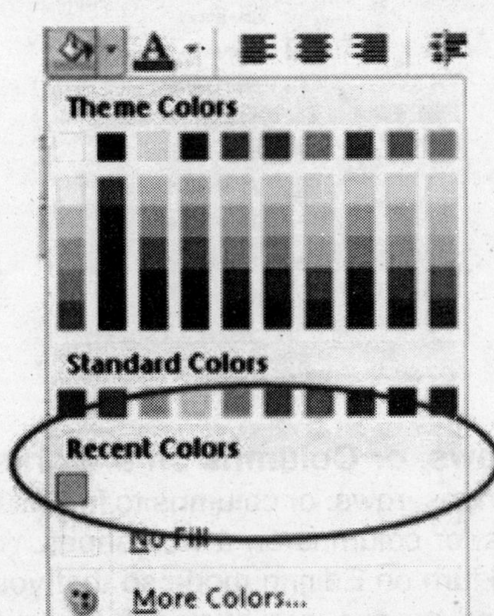

Microsoft Excel saves your 10 most recently selected custom colours. To quickly apply one of these colours, click on the **arrow** next to **Fill Colour**, and then click on the colour that you want under **Recent Colours**.

Remove Cell Fill

1. Select the **cells** that contain a **fill colour** or **fill pattern**.
2. On the **Home tab**, in the **Font group**, click on the **arrow** next to **Fill Colour**, and then click **No Fill**.

Text Colour

1. Select the **cell, range of cells, text**, or **characters** that you want to format with a different text colour.
2. On the **Home tab**, in the **Font group** select one of the following options.
   - To apply the most recently selected text colour, click on **Font Colour**.
   - To change the text colour, click on the **arrow** next to **Font Colour**, and

then under **Theme Colours** or **Standard Colours**, click on the colour that you want to use.

Bold, Underline and Italics Text

1. Select the **cell, range of cells**, or **text**.
2. Go to the **Home tab**, in the **Font group**.
3. Click on the **Bold** (**B**), **Italics** (**I**), or **Underline** (**U**) commands.
4. The selected command will be applied.

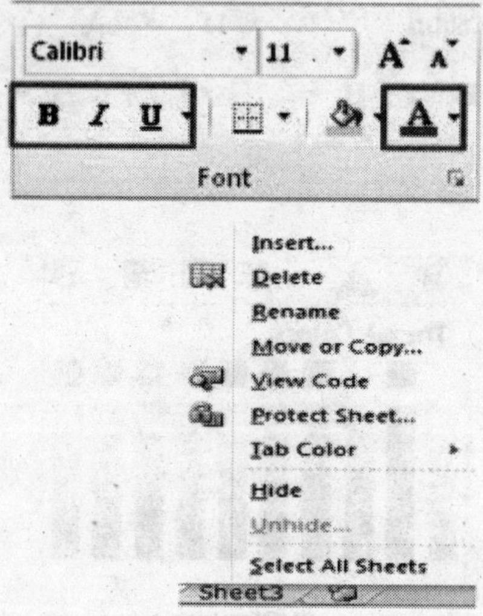

Select Cells, Ranges, Rows, or Columns on a Worksheet

You can select cells, ranges, rows, or columns to format the data in the selection, or to insert other cells, rows, or columns on a worksheet. You can also select all or part of the cell contents and turn on Editing mode so that you can modify the data.

You can select cells and ranges in a Microsoft Excel table just as you would select them in a worksheet, but selecting table rows and columns is different from selecting worksheet rows and columns.

To Select a Single Cell

Click on the cell, or press the arrow keys to move to the cell.

To Select a Range of Cells

Click on the first cell in the range, and then drag to the last cell, or hold down **SHIFT** while you press the arrow keys to extend the selection.

You can also select the first cell in the range, and then press **F8** to extend the selection by using the arrow keys. To stop extending the selection, press **F8** again.

To Select a Large Range of Cells

Click on the first cell in the range, and then hold down **SHIFT** while you click the last cell in the range. You can scroll to make the last cell visible.

To Select a Large Range of Cells Without Scrolling

Click on the first cell in the range to select it, and then click on the **Name** box at the left end of the formula bar.

To Select a Name box

Type the cell reference of the last cell in the range that you want to be selected, and then hold down **SHIFT** while you press **ENTER**.

- **To select All cells on a worksheet**

Click on the **Select All** button.

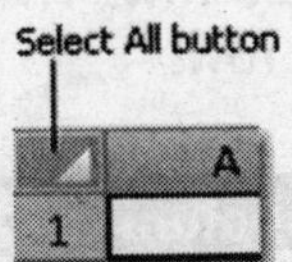

To select the entire worksheet, you can also press **CTRL+A**.

- **To select an entire row or column**

Click on the row or column heading.

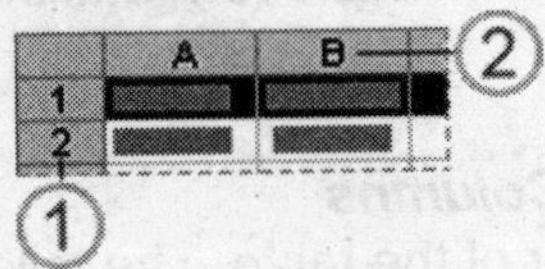

1. Row heading
2. Column heading

You can also select cells in a row or column by selecting the first cell and then pressing **CTRL+SHIFT+ARROW** key (RIGHT ARROW or LEFT ARROW for rows, UP ARROW or DOWN ARROW for columns).

To Select the First or Last Cell in a Row or Column

Select a cell in the row or column, and then press **CTRL+ARROW** key (RIGHT ARROW or LEFT ARROW for rows, UP ARROW or DOWN ARROW for columns).

To Select the First or Last Cell on a Worksheet or in a Table

Press **CTRL+HOME** to select the first cell on the worksheet or in an Excel list.

Press **CTRL+END** to select the last cell on the worksheet or in an Excel list that contains data or formatting.

To Select Rows and Columns in a Table

You can select cells and ranges in a table just as you would select them in a worksheet, but selecting table rows and columns is different from selecting worksheet rows and columns.

To Select a Table Column with or without Table Headers

Click the top edge of the column header or the column in the table. The following selection arrow appears and indicates that clicking selects the column.

You can also click anywhere in the table column, and then press **CTRL+SPACEBAR**, or you can click on the first cell in the table column, and then press **CTRL+SHIFT+DOWN ARROW**.

To Select a Table Row

Click on the left border of the table row. The following selection arrow appears, and indicates that clicking selects the row.

You can click on the first cell in the table row, and then press **CTRL+SHIFT+RIGHT ARROW**.

To Select all Table Rows and Columns

Click on the upper-left corner of the table. The following selection arrow appears, and indicates that clicking selects the table data in the entire table.

Click on the upper-left corner of the table two times to select the whole table, including the table headers.

You can also click anywhere in the table, and then press **CTRL+A** to select all table data in the table, or you can click the upper-left most cell in the table, and then press **CTRL+SHIFT+END**.

Press **CTRL+A** two times to select the whole table, including the table headers.

Set a Column to a Specific Width

1. Select the column or columns that you want to change.
2. On the **Home** tab, in the **Cells** group, click on **Format**.

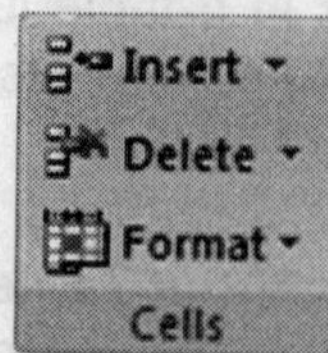

3. Under **Cell Size**, click on **Column Width**.
4. In the **Column width** box, type the value that you want.

Change the Column Width to Automatically Fit the Contents (Auto Fit)

1. Select the column or columns that you want to change.
2. On the **Home** tab, in the **Cells** group, click on **Format**.

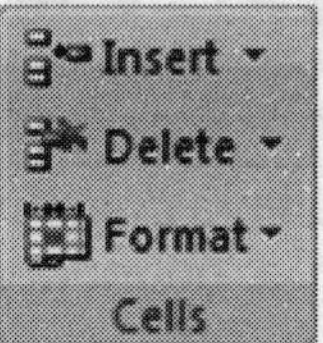

3. Under **Cell Size**, click on **AutoFit Column Width**.

Match the Column Width to Another Column

1. Select a cell in the column that has the width that you want to use.
2. On the **Home** tab, in the **Clipboard** group, click on **Copy**.

(To use the keyboard shortcut, you can also select a cell in the column that has the width you want to use, and then press **CTRL+C**.)

3. Right-click on a cell in the target column, point to **Paste Special**, and then click on the **Keep Source Columns Widths** button.

Change the Default Width for All Columns on a Worksheet or Workbook

The value for the default column width indicates the average number of characters of the standard font that fit in a cell. You can specify a different number for the default column width for a worksheet or workbook.

1. Do one of the following:
   - To change the default column width for a worksheet, click on its sheet tab.
   - To change the default column width for the entire workbook, right-click on a sheet tab, and then click on **Select All Sheets** on the shortcut menu.

2. On the **Home** tab, in the **Cells** group, click on **Format**.

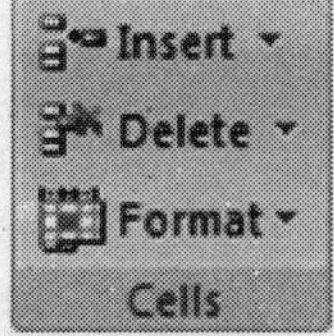

3. Under **Cell Size**, click on **Default Width**.
4. In the **Standard column width** box, type a new measurement.

Change the Width of Columns by using the Mouse

1. Do one of the following:

- To change the width of one column, drag the boundary on the right side of the column heading until the column is the width that you want.

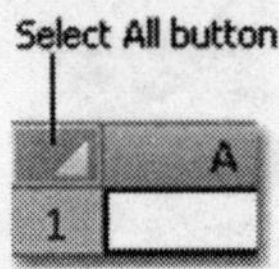

- To change the width of multiple columns, select the columns that you want to change, and then drag a boundary to the right of a selected column heading.
- To change the width of columns to fit the contents, select the column or columns that you want to change, and then double-click the boundary to the right of a selected column heading.
- To change the width of all columns on the worksheet, click the Select All button, and then drag the boundary of any column heading.

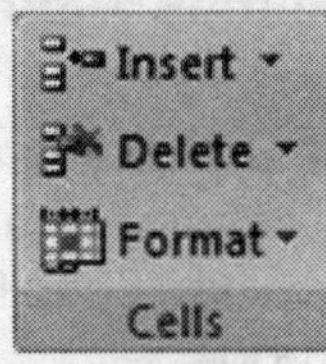

Set a Row to a Specific Height

1. Select the row or rows that you want to change.
2. On the **Home** tab, in the **Cells** group, click on **Format**.

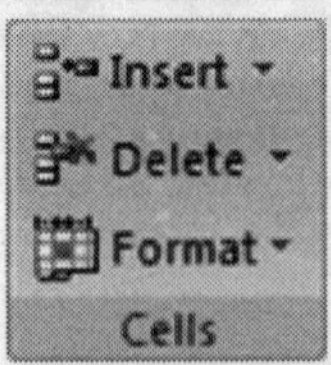

3. Under **Cell Size**, click on **Row Height**.
4. In the **Row height** box, type the value that you want.

Change the Row Height to Fit the Contents

1. Select the row or rows that you want to change.
2. On the **Home** tab, in the **Cells** group, click on **Format**.

3. Under **Cell Size**, click on **AutoFit Row Height**.

Change the Height of Rows by using the Mouse

1. Do one of the following:
   - To change the row height of one row, drag the boundary below the row heading until the row is the height that you want.

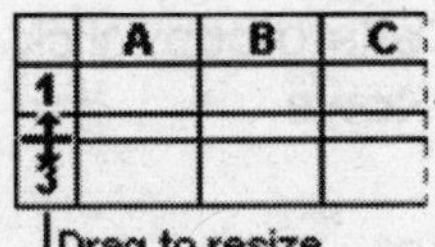

- To change the row height of multiple rows, select the rows that you want to change, and then drag the boundary below one of the selected row headings.
- To change the row height for all rows on the worksheet, click the **Select All** button, and then drag the boundary below any row heading.

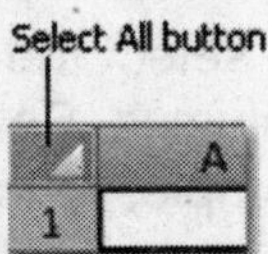

- To change the row height to fit the contents, double-click on the boundary below the row heading.

Insert Blank Cells on a Worksheet

1. Select the cell or the range of cells where you want to insert the new blank cells. Select the same number of cells as you want to insert. For example, to insert five blank cells, select five cells.
2. On the **Home** tab, in the **Cells** group, click on the arrow next to **Insert**, and then click on **Insert Cells**.

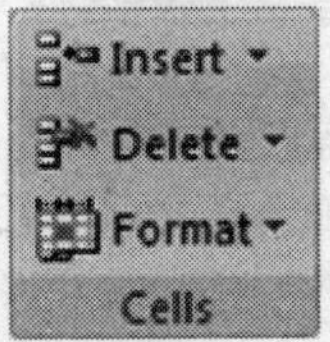

3. In the **Insert** dialog box, click on the direction in which you want to shift the surrounding cells.

Insert Rows on a Worksheet

1. Do one of the following:
   - To insert a single row, select either the whole row or a cell in the row above which you want to insert the new row. For example, to insert a new row above row 5, click a cell in row 5.
   - To insert multiple rows, select the rows above which you want to insert rows. Select the same number of rows as you want to insert. For example, to insert three new rows, you select three rows.
   - To insert nonadjacent rows, hold down **Ctrl** while you select nonadjacent rows.

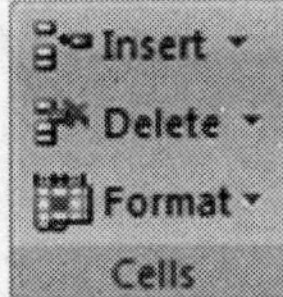

2. On the **Home** tab, in the **Cells** group, click on the arrow next to **Insert**, and then click on **Insert Sheet Rows**.

Insert Columns on a Worksheet

1. Do one of the following:
   - To insert a single column, select the column or a cell in the column immediately to the right of where you want to insert the new column. For example, to insert a new column to the left of column B, click a cell in column B.
   - To insert multiple columns, select the columns immediately to the right of where you want to insert columns. Select the same number of columns as you want to insert. For example, to insert three new columns, you select three columns.
   - To insert nonadjacent columns, hold down **Ctrl** while you select nonadjacent columns.
2. On the **Home** tab, in the **Cells** group, click on the arrow next to **Insert**, and then click on **Insert Sheet Columns**.

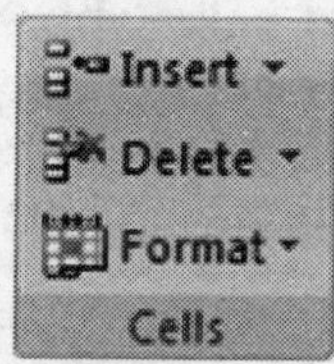

Delete Cells, Rows, or Columns

1. Select the cells, rows, or columns that you want to delete.
2. On the **Home** tab, in the **Cells** group, click on the arrow next to **Delete**, and then do one of the following:

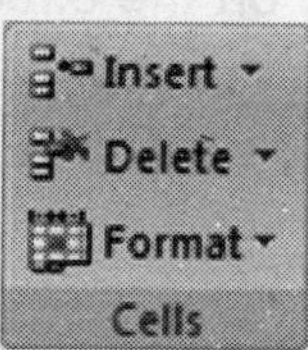

   - To delete selected cells, click on **Delete** Cells.
   - To delete selected rows, click on **Delete Sheet Rows**.
   - To delete selected columns, click on **Delete Sheet Columns**.

Hide One or More Rows or Columns

1. Select the rows or columns that you want to hide.
2. On the **Home** tab, in the **Cells** group, click on **Format**.

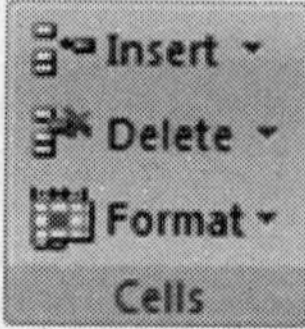

3. Do one of the following:
   - Under **Visibility**, point to **Hide & Unhide**, and then click on **Hide Rows** or **Hide Columns**.
   - Under **Cell Size**, click on **Row Height** or **Column Width**, and then type **0** in the **Row Height** or **Column Width** box.

Display One or More Hidden Rows or Columns

1. Do one of the following:
   - To display hidden rows, select the row above and below the rows that you want to unhide.
   - To display hidden columns, select the columns adjacent to either side of the columns that you want to unhide.
   - To display the first hidden row or column on a worksheet, select it by typing **A1** in the **Name Box** next to the formula bar.
2. On the **Home** tab, in the **Cells** group, click on **Format**.

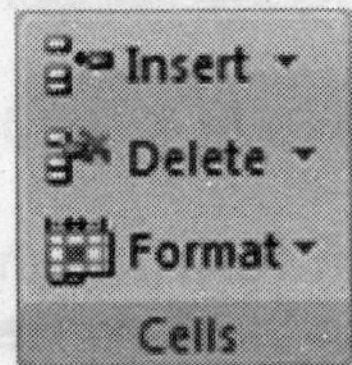

3. Do one of the following:
   - Under **Visibility**, point to **Hide & Unhide**, and then click on **Unhide Rows** or Unhide **Columns.**
   - Under **Cell Size**, click on **Row Height** or **Column Width**, and then type the value that you want in the **Row Height** or **Column Width** box.

Display all Hidden Rows and Columns at the Same Time

1. To select all cells on a worksheet, do one of the following:
   - Click the Select All button.

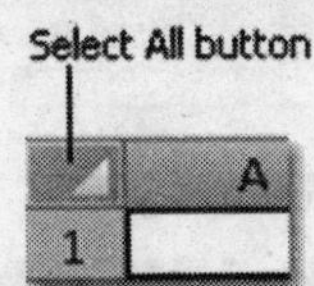

   - Press **Ctrl+A**
2. On the **Home** tab, in the **Cells** group, click on **Format**.

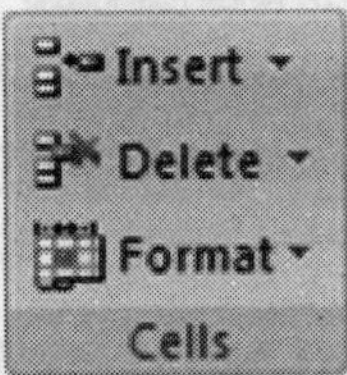

3. Do one of the following:
   - Under **Visibility**, point to **Hide & Unhide**, and then click on **Unhide Rows** or **Unhide Columns**.

- Under **Cell Size**, click **Row Height** or **Column Width**, and then type the value that you want in the **Row Height** or **Column Width** box.

Unhide the First Row or Column of the Worksheet

1. To select the first hidden row or column on the worksheet, do one of the following:
   - In the **Name Box** next to the formula bar, type **A1**.
   - On the **Home** tab, in the **Editing** group, click on **Find & Select**, and then click on **Go To**. In the **Reference** box, type **A1**, and then click on **OK**.
2. On the **Home** tab, in the **Cells** group, click on **Format**.

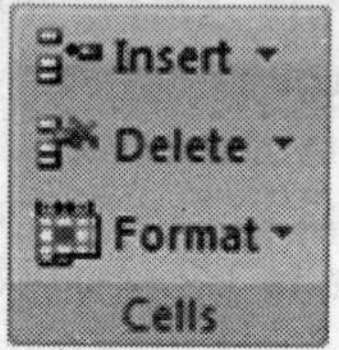

3. Do one of the following:
   - Under **Visibility**, point to **Hide & Unhide**, and then click on **Unhide Rows** or **Unhide Columns**.
   - Under **Cell Size**, click on **Row Height** or **Column Width**, and then type the value that you want in the **Row Height** or **Column Width** box.

To Change the Font

1. Select the cells you want to modify.
2. Click on the **drop-down arrow** next to the **Font** command on the **Home** tab. The font drop-down menu appears.
3. Move your mouse over the various fonts. A live preview of the font will appear in the worksheet.

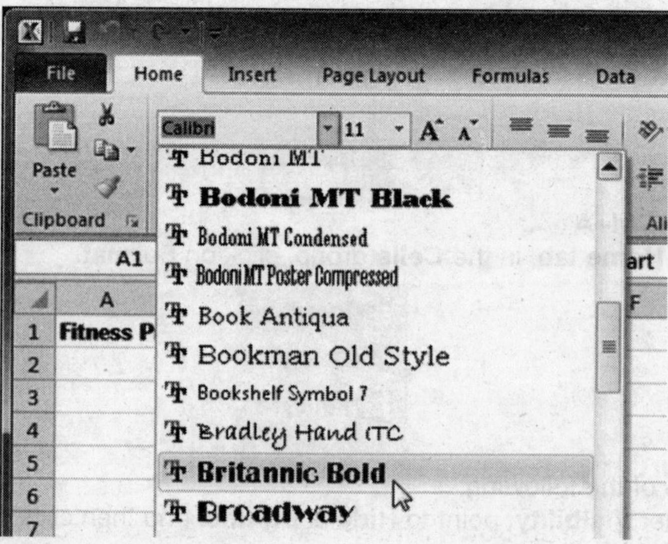

4. Select the font you want to use.

To Change the Font Size

1. Select the cells you want to modify.
2. Click on the **drop-down arrow** next to the **font size** command on the **Home** tab. The font size drop-down menu appears.
3. Move your mouse over the various font sizes. A live preview of the font size will appear in the worksheet.

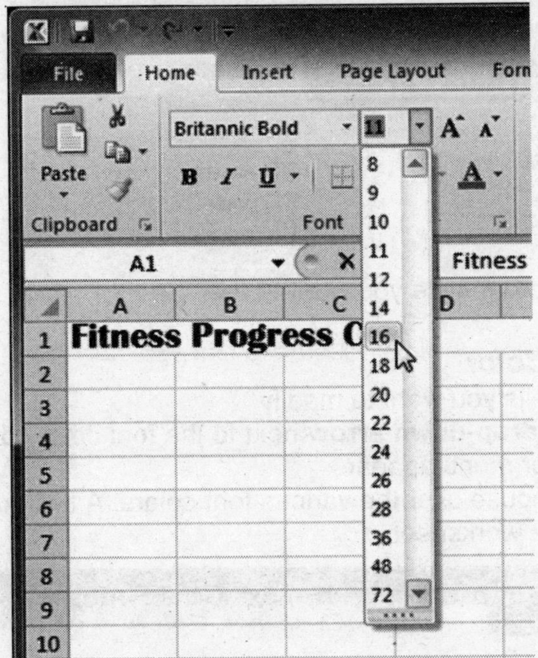

4. Select the font size you want to use.

To use the Bold, Italic and Underline Commands

1. Select the cells you want to modify.
2. Click on the **Bold**, *Italic*, or Underline command on the **Home** tab.

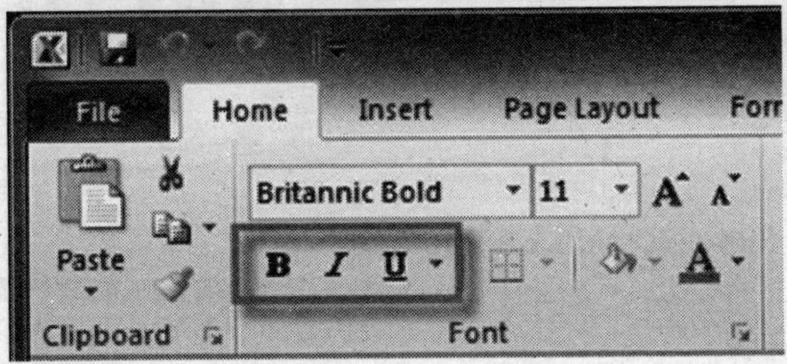

To Add a Border

1. Select the cells you want to modify.
2. Click on the **drop-down arrow** next to the **Borders** command on the **Home** tab. The border drop-down menu appears.

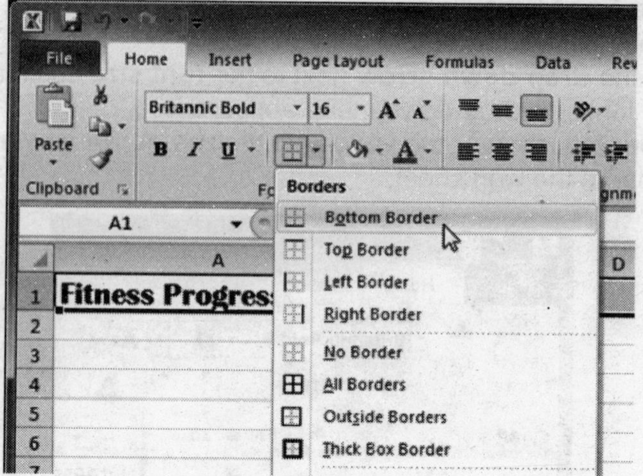

3. Select the border style you want to use.

To Change Font Color

1. Select the cells you want to modify.
2. Click on the **drop-down arrow** next to the font color command on the **Home** tab. The color menu appears.
3. Move your mouse over the various font colors. A live preview of the color will appear in the worksheet.

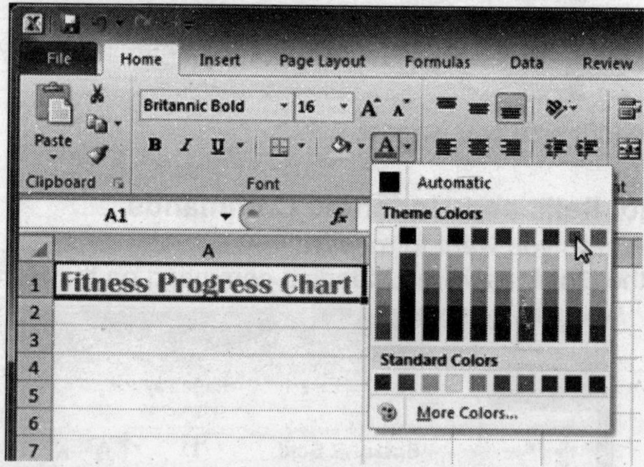

4. Select the font color you want to use.

To Add a Fill Color

1. Select the cells you want to modify.
2. Click the **drop-down arrow** next to the fill color command on the **Home** tab. The color menu appears.
3. Move your cursor over the various fill colors. A live preview of the color will appear in the worksheet.

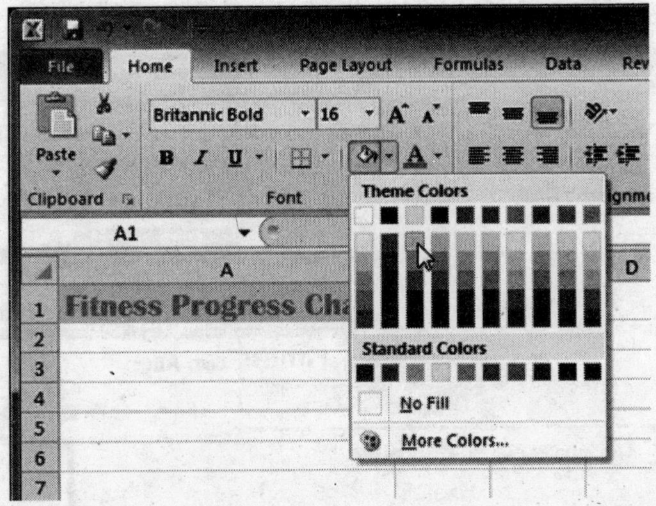

4. Select the fill color you want to use.

To Change Horizontal Text Alignment

1. Select the cells you want to modify.
2. Select one of the three horizontal **Alignment** commands on the **Home** tab.
   - **Align Text Left**: Aligns text to the left of the cell
   - **Center**: Aligns text to the center of the cell
   - **Align Text Right**: Aligns text to the right of the cell

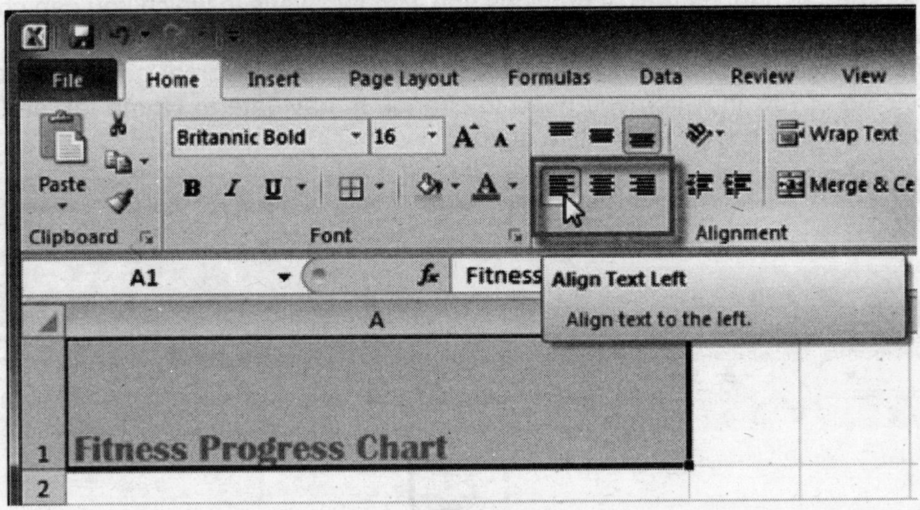

To Change Vertical Text Alignment

1. Select the cells you want to modify.
2. Select one of the three vertical **Alignment** commands on the **Home** tab.
   - **Top Align**: Aligns text to the top of the cell
   - **Middle Align**: Aligns text to the middle of the cell

- **Bottom Align**: Aligns text to the bottom of the cell

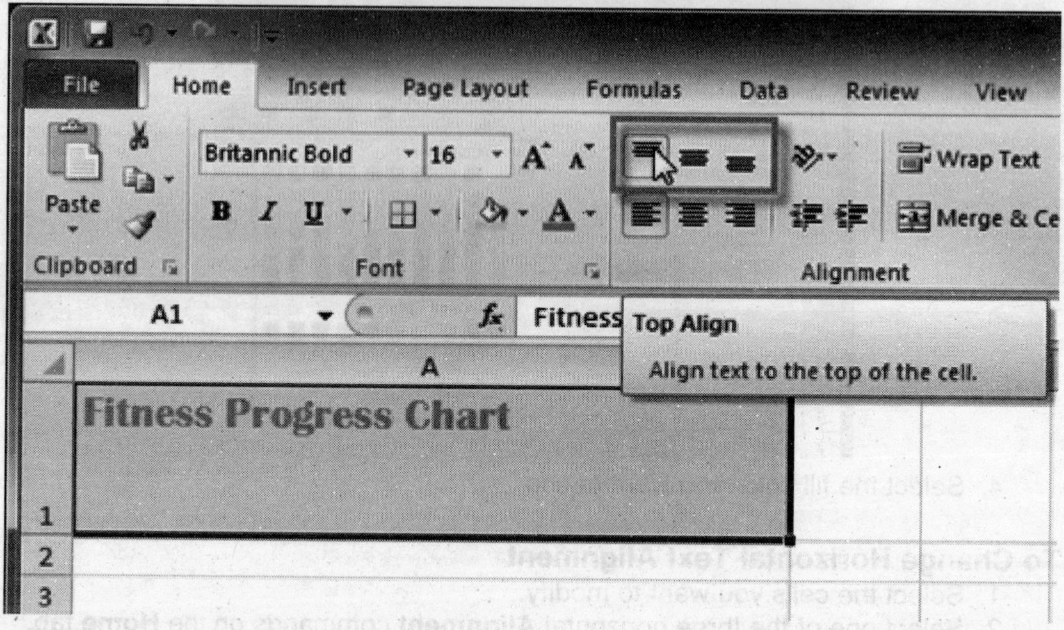

Increase/Decrease Decimal Places

In Excel 2010, you can set (increase/decrease) decimal places according to the required spreadsheet pattern. It provides you with two ways in which you can change the decimal places.

For changing decimal places, i.e. increase/decrease decimal points, select the cell, column or row in which you need to change it, navigate to **Home** tab and from **Numbers** group, click on respective option.

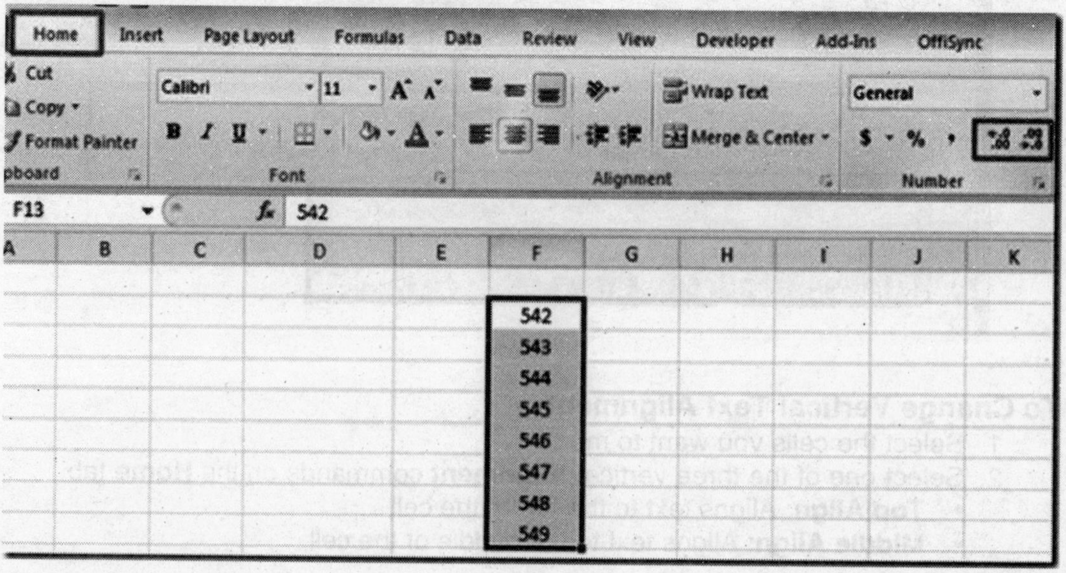

It will change the decimal place in the selected cell(s) as specified.

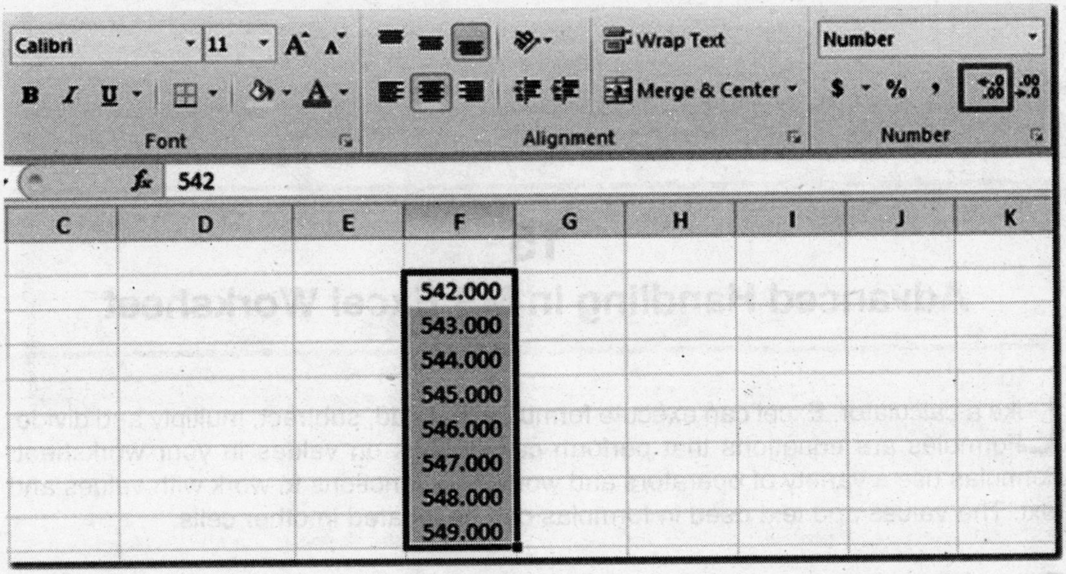

15

Advanced Handling in MS Excel Worksheet

Like a calculator, Excel can execute formulas that add, subtract, multiply and divide. Formulas are equations that perform calculations on values in your worksheet. Formulas use a variety of operators and worksheet functions to work with values and text. The values and text used in formulas can be located in other cells.

Formulas in Excel

Excel uses standard operators for equations, such as a plus sign for addition (+), minus sign for subtraction (–), asterisk for multiplication (*), forward slash for division (/) and caret (^) for exponents.

Always remember that Formulas in Microsoft Excel begin with an equal sign (=).

Addition	+	=5+5
Subtraction	-	=5-5
Multiplication	*	=5*5
Division	/	=5/5
Exponents	^	=5^5

STATISTICAL FUNCTIONS IN EXCEL 2010

Average

To calculate the average of a range of cells, use the **AVERAGE** function.

A3 | fx | =AVERAGE(A1:O1)

	A	B	C	D	E	F	G	H	I	J	K	L	M	N	O	P
1	0	7	8	6	5	9	8	7	4	8	0	3	5	6	8	
2																
3	5.6															
4																

Averageif

To average cells based on one criteria, use the **AVERAGEIF** function.

A3 `=AVERAGEIF(A1:O1,"<>0")`

	A	B	C	D	E	F	G	H	I	J	K	L	M	N	O	P
1	0	7	8	6	5	9	8	7	4	8	0	3	5	6	8	
2																
3	6.46															
4																

Median

To find the median (or middle number), use the **MEDIAN** function.

A3 `=MEDIAN(A1:O1)`

	A	B	C	D	E	F	G	H	I	J	K	L	M	N	O	P
1	0	7	8	6	5	9	8	7	4	8	0	3	5	6	8	
2																
3	6															
4																

Check:

	A	B	C	D	E	F	G	H	I	J	K	L	M	N	O	P
1	0	0	3	4	5	5	6	6	7	7	8	8	8	8	9	

Mode

To find the most frequently occurring number, use the **MODE** function.

A3 `=MODE(A1:O1)`

	A	B	C	D	E	F	G	H	I	J	K	L	M	N	O	P
1	0	7	8	6	5	9	8	7	4	8	0	3	5	6	8	
2																
3	8															
4																

Standard Deviation

To calculate the standard deviation, use the **STEDV** function.

A3 `=STDEV(A1:O1)`

	A	B	C	D	E	F	G	H	I	J	K	L	M	N	O	P
1	0	7	8	6	5	9	8	7	4	8	0	3	5	6	8	
2																
3	2.82															
4																

Min

To find the minimum value, use the **MIN** function.

A3 =MIN(A1:O1)

	A	B	C	D	E	F	G	H	I	J	K	L	M	N	O	P
1	0	7	8	6	5	9	8	7	4	8	0	3	5	6	8	
2																
3	0															
4																

Max

To find the maximum value, use the **MAX** function.

A3 =MAX(A1:O1)

	A	B	C	D	E	F	G	H	I	J	K	L	M	N	O	P
1	0	7	8	6	5	9	8	7	4	8	0	3	5	6	8	
2																
3	9															
4																

Large

To find the third largest number, use the following **LARGE** function.

A3 =LARGE(A1:O1,3)

	A	B	C	D	E	F	G	H	I	J	K	L	M	N	O	P
1	0	7	8	6	5	9	8	7	4	8	0	3	5	6	8	
2																
3	8															
4																

Check:

	A	B	C	D	E	F	G	H	I	J	K	L	M	N	O	P
1	0	0	3	4	5	5	6	6	7	7	8	8	8	8	9	

Small

To find the second smallest number, use the following **SMALL** function.

A3 =SMALL(A1:O1,2)

	A	B	C	D	E	F	G	H	I	J	K	L	M	N	O	P
1	0	7	8	6	5	9	8	7	4	8	0	3	5	6	8	
2																
3	0															
4																

Check:

	A	B	C	D	E	F	G	H	I	J	K	L	M	N	O	P
1	0	0	3	4	5	5	6	6	7	7	8	8	8	8	9	

Define and use Names in Formulas

By using names, you can make your formulas much easier to understand and work on. You can define a name for a cell range, function, constant, or table.

Define a Name for a Cell or Cell Range on a Worksheet

1. Select the cell, range of cells, or nonadjacent selections that you want to name.
2. Click the **Name** box at the left end of the formula bar.

3. Type the name that you want to use to refer to your selection. Names can be up to 255 characters in length.
4. Press **Enter**.

Define a Name by using a Selection of Cells in the Worksheet

You can convert existing row and column labels to names.

1. Select the range that you want to name, including the row or column labels.
2. On the **Formulas** tab, in the **Defined Names** group, click on **Create from Selection**.

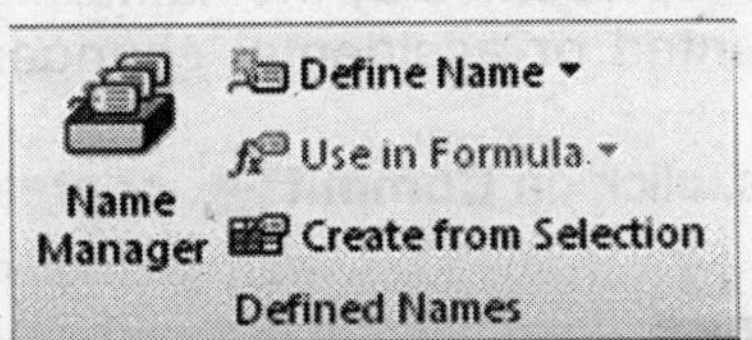

3. In the **Create Names from Selection** dialog box, designate the location that contains the labels by selecting the **Top row**, **Left column**, **Bottom row**, or **Right column** check box.

Define a Name by using the New Name Dialog Box

1. On the **Formulas** tab, in the **Defined Names** group, click on **Define Name**.

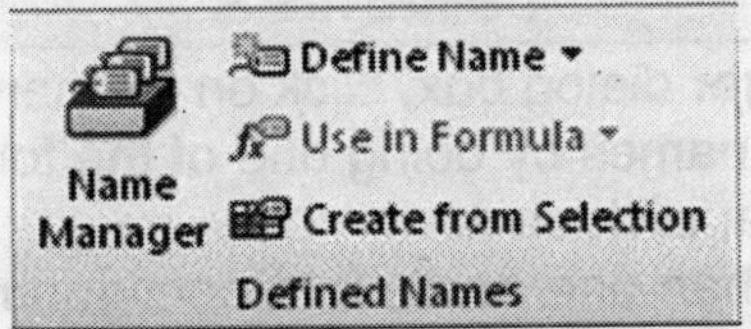

2. In the **New Name** dialog box, in the **Name** box, type the name that you want to use for your reference.
3. To specify the scope of the name, in the **Scope** drop-down list box, select **Workbook** or the name of a worksheet in the workbook.
4. Optionally, in the **Comment** box, enter a descriptive comment up to 255 characters.

5. In the **Refers to** box, do one of the following:
    - To enter a cell reference, type the cell reference.
    - To enter a constant, type = (equal sign) and then type the constant value.
    - To enter a formula, type = and then type the formula.
    - To finish and return to the worksheet, click on **OK**.

Change a Name

If you change a defined name or table name, all instances of that name in the workbook are also changed.

1. On the **Formulas** tab, in the **Defined Names** group, click on **Name Manager**.

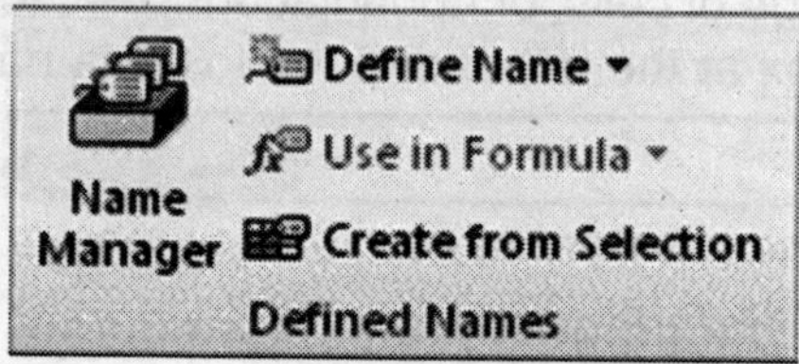

2. In the **Name Manager** dialog box, click on the name that you want to change, and then click on **Edit**.
3. In the **Edit Name** dialog box, in the **Name** box, type the new name for the reference.
4. In the **Refers to** box, change the reference, and then click on **OK**.
5. In the **Name Manager** dialog box, in the **Refers to** box, change the cell, formula, or constant represented by the name.
    - To cancel unwanted or accidental changes, click on **Cancel** ✖, or press **Esc**.
    - To save changes, click on **Commit** ✔, or press **Enter**.

Delete One or More Names

1. On the **Formulas** tab, in the **Defined Names** group, click on **Name Manager**.

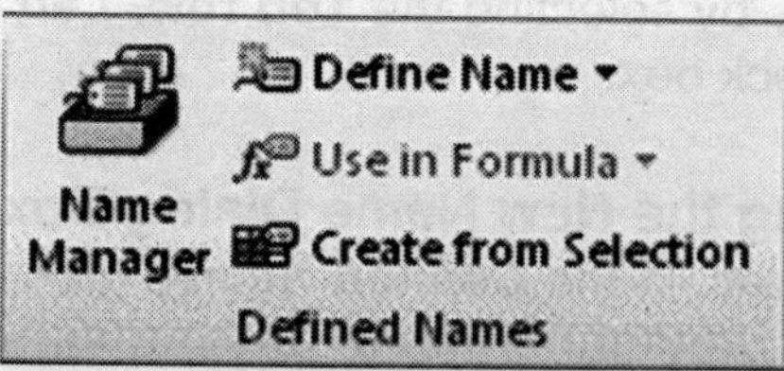

2. In the **Name Manager** dialog box, click on the name that you want to change.
3. Select one or more names by doing one of the following:
    - To select a name, click on it.
    - To select more than one name in a contiguous group, click and drag the names, or press **Shift** and click on the mouse button for each name in the group.
    - To select more than one name in a noncontiguous group, press **Ctrl** and click on the mouse button for each name in the group.
4. Click on **Delete**. You can also press the **Delete** key.
5. Click on **OK** to confirm the deletion.

Elements of Formulas

A formula can consist of any of these elements:

- Mathematical operators, such as + (for addition) and * (for multiplication).
  Example:
  =A1+A2 adds the values in cells A1 and A2.
- Values or text
  Example:
  =200*0.5 multiplies 200 times 0.15. This formula uses only values, and it always returns the same result as 100.
- Cell references (including named cells and ranges)
  Example:
  = A1 = C12 Compares cell A1 with cell C12. If the cells are identical, the formula returns TRUE; otherwise, it returns FALSE.
- Worksheet functions (such as SUM or AVERAGE)
  Example:
  = SUM(A1:A12) adds the values in the range A1:A12.

To Create a Simple Formula in Excel

1. Select the **cell** where the answer will appear (B4, for example).

B4 | fx

	A	B	C
1	Estimated painting cost per square foot		
2	Total cost	75.00	
3	Square Feet	250	
4	Total/Sq Ft		
5			

2. Type the **equal sign** (=).
3. Type in the **formula** you want Excel to calculate. For example, “75/250”.

MAX | × ✓ fx | =75/250

	A	B	C
1	Estimated painting cost per square foot		
2	Total cost	75.00	
3	Square Feet	250	
4	Total/Sq Ft	=75/250	
5			

4. Press **Enter**. The formula will be calculated, and the value will be displayed in the cell.

B4 | fx | =75/250

	A	B	C
1	Estimated painting cost per square foot		
2	Total cost	75.00	
3	Square Feet	250	
4	Total/Sq Ft	0.30	
5			

AutoSum

To summarise values quickly, you can also use AutoSum.

1. Select the **cell** where you would like your formulas solution to appear.
2. Go to the **Home tab**, in the **Editing group**.
3. Click on **AutoSum** to sum your numbers or click on the **arrow** next to **AutoSum** to select a function that you want to apply.

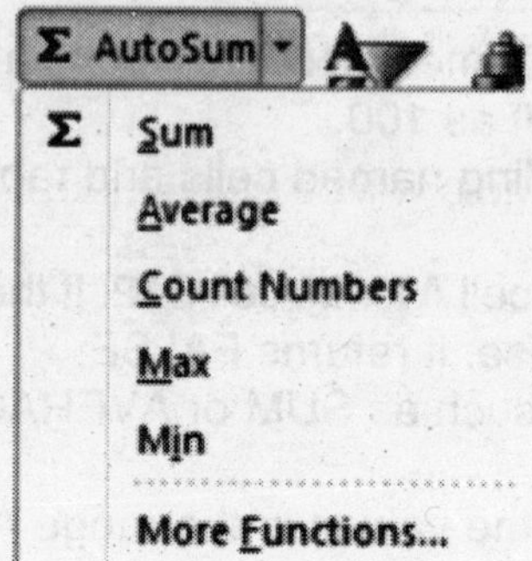

Creating Formulas with Cell References

When a formula contains a cell address, it is called a **cell reference**. Creating a formula with cell references is useful because you can update data in your worksheet without having to rewrite the values in the formula.

To Create a Formula Using Cell References

1. Select the **cell** where the answer will appear (B3, for example).

B3 | *fx*

	A	B	C	D
1	Budget for June	400.00		
2	Budget for July	300.00		
3	**Total Budget**			
4				

2. Type the **equal sign** (=).
3. Type the **cell address** that contains the first number in the equation (B1, for example).

SUM | × ✓ *fx* | =B1

	A	B	C	D
1	Budget for June	400.00		
2	Budget for July	300.00		
3	**Total Budget**	=B1		
4				

4. Type the **operator** you need for your formula. For example, type the addition sign (+).

5. Type the **cell address** that contains the second number in the equation (B2, for example).

SUM ▾ × ✓ f_x =B1+B2

	A	B	C	D
1	Budget for June	400.00		
2	Budget for July	300.00		
3	**Total Budget**	=B1+B2		
4				

6. Press **Enter**. The formula will be calculated, and the value will be displayed in the cell.

B3 ▾ f_x =B1+B2

	A	B	C	D
1	Budget for June	400.00		
2	Budget for July	300.00		
3	**Total Budget**	**700.00**		
4				

Charts in Excel

A chart is a visual representation of numeric values. Excel provides with the tools to create a wide variety of highly customisable charts.

To create a chart in Excel, you start by entering the numeric data for the chart on a worksheet.

1. Worksheet data
2. Chart created from worksheet data

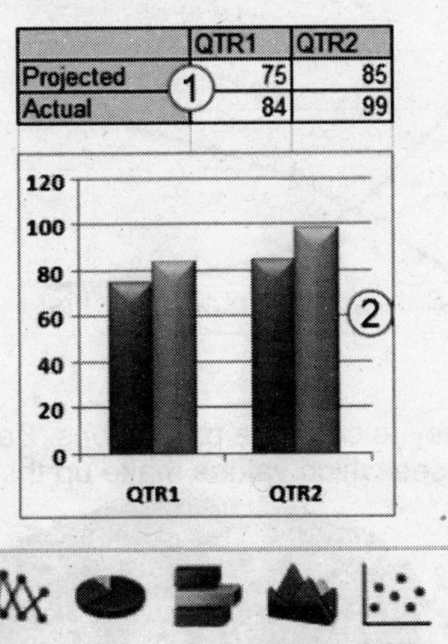

	QTR1	QTR2
Projected	75	85
Actual	84	99

Column ▾ Line ▾ Pie ▾ Bar ▾ Area ▾ Scatter ▾ Other Charts ▾

Charts

Types of Charts

There are various chart types available in MS Excel.

Column Chart

Column charts use vertical bars to represent data. They can work with many different types of data, but they are most frequently used for comparing information.

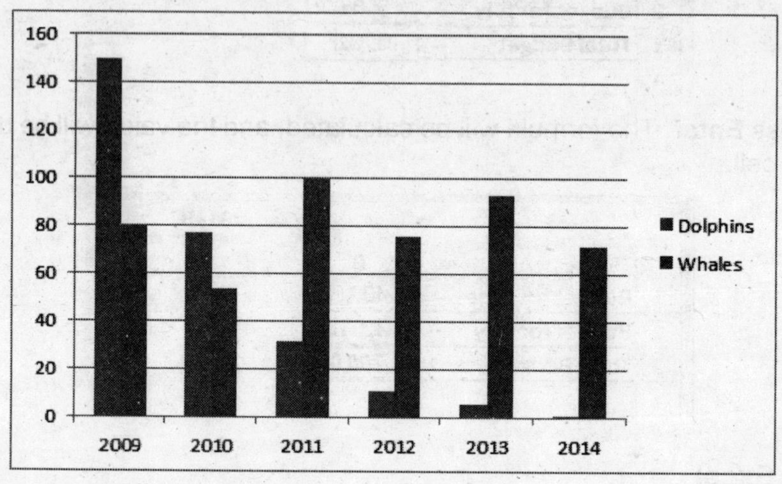

Line Chart

Line charts are ideal for showing trends. The data points are connected with lines, making it easy to see whether values are increasing or decreasing over time.

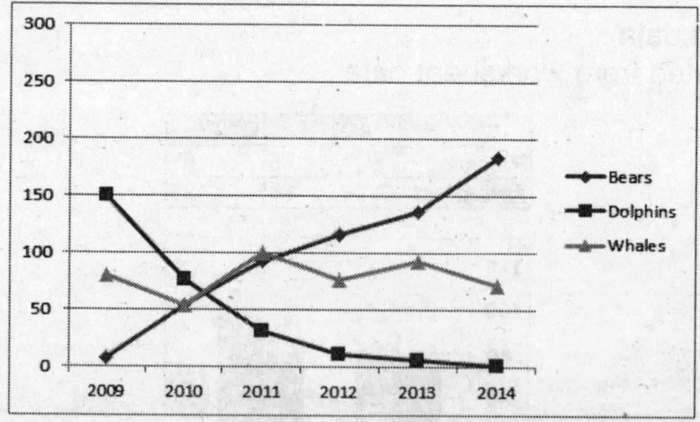

Pie Chart

Pie charts make it easy to compare proportions. Each value is shown as a slice of the pie, so it is easy to see which values make up the percentage of a whole.

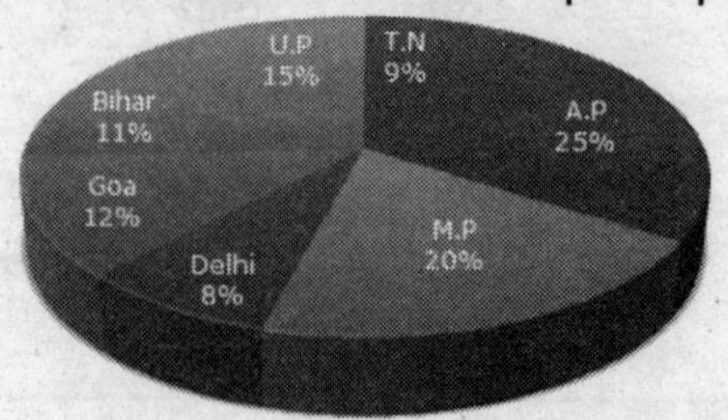

Bar Chart

Bar charts work just like Column charts, but they use horizontal bars instead of vertical bars.

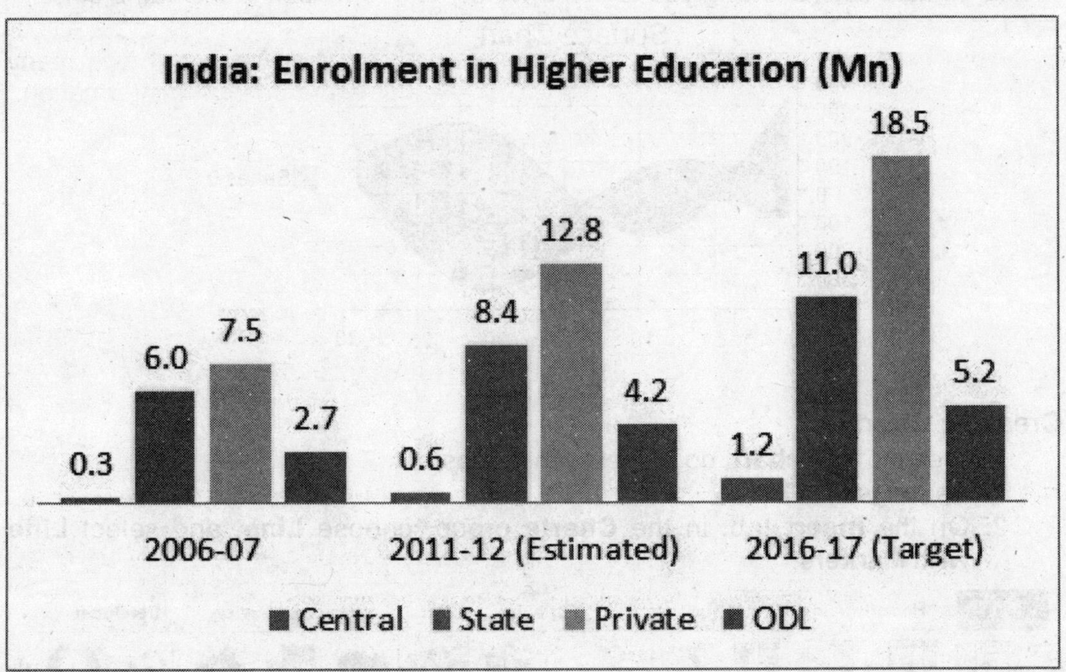

Area Chart

Area charts are similar to line charts, except that the areas under the lines are filled in.

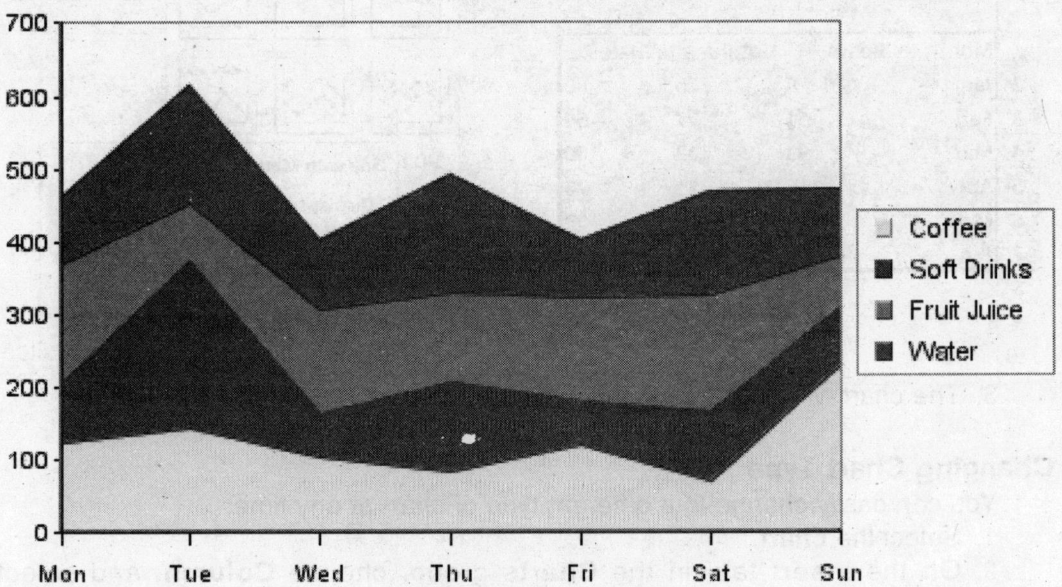

Surface Chart

Surface charts allow you to display data across a 3D landscape. They work best with large data sets, allowing you to see a variety of information at the same time.

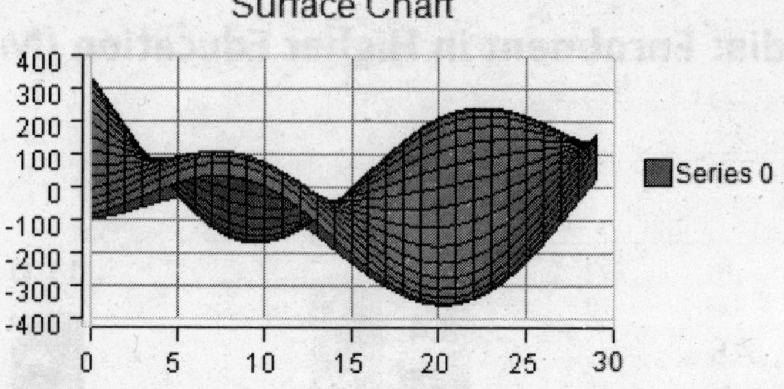

Creating Chart

To create a **line chart**, do the following steps.

1. Se range **A1:D7**.
2. On the **Insert** tab, in the **Charts** group, choose **Line**, and select **Line with Markers**.

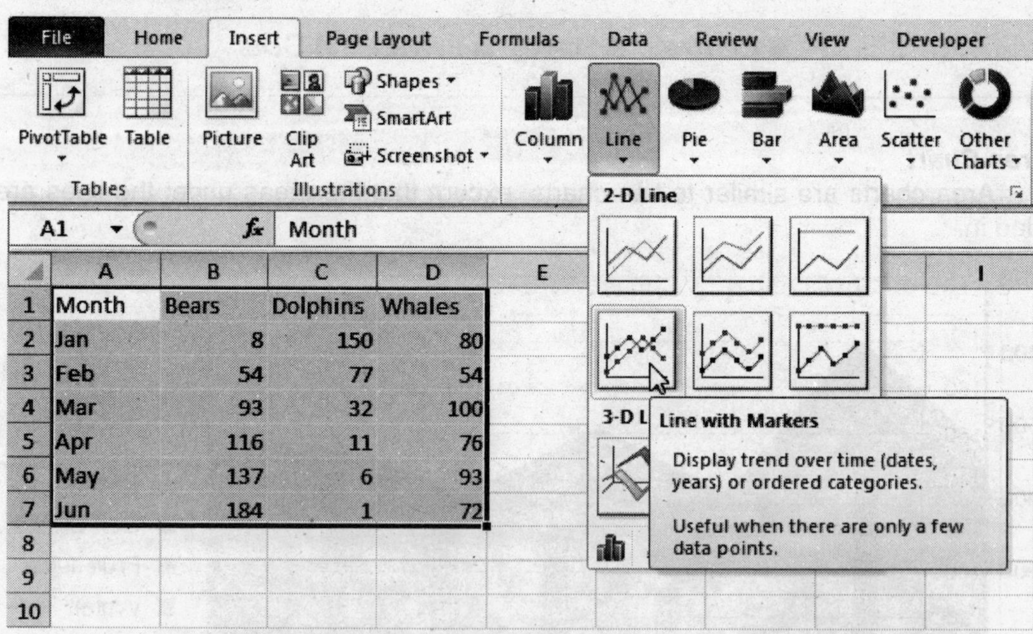

	A	B	C	D
1	Month	Bears	Dolphins	Whales
2	Jan	8	150	80
3	Feb	54	77	54
4	Mar	93	32	100
5	Apr	116	11	76
6	May	137	6	93
7	Jun	184	1	72

3. The chart will appear in the worksheet.

Changing Chart Type

You can easily change to a different type of chart at any time.

1. Select the **chart**.
2. On the **Insert** tab, in the **Charts** group, choose **Column**, and select **Clustered Column**.

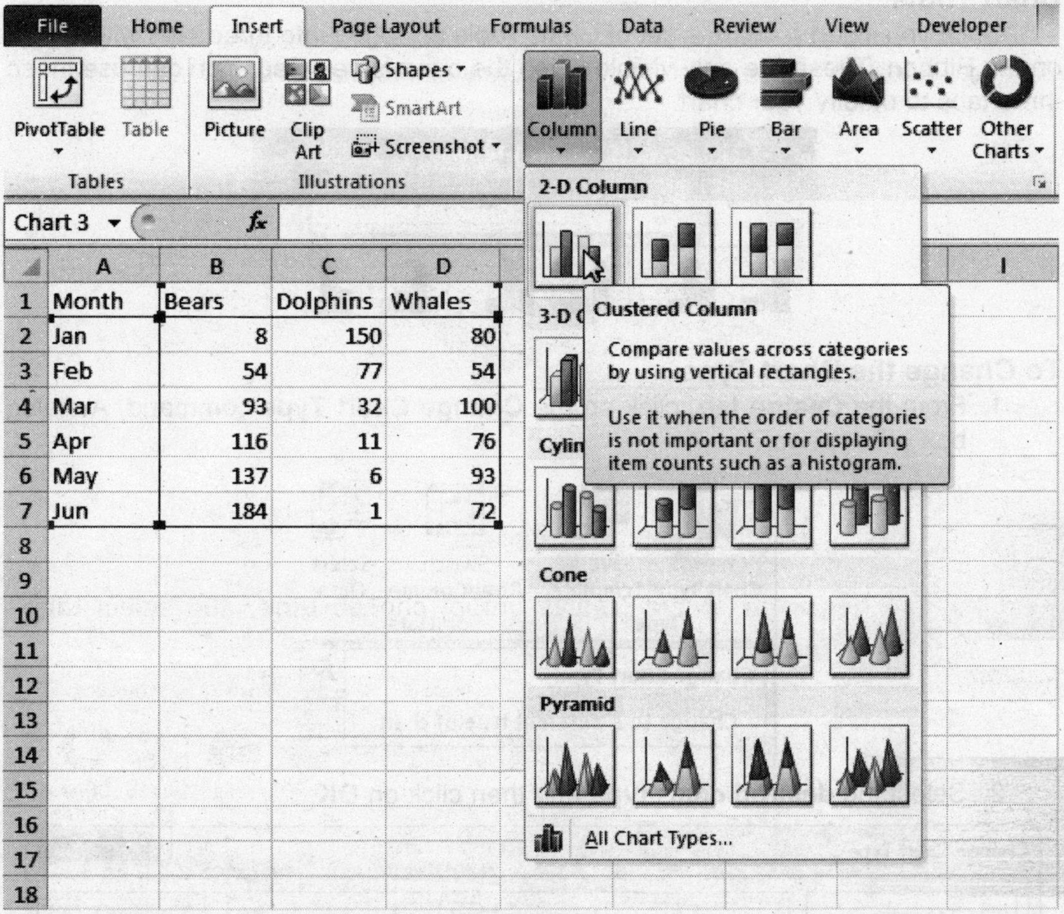

File
Home
Insert
Page Layout
Formulas
Data
Review
View
Developer
PivotTable
Table
Tables
Picture
Clip Art
Shapes
SmartArt
Screenshot
Illustrations
Column
Line
Pie
Bar
Area
Scatter
Other Charts
Chart 3
2-D Column
3-D C
Cylin
Cone
Pyramid
All Chart Types...
Clustered Column
Compare values across categories by using vertical rectangles.
Use it when the order of categories is not important or for displaying item counts such as a histogram.
A B C D I
1 Month Bears Dolphins Whales
2 Jan 8 150 80
3 Feb 54 77 54
4 Mar 93 32 100
5 Apr 116 11 76
6 May 137 6 93
7 Jun 184 1 72
8
9
10
11
12
13
14
15
16
17
18

3. The chart will appear in the worksheet.

200
180
160
140
120
100
80
60
40
20
0
Jan
Feb
Mar
Apr
May
Jun
Bears
Dolphins
Whales

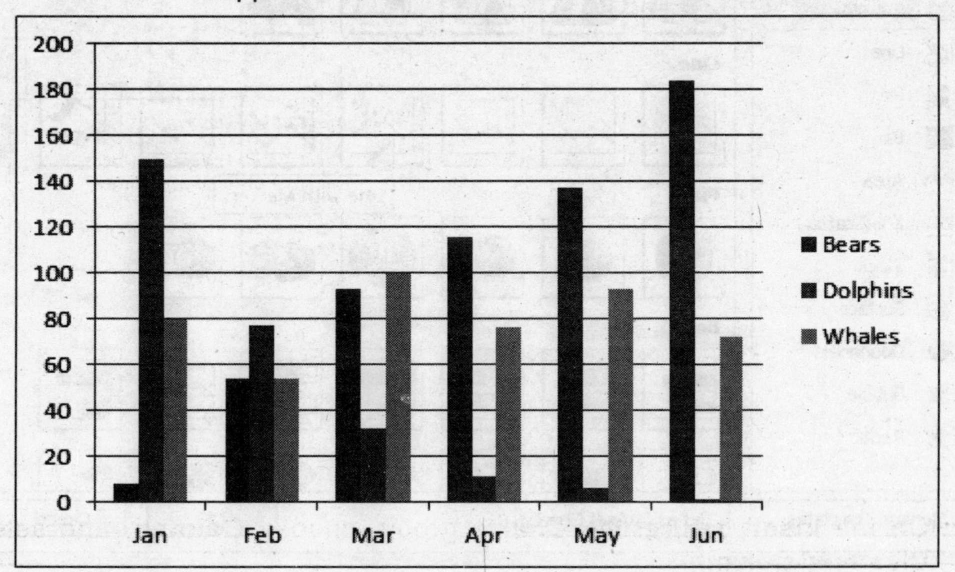

Chart Tools

Once you insert a chart, a set of Chart Tools arranged into three tabs will appear on the Ribbon. These are only visible when the chart is selected. You can use these three tabs to modify your chart.

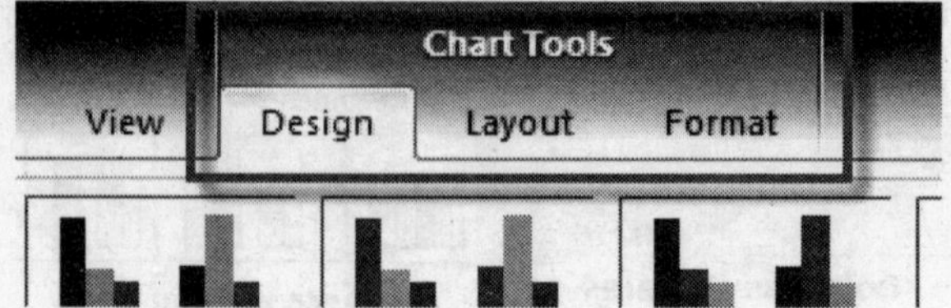

To Change the Chart Type

1. From the **Design tab**, click on the **Change Chart Type** command. A dialog box will appear.

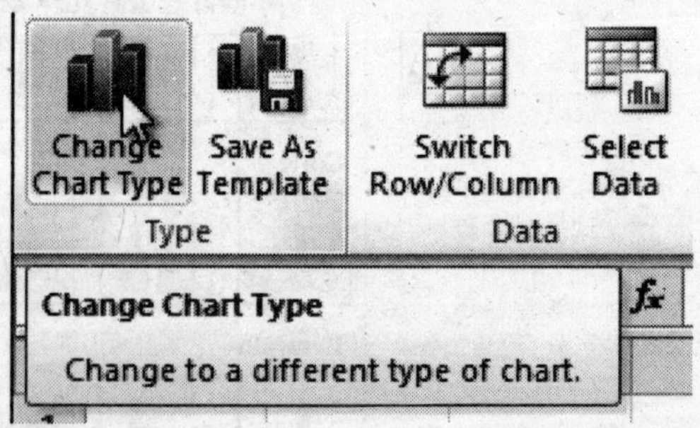

2. Select the **desired chart type** and then click on **OK**.

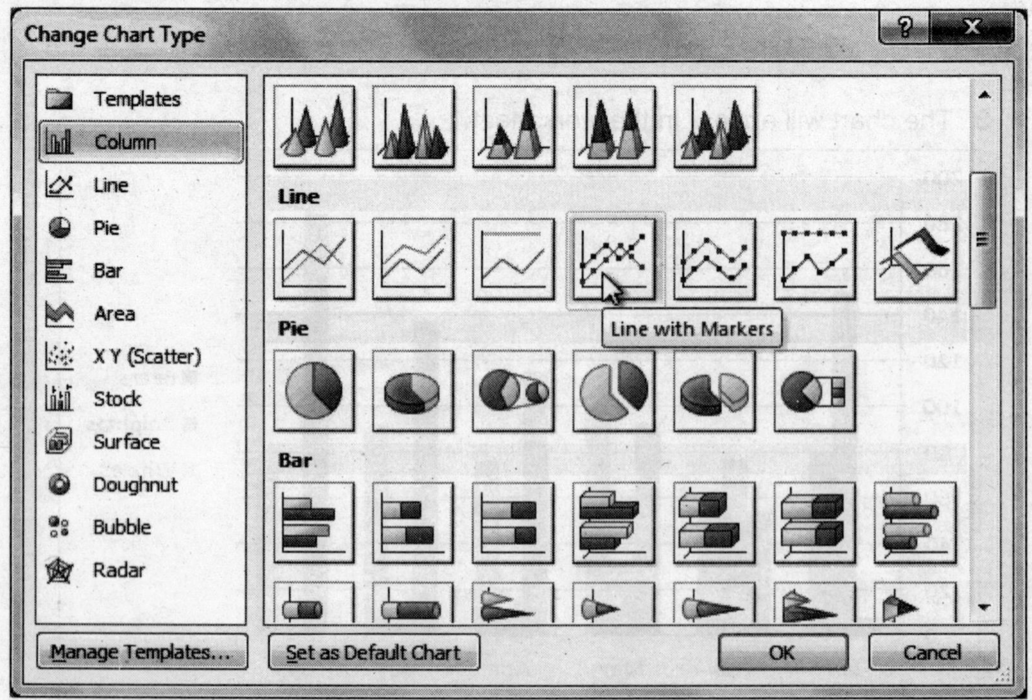

To Change the Chart Layout

1. Select the **Design tab**.
2. Click on the **More drop-down arrow** in the **Chart Layouts group** to see all of the available layouts.

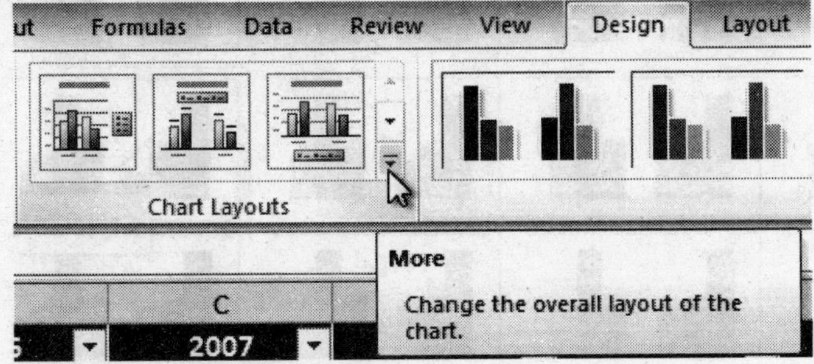

3. Select the **desired layout**.

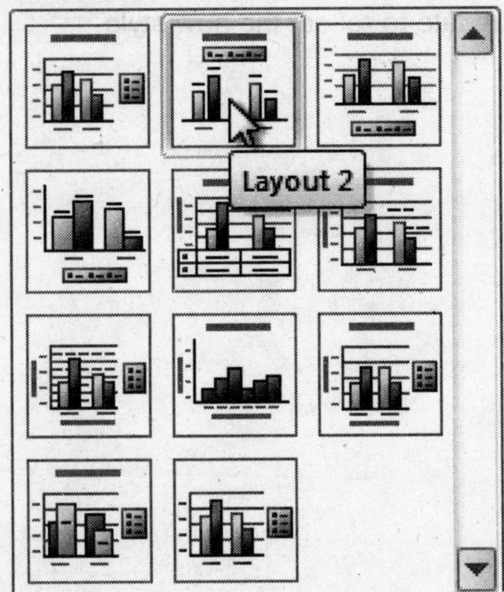

4. The chart will update to reflect the new layout.

To Change the Chart Style

1. Select the **Design tab**.
2. Click on the **More drop-down arrow** in the **Chart Styles group** to see all of the available styles.

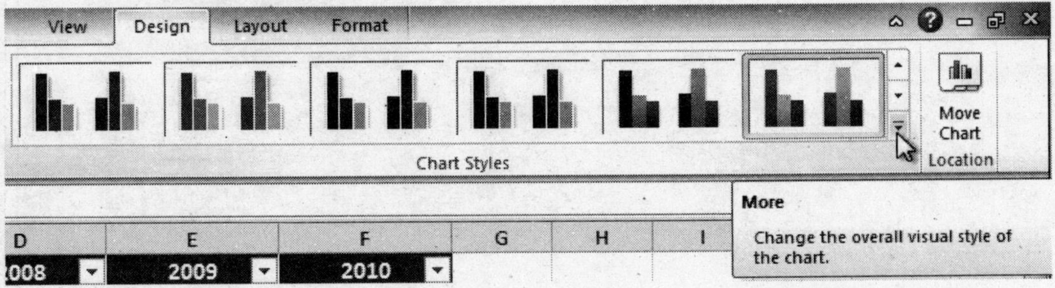

3. Select the **desired style**.

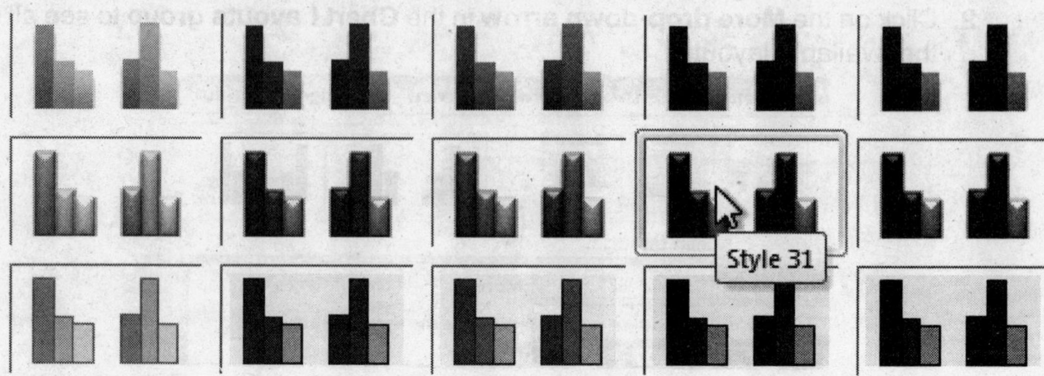

4. The chart will update to reflect the new style.

□

16

An Introduction to Microsoft Access 2010

Microsoft Access 2010 is a computer application used to create and manage computer-based databases. It is a relational database application in the Microsoft 2010 Office Suite that allows users to enter, manage and run reports on large amounts of data.

A database is a collection of data that is stored in a computer system. Databases allow users to enter, access and analyse data quickly and easily.

The features in Access 2010 are quite familiar with Access 2007, except than the addition of the Backstage view.

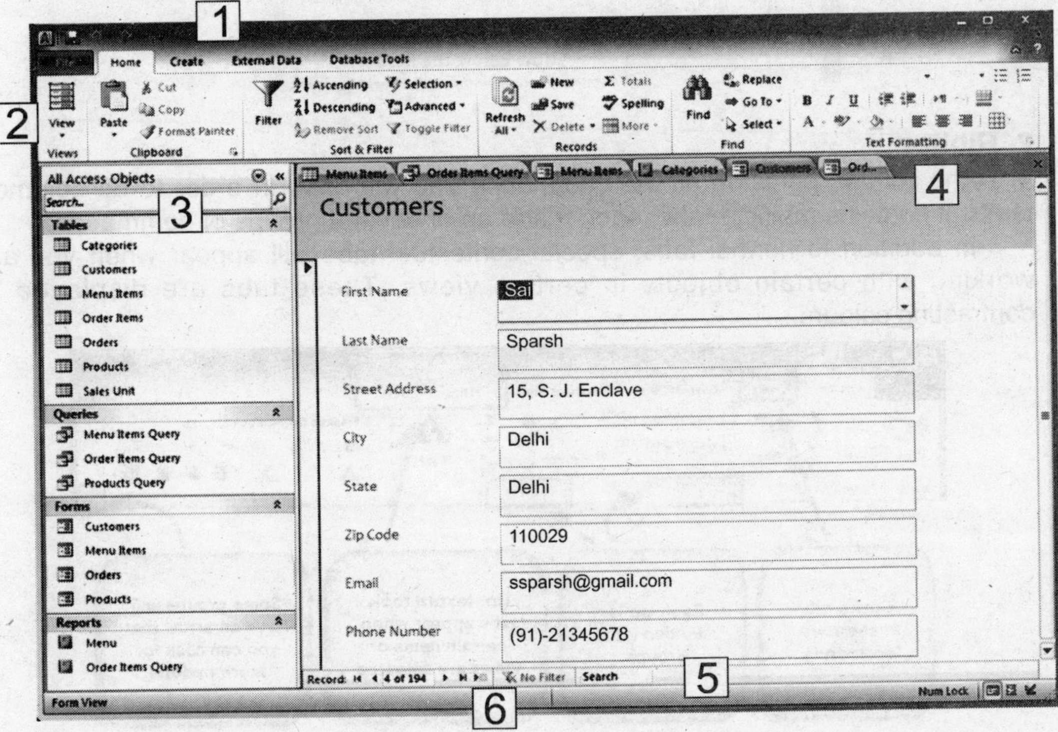

The different features found in MS Access 2010 are as follows:

1. Quick Access Toolbar

The Quick Access Toolbar lets you access common commands, no matter which tab you have selected in the Ribbon. By default, it shows the **Save, Undo** and **Redo** commands. If you wish, you can add additional commands to the toolbar by clicking the **drop-down arrow**.

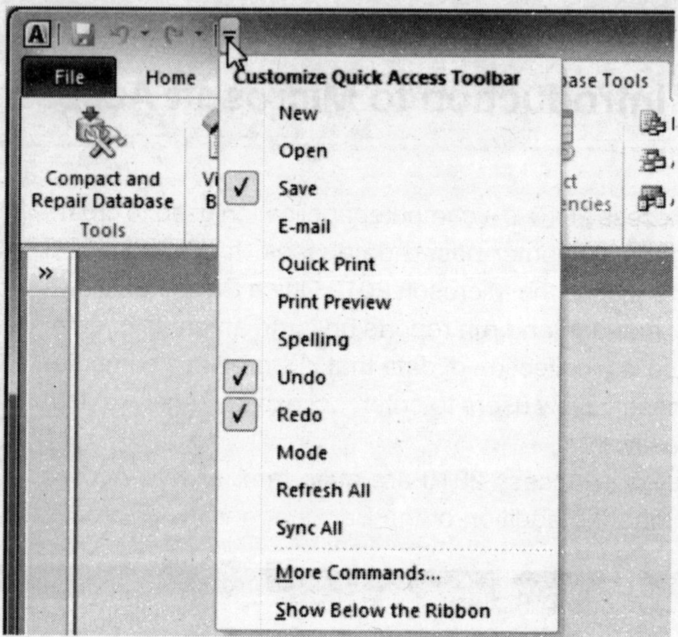

2. Ribbon

The Ribbon contains all the commands you will need in order to do common tasks. It contains multiple tabs, each made up of several groups of commands.

In addition to normal tabs, special contextual tabs will appear when you are working with certain objects in certain views. These tabs are displayed in contrasting colours.

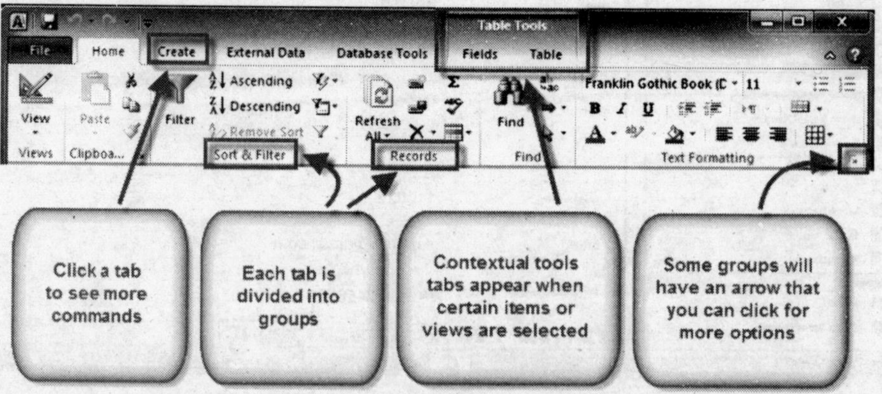

3. Navigation Pane

The Navigation Pane displays all the objects contained in your database. The objects are grouped by type. To open an object, double-click on it.

If you like, you can hide the Navigation Pane by clicking on the double arrows in the top right corner.

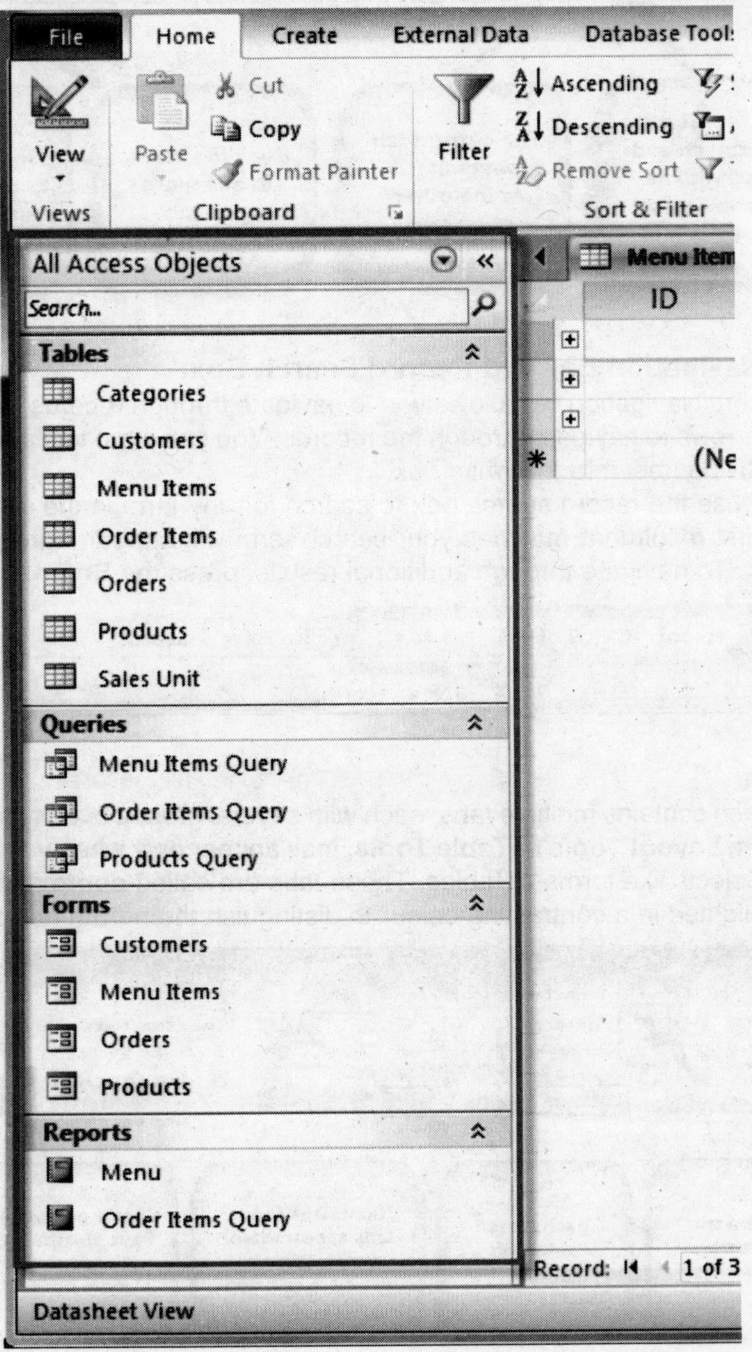

4. Document Tabs Bar

All open objects are displayed on the Document Tabs bar. To view an object, click on its tab. Click on × on the right end of the bar to close the current tab. To see more tabs, click on the **arrow**.

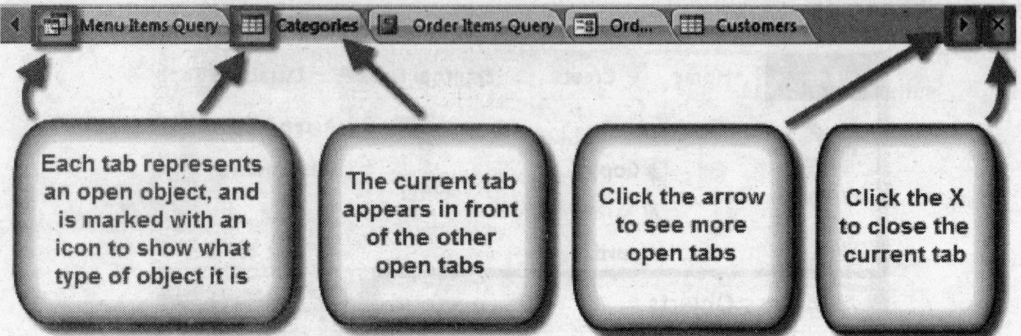

5. Record Navigation Bar and Record Search Box

The Record Navigation bar allows you to navigate through records one at a time. Click on the arrows to navigate through the records. You can jump to a specific record by typing its ID number into the white box.

You can use the record search box to search for any term in the currently open object. The first result that matches your search term will appear highlighted with a yellow border. To navigate through additional results, press the **Enter** key.

The Ribbon

The Ribbon contains multiple tabs, each with several groups of commands. Some tabs, like **Form Layout Tools** or **Table Tools**, may appear only when you are working with certain objects like forms or tables. These tabs are called **contextual tabs**, and they are highlighted in a contrasting colour to distinguish them from normal tabs.

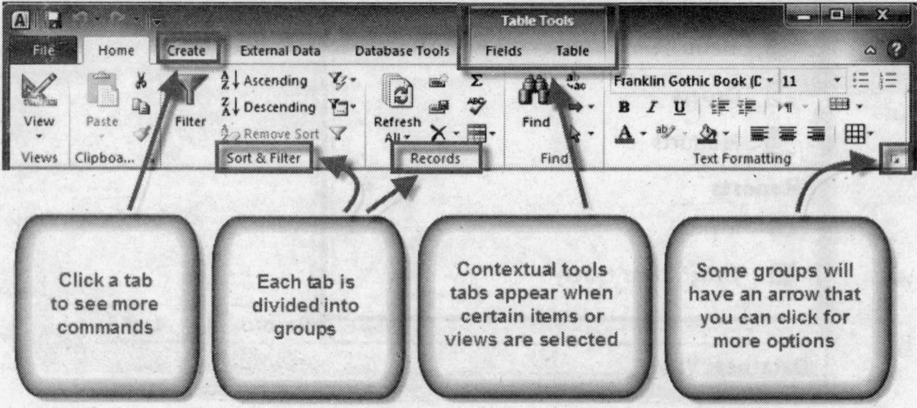

To Minimize and Maximize the Ribbon

The Ribbon is designed to be easy to use and responsive to your current task, but if you feel that it is taking up too much of your screen space, you can minimise it.

1. Click on the **arrow** in the upper-right corner of the **Ribbon** to minimise it.

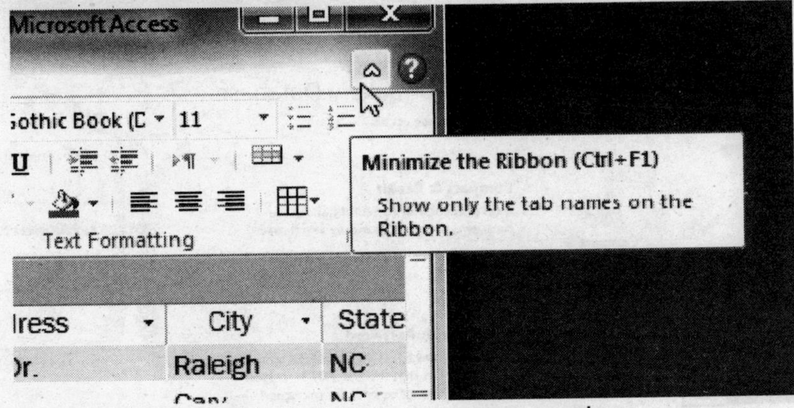

2. To maximise the **Ribbon**, click on the **arrow** again.

Backstage View

The Backstage view gives you various options for opening, saving, printing and viewing more information about your database. It is similar to the **Office Button Menu** from Access 2007 or the **File Menu** from earlier versions of Access. However, unlike those menus, it is a full-page view, which makes it easier to work with.

To get to Backstage view:

1. Click the **File tab**.

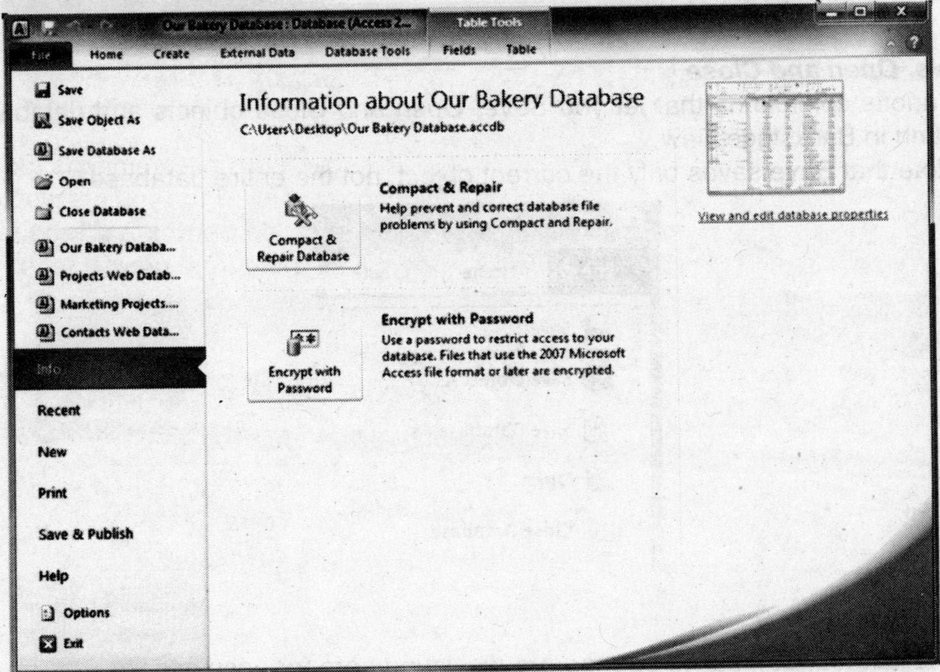

2. You can choose an option on the left side of the page.
3. To get back to your database objects, just click on **any tab** on the **Ribbon**.

The different Backstage features in **Backstage View** is shown below.

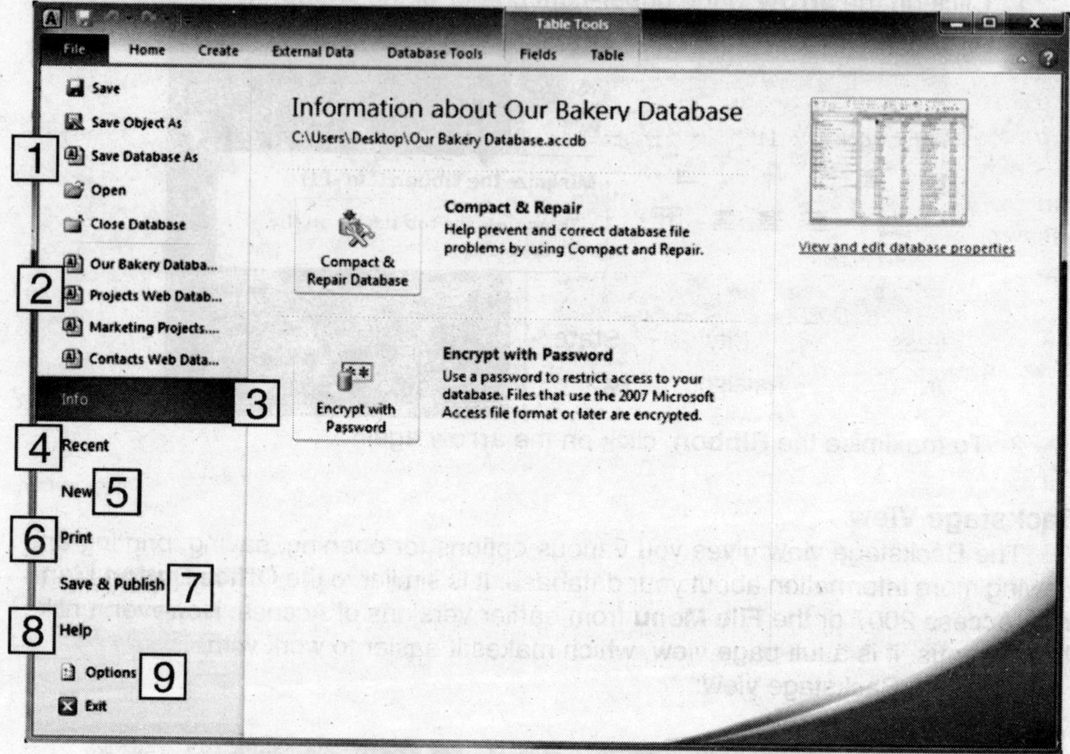

1. Save, Open and Close

Various commands that let you Save, Open and Close objects and databases are found in Backstage view.

Note that **Save** saves only the current object, not the entire database.

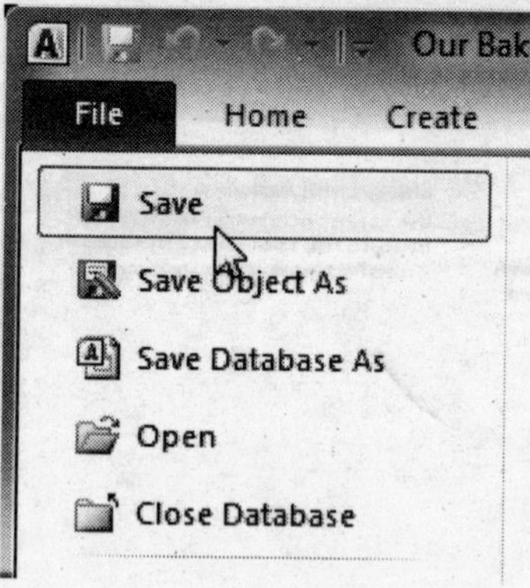

2. Recently Opened

The last four databases opened are displayed here for easy access.

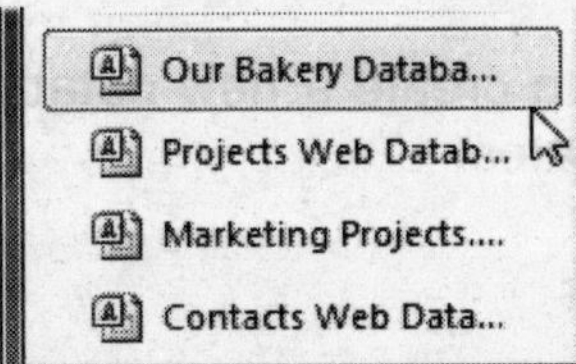

3. Info

Info contains **information** about your database. It also contains options that let you **Compact** and **Repair** your database to fix file problems and **Encrypt** it with a password.

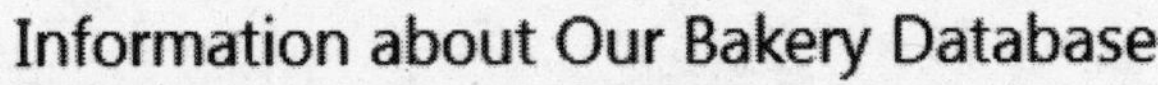

C:\Users\elizabeth\Desktop\Our Bakery Database.accdb

Compact & Repair
Help prevent and correct database file problems by using Compact and Repair.

Encrypt with Password
Use a password to restrict access to your database. Files that use the 2007 Microsoft Access file format or later are encrypted.

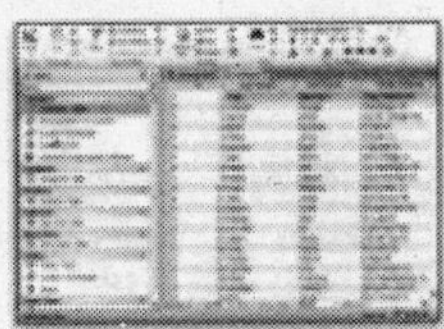

View and edit database properties

4. Recent

The Recent pane displays a more complete list of recently opened databases. It also contains an option to change the number of recent databases that are displayed in the shortened list above.

Recent Databases

Our Bakery Database.accdb
Desktop

Projects Web Database.accdb
Desktop

Marketing Projects.accdb
Desktop

Contacts Web Database.accdb
Desktop

screenshot bakery.accdb
Desktop

5. New

From the New pane, you can create a new database from scratch, or you can choose from a selection of templates.

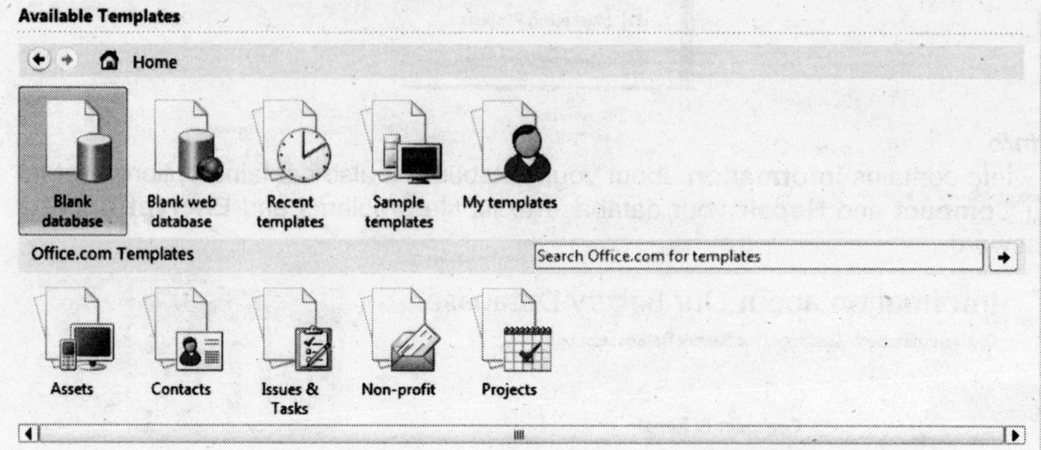

6. Print

The Print pane contains options for printing the current object in your database.

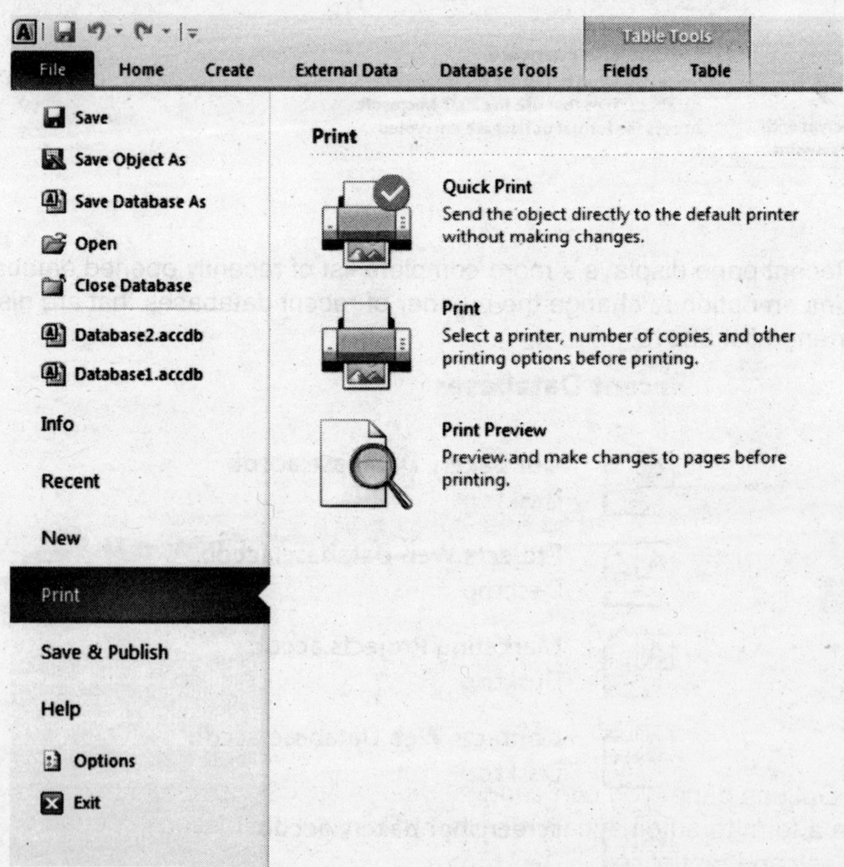

7. Save and Publish

Save and Publish provides advanced options for saving your database.

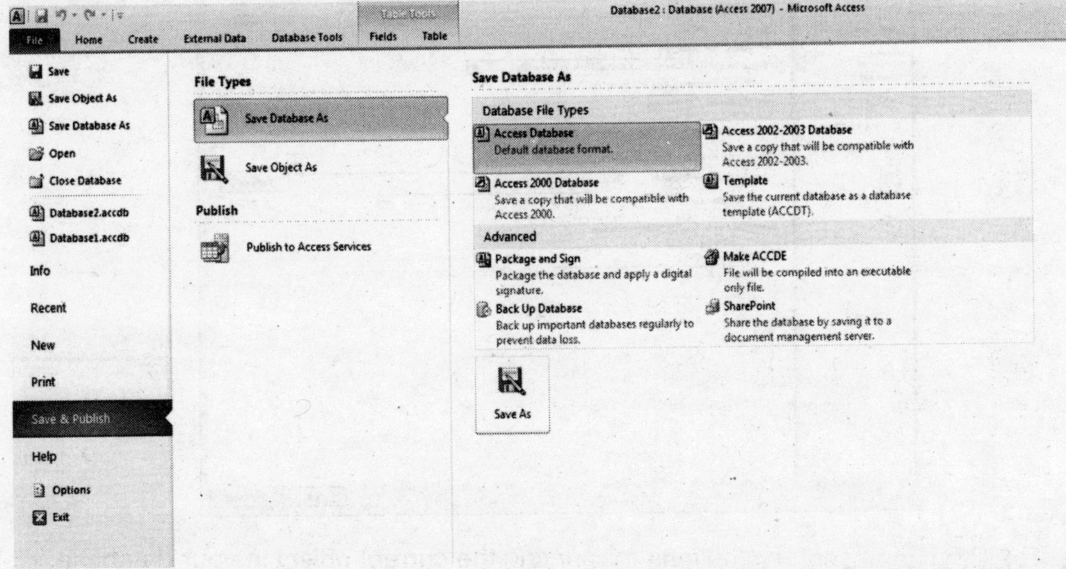

8. Help

From the Help pane, you can access Microsoft Office Help or check for updates to your software.

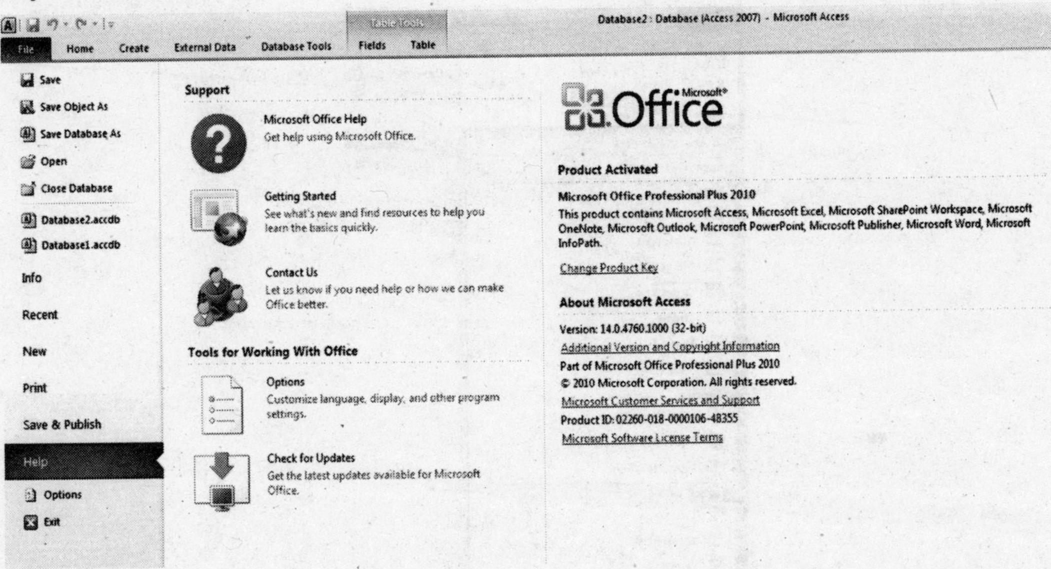

9. Options

In the Options pane, you can change various Access options. For example, you can choose a form to automatically display when your database is opened or modify the default cell and font style.

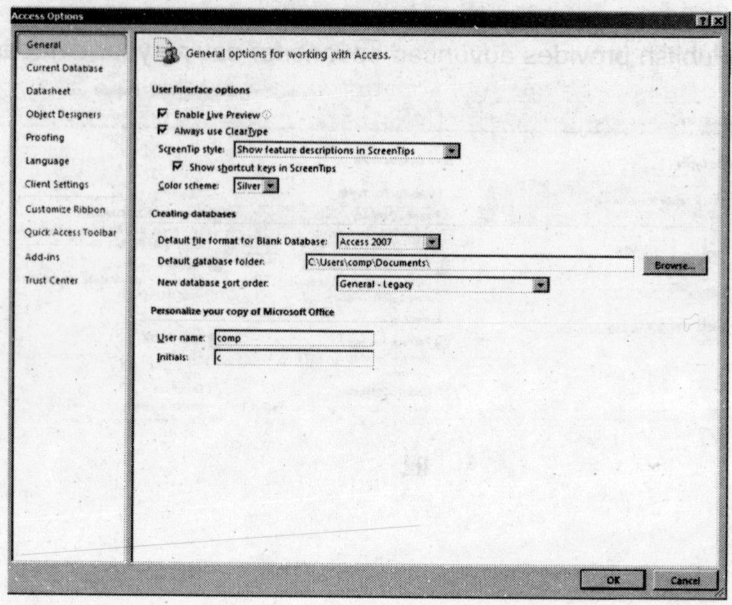

The Navigation Pane

The Navigation Pane is a list containing every object in your database. For easier viewing, the objects are organised into groups by type. You can open, rename and delete objects using the Navigation Pane.

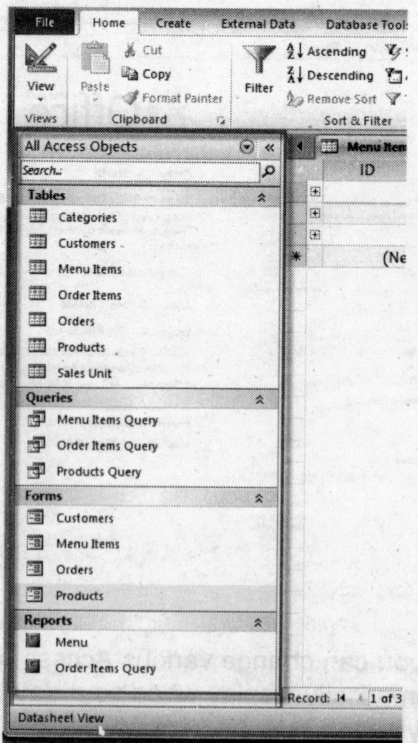

To Minimize and Maximize the Navigation Pane

The Navigation Pane is designed to help you manage all of your objects, but if you feel that it takes up too much of your screen space, you can minimise it.

1. Click on the **double arrow** in the upper-right corner of the **Navigation Pane** to **minimise** it.

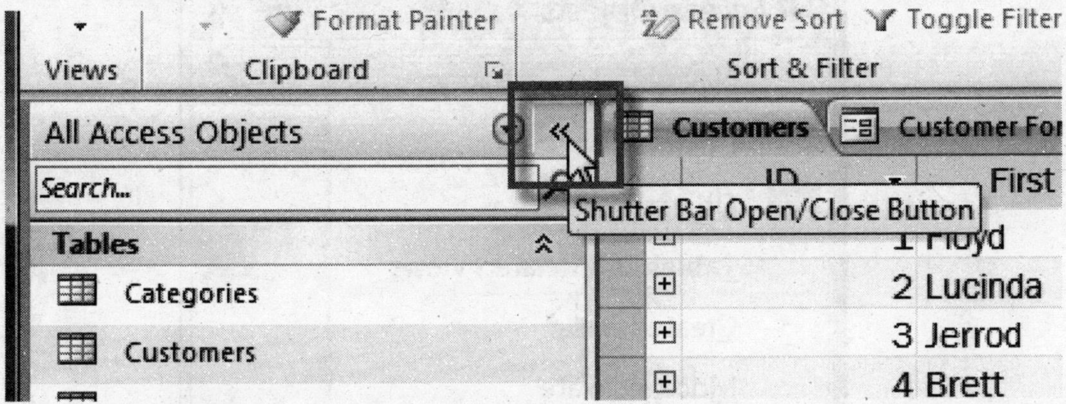

2. To make the **Navigation Pane** visible again, click on the **double arrow** to **maximise** it.

To Sort Objects in the Navigation Pane

By default, your objects are sorted by type, with the tables in one group, the forms in another, and so on. However, if you wish, you can sort the objects in the Navigation Pane into groups of your choosing.

1. Click on the **drop-down arrow** to the right of the words **All Access Objects**.

2. In the drop-down menu, select the desired sorting:
   - Select **Custom** to create a custom group for sorting the objects. After applying the sort, simply drag the desired objects to the new group.
   - Select **Object Type** to group the objects by type. This is the default setting.

- Select **Tables and Related Views** to group forms, queries and reports together with the tables they refer to.
- Select **Created Date or Modified Date** to sort the objects from most to least recently created or modified.

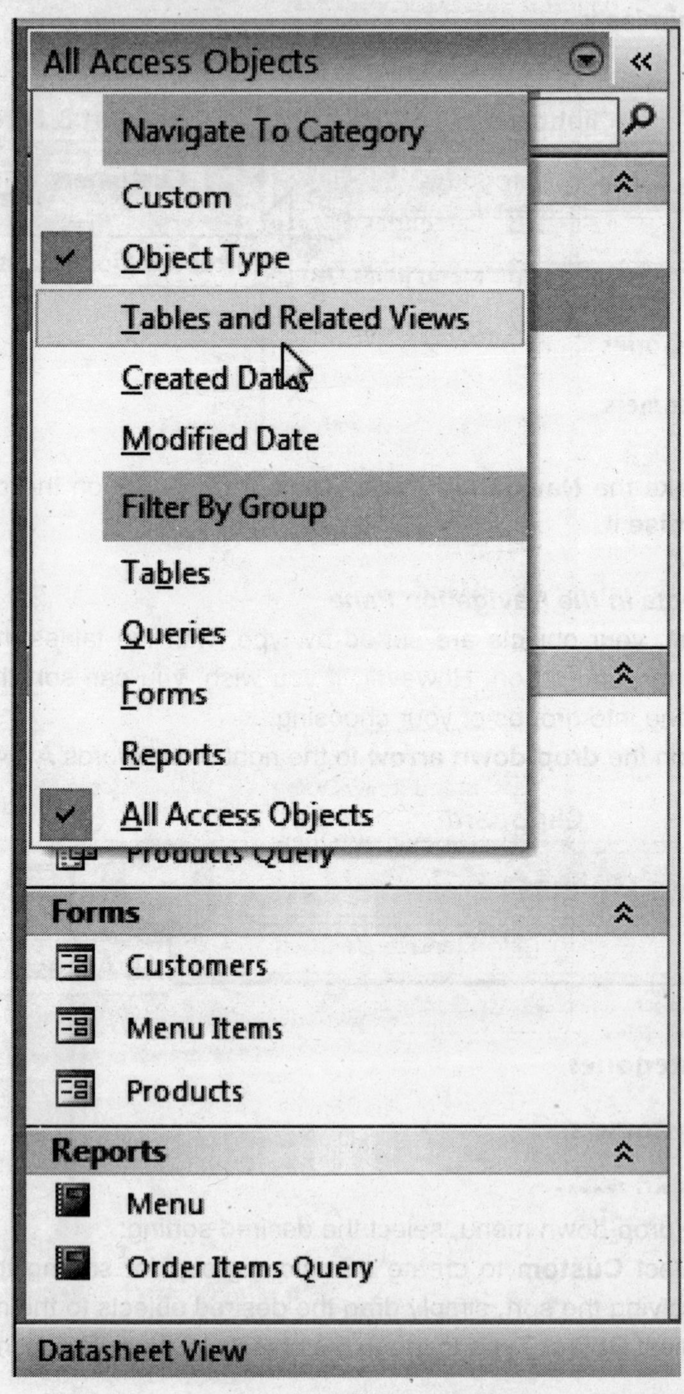

3. The objects in the Navigation Pane will now be sorted to reflect your choice.

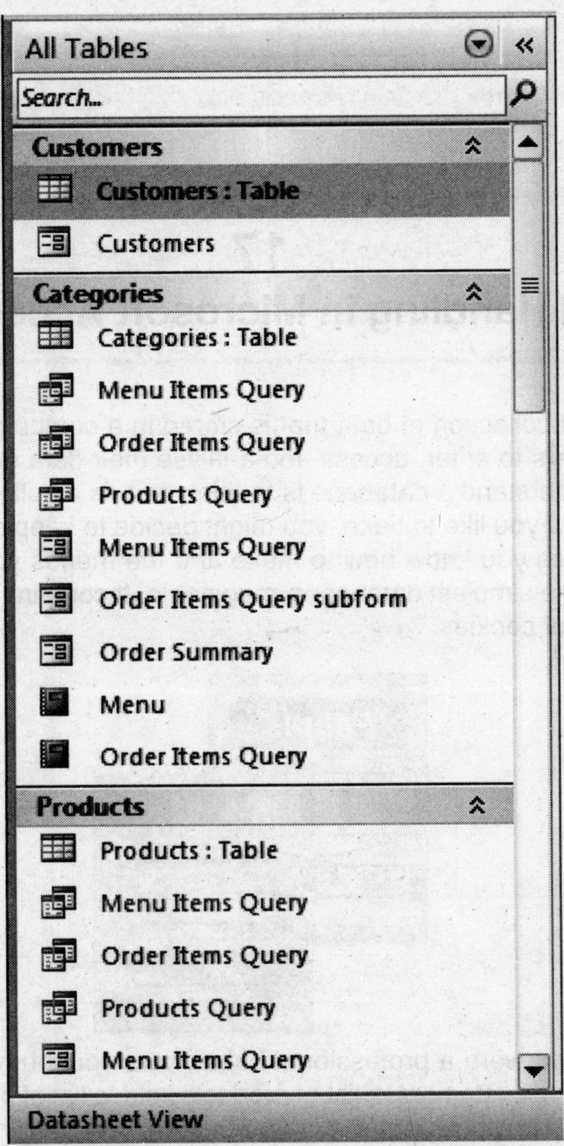

□

17

Advanced Handling in Microsoft Access Database

A database is a collection of data that is stored in a computer system. Databases allow their users to enter, access and analyse their data quickly and easily. The easiest way to understand a database is to think of it as a collection of lists.

For example, if you like to bake, you might decide to keep a database containing the types of cookies you know how to make and the friends you give those cookies to. This is one of the simplest databases imaginable. It contains two lists: a list of your friends, and a list of cookies.

However, if you were a professional baker, you would have many more lists to keep track of: a list of customers, a list of products sold, a list of prices, a list of orders... it goes on and on. The more lists you add, the more complex the database will be.

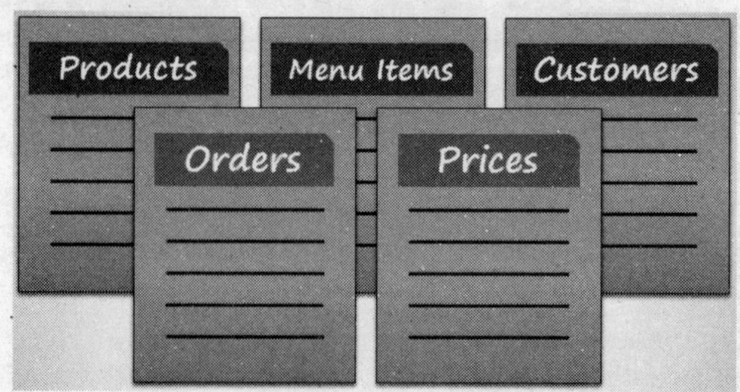

In Access, lists are a little more complex than the ones you write on paper. Access stores its lists of data in tables, which allow you to store even more detailed information. In the table below, the 'People' list in the baker's database has been expanded to include other relevant information about the baker's friends.

ID	Name	Cell Phone	Birthday	Nut Allergy?
1	Dad	555-0404	June 3	Yes
2	Aunt Aida	555-9890	July 8	No
3	Joakim	555-0462	September 19	No
4	Dwane	555-9975	January 5	No
5	Allegra	555-0099	January 14	Yes

Each Access database consists of multiple objects that let you interact with data. Databases can include forms for entering data, queries for searching within it, reports for analysing it, and, of course, tables for storing it. Whenever you work with your database, you are working with many of these objects at once.

Creating Forms in Access 2010

Access makes it easy to create a form from any table in your database. Creating forms for your database can make entering data much more convenient. When you create a form, you can design it in a way that works with your database.

Once you've created a form, you can also modify it by adding additional fields and design controls such as combo boxes.

To Create a Form

- In the Navigation Pane, select the table you would like to use to create a form. You do not need to open the table.

1. Select the **Create** tab on the **Ribbon.** and locate the **Forms** group.

2. Then click on the **Form** command.

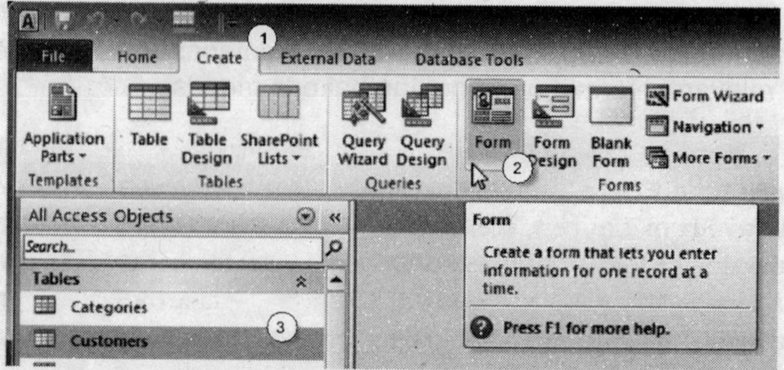

3. Your form will be created and opened in **Layout View**.

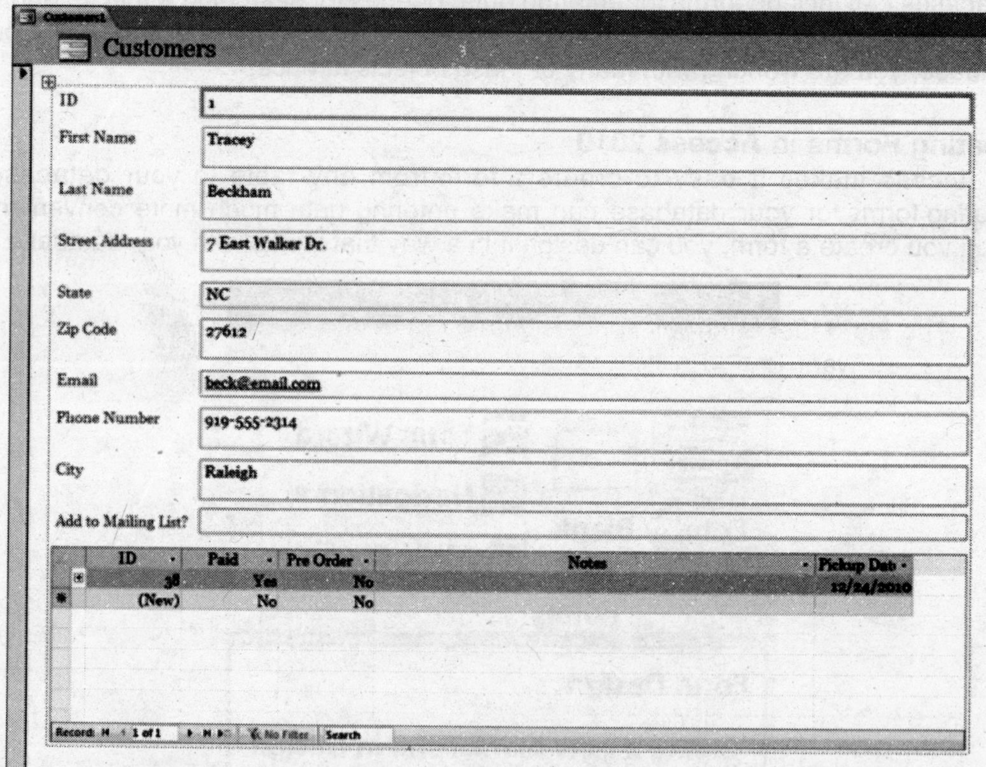

4. To save the form, click on the **Save** command on the **Quick Access** toolbar. When prompted, type a name for the form, then click on **OK**.

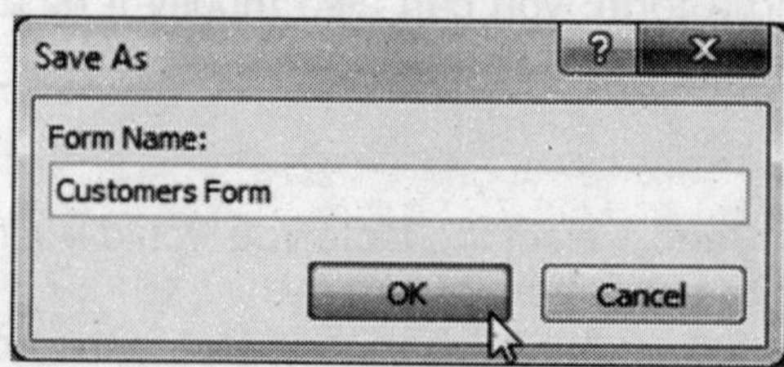

Adding Additional Fields to a Form

When you use the Form command on an existing table, all of the fields from that table are included in that form. However, if you later add additional fields to that table, those fields will not automatically show up in existing forms. In situations like this, you can add additional fields to a form.

To Add a Field to a Form

1. Select the **Form Layout Tools Design** tab, then locate the **Tools** group on the right side of the Ribbon.
2. Click on the **Add Existing Fields** command.

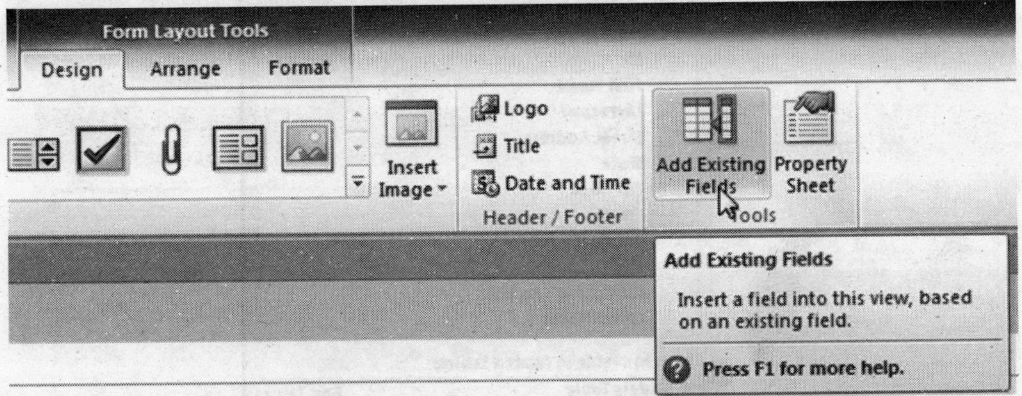

3. The **Field List** pane will appear. Select the field or fields to add to your form.

- If you want to add a field from the same table you used to build the form, simply double-click on the name of the desired field.

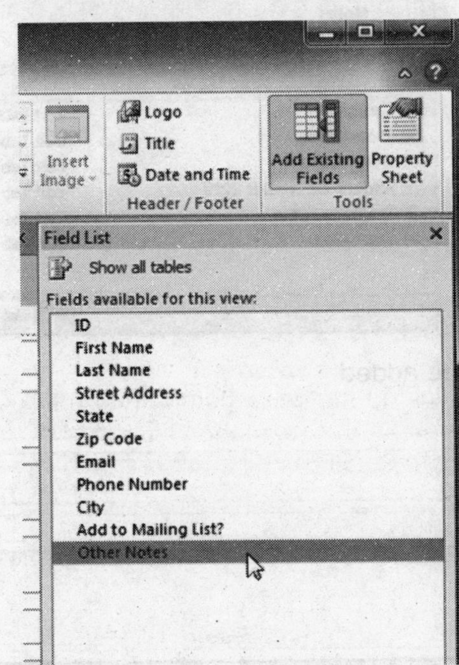

- To add a field from a different table:
  - ➤ Click on **Show All Tables**.
  - ➤ Click on the **plus sign** (+) next to the table containing the field you wish to add.
  - ➤ Double-click on the desired field.

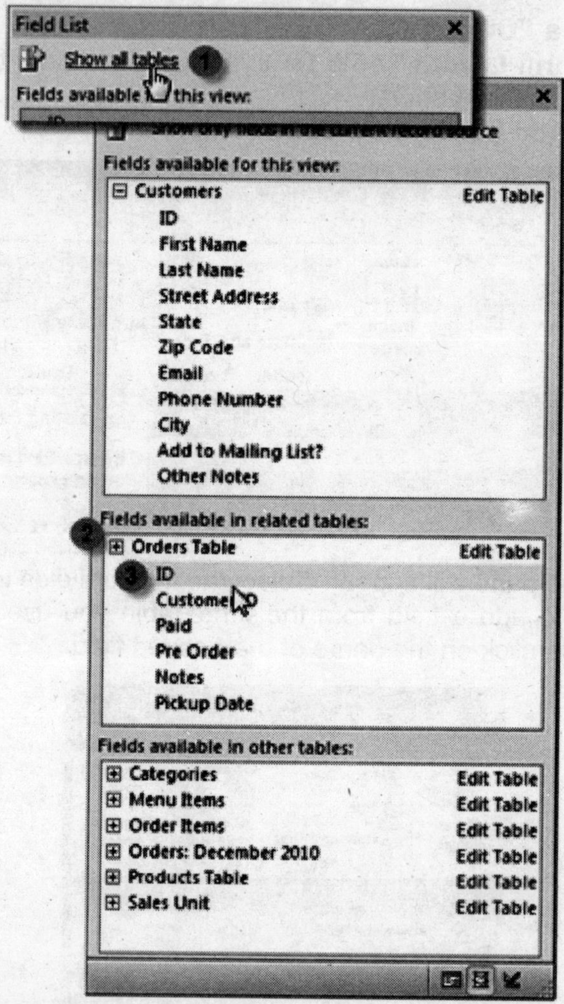

4. The new field will be added.

City Raleigh

Add to Mailing List?

Other Notes

To Open an Existing Database

1. Click on the **File tab**. This takes you to **Backstage View**.
2. Select **Open**. A dialog box will appear.

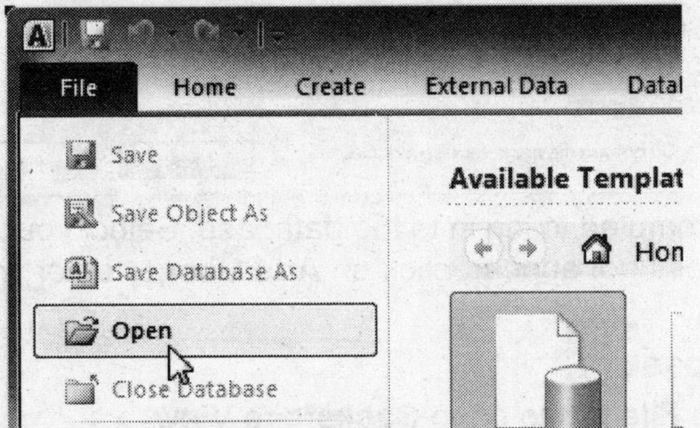

3. Locate and select the desired database, then click on **Open**.

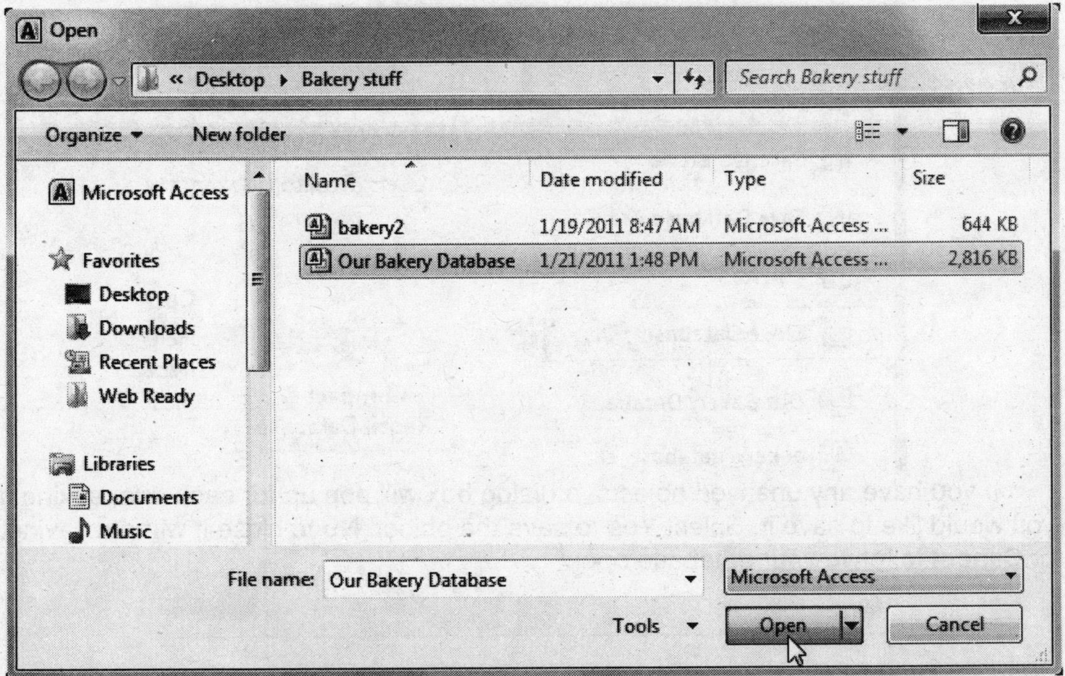

One or more warning messages may appear when you open your database. If the database contains customised functions, a yellow bar with a security warning may appear below the Ribbon. If you trust the source of your database, click on **Enable Content** for your database to display correctly.

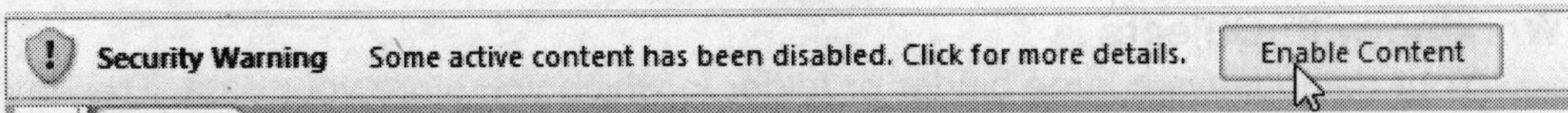

After enabling all content in the database, you may see a message asking, **Do you want to make this file a Trusted Document?** Click on **Yes** if you would like all content to be automatically enabled each time you open the database.

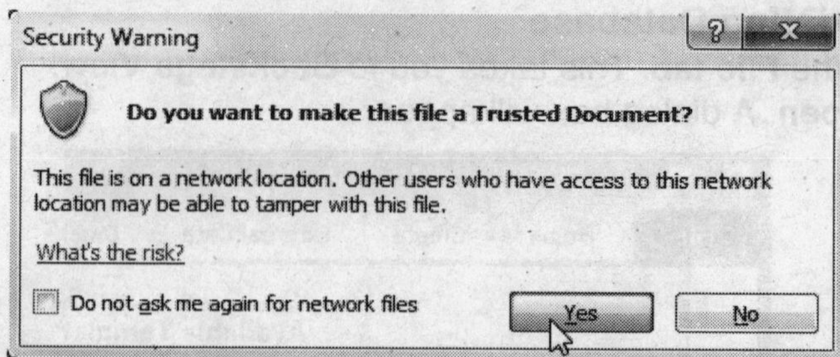

You may be prompted to log in to the database. Select your name from the log in list. If your name does not appear, click on **Add User** to enter your information.

To Close a Database

1. Click on the **File tab** to go to **Backstage View**.
2. Select **Close Database**.

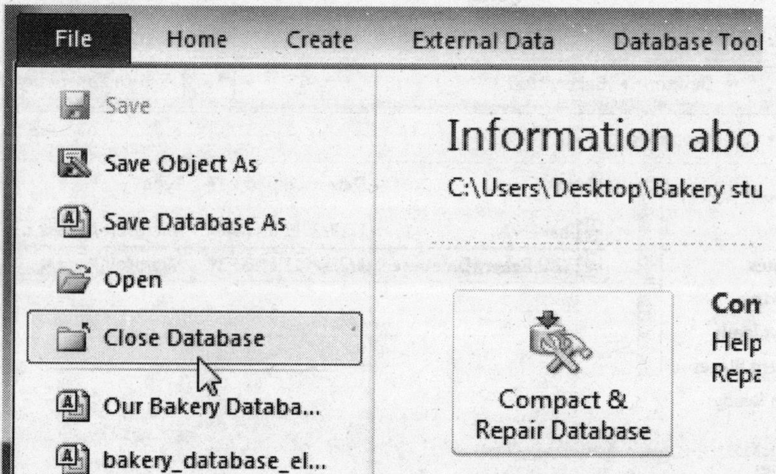

If you have any unsaved objects, a dialog box will pop up for each one, asking if you would like to save it. Select **Yes** to save the object, **No** to close it without saving, or **Cancel** to leave your database open.

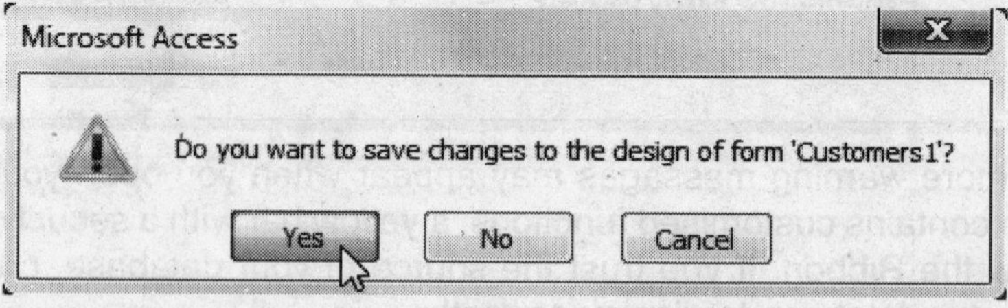

Working with Objects

Your database is a large binder or folder in which you store your data. The data itself is contained in database objects. Access 2010 treats each of these objects as separate documents, which means you will have to open and save them individually in order to work with them.

To Open an Object

1. In the **Navigation Pane**, locate the **object** you would like to open.

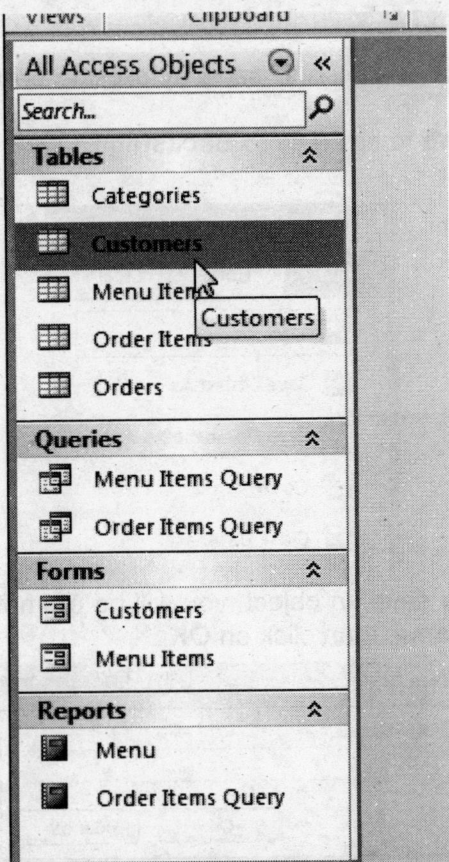

2. **Double-click** on the **desired object**. It will open and appear as a tab in the **Document Tabs** bar.

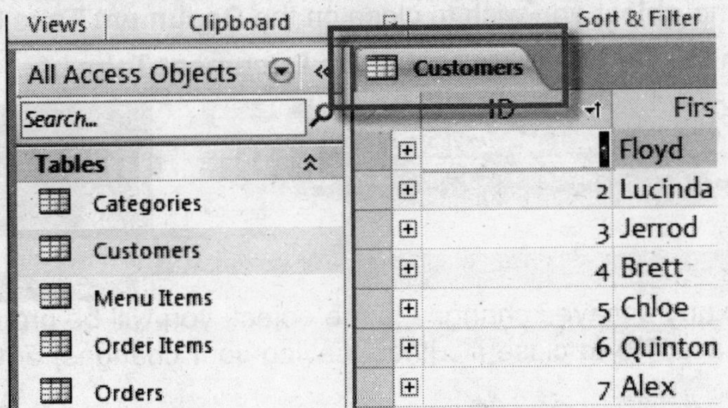

Saving Objects

As in other Microsoft Office programmes, you will be prompted to save any unsaved work when you attempt to close your database. However, it is a good idea to save your work as you go along. Saving your work often is the best way to ensure you do not lose any information if your computer crashes.

To Save a New Object

1. Select the **object** you wish to **save** by clicking on its **tab** in the **Document Tabs** bar.
2. Select the **File tab** to navigate to **Backstage View**.
3. Click on **Save**.

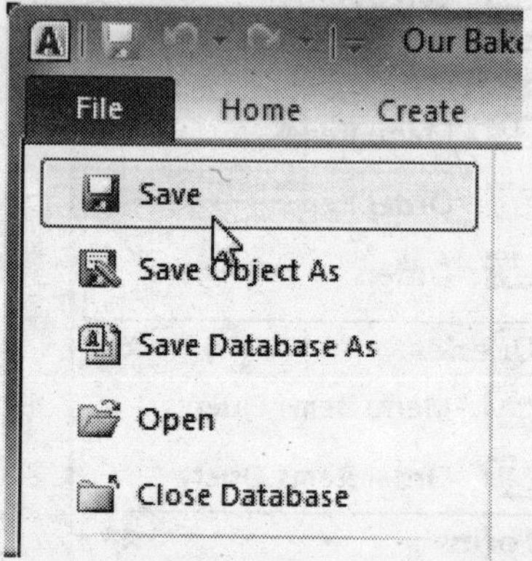

4. The first time you save an object, you will be prompted to name it. Enter the desired **object name**, then click on **OK**.

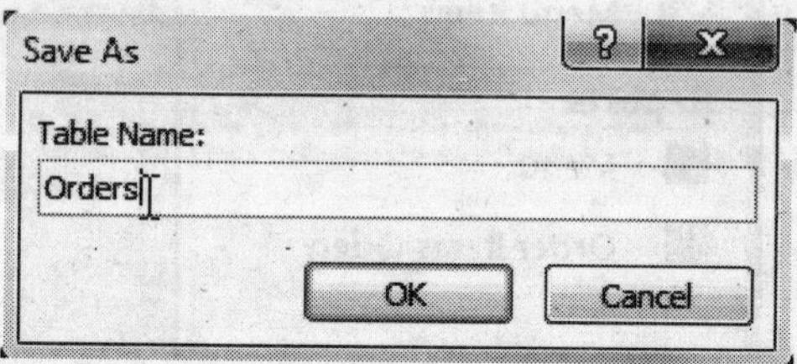

To Close an Object

1. Select the **object** you wish to close on the **Document Tabs** bar.
2. Click on the × on the far right of the **Document Tabs** bar.

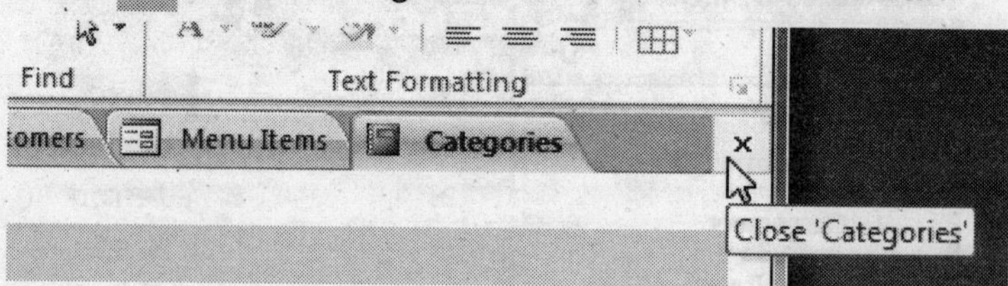

If there are any unsaved changes to the object, you will be prompted to save it. Select **Yes** to save, **No** to close it without saving your changes, or **Cancel** to leave the object open.

To Rename an Object

1. If the **object** you wish to **rename** is open, **close** it.
2. In the **Navigation Pane**, **right-click** on the **object** you would like to rename.

3. Select **Rename**.

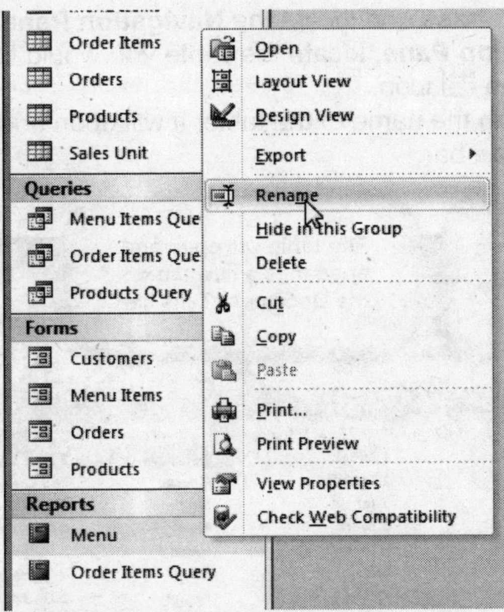

4. Type the **new name**, then press **Enter**.

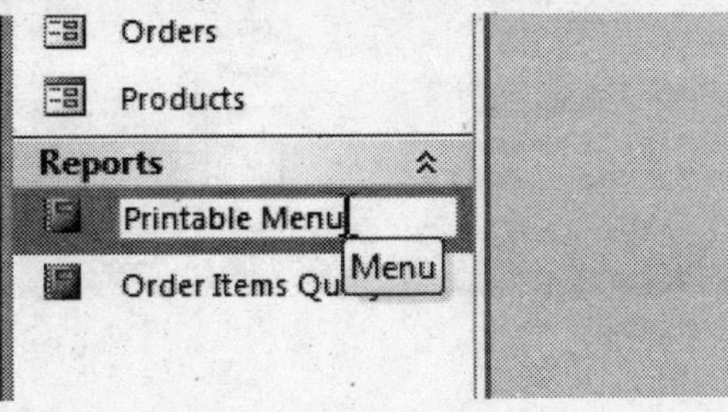

Tables

While there are four types of database objects in Access 2010, tables are arguably the most important. Even when you are using forms, queries and reports, you are still working with tables, since that is where all your data are stored. Tables are at the heart of any database, so it is important to understand how to use them.

Because the table is the primary object of a database, when you create a table and save it by giving it a name, Microsoft Access creates a section labelled **Tables** in the Navigation Pane and displays the name of thenew table in that section. In the same way, you can have as many tables as possible in the **Tables** section.

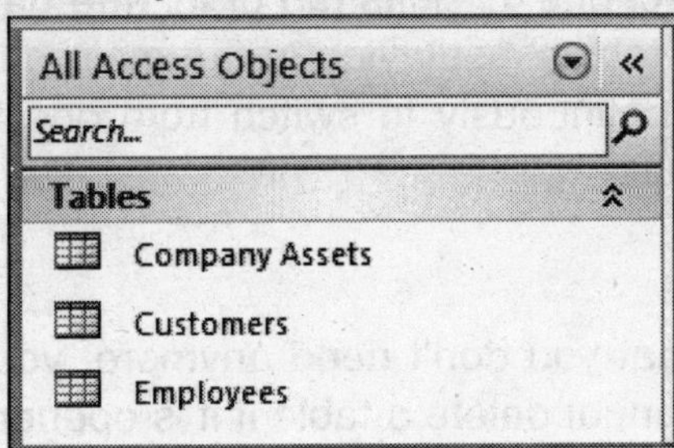

To Open an Existing Table

1. Open your **database** and locate the **Navigation Pane**.
2. In the **Navigation Pane**, locate the **table** you would like to open. Tables are marked with the ▦ icon.
3. **Double-click** on the name of the table. It will open and appear as a tab in the **Document Tabs** bar.

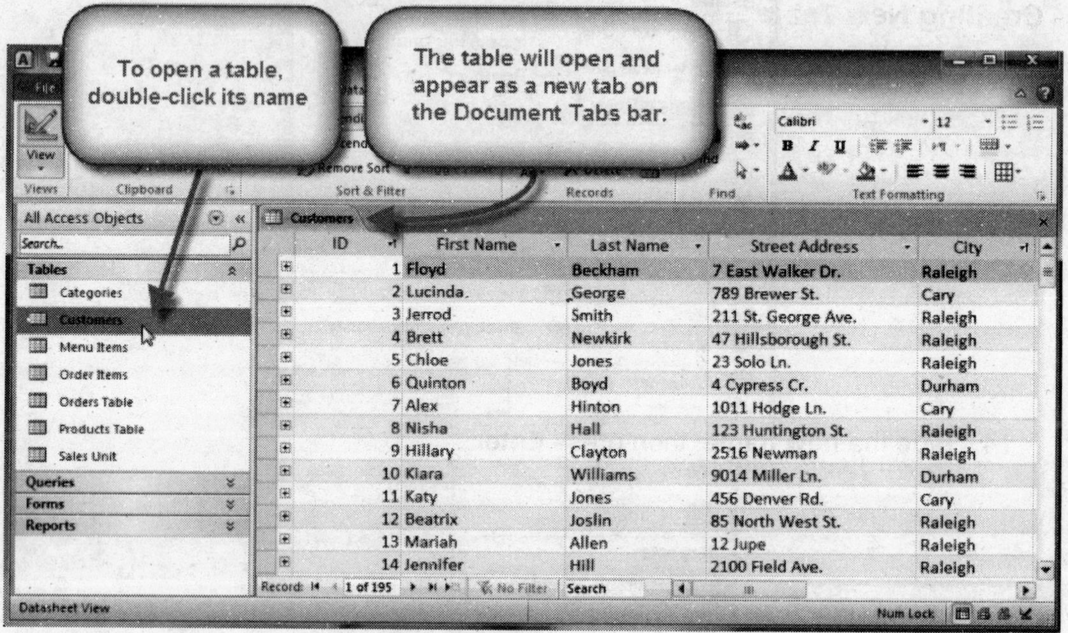

Closing a Table

After using a table, you can close it. Before closing a table, first select its tab. To close a table:

1. You can click the **close** button × on the right side of the tab.
2. You can press **Ctrl + Shift + F4**.

Selecting a Table

To select a table in the **Navigation Pane**, simply click on it.

- If you had opened many tables and they are displaying in the main area of the screen, to select one, click its **tab** or its **title bar**.
- If you have many tables displaying in the main area of the screen, you can press **Ctrl + F6** continuously to switch from one table to the next until the desired one displays.

Deleting a Table

If you have a table that you don't need anymore, you can remove it from your database. Because you cannot delete a table if it is opened, you must first close it.

To remove a table from your database:

1. In the **Navigation Pane**, **right-click** on the **table** and click on **Delete**.
2. In the **Navigation Pane**, click on the **table** to select it. Then, on the **Ribbon**, click on **Home**. In the **Record** section, click on **Delete**.
3. In the **Navigation Pane**, click on the **table** to select it and press **Delete**.

Creating New Table

To create a new table:

1. Click on **Create tab.**
2. Click on **Table Design button.**

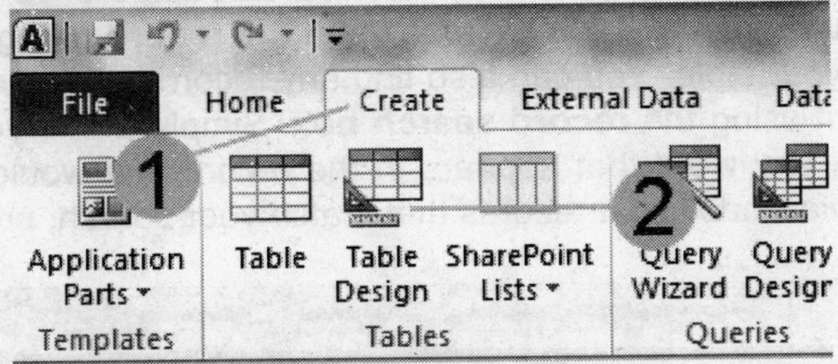

- You will see the table designation windows appear.
- Enter **fields name** and its **data type** as below.

Table1

Field Name	Data Type
stdid	Number
stdname	Text
gender	Text
phone	Text
address	Text

3. Set field **stdid** to Primary Key by **right-clicking** on that field and choose **Primary Key**.

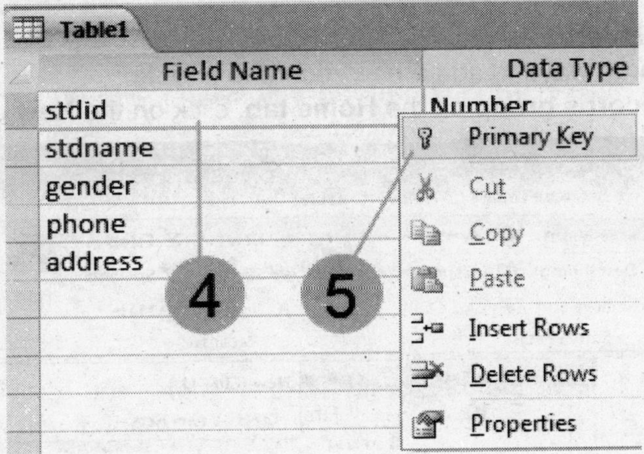

6. Click on **Ctrl + S** to Save the table.

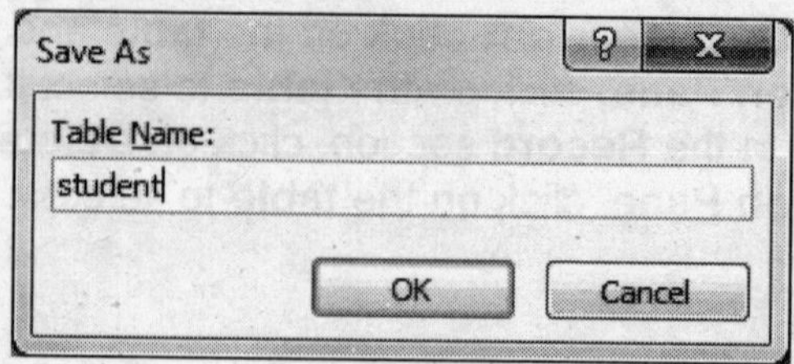

Navigating within Tables

To navigate through records in a table, you can use the **up and down arrow** keys, **scroll up and down**, or use the **arrows in the record navigation bar** located at the bottom of your table. You can also find any record in the currently open table by searching for it using the **record search box**. Simply **place your cursor** in the search box, **type** any word that appears in the record you would like to find, and press **Enter**. To view additional records that match your search, press **Enter** again.

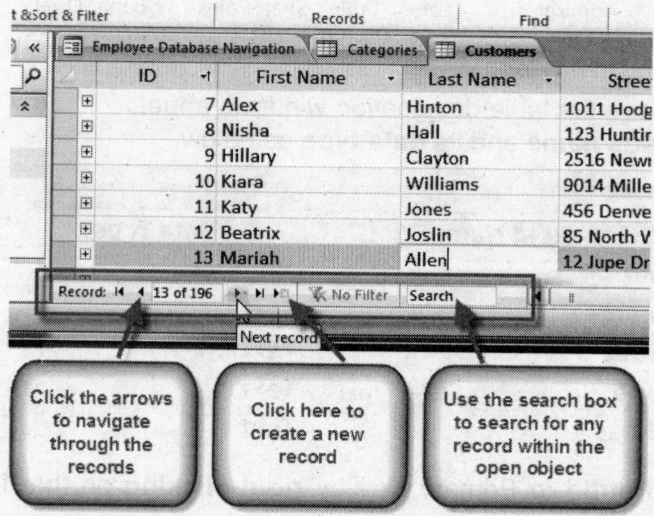

To Add a New Record

There are three ways to add a new record to a table:

1. In the **Records group** on the **Home tab**, click on the **New** command.

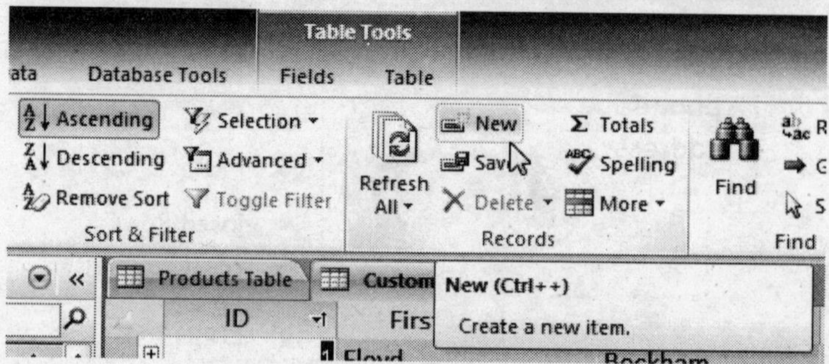

2. In the **Record Navigation bar** at the bottom of the window, click on the **New Record** button.

3. Simply begin typing in the row below your last added record.

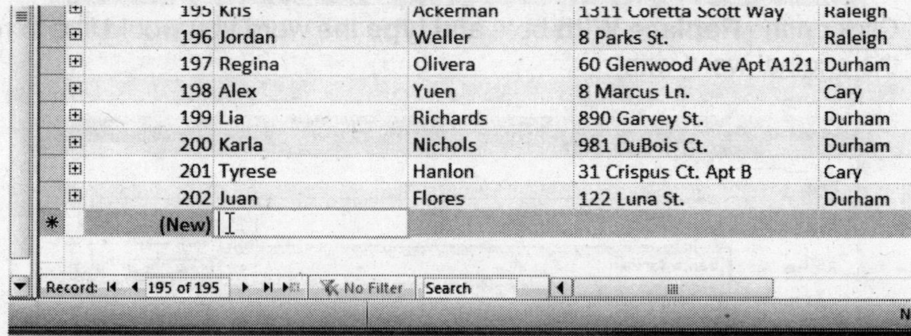

To Save a Record

1. Select the **Home tab**, and locate the **Records group**.
2. Click on the **Save** command.

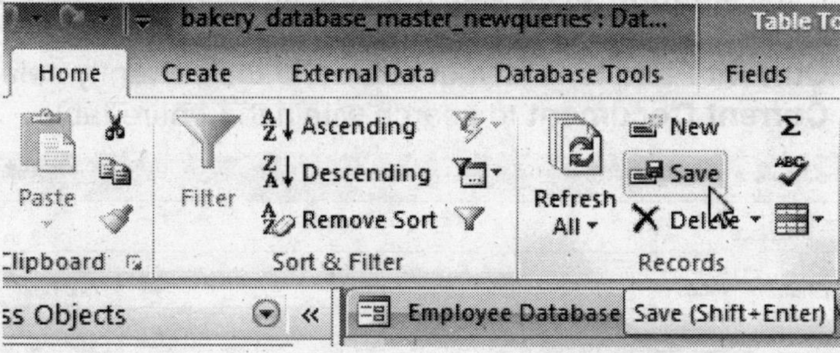

To Replace a Word within a Record

You can edit multiple occurrences of the same word by using **Find and Replace**, which searches for a term and replaces it with another term.

1. Select the **Home tab** and locate the **Find group**.
2. Select the **Replace** command. The **Find and Replace** dialog box will appear.

3. Click on the **Find What** box and **type** the word you would like to find.

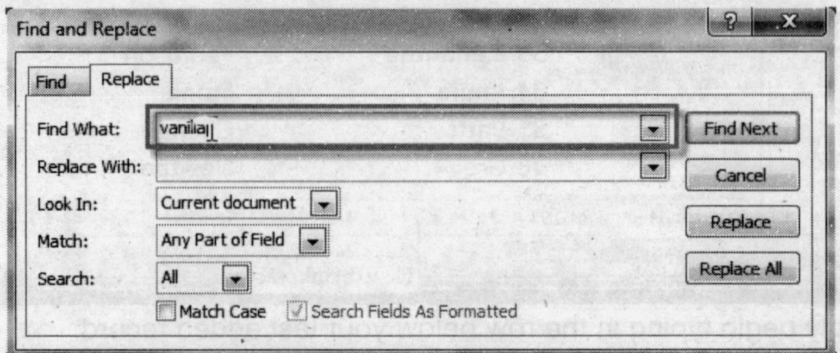

4. Click on the **Replace With** box, and **type** the word you would like to replace the original word with.

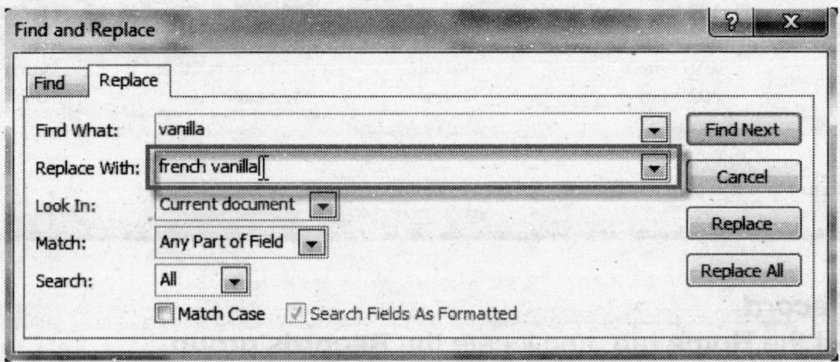

5. Click on the **Look In drop-down** arrow to select the area you would like to search.
6. Select **Current Field** to limit your search to the currently selected field.
7. Select **Current Document** to search within the entire table.

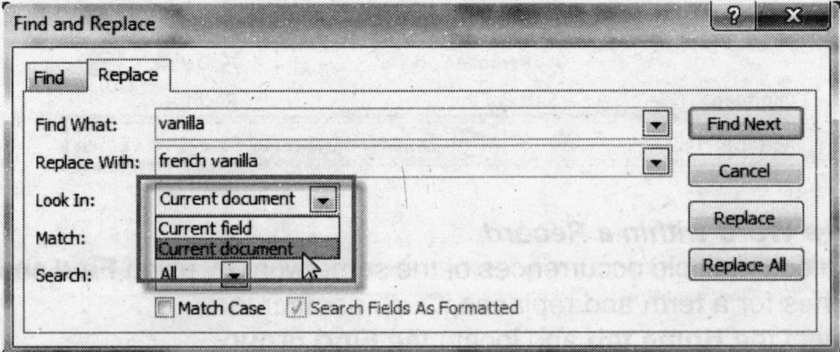

8. Click on the **Match drop-down** arrow to select how closely you would like results to match your search.
9. Select **Any Part of Field** to search for your search term in any part of a cell.
10. Select **Whole Field** to search only for cells that match your search term exactly.
11. Select **Beginning of Field** to search only for cells that start with your search term.

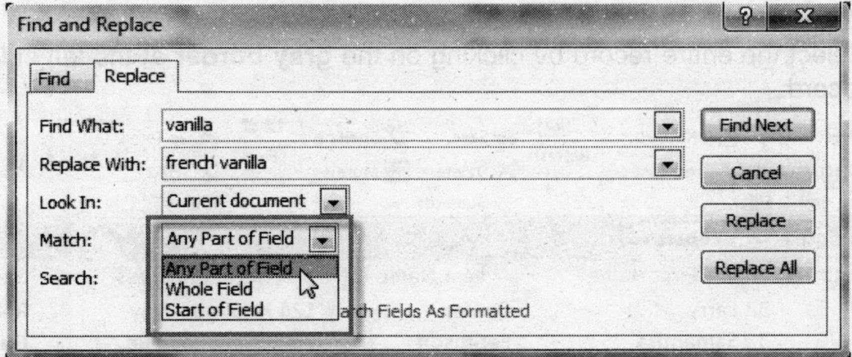

12. Click on **Find Next** to find the next occurrence of your search term.

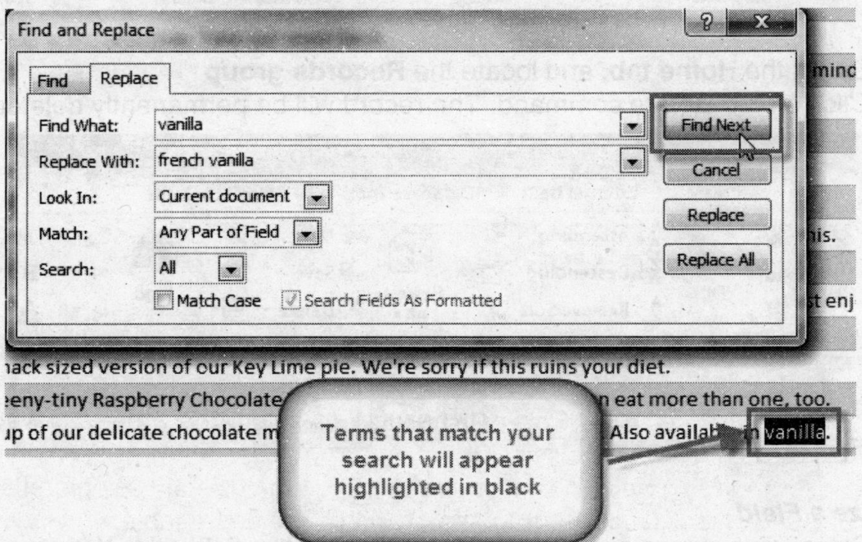

13. Click on **Replace** to replace the original word with the new one.

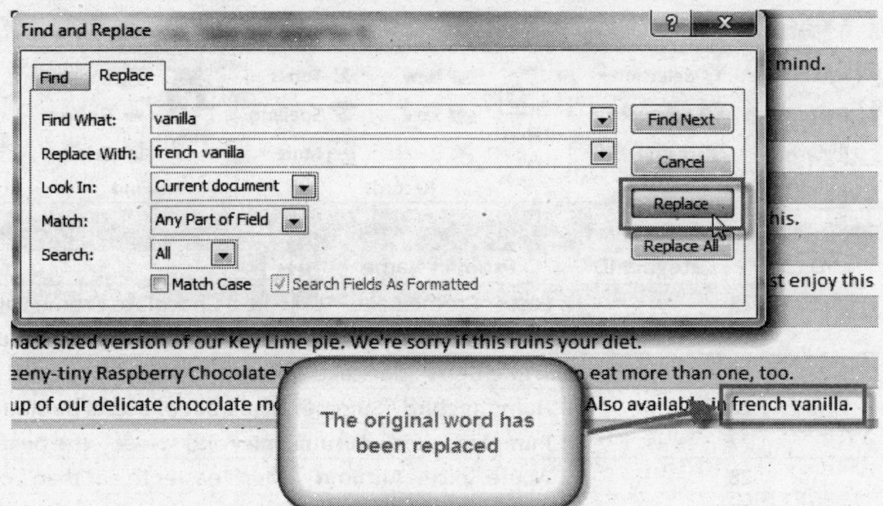

To Delete a Record

1. Select the entire record by clicking on the **gray border** at the left side of the record.

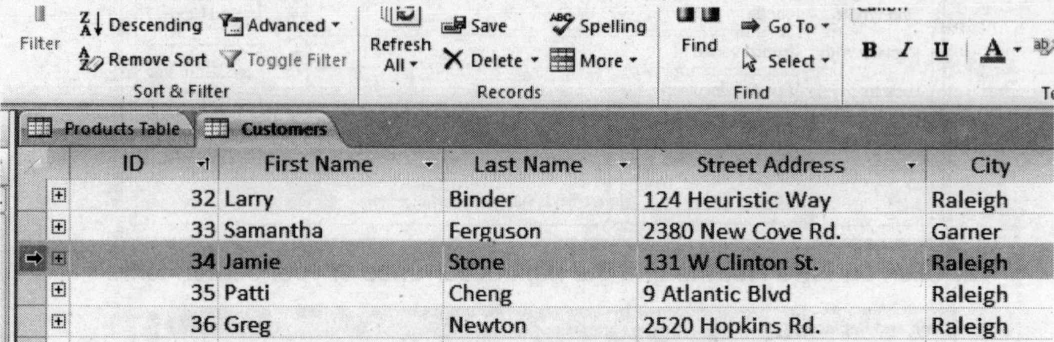

2. Select the **Home tab**, and locate the **Records group**.
3. Click on the **Delete** command. The record will be permanently deleted.

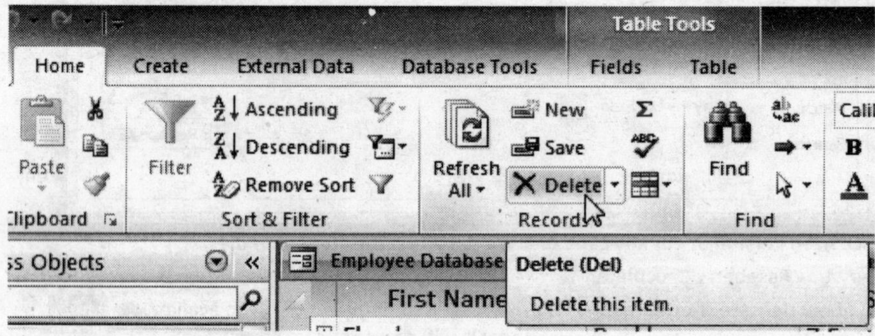

To Resize a Field

1. Place your cursor over the **right gridline** in the field title. Your mouse will become a double arrow ↔.

2. Click on the **gridline** and drag it to the right to increase the field width or to the left to decrease the field width.
3. Release the mouse. The field width will be changed.

ernal Data Database Tools Fields Table

Filter · Ascending · Descending · Remove Sort · Selection · Advanced · Toggle Filter · Sort & Filter · Refresh All · New · Save · Delete · Totals · Spelling · More · Records · Find · Replace · Go To · Select · Find · Calibri (D · B I

Products Table · Customers

ID	Category ID	Product Name	
23	2	Easter Creme Cake- Spring	Like a Chocola
24	2	Lemon Blueberry - Summer	Summer sunsl
25	2	Triple Berry Shortcake - Summer	Strawberries,
26	2	Hummingbird - Summer	Made out of a
27	2	Pumpkin Spice - Autumn	Spicy and swe
28	2	Apple Spice - Autumn	Much easier t
29	2	Gingerbread - Winter	A bite of this c

To Resize a Row

1. Place your cursor over the **bottom gridline** in the gray area to the left of the row. Your mouse will become a double arrow.

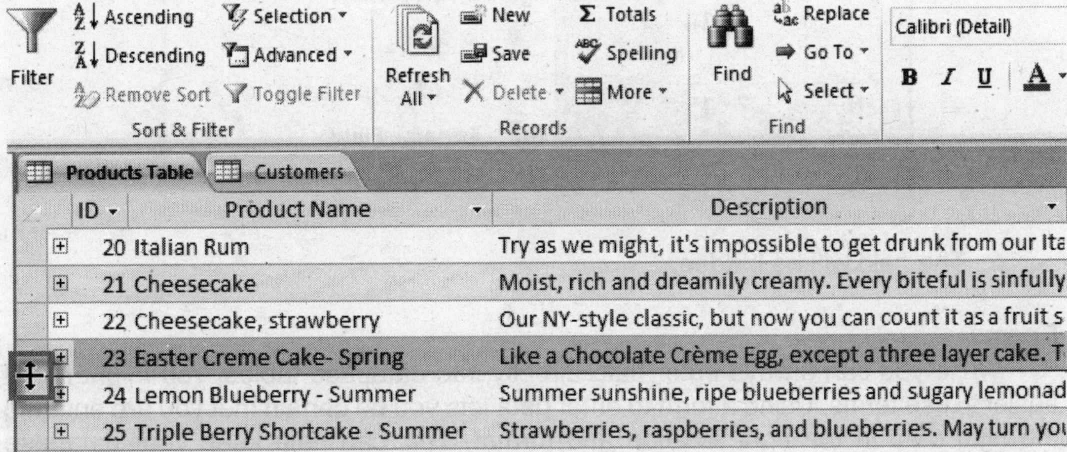

2. Click on the **gridline** and drag it downward to increase the row height or upward to decrease the row height.
3. Release the mouse. The row height will be changed.

To Hide a Field

1. **Right-click** on the field title.

2. From the drop-down menu, select **Hide Fields**.

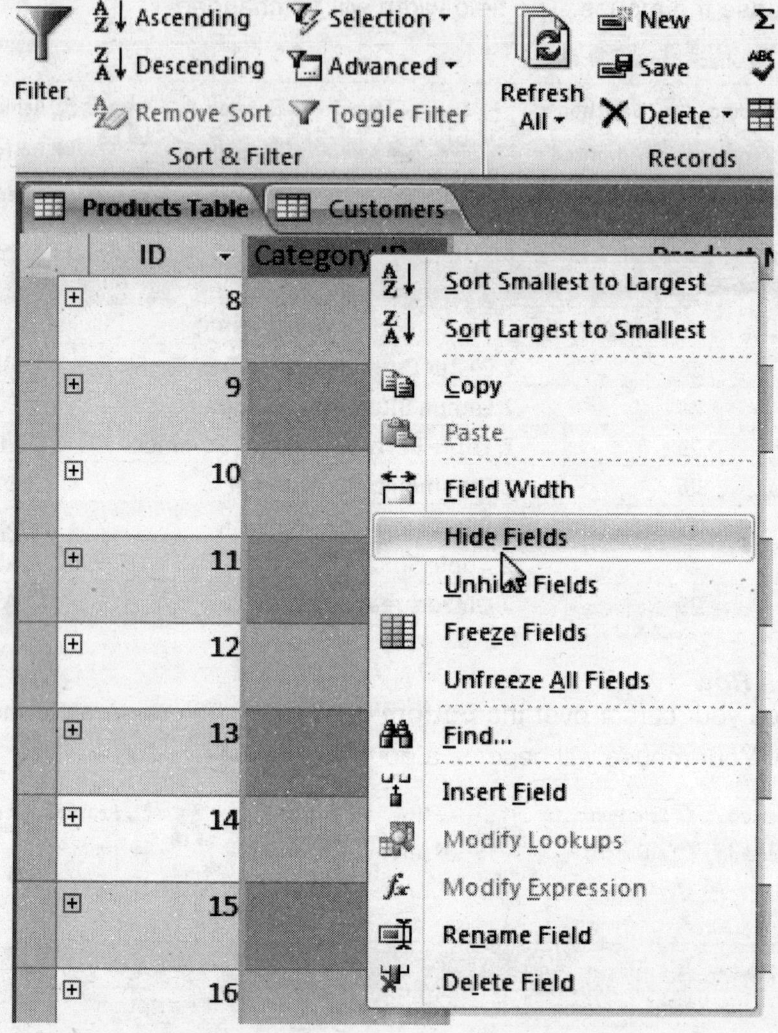

3. The field will be hidden.

Forms

While you can always enter data directly into database tables, you might find it easier to use forms. Using a form to enter data lets you be certain that you are entering the right data in the right location and format. This can help keep your database accurate and consistent.

To Open an Existing Form

1. Open your database, and locate the **Navigation Pane**.
2. In the **Navigation Pane**, locate the **form** you would like to open. Forms are marked with the icon.

3. **Double-click** on the name of the form. It will open and appear as a tab in the **Document Tabs** bar.

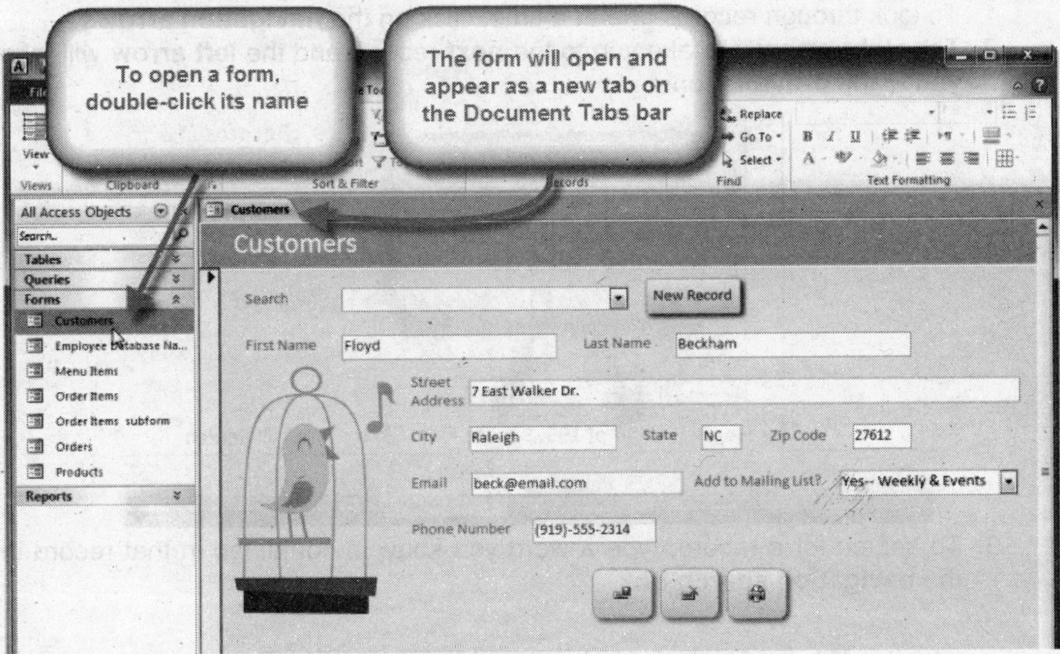

To Add a New Record

There are two ways to add a new record to a form:

1. In the **Records group** on the **Home tab** of the **Ribbon**, click on the **New** command.

2. On the **Record Navigation** bar at the bottom of the window, click on the **New Record** button.

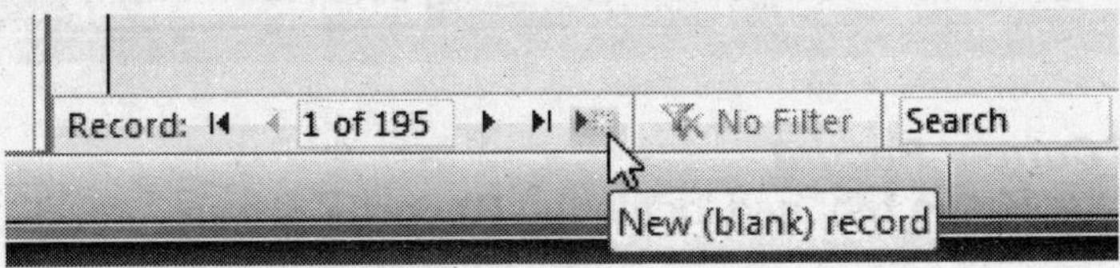

To Find an Existing Record to View or Edit

There are two ways to find and view an existing record using a form, and they both use the Navigation Bar at the bottom of the screen.

1. To look through records one at a time, click on the **navigation arrows**.
2. The **right arrow** will take you to the **next** record, and the **left arrow** will take you to the **previous** one.

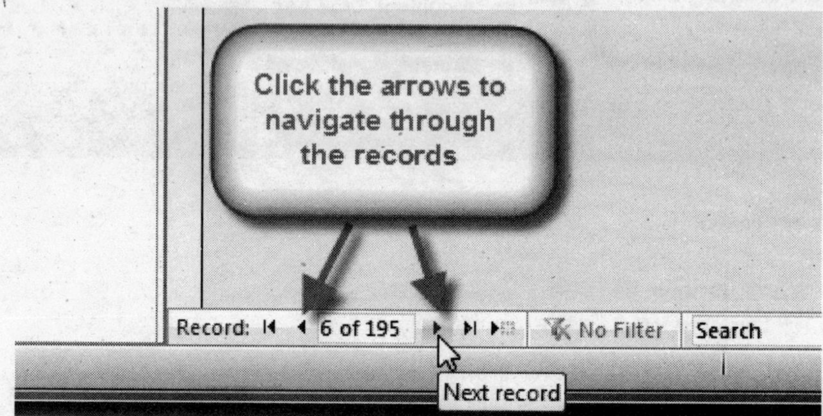

3. To search for a record, type a word you know is contained in that record in the **navigation search box**.

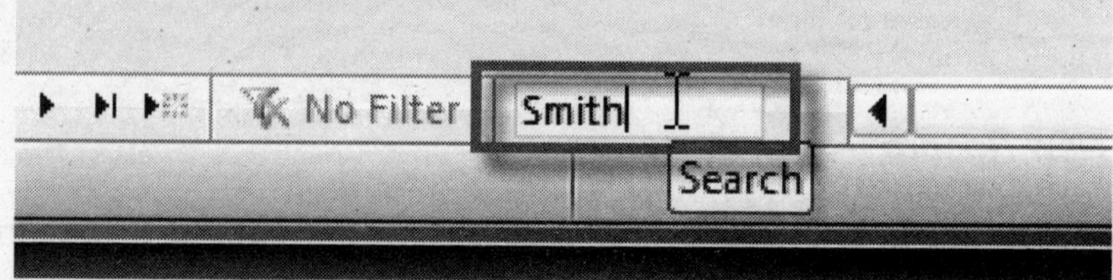

To Save the Current Record

1. Select the **Home tab**, and locate the **Records group**.
2. Click on the **Save** command. The current record will be saved.

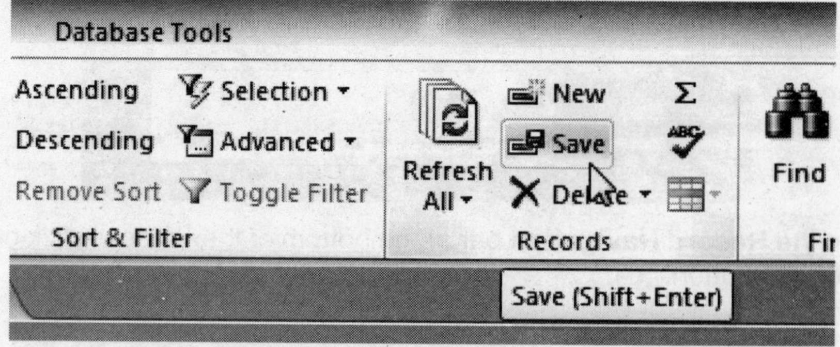

To Delete the Current Record

1. Select the **Home tab**, and locate the **Records group**.

2. Click on the **Delete** command. The record will be permanently deleted.

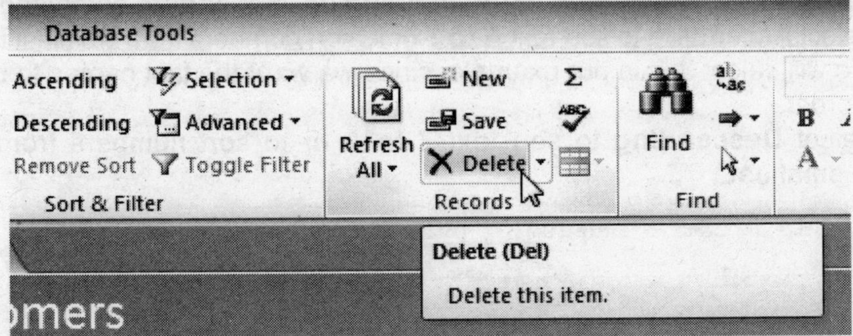

Sorting and Filtering

Sorting and filtering are tools that let you organise your data. When you sort data, you are putting it in order. Filtering data lets you hide unimportant data and focus only on the data you are interested in.

To Sort Records

1. Select a field in the cell you wish to sort by. In this example, we will sort by customers' last names.

rt & Filter | Records

se Navigation | Customers

	First Name	Last Name	
1	Tracey	Beckham	7 I
2	Lucinda	George	78
3	Jerrod	Smith	21
4	Brett	Newkirk	47
5	Chloe	Jones	23
6	Quinton	Boyd	4 (
7	Alex	Hinton	10
8	Nisha	Hall	12
9	Hillary	Clayton	25
10	Kiara	Williams	90
11	Katy	Jones	45
12	Beatrix	Joslin	85
13	Mariah	Allen	12
14	Jennifer	Hill	21
15	Jaleel	Smith	12
16	Cody	Hayes	65
17	Amaya	Gibson	5 \
18	Cynthia	Love	78

2. Click on the **Home tab** on the **Ribbon**, and locate the **Sort & Filter group**.
3. Sort the field by selecting the **Ascending** or **Descending** command.
4. Select **Ascending** to sort text **A to Z** or to sort numbers from smallest to largest. We will select this in our example, since we want the last names to be in A to Z order.
5. Select **Descending** to sort text **Z to A** or to sort numbers from **largest to smallest**.

Home
Create
External Data
Database Tools
Fields
Table
Cut
Copy
Paste
Format Painter
Clipboard
Filter
Ascending
Descending
Remove Sort
Selection
Advanced
Toggle Filter
Sort & Filter
Refresh All
New
Save
Delete
Records
Customers
ID
First Name
Last Name
1 Tracey Beckham
2 Lucinda George
3 Jerrod Smith
4 Brett Newkirk

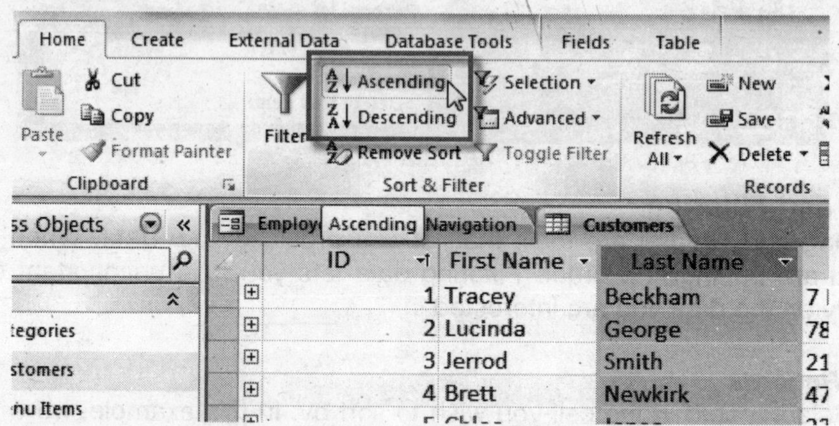

6. The table will now be sorted by the selected field.

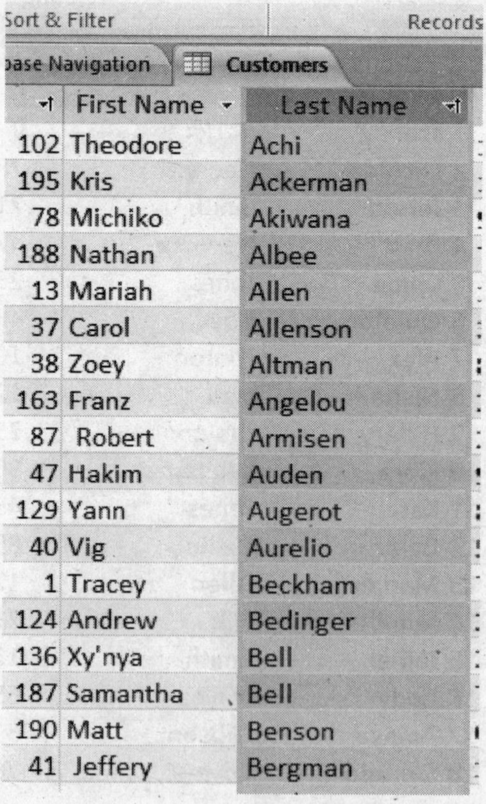

Sort & Filter
Records
Customers
First Name
Last Name
102 Theodore Achi
195 Kris Ackerman
78 Michiko Akiwana
188 Nathan Albee
13 Mariah Allen
37 Carol Allenson
38 Zoey Altman
163 Franz Angelou
87 Robert Armisen
47 Hakim Auden
129 Yann Augerot
40 Vig Aurelio
1 Tracey Beckham
124 Andrew Bedinger
136 Xy'nya Bell
187 Samantha Bell
190 Matt Benson
41 Jeffery Bergman

7. To save the **new sort**, click on the **Save** command on the **Quick Access toolbar**.

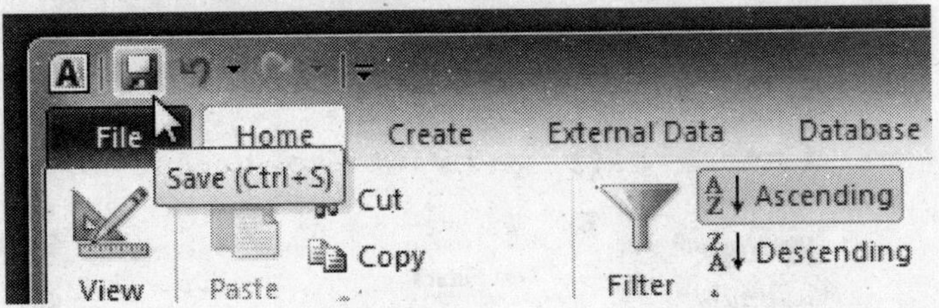

Filtering Records

Filters allow you to view only the data you want to see. When you create a filter, you set criteria for the data you want to display. The filter then searches all of the records in the table, finds the ones that meet your search criteria, and temporarily hides the ones that do not.

To Create a Simple Filter

1. Click on the **drop-down arrow** next to the field you would like to filter by. We will filter by city, as we want to see a list of customers who live in a certain city.

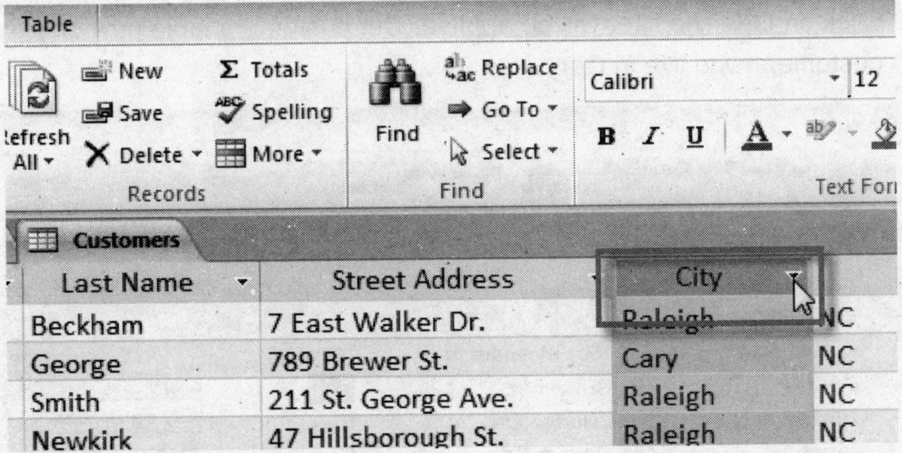

2. A **drop-down menu** with a checklist will appear. Only checked items will be included in the filtered results. Use the following options to determine which items will be included in your filter:
   - Select and deselect items one at a time by clicking their check-boxes. Here, we will deselect all the options except for Cary.
   - Click on **Select All** to include every item in the filter. Clicking on **Select All** a second time will deselect all items.
   - Click on **Blank** to set the filter to find only the records with no data in the selected field.

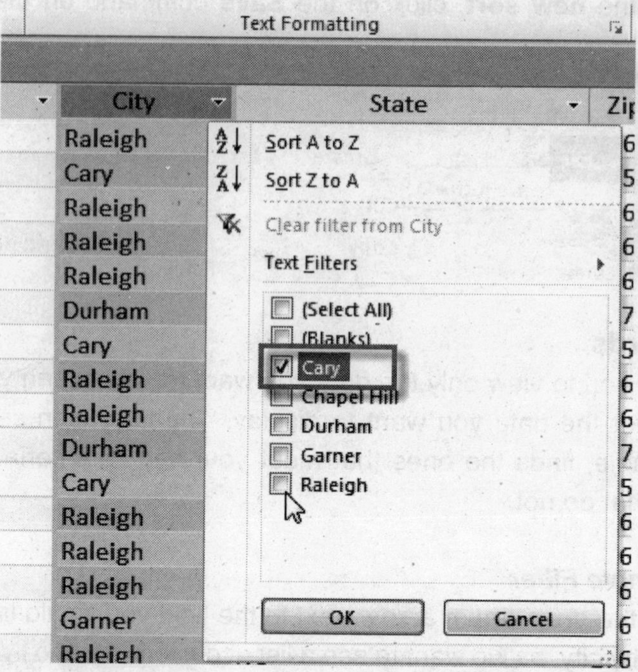

3. Click on **OK**. The filter will be applied. Our customers table now displays only customers who live in Cary.

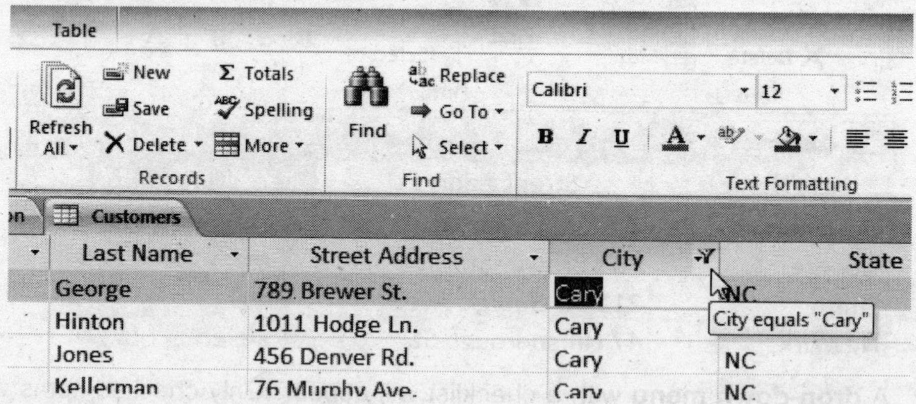

Queries

Queries are a way of searching for and compiling data from one or more tables. Running a query is like asking a detailed question of your database. When you build a query in Access, you are defining specific search conditions to find exactly the data you want.

To Apply a Simple One-table Query

1. Select the **Create tab** on the **Ribbon**, and locate the **Queries group**.
2. Select the **Query Design** command.

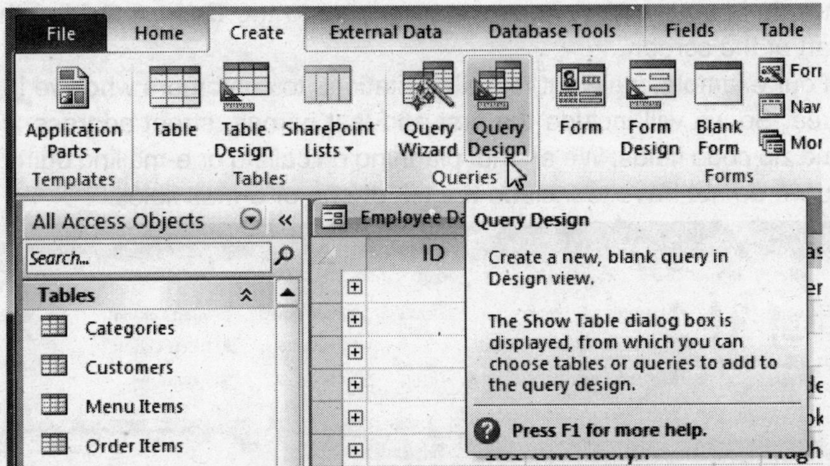

3. Access will switch to **Query Design view**. In the **Show Table dialog box** that appears, select the table you would like to run a query on. Click on **Add**, then click on **Close**. We are running a query about our customers. So we will add the **Customers table**.

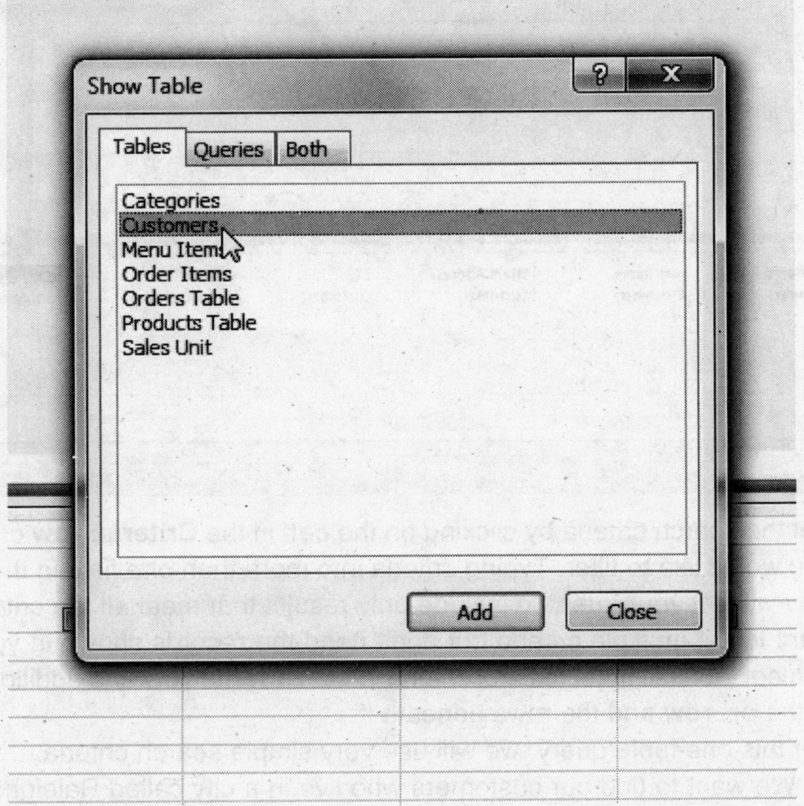

4. The selected table will appear as a small window in the **Object Relationship Pane**. In the table window, **double-click** on the **field names** you would like to

include in your query. They will be added to the **Design Grid** in the bottom part of the screen.

In our example, we want to mail invitations to customers who live in a certain area. So we will include the first and last names, street address, city, state, and zip code fields. We are not planning on calling or e-mailing our customers, so we do not have to include the telephone or e-mail fields.

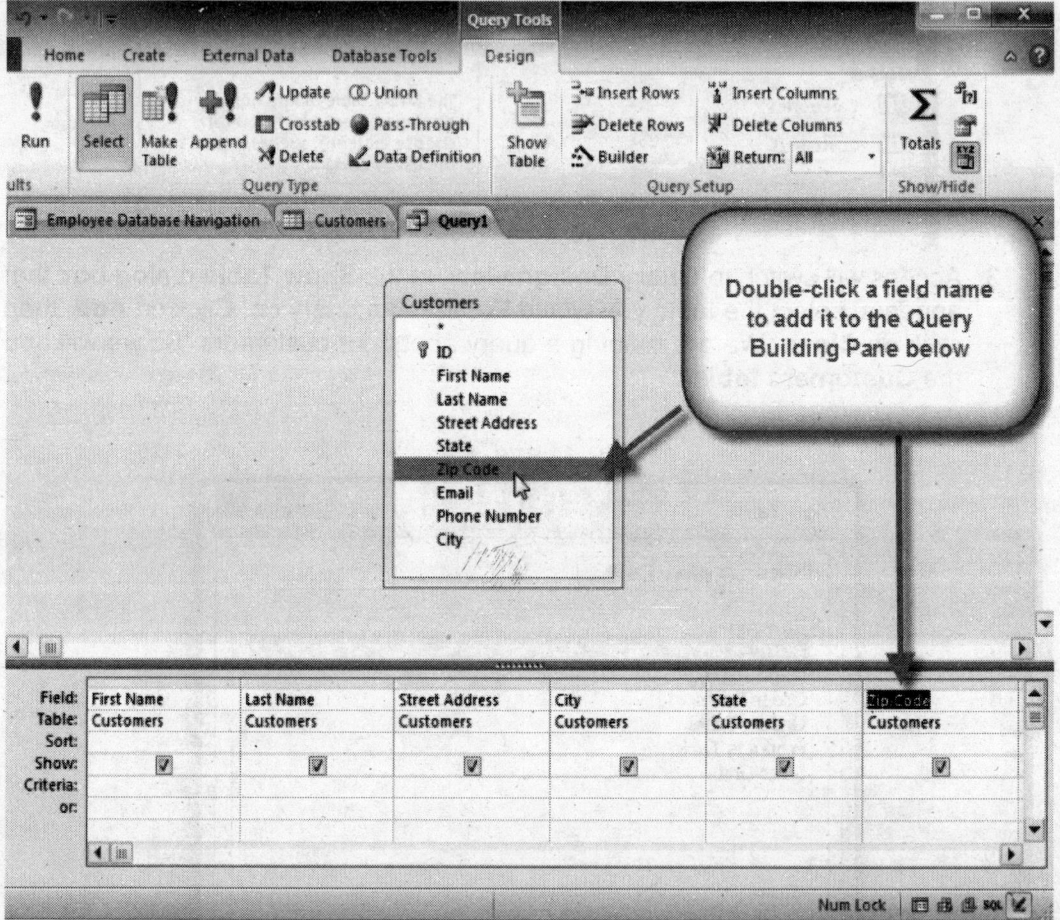

5. Set the search criteria by clicking on the **cell** in the **Criteria: row** of each field you would like to filter. Typing criteria into more than one field in the **Criteria: row** will set your query to include only results that meet all the criteria. If you want to set multiple criteria but don't need the records shown in your results to meet them all, type the first criteria in the **Criteria: row** and additional criteria in the **or: row** and the rows beneath it.
6. For this one-table query, we will use very simple search criteria.
   - We want to find our customers who live in a city called Raleigh. So in our City field, we will type "Raleigh". Typing "Raleigh" in quotation marks will retrieve all records with an exact match for "Raleigh" in the City field.

- Some customers who live in the suburbs live fairly close, and we would like to invite them as well. We will add their zip code, 27513, as another criteria. Since we want to find customers who either live in Raleigh or in the 27513 zip code, we will type "27513" in the or: row of the Zip Code field.

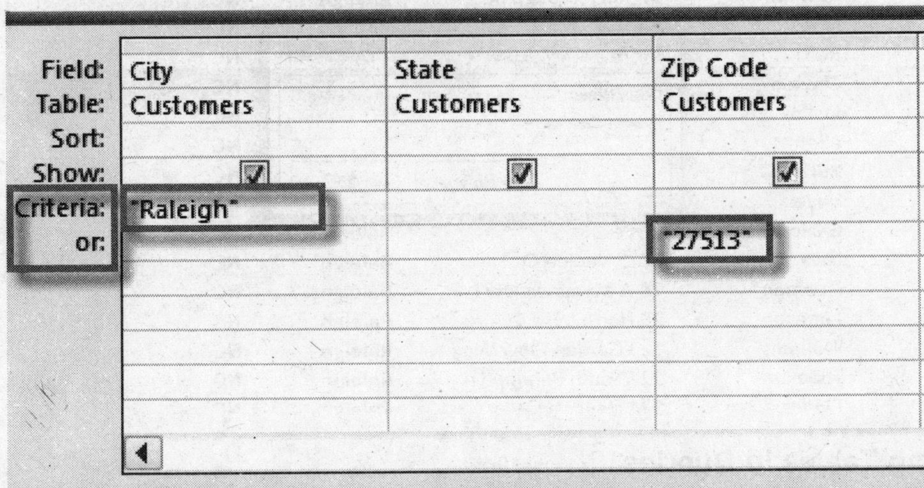

1. After we have set our criteria, we will run the query by clicking on the **Run** command on the **Query Tools Design tab**.

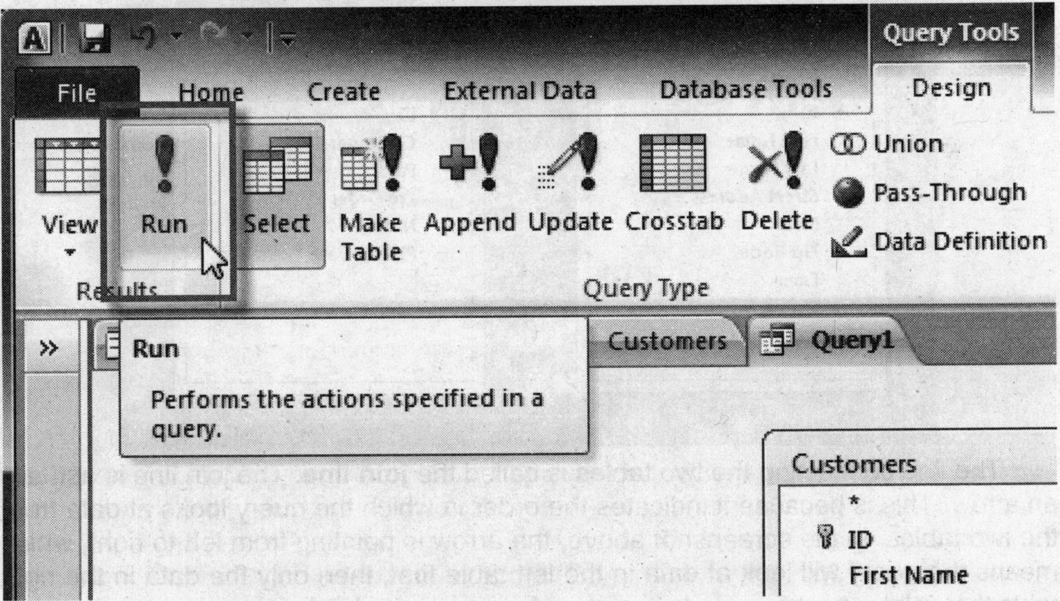

2. The query results will be displayed in the query's **Datasheet View**, which looks like a table. If desired, save your query by clicking on the **Save** command in the **Quick Access Toolbar**. When prompted to name it, type in the desired name. Then click on **OK**.

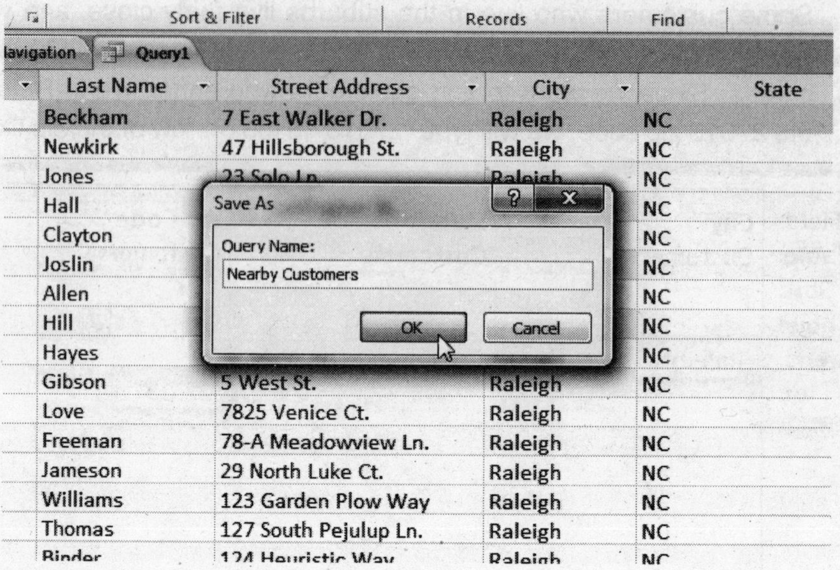

Joining Tables in Queries

When we add two tables to an Access query, this is what we will see in the **Object Relationship Pane**.

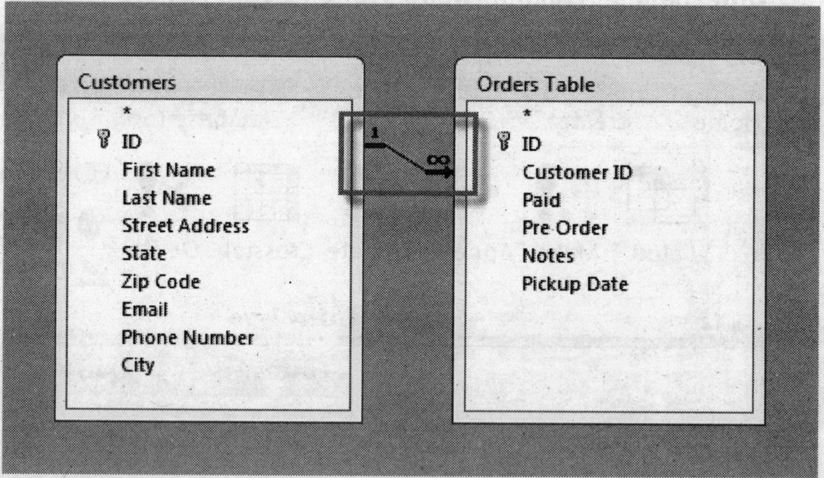

The line connecting the two tables is called the **join line**. The join line is actually an arrow. This is because it indicates the order in which the query looks at data from the two tables. In the screenshot above, the arrow is pointing from left to right, which means the query will look at data in the left table first, then only the data in the right table that relates to the records it is already seen in the left table.

Creating a Multi-table Query

Now that you have planned our query, you are ready to design and run it. If you have created written plans for our query, be sure to reference them often throughout the query design process.

To Create a Multi-table Query

1. Select the **Query Design** command from the **Create tab** on the **Ribbon**.

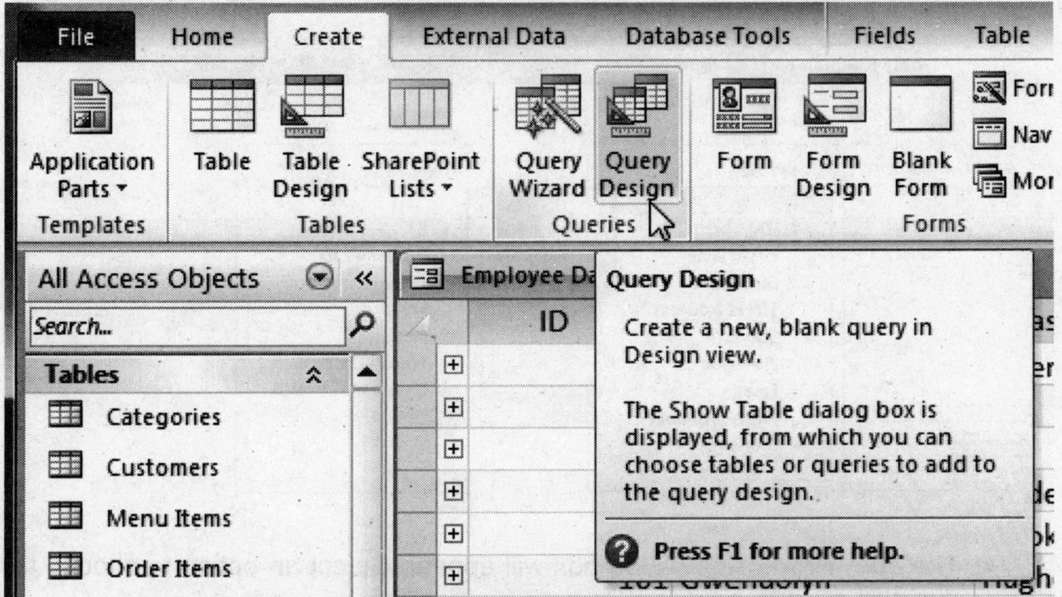

2. In the **Show Table** dialog box that appears, select each table you would like to include in your query, then click on **Add**. After you have added all the tables you want, click on **Close**. When we planned our query, we decided that we needed information from the **Customers and Orders table**, so we will add those.

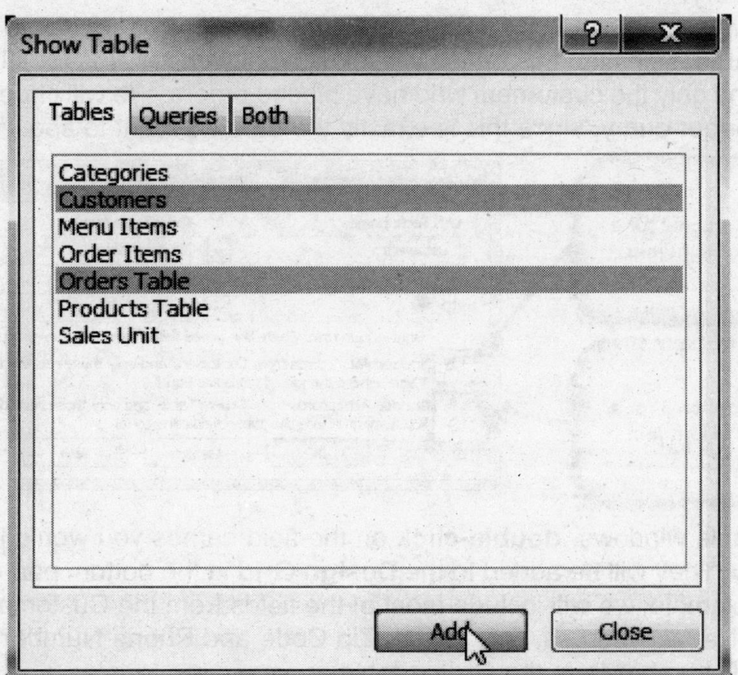

3. The tables will appear in the **Object Relationship Pane**, which is linked by a join line. **Double-click** on the thin section of the join line between two tables to edit its join direction.

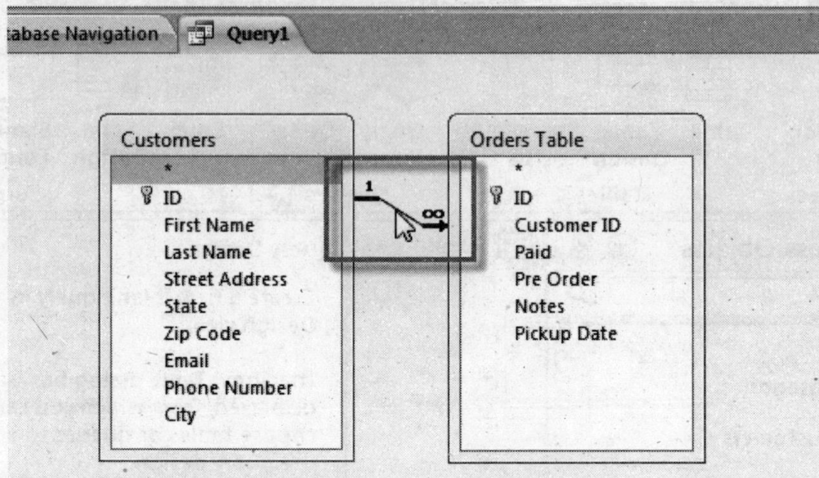

4. The **Join Properties** dialog box will appear. Select an option to choose the direction of your join.
   - Choose **option 2:** for a **Left to Right** join. In our query, the left table is the **Customers table**. So choosing this would mean all the customers who met our location criteria, whether or not they had placed an order, would be included in our results. We do not want to choose this option for our query.
   - Choose **option 3:** for a **Right to Left** join. Since our right table is our **Orders table**, selecting this option will let us work with records for all of the orders and only the customers who have placed orders. We will choose this option for our query, since this is exactly the data we want to see.

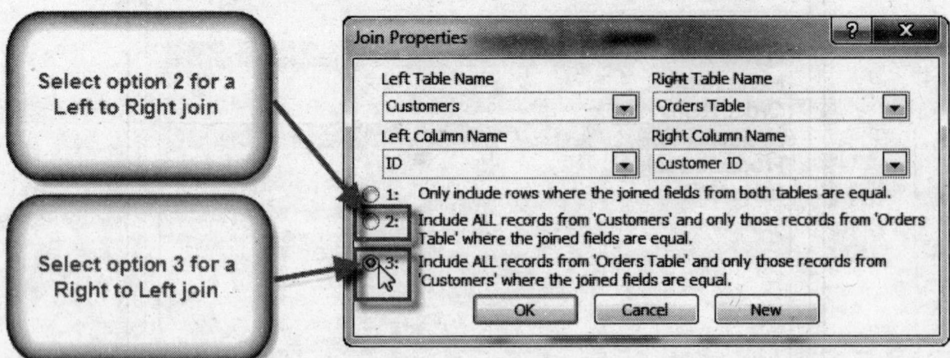

In the table windows, **double-click** on the field names you would like to include in your query. They will be added to the **Design Grid** in the bottom part of the screen.

In our example, we will include most of the fields from the Customers table: First Name, Last Name, Address, City, State, Zip Code and Phone Number. We will also include the ID number from the Orders table.

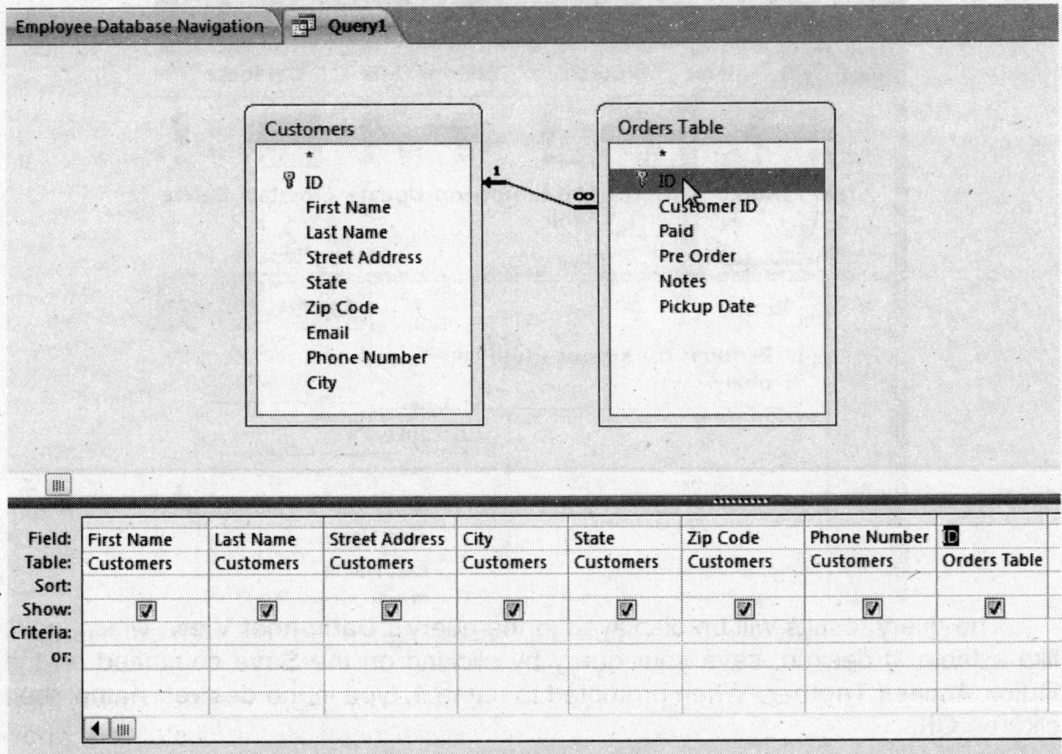

Set field criteria by entering the desired criteria in the criteria row of each field. We want to set two criteria:

- First, to find customers who do not live in Raleigh, we will type **Not In** ("Raleigh") in the **City field**.
- Second, to find customers who have a phone number beginning with the area code 919, we will type **Like** ("919*") in the Phone Number field.

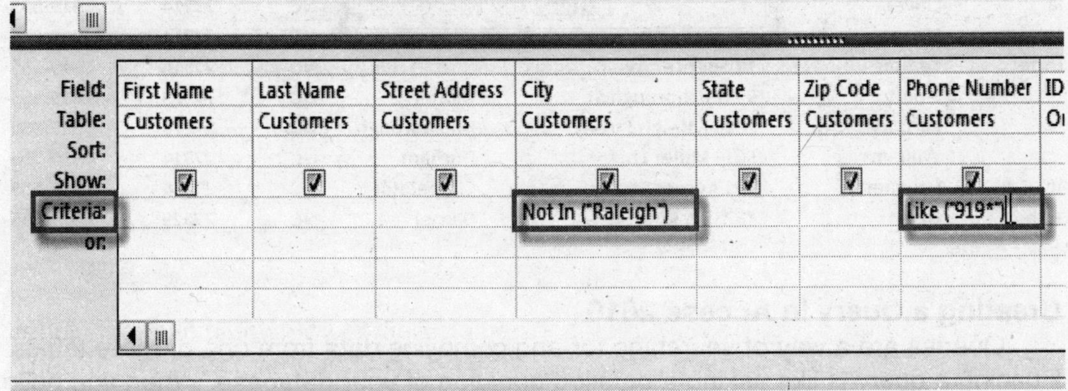

After you have set your criteria, run the query by clicking on the **Run** command on the **Query Tools Design tab**.

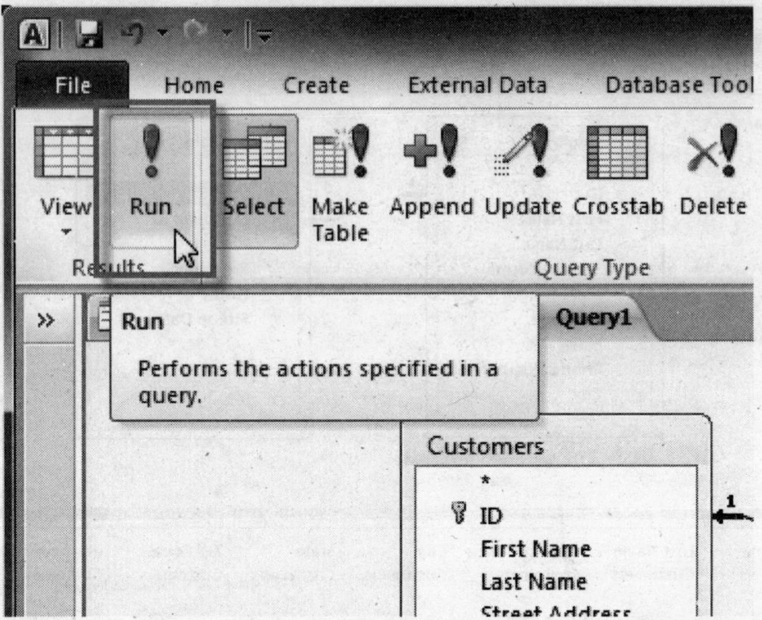

The query results will be displayed in the query's **Datasheet View**, which looks like a table. If desired, save your query by clicking on the **Save** command on the **Quick Access Toolbar**. When prompted to name it, type in the **desired name**, then click on **OK**.

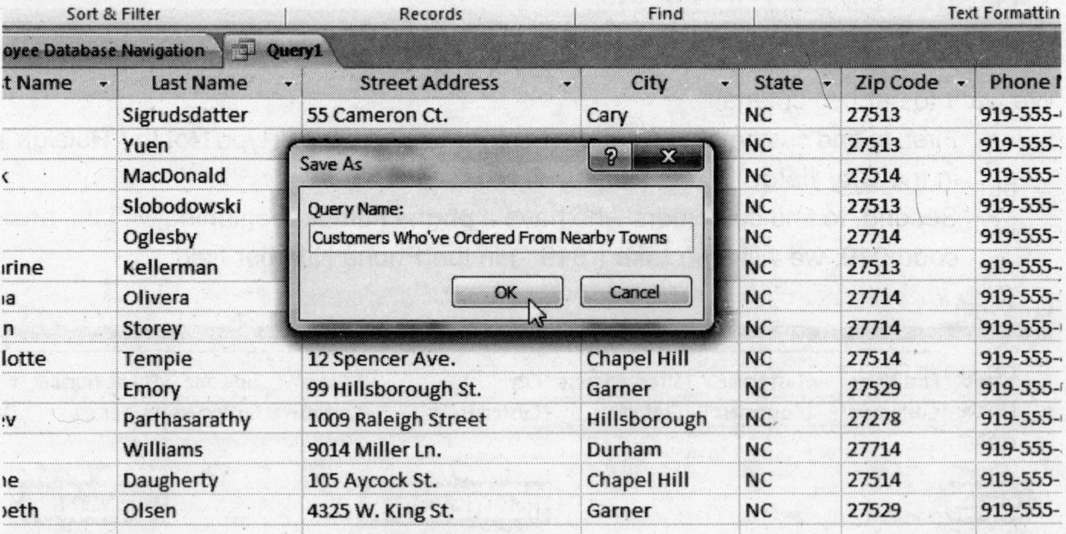

Creating a Query in Access 2010

Queries are a way of searching for and compiling data from one or more tables. Running a query is like asking a detailed question of your database. When you build a query in Access, you are defining specific search conditions to find exactly the data you want.

Queries are far more powerful than the simple searches or filters you might use to find data within a table. This is because queries can draw their information from multiple tables. A well-designed query can give information you might not be able to find out simply by examining the data in your tables.

When you run a query, the results are presented to you in a table, but when you design one you use a different view. This is called Query Design view, and it lets you see how your query is put together.

Here, let's create a query listing the names of all of our company's products, our desired target inventory levels and the list price for each item. (Suppose that you have a Access database existing in your computer named 'North India'.)

1. Open Your Database

Go to the **File** tab, select **Open** and locate the North India database on your computer.

2. Switch to the Create tab

In the Access ribbon, change from the **File** tab to the **Create** tab. This will change the icons presented to you in the ribbon.

3. Click the Query Wizard Icon

The query wizard simplifies the creation of new queries. We'll use it to introduce the concept of query creation. The alternative is to use the **Query Design view**, which facilitates the creation of more sophisticated queries but is more complicated to use.

4. Select a Query Type

Access will ask you to choose the type of query you wish to create. For our purposes, we will use the **Simple Query Wizard**. Select this and click on **OK** to continue.

5. Select the Appropriate Table from the Pull-down Menu

The **Simple Query Wizard** will open. It includes a pull-down menu that should be defaulted to 'Table: Customers'. When you select the pull-down menu, you'll be presented with a listing of all the tables and queries currently stored in your Access database. These are the valid data sources for your new query.

6. Choose the Fields You Wish to Appear in the Query Results

You can do this by either double-clicking on them or by single clicking first on the **field name** and then on the '>' icon. As you do this, the fields will move from the **Available Fields** listing to the **Selected Fields** listing. Notice that there are three other icons offered. The '>>' icon will select all available fields. The '<' icon allows you to remove the highlighted field from the **Selected Fields** list while the '<<' icon removes all selected fields.

7. Repeat Steps 5 and 6 to Add Information from Additional Tables, as Desired

Here, we're pulling information from a single table. However, we're not limited to using only one table. That's the power of a query. You can combine information from multiple tables and easily show relationships. All you have to do is select the fields. Note that this works because the North India database has predefined relationships between tables. If you're creating a new database, you'll need to establish these relationships yourself.

8. Click on Next

When you're finished adding fields to your query, click on the **Next** button to continue.

9. Choose the Type of Results You would Like to Produce

We want to produce a full listing of products and their suppliers, so choose the Detail option here and click on the **Next** button to continue.

10. Give Your Query a Title

Now you're almost done. On the next screen you can give your query a title. Select something descriptive that will help you recognize this query later. We'll call this query 'Product Supplier Information'.

11. Click on Finish

You'll be presented with the query results which will contain a list of our company products, desired target inventory levels and list prices.

Create a Report by using the Report Tool

The Report tool provides the fastest way for you to create a report, because it generates a report immediately without prompting you for information. The report displays all the fields from the underlying table or query. The Report tool may not create the final product that you ultimately want, but it is quite useful as a means to quickly look at the underlying data. You can then save the report and modify it in **Layout** view or **Design** view so that it better serves your purposes.

1. In the **Navigation** pane, click on the **table** or **query** on which you want to base the report.
2. On the **Create** tab, in the **Reports** group, click on **Report**. Access builds the report and displays it in **Layout** view.
3. After viewing the report, you can save it and then close both the report and the underlying table or query that you used as a record source.

Default Values in Access 2010

You add the default value by opening the table in Design view and then entering a value in the Default Value property for the field. If you set a default value for a table field, Access applies your value to any controls that you base on that field. If you don't bind a control to a table field, or you link to data in other tables, you set a default value for your form controls itself.

You can set a default value for table fields set to the Text, Memo, Number, Date/Time, Currency, Yes/No, and Hyperlink data types. If you don't supply a value, the field remains null (blank) until you enter a value. After you define a default value, Access applies that value to any new records that you add.

Set a Default Value for a Table Field

When you set a default value for a table field, any controls that you bind to that field will display the default value.

1. In the **Navigation** Pane, right-click on the table that you want to change, and then click on **Design View**.
2. Select the field that you want to change.
3. On the **General** tab, type a value in the **Default Value** property box.
   - The value you that you can enter depends on the data type that is set for the field. For example, you can type=Date() to insert the current date in a Date/Time field.
4. Save your changes.

Set a Default Value for a Control

You set a default value for a control only when you don't bind that control to a table field, or when you link to data in another table.

1. In the **Navigation** pane, right-click on the form that you want to change, and then click on **Design View**.
2. Right-click on the control that you want to change, and then click on **Properties** or press **F4**.
3. Click on the **All** tab in the property sheet, locate the **Default Value** property, and then enter your default value.
4. Press **Ctrl+S** to save your changes.

Create a Field Validation Rule

A field validation rule checks input to a field, and is applied when the focus leaves the field.

1. Select the field that you want to validate.
2. On the **Fields** tab, in the **Field Validation** group, click on **Validation**, and then click on **Field Validation Rule**.
3. Use the Expression Builder to create the rule.

Create a Message to Display for Field Input that is not Valid

1. Select the field that needs a message for input that is not valid. The field should already have a validation rule.
2. On the **Fields** tab, in the **Field Validation** group, click on **Validation**, and then click on **Field Validation Message**.
3. Enter an appropriate message. (For example, if the validation rule is >10, the message might be "Enter a value that is less than 10.")

Create a Record Validation Rule

A record validation rule checks input to one or more fields is applied when the focus leaves the record. Usually, a record validation rule compares the values of two or more fields.

1. Open the table for which you want to validate records.
2. On the **Fields** tab, in the **Field Validation** group, click on **Validation**, and then click on **Record Validation Rule.**
3. Use the Expression Builder to create the rule.

Create a Message to Display for Record Input that is not Valid

1. Open the table that needs a message for input that is not valid. The table should already have a record validation rule.
2. On the **Fields** tab, in the **Field Validation** group, click on **Validation**, and then click on **Record Validation Message**.
3. Enter an appropriate message. (For example, if the validation rule is [StartDate]<[EndDate], the message might be "StartDate must precede EndDate.")

Sorting Records

When you sort records, you are putting them into a logical order, with similar data grouped together. As a result, sorted data is often simpler to read and understand than unsorted data. By default, Access sorts records by their ID numbers.

To Sort Records

1. Select a field in the cell you wish to sort by. In this example, we will sort by customers' last names. 
2. Click on the **Home** tab on the **Ribbon**, and locate the **Sort & Filter** group.
3. Sort the field by selecting the **Ascending** or **Descending** command.
   - Select **Ascending** to sort text A to Z or to sort numbers from smallest to largest. We will select this in our example, since we want the last names to be in A to Z order.

- Select **Descending** to sort text Z to A or to sort numbers from largest to smallest.

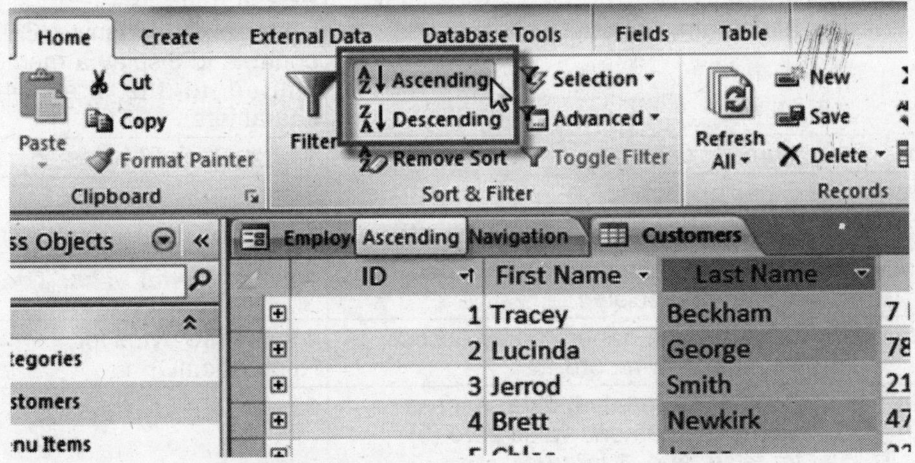

4. The table will now be sorted by the selected field.

ID	First Name	Last Name
102	Theodore	Achi
195	Kris	Ackerman
78	Michiko	Akiwana
1	Tracey	Beckham
124	Andrew	Bedinger
136	Xy'nya	Bell
187	Samantha	Bell
190	Matt	Benson
41	Jeffery	Bergman

5. To save the new sort, click on the **Save** command on the **Quick Access** toolbar.

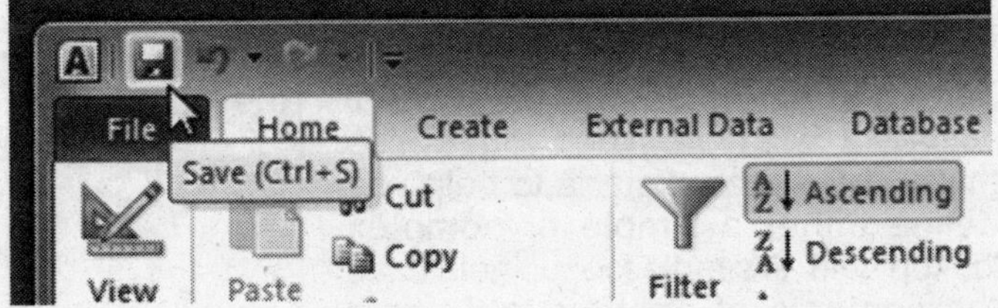

Understanding Field Data Types

Access 2010 supports 11 types of data, each with a specific purpose. However, there is the 12th option, Lookup Wizard, to help you define the characteristics of foreign key fields that link to other tables.

Here are the following data types:

Data Type	Usage	Size
Text	Alphanumeric data	Up to about 1 gigabyte (GB), but controls to display a memo are limited to the first 64,000 characters
Memo	Numeric data	1, 2, 4, 8, or 16 bytes
Number	Dates and times	8 bytes
Data/Time	4 bytes (16 bytes for ReplicationID)	8 bytes
Currency	Monetary data, stored with 4 decimal places of precision	8 bytes
AutoNumber	Unique value generated by Access for each new record.	4 bytes (16 bytes for ReplicationID).
Yes/No	Boolean (true/false) data; Access stores the numeric value zero (0) for false, and -1 for true.	1 byte
OLE Object	Pictures, graphs, or other ActiveX objects from another Windows-based application.	Up to about 2 GB
Hyperlink	A link 'address' to a document or file on the Internet, on an intranet, on a local area network (LAN), or on your local computer	Up to 8,192 (each part of a Hyperlink data type can contain up to 2048 characters)
Attachment	You can attach files such as pictures, documents, spreadsheets, or charts; each Attachment field can contain an unlimited number of attachments per record, up to the storage limit of the size of a database file	Up to about 2 GB
Calculated	You can create an expression that uses data from one or more fields. You can designate different result data types from the expression.	Dependent on the data type of the Result Type property. Text data type result can have up to 243 characters. Memo, Number, Yes/No, and Date/Time should match their respective data types.
Lookup Wizard	The Lookup Wizard entry in the Data Type column in Design view is not actually a data type. When you choose this entry, a wizard starts to help you define either a simple or complex lookup field. A simple lookup field uses the contents of another table or a value list to validate the contents of a single value per row. A complex lookup field allows you to store multiple values of the same data type in each row.	Dependent on the data type of the lookup field

Note that for each field in your table, select the data type that is best suited to how you will use that field's data.

- For character data, you should normally select the Text data type. You can control the maximum length of a Text field by using a field property.
- Use the Memo data type only for long strings of text that might exceed 255 characters or that might contain formatting characters such as tabs or line endings.
- When you select the Number data type, you should think carefully about what you enter as the Field Size property because this property choice will affect precision as well as length.
- The Date/Time data type is useful for calendar or clock data and has the added benefit of allowing calculations in seconds, minutes, hours, days, months, or years.
- You should use the Currency data type for storing money values. Currency has the precision of integers, but with exactly four decimal places. When you need to store a precise fractional number that's not money, use the Number data type and choose Decimal for the Field Size property.
- The AutoNumber data type is specifically designed for automatic generation of primary key values. Depending on the settings for the Field Size and New Values properties you choose for an AutoNumber field, you can have Access 2010 create a sequential or random long integer. You can include only one field using the AutoNumber data type in any table. If you define more than one AutoNumber field, Access displays an error message when you try to save the table.
- Use the Yes/No data type to hold Boolean (true or false) values. This data type is particularly useful for flagging accounts paid or not paid, or orders filled or not filled.
- The OLE Object data type allows you to store complex data, such as pictures, graphs, or sounds, which can be edited or displayed through a dynamic link to another Windows-based application.
- The Hyperlink data type lets you store a simple or complex 'link' to an external file or document. (Internally, Hyperlink is a memo data type with a special flag set to indicate that it is a link.) This link can contain a Uniform Resource Locator (URL) that points to a location on the World Wide Web or on a local intranet. It can also contain the Universal Naming Convention (UNC) name of a file on a server on your LAN or on your local computer drives. The link can point to a file that is in Hypertext Markup Language (HTML) or in a format that is supported by an ActiveX application on your computer.
- The Attachment data type is very similar to the OLE Object data type where you can use it to store complex data. However, unlike the OLE Object data type, you can store multiple attachments in a single record. These files are stored in a binary field in a hidden system table.
- The Calculated data type allows you to create a calculated result using an expression. The expression can include data from one or more fields.

□

18
An Introduction to Tally

Tally is a complete business accounting software developed by Tally Solutions Pvt. Ltd. in Bengaluru. Tally software is mainly used for vouchers, financial statements and taxation in many industries. It also has specialised packages for retail businesses.

Tally.ERP 9 has advanced integration capabilities in the form of Application programming interfaces to make the software extensible.

Once Tally is installed, you need to double click on the Tally ERP.9 icon. You will then see the screen as follows:

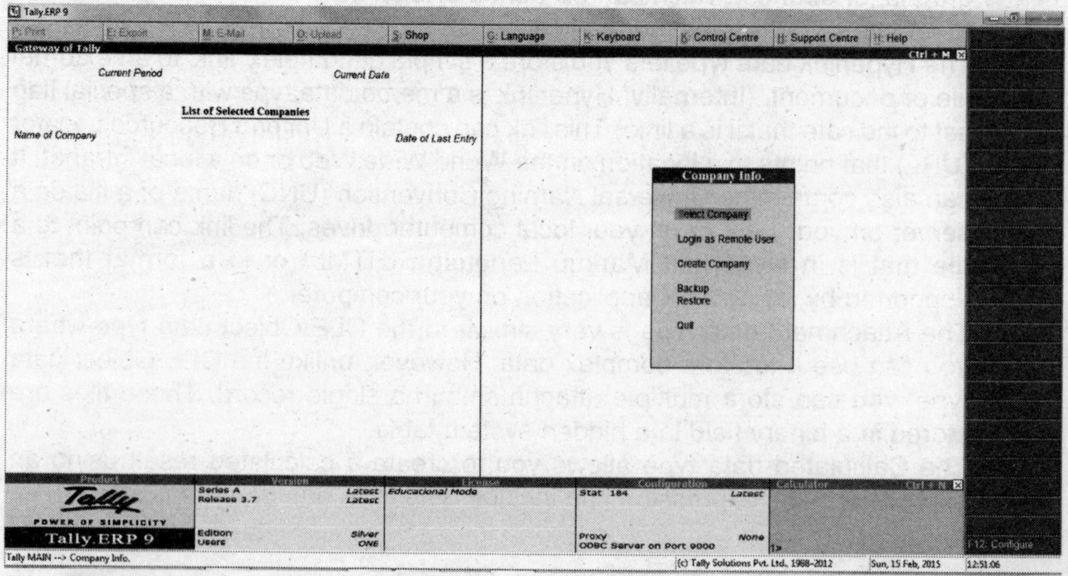

Now you have to create a company.

Creating a Company

To create the company click on **Create Company**.

The following screen will appear.

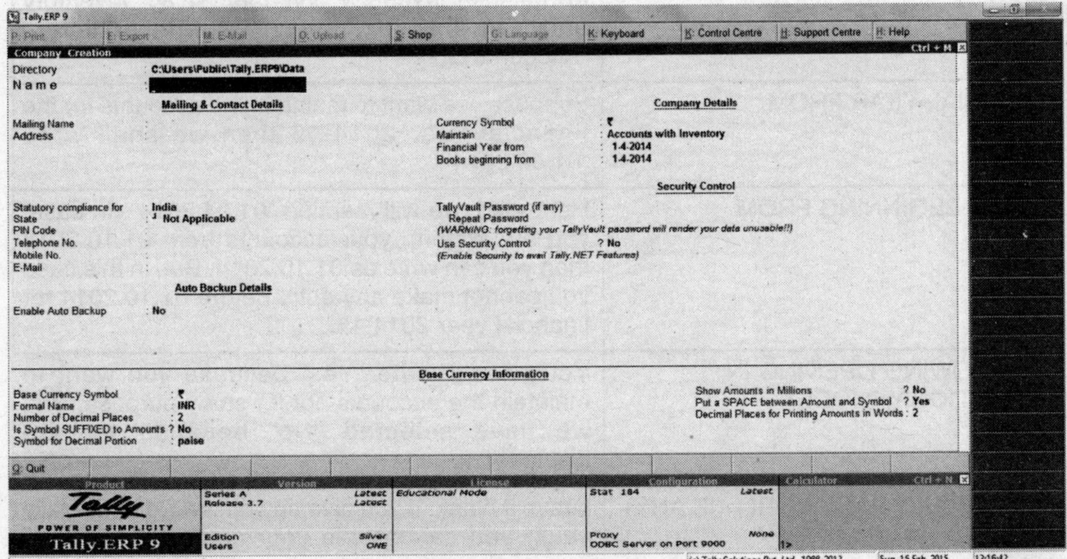

Now, to create new company you have to fill up all the details as required by tally program as under:

NAME	Write the name of company for whom the accounts are to be maintained. For example, company's name is M/S Saisparsh Media, we shall write M/S Saisparsh Media
MAILING ADDRESS	Name of company shall appear automatically. If you want to mention other name you can. In above example we are not changing the name. You have to write the address also. Say, the address is 15, Safdarjung Enclave, New Delhi – 110029
STATUTORY COMPLIANCE FOR	INDIA (It cannot be changed)
STATE	When we fill up this detail then a list of all Indian States will appear. Select any one. For this example we have selected Delhi being the state of the company.
TELEPHONE NUMBER	Give the telephone number of the company. Say – 12345678
CURRENCY SYMBOL	Already given as (₹). We need not to change the same.
MAINTAIN	There are three options given. 1. Accounts only. 2. Accounts with inventory. If you want to do

	accounts only then select accounts only and if you want to maintain stock, raising the bills, then select option "Accounts with Inventory" and if you want to maintain inventory only then select Inventory only. In this example, we are selecting "Accounts Only".
FINANCIAL YEAR FROM	Suppose, we want to maintain the accounts for the financial year 2014-15 then we shall write "01.04.2014"
BOOKS BEGINNING FROM	Here also, we will mention "01.04.2014". In case, you are starting your accounts from 01.10.2014 then you can write as 01.10.2014. But, in this case you cannot make any entry before 01.10.2014 for financial year 2014-15.
DISALLOWING OPENING IN EDUCATIONAL MODE	You should write "Yes" because you want to maintain the accounts not for study purpose. But, we have selected "No" because we are just learning.
TALLY VAULT PASSWORD, (IF ANY)	Leave it blank. If you give any password under tally vault, you cannot see your company in list of companies whenever you open the tally. It is advisable not to give any password under this column.
USE SECURITY CONTROL	In this column say "Yes". Because you must have some password for your company so that the person who knows the password, he only can open the company.
NAME OF ADMINISTRATOR	Write anything but remember, if you have written anything in capital letters, then at the time of opening company you have to write you administration name in capital letter only otherwise you would not be able to open the tally. Here we are writing XYZ as administrator's name in capital letters.
PASSWORD	You have to follow the procedure as given in administrator's name. Here also, we are writing XYZ as password in capital letters.
REPEAT PASSWORD USE TALLY AUDIT FEATURES	You should again write your password as written in Password Column. So write - XYZ in capital letters. You cannot see what you have written. It is just to test you whether you can remember your password or no. So, be very careful regarding your password. If you forget your password then you have not option to open your company. In that case you have to contact to Tally people only. Write "No". Basically this feature is required by auditors or senior persons. So for the time being

	for learners, it is advisable to select "No" against this column.

After filling all the columns your screen will appear as below:

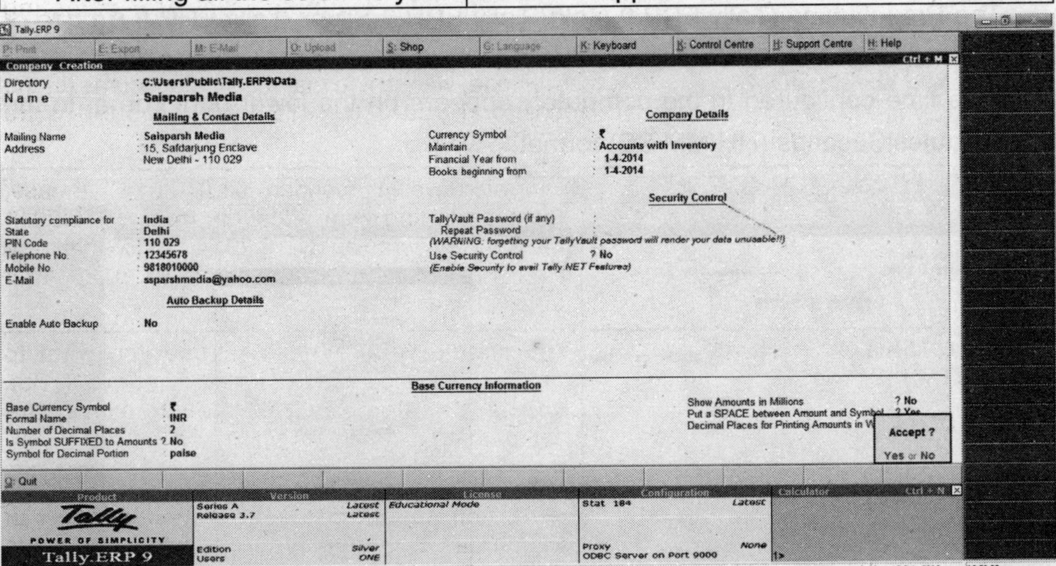

Finally it asks, Yes or No. If you select "Yes," then the company shall be created as per the details given by you. It is advisable that before selection of "Yes", once again, you must go through all the details given by you in the form. Suppose, instantly, you want to change any thing, and then select "No". You can change any thing now. Finally, you have to select "Yes".

After you select "Yes", your company is created. It will take few seconds to create the company. So, wait and watch.

For alteration or modification in company structure, refer to "Alteration of Company in Tally".

Sections of Gateway of Tally.ERP 9

You can load Tally.ERP 9 by using shortcut stores on the desktop.

- **Start ➢ Program ➢ Tally.ERP 9**

The first screen is called Gateway of Tally.ERP 9

The screen window is divided into the following three sections.

Section-1: Title/Bottom Area/Calculator Area (Ctrl+N)

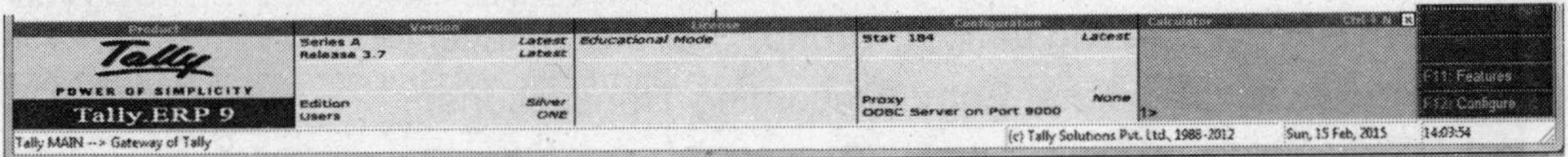

The Bottom Area contains Version number, Release details and Current Date.

The name of the day, date, month and year is displayed in the DD, MM, YYYY format on the left-hand side.

Tally.ERP 9 logo is displayed at the left of the Bottom Area.

The Product type (Tally.ERP 9 Gold, Tally.ERP 9 Silver, Tally.ERP 9 Bronze or Educational) and Tally.ERP 9 Serial Number appear on the Buttom Area. System time (the time configured in the computer) appears on the lower-right corner in the Hour:Minutes:Seconds (HH/MM/SS) format.

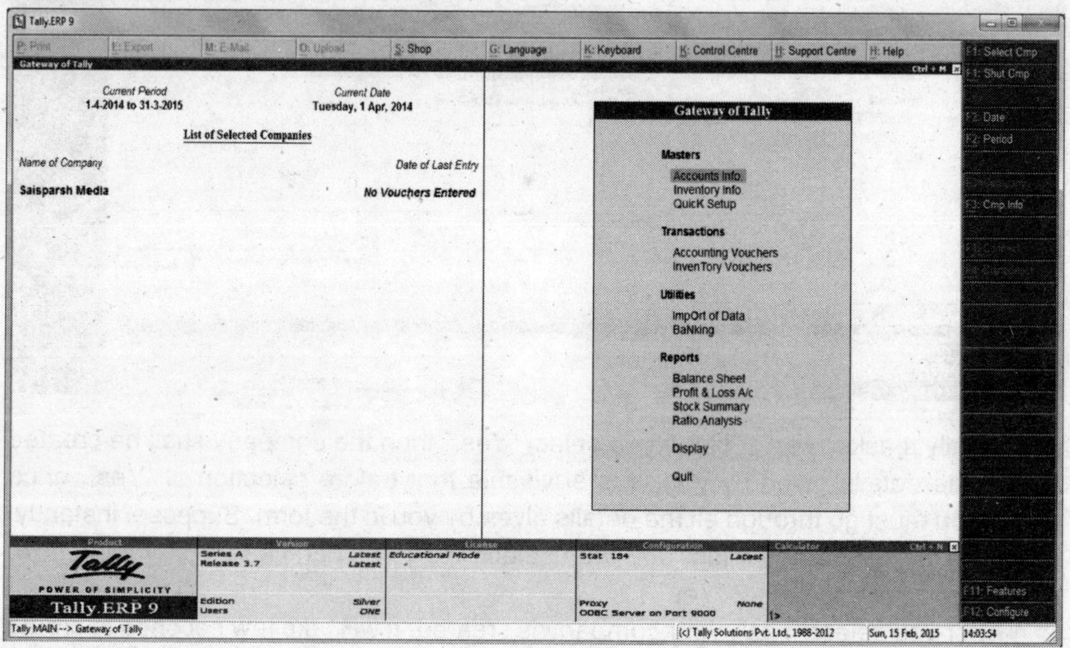

Section-2: Main Area (Ctrl+M)

The Main Area is separated into the following two areas.

- Left-hand side area
- Right-hand side area

The left-hand side area in the Main Area provides information of Current Period, Current Date and List of Selected Companies and Date of Last Entry.

In the right-hand side, you get more detailed information on the Company. The Company information menu consists of the following.

1. List of activated company (Company already created)
2. Masters (for defining Ledger, Group, Sub-group, Inventory)
3. Transactions/Voucher Entry (Recording Transactions)
4. Reports (Viewing the Balance Sheet, P&L and other Reports)

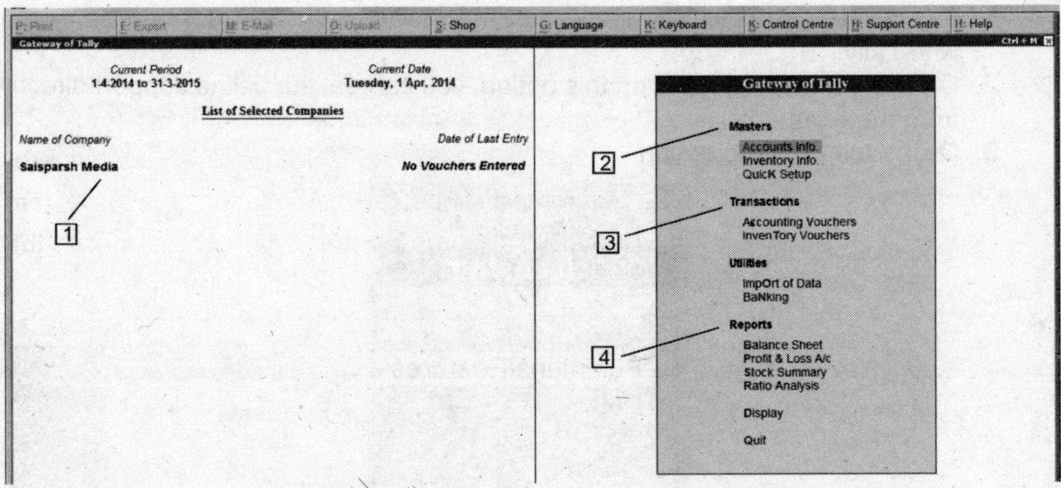

Section-3: Button Bar

By using these Buttons, you can access different utilities of Tally.

For example:

By pressing F1, you can select the Company which has already been created in Tally.

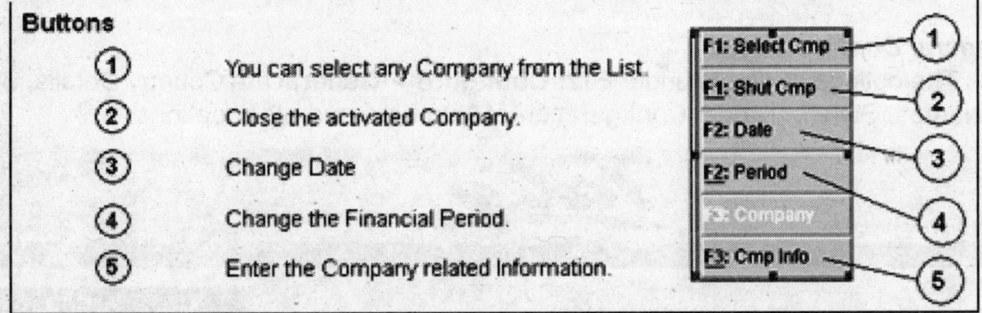

Selection Procedure of Menu Options

You can select the Menu options using any one of the following procedures.

- By **double-clicking** on the **left mouse** button
- By pressing the **Function** keys
- By pressing the **Highlighted** character (it appears in Red and Bold)
- By selecting **Up/Down arrow** key, then using the **Enter** key

Configure (F12) Your Company in Tally.ERP 9

Before you start work, it is advisable to check the company configuration. You can check the configuration from **Gateway of Tally ➢ F12: Configure**, as some configuration is required before you start your operation.

Licensing

This option is available under **F12: Configure ➢ Licensing**

1. **Function/Features:** Will show you the List of activities you can carry out with Tally.
2. **Online/Offline:** By enabling this option, you can get the online support directly from the company.
3. **Quit:** Quit from the option.

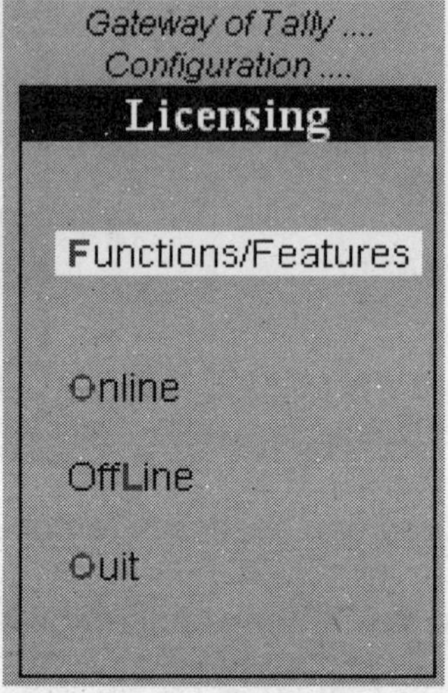

General Configuration

The options available under **F12: Configure ➢ General** are Country Details, Style of Names, Style of Dates, Configuration of Numbers and other options.

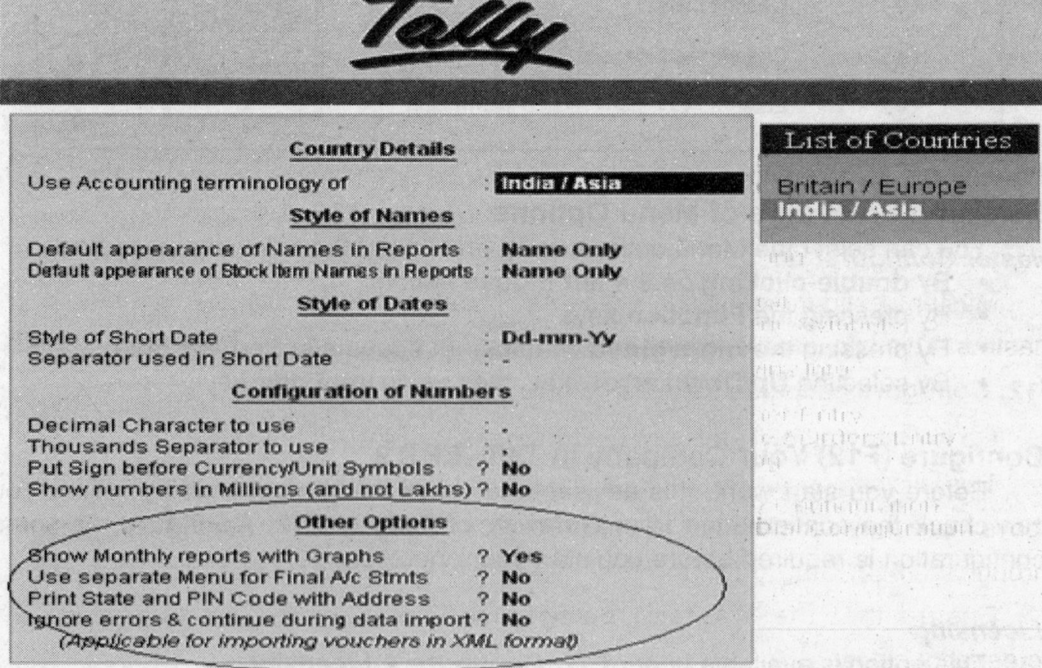

The Configuration settings of Country Details, Style of Names, Style of Dates and Configuration of Numbers are self-explanatory.

The configuration options given under Other Options are explained as follows:

- **Show Monthly Reports with Graphs**

This option is set to YES by default. Here, the reports are configured to display the Graphs in accordance with the numeric information displayed. The graphs are not displayed if this option is set to NO.

- **Use Separate Menu for Final A/c Statements**

By default, this option is set to YES. Setting this to NO-Tally displays the final statements of Balance Sheet and Profit & Loss A/c directly on the Gateway of Tally menu. However, setting this option to YES – the final statements of Balance Sheet and Profit & Loss A/c can be accessed from **Gateway of Tally menu ➢ Final Accounts**.

- **Print State and PIN Code and Address**

By default, this option is set to NO. Setting this option to YES, will allow you to print the reports with State and PIN code details entered in the company creation screen.

- **Ignore Errors & Continue During Data Import**

By default, this option is set to NO. Setting this option to YES will continue to import even if an error is reported.

Numeric Symbols

This enables you to set the number styles. Defaults are also given. You may change them by overwriting. For example, change negative sign from (–) to only ().

Master Configuration

Master Configuration is used to set the details that should appear in the account masters. This is available in the accounts and inventory master screens through the **F12: Configure** button and can be modified as per requirement.

Go to **Gateway of Tally ➢ F12: Configure ➢ Accts/Inv Info**

This allows you to decide what details should appear in the masters over and above those provided. This is available in the **Accounts and Inventory Master** screens through the **F12: Configure** and can be modified according to your need at any time.

Ensure that the **Master Configuration** settings are as shown in the screenshot below.

Master Configuration

Allow ALIASES along with Names	? Yes
Allow Language ALIASES along with Names	? No

Accounts Masters

Allow ADVANCED entries in Masters	? Yes
Add NOTES for Ledger Accounts	? Yes
Use ADDRESSES for Ledger Accounts	? Yes
Use CONTACT DETAILS for Ledger Accounts	? Yes

Inventory Masters

Allow ADVANCED entries in Masters	? No
Calculate VAT on MRP/Marginal	? No
Use PART NUMBERS for Stock Items	? No
Use Description for Stock Items	? No
Use REMARKS for Stock Items	? No
Specify Default Ledger Allocation for Invoicing	? No
Use ALTERNATE UNITS for Stock Items	? No
Allow Std. Rates for Stock Items	? No
Allow Component list details (Bill of Materials)	? No
Use ADDRESSES for Godowns	? No

Voucher Configuration

This is used to configure features while making voucher entry.

Go to **Gateway of Tally ➢ F12: Configure ➢ Voucher Entry**

Ensure that the **Voucher Configuration** settings are as shown in the screenshot below.

Accounting Vouchers

Skip Date field in Create Mode (faster entry!)	? Yes
Use Single Entry mode for Pymt/Rcpt/Contra	? No
Show Inventory Details	? Yes
Show Table of Bill Details for Selection	? Yes
Show Bill-wise Details	? Yes
Expand into multiple lines	? Yes
Show Ledger Current Balances	? Yes
Show Balances as on Voucher Date	? Yes
Use Payment/Receipt as Contra	? No
Allow Cash Accounts in Journals	? Yes
Use Cr/Dr instead of To/By during entry	? Yes
Warn on Negative Cash Balance	? Yes
Pre-Allocate Bills for Payment/Receipt	? No
Allow Expenses/Fixed Assets in Purchase Vouchers	? No
Allow Income Accounts in Sales Vouchers	? No
Activate 'E1' or 'E2' Transaction	? No

Inventory Vouchers

Show Godown -wise Details	? No
Use Ref. Number in Stock Journal	? No
Allow selection of VAT/Tax Class during entry	? No
Warn on Mismatch in VAT Rates	? No
Warn on Negative Stock Balance	? No
Honor Expiry Dates usage for Batches	? No
Show Balances as on Voucher Date	? No

Statutory and Taxation Features in Tally.ERP 9

This feature enables you to set the Statutory Features required for the Company Operations. This option is enabled only if a country is selected from the list of countries under the field **Statutory Compliance** for in the **Company Creation** screen.

Go to **Gateway of Tally ➢ F11 ➢ F3: Statutory & Taxation**

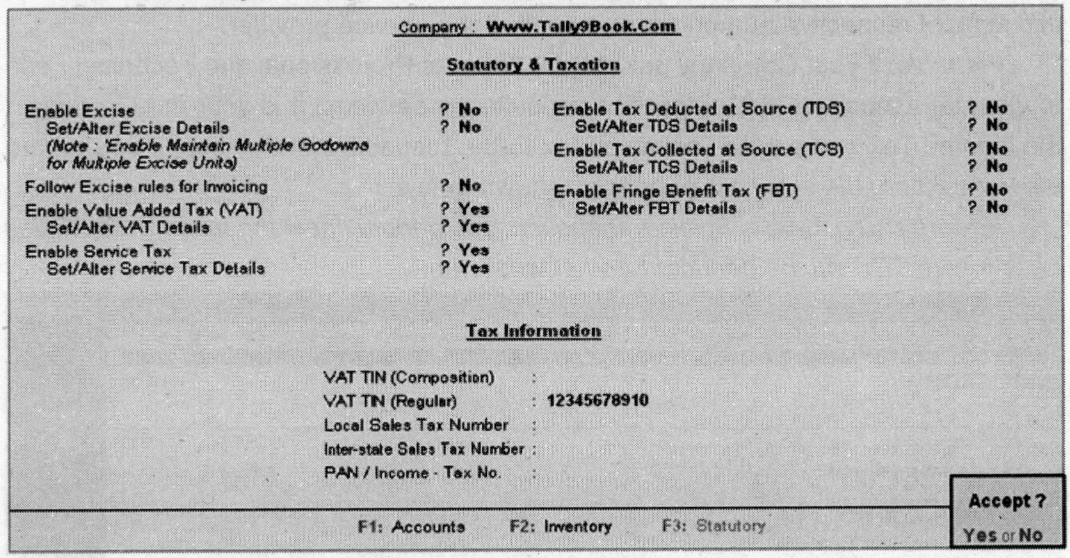

Company : Www.Tally9Book.Com

Statutory & Taxation

Enable Excise	? No	Enable Tax Deducted at Source (TDS)	? No
Set/Alter Excise Details	? No	Set/Alter TDS Details	? No
(Note : 'Enable Maintain Multiple Godowns for Multiple Excise Units)		Enable Tax Collected at Source (TCS)	? No
		Set/Alter TCS Details	? No
Follow Excise rules for Invoicing	? No	Enable Fringe Benefit Tax (FBT)	? No
Enable Value Added Tax (VAT)	? Yes	Set/Alter FBT Details	? No
Set/Alter VAT Details	? Yes		
Enable Service Tax	? Yes		
Set/Alter Service Tax Details	? Yes		

Tax Information

VAT TIN (Composition) :
VAT TIN (Regular) : 12345678910
Local Sales Tax Number :
Inter-state Sales Tax Number :
PAN / Income - Tax No. :

F1: Accounts F2: Inventory F3: Statutory

Accept ?
Yes or No

Note that the different features are available depending on the country you have selected in the **Company Creation** screen.

The following features are available on selecting India in the Company Creation screen.

Enable Dealer

Excise (Set /Alter Dealer-Excise Details)

Set these options to Yes to enable/alter the Excise for Dealers feature.

Follow Excise Rules for Invoicing

Set this option to Yes to follow Excise rules for invoicing. Provide the above Excise information for it to be printed on invoices and Accept, Yes to save.

Enable Value Added Tax (VAT)

Set /Alter VAT Details

Set these options to Yes to enable the VAT features for the company.

Enable Service Tax

Set /Alter Service Tax Details

Set these options to Yes to enable the Service Tax features for the company.

Enable Tax Deducted at Source (TDS) – Enable TDS

This is one of the unique features of Tally 9.0. This facility will allow you to deduct Income Tax at source (TDS) on behalf of the government as per specified rates in the IT Act on specified types of services, incomes, gains and would deposit it into the accounts of respective authorities on behalf of the service provider.

Example: If your Company paid ₹ 2,00,000/- as Professional and Technical Fees to Oriental Associates & Co. for their consultancy services, it is your duty to deduct the Income Tax and pay the collected tax to the respective authorities. If you record the transaction, the entry will appear as shown below.

(Before carrying on with this transaction, you should know the Income Tax Rules as to where TDS will be deducted and at what rate.)

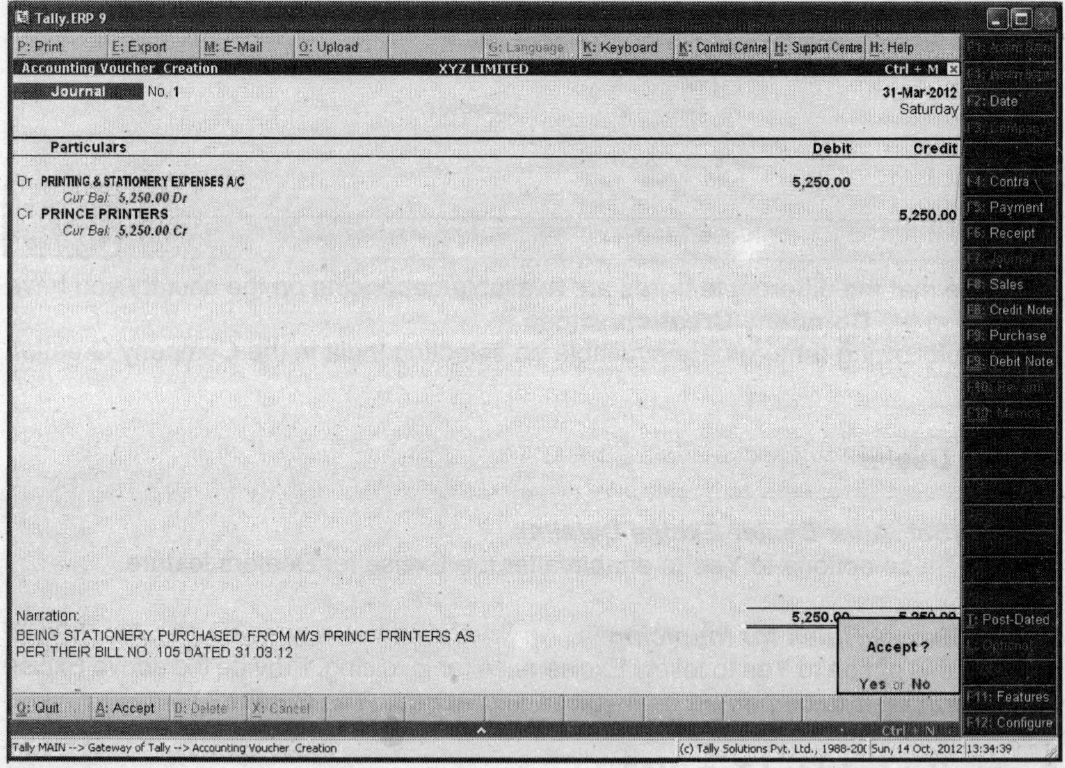

Enable Tax Collected at Source (TCS)

Set /Alter TCS Details

Set these options to Yes to enable the TCS features for the company.

Enable Fringe Benefit Tax (FBT)

Set /Alter FBT Details

Set these options to Yes to enable the FBT features for the company.

Tax Information

VAT TIN (Composition)	:
VAT TIN (Regular)	: 12345678910
Local Sales Tax Number	:
Inter-state Sales Tax Number	: BLS-123 Dt.1-1-2000
PAN / Income - Tax No.	: BLS1254ABC

Set this option to Yes to enter the Tax details of the Company.

Local Sales Tax Number

The Local Sales Tax Number entered during the Company Creation is automatically displayed in this field.

Inter-State Sales Tax Number

The details given here comprise of a number and date of registration. This information, if given, can be printed on invoices.

It is not compulsory to give this information and you may leave it blank.

PAN/Income-Tax Number

The PAN/Income Tax Number is the number allotted by the Income Tax Authorities. This number comprises of 10 digits and may be alphanumerical.

The information entered here will appear in **Account Confirmation Statements**. It is not compulsory to provide this information – this field can also be left blank.

Accounting Features in Tally.ERP 9

The options available in **Section-1** are the common features, which are applicable for all types of companies. The utility of its features is stated below.

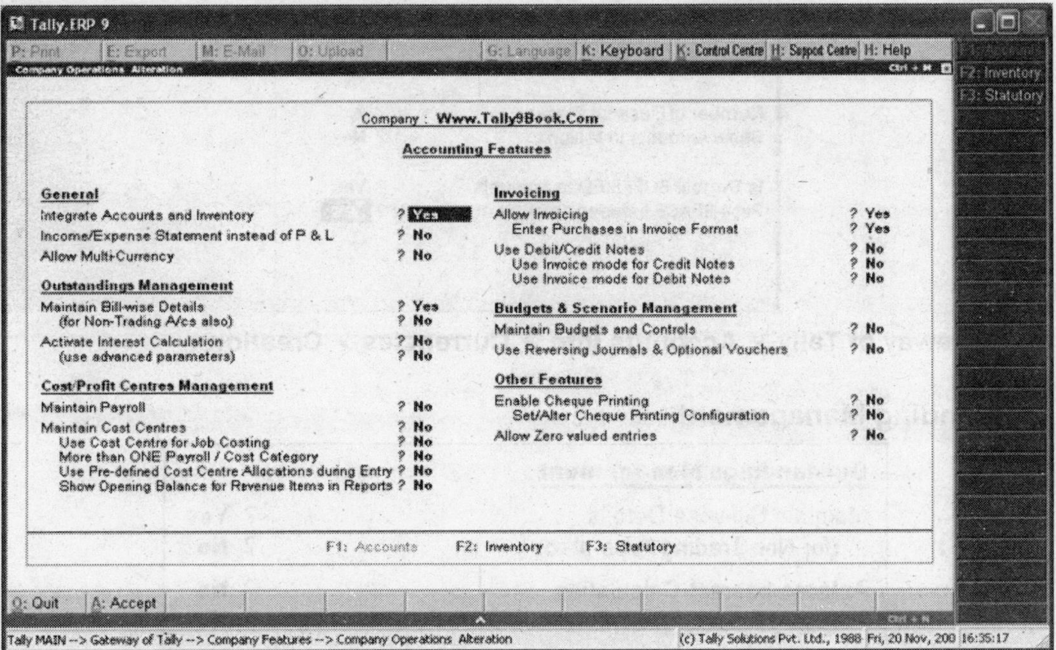

General	
Integrate Accounts and Inventory	? Yes
Income/Expense Statement instead of P & L	? No
Allow Multi-Currency	? No

Integrates Accounts with Inventory

Set the option Yes which enables the closing stock value to automatically come in the Balance Sheet and Profit and Loss Account.

Example: If you define a stock item in Tally 9.0, like 10 pcs @ ₹ 11,000/-, the value of stock (₹ 1,10,000/-) will transfer automatically in the opening stock, closing stock of the P&L Account and also in the Closing Stock of the Balance Sheet.

Income Expense Statement Instead of P&L

By saying Yes, the option will enable you to create the Income and Expenditure Statement instead of Profit and Loss Account.

Allows Multi-Currency

Set the option Yes, which allows you to record the transaction in foreign currency also. The currency option will be available in the **'Account Info'** menu and at the time of ledger creation, you can specify a currency on which accounts will be maintained.

Example: You want to create American Dollar for recording the transaction of an American Customer.

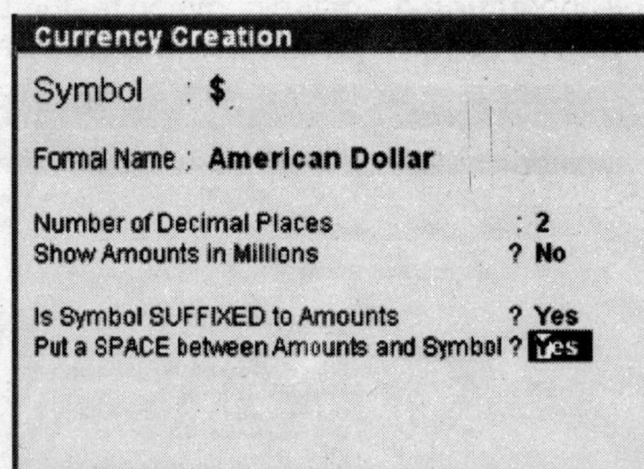

Gateway of Tally ➢ Accounts Info ➢ Currencies ➢ Creation

Outstanding Management

Outstandings Management	
Maintain Bill-wise Details	? Yes
(for Non-Trading A/cs also)	? No
Activate Interest Calculation	? No
(use advanced parameters)	? No

Maintain Billwise Details

Say Yes if you want to maintain party Bill details (Sundry Debtors and Sundry Creditors). Here, you will be able to maintain all details of Receivables and Payables from the party, for example, Acceptance of Bill, Payment of Bill, Pending Bill, Overdue Bill, etc. Otherwise say No.

Example: Assume that Mr. Siddharth is a customer of your company. Last year's Balance due on his name is ₹ 2,50,000/- of which one Bill (No. SE/13-14/150) is for ₹ 15,000/- and another Bill (No. SE/13-14/250) is for ₹ 2,35,000/-. The benefits for maintaining records in this manner allow you to calculate the amount. Billwise, you can charge interest individually or also make an aging analysis. If you record the transaction in Tally, it will appear as shown below.

Mr. Siddharth

Bill-wise Details

Page 1

Date	Ref. No.	Opening Amount	Pending Amount	Due on	Overdue by days
1-Nov-2013	SE/13-14/150	15,000.00 Dr	15,000.00 Dr	31-Dec-2013	268
15-Dec-2013	SE/13-14/200	2,35,000.00 Dr	2,35,000.00 Dr	15-Jan-2014	253
		2,50,000.00 Dr	2,50,000.00 Dr		

Gateway of Tally ➢ Accounts Voucher ➢ Ledger ➢ Create

Non-Trading a/c: Say Yes to these accounts. It enables you to maintain the reference details for other ledger also, for example, Loans, Advances, etc.

Active Interest Calculation

To calculate the interest for party ledger (like Sundry Debtors or Sundry Creditors as per their balance) or other ledgers (like Loans, Advances, etc.) option required here would be Yes.

Advance Parameters

This option is required when you want to define different interest rates based on different time spans, different type or Balance (such as Debt Balance, Credit Balances, Date of Applicability, etc.). For both the party ledger and other ledger, say Yes, otherwise No.

Cost/Profit Centres Management

Cost/Profit Centres Management

Maintain Payroll	? **No**
Maintain Cost Centres	? **No**
Use Cost Centre for Job Costing	? **No**
More than ONE Payroll / Cost Category	? **No**
Use Pre-defined Cost Centre Allocations during Entry	? **No**

Maintain Cost Centres

Say Yes to this option if you want to maintain allocation of amounts into different Cost Heads, otherwise say No.

Gateway of Tally ➢ Accounts Info ➢ Cost Center ➢ Single Create

More than One Cost Category

Say Yes when you want to form a club/group with similar kinds of cost centers.

Example: Suppose you want to maintain different types of categories in Tally, such as Branches, Departments, Members, Managers, etc. for analysis of different types of Incomes and Expenditures, it would appear as shown below.

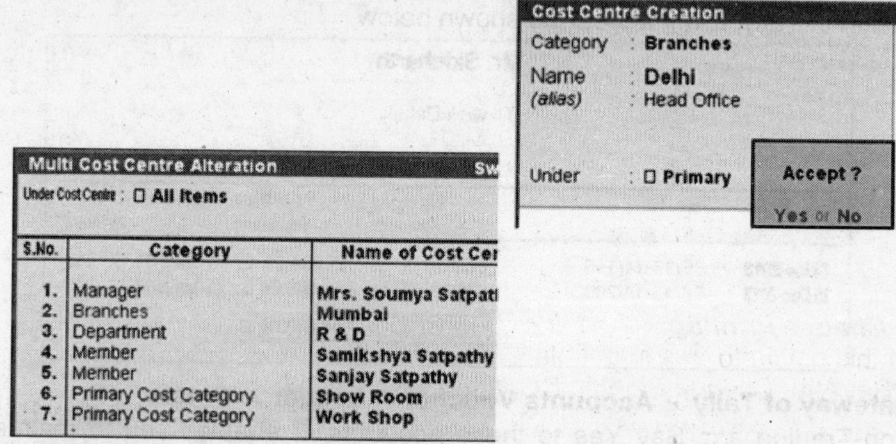

- **Use Cost Center for Job Costing**

To track all income and expenses for a project, set this option to Yes.

- **More than One Cost Category**

To create more than one Payroll or Cost Category, set this option to Yes.

- **Use Pre-defined Cost Centre Allocations During Entry**

Set this option to Yes to define Cost Centre Allocations.

Invoicing

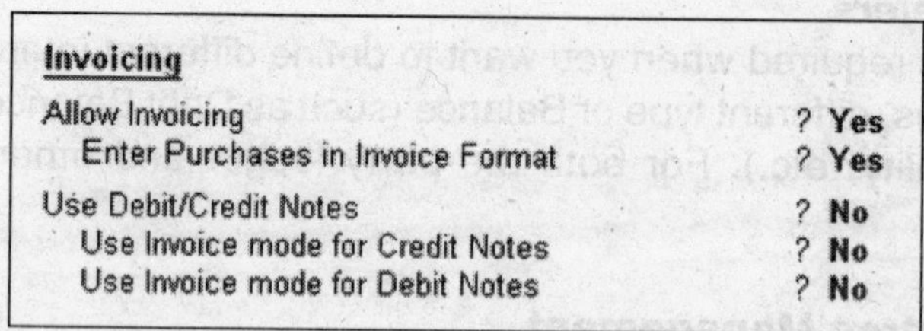

Allow Invoicing

Set this option to Yes to create Sales and Purchase vouchers in invoice format. The advantage of using the invoice format for sales invoice entry is that it enables automatic calculations of Duties and Taxes accounts.

- **Enter Purchases in Invoice Format**

Set this option to Yes to make the invoice mode as the default voucher mode for purchase vouchers.

Use Debit/Credit Notes

These types of vouchers are necessary for entries of the **Purchase Return** and **Sales Return** of goods. Say Yes to maintain the same, otherwise say No to pass these types of entries through a proper journal.

Example: You want to return 2 pieces of Sony 1 TB hard disk to Mr. Siddharth against your previous purchase, you can use the Debit Note for returning this good and deduct the amount against the party's bill.

- **Use Invoice Mode for Credit Notes**

Set this option to Yes to create Credit Notes in Invoice Mode.

- **Use Invoice Mode for Debit Notes**

Set this option to Yes to create Debit Notes in Invoice Mode.

Other Features

Other Features	
Enable Cheque Printing	? **No**
Set/Alter Cheque Printing Configuration	? **No**
Allow Zero valued entries	? **No**

Enable Cheque Printing

Set this option to Yes to enable Cheque Printing.

- Set/Alter Cheque Printing Configuration

Setting this option to Yes, Tally will allow you to alter the **Cheque Printing Configuration.**

Inventory Features in Tally.ERP 9

This feature enables you to set the Inventory Features required for the transactions.

Go to **Gateway of Tally ➢ F11: Features ➢ F2: Inventory**

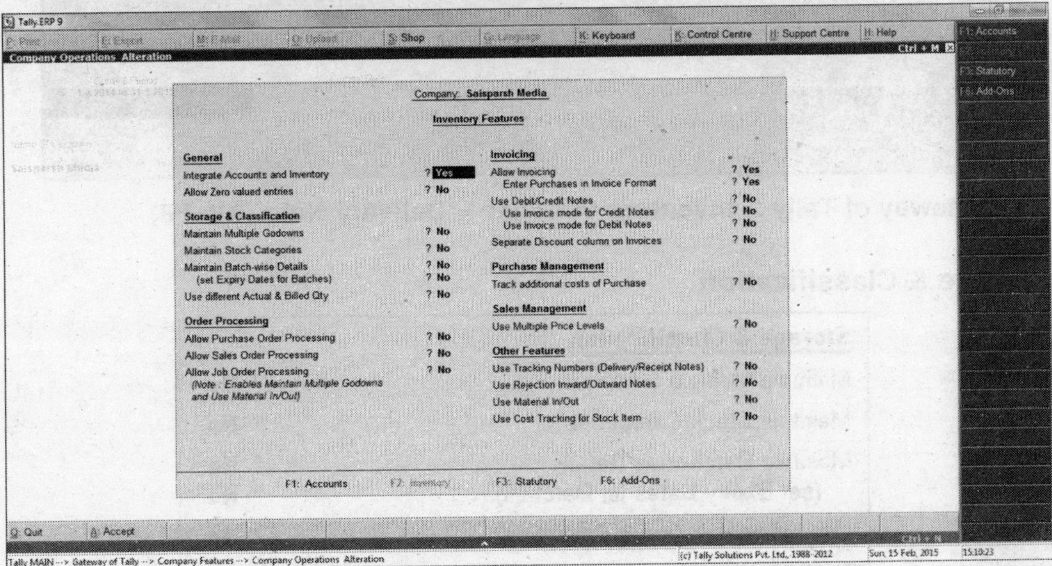

Tally.ERP 9
P: Print | E: Export | M: E-Mail | O: Upload | S: Shop | G: Language | K: Keyboard | K: Control Centre | H: Support Centre | H: Help
Company Operations Alteration

Company: Saisparsh Media

Inventory Features

General		Invoicing	
Integrate Accounts and Inventory	? Yes	Allow Invoicing	? Yes
Allow Zero valued entries	? No	Enter Purchases in Invoice Format	? Yes
Storage & Classification		Use Debit/Credit Notes	? No
Maintain Multiple Godowns	? No	Use Invoice mode for Credit Notes	? No
Maintain Stock Categories	? No	Use Invoice mode for Debit Notes	? No
Maintain Batch-wise Details	? No	Separate Discount column on Invoices	? No
(set Expiry Dates for Batches)	? No	**Purchase Management**	
Use different Actual & Billed Qty	? No	Track additional costs of Purchase	? No
Order Processing		**Sales Management**	
Allow Purchase Order Processing	? No	Use Multiple Price Levels	? No
Allow Sales Order Processing	? No	**Other Features**	
Allow Job Order Processing	? No	Use Tracking Numbers (Delivery/Receipt Notes)	? No
(Note : Enables Maintain Multiple Godowns and Use Material In/Out)		Use Rejection Inward/Outward Notes	? No
		Use Material In/Out	? No
		Use Cost Tracking for Stock Item	? No

F1: Accounts | F2: Inventory | F3: Statutory | F6: Add-Ons

Q: Quit | A: Accept

Tally MAIN --> Gateway of Tally --> Company Features --> Company Operations Alteration | (c) Tally Solutions Pvt. Ltd., 1988-2012 | Sun, 15 Feb, 2015 | 15:10:23

General

General	
Integrate Accounts and Inventory	? Yes
Allow Zero valued entries	? No

Integrate Accounts and Inventory

This field performs the same function as explained in Accounting Features.

Allow Zero Valued Entries in Vouchers

If your requirement is to pass an entry whose monetary transaction value is '0', set it as Yes. For example, in cases where you do not want to show the value amount in goods Delivery Note/Challan, or goods distributed as free sample with other goods.

Example: You want to send the Challan for delivery of goods to your customer Mr. Siddharth, which will only consist of the name of product and their delivered quantities. If you record the transaction in Tally, it will appear as follows.

Inventory Voucher Creation Ctrl + M

Delivery Note No. 1 25-Sep-2013
Ref: CH-001 Wednesday

Party's A/c Name : Mr. Siddharth
Current Balance :
Sales Ledger : SALE-12.5%
VAT/Tax Class : Sales @ 12.5%

Name of Item	Quantity	Rate per	Amount
FRZ-100 LTR.	5 NOS.		
52X DVD WRITER	3 pc		

Gateway of Tally ➢ Inventory Voucher ➢ Delivery Note (Alt+F8)

Storage & Classification

Storage & Classification	
Maintain Multiple Godowns	? No
Maintain Stock Categories	? No
Maintain Batch-wise Details	? No
(set Expiry Dates for Batches)	? No
Use different Actual & Billed Qty	? No

Maintain Multiple Godowns

Set this option to Yes, if you have more than one stock points/storage Locations/ Godowns, and you want to track stock movement in these locations. You can create any number of Stock Locations/Godowns. The Godowns/Locations option is displayed in **Gateway of Tally ➢ Inventory Info Menu** only if you set this option to Yes. You will be able to know your stocks at each location as well as assign stock movement to one or more locations during voucher entry.

Maintain Stock Categories

This offers parallel category of stocks. For example, you are dealing with different companies that sell Hard Disks, such as Sony, Seagate and Samsung. Here you can specify the entire stock item in the stock category under Hard Disk.

Name of the Item	Categories
Sony 1 TB	Hard Disk
Seagate 1 TB	Hard Disk
Samsung 1 TB	Hard Disk

Maintain Batchwise Details

This feature is required if you want to maintain the Stock item batchwise and you can also maintain the expiry date of the products.

Name of the Item	Batch No.	Mfg. Date	Expiry Date
Sony 1 TB	DG/150/14	01-07-2014	

Note that Batches should be used where they are small in number and remain constant. It is not wise to use the batch option for tracking of lots through manufacturing processes. If that is done, you will soon have a large number of batches that are not deleted. You will not be able to assign costs to particular lots, as may be the intention.

- **Set Expiry Dates for Batches**

Set this option to Yes if you want to set expiry dates for the batches. This displays an additional field **Use Expiry Dates** in the **Stock Item Creation** screen.

This is useful for businesses that deal in goods that have expiry dates, like medicines, food and other perishables. During voucher entry, date of manufacture of the product by default takes the date of the voucher. This date can be changed, but not to a date later than the voucher date. Expiry date cannot be a date prior to the voucher date.

Use Different Actual and Billed Quantity

Set this option to Yes if you want to specify quantities that are different from that delivered/received when invoicing.

For example, you have delivered goods but some of them are in disagreement. So, your customer wants to be invoiced only for the undisputed quantity. He/She might consider the rest later and would then like to be invoiced. On the other hand, the rest might be so bad that it is useless even for you to take it back. Hence, you can record the fact while raising the invoice without altering the delivery note or passing a rejection entry.

Order Processing

Order Processing
Allow Purchase Order Processing ? **No**
Allow Sales Order Processing ? **No**

Processing the Purchase Order

Set it as Yes if you want to maintain the Purchase Order. This option would be available at 'Inventory Voucher', otherwise set it as No.

Example: If you want to place an order for an item to your supplier Mr. Siddharth with specification of your order number, name of the item and their acceptable price and record the transaction in Tally will appear as shown below.

Inventory Voucher Creation Ctrl + M

Purchase Order No. **1** **20-Aug-2014** Wednesday

Party's A/c Name : **Mr. Siddharth** Order No. : **PO-001/08-09**
Current Balance :
Purchase Ledger : **PURCHASE-12.5%**
VAT/Tax Class: **Purchases @ 12.5%**

Name of Item	Quantity	Rate per		Amount
17" CLR MONITOR	2 pc	3,400.00	pc	6,800.00
LG PC -X-7170	1 NOS.	30,000.00	NOS.	30,000.00
				36,800.00

Gateway of Tally ➢ Inventory Voucher ➢ Purchase Order (Alt+F4)

Allow Sales Order Processing

Set it as Yes if you want to maintain the Sales Order, otherwise set it as No. This option is available at **'Invoice Voucher'**.

Example: If you want to record an order of 10 pieces of 17" Colour Monitor @ ₹ 4,420 from the customer Mr. Siddharth, then the recorded transaction in Tally will appear as shown below.

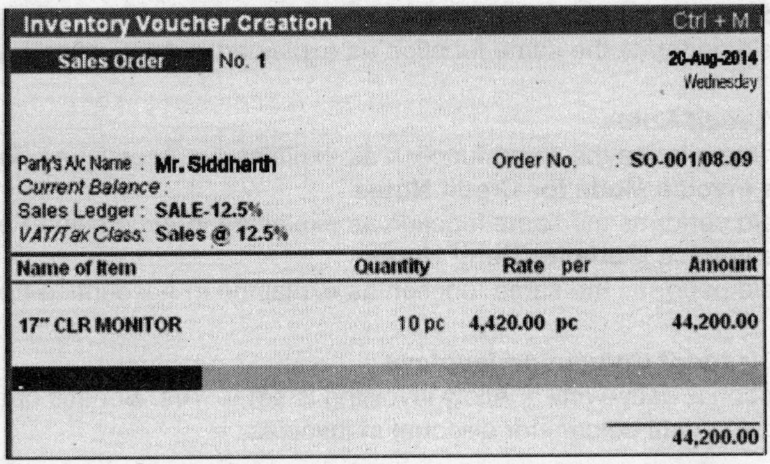

Inventory Voucher Creation Ctrl + M

Sales Order No. 1 20-Aug-2014 Wednesday

Party's A/c Name : **Mr. Siddharth** Order No. : **SO-001/08-09**
Current Balance :
Sales Ledger : **SALE-12.5%**
VAT/Tax Class: **Sales @ 12.5%**

Name of Item	Quantity	Rate per	Amount
17" CLR MONITOR	10 pc	4,420.00 pc	44,200.00
			44,200.00

Gateway of Tally ➢ Inventory Voucher ➢ Sales Order (Alt+F5)

Invoicing

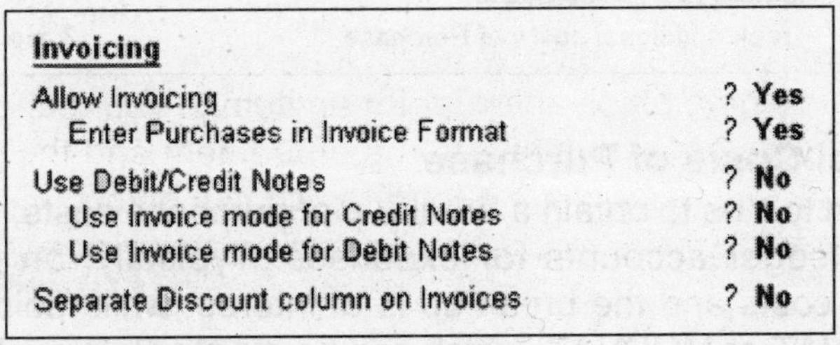

Invoicing

Allow Invoicing	? **Yes**
Enter Purchases in Invoice Format	? **Yes**
Use Debit/Credit Notes	? **No**
Use Invoice mode for Credit Notes	? **No**
Use Invoice mode for Debit Notes	? **No**
Separate Discount column on Invoices	? **No**

Sales Voucher in Invoice Format

Setting the option as Yes will allow the Invoice Format for Sales Voucher and for Purchase, otherwise say No.

Example: If you want to issue an invoice to your customer Mr. Siddharth for sale of LG PC-X-7170 Computer System, 2 nos. @ 39,000 and record the transaction in Tally, it will appear as shown below.

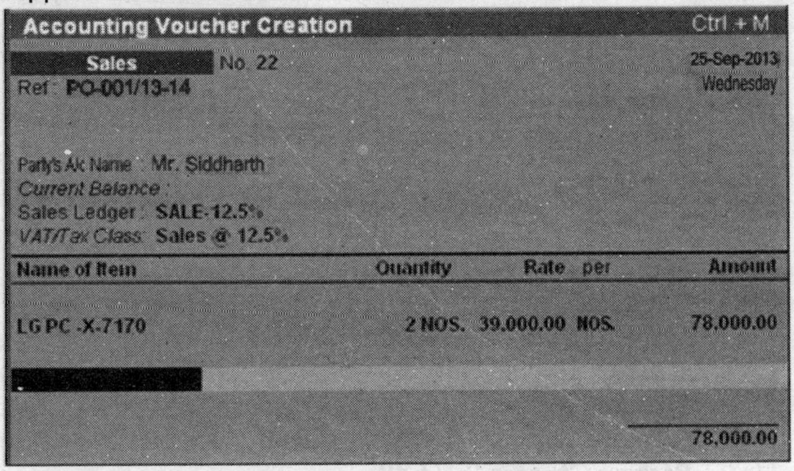

Accounting Voucher Creation Ctrl + M

Sales No. 22 25-Sep-2013 Wednesday
Ref : PO-001/13-14

Party's A/c Name : Mr. Siddharth
Current Balance :
Sales Ledger : SALE-12.5%
VAT/Tax Class: Sales @ 12.5%

Name of Item	Quantity	Rate per	Amount
LG PC -X-7170	2 NOS.	39,000.00 NOS.	78,000.00
			78,000.00

Gateway of Tally ➢ Accounting Voucher ➢ Sale

Enter Purchases in Invoice Format

This field performs the same function as explained in Accounting Features.

Use Debit/Credit Notes

This field performs the same function as explained in Accounting Features.

- **Use Invoice Mode for Credit Notes**

This field performs the same function as explained in Accounting Features.

- **Use Invoice Mode for Debit Notes**

This field performs the same function as explained in Accounting Features.

Separate Discount Column on Invoices

This option is active only if Allow invoicing is set to Yes. Set this option to Yes if you want to separate column for discount in invoices.

Purchase Management

Purchase Management	
Track additional costs of Purchase	? **No**

Track Additional Costs of Purchase

Set this option to Yes to obtain a break-up of purchase costs, without the need to separately debit ledger accounts for expenses. Typically, on purchases, one is interested in total costs and the break-up is of interest while doing analysis (except for expenses like VAT or MODVAT, which can be claimed). In such cases, passing of accounting entries for expenses will have no consequences other than lengthening your ledgers.

Example:

Purchases from ABC & Co: 10 pieces of Widgets @ ₹ 20 = ₹ 200. Expenses incurred = Tax – ₹ 20, Packing charges – ₹ 15.40, Total purchase cost – ₹ 235.

If you activate Track additional costs, you can pass the entry in any of the following methods.

Cr	*ABC & Co*				*235.40*
Dr	*Purchases*			*235.40*	
	Widgets 10 pcs	*23.50*	*235.40*		
(or)					
Cr	*ABC & Co*				*235.40*
Dr	*Purchases*			*235.40*	
	Widgets 10 pcs	*20.00*	*200.00*		
	Actuals:		*23.50*	*(235.40)*	
	Allocated As				
	Purchase Tax	*10%*	*20.00*		
	Packing Charges	*15.40*			

Cr	*ABC & Co*				*235.40*
Dr	*Purchases*			*235.40*	
	Widgets 10 pcs	*23.50*	*235.40*		

(or)

Cr	*ABC & Co*				*235.40*
Dr	*Purchases*			*235.40*	
	Widgets 10 pcs	*20.00*	*200.00*		
	Actuals:		*23.50*	*(235.40)*	
	Allocated As				
	Purchase Tax	*10%*	*20.00*		
	Packing Charges	*15.40*			

From an accounting perspective, both entries are identical. The ledger accounts **Purchase Tax** and **Packing charges** are not debited with the amounts. Hence, these figures are reflected only as break-up or analysis figures of **Purchase account**. The Actual figure reveals the total cost incurred on the Purchase and will also affect the stock value.

You may also allocate additional costs on Purchases through subsequent entries or vouchers.

The rules for including subsequent vouchers in purchase costs that Tally follows are:

Basic cost + **Additional costs allocated** (if any) + **All costs in subsequent vouchers that have zero quantity, up to the first voucher that has a non-zero quantity.**

Sales Management

Use Multiple Price Levels

Set this option to Yes to create Multiple Price Levels.

Additional Inventory Vouchers

Additional Inventory Vouchers	
Use Tracking Numbers (Delivery/Receipt Notes)	? **No**
Use Rejection Inward/Outward Notes	? **No**

Use Tracking Numbers (Delivery/Receipt Notes)

You will use the Tracking Number to link this Receipt Note with the Supplier's Invoice that will be received later. Tracking numbers link the different accounting and inventory vouchers as follows:

- Receipt Note/Goods in vouchers with Purchase Vouchers

- Goods Out/Delivery Note with sale voucher/invoice
- Rejection-in with Credit Note
- Rejection-out with Debit Note

Use Rejection Inward/Outward Notes

Set this option to Yes if you wish to record rejection of goods separately and not through a common Debit Note or Credit Note.

□

19
CorelDRAW X6

CorelDRAW is a graphic design software programme developed by Corel Corporation. CorelDRAW is a part of the CorelDRAW Graphics Suite used for professional graphic designing, photo-editing and website designing.

Document Set-up

1. To create a new document, go up to the **Menu Bar** and select **File ➤ New.**

2. This opens the **Create a New Document** window.

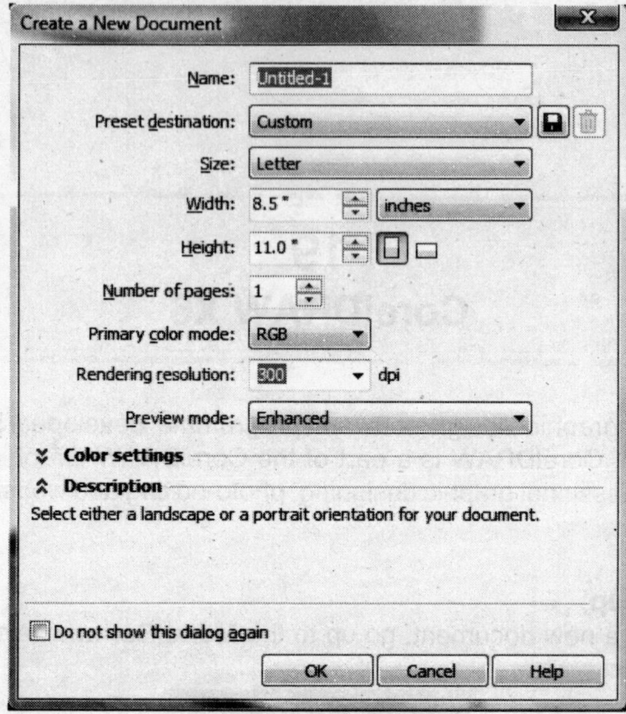

3. Make sure that **Size** is set to **Letter**. Here the **Primary Colour Mode** has been changed to **RGB** instead of **CMYK**.
4. Click on **OK**.

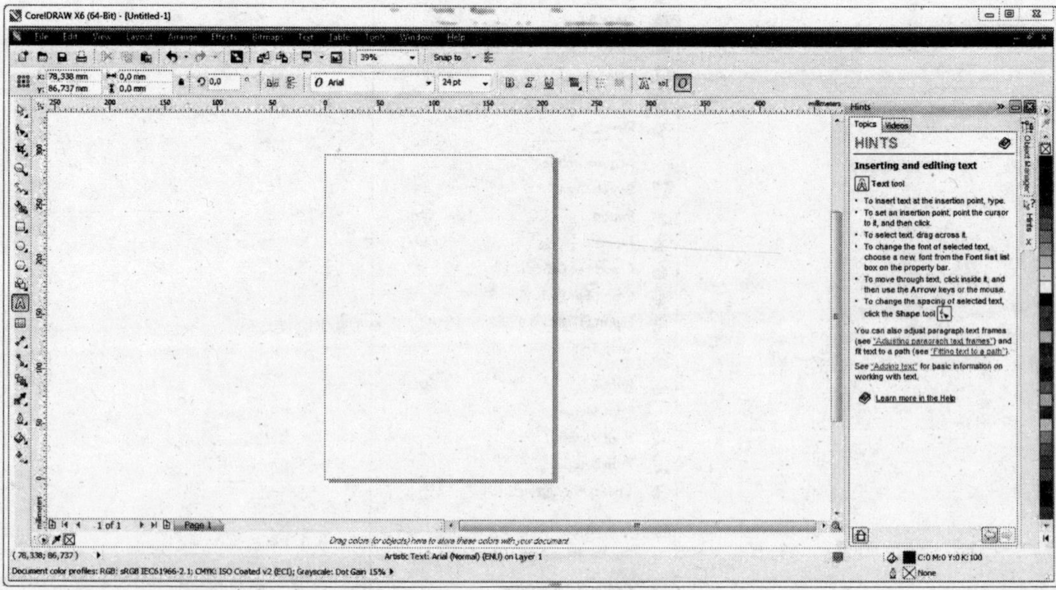

5. A blank window opens.

Create Rectangle

1. Select the **Rectangle Tool** from the **Toolbox** to the left of the screen.
2. Draw a **Rectangle** on the page.

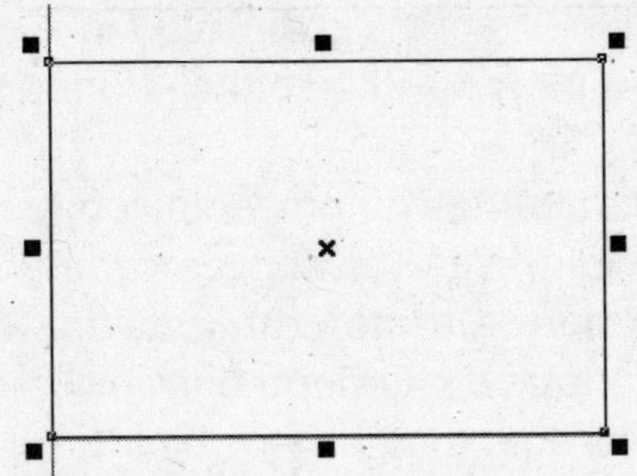

Convert to Curves

1. With the Rectangle still selected, **right click** over it to reveal a menu.
2. Select **Convert to Curves**.

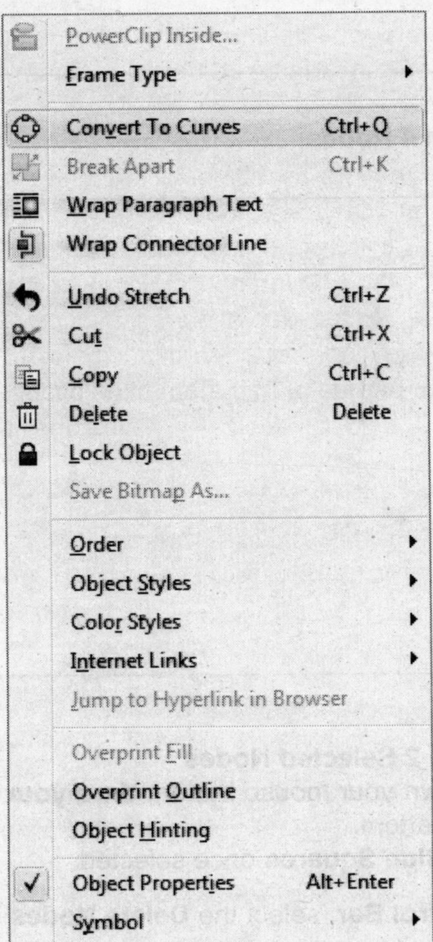

Shape Tool-Delete Nodes

1. The Rectangle will now have **4 Tiny Nodes** at each corner.

- Rectangle with **4 Nodes**

- Rectangle with **2 Selected Nodes**

2. While holding down your mouse button, **drag your cursor** over the **2 Right Nodes**, top and bottom.
3. They will turn to **Blue Squares** once selected.
4. On the **Tool Control Bar**, select the **Delete Nodes** icon. 

5. Once the Nodes are deleted, the shape changes.

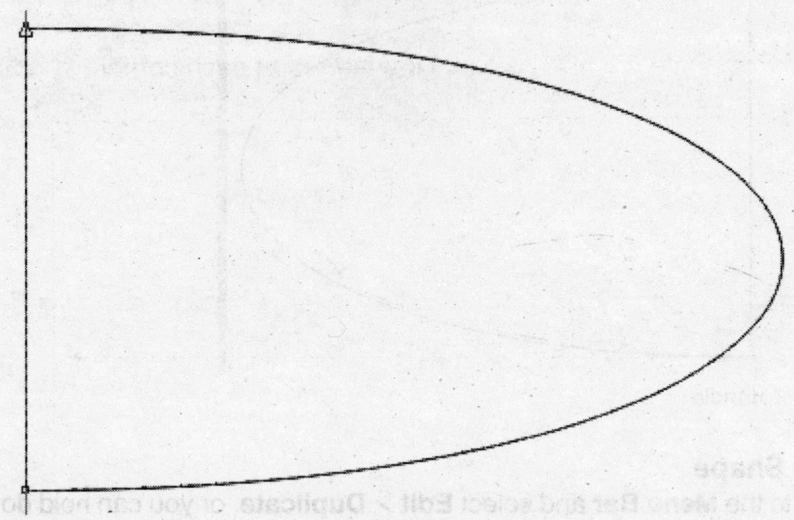

Adjust Control Handles

1. To change the curve of the shape, select either of the remaining **2 Nodes**.

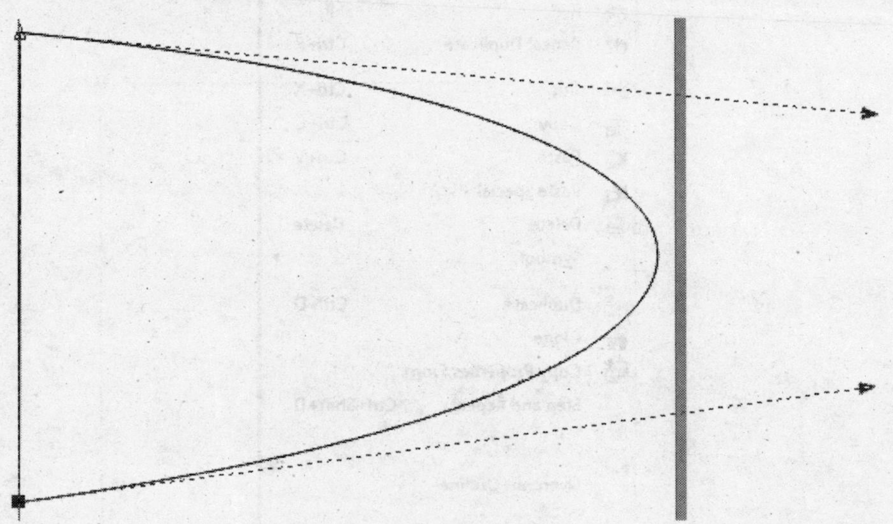

Handles Shape with Adjusted Control

2. You will see **2 Control Handles** (solid blue arrowheads).

Control Handle

3. Decrease the distance between the **Control Handles** by dragging each handle closer to the other.
4. Select the **Top Left Node** and **drag** to the **Top Left Corner** of the page.
5. Select the **Pick Tool** and then **click** on the **shape.** 

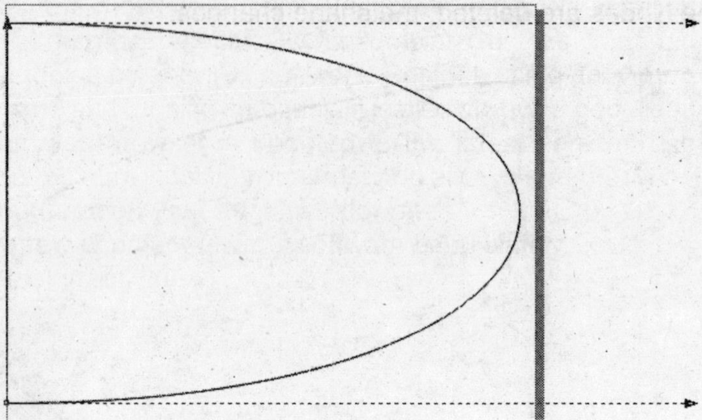

Shape Control Handle

Duplicate Shape

1. Go to the **Menu Bar** and select **Edit ➢ Duplicate**, or you can hold down **Ctrl+D** keys together.

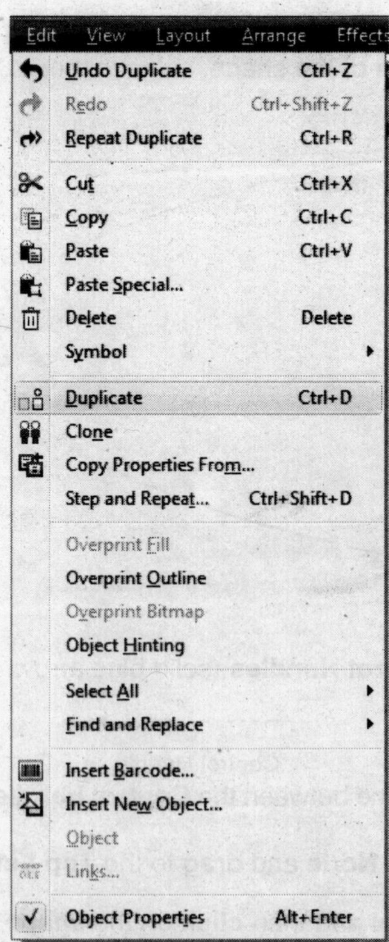

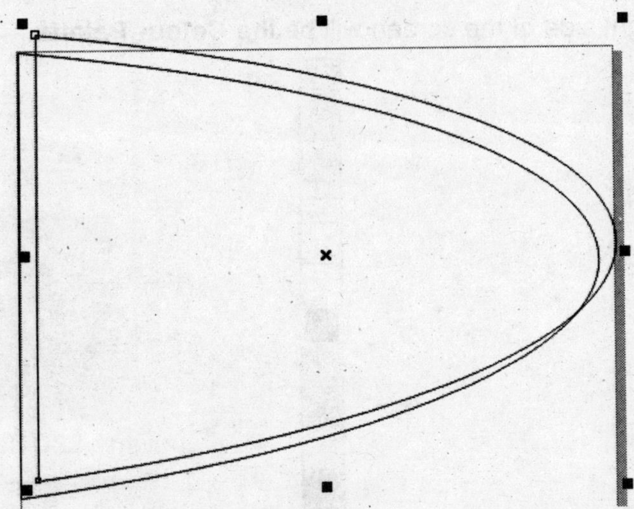

2. An exact copy of your shape will appear.

Mirror Image

1. On the **Tool Control Bar**, select the **Mirror Horizontally** icon to flip the shape.

2. Move the **duplicate shape** so that it lines up with the bottom of the page.
3. Then alternate between the **Pick Tool** and **Shape Tool** to make adjustments to the **size** of the **2 shapes**.
4. The **Duplicate Shape** should be slightly **smaller** than the original.

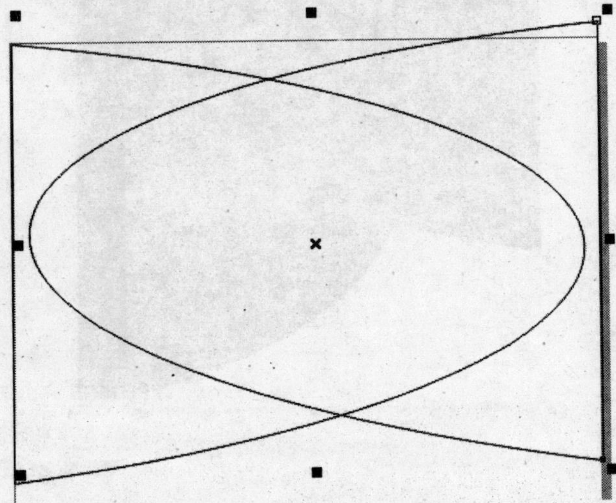

Add Fill & Outline Colour

To make the shapes a little easier to work with, let us add some colour to them.

1. You can select both shapes by **dragging** the **cursor** over them while **holding** down the **mouse button**.

2. On the right side of the screen will be the **Colour Palette.**

3. Select any colour you choose. Simply click on your **desired colour** in order to **Fill the shape** and **right click** over the **same colour** to set the **Stroke/Outline** of the shape.

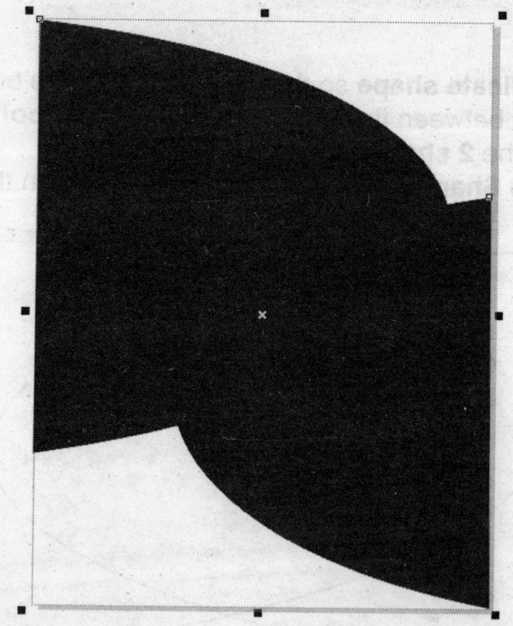

Arrange Order

1. Using the **Rectangle Tool** again, draw a **Rectangle** that completely covers the page, including the **2 shapes.**
2. Set its **Fill Colour** to something different so that you are able to distinguish between the **2 layers.**
3. Now we will send this **layer behind the first** by changing the order.

4. On the **Menu Bar** select **Arrange ➢ Order ➢ To Back of Page**.

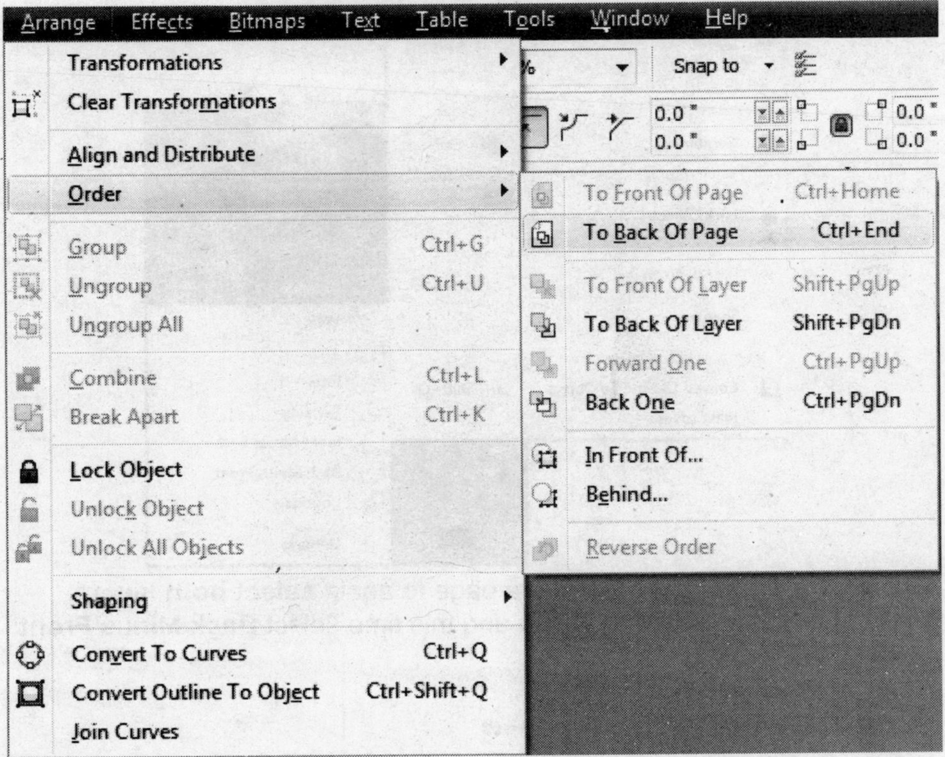

Shaping

1. Select both the blue shapes. Do this by **selecting** 1, then **hold down** the **Shift** key and **select** the other.

2. We will **merge** these **2 shapes** together, so that they become **1 shape**.

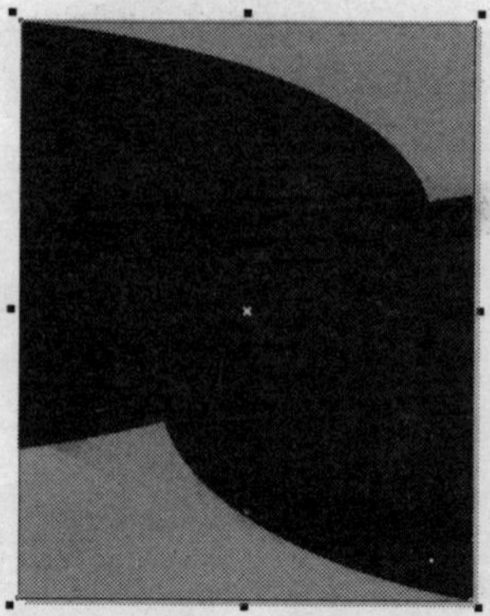

3. On the **Menu Bar** select **Arrange ➤ Shaping ➤ Weld**.

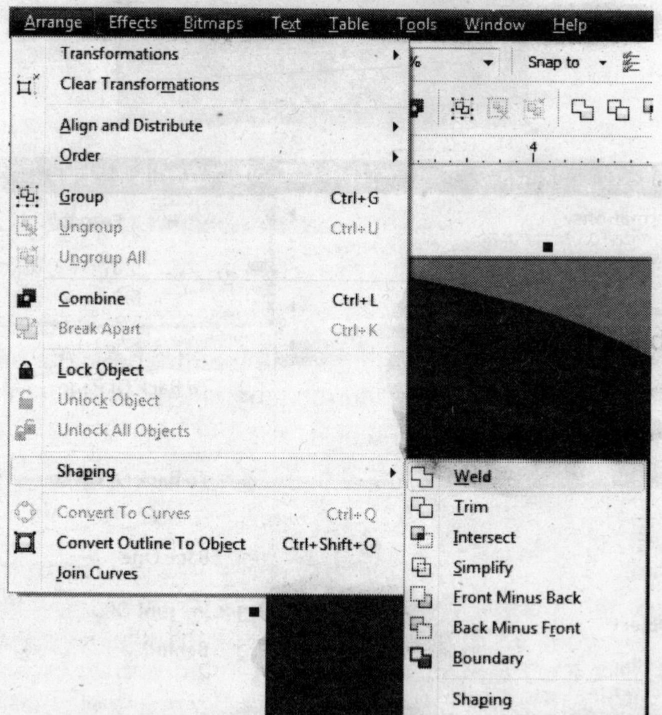

4. **Drag** the **cursor** over the entire page to again **select both layers**.
5. Go back to the **Shaping Menu** and this time select **Back Minus Front**.

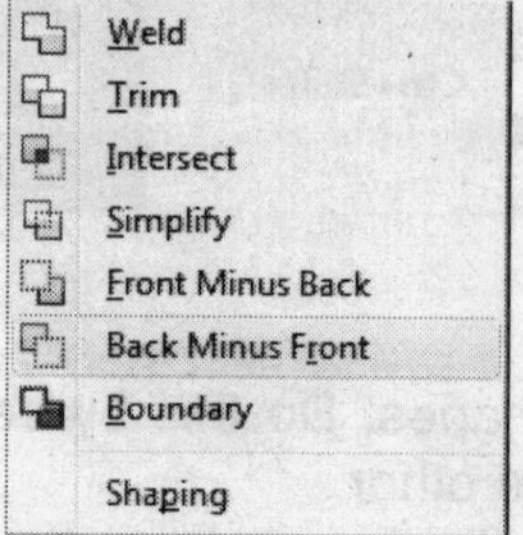

6. Your new shape should look something like this one.

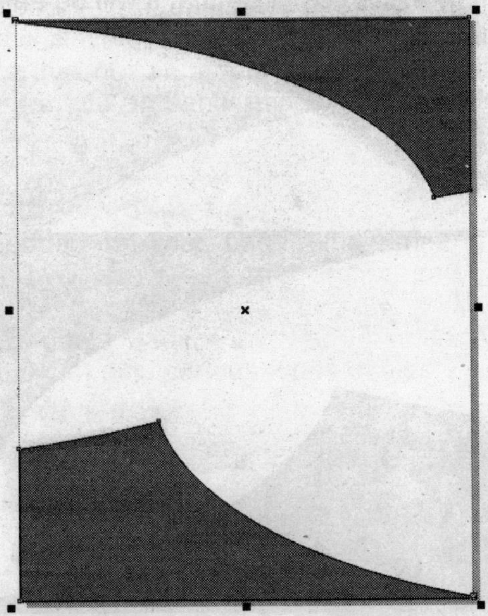

Break Curve Apart

1. We will break this shape apart by going to the **Menu Bar** and selecting **Arrange ➢ Break Curve Apart**.

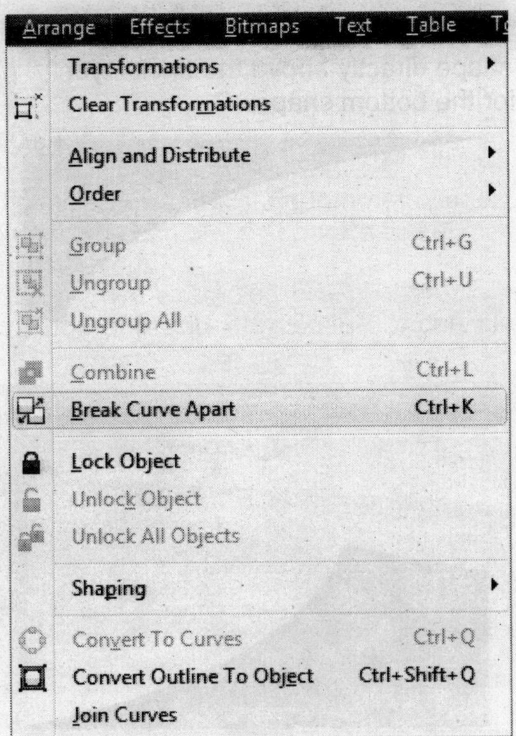

2. Now you will be able to freely move each piece around.
3. Remember to change the colour so that it will be easier for you to spot which layer you are working with.

4. Move the top shape directly above the back layer.
5. Do the same for the bottom shape.

6. Select both shapes, and on the **Menu Bar** select **Arrange ➢ Order ➢ To Back of Page** to send them to **Back of Layer**.

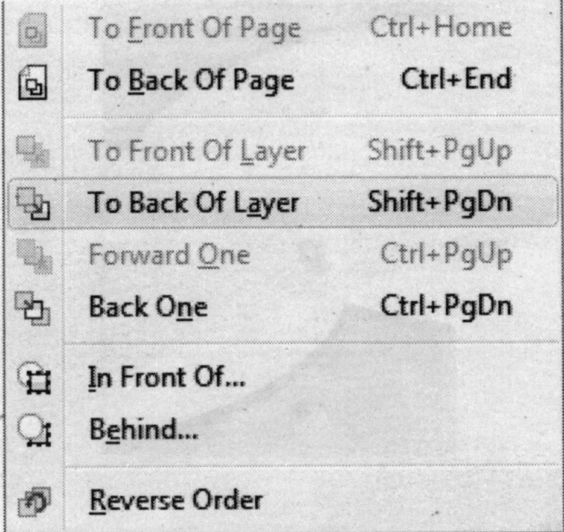

7. Then using the **Arrow keys** on your keyboard, move the shape downward until it is in the desired location on the flyer.
8. Click on **any white area** to **deselect both shapes**, then reselect the bottom shape and move upward to desired location.

Adjust Triangular Handle

Notice there is still some white space separating the 2 layers at the corner.

1. To fix this, select the **Shape Tool**, then click on the **2nd layer** and **drag** the **Blue Triangular Handle** upward to meet the top layer.

2. Repeat this for the shape at the bottom of the page but select the **Blue Square Handle** instead and drag downward toward the **1st layer**.

CMYK to RGB Colour

Next we will set the colour for each layer.

1. To open the **Colour Docker**, go up to the **Menu Bar** and select **Window ➢ Dockers ➢ Colour**.

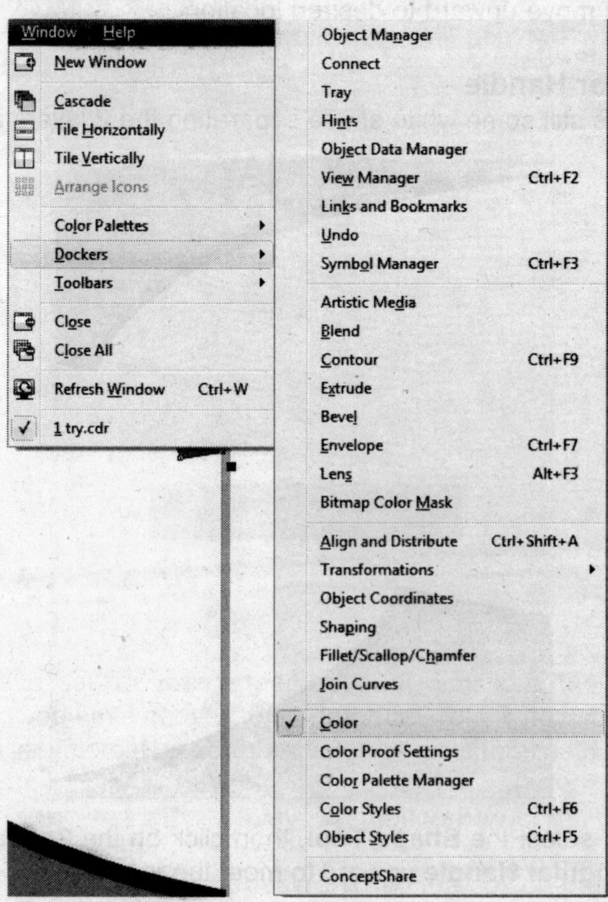

2. The **Colour Docker** will appear on the right side of the screen.

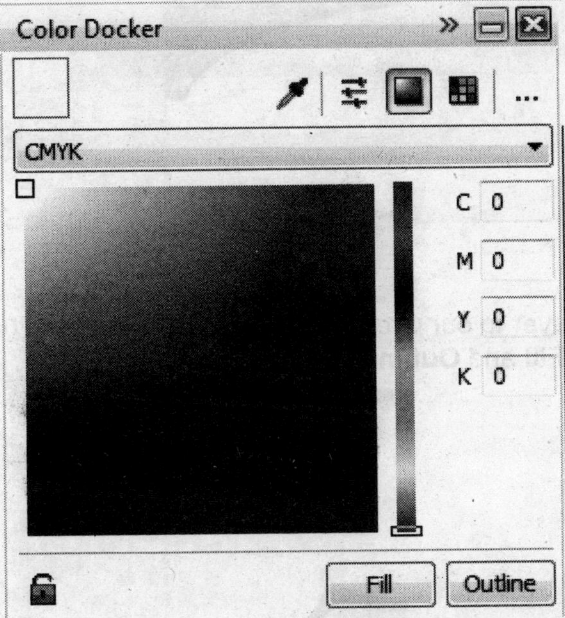

3. Click on the down arrow to the right of **CMYK** and change to **RGB**.

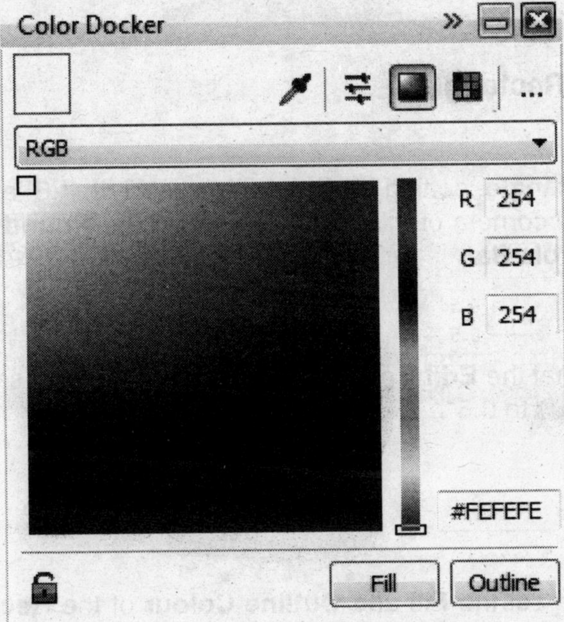

Set RGB Colour Values

1. Change R to 128, G to 0 and B to 0.
2. Then click on the **New Colour** on the top left of the **Colour Docker** to apply to shape.

3. You can also select the **Fill** and **Outline** buttons at the bottom of the **Docker**.

4. Set the top layer to our Green Colour – R to 153, G to 204 and B to 153.
5. Then select **Fill** and **Outline**.

Create Rounded Rectangle

1. Draw a **Rectangle**, setting its dimensions to Width 1.6" and Height 1.75".
2. To round the corners of this rectangle, select the **Round Corner** icon on the **Tools Controls Bar**.

3. Make sure that the **Edit Corners Together** icon is also selected, then set the Corner Radius to 0.5".

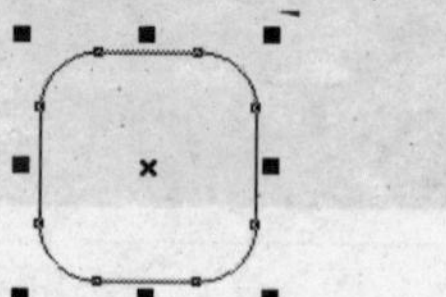

4. Now you can set the **Fill** and **Outline Colour** of the **Rectangle** by selecting the Red Colour that was already used.

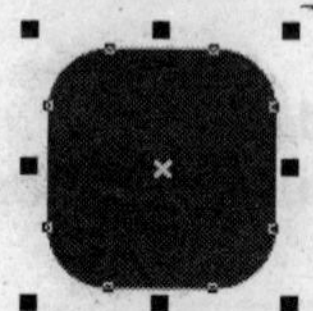

5. If you look at the bottom of the screen, you will see a **Colour Palette** called the **Document Palette**.

6. It shows all the previously used colours within the document. This way you do not have the trouble of re-entering all those colour values again.

Convert To Bitmap

1. Now we will have to add a **Gaussian Blur** to this shape.
2. With the Rectangle selected, go up to the **Menu Bar** and select **Bitmaps ➢ Convert to Bitmap**.

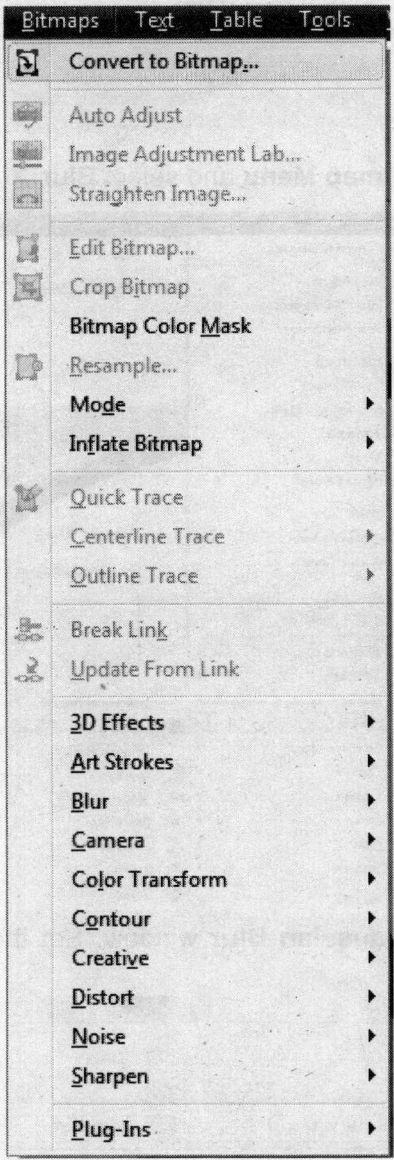

3. A **Convert to Bitmap** window appears.
4. Click on **OK**.

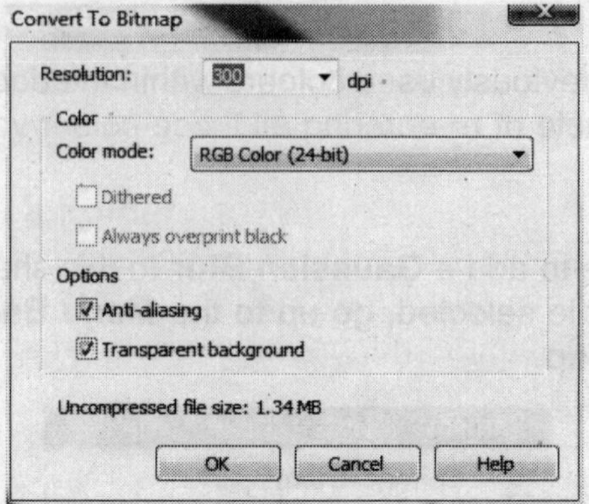

Set Gaussian Blur

1. Go back to the **Bitmap Menu** and select **Blur ➢ Gaussian Blur**.

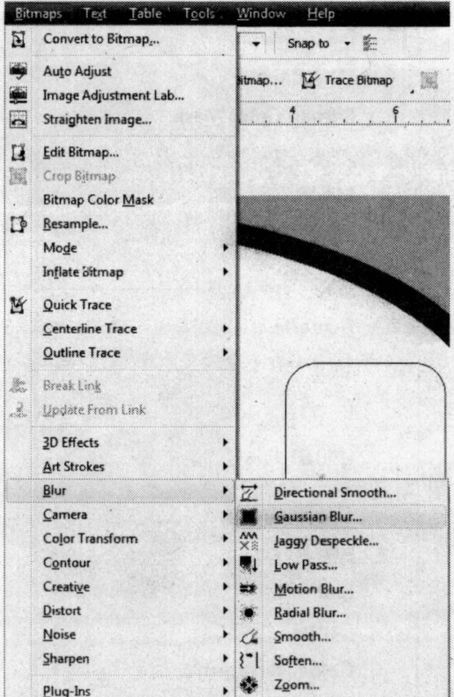

2. This opens the **Gaussian Blur** window. Set the Radius to 20, then click on **OK**.

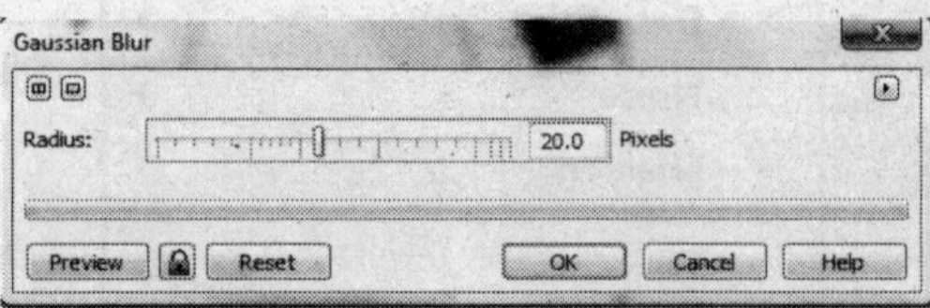

3. This creates a rectangle with Gaussian Blur.

4. **Duplicate** this shape.
5. **Recreate** a smaller White Rectangle and place inside each of the Red Rectangles.
6. Set Width to 1.55" and Height to 1.7".
7. Then set **Corner Roundness** to 0.258".
8. Create a **Duplicate** of this shape and place on top of the other Red Rectangle.

9. This creates a white rectangle with red background.
10. Draw another rectangle with the following dimensions – Width 3.55" and Height 3.8".
11. Set its **Corner Roundness** to 0.6".
12. Set its **Fill and Outline Colour** to our already used Green.

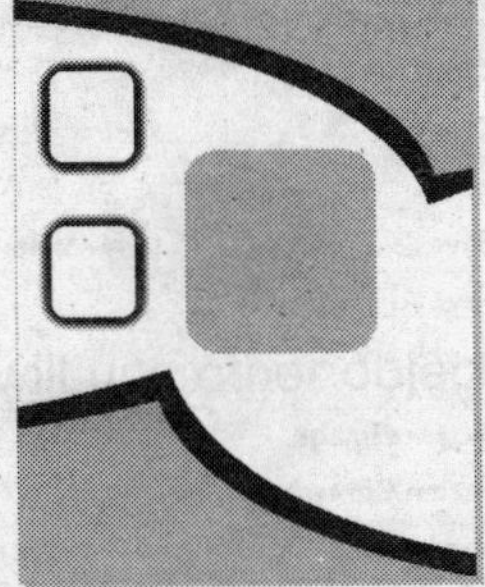

(Rectangle before Gaussian Blur)

13. Repeat the process to set the **Gaussian Blur**.

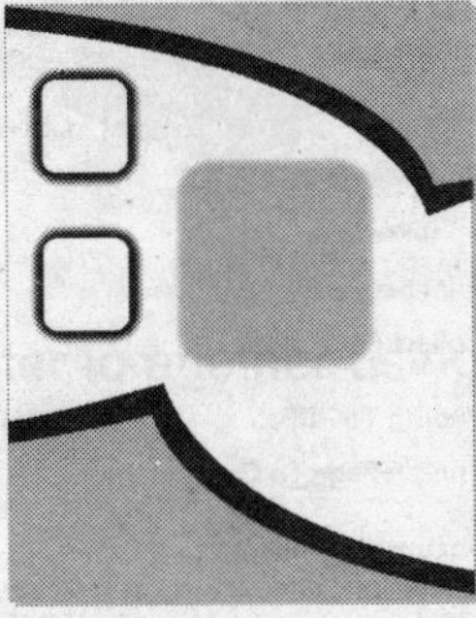

(Rectangle after Gaussian Blur)

14. Draw another White Rectangle to place above the Green Rectangle setting Width to 3.25" and Height to 3.5".
15. Set **Corner Roundness** to 0.55".

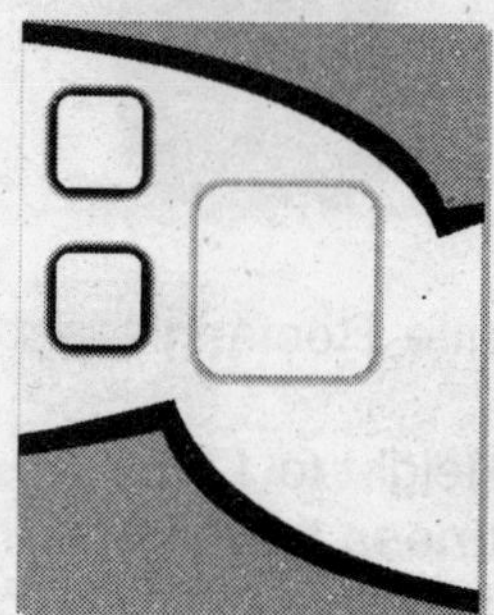

16. You will get a new product flyer-coloured background.

Insert Images

1. Once you have downloaded the images, you will need to place them into the flyer.
2. Starting with the White Teddy Bear, go to the **Menu Bar** and select **File ➢ Import**.

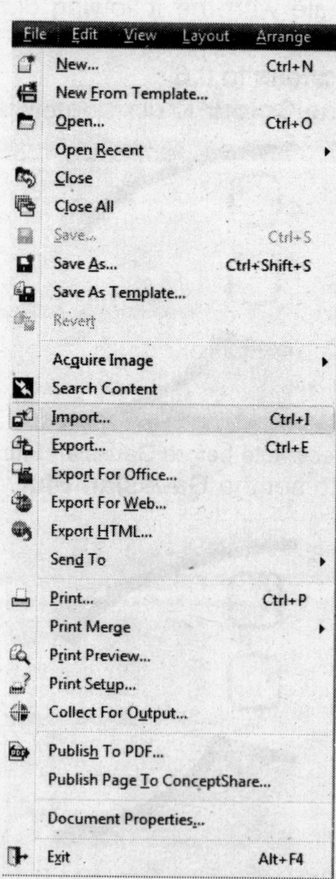

3. This opens the **Import** window.

4. Browse to where you saved the file.
5. Select it and then click on **Import** on the bottom right of the window.
6. You will see the **Image Name** along with some more details about the image next to your cursor.
7. Click **anywhere on the screen** to place the image.

Crop Images

1. With the image selected, click on the **Shape Tool** icon on the **Toolbox**.
2. The **8 Black Square Handles** around your image will change to **4 Nodes**.

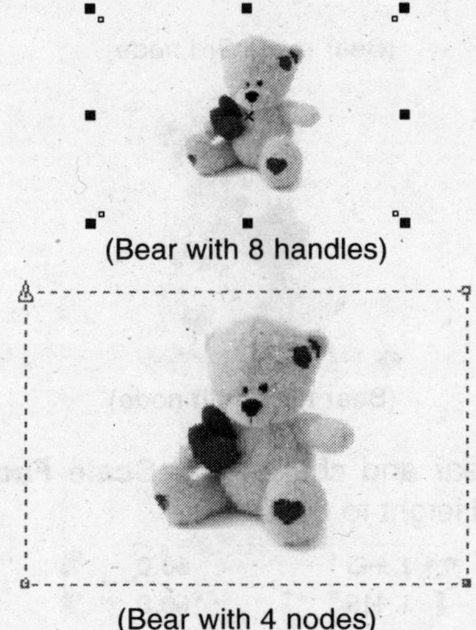

(Bear with 8 handles)

(Bear with 4 nodes)

3. Select a **Node** and **drag Inwards** toward the image without cutting off any part of it and then release.

(Bear move 1st node)

4. Continue to move each **Node** wherever necessary.

(Bear move 2nd node)

(Bear move 3rd node)

(Bear move 4th node)

5. Select the White Bear and change the **Scale Factor** of the image, setting both the Width and Height to 60%.

↔ 1.445 "	60.0	%
↕ 1.415 "	60.0	%

6. Place the newly **cropped image** in the White Box.

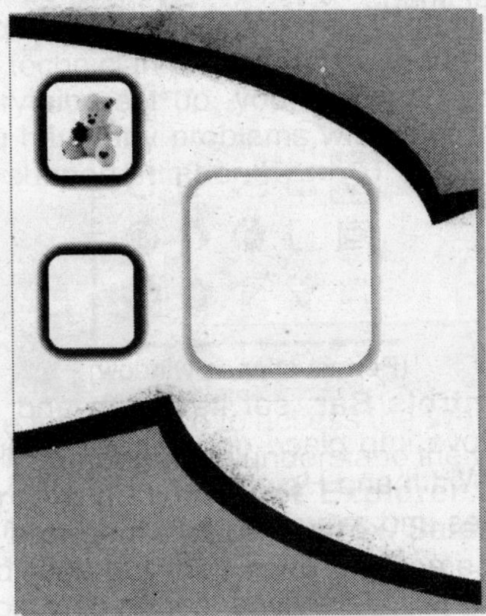

7. **Repeat** the steps to add the other 2 images, **crop** them and place them where they need to be.
8. Set the **Scale Factor** for the Gray Bear to 65% and the image of the 2 Bears to 120%.

Basic Shapes Tool-Heart

Next we will add some Hearts to the Flyer.

1. On the **Toolbox**, select the **Basic Shapes Tool**.
2. On the **Tool Controls Bar**, you will see what looks like a **Parallelogram**. Click on the **down arrow** on the right and select the Heart Icon from the menu that appears.

3. While holding down your **Ctrl** key, draw a Heart on the screen, this gives you a proportional image.

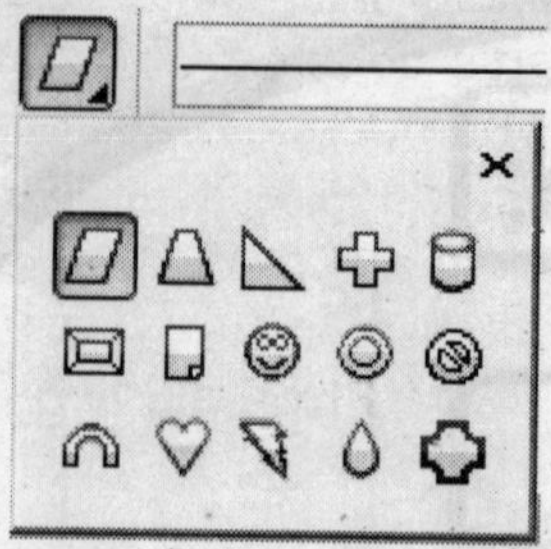

(Perfect shapes window)

4. On the **Tool Controls Bar**, set its Width and Height to 0.6". Create a **Duplicate** and move into place on the flyer. Adjust the dimensions of the 2nd Duplicate to Width and Height 0.4".
5. Create 3 Duplicates and move them into place on the flyer.

6. Adjust the dimensions of the 3rd Duplicate to Width and Height 0.2" and place on the flyer.
7. Place 4 Hearts on the Red Layer.
8. Set their Width and Height to 0.3".

9. Repeat the steps to apply colour, set the Hearts on the White Background to Solid Red and the Hearts on the Red Background to Solid White.
10. You can set each Heart's colour 1 by 1, or hold down the **Shift** key and select each Heart that you need to apply the change to.
11. You can also drag your cursor over all the Hearts you wish to select at once, just be careful not to select any other shapes.
12. Then set the White Hearts.
13. Next we will apply text to the Flyer, starting with the **Gradient Filled Title**.

Fonts

You can use any font of your choice from the font list.

For a newly downloaded Font to be usable on your machine, you must first install it. Any Font installed while CorelDRAW is open, will not be visible in the **Font List**. To correct this, you will have to **restart** the CorelDRAW programme after **Font(s) installation**.

Insert Text on a Path

1. Select the **Text Tool** from the **Toolbox**.
2. Notice that the cursor changes to an **X** with an **A**. Move the cursor over the edge of the **Top Red Layer**. The cursor changes to an uppercase **I** and the word **'Edge'**.
3. When you see this, it means that you are on the edge of the layer. Click there and **start typing** 'New Products'.

4. Click on **OK**, so the text appears upside down.

Mirror Text

1. Go up to the **Tools Control Bar** and select the **Mirror Text Vertically** icon.

2. The text is now right side up, however it is facing the wrong direction.
3. Then click on the **Mirror Text Horizontally** icon.

4. The text will now be right side up.

Format Text

1. **Triple click** to select **all text**.
2. On the **Tools Control Bar** select the **down arrow** on the **Font List** and choose the **NotMaryKate Font**.

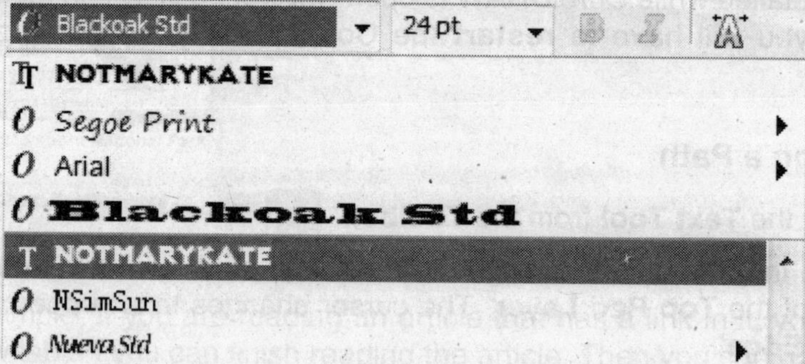

3. In the box on the right side of the **Font List box**, click on the **down arrow** and set the **Font Size** to 48 pt.

4. Select the text by **triple clicking** over it and set the **Outline/Stroke Colour** to White.

Set Gradient with Fountain Fill

1. Go over to the **Toolbox** and select the **Fill Tool** icon.
2. Scroll over to the **Pop-up Menu** and select **Fountain Fill**.

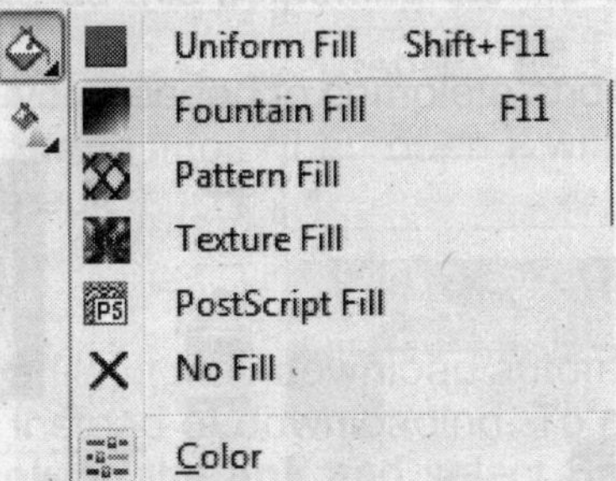

3. This opens the **Fountain Fill** window.

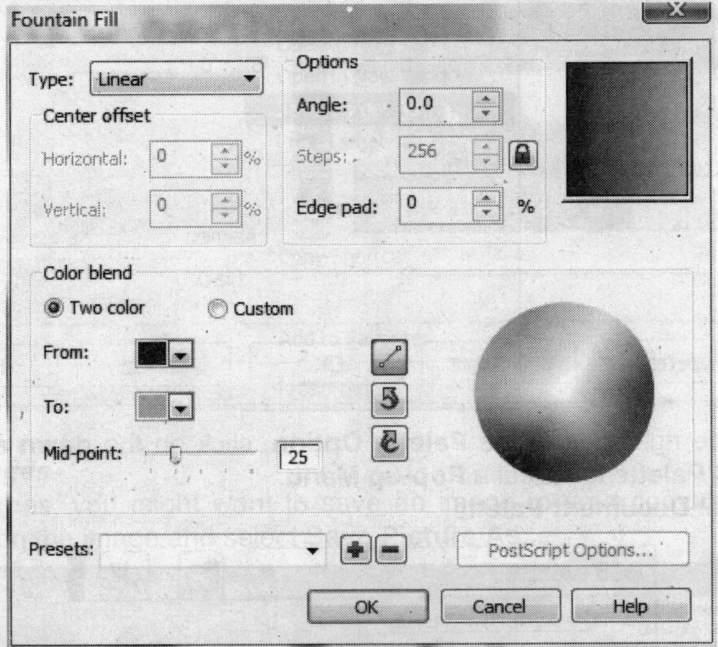

4. In the Colour Blend Section, Two Colour should be checked. To the right side of the **From** option, select the **down arrow** and choose **More** at the bottom of the **Colour Palette**.

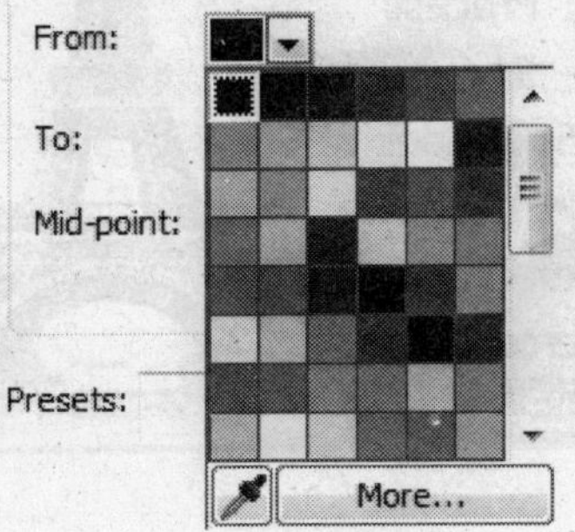

5. This opens the **Select Colour** window.

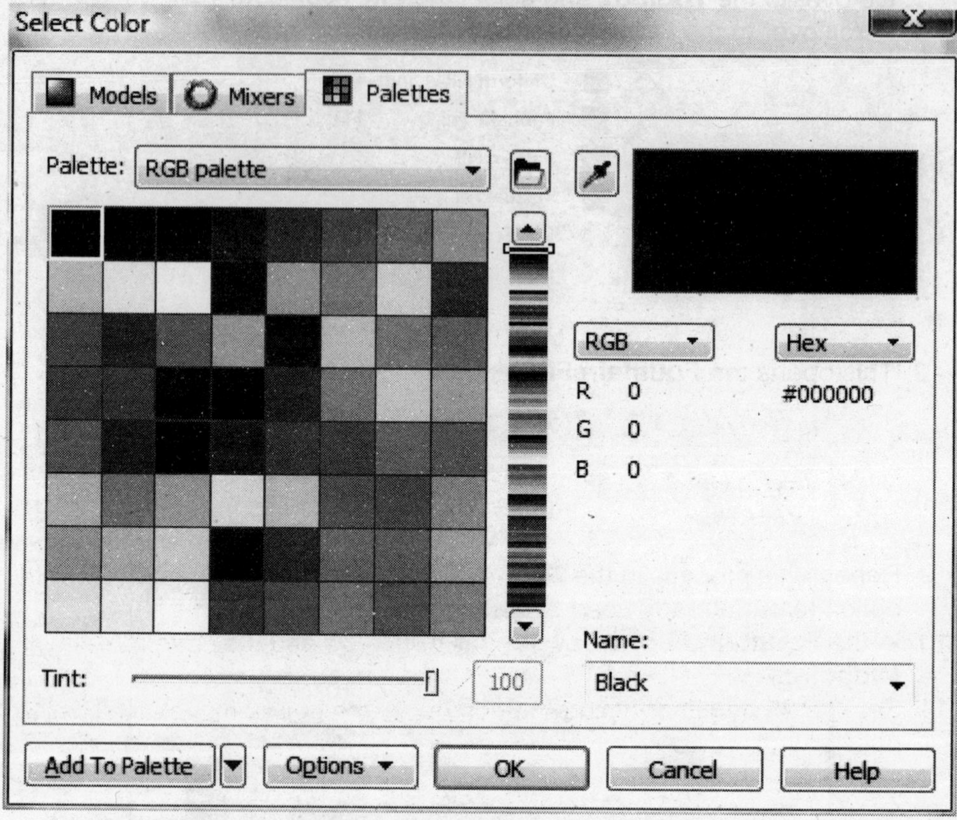

6. To the right side of the **Palette Option**, click on the **down arrow** next to **RGB Palette** to reveal a **Pop-up Menu**.
7. Select **Document Palette**.

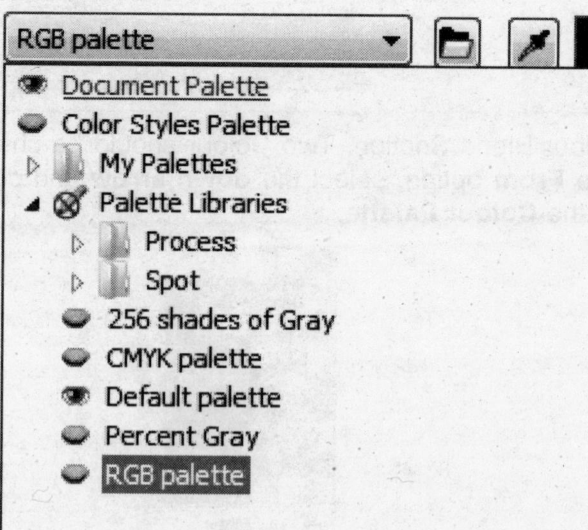

8. Select the Red colour that has been used on the flyer and click on **OK**.

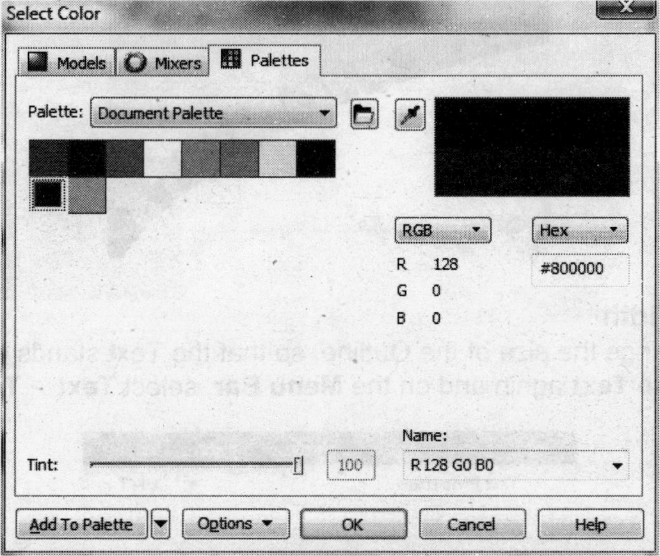

9. Repeat this process in the **Fountain Fill** window to set the colour for the **To** option to our already used Green.
10. In the **Fountain Fill** window, under the **From** and **To** options, you will see **Midpoint**.
11. Set it to 25 by either typing the number in the box or move the slider to that position.
12. Then click on **OK**.

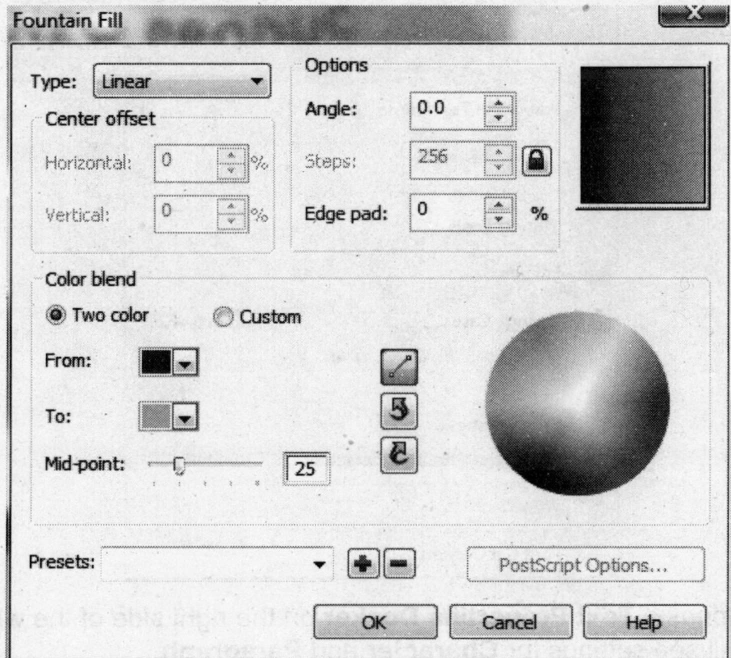

13. The **Title Text** will now have a **Gradient Fill**.

Set Outline Width

We can change the size of the Outline, so that the Text stands out.

1. Select the **Text** again and on the **Menu Bar**, select **Text ➢ Text Properties**.

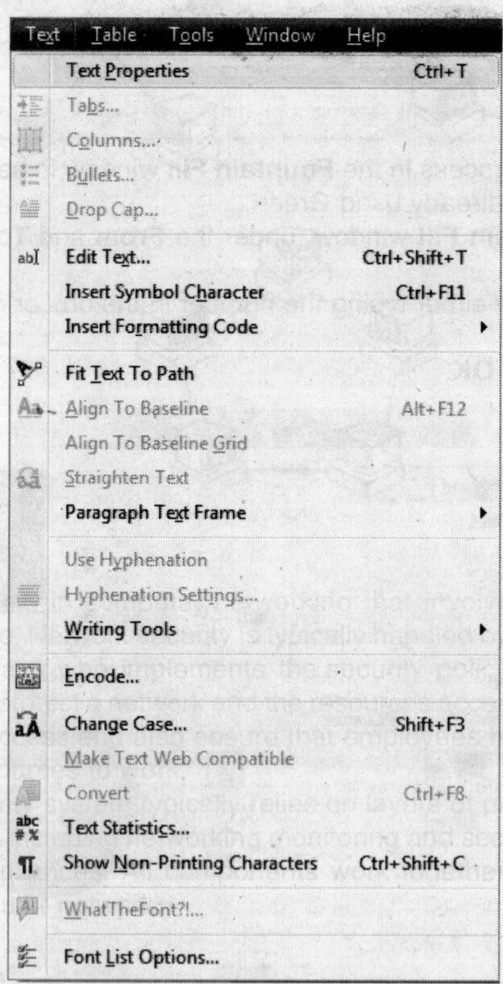

2. This opens a **Text Properties Docker** on the right side of the window.
3. You will see settings for **Character** and **Paragraph**.

4. Set the **Outline Width**, represented by this icon 🖋 to 2.5 pt.

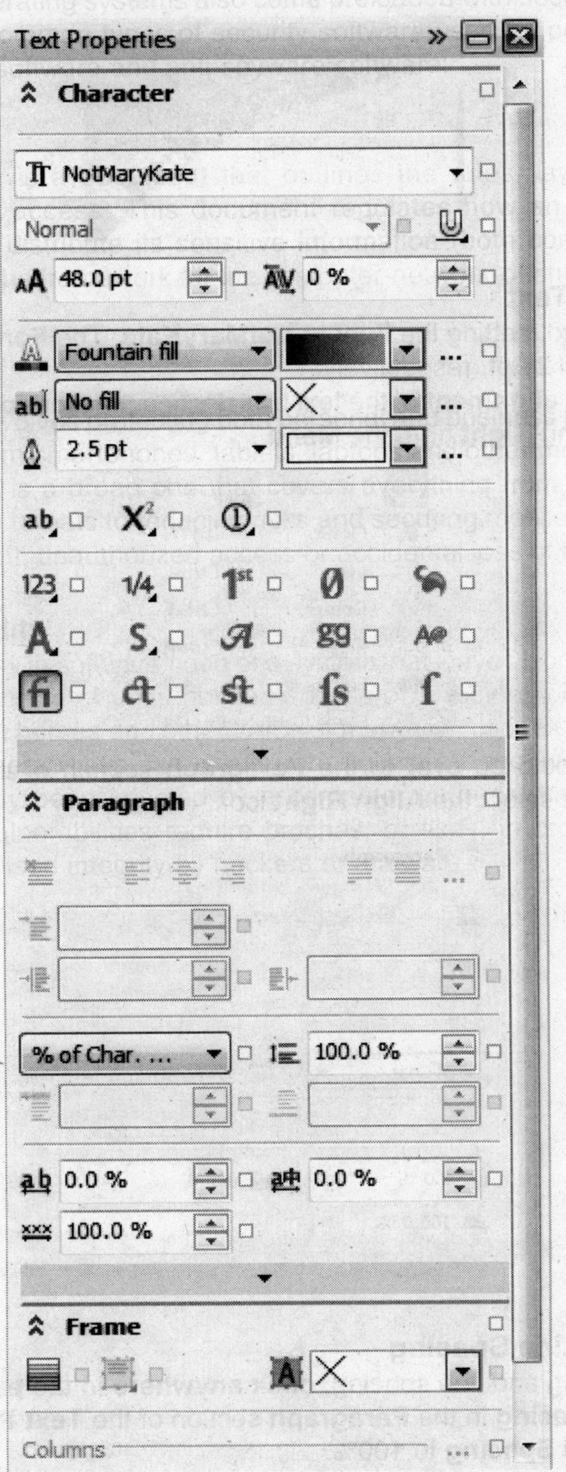

5. Then click on **any white area** on the canvas to see the change applied to the text.

Add Remaining Text

1. Type the text, setting the Font to **NotMaryKate**. The **Font Size** should be set to 18 pt and 24 pt, respectively.
2. Change the **alignment** of the text by selecting the **Horizontal Alignment** icon and choosing **Right** from the **Menu**.

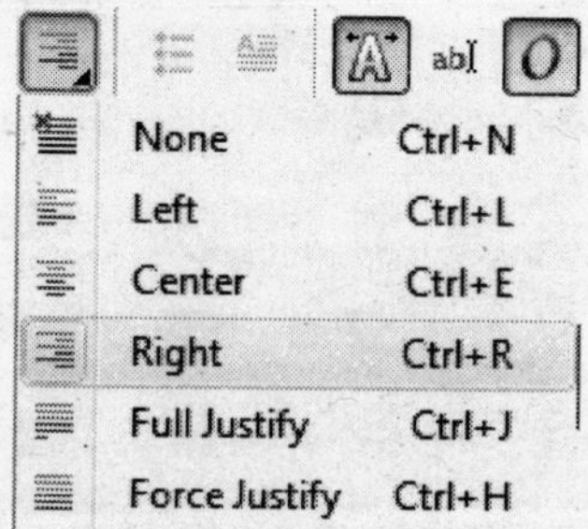

3. You also could go over to the **Paragraph** section of the **Text Properties Docker** and select the **Align Right** icon.

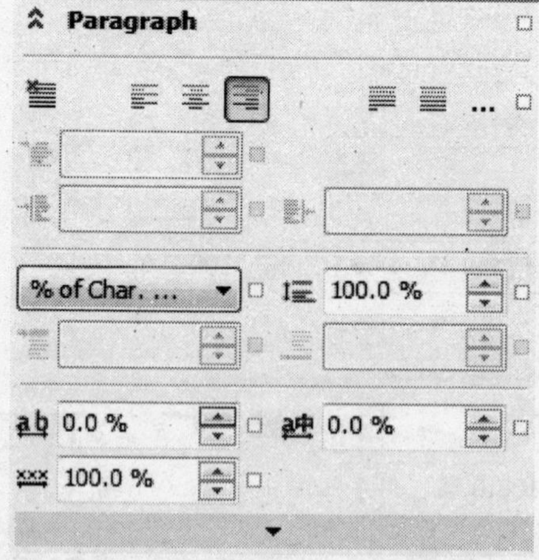

Adjust Leading/Line Spacing

1. To fix leading and line spacing, **click anywhere** in the paragraph and adjust the **Line Spacing** in the **Paragraph** section of the **Text Properties Docker**.
2. Set the **Line Spacing** to 100%.

Save File

To Save your file:

1. Go to the **Menu Bar** and select **File** ➢ **Save**.

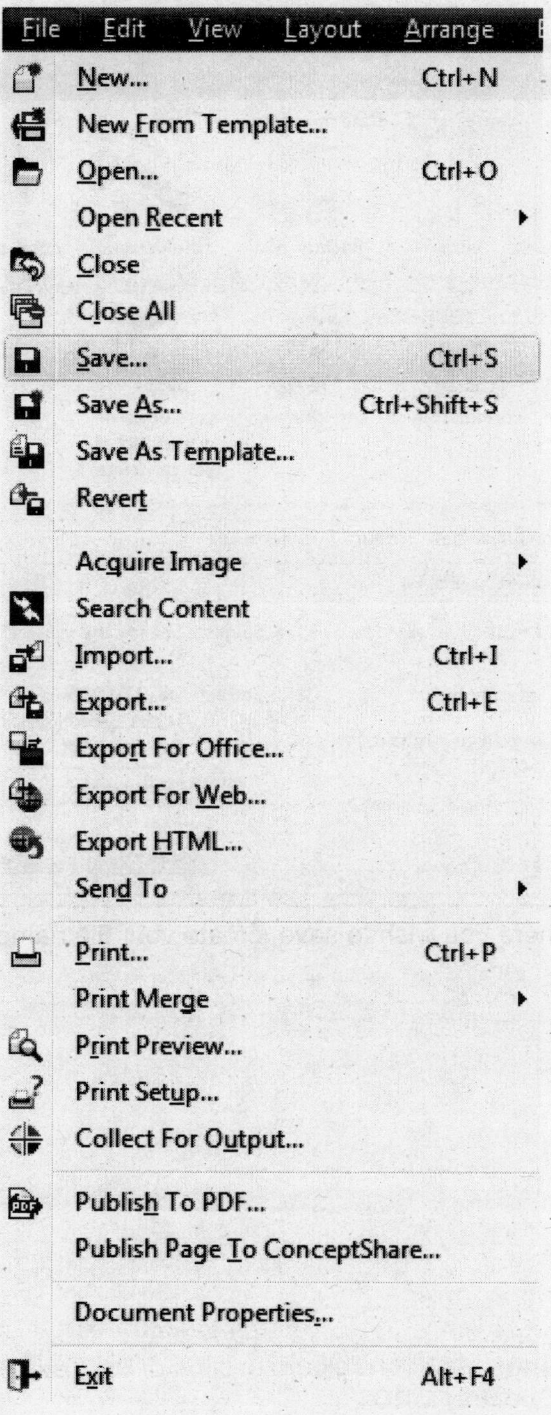

2. This opens the **Save Drawing** window.

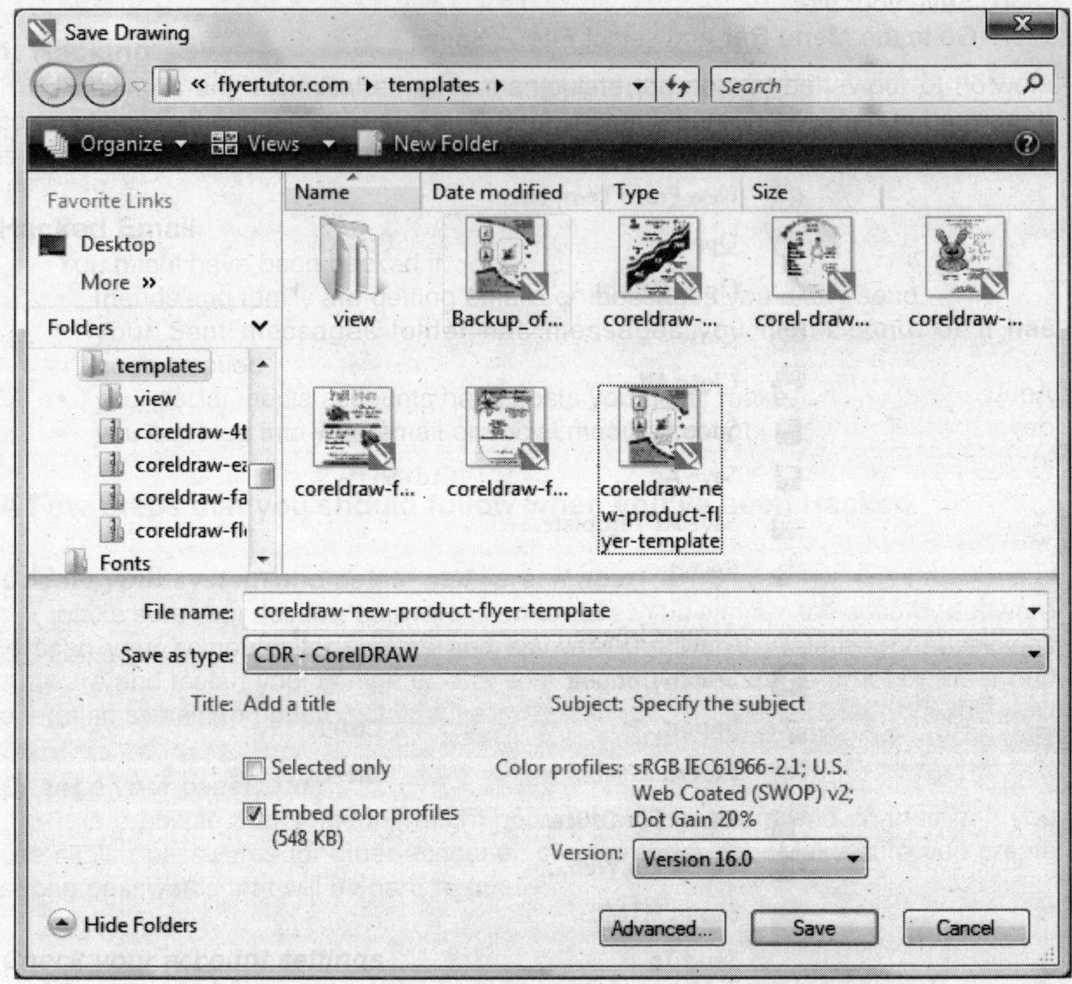

3. Browse to where you wish to save, create your file name, and click on **Save**. ☐

20
Adobe PageMaker 7.0

Adobe PageMaker 7.0 is an ideal page layout programme developed by Adobe Corporation. This programme is used in desktop publishing to create high-quality publications.

Getting Started with Adobe PageMaker 7.0

1. Click on the **Start** button.
2. Click on **All Programs** option from the menu.
3. Search for **PageMaker 7.0** from the submenu and click on it.

PageMaker 7.0 will open for you. Look at the PageMaker window and its various features.

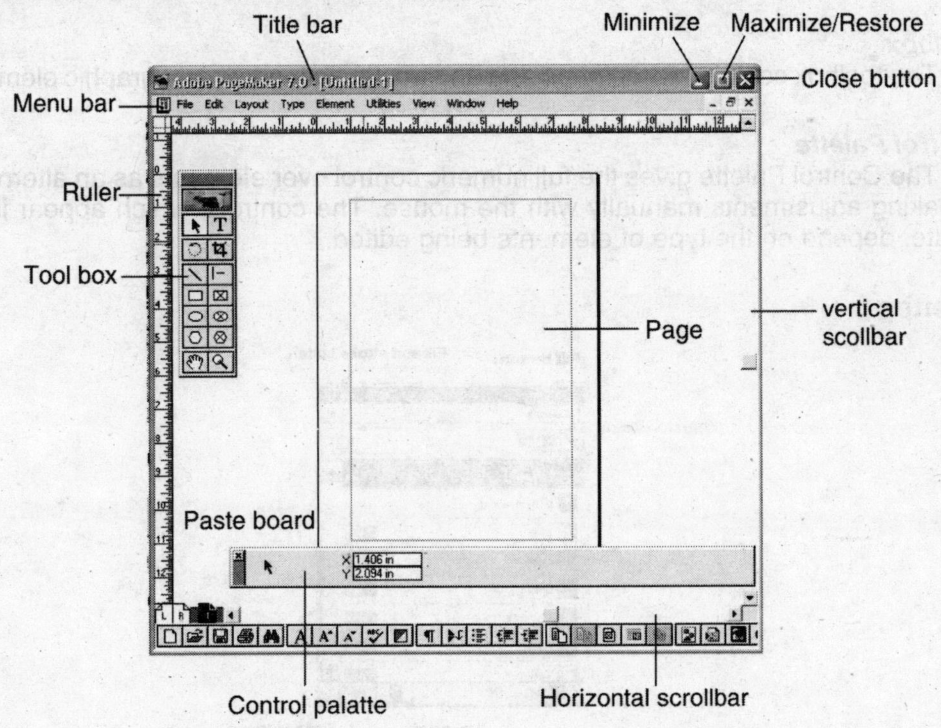

Restore Button

The Restore button is used to restore the PageMaker window to its original size.

Close Button

The Close button is used to close the PageMaker window.

Menu Bar

Below the Title bar is the Menu bar.The Menu bar cannot be moved from its default position on the screen. When we click on a menu, a dropdown list of command appears.

Page and Pasteboard

All items positioned on the page will normally be printed. The surrounding pasteboard is the work area. Items positioned on the pasteboard will not be printed.

The Rulers

The Rulers help us to make measurements on screen. Dotted line markers in each ruler indicate your current position.

Vertical Scroll Bar

The vertical scroll bar is used to move the document upward and downward.

Horizontal Scroll Bar

The horizontal scroll bar is used to move the document side to side.

Toolbox

The toolbox contains tools for adding and manipulating text and graphic elements.

Control Palette

The Control Palette gives the full numeric control over elements as an alternative to making adjustments manually with the mouse. The controls, which appear in the palette, depend on the type of elements being edited.

Palettes

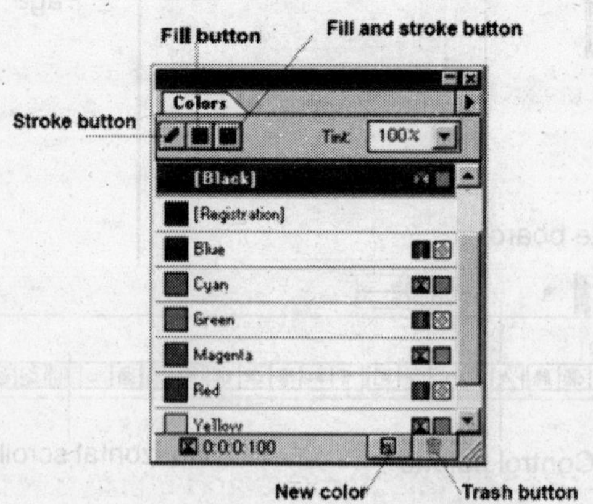

Colours Palette

The highlighted colour in the Colour Palette indicates the colour of the currently selected element.

Stroke Button

We click on the Stroke button to apply a colour to the line on a rectangle, polygon, ellipse or frame.

Fill Button

We click on the Fill button to change the fill colour of a rectangle, polygon, ellipse or frame.

Fill and Stroke

We click on the Fill and Stroke button to apply the same colour to both the stroke and the fill.

Tint

It is used to specify a tint percentage to apply object-level tints of the base colour applied to the selection.

New Colour

Click on the New Colour button to create a new colour and add it to the palette.

Trash Button

Click on the Trash button to delete a selected colour from the palette.

Toolbox

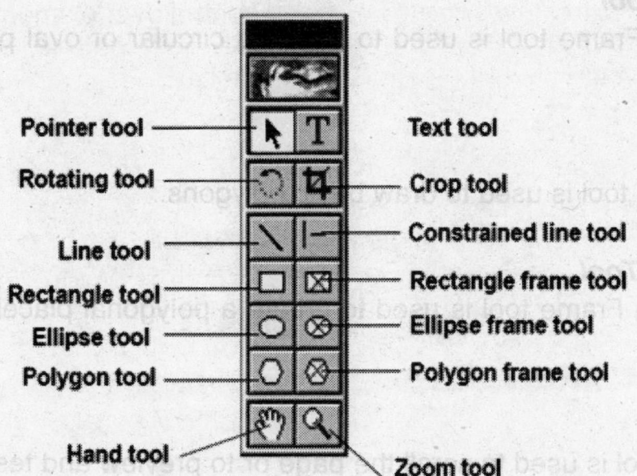

Pointer Tool

The Pointer tool is used to select, move and resize text blocks and graphics.

Text Tool

The Text tool is used to type, select and edit text.

Rotating Tool

The Rotating tool is used to select and rotate objects.

Cropping Tool

The Cropping tool is used to trim imported graphics.

Line Tool

The Line tool is used to draw straight lines in any direction.

Constrained Line Tool

The Constrained Line tool is used to draw vertical or horizontal lines.

Rectangle Tool

The Rectangle tool is used to draw rectangles and squares.

Rectangle Frame Tool

The Rectangle Frame tool is used to create a rectangular placeholder for text and graphics.

Ellipse Tool

The Ellipse tool is used to draw ellipses and circles.

Ellipse Frame Tool

The Ellipse Frame tool is used to create a circular or oval placeholder for text and graphics.

Polygon Tool

The Polygon tool is used to draw basic polygons.

Polygon Frame Tool

The Polygon Frame tool is used to create a polygonal placeholder for text and graphics.

Hand Tool

The Hand tool is used to scroll the page or to preview and test hyperlinks.

Zoom Tool

The Zoom tool is used to magnify or reduce an area of the page.

Control Palette in Character View

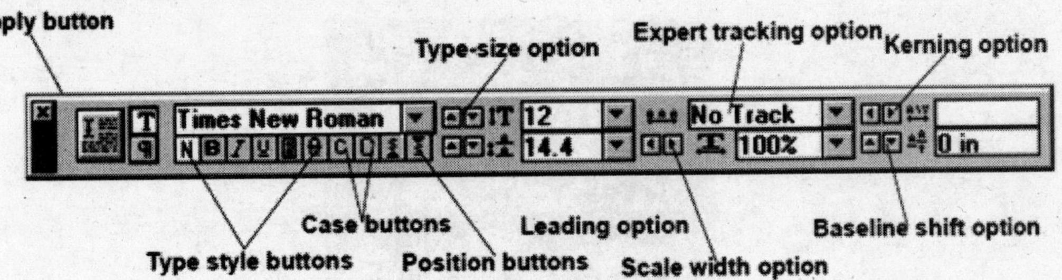

Apply Button

We click on the Apply button to apply formatting to the selected text.

Type Style Buttons

We click on the Type Style buttons to apply styles, such as Normal, Bold, Italic, Underline, Reverse or Strikethrough to the selected text.

Case Buttons

We click on the Case buttons to specify small caps or all caps to the selected text, or deselect both buttons for normal case.

Position Buttons

We click on the Position buttons to specify Superscript or Subscript type to the selected text, or deselect both buttons for normal position.

Type-size Option

This is used to specify type size in points. Nudge amount is 0.1 point.

Leading Option

This is used to specify the vertical space between lines of type in a paragraph. Auto turns on automatic leading at 120% of type size. Nudge amount is 0.1 point.

Expert Tracking Option

We type or select the amount of space between letters and words that apply to the selected text.

Kerning Option

The Kerning option is used to increase, decrease or view kerning increments, accurate to 0.001 of an em space. Nudge amount is 0.01 em.

Baseline Shift Option

The Baseline Shift option is used to specify the baseline alignment of the text.

File Menu

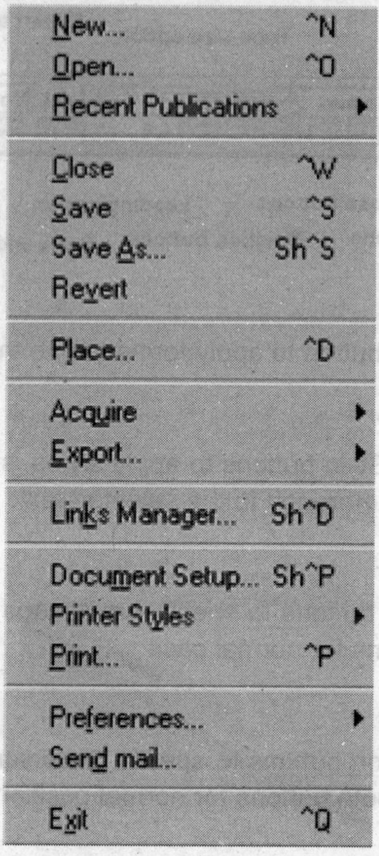

New

This option helps you to open a new PageMaker publication or template file.

To Start a New Publication

1. Choose **File ➢ New.**
2. Specify options in the **Document Set-up** dialog box.

You specify page layout details, number of text columns, page-numbering scheme and the basic design of the publication in the publication itself.

Open

It opens an existing PageMaker publication or template file. By default, it opens the original publication or a copy of the template file.

To Open a Publication

1. Choose **File ➢ Open**.
2. Select the publication you want to open.
3. Select **Original** or a **Copy**.

When you select a template or a PageMaker publication, PageMaker automatically selects **Copy**. To open the original of a template instead, click on **Original.**

4. Click on **OK**.

Recent Publications

It lists the last eight PageMaker publications that you opened and saved.

Close

To close the active publication without exiting PageMaker, choose **File ➢ Close.** To close all open publications without exiting PageMaker, hold down **Shift** and then choose **File ➢ Close All**.

If you have made changes since you saved the publication, PageMaker will ask if you want to save those changes. You can **save** changes, **ignore** them, or **cancel** the **Close** command.

Save

Save stores the active publication in a file with the same name or prompts you for a name if the file has not been saved yet. After saving, you can continue to work in your publication.

To Save a Publication for the First Time

1. Choose **File ➢ Save a File ➢ Save As.**
2. Select a folder in which to store the **saved file.**
3. Type a **name for the publication**, and then click on **Save.**

PageMaker saves your publication in the current location unless you specify a different folder.

To Save all Open Publications

Press **Shift** and choose **File ➢ Save All**.

Save As

It lets you rename your publication or template, or save it to a different disk or folder. Unlike the **Save** command, **Save As** also compresses your file, making its file size as small as possible.

To Save a Publication with a New Name or in a Different Location

1. Choose **File ➢ Save As**.
2. Type a **new name** or specify a **new location.**
3. Click on **Save.**

Changing a publication's name or location using **Save As** creates a new copy of the publication, so two versions of the publication exist: one with the old name or location and one with the new.

Revert

It removes all changes to the active publication since you last saved it. Press **Shift** as you choose Revert to cancel changes since the last mini-save. Several operations cause mini-saves, including turning, deleting or inserting pages, printing and copying or pasting objects to the **Clipboard**.

Place

It imports text, graphics and spreadsheet or database files into the active publication. The options available depend on what is selected when you choose this command. The files you can place depend in part on the import filters installed.

To Place Text or a Graphic in Layout View

1. Choose **File ➢ Place.**
2. Select the file you want to **import**, then select **Importing** options and then click on **OK** or **Open**.

Acquire

Use Acquire options to **import TIFF images** created in a separate device into your publication.

PageMaker supports **TWAIN**, a cross-platform interface that lets you create a TIFF image using a device (such as a scanner, video-capture board, or digital camera) attached to your computer and **import** the image into your publication without leaving PageMaker.

To Select a TWAIN-compatible Device

1. Choose **File ➢ Acquire ➢ Select Source.**
2. Select the **input device**.
3. Click on **OK**.

To Create and Import a TIFF Image

1. Choose **File ➢ Acquire ➢ Acquire Image.**
2. Specify a **name, location** and other available options for the image, and then click on **OK**.

Export

This option is used for **creating new files** from elements within a publication.

Links Manager

It lets you **view link status**, update and **manage linked files** in the active publication.

Document Setup

This lets you **change settings** for a publication, first defined when you chose New, such as page size, number of pages and page-numbering. Margins are applied to the document master page.

When we choose **File ➢ New** to begin a new publication, the **Document Setup** dialog box appears. We can define the basic parameters of the publication, such as page size, orientation, margins and the number of sides on which you print.

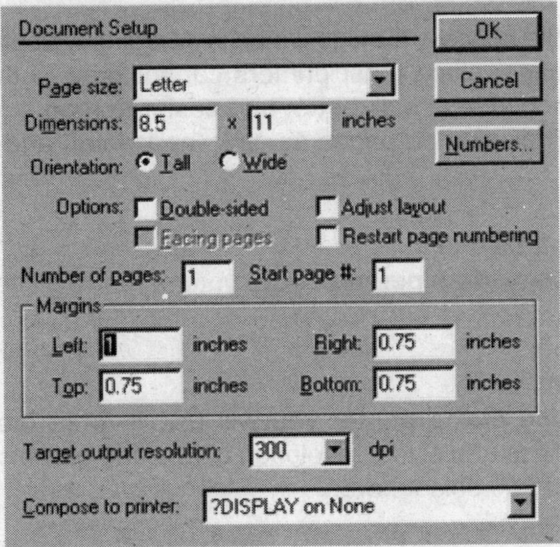

Page Size

Select a standard page size from the Page Size pop-up menu. When we select a page size, its dimensions appear in the **Dimensions** text boxes.

Dimensions

Use the Dimensions text boxes to specify a custom page size up to 42 by 42 inches (1065 by 1065 mm).

Orientation

Select **Tall** for a page that is taller than it is wide (Portrait orientation), or select **Wide** for a page that is wider than it is tall (Landscape orientation).

Options

Double-sided

Click on Double-sided to set **Inside and Outside margins** to accommodate binding on pages that will be printed on two sides.

Facing Pages

Click on Facing Pages, if you want left and right pages displayed together.

Adjust Layout

Adjust Layout in the **Document Setup** dialog box helps to reposition or resize objects and guides when you change margins, page size or orientation.

Number of Pages

Enter the Number of Pages you initially plan for the publication.

Margin

Margin is the white space around text blocks. Margins typically need to be created on the edges of a page, since most printers cannot print to the very edge. White space also makes a document look better and easier to read.

The margins will display on pages as pink (horizontal) and blue (vertical), non-printing lines.

Target Output Resolution

Select the number of **dots per inch (dpi)** your printer will use for the final printing of the publication.

Compose to Printer

Choose the name of the printer you will use to print the final copy of your publication. Font choices and sizes, resolution of text and graphics, and the print area depend on the printer you select here.

Preferences

It controls various settings that apply to publication-wide behaviour.

Exit

Exit ends your PageMaker session. If you have not saved the current publications since you last edited them, PageMaker prompts you to save changes before quitting.

Edit Menu

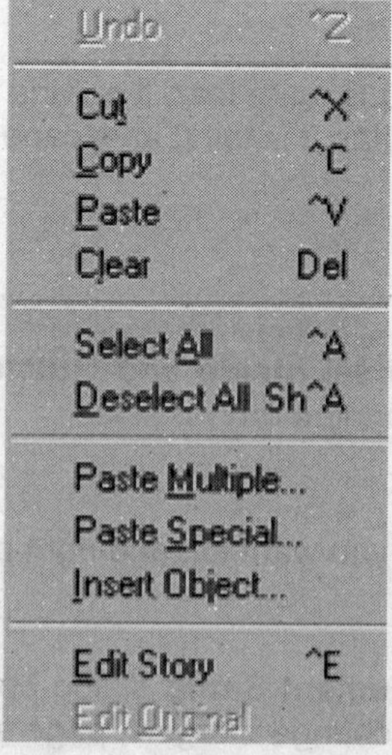

Undo

Undo lets you reverse your last action. The Undo command reverses only the most recent action. For example, if you use **Cut** three times, you will only be able to undo the **last Cut**.

PageMaker remembers your last action and lets you reverse it by choosing **Edit ➢ Undo**. PageMaker provides two ways to correct mistakes or to reverse actions you have taken: Choose **Edit ➢ Undo** or **File ➢ Revert**.

Cut

This command moves the selected text or objects from the publication to the Clipboard, removing them from the page.

Copy

This command copies the selected text or graphics to the Clipboard. The original objects remain on the page or in the story view window.

Paste

This command places the contents of the Clipboard (the last thing you cut or copied) into your publication. The contents of the Clipboard can be pasted repeatedly. Pasting does not affect the contents of the Clipboard.

To Cut, Copy and Paste an Object

1. Select one or more objects.
2. Choose **Edit ➢ Copy** or **Cut**.

Use any of the following options:

To offset the pasted copy, choose **Edit ➢ Paste**.

- To **paste the copy** directly over the original object, press **Ctrl+Alt+V**.
- To quickly **paste copies** of an object at a specific offset, press **Ctrl+Alt+V**, **drag the copy** in the direction and to the distance you want subsequent copies to be offset, and **repeat this step** as needed to create the effect you want.

Clear

This command deletes the selected text or graphic. Choosing **Clear** is the same as pressing the **Delete** key. You cannot paste a cleared object, because it is not on the Clipboard.

Select All

It selects everything on the visible page or facing pages, and the pasteboard. Each selected object has visible handles, and all selected objects can be cut or copied to the Clipboard or cleared.

Deselect All

It deselects everything on the visible page or facing pages, and the pasteboard.

Paste Multiple

This option lets you duplicate selected objects by specifying the number of copies you want and their numerical offset from the original object.

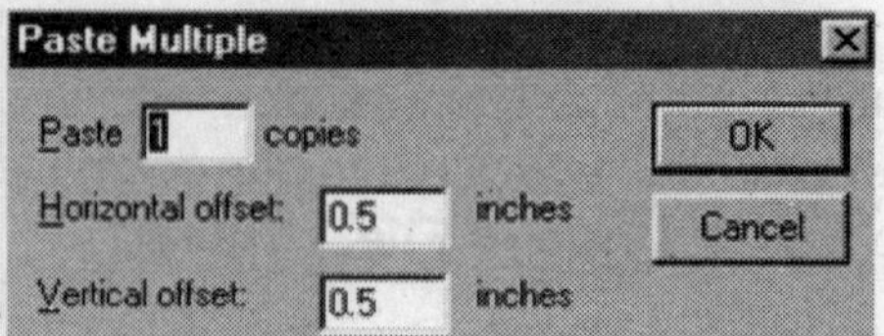

To Paste Several Copies of an Object

1. Select the **object** you want to **duplicate**.
2. Choose **Edit ➢ Copy**.
3. Choose **Edit ➢ Paste Multiple**.
4. Specify the **number of copies to paste** and the offset distance between each.

Note that you cannot use the **Undo** command to reverse multiple-paste actions.

Edit Story

Opens the story editor to show the story currently selected, or opens a new story window if no text is selected.

- In story editor, you work only on the text, not the layout, so revising text is fast and easy. Working in story editor is a convenient way to type or edit lengthy blocks of text.
- You can apply formatting to text in story editor, but you would not see most of the formatting until you return to layout view.

To Work in Story Editor

1. Click on a **story** with the **text tool** or the **pointer tool**.
2. Choose **Edit ➢ Edit Story**.
3. When you are finished working in the story editor, choose **Edit ➢ Edit Layout** to return to layout view.

Edit Original

It opens the source application to which the selected object is linked. Press **Shift + Edit Original** to choose an application (other than the original source application) to edit the object.

Layout Menu

Go to Page

This command turns to another page or master page in the active publication. Choose:

Layout ➢ Go to Page and **type the page number** you want.

Moving Between Pages

You can easily move from one page to another when you are working on a publication with multiple pages. Click on the **left** or **right arrows** to view lower or higher numbered page icons.

To Move Between Publication Pages

Use the technique that suits your needs.

- Click on a **page icon** along the bottom of the **layout window**. (Click on the left or right arrows to view lower-or higher-numbered page icons.)
- To go to the **previous page**, press the **Page Up** key; to go to the **next page**, press the **Page Down** key.
- To go to the **first page**, press the **Home key**; to go to the **final page**, press the **End key**.

Insert Pages

It lets you add pages to a publication before or after the current page, or insert new pages between two facing pages and specifies the master applied to new pages.

- If you choose **File ➢ Document Setup** to alter the number of pages, PageMaker adds or deletes pages from the end of the publication Shortcut to add a page to the end of the publication, press **Ctrl + Alt + Shift + G**.

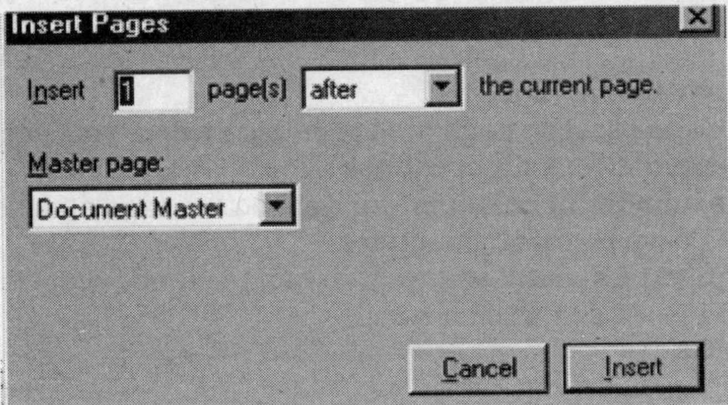

- If you choose **Layout ➢ Insert Pages** and also specify which master to apply to new pages you insert.

To Add Pages Anywhere in the Publication

1. Go to the **place** where you want to insert pages.
2. Choose **Layout ➢ Insert Pages**.
3. Type the **number of pages** you want to add, and **select a location** for the new pages.
4. Specify the **master pages** you want to apply, and then click on **Insert**.

Remove Pages

This deletes the designated range of pages in a publication, including the text and graphics on those pages.

To Remove Pages

1. Choose **Layout ➢ Remove Pages.**
2. Type the **range of pages** you want to remove, and then click on **OK.**

Sort Pages

You can move pages from one position to another in the active publication simply by arranging thumbnail representations of your pages in the page order you want.

To Move Pages

1. Choose **Layout ➢ Sort Pages.**
2. Select the page or pages you want to move, as follows:
   - To select **either a single-sided page** or a pair of facing pages, click on the **page** icon.
   - To select **one page** in a pair of facing pages, press **Ctrl** and click on the **page**.
3. Drag the selection to the location you want. To insert a selection between a pair of facing pages, press **Ctrl** and **drag the selection** over the facing pages.

A black bar indicates where the selected pages will be inserted.

Column Guides

This specifies the number of columns and the amount of space between the columns on the page.

To Set Up Columns on a Page

1. Turn to the publication page or master page where you want the columns.
2. Choose **Layout ➢ Column Guides.**
3. Enter the **number of columns** you want on the page and the space you want between columns, called the **gutter**.
4. Select **Adjust Layout** if you want existing text and graphics on the page to adjust to the revised column setup.
5. Click on **OK.**

Copy Master Guides

It displays on the current page(s) the non-printing guides on the **Master page** currently applied. It is useful if you have moved the guides on the page and want to reset them quickly.

Autoflow

When checked, text flows into available columns until there is no more text to place. Pages are added to the end of the publication, if necessary. Switch between manual and automatic flow by pressing **Ctrl** while text is flowing.

Type Menu

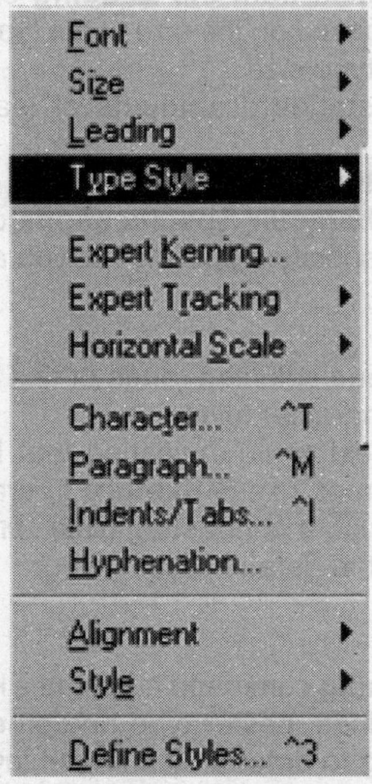

Font

You select the font for a selected range of text, a default for a single publication, a default for all future publications or the next text you place or type in.

To Format Text

1. Using the **text tool**, select the **text** you want to format.
2. Choose the **formatting attribute** you want from the **Type menu** or use the **Control palette**.

Size

You specify text font size in points for a selected range of text as a default for a single publication, or as a default for all future publications. Use the **Other** command to specify text font size from 4 to 650 points in 0.1 point increments.

Leading

This sets the space, measured in points, between consecutive lines of type. Leading can be selected for a range of text, as a default for a single publication, or as a default for all future publications.

Use the **Other** command to **set leading values** ranging from 0 to 1300 points. Leading is applied at the character level.

You can change the **default for autoleading** in the **Spacing Attributes** dialog box, available from the **Paragraph Specifications** dialog box.

You can specify leading as follows:

- Choose the **Auto** option from the **Leading** submenu to have PageMaker calculate the leading based on the size of the type. By default, the **autoleading** value is 120% of the type size.
- Choose any of the standard amounts of leading listed on the **Leading** submenu.
- Type a **custom leading value** (in one-tenth of a point increments) in the **Control palette** or **Character Specifications** dialog box, or choose **Type ➢ Leading ➢ Other** to specify a specific leading amount.

Type Style

It lets you set the style for a selected range of text or the next text you type. Text formatting is applied at the character level.

For example, to show text while indicating that it has been deleted from the paragraph, as in a legal contract, use **Strikethru** to draw a line through the text. Or, to create paper-coloured text on a contrasting black, tinted, or coloured background, use **Reverse**, which applies the default paper colour.

Expert Kerning

The **Type ➢ Expert Kerning** command automates kerning to give you tight control over letter spacing for headlines, poster type and other display type at large sizes. You can use **Expert Kerning** to determine fine kerning values even if you've mixed fonts and sizes in the same line. You can adjust kerning tightness by specifying a kern strength. Values for kern strength range from 0.00 to 1.00; the higher the value, the tighter the spacing. (The default value is 0.50.).

To Use Expert Kerning

1. Use the **text tool** to select the text to be kerned.
2. Choose **Type ➢ Expert Kerning.**
3. Type the **Kern Strength** (from 0.00 to 1.00) you want PageMaker to use when creating **kerning pairs**. Alternatively, use the slider bar to set the value.
4. Click on **OK**.

Expert Tracking

It allows you to apply size-dependent letter spacing over a range of text instead of adjusting the spacing between pairs of letters.

To Apply a Track

1. Using the **text tool**, select the text you want to track.
2. Choose **Type ➢ Expert Tracking**.
3. Choose one of the five **built-in tracks** from the menu, or choose **No**.

Edit Tracks

It displays tracking values as lines plotted on a grid, with each line representing one track. It also allows you to customize tracking for specific fonts at specific sizes.

Horizontal Scale

Use Horizontal Scale to adjust the width of characters. You can specify a scaling percentage between 5 and 250% (in increments of a tenth of 1%) or choose from commonly used character-width percentages on the **Horizontal Scale submenu**.

Character

It controls the font, size and other attributes of a selected range of text, part of the default, or part of a style.

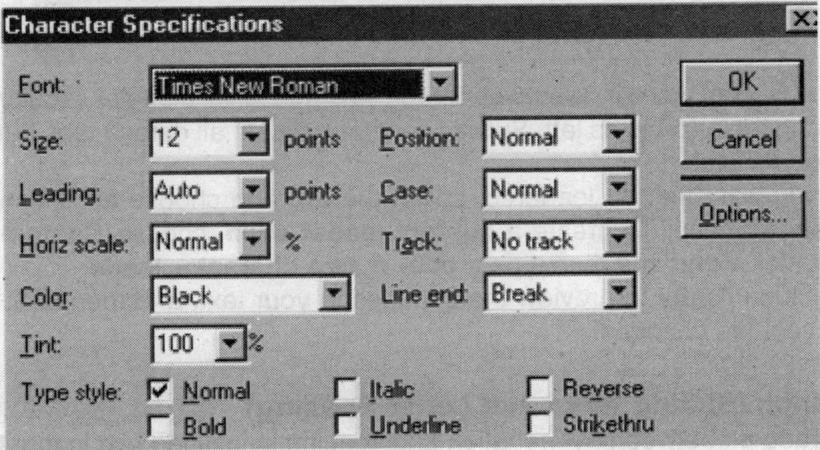

To Format Several Texts Attributes at Once

1. With the **text tool**, select the text you want to format.
2. Choose **Type ➢ Character**, or click on the **Control palette** to activate it.
3. Change settings in the **Character Specifications** dialog box or on the **Control palette.**

Paragraph

It sets the paragraph-level attributes for a single paragraph, for text placed into PageMaker, for part of a style, or for the default settings.

To Format Paragraphs

1. Using the **text tool**, click on an **insertion point** in a **single paragraph** or select **a range of paragraphs**.
2. Choose **Type ➢ Paragraph.**
   The **Paragraph Specifications** dialog box lets you apply formatting which is not available on the **Control palette**.
3. Select **formatting** options.

To Set Tabs with the Indents/Tabs Ruler

1. In **layout view**, click on an **insertion point** in a **paragraph**, or select a **group of paragraphs.**
2. Choose **Type ➢ Indents/Tabs.**

3. Click on a **tab-alignment** icon (left, right, center, or decimal) for the first tab you want to set.
4. Click on a **tab location** on the ruler to position the new tab, or move an existing tab by dragging its marker along the ruler.

The first tab you set deletes all default tabs (the small triangles regularly spaced along the ruler) to its left. Subsequent tabs delete all default tabs between the tabs you set.

5. If you want the tab leadered, select the **tab** and choose an option from the **Leader** menu. To create a **custom leader style**, choose **Custom** from the **Leader menu** and then type a **one-** or **two-character leader**.
6. Click on **Apply** to preview the changes to your text, and then click on OK to accept the changes.

Hyphenation (Setting Word and Letter Spacing)

The trade-off between hyphenation and spacing in justified text is that the closer you come to ideal spacing between letters and words, the more likely it is that words will need to be hyphenated.

Alignment

It allows you to change the alignment of text at the paragraph level. You can align text with the left or right edges of a text block.

- Alignment is a **paragraph attribute**, so all text in a paragraph shares the same alignment.
- To change **paragraph alignment**, you must select the text with the **text tool**.

Align Left text lines line up along with left edge.
Align Centre text lines are centred.
Align Right text lines line up along the right edge.
Justified Text is aligned with both the left and right edges of a text block.
Force Justify text is spaced. So it fills the space between the left and right edges of a text block.

To Apply a Style

1. Using the **text tool**, click on an **insertion point** in a paragraph, or select a **range of paragraphs**. Then use one of the following methods to apply a style:
   - In the **Styles palette**, click on the **name of the style** you want to apply.
2. In the **Style Options** dialog box, from the **Next Style** menu, choose the **name of the style** to follow this paragraph style (for example, Caption), and then click on **OK**.

Text Wrap

This lets you determine how text flows when it encounters a graphic object.

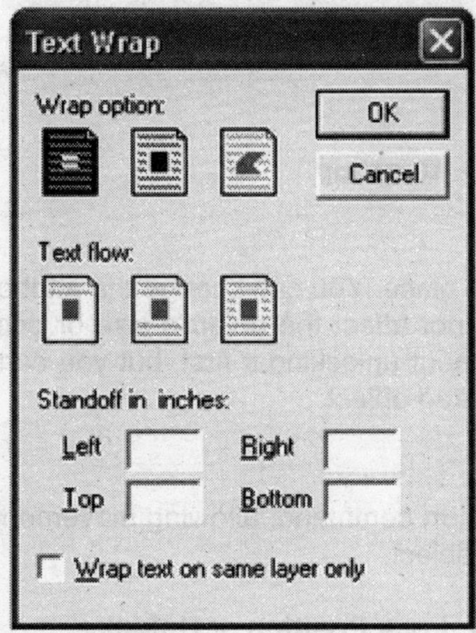

To Wrap Text Around a Graphic

1. Select a **graphic** or **image**.
2. Choose **Element ➢ Text Wrap**.
3. Click on a **Wrap option**.
4. Specify a **Text Flow** option.
5. Enter **standoff values** for the boundary.
6. Select **Wrap Text** on **Same Layer Only** if you want text on other layers to ignore the text wrap boundary.
7. Click on **OK**.

Group Objects

One or more of the objects you select can be a group, but if you select two or more groups, note that all selected objects (including those within groups) form a single, unnested group.

To Group Objects

1. Using the pointer tool, press **Shift** and select the objects to be grouped.
2. Choose **Element ➢ Group**.

To Select Text or an Individual Object Within a Group

1. Select the **pointer tool** (to select graphics or text objects), or the **text tool** (to edit text).
2. If you are selecting an object within the group, press **Ctrl** and select the object. To select text, click on an **insertion point** in the text.

The objects retain the changes you made while the objects were grouped.

Ungroup

It separates grouped object into constituent objects. The objects retain the changes you made while the objects were grouped.

To Ungroup Objects

1. Select the **group**.
2. Choose **Element ➢ Ungroup**.

Lock Position

It maintains objects in place. You can change the attributes of a locked object as long as the change does not affect the object's size or position. You cannot cut or delete a locked object without unlocking it first, but you can copy a locked object; it will be pasted as an unlocked object.

Unlock

It undoes **Lock Position** command, allowing movement of selected object.

To lock or unlock an object:

1. Select the **object**.
2. Choose **Element ➢ Lock Position** or **Unlock**.

Mask

This lets you cover part of an object so that only a portion of it appears through a shape drawn with the rectangle, ellipse, or polygon tool. You mask objects by positioning the mask or masking object on the objects you want to mask, selecting both objects and choosing the **Element ➢ Mask** command.

Unmask

This lets you undo a mask by selecting the masking object or the masked object, and choosing the **Element ➢ Unmask** command.

Rounded Corners

This lets you select the shape of corners when a PageMaker-drawn box is selected. With no object selected, the chosen setting becomes the default.

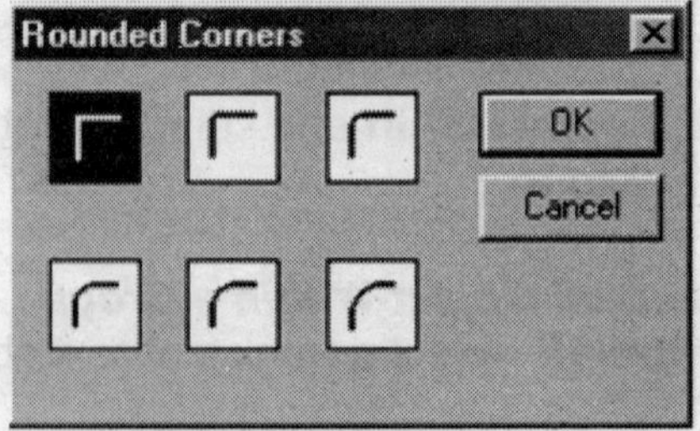

Bullets and Numbering

This helps you to adding bullets and numbers in front of paragraphs.

Change Case

PageMaker provides three type-case attributes.

Normal leaves uppercase and lowercase letters as typed.

All Caps displays letters as full-sized capitals.

Small Caps displays lowercase letters as small capitals.

Drop Cap

This helps you to format a letter, word or selected text as a large initial.

Find

It locates specified text, characters, or formatting (Font, Size, and so on) in the selected text, in an entire story, in all stories in the active publication, or in all stories in all open publications.

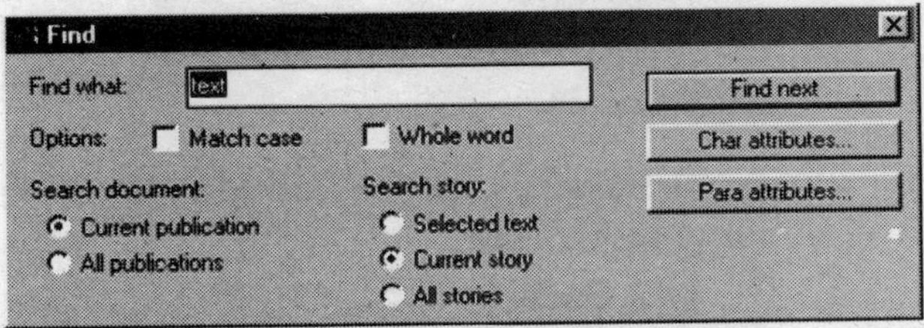

Find Next

This command finds the next instance. This option is available only in **Story view** after you've used the **Find** command.

Change

It locates and replaces specified text, characters, or formatting (Font, Size, and so on) in the selected text.

Spelling

It checks and helps correct spelling and basic grammatical error in the selected text, in an entire story. This option is available only in **Story view**.

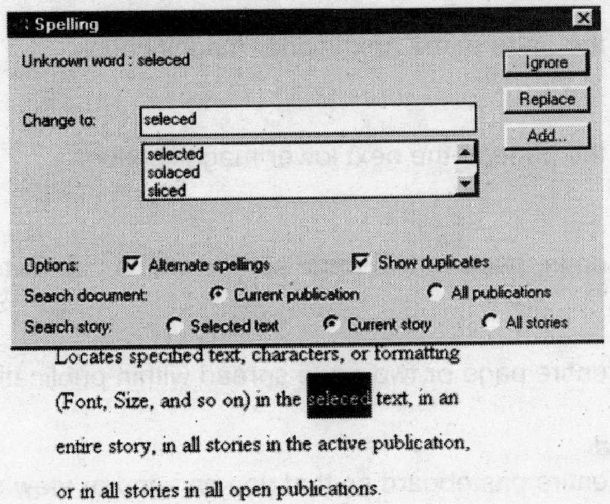

View Menu

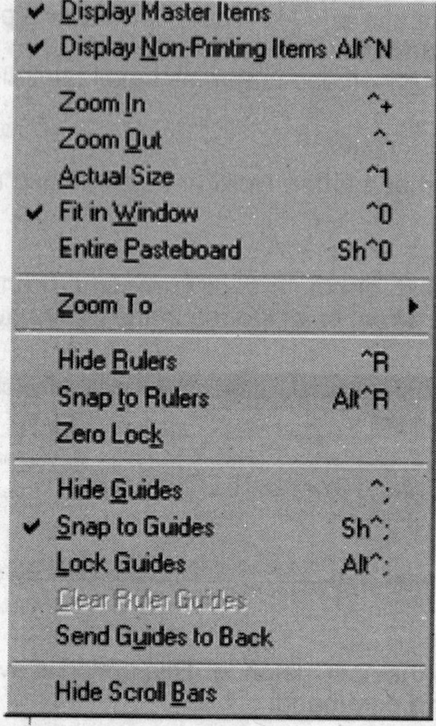

Display Master Items

This makes master page objects all visible or all invisible on a page.

Display Non-Printing Items

This shows or hides the objects defined as non-printing.

Zoom In

This displays the page at the next higher magnification.

Zoom Out

This displays the page at the next lower magnification.

Actual Size

This displays entire page or two-page spread within publication window.

Fit In Window

This displays entire page or two-page spread within publication window.

Entire Pasteboard

This displays entire pasteboard so that you can find or view objects.

Zoom To

This displays options for zooming directly to one of six magnifications between 25% and 400%.

Show/Hide Rulers

This turns the rulers on and off.

Snap to Rulers

This lets you precisely position text or graphics by pulling them to the increments shown on the ruler. Snap to Rulers does not work unless the rulers are turned on.

Zero Lock

This removes the crosshairs from the upper-left corner of the screen so that you cannot change the zero point of the rulers.

Show/Hide Guides

This hides or displays the column ruler and margin guides.

Snap to Guides

This lets you precisely position text or graphics by pulling them to the nonprinting column and ruler guides.

Lock Guides

This prevents you from accidentally moving the non-printing guides when you reposition adjacent text or graphics. Lock Guides is available only when the guides are turned on.

- To adjust **column widths**, you can move the **column guides** by dragging them. The two lines forming the **gutter** between columns move together. Text and graphics already on the page are not changed in any way when you drag column guides. (Moving these column guides does not affect the margin guides.)
- Once you have set up your columns, you can lock them in place to prevent accidental moving.

To Lock or Unlock Column and Ruler Guides

Choose **View ➢ Lock Guides**.

Clear Ruler Guides

This removes all ruler guides on the current page or two-page spread.

Send Guides to Back/Bring Guides to Front

This sets guides to display in back of page elements throughout the current publication. Sending Guides to the back makes selection of objects easier. Bringing guides to the front makes selection and moving of guides easier.

Show/Hide Scroll Bars

This displays or hides the scroll bars.

Window Menu

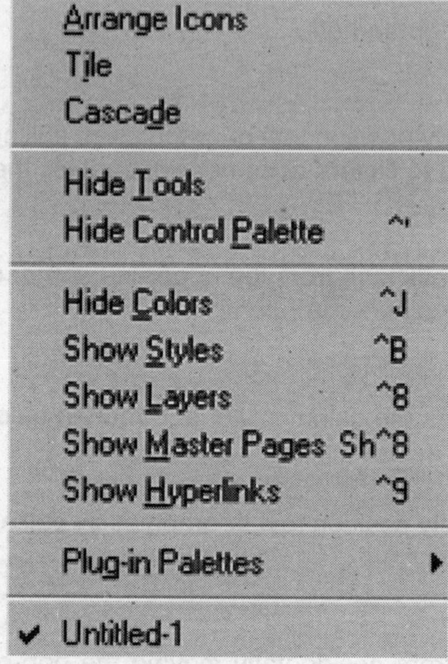

Tile

This places open publication or story windows side-by-side. To tile all, open **story windows** in all **open publications** at once.

Cascade

This rearranges open publication or story windows by overlapping them so that title bars are visible. To cascade all, open **story windows** in all **open publications** at once.

Show/Hide Tools

This displays or hides the **floating palette** from which you select PageMaker's drawing and editing tools.

Show/Hide Control Palette

This displays or hides the palette for manipulating objects or (when text is selected) applying **text and paragraph styles** and **attributes**.

Show/Hide Colours

This displays or hides the palette which lists the defined colours.

Show/Hide Styles

This displays or hides the **Styles palette**.

Show/Hide Master Pages

This displays or hides the **Master Pages palette**.

Show/Hide Hyperlinks

This displays or hide the **Hyperlinks palette**.

Plug-in Palettes

This shows or hides palettes made available by PageMaker **plug-in modules**.

WORKING WITH PALETTES

PageMaker includes several palettes, like the Control palette, the Colors palette, the Hyper-links palette, the Layers palette, the Master Pages palette and the Styles palette.

1. The Control Palette

The control Palette displays the properties for the selected paragraph, character or object. It is a sort of shortcut to the object, text and paragraph properties. You can choose Window and select Show Control Palette to display the Control palette.

The Control Palette in Object Mode

The Control Palette, when it has an object selected, displays the object properties, such as the reference point, position, size, scaling, cropping, printer resolution, rotating, skewing, and horizontal and vertical reflection.

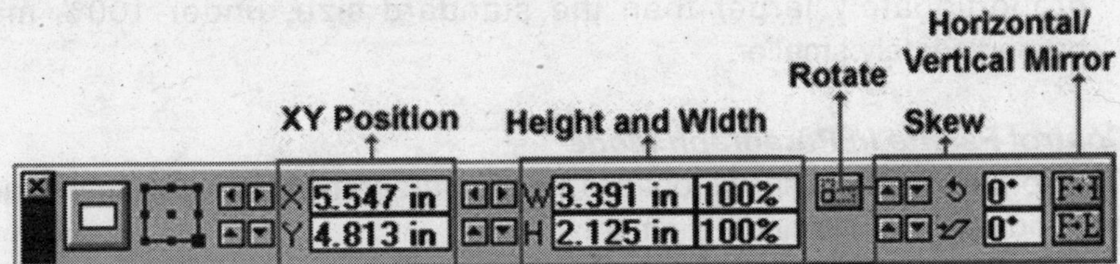

- Horizontal/vertical mirror mirrors the currently selected object along the x or y-axis.
- Height/width sets the height and width of the currently selected object, either numerically in inches or in percentages of the current size.
- Rotate is used to rotate the selected object around an axis. The center of rotation is set as the object's center and exact measurements can be used.

- Skew is used to skew the currently selected object in degrees.
- XY position sets the horizontal and vertical position of the upper-left corner of the currently selected object.

The Control Palette in Character Mode

The Character Palette is displayed when the text tool is selected. It has options for changing text styles, size, leading, tracking, width and kerning. There is a toggle button to shift between paragraph view and character view.

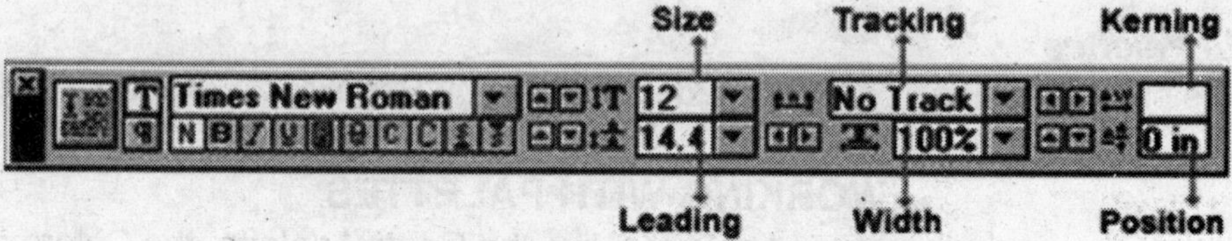

- Kerning: Text Kerning adjusts the space between characters in text. It is selective, so you can adjust just one or two characters, or whole sections of text. Negative numbers move characters closer together, whereas Positive numbers space them out.
- Leading: Text Leading adjusts the spacing between lines of text. This is applicable on line-by-line basis. Positive and Negative numbers have the same effect as they have on Kerning, except that the spacing is between the lines of text.
- Tracking: Text Tracking adjusts how closely characters follow each other. Very tight tracking brings text closer together, very loose spreads it out a bit.
- Size: Text Size adjusts point size of text.
- Position: Text Position adjusts the placement of the text on a given line. Positive Numbers move the text into a super text position (above the line), and Negative numbers move it into a subtext position (below the line).
- Width: Text Width adjusts the character width and does not affect height. The larger the percentage, the wider the word. Percentages over 100% make it proportionately larger than the standard size, under 100% make it proportionately smaller.

The Control Palette in Paragraph Mode

The Control Palette displays options for the paragraph style, alignment, indents, spacing, grid spacing and grid alignment

2. The Color palette

You use the Color palette in PageMaker to assign spot, process and tints for all objects and text within the document.

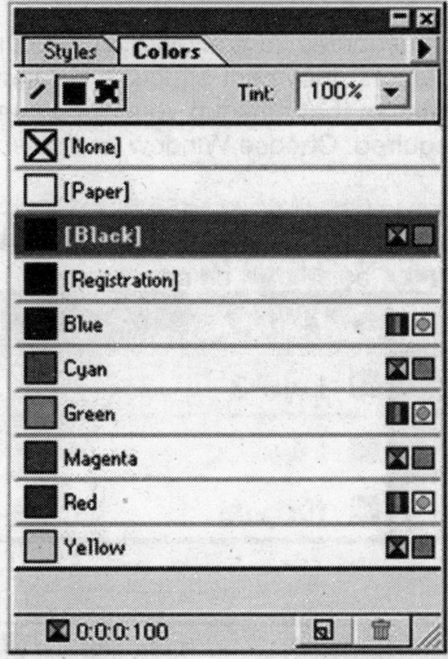

3. The Style Palette

The Style palette contains styles which are applied to the corresponding items in the text (e.g. chapter heading, caption) in order to give them their distinctive appearance in the publication.

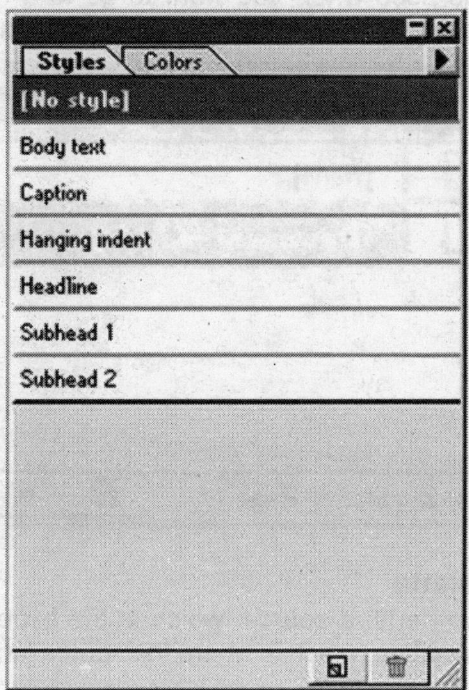

4. The Layer Palette

Layers offer you unprecedented control over your documents. The Layer Palette is used where a multiple layers document structure is required. Layers allow you to separate the different elements that makeup your document. You can hide, display, add or delete layers as required. Choose Window and select Show Layers to display the Layers Palette.

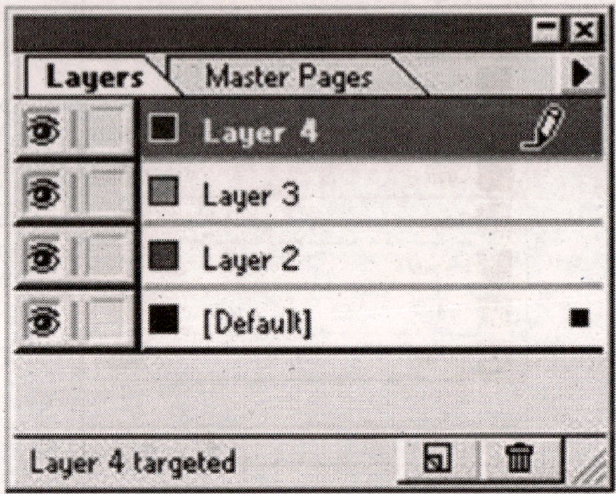

5. The Master Pages Palette

The Master Pages palette is used to create and apply masters. It displays a list of available master pages for a particular document. The master page icon at the bottom of the window is used when you want to go to a master page for editing. Choose Window and select Show Master pages to display the master Pages palette.

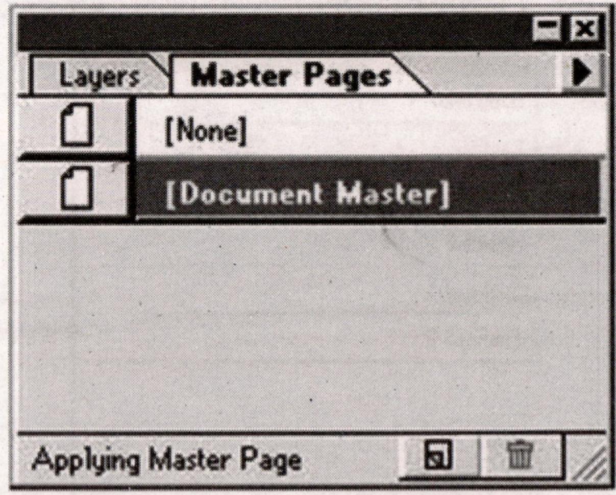

6. The Hyperlinks Palette

A hyperlink has two parts: a source, which is the hyper linked text, or graphic that you click, and a destination, which is where the source jumps. Inside a PageMaker publication, destinations are called anchors. You can also give a valid web hyperlink. Choose Window and select Show Hyperlinks to display the Hyperlinks palette.

Working with Text in Adobe PageMaker

Working with text is very similar to working with a word processor program such as Microsoft Word. Two key differences, however, are that in PageMaker 7.0, you will use the Text tool and enter all your text into a text box.

PageMaker's Text Boxes

A text box is a 'container' for your text. It is a confined area on your document that is designed to hold text. The text you type into your document will automatically be enclosed in a text box. You can determine the size by creating the text box before you begin typing. You can also resize and reposition your text boxes using the **Pointer** tool.

Creating a New Text Box

1. Click on the **Text** tool in the toolbox.
2. Move your cursor back to your document. Your cursor will turn into an I-Beam once you move it over your document.
3. Click anywhere on your document within the margin guides, and then drag the mouse to the right to create a rectangular box.
4. Release your mouse when you have a text box of the size you want. Your cursor will automatically position itself inside the box.
5. Begin typing in your text. You may also paste text into the text box.
6. Once you are done typing in your text, simply click on the **Pointer** tool in the toolbox to de-select the text box.

Using the Text Tool to Edit your Text

Once you have created a text box and entered your text, you can then edit it. For this purpose, you will primarily use the **Text** tool and the **Type** menu.

1. Click on the **Text** tool from the toolbox.
2. Position the cursor at the beginning of the text you want to format.
3. Click and drag the I-beam across the text to select it.
4. Edit the selected text as follows:

To Delete Text

- Tap the **Delete** key or simply start typing, which will replace the selected text.
- Click on the **Edit** menu, and then select **Clear**.

To Copy or Move the Text

- Click on the **Edit** menu.
- Select the **Cut**, **Copy** or **Paste** command.

To Change the Type Style

- Click on the **Type** menu.
- Select your desired option.

Linking Graphics in PageMaker

Graphics that are placed in PageMaker are linked files. The linked files can be stored in the publication, or another drive, or they can be unlinked from the publication. Linking allows you to save more versions on your hard drive while using less space.

Link Manager

The Link Manager command lets you view or modify links for single and multiple objects through out a publication. Follow these steps to link an object in a PageMaker document:

1. Insert the picture.
2. Click on file menu.
3. Click on link manager command.
4. Then its dialog box will appear.
5. Click on 'info' button.
6. Choose anyone picture.
7. Click on open button.
8. Click on ok button.

When a graphic is changed, the link should be updated to the new name, or the old file should be deleted and the new file contains the same name of the previous file.

To check the status of the linked files:

1. Click on **File**.
2. Click on **Links Manager**.
3. Look at each line showing the status of linked files.
4. Click on a line.

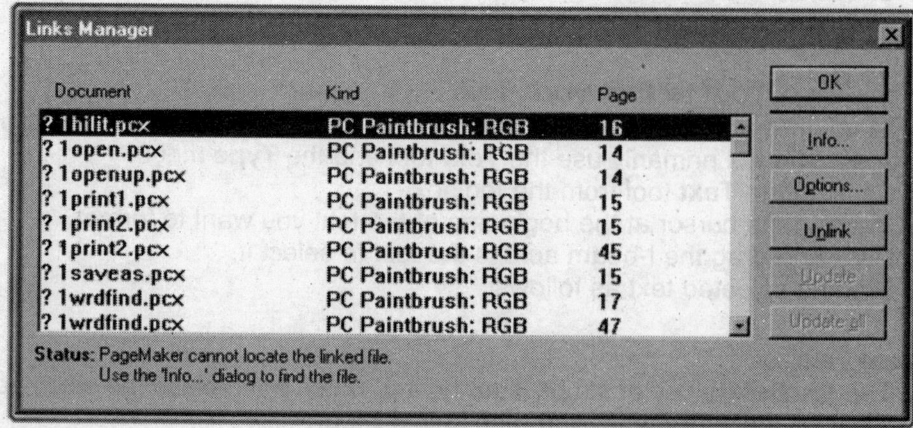

5. Click on **Info** to see where the link should be.

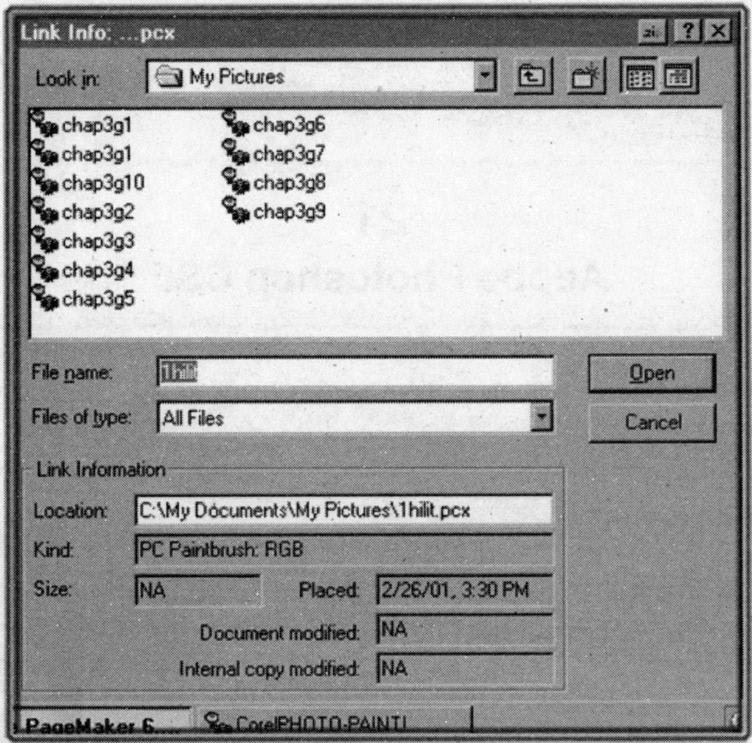

6. Click on **Options** to **Store copy in Publication** or to **Update automatically**.

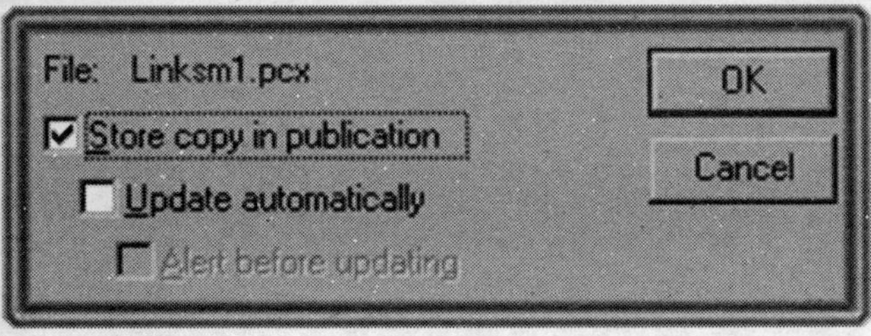

□

21
Adobe Photoshop CS5

When you first open Photoshop, you have a blank working space with various menus.

The Photoshop work area is designed to help you maximize your workspace and have easy access tools, options and palettes. The default work area with a new blank document is sometimes referred to as the active image area. In the default work area, the toolbox is located on the left, the menu bar and options bar at the top, and the palettes on the right.

Basic Operations

You can control the options bar, palettes and toolbox as follows:

- To move and float the options bar, point to the vertical dotted line along the left edge, which is called the gripper bar. Drag and drop the options bar into the work area. You can also place it along the bottom of the work area. You may find this location works better if you tend to focus your attention on the middle and lower half of the screen as you work.
- To return the options bar to its default position, simply drag and drop it back into place just below the menu bar.
- To reset all of the settings in the options bar back to the original defaults, right-click on the dashed-square icon on the options bar, and then select either **Reset Tool** or **Reset All Tools**. You can collapse the options bar, toolbox, or any of the palettes by double-clicking the top or left edge of the bar. To expand them, simply double-click the bar.
- Press **Tab** to hide the options bar, toolbox and palettes. Press **Tab** again to make them visible.
- You can also access the options bar, toolbox and palettes from the **Window** menu, as follows: Press **Shift+Tab** to hide the palettes in the work area. Press **Shift+Tab** again to make the palettes visible.
- To move the palette groups in the work area, press and drag the top bar of the group. To move back to the original location, select **Window → Workspace → Reset Palette Locations**.
- To separate a palette from its group, select the name of the palette or click anywhere on the tab and drag it outside of the group. To place it back, drag the tab and drop it in the group. You can use the **Reset Palette Locations** command to put all of the palettes back in the group at once and in the default order.
- You can store individual palettes (not as a group) in the palette well. Simply point to the name of the palette or anywhere on the tab, and then drag and drop it into the palette well. You can also select the **Menu** option **Dock to Palette Well** from the palette shortcut menu.

Exploring the Toolbox

The toolbox in Photoshop CS2 contains a total of 58 basic tools, with 22 visible in the toolbox by default. There are two new tools in Photoshop CS2: Spot Healing Brush tool and Red Eye tool. They are both in the **Healing Brush** tool group, and the new **Spot Healing Brush** is the default tool.

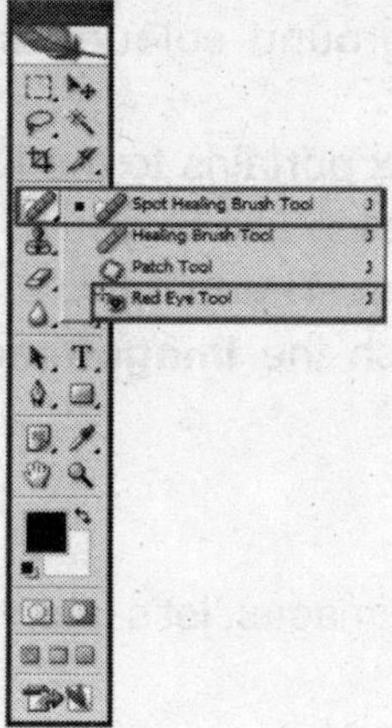

When you move your mouse pointer over each of the tools in the toolbox, a **ToolTip** appears and displays the name of the tool and its keyboard shortcut. You can view the hidden tools of a tool group by clicking on the small triangle at the lower-right corner of the tool. You can also cycle through the tools in a group without expanding them by pressing **Shift** and the shortcut for the tool. For example, to cycle through the tools in the **Lasso** group, press **Shift+L**. Press **Shift+L** again to reveal the next tool in the group.

Now focus your attention on the lower portion of the toolbox. Notice the large black and white squares. They are the colour selection boxes. The upper colour selection box represents the current foreground colour; the lower one represents the current background colour.

You should learn two shortcuts for these boxes, as follows:

- Press **D** or click on the small black and white squares under the **colour selection** boxes to change the colour selection boxes back to the defaults of black and white.
- Press **X** or click on the curved arrow above the **colour selection** boxes to switch the foreground and background colours.

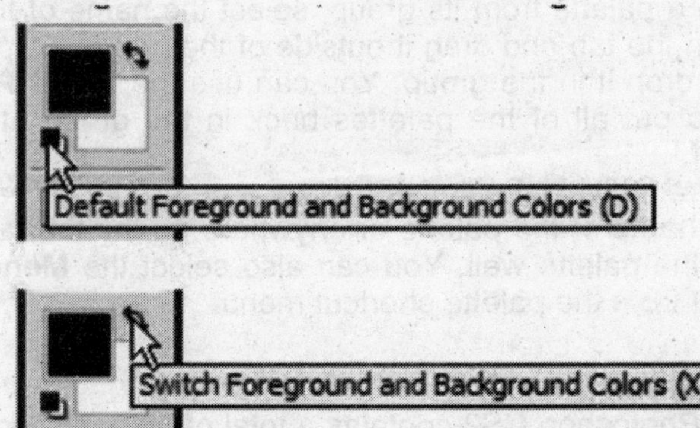

You'll also notice that the same colour selection boxes appear in the Colour palette. The foreground colour is also used with the paint and stroke functions. The background colour is associated with gradient fills and with the **Eraser** tool. In addition, both the foreground and background colours are used by some of the special effect filters.

The next group in the toolbox pertains to the **Quick Mask** mode.

The next group of three buttons allows you to switch to different screen modes while you're working in Photoshop. The last two icons, positioned on top of a larger button, are a quick way to launch the **ImageReady** application, which you use to create Web graphics.

Create a New Image File

Before you start working with images, let's learn more about some basic operations using a new blank file.

1. Select **File → New** (or press **Ctrl+N**). The **New** dialogue box appears.

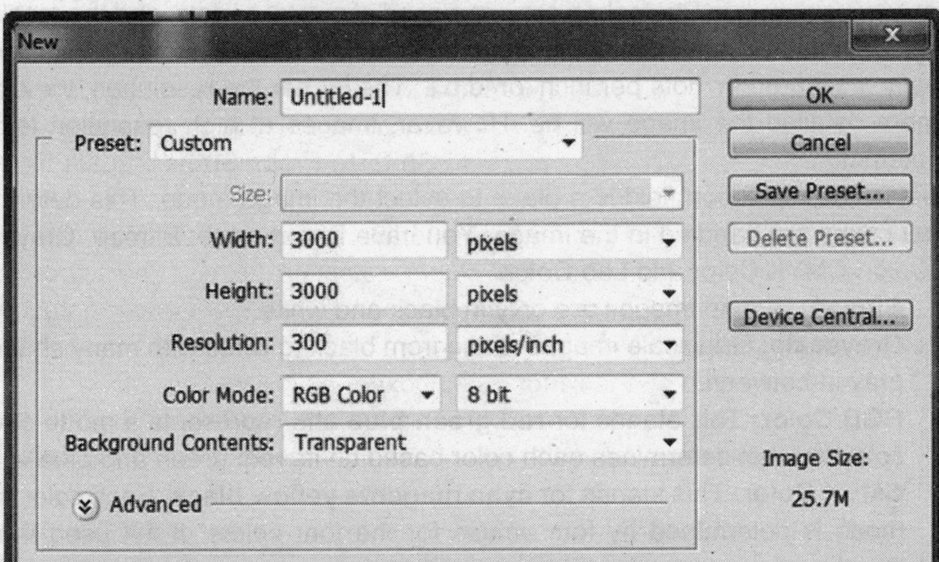

2. Select the **Presets** drop-down list arrow to view the **Presets** menu. You'll notice several different preset sizes for print, Web and video. You can even create your own custom size and save it as a preset. If necessary, select **Photoshop Default Size** from the **Presets shortcut** menu.
3. Read the **ToolTips** for the different settings and options in the dialogue box.
4. Notice that the mouse changes to a pointing finger with a double-arrow over the words Width, Height and Resolution. This is called a scrubby slider. As you press the mouse and move to the right or left, the numbers or values in the box increase or decrease. Scrubby sliders are also available to change values in the options bar and palettes.

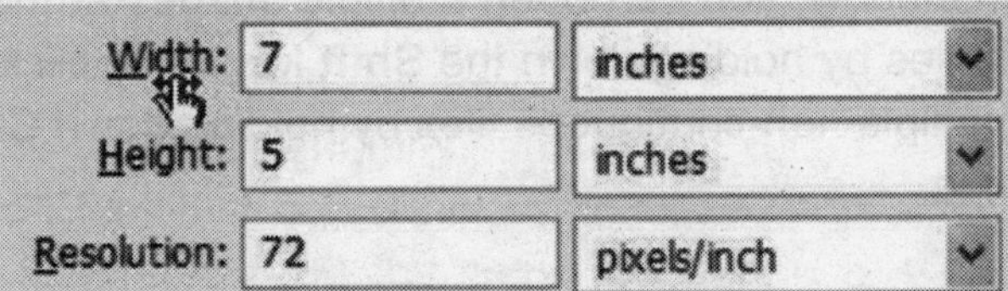

5. Change the units for both the width and height to pixels. Notice that when you change one unit, both units change.

To change only one unit, press **Shift** while making the change. With the addition of **Alt** or **Shift**, you have a little more control over the scrubby sliders. Move your mouse pointer over the words until the pointer changes to the pointing finger. Press **Alt** and then move the mouse slowly to increase the numbers one at a time. Press **Shift** and then move the mouse slowly to increase the units by 10. This function works in several of the dialogue boxes, tool options and palettes.

The next section deals with the size of the image. You can manually enter values for the width and height, choosing from a selection of different units, including pixels, millimeters and inches.

Below the width and height fields is a place to enter the desired resolution. The images you work with in Photoshop are composed of pixels, or dots, and the resolution determines how many of these dots will be assigned per inch of the image. Resolution is usually measured in 'dots per inch' or 'd.p.i.' The higher the resolution, the clearer and more detailed the image will be. However, images at high resolution take up more memory.

Below the resolution field is a place to select the image mode. This determines the way colors are handled in the image. You have five choices: Bitmap, Grayscale, RGB Color, CMYK Color and Lab Color.

- **Bitmap:** Bitmap images are only in black and white.
- **Grayscale:** Grayscale images range from black to white with many shades of gray in between.
- **RGB Color:** This stands for **red green blue** and represents a mode of color selection that determines each color based on its red, green and blue values.
- **CMYK Color:** This stands for **cyan magenta yellow black**. Each color in this mode is determined by four values for the four colors of ink used in color printers.
- **Lab Color:** This is a mode in which the colors are based on the three factors of luminosity, green-red and blue-yellow.

Once you choose the size, resolution and mode that you desire for your image, you may select what color (if any) you want for the background.

If, rather than creating a new image, you wish to open a stored image, click on **Open**, instead of **New** in the **File** menu. The shortcut for this command is **Ctrl + O**. When you do so, an explorer window will open that allows you to browse through the contents of your computer for files. Simply click on the desired image and press the **Enter** key or click on **Open**.

In the explorer window, you can open multiple images at the same time. Open multiple contiguous files by holding down the **Shift** key while clicking on the first and last image. Open multiple non-contiguous files by holding down **Ctrl** while clicking on each individual image.

Select an Entire Image

Select All

This command selects the entire image inside the document window. You may have used **Select All** in other programs. Let's see how it works in the pixel-based environment of Photoshop.

You can practice this method even on a blank document:

1. Select **Select → Select All** (**Ctrl+A**). An animated (moving) dashed line appears inside the area of the document window. This line is referred to as a marquee, and the motion is referred to as marching ants.

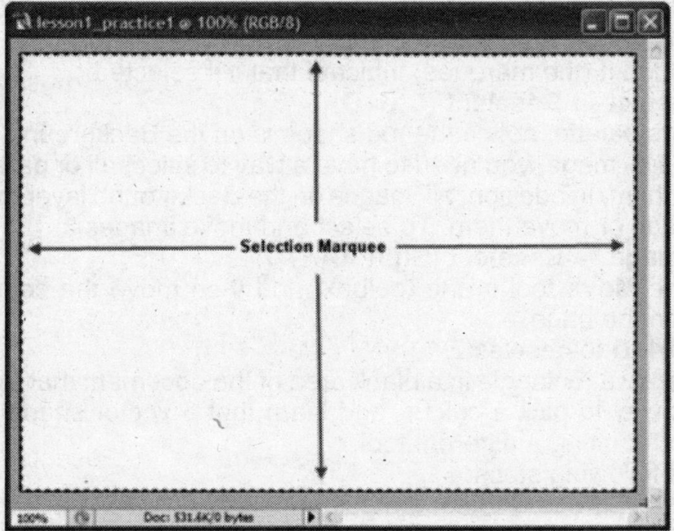

2. To deselect the image area, select **Select → Deselect** (**Ctrl+D**). You can also temporarily hide the line from view by pressing **Ctrl+H**. Change it back immediately by pressing **H** to avoid problems because the active selection is hidden.

Draw Pixel and Vector Shapes

Here, you'll use the Rectangular Marquee selection tool to both draw and select pixels. You'll also draw a vector shape rectangle with the Rectangle tool, which can draw both vector shapes and pixel shapes.

1. Select the **Rectangular Marquee** tool in the toolbox. Draw a small rectangle in the upper-left area of the new blank document by dragging the mouse down and to the right. You can also press **Shift** to constrain the rectangle to a square.
2. Select **Edit → Fill** (**Shift+F5**). The **Fill** dialogue box appears.
3. Select **Colour** from the **Use drop-down** menu. The **Adobe Colour Picker** appears.
4. Select a colour either by moving the small circle in the large colour field, moving the colour sliders along the vertical colour bar, or typing the colour values.

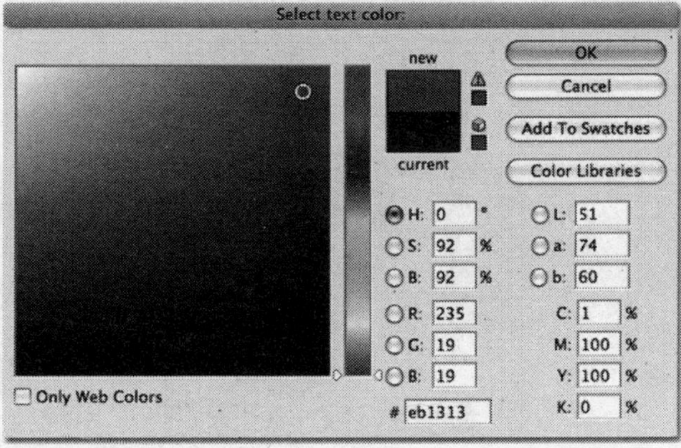

1. Click on **OK** to close the **Colour Picker**, and then click on **OK** again to close the **Fill** dialogue box. The rectangle is now filled with a red colour and the lines around it (the marquee) indicate that it's selected.
2. Select **Select → Deselect** (**Ctrl+D**).

In the **Layers** palette, notice the red shape is on the Background layer. Because this image is a pixel image, you need to have a way to select all or part of the pixels to change or move them. In addition, all images on the Background layer must be selected before you can edit or move them. To select and move images:

1. Select **Image → Reselect** (**Shift+Ctrl+D**)
2. Select the **Move** tool in the toolbox, and then move the coloured rectangle around on the page.
3. Press **Ctrl+D** to deselect.

Now you'll draw a rectangle in a blank area of the document that's a vector shape, learn a different way to pick a colour, and learn that a vector shape has a different type of selection requiring a different tool.

Perform the following steps:

1. If necessary, press **D** to set the colour selection boxes back to the defaults.
2. In the **Colour** palette, pick a colour from the **Colour Spectrum** bar at the bottom, move the slider bars for the colours, or type in the colour values.

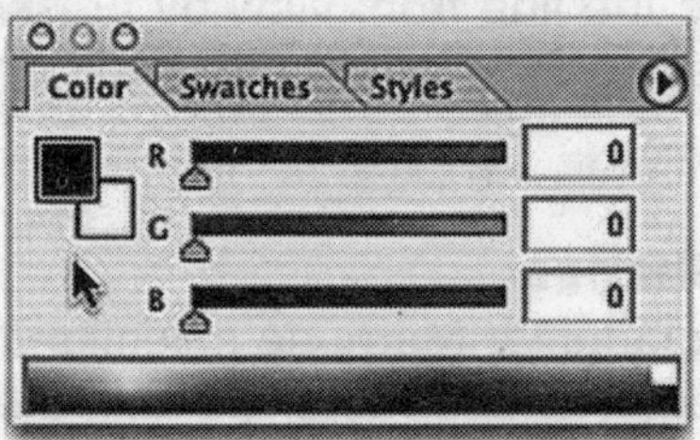

1. Select the **Rectangle** tool in the toolbox. It's located just below the **Text** tool.
2. On the options bar, make sure the **Shape layers** button is selected, or right-click and select **Reset** tool.
3. Drag and draw a rectangle below the first one or anywhere in a blank area.
4. Select the **Path Selection** tool in the toolbox, located to the left of the **Text** tool, and then click on the rectangle. It's now selected and you can move it around on the page.

This second rectangle is a vector shape object, which is different than the first pixel image. There's an indicator that this shape is different. Look at the Layers palette – there's a new **Shape** layer with different types of thumbnails.

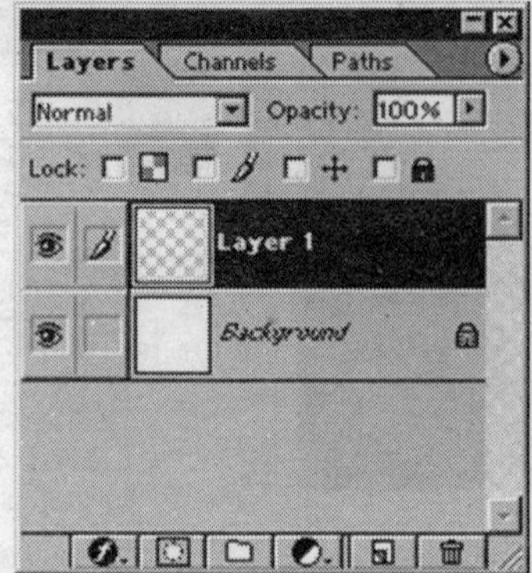

The two rectangles (pixel and vector) require different methods to select each one to make changes to them. Use the **Path Selection** tool to select the vector shape and one of the **marquee selection** tools to select the pixel shape.

Before you save the file, let's explore the different full-screen viewing modes, as follows:

1. Select the **Zoom** tool, and then click on the **Fit On Screen** button on the options bar, or press **Ctrl+0** (zero).
2. Select the middle of the three **Screen Mode** tools in the toolbox, or press **F**. This shows your image on the screen with the menu bar at the top and a 50% grey background.
3. Press **Tab** to hide the toolbox and palettes and, if necessary, go to the **Window** menu and deselect **Options** to hide the options bar.
4. Move the image around by pressing the spacebar to temporarily activate the **Hand** tool.
5. Press **F** again to display your image onscreen with no menu bar and a black background. You can cycle through several open images by pressing **Ctrl+Tab**.
6. To return to the standard mode, press **F**, or press **Tab** to display the toolbox and then click on the **Standard Screen Mode** tool.

You can save your file in a new folder. Select **File → Save**, type the File name in the **File name** text box, and then select **Photoshop (*.PSD;*.PDD)** in the **Format** text box. This allows you to save the file as a Photoshop file rather than a JPEG (Joint Photographic Experts Group).

CAPTURE, CROP AND TRANSFORM

Capture a Screen Image

To capture a screen image, do the following:

1. If Photoshop is open, minimize the programme and open **My Computer** to locate a file folder with images.
2. If necessary, change to the **Thumbnails view**.
3. Press **Alt+Print Screen**. This takes a picture or screen capture of the active window, and the image is saved as data to the **Clipboard**. You'll not see the image until you paste it into Photoshop.
4. Close the window and maximize Photoshop.
5. Select **File → New**. Notice the **Preset** field in the **New** dialogue box that displays Clipboard. Photoshop automatically opens a new file with the dimensions and resolution based on the Clipboard data.
6. Click on **OK**, and then select **Edit → Paste** (**Ctrl+V**) to paste the image into the new blank window.

Crop Tool and Navigator Palette

You can use the Navigator palette to help zoom in on the area for your crop, as follows:

1. In the **Navigator** palette, experiment with the zoom slider. When you zoom greater than 100% and move the mouse pointer over the small thumbnail of

your image, you can move the coloured box (rectangle) to isolate an area of your image. You can also use the **Zoom** tool to accomplish the same task.
2. Select the **Crop** tool in the toolbox.
3. In the document window, drag a rectangle around the part of the image you want to keep. Notice the marquee around the area. You can adjust the area by moving the whole selection area or dragging the handles.
4. Release the mouse. The image area that falls outside of the crop marks is darker in colour, showing you the parts of the image that will be deleted.

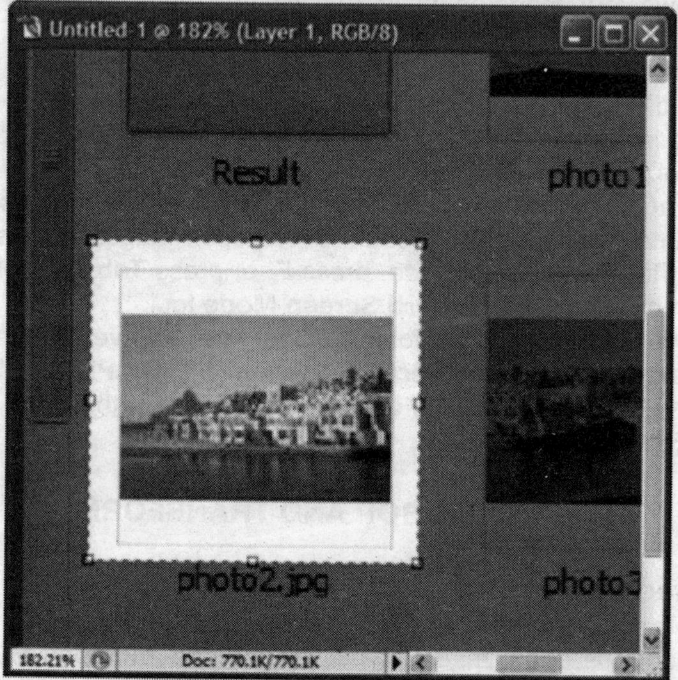

1. To finish the cropping task, either right-click and select **Crop**, double-click inside the marquee, click on the tick mark near the right side of the options bar, or press **Enter**.
2. To cancel the crop before you complete the task, either right-click and select **Cancel**, click on the **Cancel** button on the options bar, or press **Esc**.

Apply a Transformation

A transformation is a change in the size, orientation, perspective, or other alteration of an image. The transformations in Photoshop are scale, rotate, skew, distort, perspective and flip. CS2 offers a new transformation called **warp**. Another new feature in CS2 is called **vanishing point**. Although you think of vanishing point and perspective together, it's not in the Transformation group. The vanishing point feature is located in the **Filters** menu, and when selected, launches in a separate window. Remember that perspective is a transformation.

You can apply transformations to an entire image or parts of an image. The image can be a pixel or vector image. If you're going to apply a transformation to the entire image or part of the pixels and the images are on the Background layer, you need to make a selection.

You can apply and execute transformations one at a time or in continuous succession. The command for continuous transformations is called **Free Transform**. If you're going to apply more than one transformation to the same image, it's best to use the **Free Transform** tool because the pixels' dimensions are changed only once. The process of changing the dimensions of pixels is called **resampling**.

To transform the cropped image, do the following:

1. Select **Edit → Transform → Flip Horizontal**. To commit to this transformation, press **Enter**. To cancel, select **Edit → Undo** (**Ctrl+Z**).
2. Select **Edit → Transform → Rotate**. Notice the handles that appear, and then look at the settings on the options bar. You can rotate the image visually or type in an angle of rotation in the options bar. To rotate visually, move the mouse cursor outside of the boundary area until it changes to a curved double arrow. Drag the image to the right or left to rotate it. Notice that you cannot make additional transformations without committing first.
3. To cancel the rotation, click **Cancel** on the options bar.
4. Select **Edit → Free Transform** (**Ctrl+T**). Notice that handles, called Transform controls, appear on the image and transform options appear on the options bar.
5. Move the mouse cursor outside the controls until it changes to the rotate symbol and then rotate the image.
6. To reduce the size of the image, right-click inside the box and select **Scale**, or press **Shift** and drag the top or bottom corner inward. Press **Enter** or click on the tick mark on the options bar to apply both the rotate and the scale.
7. To skew the image, right-click and select **Skew** from the transform menu or press **Shift+Ctrl**. Grab a top or bottom centre handle and drag right or left.

Note that the display may appear somewhat pixilated. It looks betters after you apply the transformation. If you have your image magnified with the zoom, you'll see the pixels.

Create a Reflection Image

You can turn a simple picture into something attractive by making a reflected image with the help of simple selection, cropping and transformation techniques along with other image-manipulation techniques.

- One way to create a reflected image is to create a duplicate image, use the **Rectangular Marquee** tool to select an area, crop and vertically flip the duplicate image, increase the canvas size of the original image, and then combine the flipped image with the original image.

To create the reflected sunset image, do the following:

1. Download a picture (Sunset.jpg). Select **File → Open**, locate and select the file, and then click on **Open**.
2. To prevent from accidentally saving over your original image, select **Image → Duplicate**. The **Duplicate Image** dialogue box appears.
3. Click on **OK**. A duplicate image, titled **Sunset copy**, appears.
4. Click on the document window of the original image, Sunset.jpg, to make it active, and then click on the **Close** button in the upper-right corner of the document window.
5. With the Sunset copy document window still open, select **File → Save As**, name it SunsetWorking, and then save it in the default Photoshop file format (**PSD**) instead of the original JPEG format. It's a good practice to save an image file in the PSD format while you're working on it. When you finish creating an image, save a copy in another format as needed.
6. Resize the document window by dragging the lower-right corner of the window until you see the grey image work area outside of your image.
7. Crop part of the lower portion of the image, just below where the large tree on the right meets the ground. Simply remove part of the dark foreground. To do so, select the **Rectangular Marquee** tool, draw a rectangle around the area you want to keep, and then select **Image → Crop**.
8. Be sure your entire image is selected, and then select **Edit → Copy (Ctrl+C)**.
9. Select **File → New**, and then click on **OK**. A new blank document opens, which should be in the same dimensions and resolution of the original image.

10. In the new blank document, select **Edit → Paste** (**Ctrl+V**).
11. Select **Edit → Transform → Flip Vertical** (**Ctrl+T**), and then press **Enter**, or click on the tick mark on the options bar, to apply the transformation.
   To accommodate the reflected image in the working copy, you need to add more canvas space to the bottom of the working copy, as follows:
12. Select the SunsetWorking document window, and then deselect the image (**Ctrl+D**), if necessary.
13. Select **Select → Image → Canvas Size** (**Alt+Ctrl+C**). The **Canvas Size** dialogue box appears.
14. The Anchor diagram in the middle includes a white square that represents the position of your image and direction arrows. Click on the arrow just above the white square, as shown below, indicating that you want to add space at the bottom.

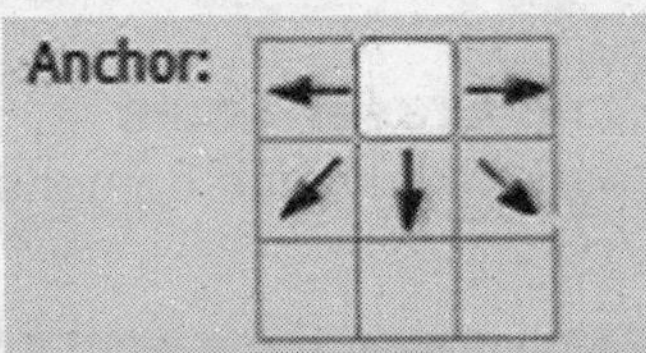

15. Change the Height setting for the amount of space to add. You can tick the **Relative** box just above the Anchor diagram and type the final height dimension. For example, typing 4 in the Height text box indicates the height of the image after you've added the extra space, as shown in the screenshot below.

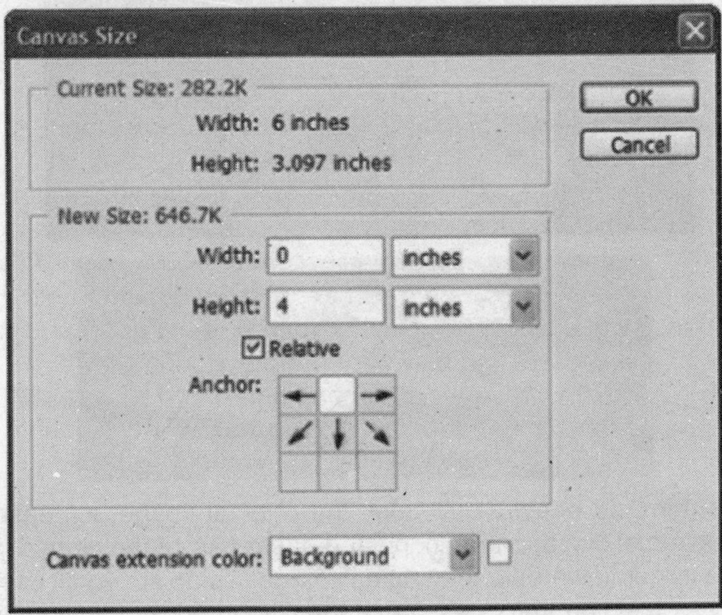

17. Switch back to document window with the flipped image.
18. Select the **Move** tool from the toolbox, and then drag the flipped image into the SunsetWorking document window.

19. Position the flipped image below the original image without any gap or overlap.
    You can use the arrow keys on the keyboard to move in small increments, which is called **nudging**.
20. In the **Layers** palette, notice that the flipped image is on a new layer. If you need to select the image, **Ctrl+**click on the thumbnail of the image in the **Layers** palette.
21. Press **Ctrl+T**, and then drag the middle bottom handle upward to shorten only the image height because, in a natural reflection, the reflected image is foreshortened. Press **Enter**, or click on the tick mark on the options bar.
22. Crop the picture, if necessary, to delete any extra white canvas.
23. Save the changes to SunsetWorking, and then close the copy of the flipped image without saving it. Your reflected picture is complete.

Use the Elliptical Marquee and Eraser Tools

Consider the following screenshots, which demonstrate the effects of mirroring an image.

To get this mirrored effect, you'll copy the original image, increase the canvas size, apply a horizontal flip, and then copy and paste part of the flipped image (in this case, one of the larger flowers) to the original image. To do so, you'll use an alternate method to copy a selection that doesn't use the Clipboard. In addition, you'll use the **Elliptical Marquee Selection** tool and anti-aliasing to soften the look of the pasted flower, along with a unique function of the **Eraser** tool to erase areas back to the original image.

To create a mirrored image, do the following:

1. Download a picture (Flower.jpg) and then open the file.
2. Press and hold the **Alt** key, and then select **Image → Duplicate**.
3. Close your original image.
4. Select **File → Save As**, and then save the duplicate image in the **PSD** format.
5. Follow the same steps as you did when creating a reflection image. Use the horizontal flip transformation and increase the width of the canvas size to accommodate the flipped image. Crop to delete any extra blank canvas.
6. Save your intermediate image with a new file name, and then close the file before you continue.

7. Open the image you saved in the previous step.
8. Select the **Elliptical Marquee** tool and, if necessary, reset the tool options. Make sure Anti-alias has a tick mark, indicating it's turned on.
9. Draw an elliptical selection around the large white flower on the right side of the image. Press **Alt** to draw from the centre and start at the green point of the leaf, as shown in the screenshot below.

   It takes a little practice and some additional techniques to draw a selection with the **Elliptical Marquee** tool. You can press the spacebar to move the selection area as you draw, and press **Alt** to draw from the centre outward. Release the mouse first and then the **Alt** key.

10. Make a copy of the flower using an alternative method that copies the image as you drag it to a new location. Select the **Move** tool, and then press and hold **Alt**. The cursor should change to one black arrow with an additional white arrow. Move the flower into the centre of the image, as shown in the screenshot below.

If you move the image without pressing **Alt**, the pixels left behind will fill with the background colour if the selection is on the Background layer. If the selection is on another layer, the area that's left will be transparent.

Here, the image is on a separate layer and placed on the right side of the canvas that has the white background. If you move the selection without copying the image, you'll see the white background. To see the difference, move your flipped image so that it overlaps the original image, and then make a selection. When you move this selection without copying, you'll see the image underneath. Notice that the surrounding area of the copied flower covers the other flowers. Because you copied the flower on the right, which resides on a new layer, you can use the **Eraser** tool and one of its options to erase back to the image that's stored in the History palette. This works similar to the **History Brush** tool.

To use the Eraser tool, do the following:

1. Look at the top of the **History** palette at the small thumbnail image just to the right of the **Brush** icon. This thumbnail should display your intermediate mirror image stage, as shown in the screenshot below.

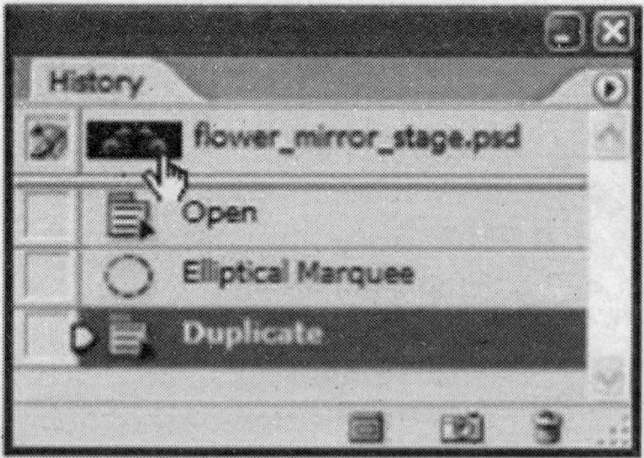

If your thumbnail doesn't display the intermediate mirror stage image, undo your copied flower, save the current file, close the file, and reopen it. If you're already familiar with the **History** palette, go back to the state without the copied flower, make a new snapshot, and change the source of the History Brush.

1. Make sure your copied flower is still selected, and then select the **Eraser** tool. Reset the tool options, if necessary.
2. On the options bar, click on **Erase to History**. This erases the part of the copied image that's covering the flowers underneath it to reveal the original image.

3. Drag the **Eraser** tool across the area you want to delete. If necessary, you can change the size of the **Eraser** tool in the **Brush pop-up** menu on the options bar using the **Master diameter slider**, or you can use a quick keyboard method. Each time you press the left bracket ([), you decrease the brush size; pressing the right bracket (]) increases the brush size. In the **Brush pop-up** menu, you can also adjust the hardness.

You can experiment with the Eraser tool to see how it works differently when **Erase to History** is turned off. The copied flower is positioned so that the selection area is over part of the image on the same layer and over part of the image on the Background layer. When you erase on the right half of the selection area, Photoshop erases to transparent so you see the white of the background. If you erase on the left side, Photoshop erases to transparent and reveals the image below on the Background layer, as shown in the screenshot below. If you're erasing on the Background layer, Photoshop erases to the background colour.

The other eraser in the Eraser group, the **Background Eraser**, works similar to the **Magic Eraser** with two major differences. One difference involves dragging instead of clicking. You drag the Background Eraser over the image to delete pixels. With the Magic Eraser, you click on the image to delete pixels. The other difference is that the Magic Eraser allows you more control with different settings on the options bar.

To complete the steps in this section, crop the extra dark areas on the left and right sides of the image, and then save your changes. You now have a completely new picture made out of an existing image.

Magic Wand and Magic Eraser Tools

As you compare the two images in the screenshot below, the image on the right is made more interesting with the addition of more balloons.

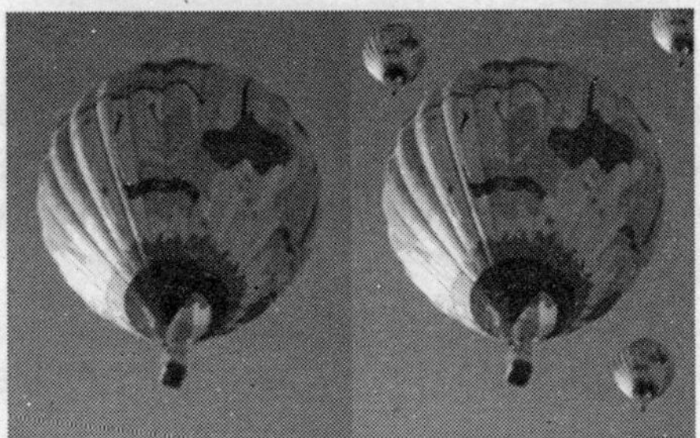

Consider the best way to select the balloon, with the **gondola**, in order to copy it. If you use the **Elliptical Marquee** tool, you'll potentially include too much of the sky with the balloon because of the position of the gondola. Notice that part of the sky is darker than other portions. When you select the sky, you can use a command to select the inverse or opposite, which in this case is the balloon. You can accomplish this with the **Magic Wand** tool.

The Magic Wand tool selects areas of colour based on the brightness of the pixel that you click with the tool. The tolerance option for the Magic Wand tool controls how closely the brightness of the colour, or range of colours, needs to match the colour of the selected pixel.

The screenshot below illustrates the concept using the RGB colour scheme. The A column shows that the Magic Wand will select colours in a range from 68 to 132 from the colour value of R100 G100 B100. In the B column, in which the tolerance range is increased, the selection includes colours in a range from 67 to 133.

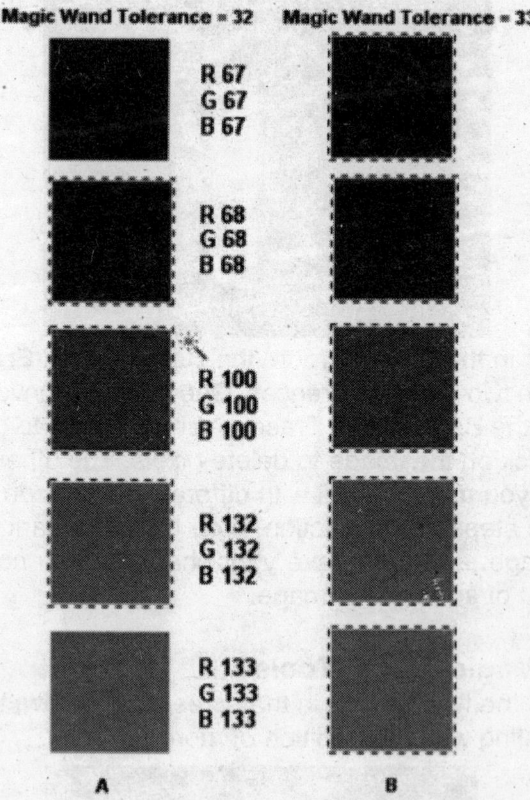

Now you'll learn two methods and some alternative approaches for selecting the balloon and the gondola. You can try each one and evaluate which is the best. Remember that there's no right or wrong way to accomplish the selection of the balloon.

Try this technique first:

1. Download a picture (Balloon.jpg) and open it.
2. Select **Image → Duplicate**. Save the duplicate file as Balloons-working in PSD format.

3. Select the **Magic Wand** tool, observe the settings on the options bar, and, if necessary, reset the tool options by right-clicking on the square tool on the options bar.

One of the options bar settings is Contiguous (means near or touching). When you tick this option, the selection of the range of pixels will be near the one you click. If you don't tick it, Photoshop selects pixels within the tolerance range in the entire image. For the next set of steps, leave it ticked.

You need to experiment with different tolerance settings to see their effects. You can use the scrubby sliders to increase or decrease the number. If your first selection doesn't include enough of the pixels, select a higher number. If you want to pick colours very close to your sample, use a low number. The Magic Wand uses the same size sample selection as the **Eyedropper** tool.

To experiment with tolerance settings, do the following:

1. Change the tolerance to 55, and then click on the Magic Wand tool in the sky area.
2. Notice there's a small area inside the balloon at the top right that's included in the selection. You'll subtract this from the selection.
3. Decrease the tolerance to 32. Then, press **Alt** and notice the Magic Wand cursor change to a minus to subtract, or click on the **Subtract** button on the options bar.
4. Click on the blue area closest to the side of the balloon to subtract it from the selection.
5. Select **Image → Inverse** (**Shift+Ctrl+I**) to select the opposite, which in this example is the balloon.
6. While the balloon is selected, you can copy and paste. Use **Copy As** instead of dragging a copy with the **Move** tool so that each copy will be on a new separate layer.
7. Press **Ctrl+T** to select **Free Transform**.
8. Press **Shift**, and then drag the upper-left or lower-right corner to scale the balloon smaller.
9. Press **Enter**, or click on the tick mark on the options bar.
10. Repeat the copy, paste and scale routine until the image looks similar to the illustration. If you don't see a copied image to move or scale, the original is positioned exactly on top of it.

Here's another method of selection that uses a combination of the Rectangular Marquee and the Magic Wand. Use the image you're currently working on or open the original image:

1. Make sure the Background layer is active or selected. (Click once on the name of the layer to activate it, if necessary.)
2. Select the **Rectangle Marquee** tool and draw a rectangle around the large balloon but not touching it. Because the smaller balloons are on separate layers, they aren't included in the selection.
3. Select the **Magic Wand** tool, and then press **Alt** to subtract from the selection. Click inside the selection square. The balloon is now selected.
4. Deselect the balloon.

You can also use the **Lasso** tool to quickly draw a selection area around one of the small balloons, followed by the **Magic Eraser** tool. The Magic Eraser tool deletes pixels of the same colour brightness as a pixel you select. The area of deletion is left transparent. You can control the tolerance and the contiguous settings for the Magic Eraser tool. It's similar to the Magic Wand tool, except the Magic Erase deletes pixels whereas the Magic Wand selects pixels. The other eraser in the Eraser tool group, the Background Eraser, deletes pixels when you drag the tool. The area's left transparent. The Background Eraser tool options are different than the Magic Eraser tools options.

You can practice this technique on your balloon image, as follows:

1. Click on the **Background layer** in the **Layers** palette to make sure it's selected.
2. Use the **Lasso** tool to quickly draw a rough circle around the large balloon that includes some of the blue sky. Reset the tool options.
3. Copy, paste, move the selected balloon image to a different location, and then scale it smaller.
4. Zoom in on the area, if necessary.
5. Select the **Magic Eraser** tool, and then reset the tool options. Click on the blue area around the balloon. It goes away, like magic.
6. Save the file with the extra added balloon, or select **Edit → Step Backward** (**Alt+Ctrl+Z**) until the extra balloon disappears.
7. Save the image of your multiple balloons.

Create a Vignette

Now you will get to know about how you can create many new images by isolating part of an existing image and adding it to different backgrounds. You can use these images in a wide variety of ways.

Remember that:

- Magnetic Lasso is used for selection.
- Eyedropper tool is used to sample a colour.
- Paint Bucket tool is used to create a pattern background.
- Gradient tool is used to create a smooth colour transition for a background.
- Magic Eraser tool is used to delete colours.

Now, do the following:

1. Download a picture (Sunflower.jpg) and open the file. Reset to program defaults or reset the tools.
2. Select **Insert → Duplicate**.
3. Save the duplicate image as SunflowerOriginal.psd.
4. To erase the background, select the **Magic Eraser** tool, reset the tool options, and then set the Tolerance to 25.
5. Using the **Magic Eraser** tool, click on each of the dark background areas to delete the pixels. The checkerboard pattern indicates a transparent background. Notice in the **Layers** palette that the Background layer automatically converts to a new active layer.

Because the Magic Eraser erases to transparent pixels, it automatically converted the Background layer to a layer with nothing underneath and named it Layer 0. If you need to change the Background layer for special effects, you can manually change it by double-clicking on the layer name in the **Layers** palette, and then clicking on **OK** in the **New Layer** dialogue box.

Now you'll use the **Feather** option in the **Magnetic Lasso selection** tool to create the soft-edged effect characteristic of a vignette. You know that feathering blurs the edge by adding a transition area between the selection and its surrounding pixels.

The Magnetic Lasso is a good tool for this selection because it works best in areas of strong contrast. It would also work well without deleting the background because there's a contrast between the yellow sunflower and the dark background.

To use the Magnetic Lasso tool, do the following:

1. Select the **Magnetic Lasso**. Reset the tool options, if necessary.
2. Set the feather option to 20.
3. Drag the mouse around the petals of the flower, and then close the selection. As you release the mouse button, you'll see that the area is a different shape than the outline of the flower. This is because of the feather setting.
4. Create a new file that's the same size and resolution as your open file. To do so, select **File → New**, and then select the **Window** menu on the menu bar outside of the dialogue box.
5. At the bottom of the Window menu, select the name of your open file. The dimensions and resolution of your open file are automatically filled in the **New document** dialogue box. Click on **OK**.
6. Create a second new blank document with the same dimensions and resolution.
7. If necessary, press **D** to change the foreground and background colours to the default.
8. Switch back to the sunflower image, and leave the sunflower selected. Select the **Eyedropper** tool, and then click on the leaf at the bottom of the image to pick up a lightgreen colour to use for a gradient background in your new file.
9. Activate one of the new files by clicking on the title bar of the document window.
10. Select the **Gradient** tool.
11. Starting on the left side, approximately in the middle of the blank canvas, draw a straight line across the width of the canvas. Press and hold **Shift** to constrain it to a straight line. This produces a linear gradient with the dark colour on the left using the foreground and background colours.

You can experiment with gradients in the **Gradient Editor** dialogue box. On the options bar, click on the icon of the gradient type (not the arrow) to the right of the icon of the gradient tool.

1. Switch back to the sunflower image, select the **Move** tool, and then drag the selected sunflower to the file with the gradient background.
2. Move the mouse pointer to a desired position, and then save the file as FlowerGradientbk.psd. Close the file.
3. In the remaining blank canvas, select the **Paint Bucket** tool. It's located with the Gradient tool. From the options bar menu, select **Pattern**.

4. Select the woven pattern from the **Pattern** menu to use as a background for this image. You can also use the **Paint Bucket** and the **Foreground** option on the options bar to fill the canvas with the foreground colour.
5. Move to the canvas, and then click to fill the canvas with the selected pattern.
6. Switch back to the sunflower file, select the **Move** tool, and then press **Shift** as you drag to drop the flower in the middle of the new file with the background pattern. Reposition if necessary.
7. Press **Ctrl+T**, scale the flower, and then press **Enter** to apply the transformation.
8. Crop the image to have approximately equal amounts of the background around the sunflower.

To add a border, do the following:

1. Select the **Background** layer, and then select **Select → All** (**Ctrl+A**).
2. Select **Select → Modify → Border**, and then type 20 pixels in the **Border Selection** dialogue box.
3. Select **Edit → Fill** (**Shift+F5**), and then select a fill colour or pattern.
4. Save the file as SunflowerPatternbk.psd.

The feathering effect on the sunflower softens the edges. Some of the area is also transparent, which helps it blend into the background. Here, the transparent effect is created because the background in the original picture became transparent with the use of the Magic Eraser tool and the creation of Layer 0 with no background beneath it. If you move the sunflower image to a new file, it'll be on a new layer. Therefore, the transparent edges allow you to see the background.

PHOTO RETOUCHING AND COLOUR ADJUSTMENTS

What is Retouching

Retouching is the process of making changes to improve your image. These changes include the removal or touch-up of artefacts that the camera or scanner introduces into an image. You may want to change or remove incongruous objects in the image, imperfections of the subject, details recorded by the camera that our eyes filter out, or imperfections of colour. The challenge in retouching is to make these changes undetectable. Some changes are quick and easy, whereas others are tedious and time-consuming.

Retouching with Selection and Deletion Tools

Here, you'll retouch a photograph using the Marquee Selection tool to make a selection, select a colour with the **Eyedropper** tool, and then delete to the background colour.

Let's start by preparing a working copy of an image file, as follows:

1. Download a picture (OldBuilding-orig.jpg) and open the file in Photoshop, and then select **Image → Duplicate**.
2. Save the duplicate copy as OldBuilding-working.psd. Keep your original file open to use as a reference.

3. If necessary, press **D** to set the foreground and background colours to the default of black and white.

Shortly, you'll sample the colour to the right of the broken glass in the window with the **Eyedropper** tool and then switch this colour to the background colour. It's a good idea to look at the colour values to get an idea of the colour in the image. Here, you'll discover that the inside of the window area is a dark colour but isn't black. Using the colour from the original image helps make the touch-up undetectable.

In this sample image, you may find it difficult to draw the selection inside the window because it's positioned at the edge of the canvas. Here's a quick way to add extra canvas without using Canvas Resize:

1. Enlarge the document window of your working copy to see the grey area around your image. You can either drag the lower-right corner of the document window or click on the **Maximize** button for the document window.
2. Select the **Crop** tool, and then draw around the complete image.
3. Drag the small square on the right further to the right to expand the width of the crop area, as shown in the screenshot below.

1. **Double-click** inside the area or press **Enter** to apply the crop.

Notice that the colour of the extended canvas is the same as the background colour. If you want the canvas to be a different colour, change the background colour before you apply the crop. After all retouching is complete, you can crop the image to delete the extra portion of canvas.

To perform some simple touch-ups on the working copy of the image, do the following:

1. Using the **Zoom** tool or the **Navigator** palette, enlarge the upper-right area of the building, focusing on the broken pane of glass, as shown in the below screenshot.

1. Select the **Eyedropper** tool from the toolbox, and then move the tool over the darkest area inside the window. Observe the RGB (red, green, blue) colour values in the **Info** palette. Black is represented by RGB 0, 0, 0.
2. Select the **Eyedropper** tool to obtain a representative colour sample. It doesn't have to be the exact one that's shown in the example.
3. Press **X** to switch the foreground colour to the background colour selection box.
4. Select the **Rectangular Marquee** tool, and then draw a rectangle inside the window area including the two vertical bars leaving the edge of the grey stucco. You can press the spacebar to move the selection as you're drawing it. If you need to add to the selection after it's made, press **Shift** and then draw a new area. This adds the new area to your current selection. To subtract an area from your selection, press **Alt**. To start over, press **Ctrl+D** to deselect.
5. Press **Delete**. The selection area fills with your sampled background colour.
6. Repeat this procedure for the second window pane and the areas of the rectangular frame at the top of the doorway that overlap the dark background of the doorway, as shown in screenshot below.

Retouching with the Move Tool

The next area to touch up or repair is located to the left of the arch area in the top-centre part of the building. You'll see a circular darker spot and a larger rectangular area with some red colour. The simple technique you'll use for the small circular area is to make a selection area just below the damaged spot, and then use the **Move** tool to drag a copy of the selected area over the detracting darker spot. Because you're selecting an area similar to the one you're replacing, it'll match seamlessly.

To retouch with the **Move** tool, do the following:

1. Enlarge the areas for repair in the top-centre of the building.

2. Using the **Rectangular Marquee** tool, draw a rectangular selection just below the small dark area, as shown in the screenshot below.

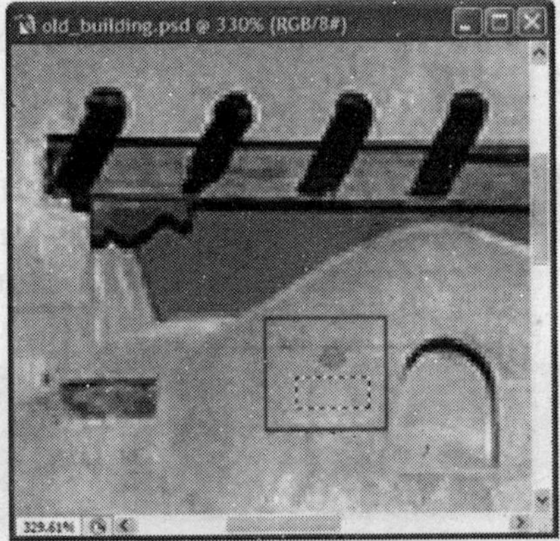

3. Select the **Move** tool, and then press **Alt**. Make sure the cursor changes to two small arrows, indicating you'll make a copy as you move the selection.
4. Move the selection into position over the area, and then press **D** to deselect.

Retouching with the Patch Tool

The **Patch** tool is located in the **Healing Brush** group in the toolbox. With this tool, you can repair an area by blending a 'patch' into the area.

To use this tool, you select the **Patch** tool, and then draw a selection around the area you want to patch. You can add or subtract to the selection just as you do with other selection tools.

Now that you know how the tool works, let's patch that other area on the front of the building, as follows:

1. Select the **Patch** tool, and then draw around the rectangular red area to the left of the arch on the building.
2. Move the **Patch** tool cursor inside the selected area, and then drag it to the right to use this area of pixels as the source. As you drag the selection, you'll see the changes live in the first selection area, as shown in the screenshot below.

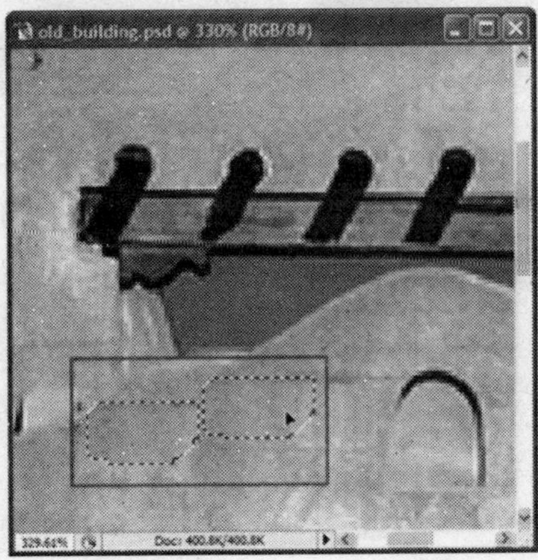

3. Release the mouse. Your patch is complete. Press **Ctrl+D** to deselect it. Feel free to complete the remainder of the retouching to eliminate the rectangle over the door and some of the tall grass at the bottom of the picture. Crop the picture as needed, and then save your changes. Close both the original image and your retouched photo.

Retouching with the Healing Brush and Clone Stamp Tools

There are countless times when you cannot avoid annoying elements in your image, such as electrical transformers and power lines. Here, let's take the picture of a icicle to experiment with retouching.

Just as each image requires different selection techniques, each image also requires different retouching techniques. Sometimes you need to use more than one tool, or a combination of tools, to make a retouched area undetectable.

Look at the image of the original icicle on your right (above). Notice that the blue sky has different values. Because it covers a large area, it'll be difficult to use some of the retouching methods you've learned. If you experiment with the Patch tool on the bottom area of the image, you'll probably get unexpected results because some of the elements you want to remove are not completely isolated. However, you can use the **Healing Brush** and **Clone Stamp** tools to retouch this image appropriately.

The icon in the toolbox for the Healing Brush tool looks like a plaster. In Photoshop CS2, the icons for the Healing Brush tool and the new Spot Healing Brush tool look very similar. The Healing Brush tool is the one without the half-circle, as shown below.

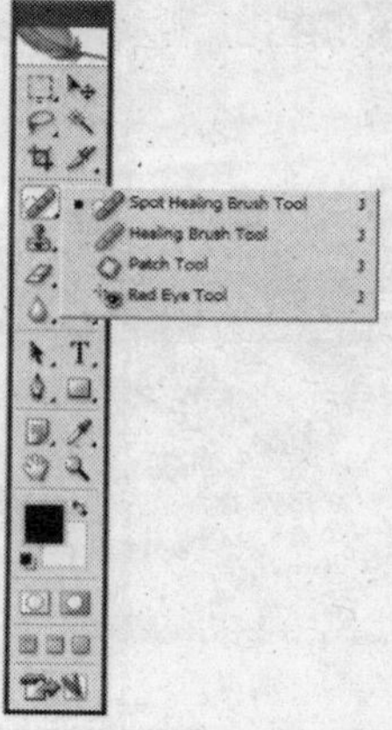

The Healing Brush tool works well for retouching small, isolated areas. You can select the size of the brush to be a little larger than the area you need to cover. If you need to work on a larger area, the Patch tool works best.

The major difference between the Healing Brush and the Patch tool is how you determine the source of the pixels you use. With the Healing Brush tool, you must first press **Alt**, and then click with the tool to establish the point of origin for the source pixels. As long as you continue to brush or paint without releasing the mouse, it uses the same point of origin. Then, you drag the mouse or paint over the area. It mixes the colour and brightness values along with texture, and any pattern from the source with the destination pixels along the outside edge area of the brush. Therefore, the resulting colour and shading in the destination area is directly related to the size of brush and its hardness.

To use the Healing Brush tool, let's remove the electrical power lines and transformer in the icicle image, as follows:

1. Download a picture (Icicle.jpg) and open it. Then select **Image → Duplicate**.
2. Save the duplicate file as WinterIcicle.psd. Keep your original image file open to use as a reference.
3. Enlarge the bottom area of the image by drawing a box around it with the **Zoom** tool.
4. Select the **Eyedropper** tool, and then move it over the area above the power line on the right side of the image. Notice that the blue colour value is fairly consistent, which is a good area to use for the source pixels.
5. Select the **Healing Brush** tool, and then move to the power line on the right side of the image.
6. Adjust the Brush size to just slightly larger than the object you are deleting. You can press and release the right bracket (]) to increase the brush in small increments or the left bracket ([) to decrease the brush. If you press and hold you can increase or decrease the size of the brush by large increments. You'll find this visual approach works well to determine the size of the brush without going to the options bar.
7. **Alt+click** in a blue area above the power line to use as your source pixels. You'll notice the cursor changes to a plus sign (+) inside a circle.
8. Drag the brush and paint over the power line. Be careful a s you brush to avoid touching the icicle as the Healing Brush mixes pixels along the outer edge of the brush and not directly on the tip of the brush. Don't worry if it doesn't look correct as you paint. You won't see the end results until you release the mouse.
9. **Alt+click** below the second power line on the right side and brush away the power line. As you near the tree branches you might want to **Alt+click** above the power line to change your origin of pixels. During the painting process you can change your point of the source as many times as you want.

To use the Healing Brush tool effectively on the power line on the left, it needs to be cut off or isolated from the electrical transformer. You can do this with the **Clone Stamp** tool.

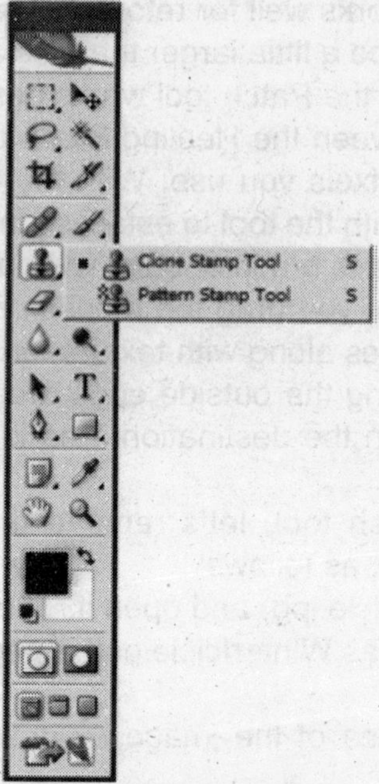

The Clone Stamp tool just uses the pixels from the source area and places the identical pixels in another area. It does not mix pixels in the destination area.

Similar to the Healing Brush, you must **Alt+click** to establish the source of the pixels sometimes referred to as sampling. You can change the size and hardness of the Clone Stamp tool and both the Clone Stamp and the Healing brush can use source pixels from one image file and paint them in a completely separate open image file.

Now let's use the Clone Stamp tool to isolate areas of the electrical transformer.

1. Select the **Clone Stamp** tool, and then **Alt+click** just above the power line to the left of the icicle to establish the origin for your pixels. You can use the right bracket and left bracket keys to increase or decrease the size of the Clone Stamp tool or use the options bar.
2. Clone the pixels to break the power line from the transformer and the icicle, as shown in the screenshot below.

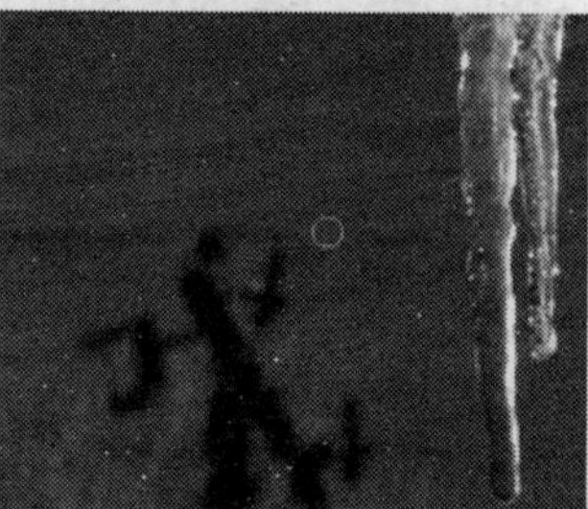

3. Switch back to the **Healing Brush** tool, **Alt+click** to establish the pixel source, and then brush away the isolated lines.
4. Continue to isolate larger pieces of the image with the Clone Stamp tool, and then use the **Patch** tool. When you use the Patch tool, be sure your selection area does not touch the edges of the image you are removing.

The screenshot below shows the transformer section isolated, and the Patch tool selection around it. Move the selection upward for the source pixels.

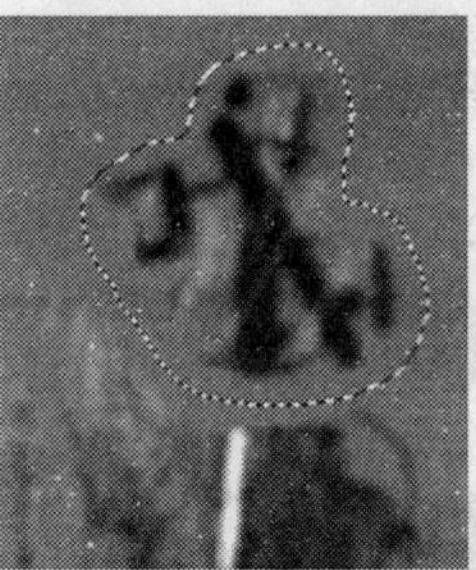

5. To complete the retouching, use the **Clone Stamp** tool and clone pixels at the bottom edge of the image to separate the tree branches from the edge of the image. Use the **Patch tool** to delete the remainder of the tree branches at the bottom.
6. For the last step, view the image at 100% by clicking the **Actual pixels** button in the **Zoom** tool or press **Ctrl+Alt+ 0** (zero). Make additional touch-ups as needed.
7. Save the changes and close this file and your original file.

Retouching Spots

The Spot Healing Brush tool works just like the Healing Brush tool except you don't have to click to establish a source for your pixels. The Spot Healing Brush tool icon looks like a small half-circle and is located next to the Healing Brush tool. It's perfect for small areas, such as dust specks or small blemishes on a face, and is a real time saver – just one mouse click and the spot's gone. Make sure the brush size is just slightly larger than the spot you're removing.

You'll use the **Spot Healing Brush** tool to remove the tiny specks on the background in the original image of the pressed flower arrangement.

To use the Spot Healing Brush tool, do the following:

1. Download a picture (PressedFlowers.jpg) and open it and make a duplicate copy.
2. Save the duplicate in as PressedFlowers.psd.
3. Move around in the image in an enlarged view to see the tiny specks on the background and on the lower light yellow flower. Press **H** or the spacebar to activate the **Hand** tool to easily move around in the image.
4. Select the **Spot Healing Brush** tool, and then click on each spot to delete them.

Restore a Photo and Vignette

An old photo in need of repair is an excellent image on which to practice all the retouching skills you've learned. As you do this type of repair, you'll learn that photo restoration is tedious and time consuming.

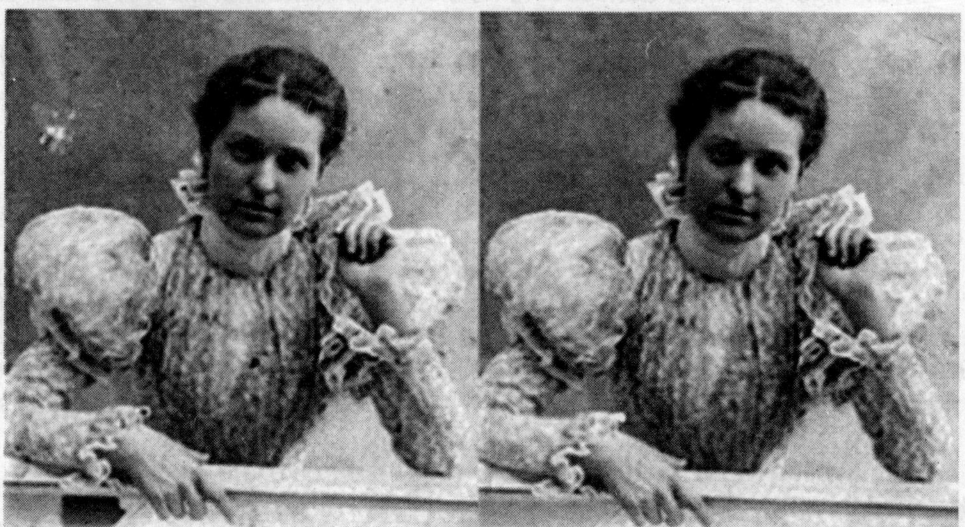

To help you have more control when cropping a small amount of the torn left edge when repairing it, turn off the **Snap To** feature (select **View → Snap To → None**). You can always turn this feature back on when you need it. It's useful to help position and align objects.

To create a vignette, do the following:

1. Download a picture (AntiquePhoto.jpg) and open and make a duplicate copy.
2. Save the duplicate as AntiquePhoto.psd. Close the original file.
3. Double-click the **Background layer** in the **Layers** palette, and then click on **OK** in the **New Layer** dialogue box.
4. Select the **Elliptical Marquee** tool and, if necessary, reset the tool options.
5. Set a Feather value of 15 on the options bar.
6. Draw an elliptical selection, as shown in the screenshot below. Be sure the top of the ellipse is not too far above the head because of the width of the Feather setting. Press **Alt** to draw from the centre outward. You can also press the spacebar to move the shape as you draw. Release the mouse before you release the keys.

1. Create a new document file at least the same size or larger than the open file.
2. Select the **Move** tool, and then drag the selected image to the new document window.
3. In the new document window, select the **Background layer** in the **Layers** palette to make it active.
4. Select **Select → All** (**Ctrl+A**) to add a border. You'll learn a new way to add a border using a Stroke applied to the selection border.
5. Select the **Eyedropper** tool, and then pick a colour for the border from the image. You can accomplish the same result by double-clicking on the foreground colour selection box, and then selecting a colour in the **Colour Picker**.
6. Select **Edit → Stroke**. The colour you picked displays in the colour box.
7. Set the width of the border.
8. Your finished vignette should look similar to the picture in the screenshot below. Save your new file as PhotoVignette.psd, and close both files.

Understand Colour Basics

Open the **Colour Picker** in by double-clicking on the **foreground colour** selection box. Notice the four areas on the lower right with a character and values, plus the large colour field on the left, as shown below.

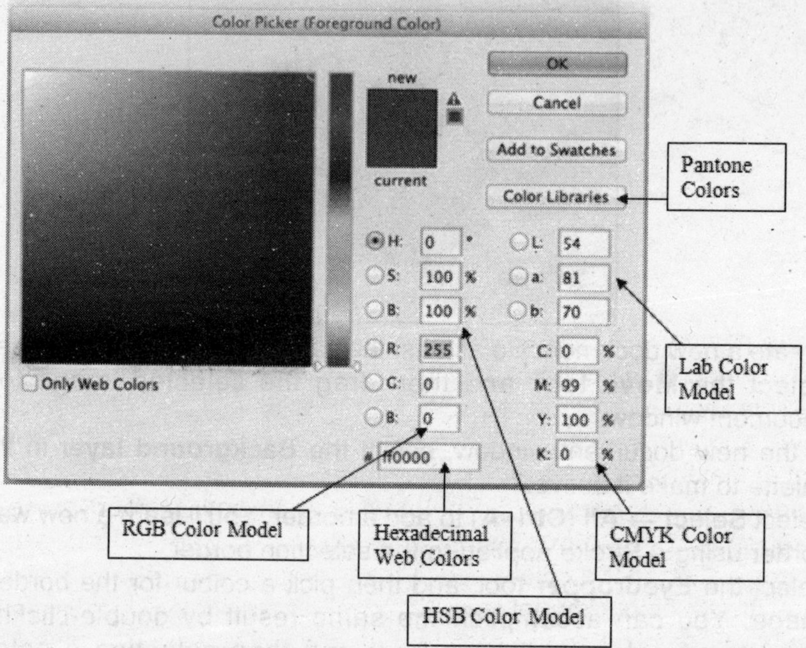

These represent different colour modes that Photoshop supports that are based on colour models. A colour model is simply another way to describe colour with a numerical value. The four colour modes in the Colour Picker are RGB, HSB, CMYK and LAB. The letters for the first three modes stand for red, green, blue; cyan, magenta, yellow, black; and hue, saturation, brightness.

All digital images start out in RGB colour mode because of the process digital cameras, scanners and digital video use to convert light into its RGB components. As a result, you must convert an RGB image to another colour mode for different types of final output.

The CYMK and LAB colour modes are used mainly for printing images on high-end PostScript printers and presses. The four-colour printing process creates the image with dots of the four ink colours – CMYK. It can also use special premixed inks. These standardized premixed inks are referred to as the Pantone Matching System.

Here are the steps to convert an RGB image to CMYK:

1. Open any digital image. Notice that RGB appears in the title bar.
2. Select **Image → Mode → CMYK**.

That's how easy it is to convert from RGB to CMYK. You may notice a difference in the colour as Photoshop simulates the printed ink colours on the RGB monitor.

RGB colour mode is based on the additive colour model. Equal portions of red, green, and blue are added to become white. The opposite happens in CMYK mode, which is based on the subtractive colour model. In this model, when you add all the colours the result is black. The range of colours in RGB colour mode is based on the spectrum of visible light. The colour slider bar in Colour Picker represents the colour spectrum. If you bend the colour spectrum into a circle, you'll have the Colour Wheel.

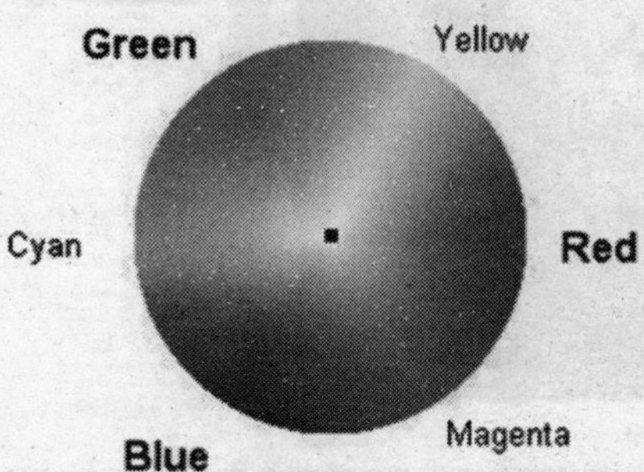

Notice the positions of the colours on the Colour Wheel. This makes it easy to see the relationships of the colours and the colour opposites.

For example, cyan is opposite red, and cyan is made from the two adjacent primary colours of blue and green.

Remember that this is the additive colour model, which is different from the pigment model. To see how this relates to Photoshop, open any of your images. Select **Image → Adjustment → Colour Balance**. In the Colour Balance dialogue box, you can see the correlation of the colour opposites.

You know that a colour model is simply another way of describing colour with a numerical value. Each pixel on the monitor has a value for each of the three colours of RGB. The numerical range is from 0 to 255. In the additive colour model, black represents the absence of colour, so the value for black is 0. White represents all the colours, so the value for white is 255. Fifty percent of all the colours is a medium grey.

The RGB values for a colour are usually written with the characters RGB and the value. A colour value in RGB mode is written with the three values for the colour. For example, the value for cyan is RGB (0, 255, 255), as shown in the Colour palette.

The other colour models that are relevant to colour adjustments in Photoshop are HSB and HSL. The HSB model represents the colours based on hue, saturation, and brightness. The HSL model is a variation of the HSB model and is based on hue, saturation and lightness. The difference between the two is that the lightness is based on linear changes of how light or dark the colour is and the brightness of the HSB model is based on non-linear changes. In Photoshop, you'll see the HSB colour model in the Colour Picker.

To see how the colour field changes in the Colour Picker when you select each one of the elements of the HSB colour model, do the following:

1. Open any image.
2. Use the **Eyedropper** tool to sample a colour.
3. Double-click on the foreground colour selection box to open the **Colour Picker**.
4. Select the **Saturation** option (labelled '**S**'). The colour field shows all the hues with the maximum saturation at the top and the minimum at the bottom, as shown in the screenshot below.

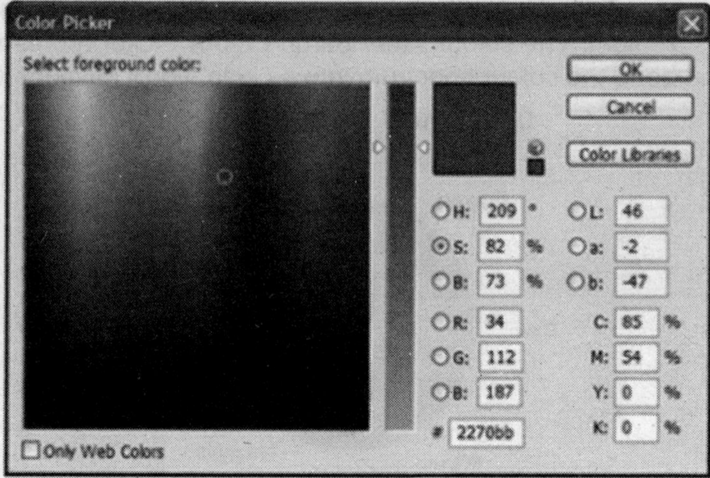

5. Select the **Brightness** option (labelled '**B**'). The colour field shows all the hues with the maximum brightness at the top and the minimum at the bottom.
6. Close the **Colour Picker**. In Photoshop, the **Hue/Saturation** dialogue box has settings for HSL (Hue, Saturation and Lightness).

To create Adjustment layers and modify the brightness, hue and colour balance of an image, do the following:

1. Download a picture (OldBuilding-rev.jpg) and open the file, and then reset all of the tool options.
2. Select **Image → Duplicate**, and then save the file as OldBuilding-working2 in PSD format.
3. Select **Layer → New Adjustment Layer**, or click on the **New Adjustment layer** button at the bottom of the **Layers** palette, and then select **Levels**. If necessary, click on **OK**. The **Levels** dialogue box appears, as shown below in the screenshot.

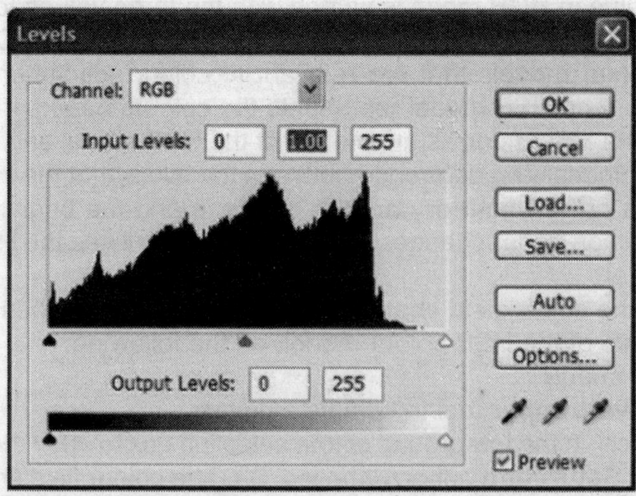

4. Move the white triangle located just below the histogram (graph) to the left until it's nearly even with the tall peak and observe the change in the image.

5. To undo your changes, press **Alt** and then click on **Reset**. (The **Cancel** button changed to **Reset** when you pressed **Alt**.) Experiment with the sliders to see the changes in the tonal range of the image. When you're satisfied with your changes, click on **OK**.
6. To compare the difference between the original tone of the image and the adjustments, click on the layer visibility icon (eye) in the left column of the **Adjustment** layer to turn off the layer and see the original.
7. Close the file without saving the changes.

Now you'll work with the Hue/Saturation adjustment to quickly change the colours (hue) of the image.

1. Open the image with the multiple balloons (illustrated under Magic Wand and Magic Eraser tools). Verify that the smaller balloons are still on separate layers. If they aren't, use a selection technique to select a balloon.
2. To select one of the smaller balloons on a layer, **Ctrl**+click the thumbnail of the layer.
3. Select **Layer → New Adjustment** layer, and then select **Hue/Saturation**. The Adjustment layer is added above the current layer.
4. Move the **Hue** slider to the left or right to see it change the colour of the balloon.
5. Repeat until you have coloured the rest of the small balloons. Be sure to select the layer for each balloon. For one of the balloons, you can use the **saturation** slider to remove the colour until it has no colour and is simply shades of black and white.
6. Select **File → Save As**, and then save the file as MultiColoursBalloon.

To make a simple colour balance adjustment, do the following:

1. Open the vignette. Be sure to reset all tool options.
2. To select the layer with the portrait (Layer 1), **Ctrl**+click the thumbnail in the **Layers** palette. Make sure Layer 1 is the active layer by clicking on the name of the layer.
3. Select **Layer → New Adjustment** layer, and then select **Colour Balance**. The layer is added above Layer 1.
4. In the **Colour Balance** dialogue box, increase the yellow by moving the slider to the left to about - 50, and then click on **OK**. Generally, an image is more pleasing with a shift toward the warmer colours (yellow, red and magenta).
5. Click on the **layer visibility icon** (eye) in the left column of the **Adjustment** layer to turn off the layer. Compare the before and after.
6. If you wish, you can select **File → Save As** and save the file with a new name.

Saving a PSD file in JPEG

Just as one image size does not fit all types of output, one file format does not work for all types. Each format has its own set of options. For example, when you save a file in JPEG format, your layers are not saved. Make sure you don't save over the original Photoshop (PSD) file that contains the layers.

To save your image in JPEG format, do the following:

1. Select **File → Save As**.

2. Change the **File format type** to **JPEG** (*.JPG; *.JPEG;*.JPE), type a new name for the file, and then click on **Save**. The **JPEG Options** dialogue box appears.
3. In the JPEG Options dialogue box, as shown in the screenshot below, adjust the quality setting, if necessary.

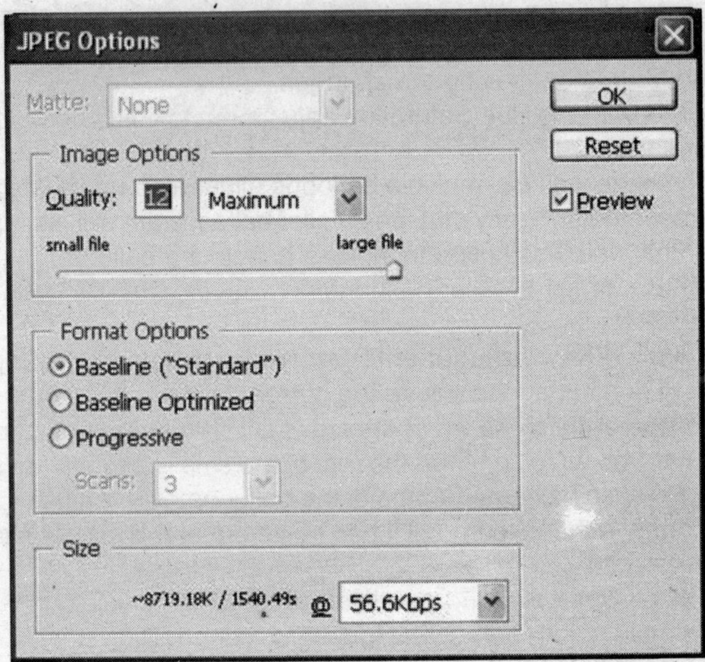

This setting determines the amount of compression. The more compression, the smaller the file size. The maximum Quality setting value is 12, which has the least amount of compression and the largest file size.

□

22
Adobe Indesign CS5

InDesign is a desktop publishing software application produced by Adobe Systems. It can be used to create works, such as posters, flyers, brochures, magazines, newspapers and books. This program has a host of tools and varied features to make working easy and smart.

1. Creating New Documents

Step 1

Open InDesign and you will be presented with an introduction screen. It is here where you will start to create the new document. But before you create a new document, you need to make sure that units used for measuring are set up correctly.

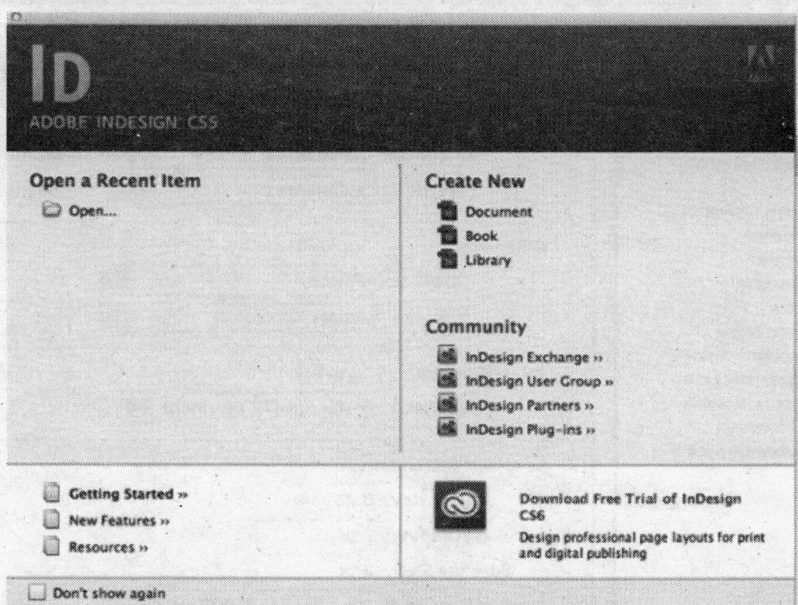

Let's work in millimetres for rulers and points for type. To change these values, go to **InDesign → Preferences → Units and increments**. Under Ruler Units change the horizontal and vertical values to the desired unit of measurement.

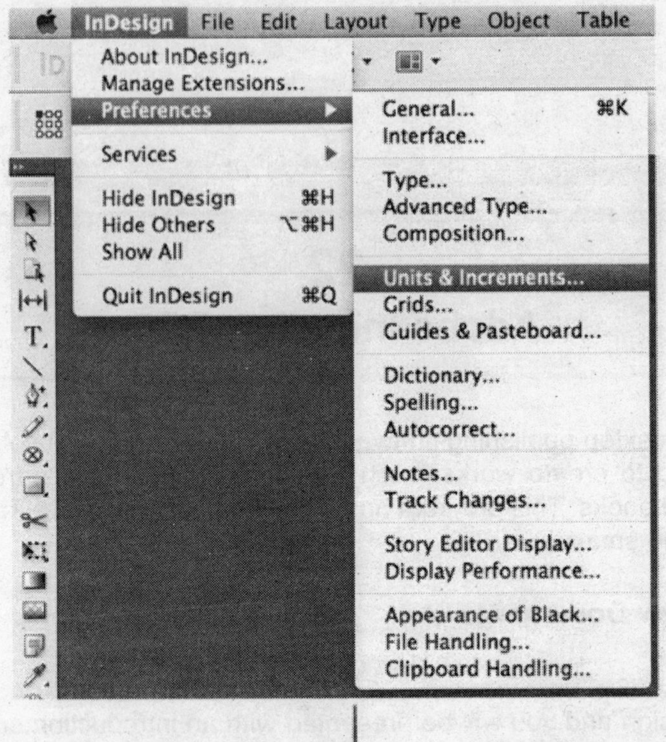
InDesign
File
Edit
Layout
Type
Object
Table
About InDesign...
Manage Extensions...
Preferences
Services
Hide InDesign ⌘H
Hide Others ⌥⌘H
Show All
Quit InDesign ⌘Q
General... ⌘K
Interface...
Type...
Advanced Type...
Composition...
Units & Increments...
Grids...
Guides & Pasteboard...
Dictionary...
Spelling...
Autocorrect...
Notes...
Track Changes...
Story Editor Display...
Display Performance...
Appearance of Black...
File Handling...
Clipboard Handling...

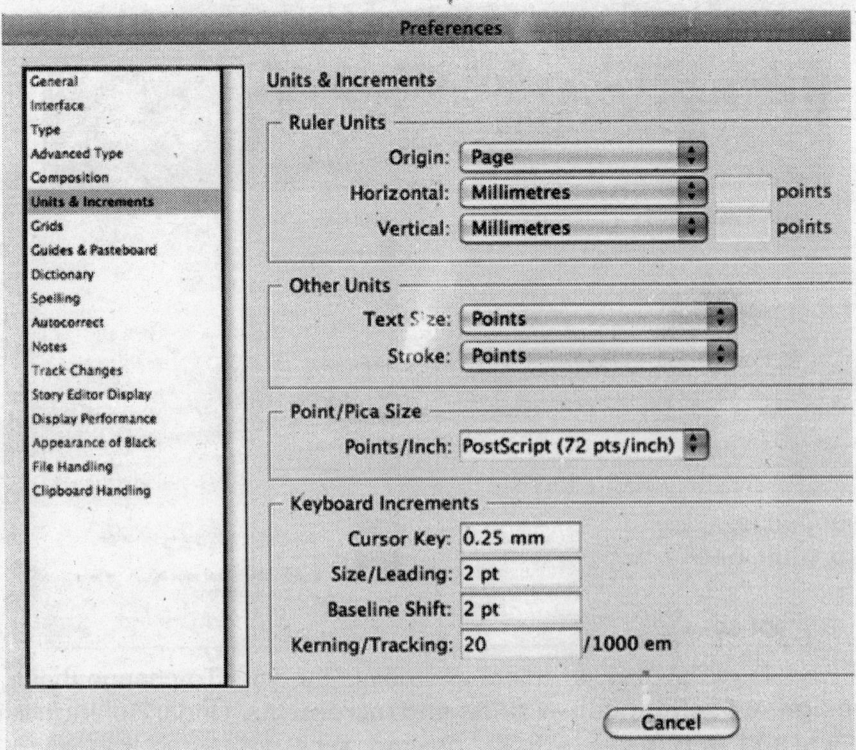
Preferences
General
Interface
Type
Advanced Type
Composition
Units & Increments
Grids
Guides & Pasteboard
Dictionary
Spelling
Autocorrect
Notes
Track Changes
Story Editor Display
Display Performance
Appearance of Black
File Handling
Clipboard Handling
Units & Increments
Ruler Units
Origin: Page
Horizontal: Millimetres points
Vertical: Millimetres points
Other Units
Text Size: Points
Stroke: Points
Point/Pica Size
Points/Inch: PostScript (72 pts/inch)
Keyboard Increments
Cursor Key: 0.25 mm
Size/Leading: 2 pt
Baseline Shift: 2 pt
Kerning/Tracking: 20 /1000 em
Cancel

Step 2

The origin of the ruler can be set to spread, page or spine. By selecting **spread**, the ruler will start from the left hand side of the document and span across the spread of the document.

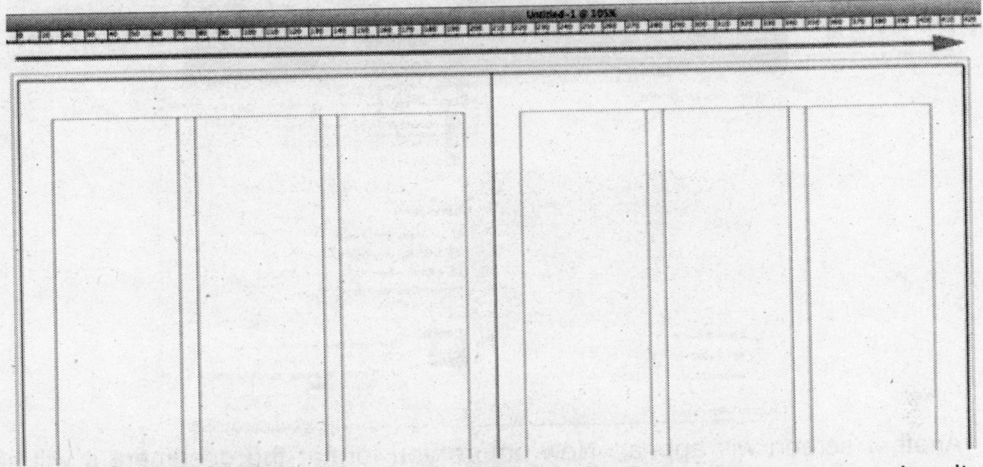

By selecting **page**, the ruler will start at the left hand side and stop when it gets to the end of the page and it will start at zero again.

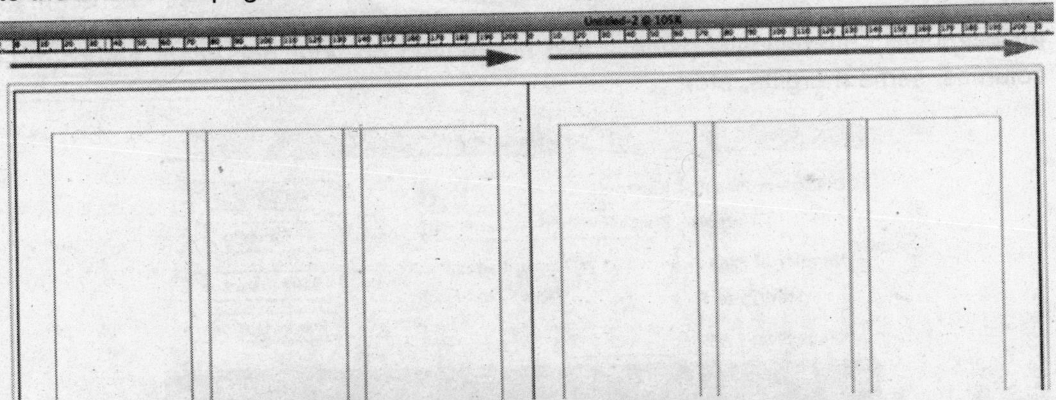

The **spine** preset is useful when you are using facing pages and of course have a spine. The ruler will start its zero point from the spine and work to the edge of the document.

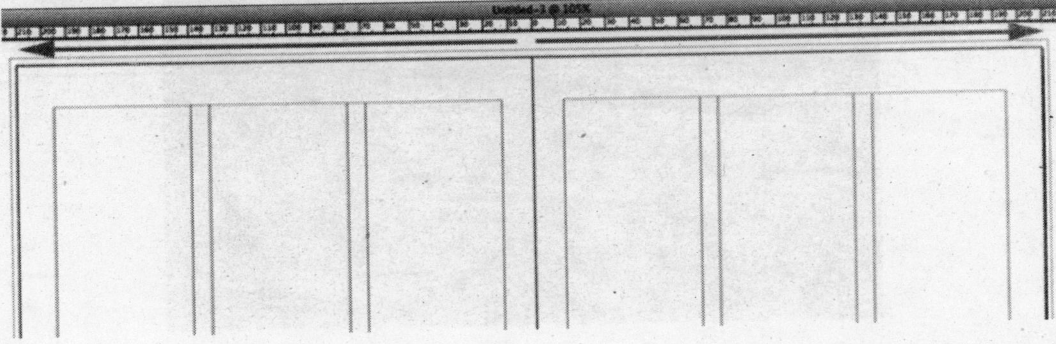

Step 3

Now, let's go back to the introduction screen. On the right hand side, select **create new document**.

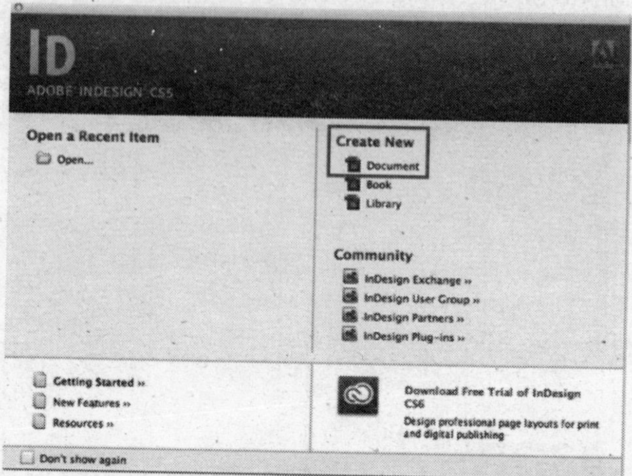

Another screen will appear. Now before you format the document it will save time to have a rough idea of the kind of document you want to set. Let's set a folded A4 eight page newsletter. The intention behind this is print, number of pages eight with facing pages ticked and start page number one. If you tick Master text frame, InDesign will automatically place a text box based on your document setup (three columns, same margins, etc).

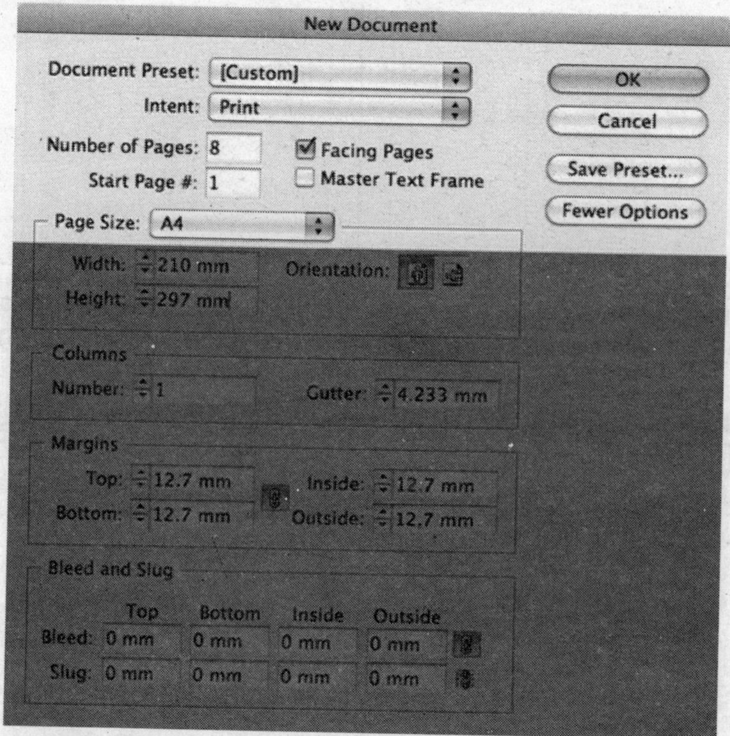

Step 4

Within the page size division you have a drop down menu with a selection of popular presets. But here you will select A4 as it is present. If you want to enter a custom size you can do so be typing directly into the width and height boxes. You can also define the orientation to portrait or landscape.

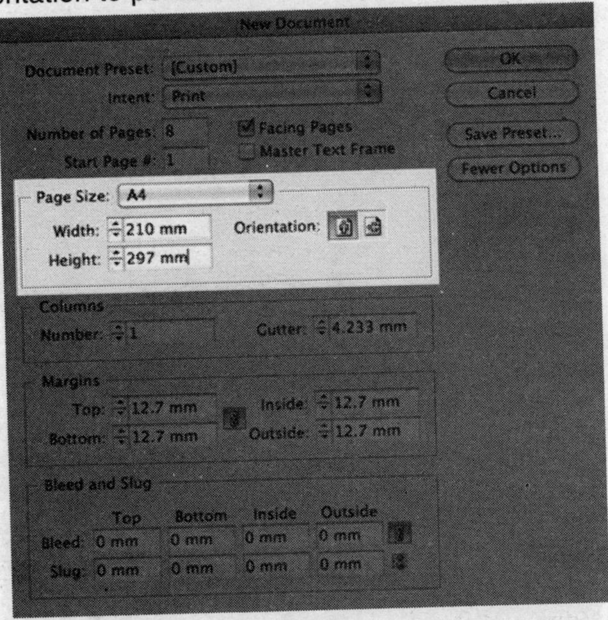

Step 5

You will need a three column structure. You would usually like to have a gutter set at half the size of the outside margins.

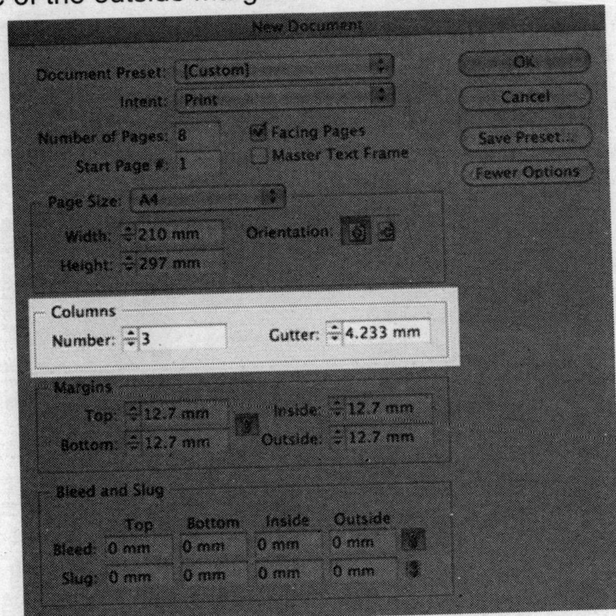

Step 6

When setting margins you would like to progress your sizes from smallest to largest in the following order: inside, outside, top, bottom. So the breakdown is as follows: inside: 12.5mm, outside 15mm, top 17.5mm and Bottom 20mm. When entering the values make sure that the link symbol at the centre of the margins column is not ticked. When ticked, it will make all the margin settings the same.

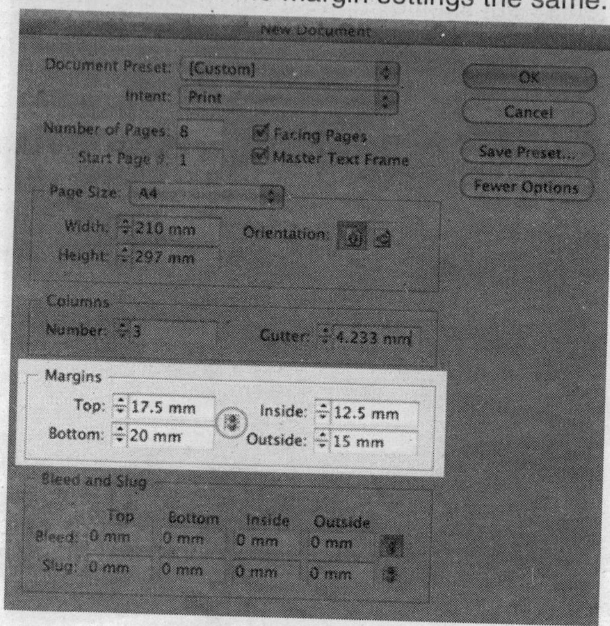

Step 7

Now, you will take the outside value and half it for the gutter, 7.5mm.

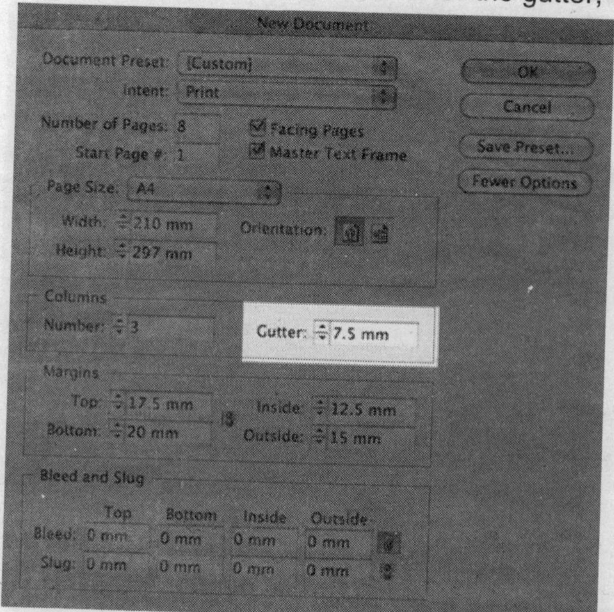

Step 8

Let's set the bleed at 3mm. Again the bleed option has a link feature which in this case is best ticked to make the bleed settings the same. You don't have to use slug. However, slug can be used to place information and notes which will be seen by a printer and then cut off along with the bleed.

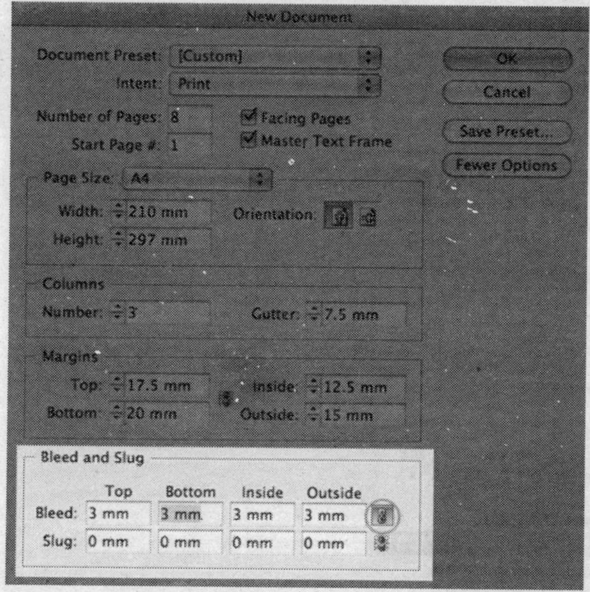

Step 9

If this is a document setup you are likely to use again in the future, navigate to the **Save Preset** button and click on it. Give it a name and click on **OK**. Next time, when you open InDesign, this preset will be set up ready.

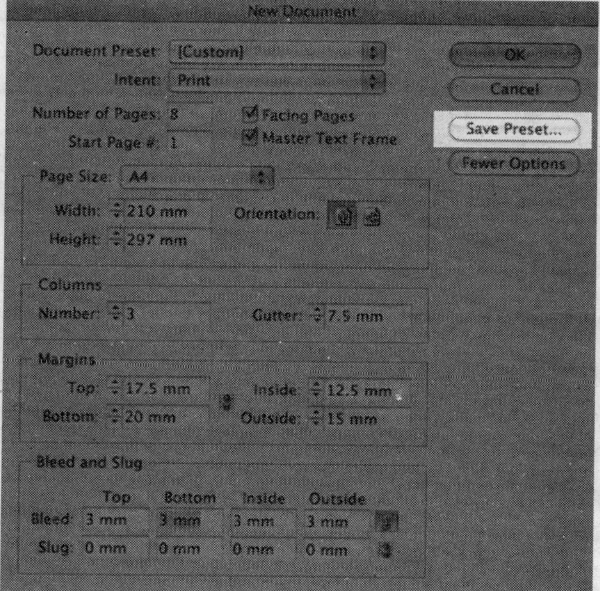

Step 10

If at any point of time, you find the need to change the document size or bleed, go to **File → Document Setup**.

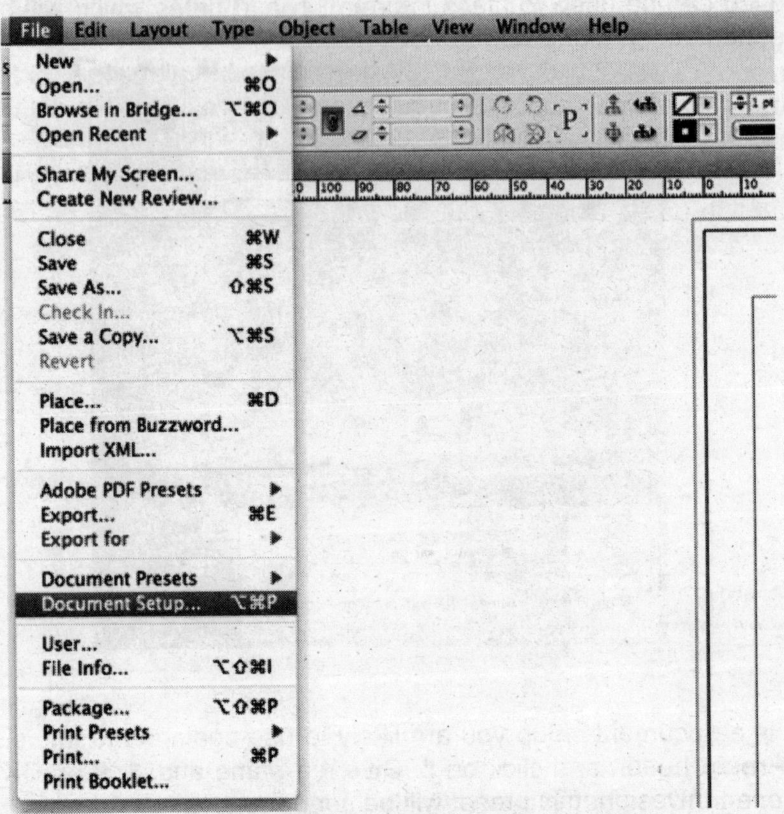

If you need to adjust the margins or columns go to **Layout → Margins and Columns**

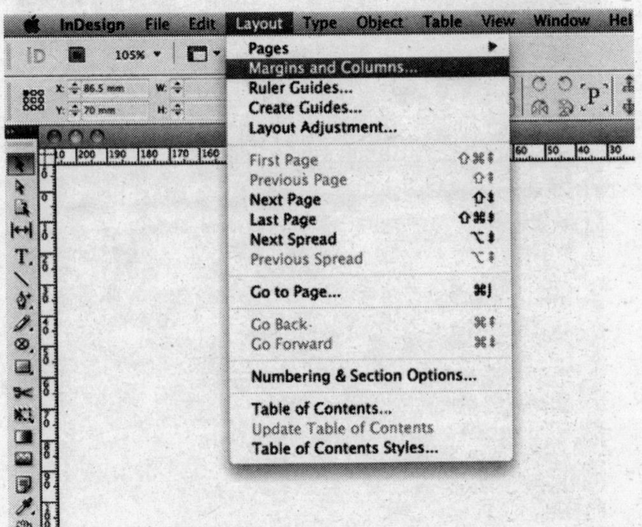

2. The Layers Panel

The layers panel in InDesign CS5 is packed with features that can really speed up your operating pace. The panel resembles Adobe's Illustrator Layer panel and has borrowed many of its useful features.

The Panel

First open an existing document that contains a lot of items. To activate the panel go to **Window → Layers**. Click once on one of the disclosure arrows to reveal the items contained within that layer.

Immediately you will notice that each individual item has been split on to an individual sub layer. These layers are automatically assigned a name. A text layer will take its name from the beginning of the text frame, a shape will be named square or rectangle, etc. and an imported graphic will be named by its source name.

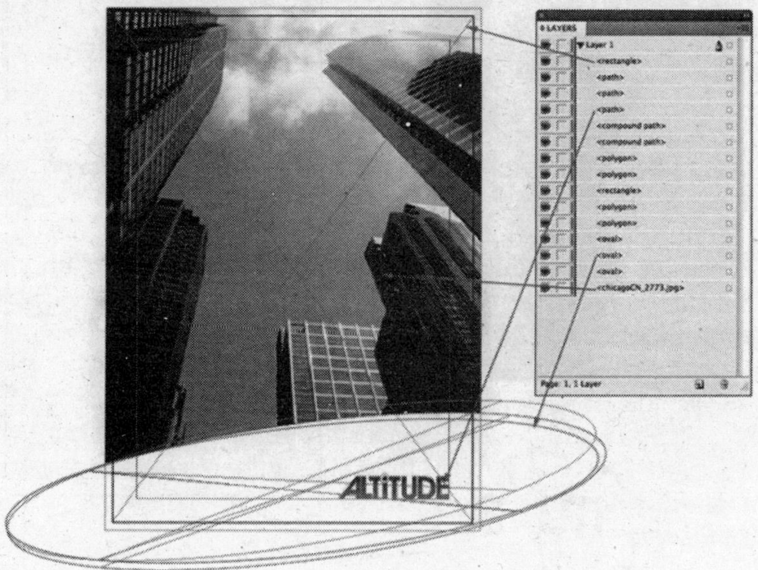

To change the name of a layer, click once on top of the actual name. (The cursor will transform into a white hand) and then again, the name will highlight blue, now enter the new name.

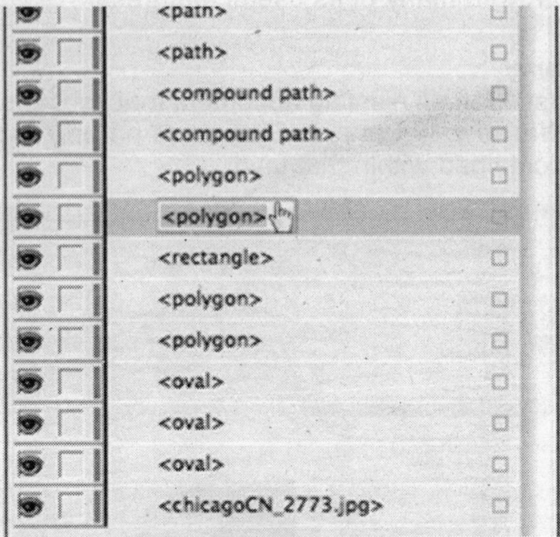

Visibility and Locking

Before the introduction of the Layers panel, InDesign would stack items on top of each other making individual selecting a bit of a headache. Now, by using the layers panel, it is possible to turn the visibility of the items on or off and in turn locate the item faster. Do this by clicking on the **visibility icon** shown below.

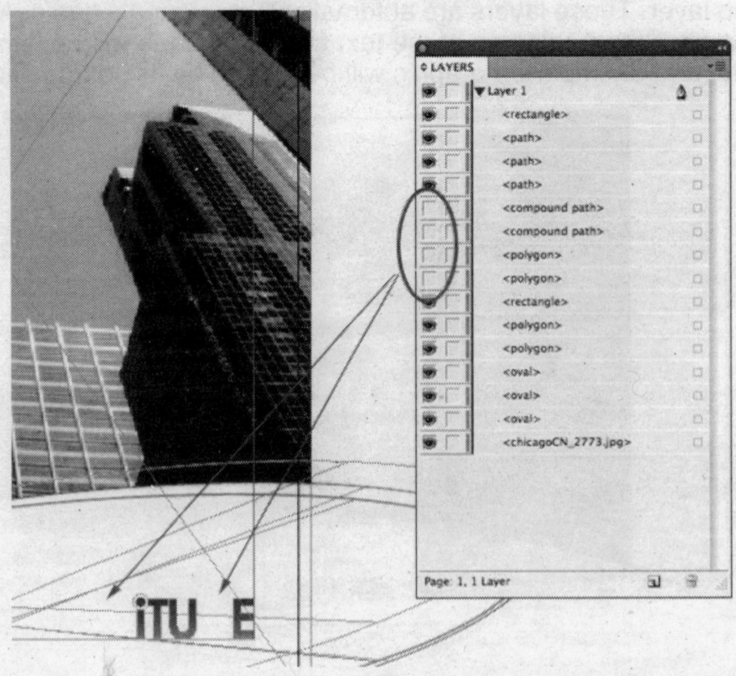

To select or deselect a few items at a time, click once on the visibility icon and drag up or down the line of icons. Alternatively, hold down the shift key to pick out layers not sitting next to each other.

Next to the visibility icon is the lock option. To lock or unlock, simply click on the **lock box**. When an item is locked and you attempt to move it, InDesign will bypass the locked item and select the item below it. To unlock the locked item, click on the **padlock** symbol attached to the item frame.

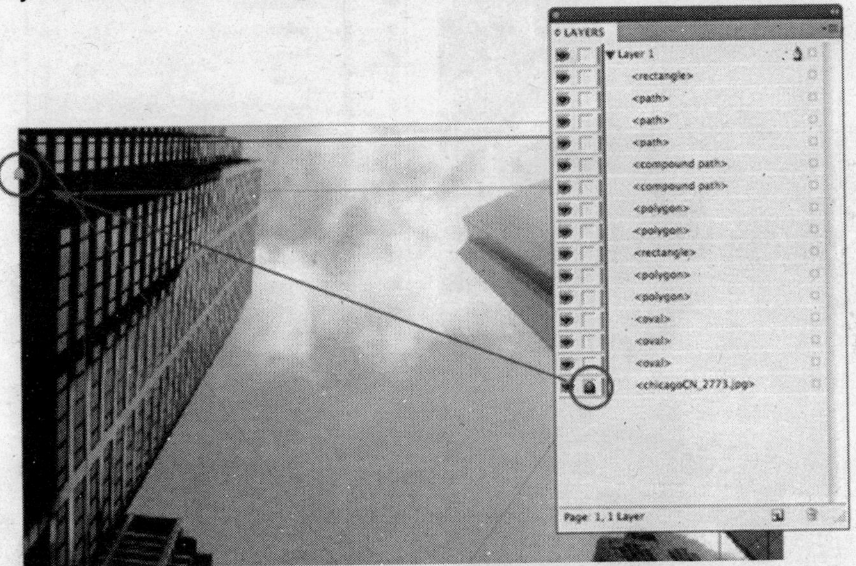

Groups

If a group has been created, it will display in the layers panel under its own disclosure arrow and named group. Again, it is possible to rename this layer to make navigating easier. Note that InDesign will continue to name groups as 'group' regardless of how many is created, so for your understanding, rename as you create.

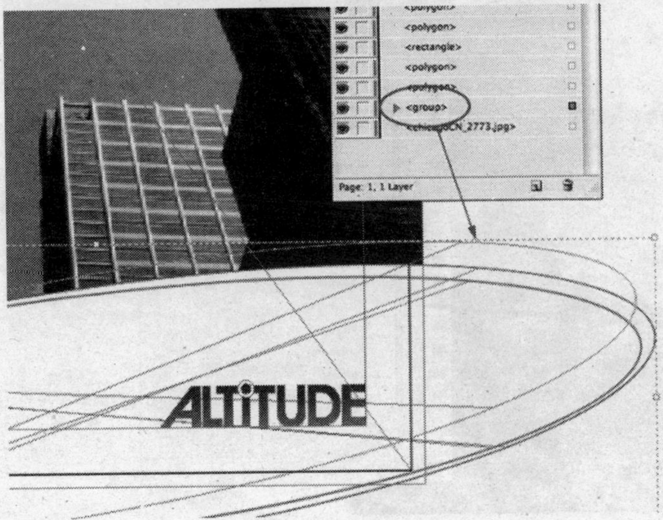

The cool feature about grouping within a layer is the ability to control the groups via the layer panel. Here you can simply select the item you want to add to the group and drag it into the group layer. This process can be reversed too; if you want to take an item out of the group, just drag it out.

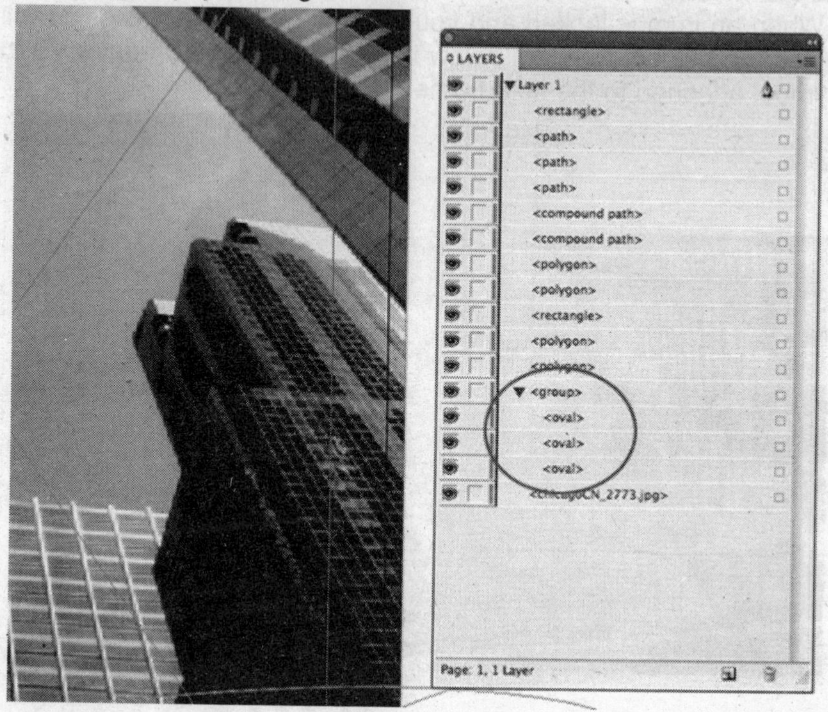

Navigating Items

If there is a particular item you want to locate and edit use the following method. Find the item in the panel list, right click → **Select and Fit Item**. InDesign will automatically select the item, center it and zoom in close.

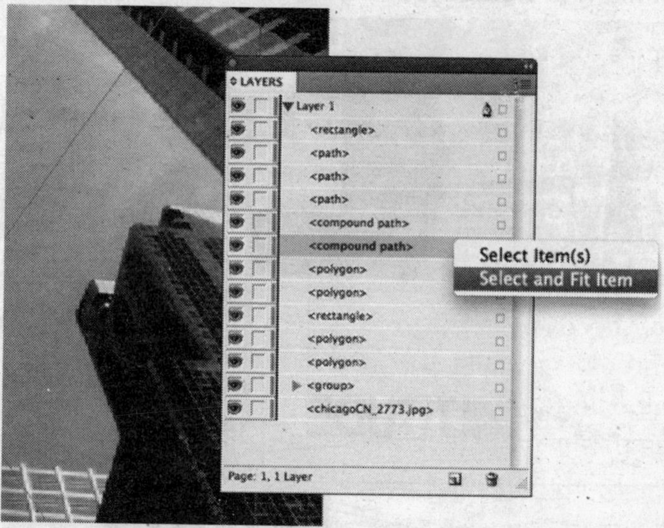

It is also possible to toggle through individual items by clicking on the square to the left of the layer name. When clicked, InDesign will select the frame. However, this method will only highlight the item and it won't be centered.

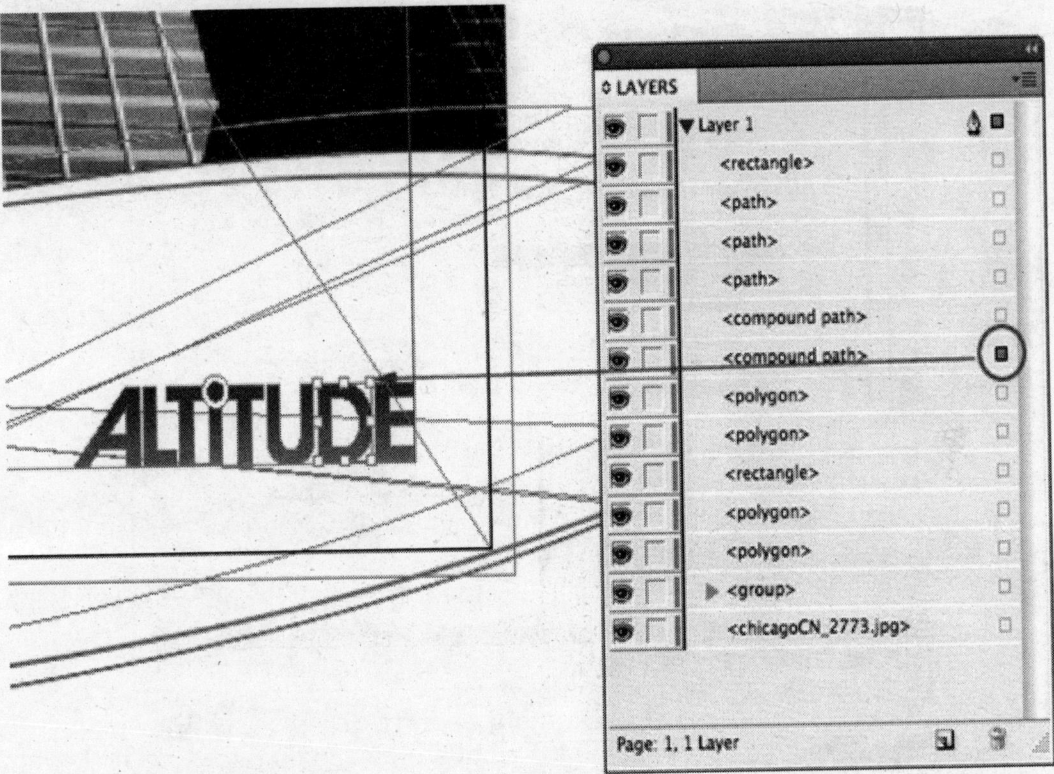

3. Importing Graphics

InDesign can handle a variety of graphics including jpg, eps, pdf, tiff, psd and most Adobe formats to name a few. InDesign doesn't actually place the graphic into the document. Instead it makes a link to the original file and generates a preview within the document. As InDesign is a layout and typesetting program, you need to edit and prepare your files within another program, for example Photoshop or Illustrator. To create a new document, go to: **File → New → Document (Command + n).**

Step 1

To start, you need to prompt InDesign to place a graphic. Do this by **File → Place** (**Command + d**) navigate to where your graphic is located, select and click on **Open**. When importing graphics, you can either import into an existing frame by selecting the frame with the **Selection** tool (**V**) before starting this step. Or import the graphic directly into the document, which will automatically create a frame for the graphic to sit in.

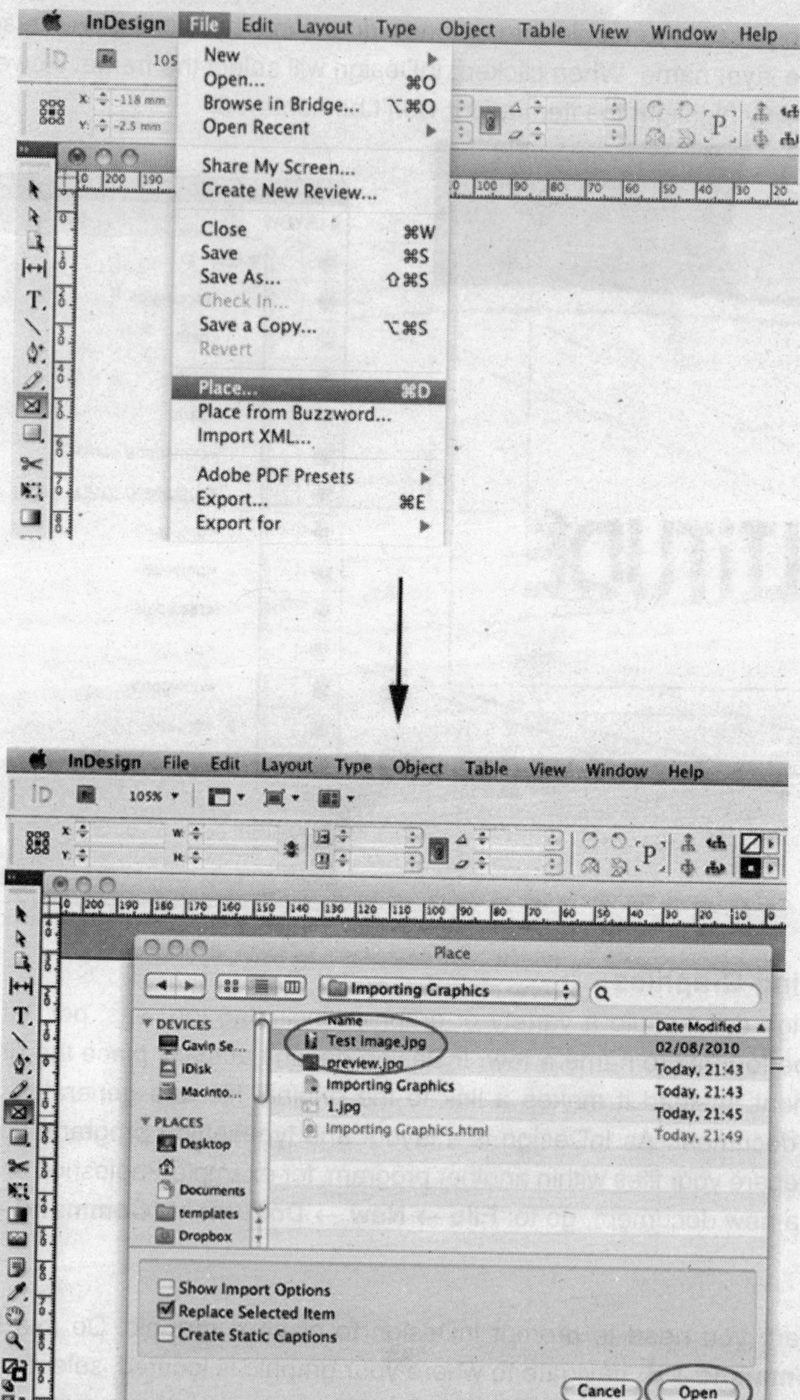

Step 2: Importing Directly into the Document

Within CS5, once you have clicked open and placed a graphic, a small transparent preview image will appear. You now have a couple of options. Firstly, clicking once will import your graphic at its original size (100%). If the frame is hanging over the edges of the working space use the **Selection** tool to drag one of the corners to resize. Hold down shift to constrain the proportions.

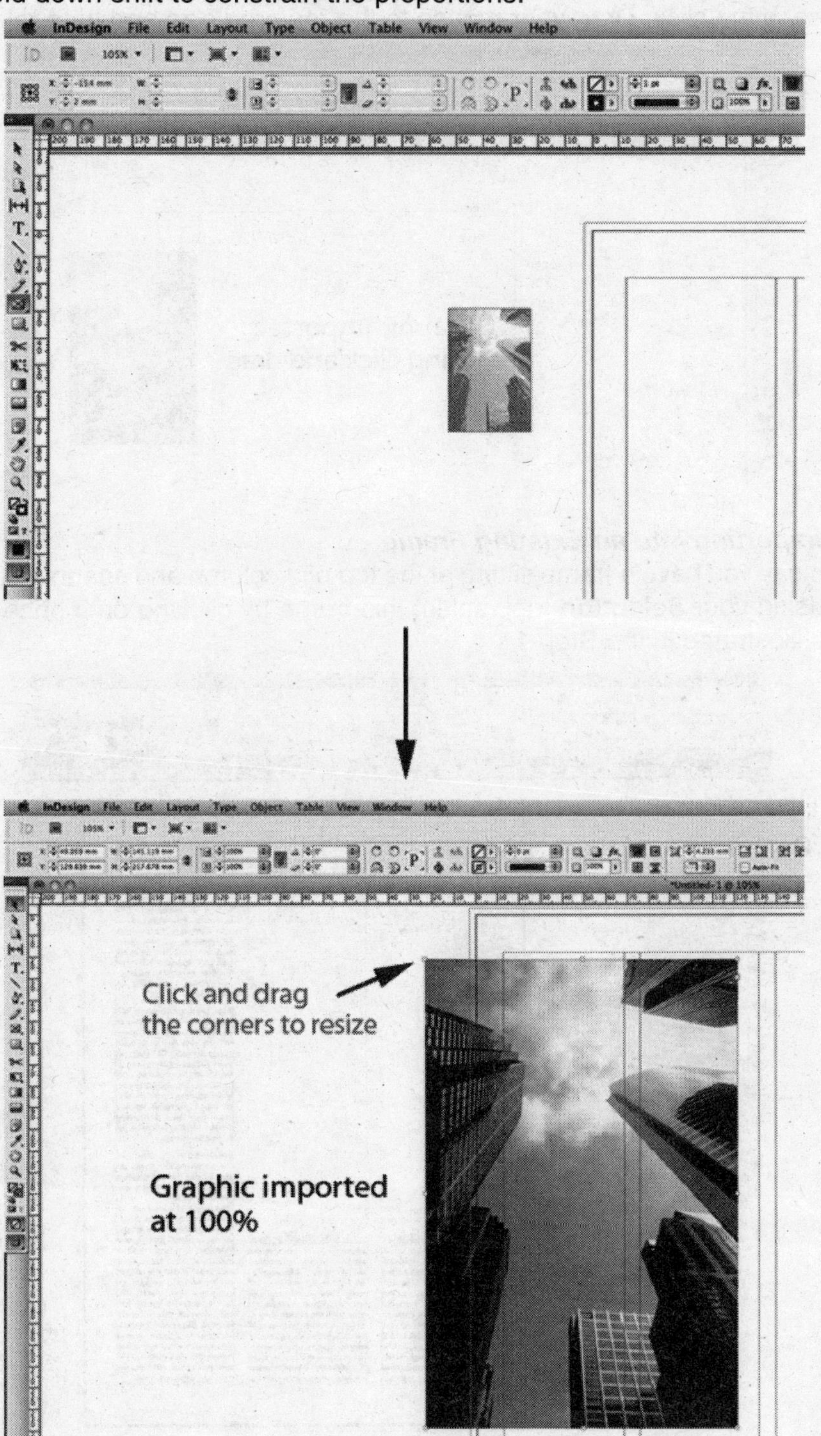

Step 3

Secondly, by clicking and holding down your mouse button, you can size the bounding box to suit the layout. After selecting **Open**, click on the document and don't release the click. Drag your mouse to the required size and then release.

Step 4: Importing into an Existing Frame

Let's say you have a frame sitting at the top of a column and spanning two column widths. Using your **Selection** tool, select this frame by clicking on it once and follow the steps illustrated in the Step 1.

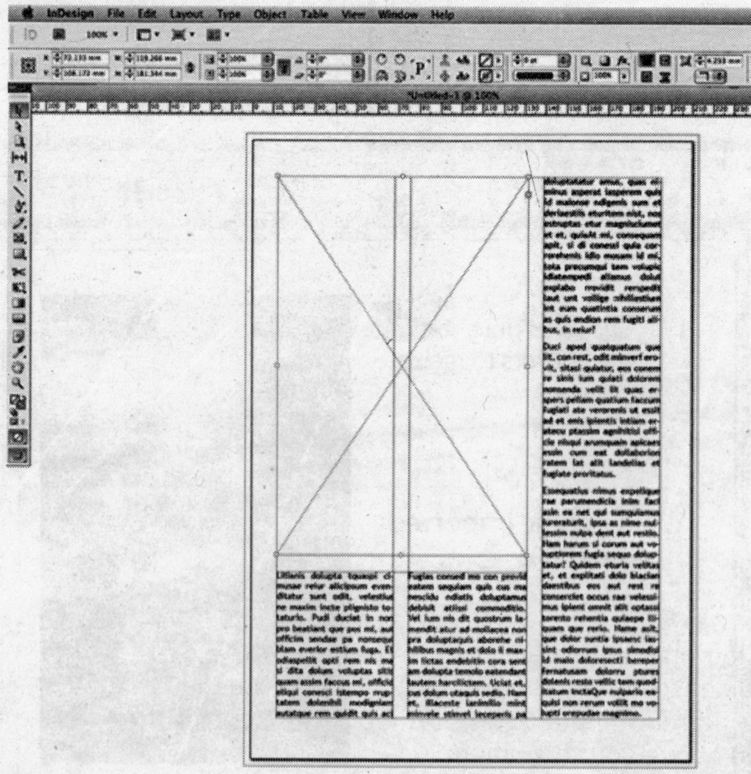

Step 5

You will notice that graphic has been imported and is cropped. InDesign has imported the graphic at 100%, which in my case is larger the frame you want to place it in.

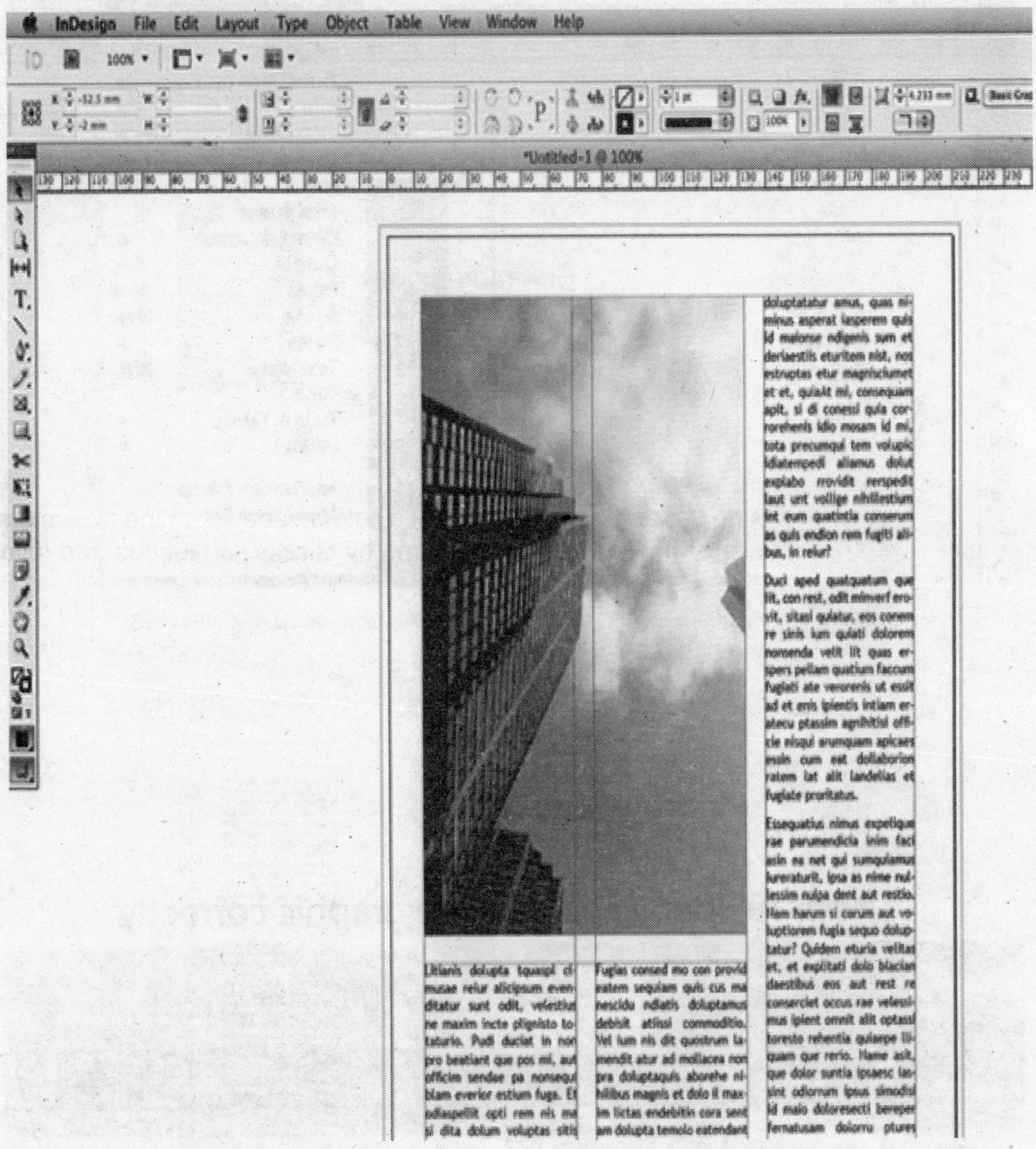

Step 6

To fit the graphic correctly, activate the **Control Dock** by going to **Window → Control**. We have highlighted the buttons that are needed below. If they are not visible select your frame with the **Selection** tool. The **Control Dock** is found at the top of your screen above your document.

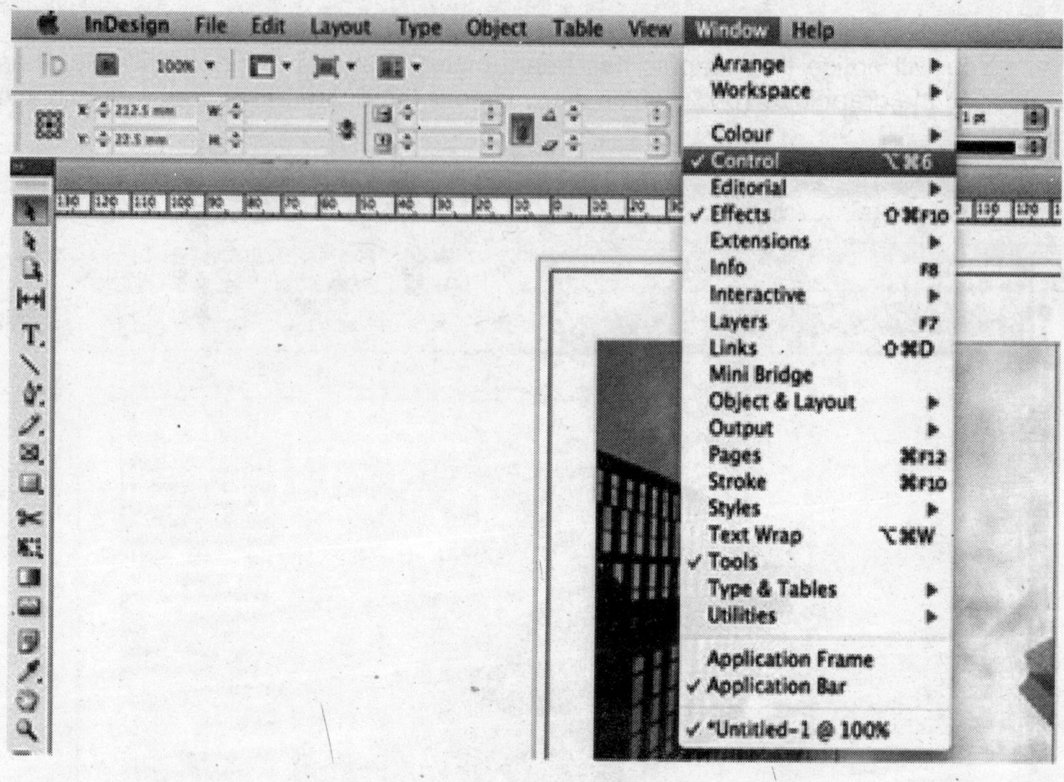

Icons needed for fitting the graphic correctly

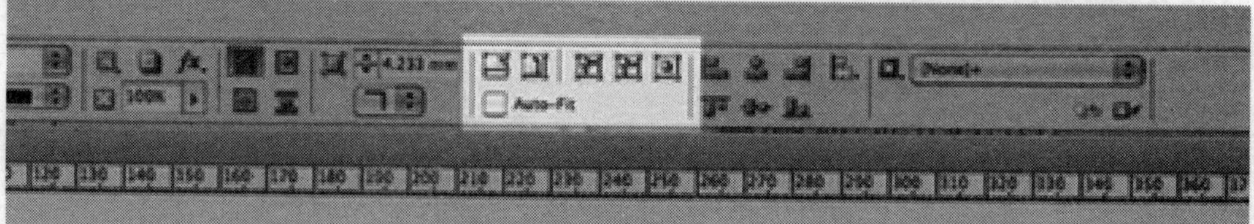

By hovering over each button with your cursor a text description will appear for each icon.

Step 7

To obtain a clearer view of the graphic we have opted to **Fit Content Proportionally** then **Center Content**. From here you can edit to suit your design.

Step 8

Once the graphic has been made easier to handle, the **Direct Selection** tool (**A**) can be employed to move, resize and position the content within the frame. Select the **Direct Selection** tool and click once inside the frame, you will notice that a brown frame will appear. This frame represents the bounding edges of the graphic you imported.

Step 9

Hover above the brown frame and the **Hand** tool will appear. To edit, either click or drag to change the position, or resize by dragging on of the corners out or in.

4. Threading Text

The process of threading text is linking two or more text frames allowing text to flow from one separate frame to another.

Step 1

Create a new document by going to **File → New → Document** and set the number columns to two or more and the remaining values to suit.

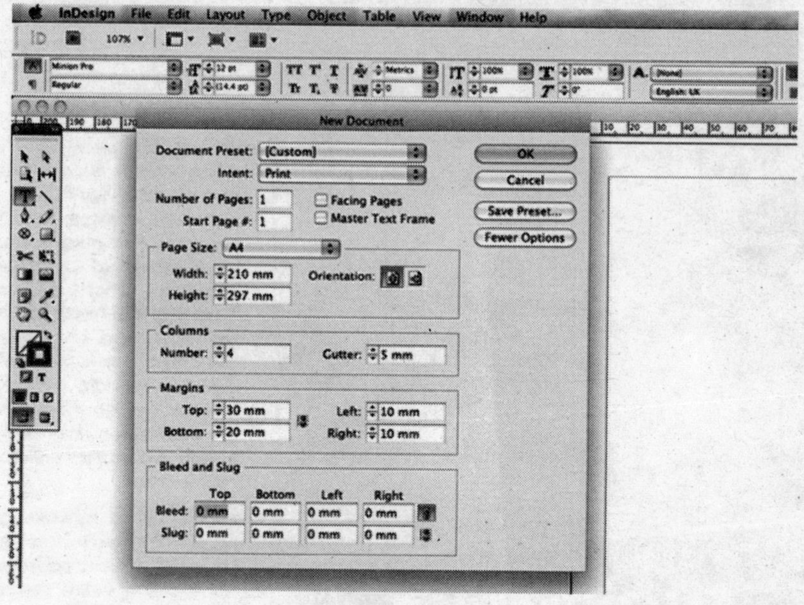

Step 2

Select the **Type** tool (**T**) from the tool box and draw a text frame over two columns by clicking and dragging over the area you want to cover.

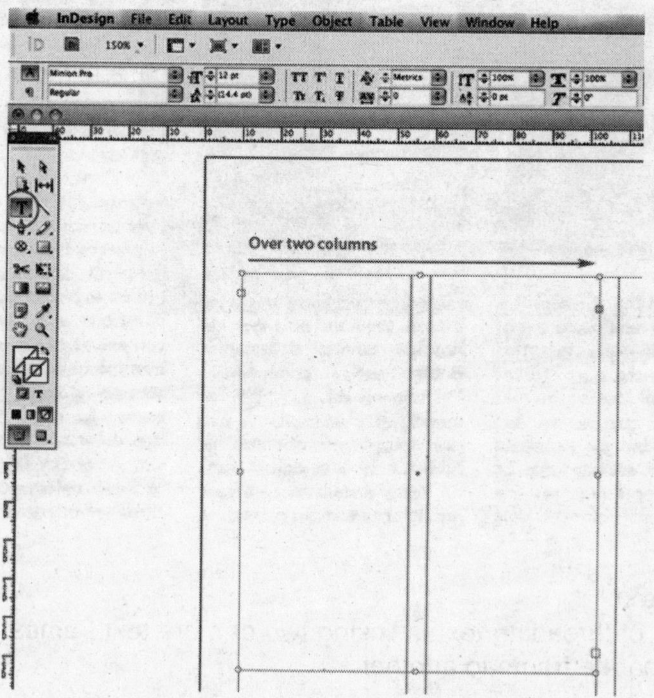

Step 3

Go to **Type → Fill with Placeholder Text**

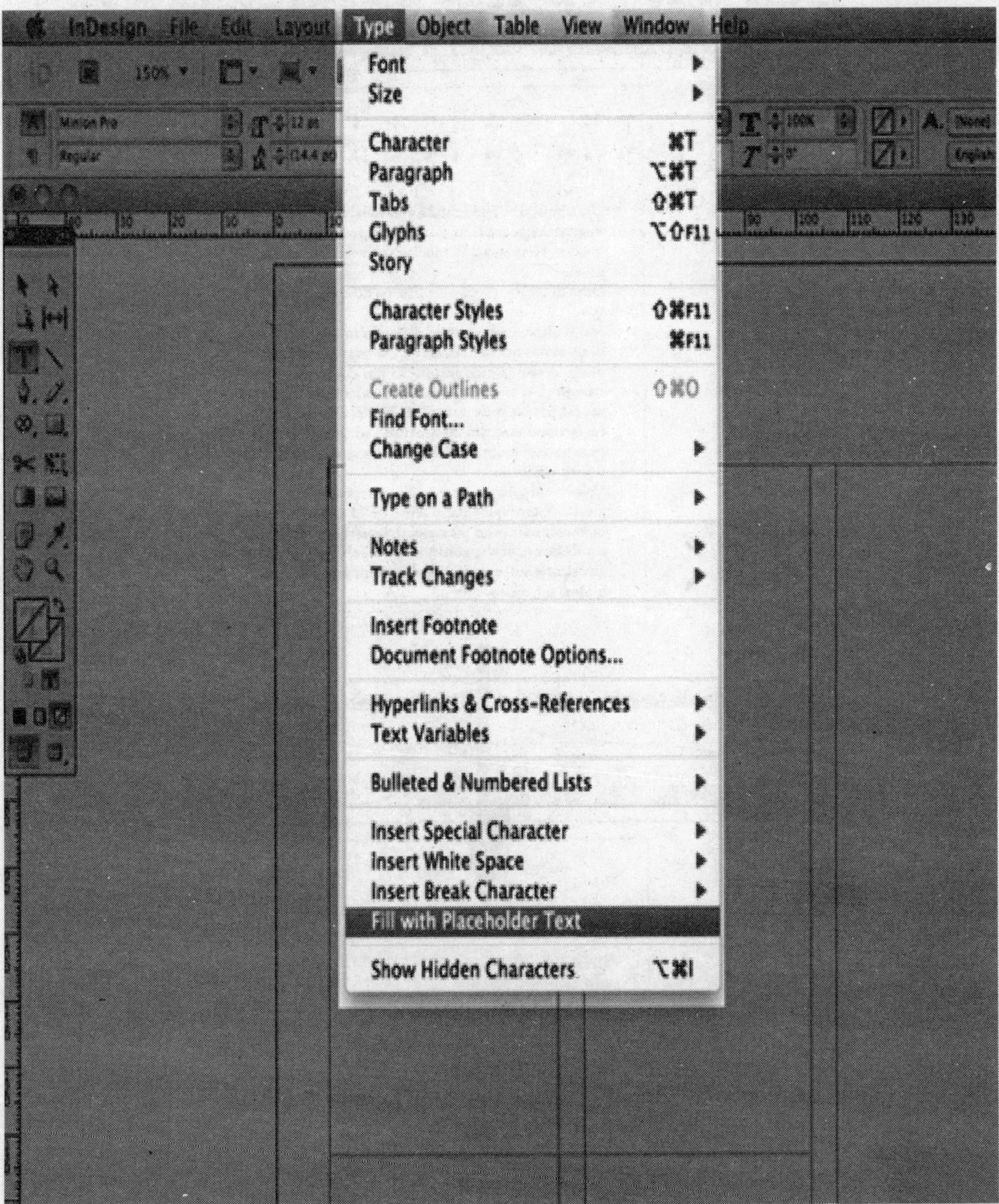

Step 4

Now reduce the text frame to one column. Do this by selecting the **Selection** tool and dragging the middle handle that sits on the vertical edge of the frame until it snaps to one column.

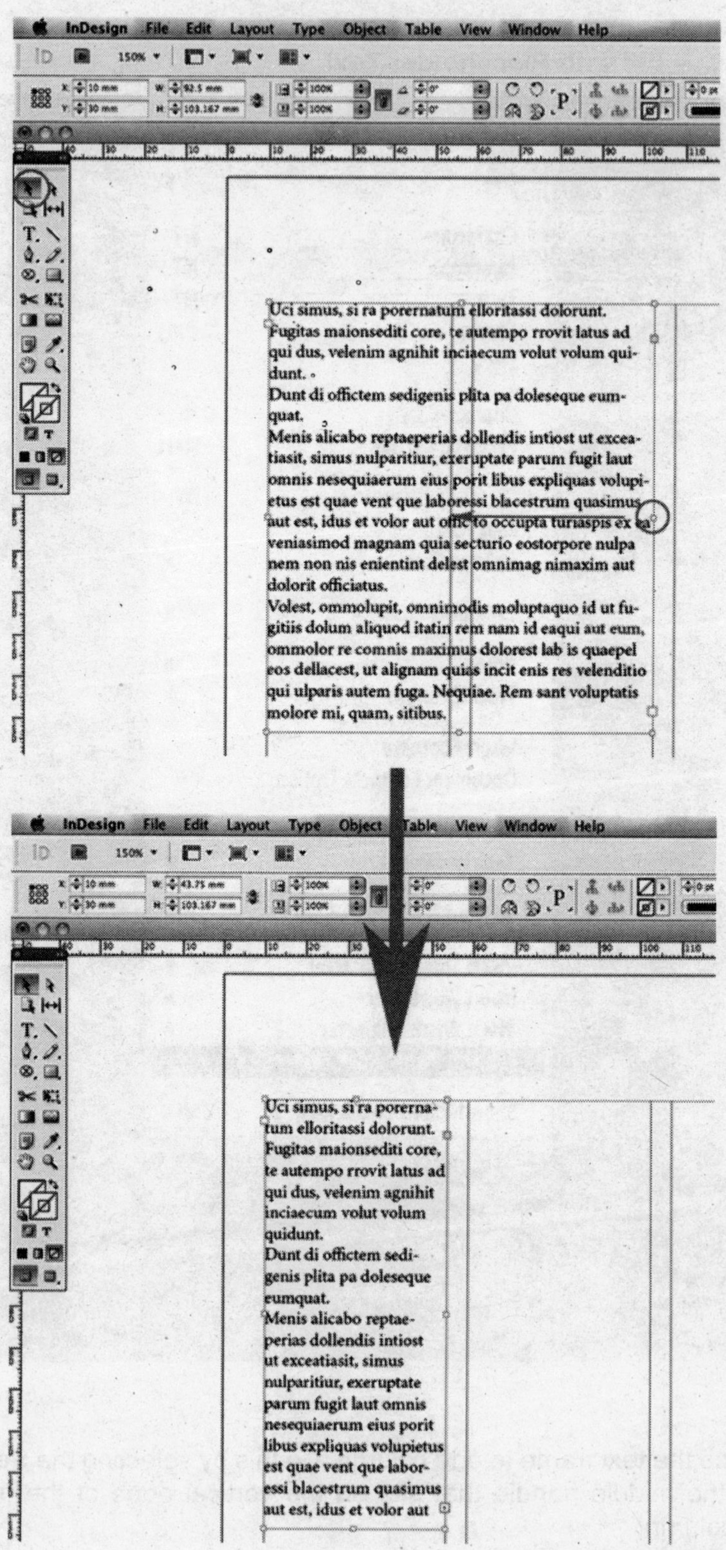
InDesign File Edit Layout Type Object Table View Window Help
Uci simus, si ra porernatum elloritassi dolorunt.
Fugitas maionsediti core, te autempo rrovit latus ad qui dus, velenim agnihit inciaecum volut volum quidunt.
Dunt di offictem sedigenis plita pa doleseque eumquat.
Menis alicabo reptaeperias dollendis intiost ut exceatiasit, simus nulparitiur, exeruptate parum fugit laut omnis nesequiaerum eius porit libus expliquas volupietus est quae vent que laboressi blacestrum quasimus aut est, idus et volor aut offic to occupta turiaspis ex ea veniasimod magnam quia secturio eostorpore nulpa nem non nis enientint delest omnimag nimaxim aut dolorit officiatus.
Volest, ommolupit, omnimodis moluptaquo id ut fugitiis dolum aliquod itatin rem nam id eaqui aut eum, ommolor re comnis maximus dolorest lab is quaepel eos dellacest, ut alignam quias incit enis res velenditio qui ulparis autem fuga. Nequiae. Rem sant voluptatis molore mi, quam, sitibus.
InDesign File Edit Layout Type Object Table View Window Help
Uci simus, si ra porernatum elloritassi dolorunt.
Fugitas maionsediti core, te autempo rrovit latus ad qui dus, velenim agnihit inciaecum volut volum quidunt.
Dunt di offictem sedigenis plita pa doleseque eumquat.
Menis alicabo reptaeperias dollendis intiost ut exceatiasit, simus nulparitiur, exeruptate parum fugit laut omnis nesequiaerum eius porit libus expliquas volupietus est quae vent que laboressi blacestrum quasimus aut est, idus et volor aut

Step 5

You will notice that a red box containing a crosshair has appeared at the bottom right hand side of the frame. This indicates that there is text overflowing and missing from view. Now draw another text frame as detailed in step two.

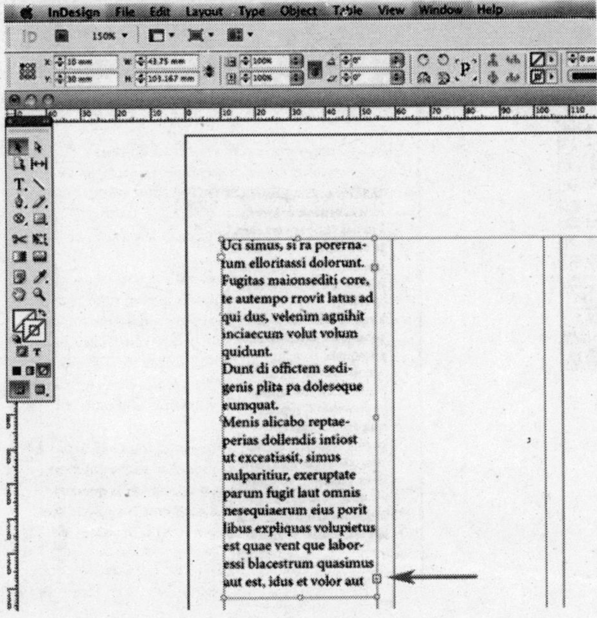

Step 6

Using the **Selection** tool, click once on the **red box** in the first frame. You will notice that the cursor will change its appearance to a thread icon and a small preview paragraph will appear, the text is now ready for threading.

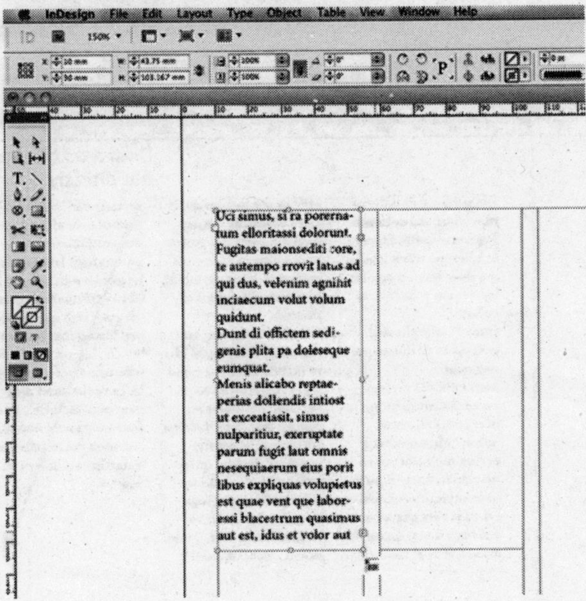

Step 7

With the cursor still loaded, hover over the second text frame, the cursor will change to a link icon. Click once and watch as the text is flowed into the second frame.

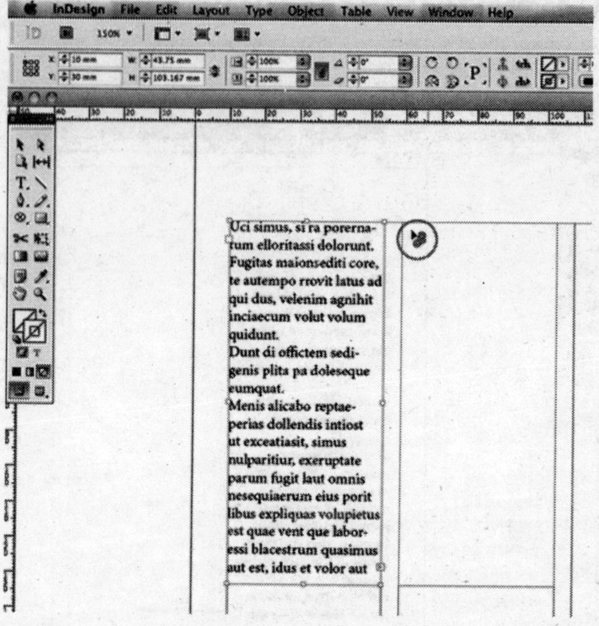

Step 8

At this point you might still be left with an indicating red box on the second text frame. Instead of creating a new text frame with the text frame tool, select the **Selection** tool, click on the **red box** and click and draw a frame with the loaded cursor. The new frame will contain the reminder of the text.

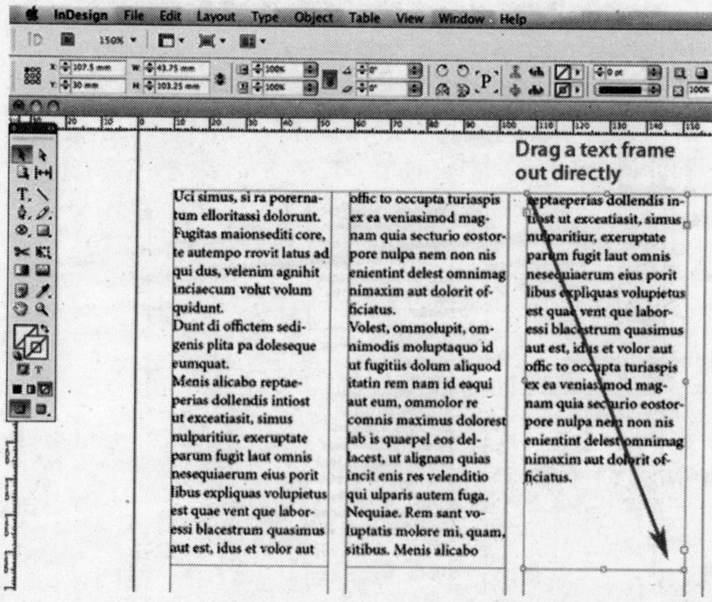

Step 9

To view text threads go to **View → Extras → Show Text Threads**

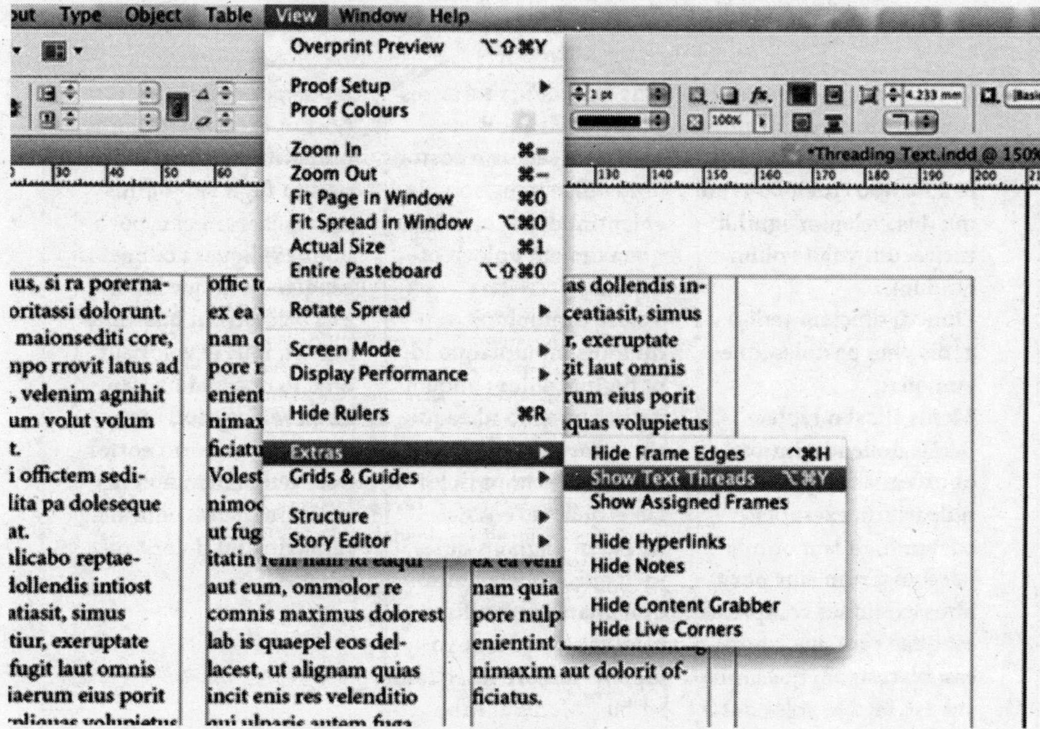

Viewing threads can be useful when working with text heavy documents.

Step 10

To undo a thread use the **selection** tool and double click on the in-port of the text frame you wish to unthread.

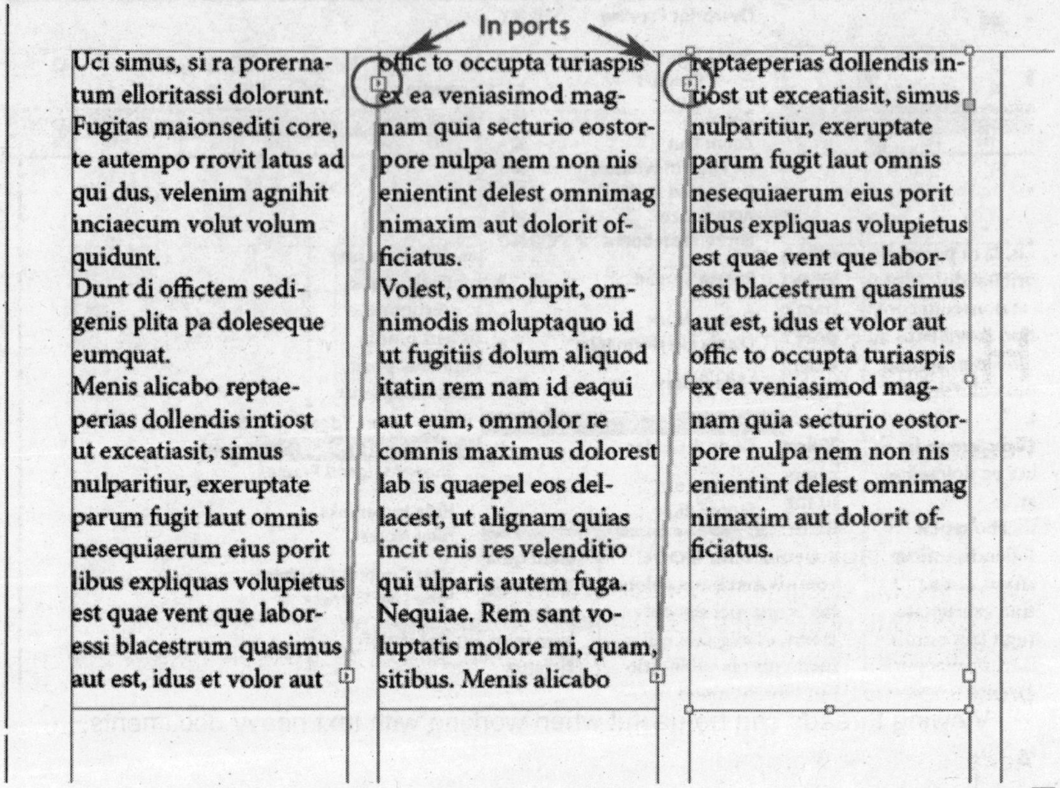

In ports

Uci simus, si ra porerna-
tum elloritassi dolorunt.
Fugitas maionsediti core,
te autempo rrovit latus ad
qui dus, velenim agnihit
inciaecum volut volum
quidunt.
Dunt di offictem sedi-
genis plita pa doleseque
eumquat.
Menis alicabo reptae-
perias dollendis intiost
ut exceatiasit, simus
nulparitiur, exeruptate
parum fugit laut omnis
nesequiaerum eius porit
libus expliquas volupietus
est quae vent que labor-
essi blacestrum quasimus
aut est, idus et volor aut

offic to occupta turiaspis
ex ea veniasimod mag-
nam quia secturio eostor-
pore nulpa nem non nis
enientint delest omnimag
nimaxim aut dolorit of-
ficiatus.
Volest, ommolupit, om-
nimodis moluptaquo id
ut fugitiis dolum aliquod
itatin rem nam id eaqui
aut eum, ommolor re
comnis maximus dolorest
lab is quaepel eos del-
lacest, ut alignam quias
incit enis res velenditio
qui ulparis autem fuga.
Nequiae. Rem sant vo-
luptatis molore mi, quam,
sitibus. Menis alicabo

reptaeperias dollendis in-
tiost ut exceatiasit, simus
nulparitiur, exeruptate
parum fugit laut omnis
nesequiaerum eius porit
libus expliquas volupietus
est quae vent que labor-
essi blacestrum quasimus
aut est, idus et volor aut
offic to occupta turiaspis
ex ea veniasimod mag-
nam quia secturio eostor-
pore nulpa nem non nis
enientint delest omnimag
nimaxim aut dolorit of-
ficiatus.

23
HTML and Web Page Designing

HTML is a standard markup language used to create web pages. HTML stands for Hypertext Markup Language.

Features of HTML

- It is a **markup language**.
- A markup language contains a **set of markup tags**.
- The tags describe **document content**.
- HTML documents contain **HTML tags** and **plain text**.
- HTML documents are also called **web pages**.

The only thing you need to make a website is a browser and a simple word processor, such as Notepad.

You can get the Notepad by clicking on: **Start ➢ All Programs ➢ Accessories ➢ Notepad**.

HTML Tags

- HTML markup tags are usually called HTML tags.
- HTML tags are keywords (tag names) surrounded by angle brackets like <html>.
- HTML tags normally come in pairs like <p> and </p>.
- The first tag in a pair is the start tag, the second tag is the end tag.
- The end tag is written like the start tag, with a slash </> before the tag name.
- Start and end tags are also called opening tags and closing tags <tagname>content</tagname>.

HTML Elements

In HTML, most elements are written with a start tag (e.g. <p>) and an end tag (e.g. </p>), with the content in between: <p>This is a paragraph</p>.

Web Browsers

The purpose of a web browser (such as Google Chrome, Internet Explorer, Firefox, Safari) is to read HTML documents and display them as web pages. The browser does not display the HTML tags, but uses the tags to determine how the content of the HTML page is to be presented/displayed to the user.

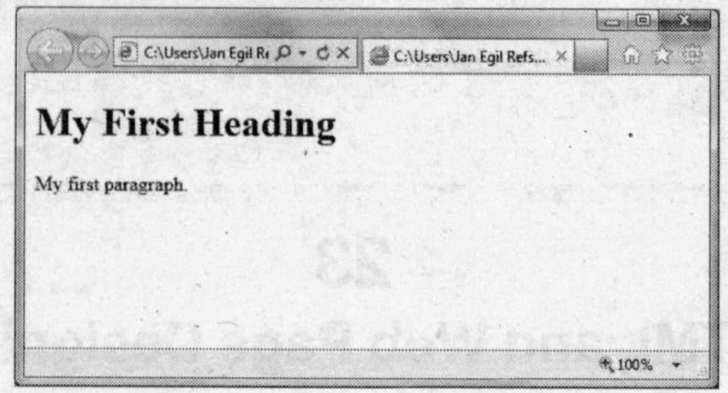

HTML Page Structure

Below is a visualization of an HTML page structure:

```
<html>
<body>
<h1>This is a heading.</h1>
<p>This is a paragraph.</p>
<p>This is another paragraph.</p>
</body>
</html>
```

1. Open **Notepad**.

To open Notepad in Windows 7 or earlier versions:

Click on **Start** ➢ **All Programs** ➢ **Accessories** ➢ **Notepad**.

To open Notepad in Windows 8 or later versions:

Open the **Start Screen** (the window symbol at the bottom left on your screen) ➢ Type **Notepad**.

2. Write or copy some HTML into Notepad.

Example:

```
<!DOCTYPE html>
<html>
<body>
<h1>My First Heading</h1>
<p>My first paragraph.</p>
</body>
</html>
```

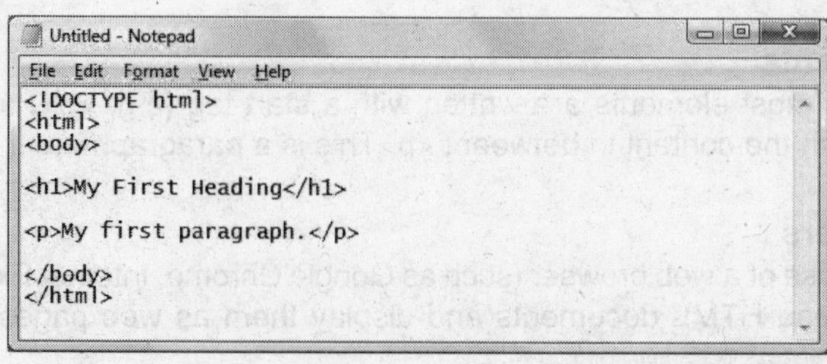

3. Save the HTML Page.

To save the file on your computer: Select **File ➢ Save as** in the **Notepad menu**.

When saving an HTML file, use either the **.htm** or the **.html** file extension. There is no difference. It is entirely up to you.

4. View HTML Page in your Browser.

Double-click on your **saved HTML file**, and the result will look much like this:

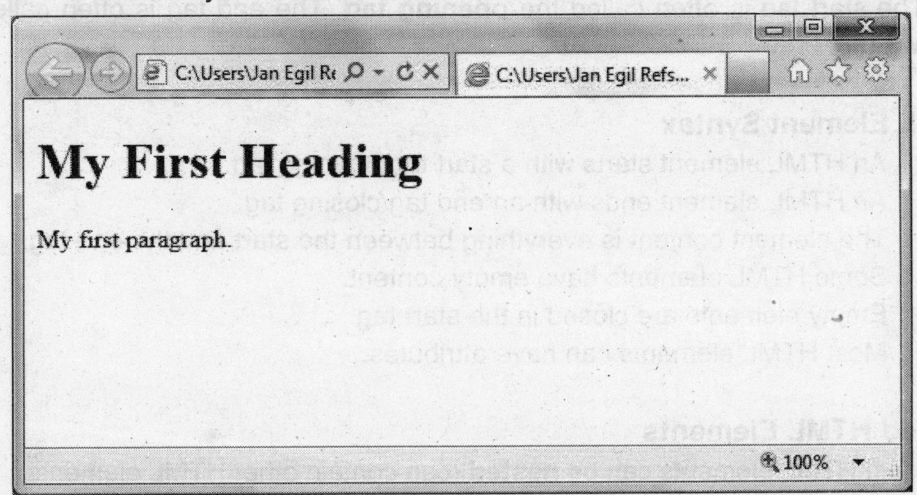

HTML Headings

HTML headings are defined with the <h1> to <h6> tags.

Example:

```
<h1>This is a heading</h1>
<h2>This is a heading</h2>
<h3>This is a heading</h3>
```

HTML Paragraphs

HTML paragraphs are defined with the <p> tag.

Example:

```
<p>This is a paragraph</p>.
<p>This is another paragraph</p>.
```

HTML Links

HTML links are defined with the <a> tag.

Example:

```
<a href="http://www.w3schools.com">This is a link</a>.
```

HTML Images

HTML images are defined with the <img> tag.

Example:

```
<img src="w3schools.jpg" alt="W3Schools.com" width="104" height="142">.
```

HTML Elements

An HTML element is everything from the start tag to the end tag.

Start tag*	Element content	End tag*
<p>	This is a paragraph	</p>
<a href='default.htm'>	This is a link	</a>

The start tag is often called the **opening tag**. The end tag is often called the **closing tag**.

HTML Element Syntax

- An HTML element starts with a start tag/opening tag.
- An HTML element ends with an end tag/closing tag.
- The element content is everything between the start and the end tag.
- Some HTML elements have empty content.
- Empty elements are closed in the start tag.
- Most HTML elements can have attributes.

Nested HTML Elements

Most HTML elements can be **nested** (can contain other HTML elements). HTML documents consist of nested HTML elements.

HTML Document

Example:

```
<!DOCTYPE html>
<html>
<body>
<p>This is my first paragraph.</p>
</body>
</html>
```

The example above contains 3 HTML elements.

HTML Example Explained

The <p> element:

<p>This is my first paragraph.</p>

The <p> element defines a paragraph in the HTML document.

The element has a start tag <p> and an end tag </p>.

The element content is:

This is my first paragraph.

The <body> element:

<body>

```
<p>This is my first paragraph.</p>
</body>
The <body> element defines the body of the HTML document.
The element has a start tag <body> and an end tag </body>.
The element content is another HTML element (a p element).
The <html> element:
<html>
<body>
<p>This is my first paragraph.</p>
</body>
</html>
The <html> element defines the whole HTML document.
The element has a start tag <html> and an end tag </html>.
The element content is another HTML element (the body element).
```

Don't Forget the End Tag

Some HTML elements might display correctly even if you forget the end tag:

```
<p>This is a paragraph
<p>This is a paragraph
```

The example above works in most browsers, because the closing tag is considered optional.

But, it is advised that you never rely on this. Many HTML elements will produce unexpected results and/or errors if you forget the end tag.

Empty HTML Elements

HTML elements with no content are called empty elements.

 is an empty element without a closing tag. (The <br> tag defines a line break.)

HTML Attributes

Attributes provide additional information about HTML elements.

- HTML elements can have attributes.
- Attributes provide additional information about an element.
- Attributes are always specified in the start tag.
- Attributes come in name/value pairs like: name ="value".

Attribute Example

HTML links are defined with the <a> tag. The link address is specified in the href attribute.

Example:

```
<a href="http://www.w3schools.com">This is a link</a>
```

HTML Headings

- Headings are important in HTML documents.
- Headings are defined with the <h1> to <h6> tags.
- <h1> defines the most important heading. <h6> defines the least important heading.

Example:

```
<h1>This is a heading</h1>
<h2>This is a heading</h2>
<h3>This is a heading</h3>
```

HTML Lines

The <hr> tag creates a horizontal line in an HTML page.

The hr element can be used to separate content:

Example:

```
<p>This is a paragraph.</p>
<hr>
<p>This is a paragraph.</p>
<hr>
<p>This is a paragraph.</p>
```

HTML Paragraphs

Paragraphs are defined with the <p> tag.

Example:

```
<p>This is a paragraph</p>
<p>This is another paragraph</p>
```

Browsers automatically add an empty line before and after a paragraph.

HTML Line Breaks

Use the <br> tag if you want a line break (a new line) without starting a new paragraph.

Example:

```
<p>This is<br>a para<br>graph with line breaks</p>
```

HTML Text Formatting

- **This text is bold**
- *This text is italic*
- This is `computer output`
- This is $_{\text{subscript}}$ and ^{superscript}

HTML Formatting Tags

HTML uses tags like <b> and <i> for formatting output, like bold or italic text.

These HTML tags are called formatting tags.
Here is a list of HTML Text Formatting Tags.

Tag	Description
<p>	Defines bold text
<em>	Defines emphasized text
<i>	Defines a part of text in an alternate voice or mood
<small>	Defines smaller text
<strong>	Defines important text
<sub>	Defines subscripted text
<sup>	Defines superscripted text
<ins>	Defines inserted text
<del>	Defines deleted text
<mark>	Defines marked/highlighted text

Example of a HTML:

```
<!DOCTYPE html>
<html>
<body>
<p><b>This text is bold</b></p>
<p><strong>This text is strong</strong></p>
<p><em>This text is emphasized</em></p>
<p><i>This text is italic</i></p>
<p><small>This text is small</small></p>
<p>This is<sub> subscript</sub> and <sup>superscript</sup></p>
</body>
</html>
```

Result:

- **This text is bold**
- **This text is strong**
- *This text is emphasized*
- This text is italic
- This text is small
- This is $_{\text{subscript}}$ and ^{superscript}

□

24
Networking

Windows 7 makes it a cinch to connect to home, work and wireless networks so that you can share your stuff, surf the web and get your work done practically anywhere.

At Home

HomeGroup is the easy way to connect the PCs running Windows 7 on your home network so you can automatically share printers and libraries (music, video, documents) with other people in your home. You can join a homegroup in any edition of Windows 7.

SET UP A NETWORK HOMEGROUP

HomeGroup is relatively easy to set up and can be useful when working with multiple computers.

1. Go to **Control Panel**, type **Home** in the search box, and when **HomeGroup** appears, select it.

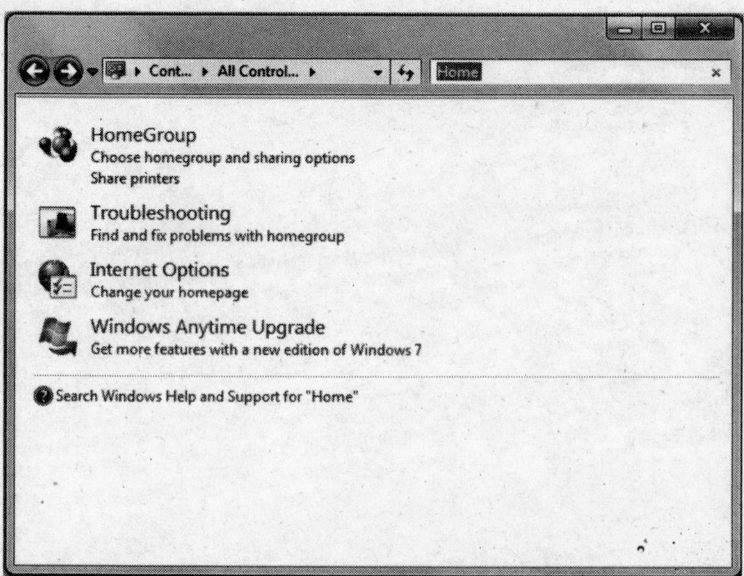

2. When the initial HomeGroup window appears, you will be informed that there is currently no HomeGroup on the network. You will also find a brief introduction to HomeGroup feature and several links.

3. Click on the **Create a Homegroup** button.

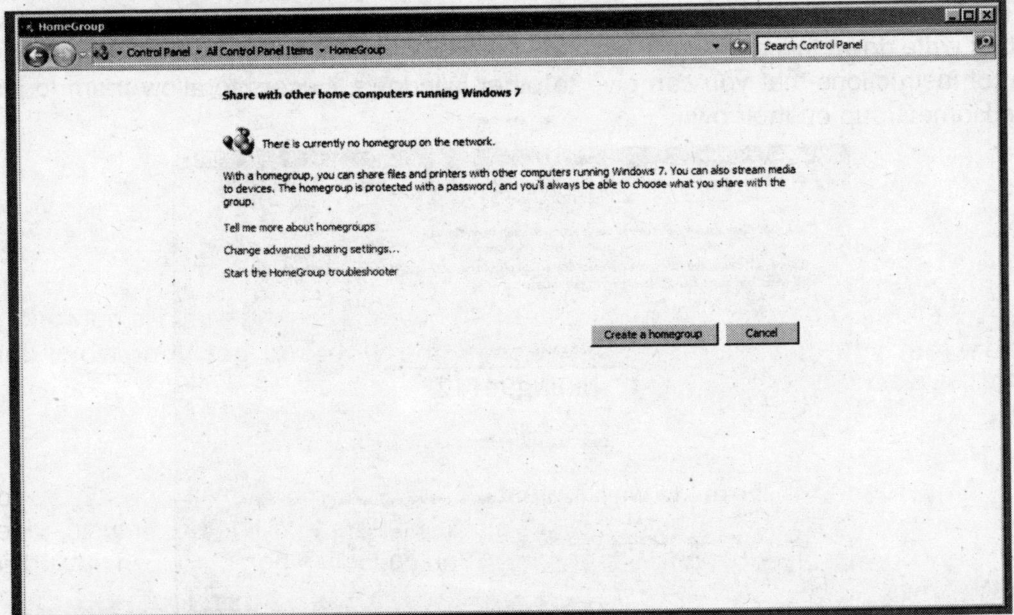

4. To launch the **Create a HomeGroup** wizard, click on the **Create a HomeGroup** button. When the first screen in the **Create a HomeGroup** wizard appears, you will be prompted to choose what libraries, or types of files, you want to share to the **HomeGroup**. You can also choose to share **printers**.

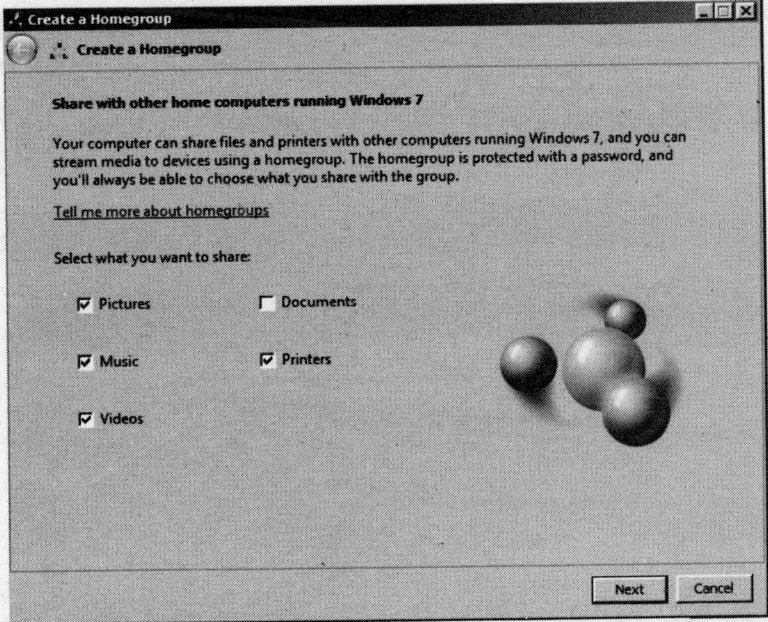

5. As you begin the process of creating the **HomeGroup**, you'll be prompted to choose what you want to share with other computers.

Once you choose what you want to share, Windows 7 will create the HomeGroup and you will then see the **HomeGroup password**. This is the password that other Windows 7 systems will need in order to **join and access** the **HomeGroup**. You can either write down this password or click on the **link** to print the password along with a set of instructions that you can give to other Windows 7 users to allow them to join the HomeGroup on their own.

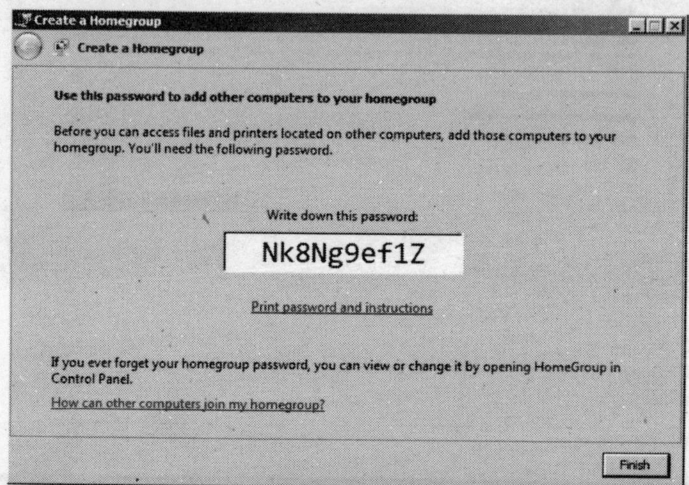

6. The second screen will provide the **password** that other Windows 7 systems will need to join the HomeGroup. When you click on **Finish**, you will see the **HomeGroup settings** window, where you can perform a host of additional operations related to the HomeGroup.

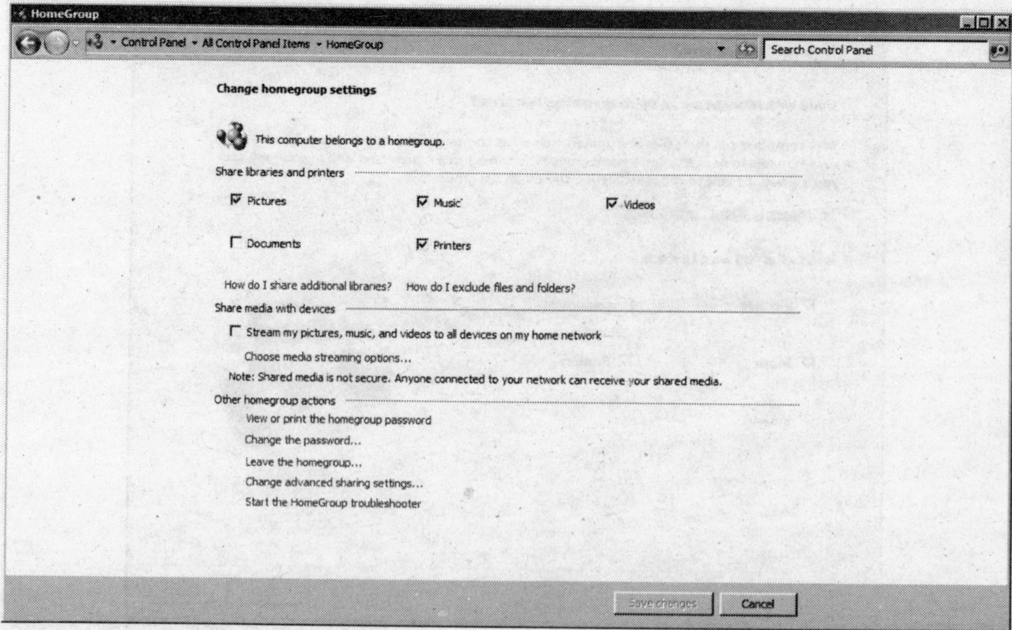

You can also use the settings in this window to perform a host of operations related to the HomeGroup.

SHARING FILES

The easiest way to share files on your network is to set up sharing with a homegroup. If you do not have a homegroup, you can share files by placing them in one of the **Public folders**. Any file or folder you put in a Public folder is automatically shared with the people connected to your network.

To turn on **Public folder sharing**, follow these steps:

Open **Advanced sharing settings** by clicking on the **Start** button, and then on the **Control Panel**.

1. In the search box, type **network**, click on **Network and Sharing Center**, and then in the left pane, click on **Change advanced sharing settings**.

2. Click on the **chevron** to expand the current network profile.

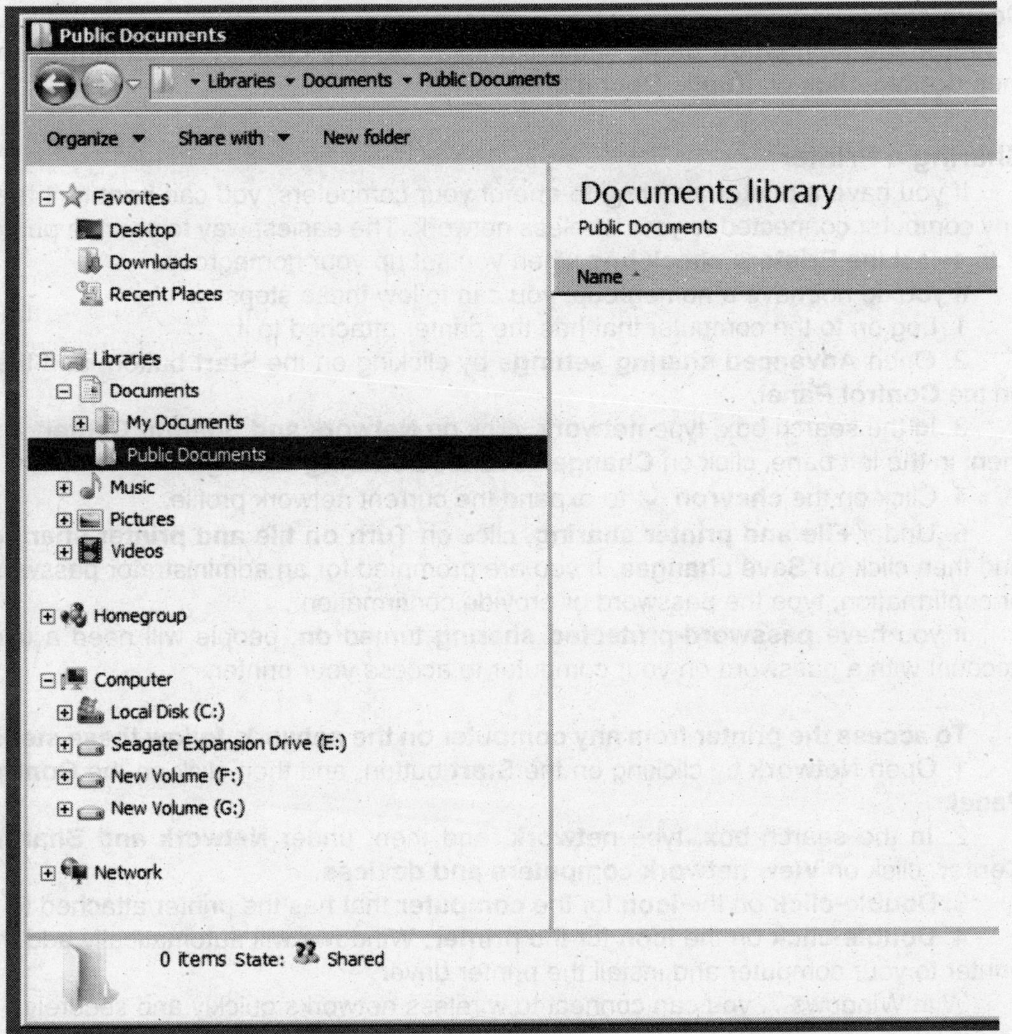

Under **Public folder sharing**, click on one of the following options:

1. **Turn on sharing so that anyone with network access can read and write files in the Public folders.**

2. **Turn off Public folder sharing (people logged on to this computer can still access these folders).**

3. Click on **Save changes**. If you are prompted for an administrator password or confirmation, type the password or provide confirmation.

4. You will need to repeat the previous steps on each computer that you want to share files from.

To share your files, save them or copy them to a **Public folder** on your computer. There is a **Public folder** for each type of library (Documents, Music, Videos, and Pictures).

Every person with a user account on the computer shares these folders. For example, to open the **Public Documents folder**:

1. Open the **Documents library** by clicking on the **Start** button, and then on **Documents**.

2. In the **navigation pane**, under Libraries, **double-click** on **Documents**, and then **double-click** on **Public Documents**.

Sharing a Printer

If you have a printer attached to one of your computers, you can print to it from any computer connected to your wireless network. The easiest way to share a printer is to select the **Printers check box** when you set up your homegroup.

If you do not have a homegroup, you can follow these steps:

1. Log on to the computer that has the printer attached to it.

2. Open **Advanced sharing settings** by clicking on the **Start** button, and then on the **Control Panel**.

3. In the search box, type **network**, click on **Network and Sharing Center**, and then, in the left pane, click on **Change advanced sharing settings**.

4. Click on the **chevron** ⌄ to expand the current network profile.

5. Under **File and printer sharing**, click on **Turn on file and printer sharing**, and then click on **Save changes**. If you are prompted for an administrator password or confirmation, type the password or provide confirmation.

If you have **password-protected sharing** turned **on**, people will need a user account with a password on your computer to access your printer.

To access the printer from any computer on the network, follow these steps:

1. Open **Network** by clicking on the **Start** button, and then click on the **Control Panel**.

2. In the search box, type **network**, and then, under **Network and Sharing Center**, click on **View network computers and devices**.

3. **Double-click** on the **icon** for the **computer** that has the printer attached to it.

4. **Double-click** on the **icon** for the **printer**. Windows will automatically add the printer to your computer and install the printer driver.

With Windows 7, you can connect to wireless networks quickly and securely.

Network Name (SSID)

- **Security type** (WEP and WPA are common types)
- **Encryption type** (Additional feature of some types of security)
- **Security key** or **passphrase**
- **Start this connection automatically** – Select this option if you want the computer to automatically log on when it is in range of the wireless network.
- To verify the wireless connection is complete, click on the available network icon to display a list of available wireless networks.

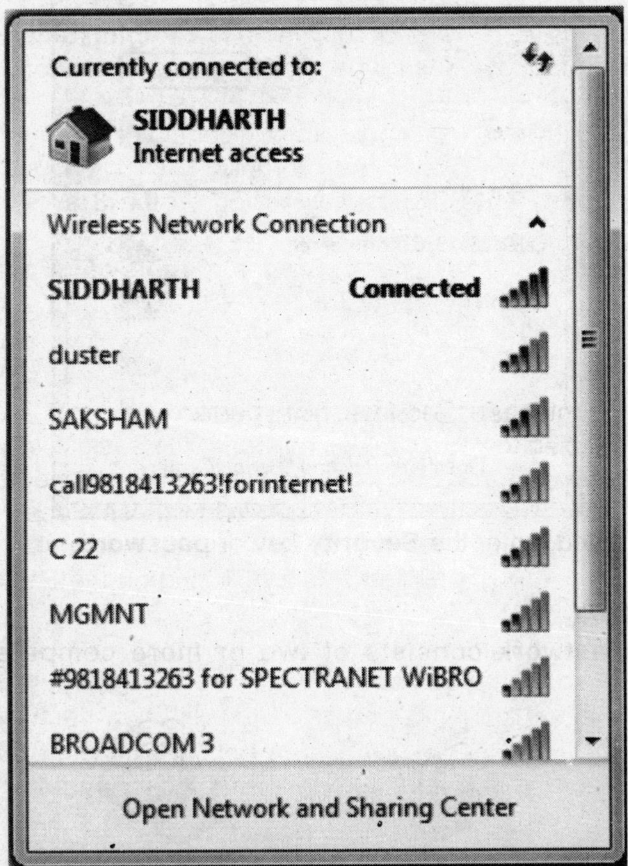

1. After you have set up a connection to your **home network**, or a **public WIFI network**, you can reconnect to that network at a later time.
2. If, during the original setup, you selected the **Start this connection automatically** option, the network connection will be made, using the values entered during the setup, when you bring your computer into the range of existing wireless network.
3. If you did not select the **automatic connection** option, do the following when the computer is within the range of the wireless network.
4. **Turn on** the **wireless device power** ⁽|⁾, and then click on the **network icon** in the **toolbar** to display a list of available wireless networks.

5. Select the desired network and click on **Connect**.

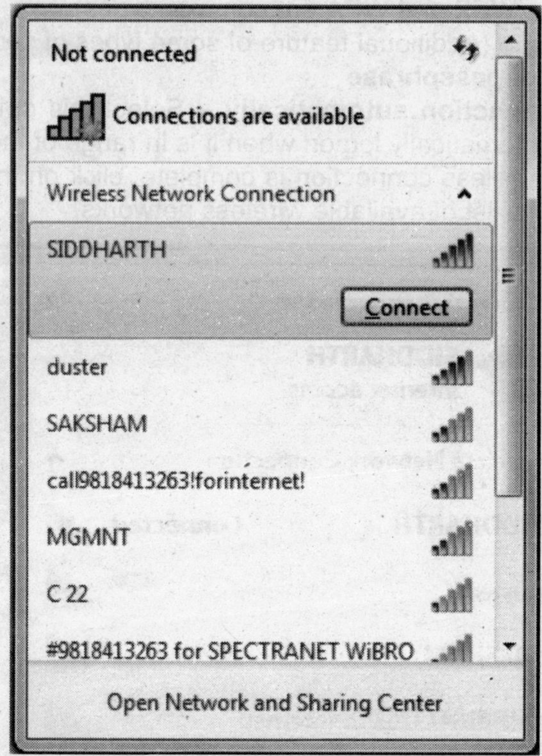

6. When prompted, enter the **Security key** or **password**.

Computer Network

A computer network consists of two or more computers intended to share resources.

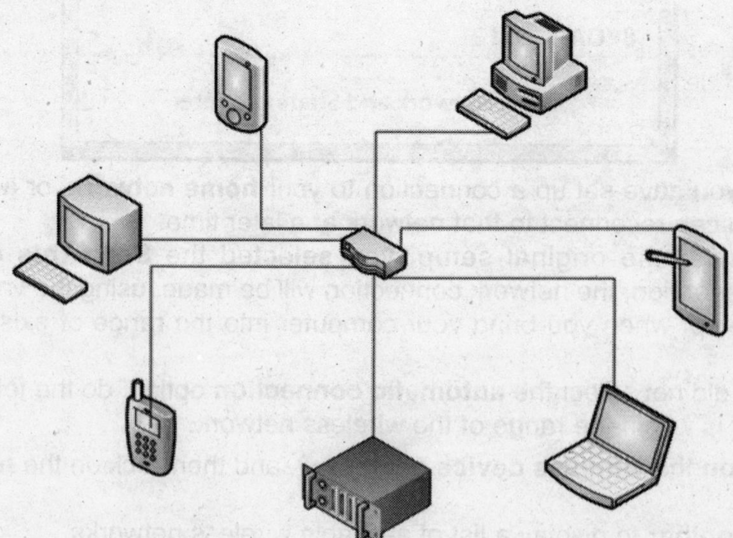

Peer-to-Peer Network

A peer-to-peer (P2P) network is created when two or more PCs are connected and share resources without going through a separate server computer. A P2P network can be an ad hoc connection, i.e. a couple of computers connected via a Universal Serial Bus to transfer files. A P2P network also can be a permanent infrastructure that links a half a dozen of computers in a small office over copper wires. Or a P2P network can be a network on a much grander scale in which special protocols and applications set up direct relationships among users over the Internet.

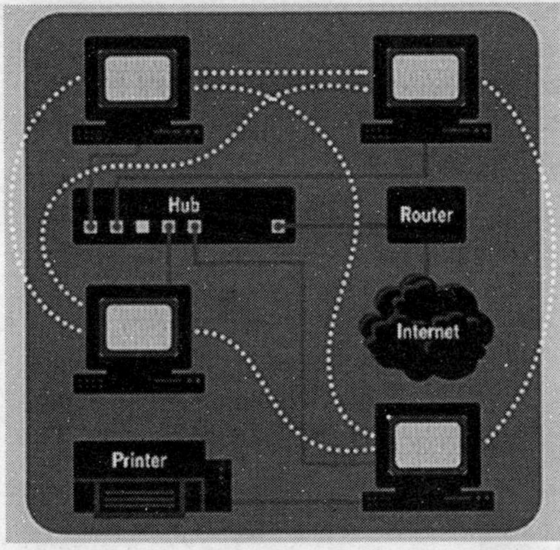

Client/Server Network

A client/server network is a system where one or more computers called 'clients' connect to a central computer named a 'server' to share or use resources. Each client computer must use an operating system that allows it to be identified to participate in the network.

A computer network is referred to as client/server if, at least one of the computers is used to 'serve' other computers referred to as 'clients'. Besides the computers, other types of devices can be part of the network.

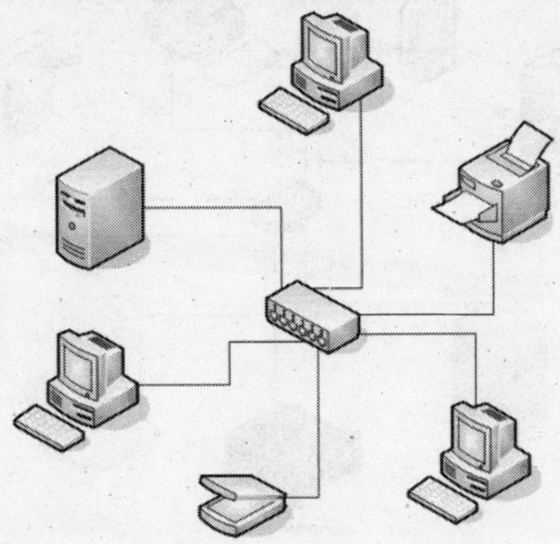

In a client/server environment, each computer still holds, or can still hold its (or some) resources and files. Other computers can also access the resources stored in a computer, as in a peer-to-peer scenario. One of the particularities of a client/server network is that the files and resources are centralized. This means that a computer, the server, can hold them and other computers can access them. Since the server is always ON, the client machines can access the files and resources without caring whether a certain computer is ON.

One of the consequences of a client/server network is that, if the server is turned OFF, its resources and sometimes most of the resources on the network are not available. In fact, one way to set up a client/server network is to have more than one server. In this case, each server can play a different role.

To access the network, a person, called a user must provide some credentials, such as a username and a password.

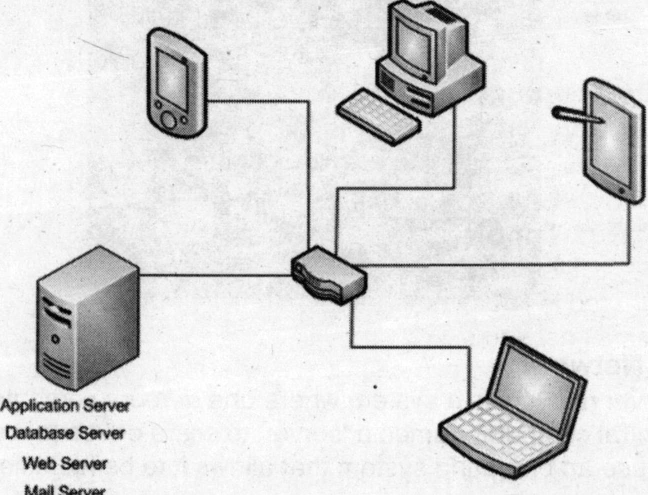

In a medium to large network, there can be many servers with each performing a different task.

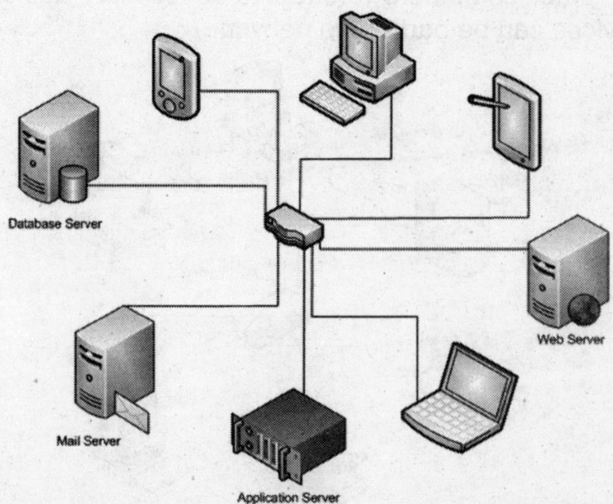

TYPES OF NETWORK TOPOLOGY

Network Topology is the schematic description of a network arrangement, connecting various nodes (sender and receiver) through lines of connection.

1. BUS Topology

Bus topology is a network type where every computer and network device is connected to single cable.

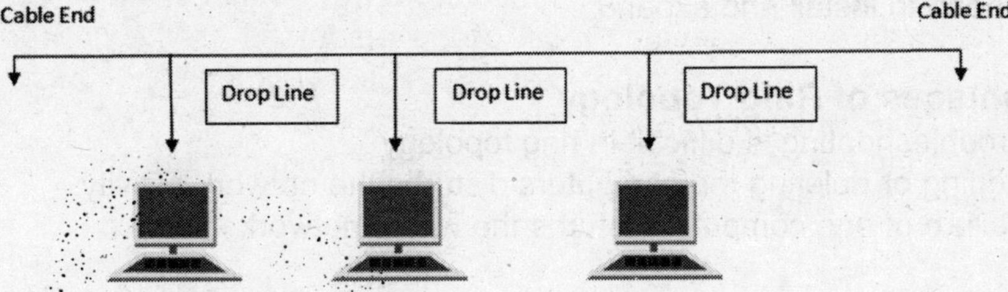

Features of Bus Topology

- It transmits data only in one direction.
- Every device is connected to a single cable

Advantages of Bus Topology

- It is cost effective.
- Cable required is least compared to other network topology.
- Used in small networks.
- Easy to expand joining two cables together.

Disadvantages of Bus Topology

- Cables fails then whole network fails.
- If network traffic is heavy or nodes are more, the performance of the network decreases.
- Cable has a limited length.
- It is slower than the ring topology.

2. RING Topology

A ring topology is called so because it forms a ring as each computer is connected to another computer, with the last one connected to the first.

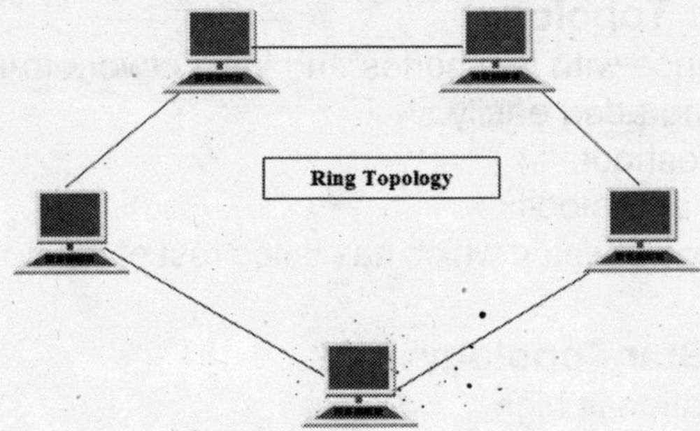

Features of Ring Topology

- A number of repeaters are used and the transmission is unidirectional.
- Date is transferred in a sequential manner that is bit by bit.

Advantages of Ring Topology

- Transmitting network is not affected by high traffic or by adding more nodes, as only the nodes having tokens can transmit data.
- Cheap to install and expand

Disadvantages of Ring Topology

- Troubleshooting is difficult in ring topology.
- Adding or deleting the computers disturbs the network activity.
- Failure of one computer disturbs the whole network.

3. STAR Topology

In this type of topology, all the computers are connected to a single hub through a cable. This hub is the central node and all others nodes are connected to the central node.

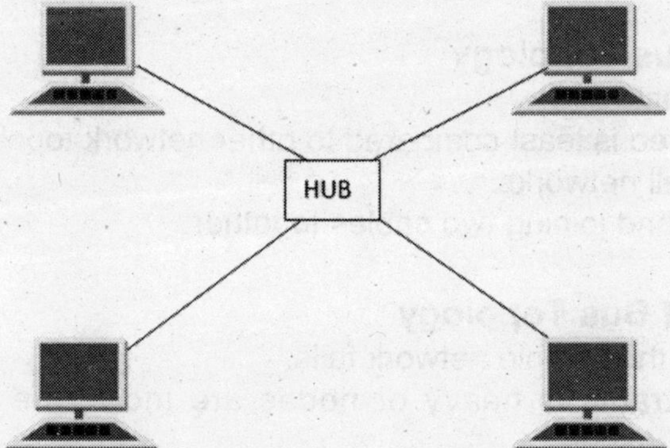

Features of Star Topology

- Every node has its own dedicated connection to the hub.
- Acts as a repeater for data flow.
- Can be used with twisted pair, Optical Fibre or coaxial cable.

Advantages of Star Topology

- Fast performance with few nodes and low network traffic.
- Hub can be upgraded easily.
- Easy to troubleshoot.
- Easy to setup and modify.
- Only that node is affected which has failed rest of the nodes can work smoothly.

Disadvantages of Star Topology

- Cost of installation is high.

- Expensive to use.
- If the hub is affected then the whole network is stopped because all the nodes depend on the hub.
- Performance is based on the hub that is it depends on its capacity

4. MESH Topology

It is a point-to-point connection to other nodes or devices. Traffic is carried only between two devices or nodes to which it is connected. Mesh has n (n-2)/2 physical channels to link hn devices.

Types of Mesh Topology

- Partial Mesh Topology: In this topology, some of the systems are connected in the same fashion as mesh topology but some devices are only connected to two or three devices.
- Full Mesh Topology: Each and every nodes or devices are connected to each other.

Features of Mesh Topology

- Fully connected.
- Robust.
- Not flexible.

Advantages of Mesh Topology

- Each connection can carry its own data load.
- It is robust.

- Fault is diagnosed easily.
- Provides security and privacy.

Disadvantages of Mesh Topology

- Installation and configuration is difficult.
- Cabling cost is more.
- Bulk wiring is required.

5. TREE Topology

It has a root node and all other nodes are connected to it forming a hierarchy. It is also called hierarchical topology. It should at least have three levels to the hierarchy.

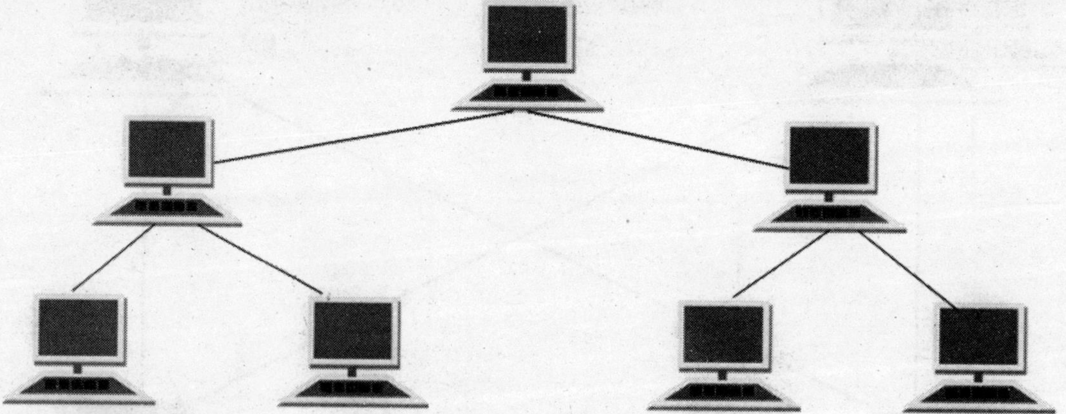

Features of Tree Topology

- Ideal if workstations are located in groups.
- Used in Wide Area Network.

Advantages of Tree Topology

- Extension of bus and star topologies.
- Expansion of nodes is possible and easy.
- Easily managed and maintained.
- Error detection is easily done.

Disadvantages of Tree Topology

- Heavily cabled.
- Costly.
- If more nodes are added maintenance is difficult.
- If the central hub fails, the whole network fails.

6. HYBRID Topology

It is two different types of topologies which is a mixture of two or more topologies. For example, if in an office in one department ring topology is used and in another star topology is used, connecting these topologies will result in Hybrid Topology (ring topology and star topology).

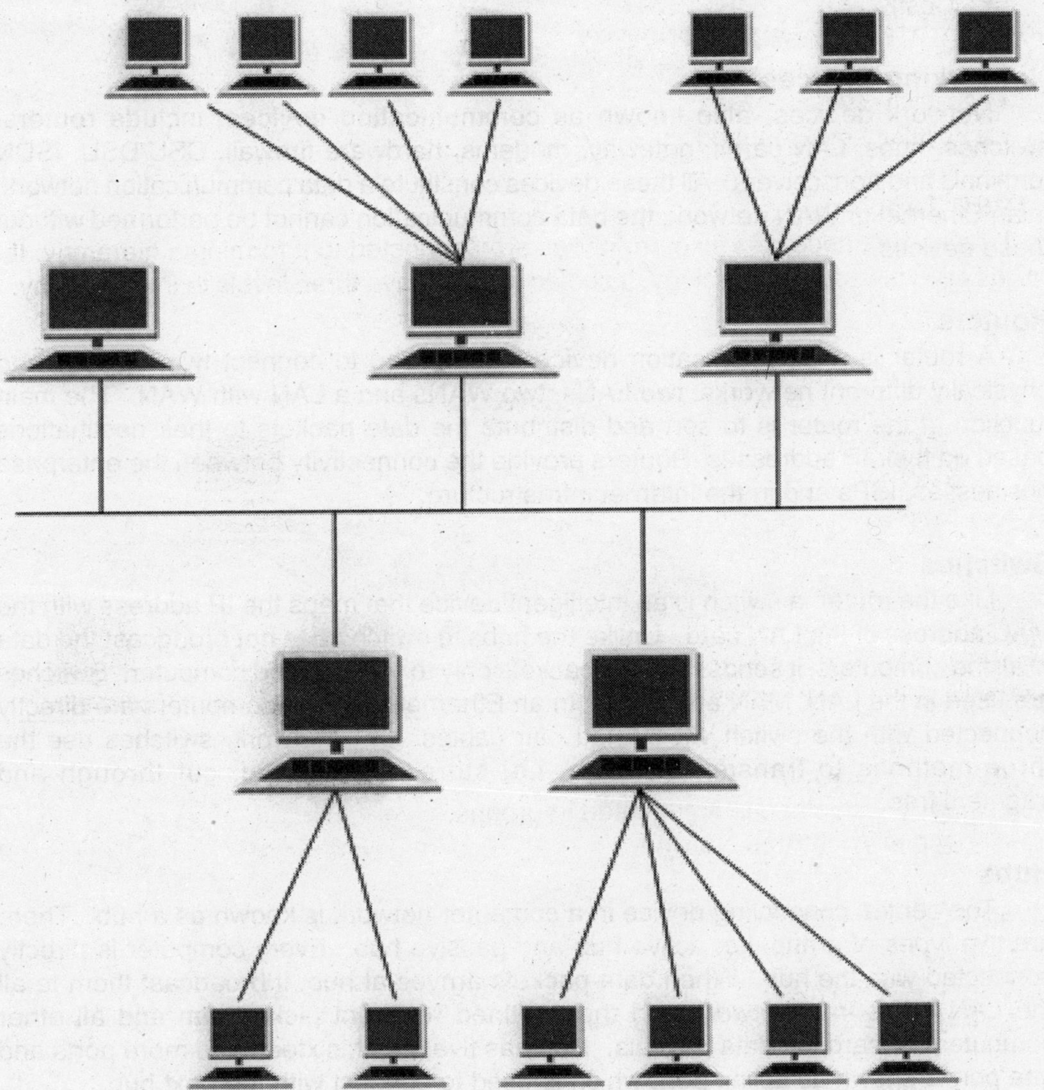

Features of Hybrid Topology

- It is a combination of two or topologies.
- Inherits the advantages and disadvantages of the topologies included.

Advantages of Hybrid Topology

- Reliable as Error detecting and trouble shooting is easy.
- Effective.
- Scalable as size can be increased easily.
- Flexible.

Disadvantages of Hybrid Topology

- Complex in design.
- Costly.

Networking Devices

Network devices, also known as communication devices, include routers, switches, hubs, LAN cards, gateway, modems, hardware firewall, CSU/DSU, ISDN terminals and transceivers. All these devices constitute a data communication network. In an Ethernet or WAN network, the data communication cannot be performed without these devices.

Routers

A router is a communication device that is used to connect two logically and physically different networks, two LANs, two WANs and a LAN with WAN. The main function of the router is to sort and distribute the data packets to their destinations based on their IP addresses. Routers provide the connectivity between the enterprise businesses, ISPs and in the internet infrastructure.

Switches

Like the router, a switch is an intelligent device that maps the IP address with the MAC address of the LAN card. Unlike the hubs, a switch does not broadcast the data to all the computers; it sends the data packets only to the destined computer. Switches are used in the LAN, MAN and WAN. In an Ethernet network, computers are directly connected with the switch via twisted pair cables. In a network, switches use the three methods to transmit the data, i.e. store and forward, cut through and fragment free.

Hubs

The central connecting device in a computer network is known as a hub. There are two types of a hub, i.e. active hub and passive hub. Every computer is directly connected with the hub. When data packets arrives at hub, it broadcast them to all the LAN cards in a network and the destined recipient picks them and all other computers discard the data packets. Hub has five, eight, sixteen and more ports and one port is known as uplink port, which is used to connect with the next hub.

Modems

A modem is a communication device that is used to provide the connectivity with the internet. Modem works in two ways, i.e. modulation and demodulation. It converts the digital data into the analog and analog to digital.

LAN Cards

LAN cards or network adapters are the building blocks of a computer network. No computer can communicate without a properly installed and configured LAN card. Every LAN card is provided with a unique IP address, subnet mask, gateway and

DNS. An UTP/STP cable connects a computer with the hub or switch. LAN cards are inserted into the expansion slots inside the computer. Different LAN cards support different speed from 10/100 to 10/1000.

Multiplexer

Multiplexer is a device that is used to combine the several electrical signals into one signal.

TCP/IP

TCP/IP — (Transmission Control Protocol/Internet Protocol) is the basic communication language or protocol of the Internet. It can also be used as a communications protocol in a private network (either an intranet or an extranet). When you are set up with direct access to the Internet, your computer is provided with a copy of the TCP/IP program just as every other computer that you may send messages to or get information from also has a copy of TCP/IP.

TCP/IP is a two-layer program. The higher layer, Transmission Control Protocol, manages the assembling of a message or file into smaller packets that are transmitted over the Internet and received by a TCP layer that reassembles the packets into the original message. The lower layer, Internet Protocol, handles the address part of each packet so that it gets to the right destination. Each gateway computer on the network checks this address to see where to forward the message.

TCP/IP uses the client/server model of communication in which a computer user (a client) requests and is provided a service (such as sending a Web page) by another computer (a server) in the network. TCP/IP communication is primarily point-to-point, meaning each communication is from one point (or host computer) in the network to another point or host computer.

WAP

WAP (Wireless Application Protocol) is a secure specification that allows users to access information instantly via handheld wireless devices, such as mobile phones, pagers, two-way radios, smartphones and communicators. WAP supports most wireless networks. These include CDPD, CDMA, GSM, PDC, PHS, TDMA, FLEX, ReFLEX, iDEN, TETRA, DECT, DataTAC and Mobitex.

WAP is supported by all operating systems. Ones specifically engineered for handheld devices include PalmOS, EPOC, Windows CE, FLEXOS, OS/9 and JavaOS. WAPs that use displays and access the Internet run what are called micro browsers, which are browsers with small file sizes that can accommodate the low memory constraints of handheld devices and the low-bandwidth constraints of a wireless-handheld network. WAP supports both HTML and XML languages.

Intranet

Intranet is the generic term for a collection of private computer networks within an organization. An intranet uses network technologies as a tool to facilitate communication between people or work groups to improve the data sharing capability and overall knowledge base of an organization's employees. Intranets utilize standard network hardware and software technologies, like Ethernet, Wi-Fi, TCP/IP, Web browsers and Web servers.

Firewall

A firewall is a system designed to prevent unauthorized access to or from a private network. Firewalls can be implemented in both hardware and software, or a combination of both. Firewalls are frequently used to prevent unauthorized Internet users from accessing private networks connected to the Internet, especially intranets. All messages entering or leaving the intranet pass through the firewall, which examines each message and blocks those that do not meet the specified security criteria.

Firewalls can be either hardware or software but the ideal firewall configuration will consist of both. In addition to limiting access to your computer and network, a firewall is also useful for allowing remote access to a private network through secure authentication certificates and logins.

Hardware firewalls are typically found in broadband routers and most hardware firewalls have a minimum of four network ports to connect other computers.

Software firewalls are installed on your computer (like any software) and you can customize it; allowing you some control over its function and protection features. A software firewall will protect your computer from outside attempts to control or gain access your computer.

Types of Firewall in Network Security

Firewalls are used to protect both home and corporate networks. A typical firewall program or hardware device filters all information coming through the Internet to your network or computer system. There are several types of firewall techniques that will prevent potentially harmful information from getting through.

Packet Filter

It looks at each packet entering or leaving the network and accepts or rejects it based on user-defined rules. Packet filtering is fairly effective and transparent to users, but it is difficult to configure. In addition, it is susceptible to IP spoofing.

Application Gateway

It applies security mechanisms to specific applications, such as FTP and Telnet servers. This is very effective, but can impose a performance degradation.

Circuit-level Gateway

It applies security mechanisms when a TCP or UDP connection is established. Once the connection has been made, packets can flow between the hosts without further checking.

Proxy Server

It intercepts all messages entering and leaving the network. The proxy server effectively hides the true network addresses.

Next Generation Firewall (NGFW)

It is a newer class of firewalls which filters network and internet traffic based upon the applications or traffic types using specific ports. Next Generation Firewalls (NGFWs) blend the features of a standard firewall with quality of service (QoS) functionalities in order to provide smarter and deeper inspection.

Wireless Networking

The term 'wireless networking' refers to technology that enables two or more computers to communicate using standard network protocols, but without network cabling.

There are two kinds of wireless networks:

1. An ad-hoc, or peer-to-peer wireless network consists of a number of computers, each equipped with a wireless networking interface card. Each computer can communicate directly with all of the other wireless enabled computers. They can share files and printers this way, but may not be able to access wired LAN resources, unless one of the computers acts as a bridge to the wired LAN using special software. (This is called 'bridging').

In Ad-Hoc or Peer-to Peer Networking, each computer with a wireless interface can communicate directly with all of the others.

2. A wireless network can also use an access point, or base station. In this type of network, the access point acts like a hub, providing connectivity for the wireless computers. It can connect (or 'bridge') the wireless LAN to a wired LAN, allowing wireless computer access to LAN resources, such as file servers or existing internet connectivity.

There are two types of access points:

- Dedicated hardware access points (HAP) offer comprehensive support of most wireless features, but check your requirements carefully.

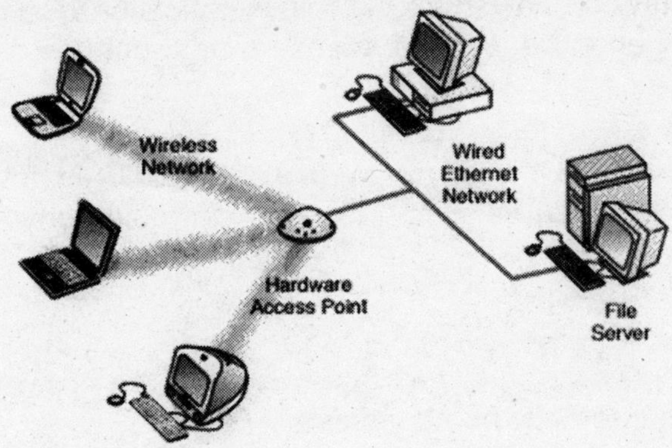

Wireless connected computers using a Hardware Access Point.

- Software Access Points run on a computer equipped with a wireless network interface card as used in an ad-hoc or peer-to-peer wireless network.

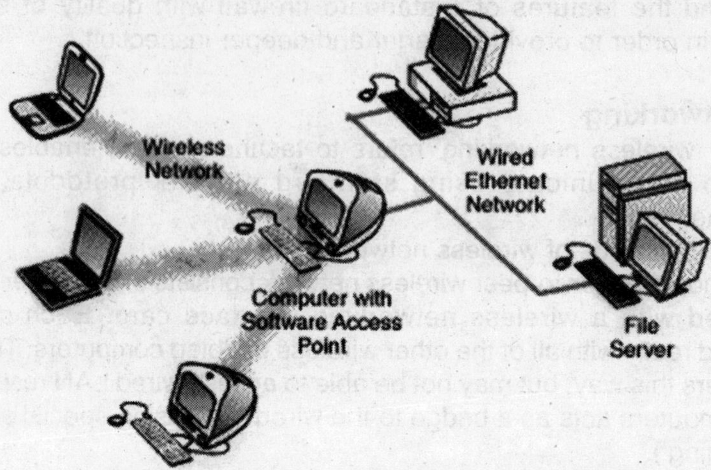

Wireless connected computers using a Software Access Point.

□

25
An Introduction to Internet

The Internet is the largest computer network in the world, connecting millions of computers. A network is a group of two or more computer systems linked together.

There are two main types of computer networks:

Local Area Network (LAN): A LAN is two or more connected computers sharing certain resources in a relatively small geographic location, often in the same building. Examples include home networks and office networks.

Wide Area Network (WAN): A WAN typically consists of two or more LANs. The computers are farther apart and are linked by telephone lines, dedicated telephone lines, or radio waves. The Internet is the largest Wide Area Network (WAN) in existence.

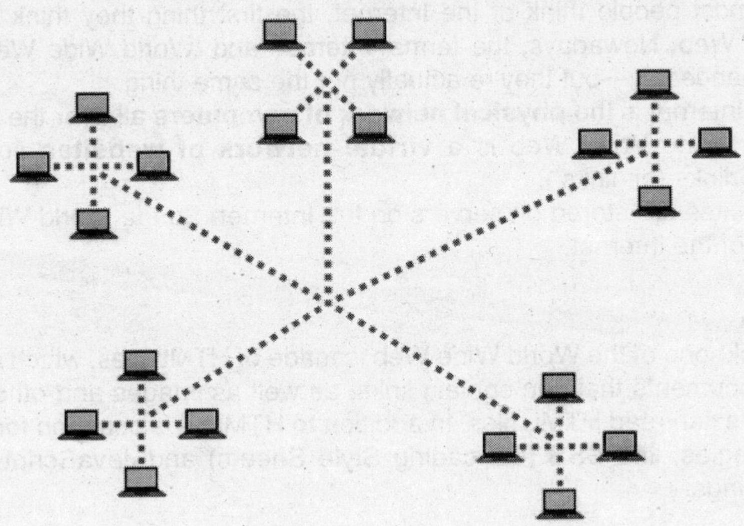

Servers and Clients

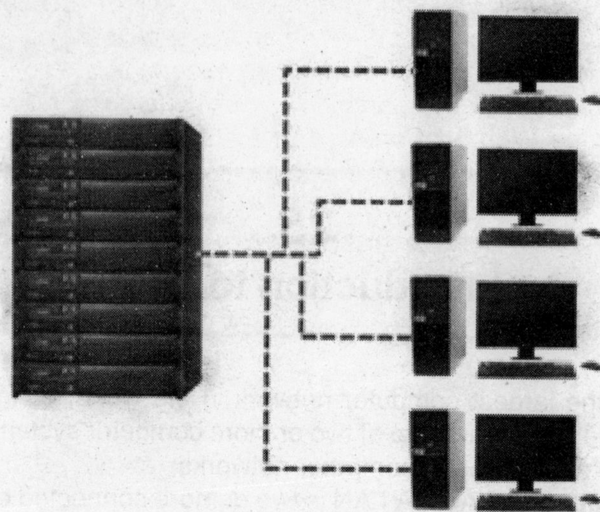

You may have heard someone say something like 'The server is down' or 'We are having problems with the e-mail server'.

A server is a computer that 'serves' many different computers in a network by running specialised software and storing information. For example, web pages are stored on servers.

When you access a web page, your computer is acting as a client. A client runs familiar software, such as web browsers or e-mail software, and it communicates with the server to get the information it requires.

In order for your browser to display a web page, it requests data from the server where the page is stored. The server processes the request and then sends the data to your browser, where it is displayed.

World Wide Web

When most people think of the Internet, the first thing they think about is the World Wide Web. Nowadays, the terms 'Internet' and 'World Wide Web' are often used interchangeably—but they're actually not the same thing.

- The Internet is the **physical network of computers** all over the world.
- The World Wide Web is a **virtual network of websites** connected by hyperlinks (or 'links').
- Websites are stored on servers on the Internet. So the World Wide Web is a part of the Internet.

HTML

The backbone of the World Wide Web is made of HTML files, which are specially formatted documents that can contain links, as well as images and other media. All web browsers can read HTML files. In addition to HTML, it is common for websites to use technologies, like CSS (Cascading Style Sheets) and JavaScript to do more advanced things.

URL

To get to a web page, you can type the URL (Uniform Resource Locator) into a browser. The URL, also known as the web address, tells the browser exactly where to find the page. However, most of the time people get to a web page by following a link from a different page, or by searching for the page using a search engine.

The World Wide Web was created in 1989 by Tim Berners-Lee, a software engineer. Before then, computers could communicate over the Internet, but there were no web pages.

Tim Berners-Lee

As the Internet has grown, it has developed into a multi-faceted tool with a vast range of uses. It is now easy to keep in touch with friends, publish your own articles, or even watch your favourite TV shows using the Internet.

Types of Internet Service

There are many different ways of connecting to the Internet:

Dial-up

This connection is slower than other Internet connection types. It connects through existing phone lines using a dial-up modem. We must dial up to connect to the Internet and disconnect when done.

DSL

This connection is called **Broadband** and are much faster than dial-up connection. It connects through phone lines, but does not necessarily require phone service. It does not require dialing up and can be kept 'Always on'.

Cable

This is also a broadband connection and much faster than dial-up and DSL. It uses cable connection and does not require dialling up.

Satellite

This is a broadband connection, faster than dial-up, but data are delayed. So, it is not good for real-time applications like gaming or videoconferencing. It connects via satellites orbiting the earth and does not require phone or cable lines.

3G and 4G

This connection is available for mobile phones, computers and tablets. It connects wirelessly through the service provider's 3G or 4G network and allows access to the Internet anywhere without a Wi-Fi connection.

Choosing an ISP

Once you have decided which type of Internet access you are interested in, you can determine which ISPs are available in your area that offer the type of Internet access you want. Then you will need to purchase Internet service from one of the available ISPs.

Below are some things to consider related to ISPs:

- Speed
- Price
- Ease of installation
- Service record
- Technical support
- Contract terms

The primary piece of hardware you need to access Internet is a **modem**.

The type of Internet access you choose will determine which type of modem you need. Dial-up access uses a telephone modem, DSL service uses a DSL modem, cable access uses a cable modem, and satellite service uses a satellite adapter. The ISPs usually give a modem during connection.

Router

A router is a hardware device that allows you to connect several computers and other devices to a single Internet connection, which is known as a home network. Many routers are wireless that allow you to easily create a wireless network.

Network Card

A network card is a piece of hardware that allows computers to communicate over a computer network. Most newer computers have a network card built into the motherboard, so it is probably not something you will need to purchase. The network card will have an Ethernet port, a wireless connection, or both.

Web Browsers

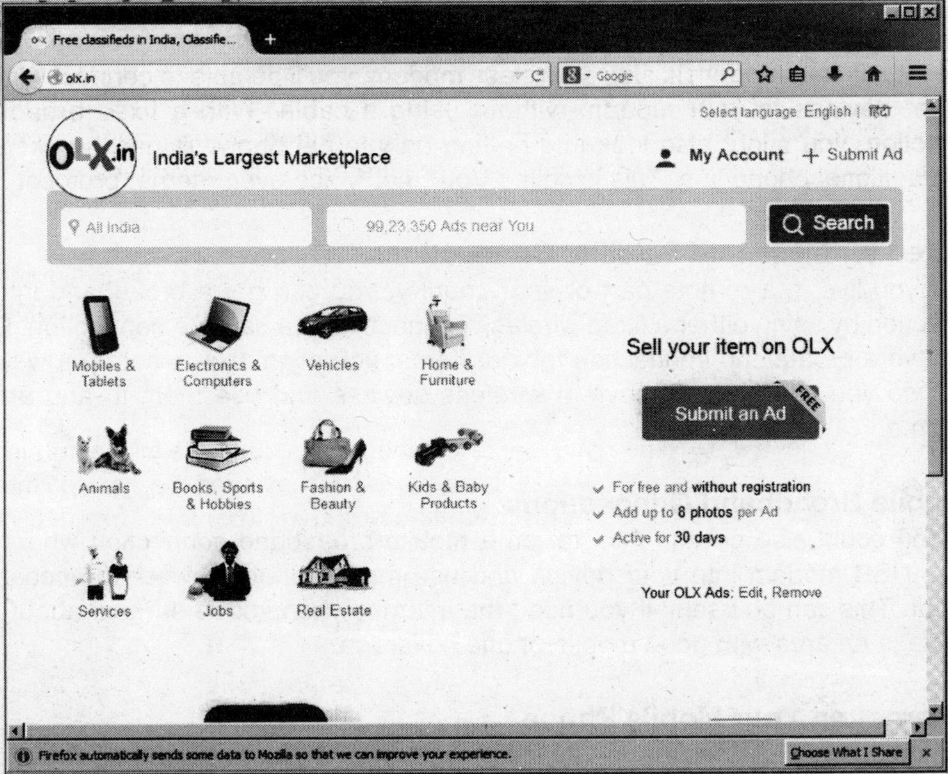

A web browser is the tool you use to access the World Wide Web. The browser's main job is to display web pages. It also lets you create bookmarks (sometimes called Favorites) for sites you like, so you can easily find them again later.

TYPES OF INTERNET CONNECTIONS

There are lots of ways to connect devices like mobile phones and computers to the internet.

1. Dial-up Connections

To get a dial-up connection, your computer will dial a phone number using your telephone line. This type of connections need a modem to connect to the internet and you pay for a call each time you dial-up. Dial-up connections are really slow compared to broadband, and are usually too slow for streaming video and making voice or video calls on the internet.

2. Broadband Connections

Broadband is a high-speed internet connection. Unlike dial-up, with broadband your phone line is not tied up. You can make a phone call and be on the internet at the same time. With broadband, you can watch live news and sport, download and share large files quickly and shop or bank online more easily.

3. Fixed Broadband Connections

A fixed broadband connection is a permanent connection to the internet. If you've got fixed broadband at home, you'll have a broadband modem that you can plug a cable into. If your modem is also a wireless modem, you'll be able to connect wireless internet devices to your modem without using a cable. With a fixed broadband connection, you might also look into getting an internet phone rather than keeping your traditional phone line. This is called VoIP, i.e. 'voice over internet protocol'.

4. Fixed Wireless and Satellite Connections

If you live in a remote part of your country, you can get a broadband internet connection by using either a fixed wireless connection or a satellite connection. Once you have a broadband connection to your home, you might like to set up a wireless router so you can connect several wireless devices and use them in and around the home.

5. Mobile Broadband Connections

You could also get the internet on a mobile broadband connection where you plug a USB modem into your device and use mobile phone towers to access the internet. This can be useful if you need the internet when you're out and about, or if you live in an area with good mobile phone coverage.

6. Internet on Your Mobile Phone

Many mobile phones let you access the internet if you've signed up for internet in your mobile phone plan. 'Smartphones' are mobile phones that are like small computers. They have software on them to make it easier for you to surf the internet, check email and use social networking sites.

7. Wireless Hotspots

If you're out and about with an internet device like a laptop, tablet or smartphone, you might want to connect at a wireless hotspot. Wireless 'hotspots' are in places like libraries and cafés, which offer you free access to their broadband connection. You need to be a member of the library or a customer at a café to get the password for the wireless connection.

Local Area Network (LAN)

A local area network (LAN) is a computer network that spans a relatively small area. Most LANs are confined to a single building or group of buildings; however, one LAN can be connected to other LANs over any distance via telephone lines and radio waves. A system of LANs connected in this way is called a wide area network (WAN). Most LANs connect workstations and personal computers. LANs are capable of transmitting data at very fast rates, much faster than data can be transmitted over a telephone line; but the distances are limited, and there is also a limit on the number of computers that can be attached to a single LAN.

Types of LANs

There are many different types of LANs. Ethernets are the most common LANs for PCs.

The following characteristics differentiate one LAN from another:

- **Topology:** It means the geometric arrangement of devices on the network. For example, devices can be arranged in a ring or in a straight line.
- **Protocols:** These are rules and encoding specifications for sending data. The protocols also determine whether the network uses a peer-to-peer or client/ server architecture.
- **Media:** These are devices that can be connected by twisted-pair wire, coaxial cables, or fiber optic cables. Some networks do without connecting media altogether, communicating instead via radio waves.

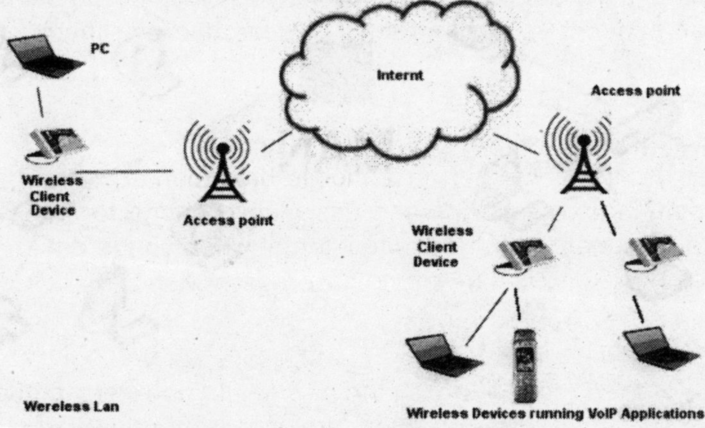

Wide Area Network (WAN)

A wide area network (WAN) is a kind of computer network that spans a relatively large geographical area. Typically, a WAN consists of two or more local area networks (LANs). Computers connected to a wide area network are often connected through public networks, such as the telephone system. They can also be connected through leased lines or satellites. The largest WAN in existence is the Internet.

A WAN spans a large geographic area, such as a state, province or country. WANs often connect multiple smaller networks, such as local area networks (LANs) or metro area networks (MANs).

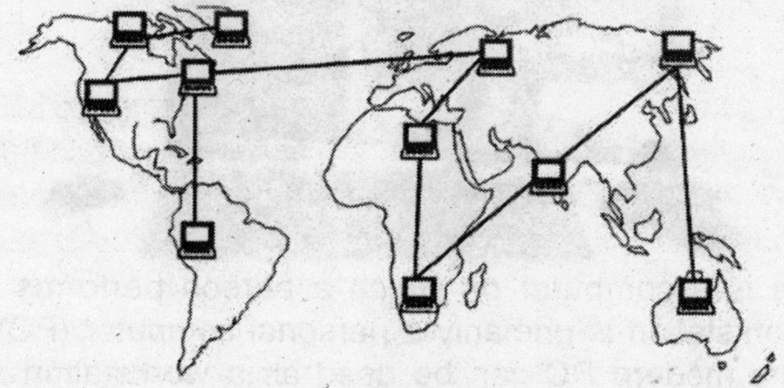

Wide area network

Metropolitan Area Network (MAN)

A metropolitan area network (MAN) is a kind of data network designed for a town or city. It is a kind of network that interconnects users with computer resources in a geographic area or region larger than that covered by even a large local area network (LAN) but smaller than the area covered by a wide area network (WAN). Thus, we can say that MANs are larger than local area networks (LANs), but smaller than wide area networks (WANs).

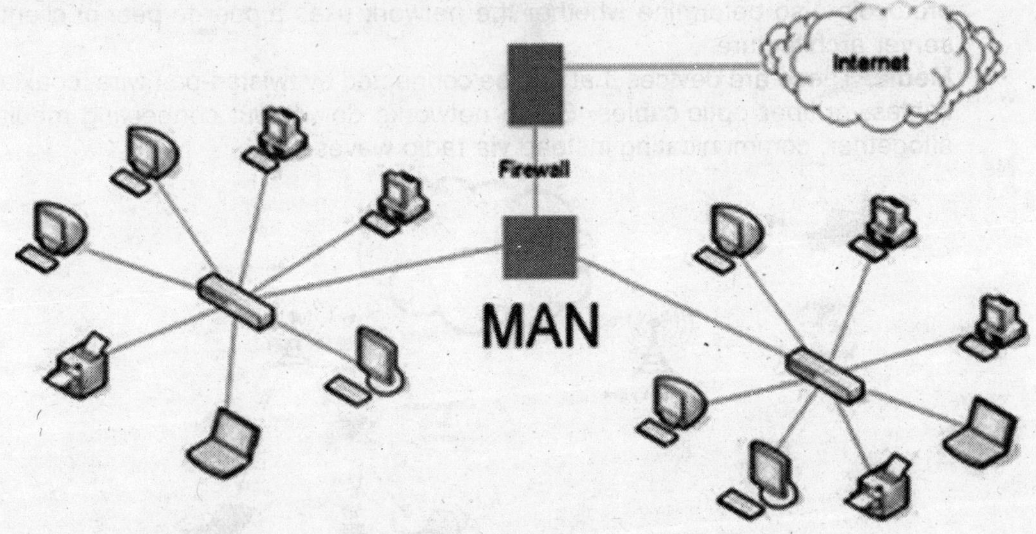

Network Hardware

In a network, computers and other devices are connected to share resources. When a computer or device — 'A' is requesting a resource from another computer or device — 'B', the item 'A' is referred to as a client. Because all or most items that are part of a network live in association or cooperation, almost any one of them can be referred to as a client. Based on this, there can be different types of clients.

A workstation is a computer on which a person performs everyday regular assignments. A workstation is primarily a personal computer (PC). It can also be a laptop. Almost any modern PC can be used as a workstation and participate to a network.

Before building a computer network, you should plan it. In some cases, you may want to use one or more computers you already have.

Network Distribution

Building a network consists partly of connecting the computers.

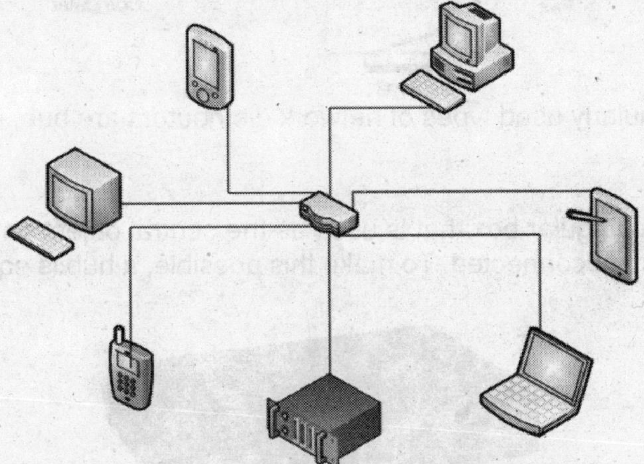

Besides the computers, you will use other objects.

Network Cables

Cable is used to connect computers. The most commonly used cable is referred to as Category 5 cable RJ-45. The ends of the cable appear as follows:

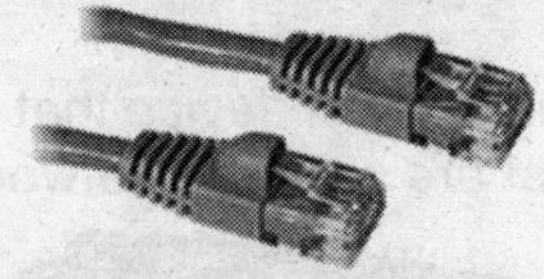

Network Distributors

You can connect one computer to another using their serial ports.

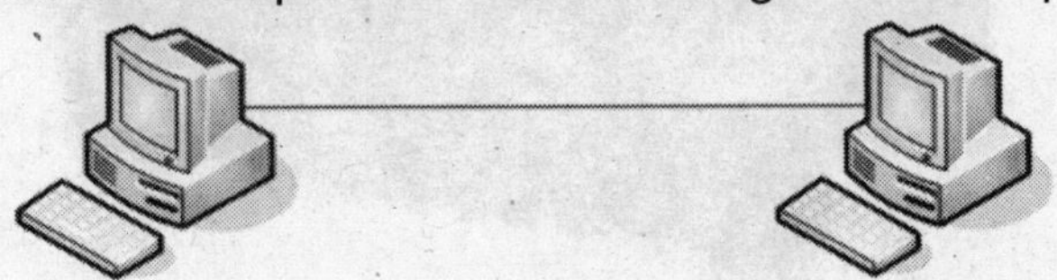

This is possible because almost every computer has a serial port. If you have to connect many computers to produce a network, this serial connection would not be practical. The solution is to use a central object that the computers and other resources can connect to, and then this object becomes responsible to 'distribute' or manage network traffic.

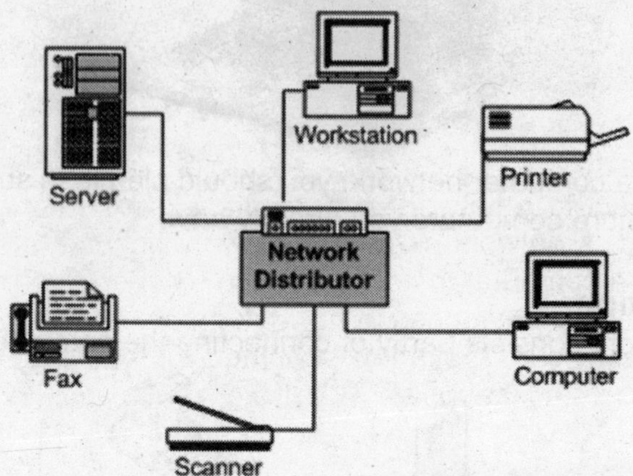

The most regularly used types of network distributors are hub, router and switch.

Hub

A hub is a rectangular box that is used as the central object on which computers and other devices are connected. To make this possible, a hub is equipped with small holes called ports.

A hub can be equipped with 4, 5, 12, or more ports depending on its type. When configuring a hub, you connect an RJ-45 cable from the network card of a computer to one port of the hub.

Routers

Like a hub, a router is another type of device that acts as the central point among computers and other devices that are part of a network.

A router functions a little differently than a hub. Like a hub, the computers and other devices are connected to a router using network cables. To make this possible, a router is equipped with holes, called ports, in the back.

Wired Network Cards

In order to connect to a network, a computer must be equipped with a device called a network card. A network card, or a network adapter, also called a network interface card allows a computer to connect to the exterior.

There are roughly two categories of network cards: internal and external.

An internal network card looks like a printed circuit board with some objects 'attached' or 'glued' to it and it appears as follows:

The area where you add a network card in your computer is called a slot. One of the most important characteristics of a network card is the speed it can use to carry information (data). The speeds are either 10 or 100 Mbps (megabits per second).

An external network card can be used or installed externally. This can be done using USB.

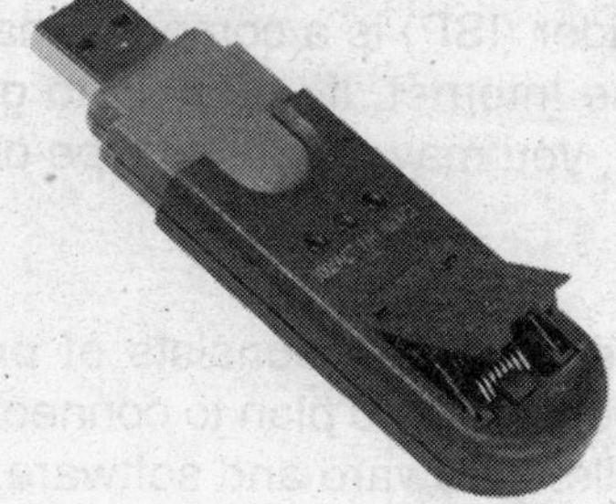

Wireless Network Cards

Instead of using a wired network card, you can use a wireless network card. Most laptops already have a wireless card built-in so you may not have to acquire one.

A wireless network card is not difficult to install. The physical installation of a wireless network card follows the same rules as that of a wired network card.

Besides the wireless network cards that can be installed inside the computer, you can use external cards. These are installed using a USB port.

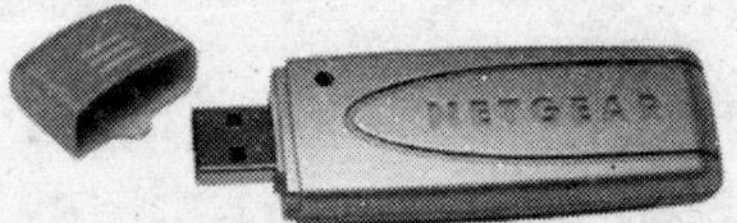

These adapters, like most USB objects, are easy to connect and use. Like the other hardware parts, when you connect these, the computer detects them and helps you get them ready for use.

Network Accessories

Printers

If you attach a printer to one computer and share it, when that computer is off, nobody can print. An alternative is to purchase a network printer. That is, a printer that will directly connect to the network and people can print to it any time.

There are two types of printers in this case:

- Some printers come equipped with a network card. In this case, you can use an RJ-45 cable to connect it to a router or a hub. Most printers nowadays have a USB port that can be used to connect them to a router.
- Many printers come equipped with wireless capability. This means that the computers can connect to the printer without using a wire and they can print.

Internet Service Provider (ISP)

An Internet Service Provider (ISP) is a company that serves as the intermediary between your network and the Internet. If you plan to give access to the Internet to the members of your network, you may need this type of company.

Firewall

Firewall is a security measure that consists of protecting your network from intruders. This is primarily important if you plan to connect your network to the Internet. There are two types of firewalls: hardware and software.

Setting Up Your Internet Connection

You can use the instructions provided by your ISP (or included with the modem) to set up your Internet connection. Depending on what type of service you have, your ISP may need to send a technician to your house to turn on the connection.

After you have everything set up, you can open your web browser and begin using the Internet. If you have any problems with your Internet connection, you can call your ISP's technical support number.

A web browser is the tool you use to access the World Wide Web. In order to get the most out of the Web, it is important to understand the various features of a browser.

- Nowadays, **Chrome** and **Internet Explorer** are the most popular web browsers. Other browsers include **Firefox, Safari** and **Opera**. Each one has its own look and feel, but they have the same goal: to display web pages correctly. For most web pages, any well-known browser will work.
- Browsers use a **Graphical User Interface (GUI)**, which means you can navigate by pointing and clicking with a mouse instead of just typing. Some devices like mobile phones use different types of GUIs, such as touchscreens.

Address Bar

Browsers have an address bar that shows the web address (also called a URL) of the page you are on. To go to a different page, you can type an address in the address bar and then press Enter (or Return).

Links

Most of the time, you will get to a different page by clicking on a link. A link can be text or an image, and it's usually formatted to stand out so you know to click on it. Many text links are blue, and they may also be underlined.

A link may lead to another web page, or it could lead to a document, video, or any other type of file. If you are not sure if something is a link, hover the mouse over it. The pointer should change to a hand symbol.

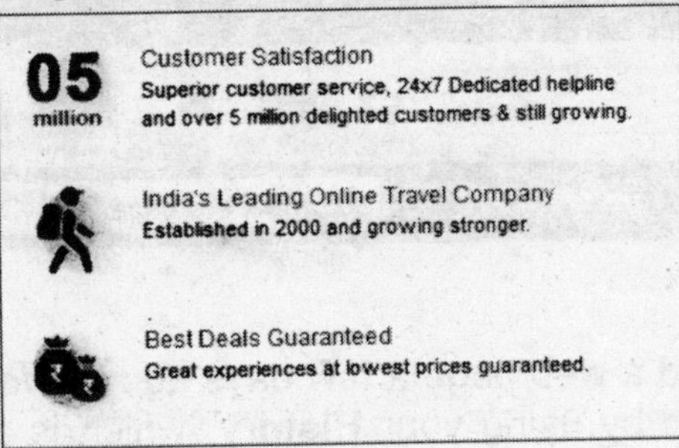

Navigation Buttons

Sometimes after you click on a link, you might want to go back to the previous page. You can do this using your browser's **Back** button. Once you've pressed the **Back** button, you can press the **Forward** button to follow the link again.

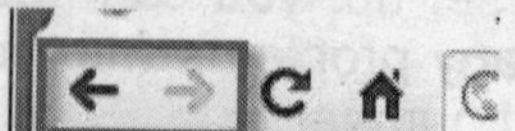

When you use the **Back** and **Forward** buttons, your browser may use its web cache to display the page. The **web cache** stores recently viewed web pages so they do not need to be downloaded again. This is good because it speeds up your web browsing, but sometimes you want to see the most up-to-date information on the page. You can use the **Refresh** button (sometimes called **Reload**) to tell the browser to load the page again.

Search Bar

Some browsers have a built-in search bar for performing web searches. However, many browsers have combined the address bar and the search bar into a single bar where you can type web addresses or search terms.

Adding Bookmarks

If you have found a page you'd like to go back to later, you can add it to your **Bookmarks** (sometimes called **Favorites**). Bookmarks make it easier to find a page later on. Instead of having to remember the exact web address, you can just scroll through your bookmarks until you see the name of the page.

- In Internet Explorer 9, you can add a bookmark by clicking on the **star** icon and then selecting **Add to Favorites**. Other browsers are similar, but they may use different wording.

Browsing History

Suppose you visited a web page a few days ago but forgot to bookmark it. You can find the page again by using your **History**, which is a list of websites you've visited. Usually, pages will stay in the history for a certain number of days. To maintain privacy, you can delete your history at any time.

Viewing Your History

To view your history in Internet Explorer 9, click on the **star** icon, then select the **History** tab.

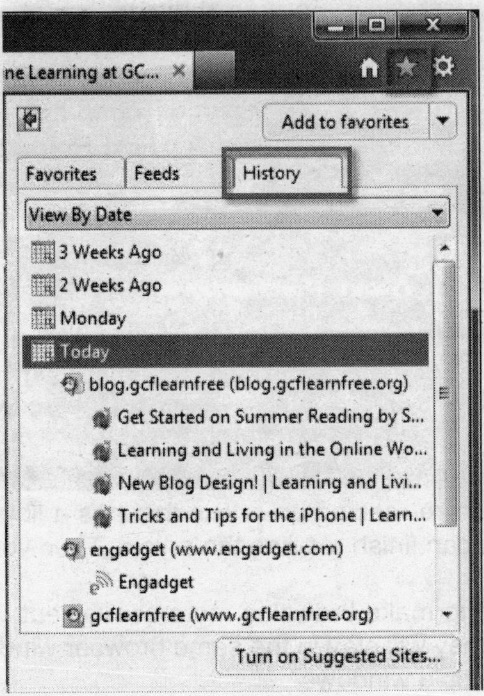

Deleting Your History

- In Internet Explorer 9, click on the **gear** icon to open the **Tools menu**.
- Click on **Safety** and then select the **Delete browsing history....**

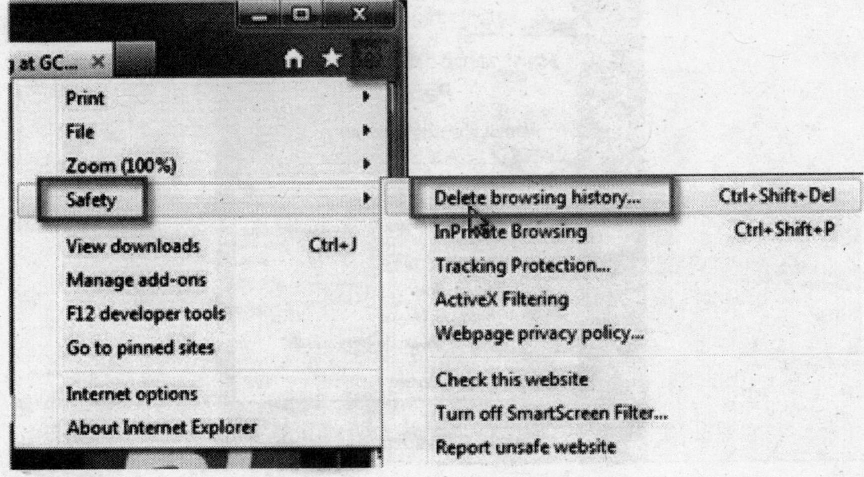

Tabbed Browsing

Many browsers allow you to open a link in a new tab. This allows you to keep the current page open instead of going directly to the new page.

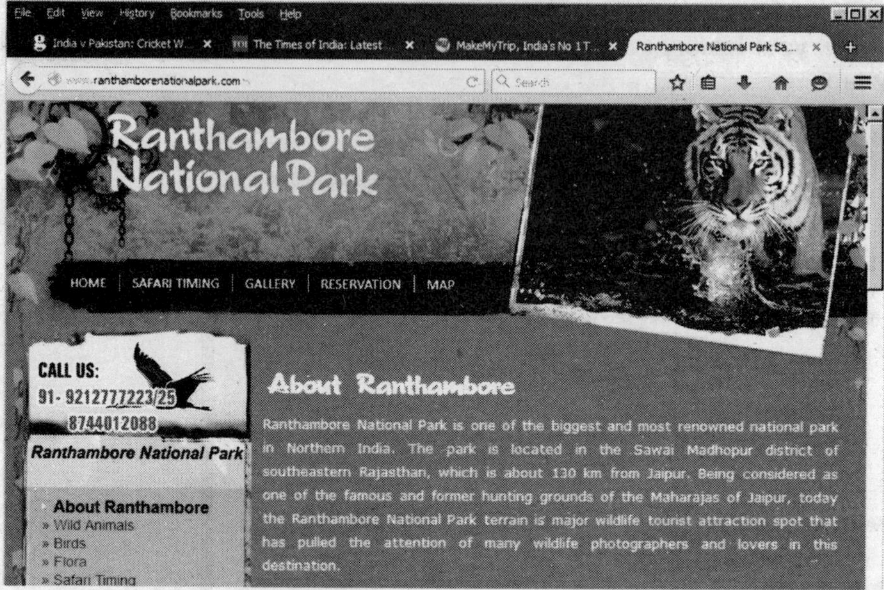

For example, if you are reading an article that has a link in it, you can open the link in a new tab so you can finish reading the article. Then you can go to the new tab to view the link.

Tabs are designed to make browsing more convenient. You can open as many links as you want, and they will stay in the same browser window instead of cluttering up your screen with multiple windows.

- To **open** a link in a new tab, **right-click** on the **link** and click on **Open in new tab**.
- To **close** a tab, click on the **'x'** on the tab.

Downloading Files

Your browser can display many different types of documents, media and other files. But there are times when you will want to access a file outside of your browser. Downloading enables you to do this by putting the file on your computer so you can access it.

For example, suppose you needed to complete and print a form you found online. You could download it to your desktop, then open it with the appropriate programme (such as Microsoft Word) to edit it.

How to Download a File

If you click on a link to a file, it may download automatically, but sometimes it just opens within your browser instead of downloading. To prevent it from opening in the browser, you can **right-click** on the **link** and select **Save Target As....** You will be able to choose the folder where the file is saved.

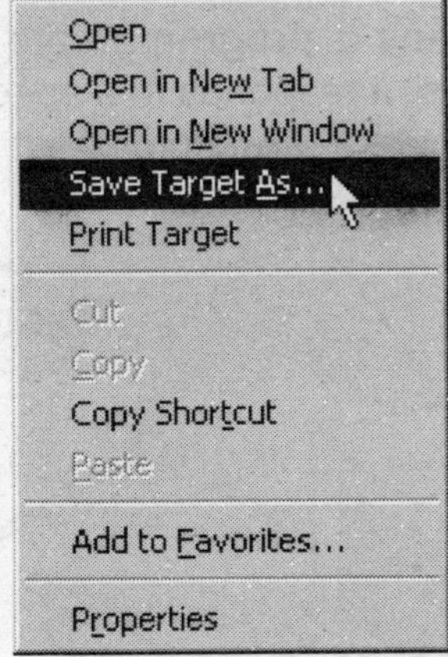

Saving Images

Sometimes, you might want to save an image to your computer. To do this, **right-click** on the image and select **Save Picture As....**

□

26
Memory Tips

Computer

Computer generally means a programmable machine. The two principal characteristics of a computer are: it responds to a specific set of instructions in a well-defined manner and it can execute a prerecorded list of instructions (a program).

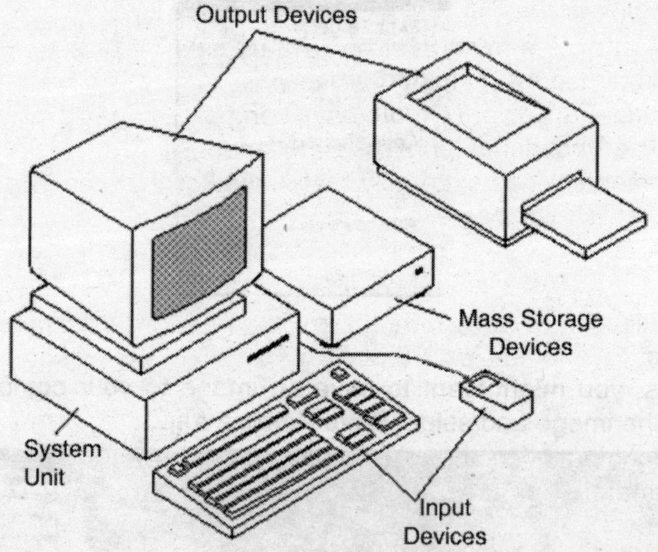

Modern Computers

Modern computers are electronic and digital. The actual machinery — wires, transistors and circuits —is called hardware; the instructions and data are called software.

All general-purpose computers require the following hardware components:

- Memory – enables a computer to store, at least temporarily, data and programs.
- Mass storage device – allows a computer to permanently retain large amounts of data. Common mass storage devices include disk drives and tape drives.
- Input device – usually a keyboard and mouse. The input device is the medium through which data and instructions enter a computer.

- Output device – a display screen, printer, or other device that lets you see what the computer has accomplished.
- Central processing unit (CPU) – the heart of the computer, this is the component that actually executes instructions.
- In addition to these components, many others make it possible for the basic components to work together efficiently. For example, every computer requires a bus that transmits data from one part of the computer to another.

Computer Classification: By Size and Power

Computers can be generally classified by size and power as follows, though there is considerable overlap:

- Personal computer – a small, single-user computer based on a microprocessor. In addition to the microprocessor, a personal computer has a keyboard for entering data, a monitor for displaying information, and a storage device for saving data.
- Workstation – a powerful, single-user computer. A workstation is like a personal computer, but it has a more powerful microprocessor and a higher-quality monitor.
- Minicomputer – a multi-user computer capable of supporting from 10 to hundreds of users simultaneously.
- Mainframe – a powerful multi-user computer capable of supporting many hundreds or thousands of users simultaneously.
- Supercomputer – an extremely fast computer that can perform hundreds of millions of instructions per second.

Bus

- It is a collection of wires through which data is transmitted from one part of a computer to another. You can think of a bus as a highway on which data travels within a computer. When used in reference to personal computers, the term 'bus' usually refers to internal bus. This is a bus that connects all the internal computer components to the CPU and main memory. There's also an expansion bus that enables expansion boards to access the CPU and memory.

  All buses consist of two parts — an address bus and a data bus. The data bus transfers actual data whereas the address bus transfers information about where the data should go. The size of a bus, known as its width, is important because it determines how much data can be transmitted at one time. For example, a 16-bit bus can transmit 16 bits of data, whereas a 32-bitbus can transmit 32 bits of data.
- In networking, a bus is a central cable that connects all devices on a local-area network (LAN). It is also called the backbone network.

Network

A network is a group of two or more computer systems linked together. There are many types of computer networks, including the following:

- Local-area networks (LANs): The computers are geographically close together, that is, in the same building.
- Wide-area networks (WANs): The computers are farther apart and are connected by telephone lines or radio waves.
- Campus-area networks (CANs): The computers are within a limited geographic area, such as a campus or military base.
- Metropolitan-area networks (MANs): A data network designed for a town or city.
- Home-area networks (HANs): A network contained within a user's home that connects a person's digital devices.

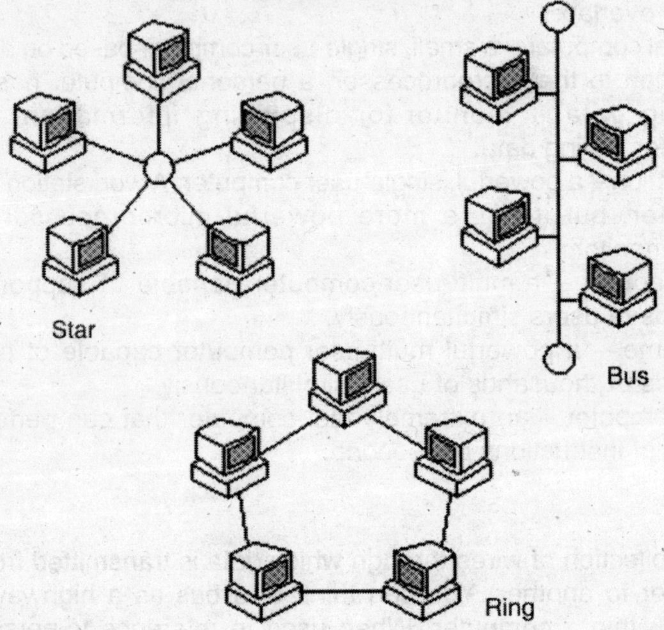

Network Security

A specialized field in computer networking that involves securing a computer network infrastructure. Network security is typically handled by a network administrator or system administrator who implements the security policy, network software and hardware needed to protect a network and the resources accessed through the network from unauthorized access and also ensure that employees have adequate access to the network and resources to work.

A network security system typically relies on layers of protection and consists of multiple components including networking monitoring and security software in addition to hardware and appliances. All components work together to increase the overall security of the computer network.

Security Software

A general phrase used to describe any software that provides security for a computer or network. There are many types of security software including antivirus software, encryption software, firewall software and spyware removal software. Additionally, many operating systems also come preloaded with security software and tools. The two most common types of security software used for personal computer security are antivirus software and anti-spyware software.

Security Policy

A security policy is a document that outlines the rules, laws and practices for computer network access. This document regulates how an organization will manage, protect and distribute its sensitive information (both corporate and client information) and lays the framework for the computer-network-oriented security of the organization.

Mobile Security

Mobile security involves protecting both personal and business information stored on and transmitted from smartphones, tablets, laptops and other mobile devices. The term 'mobile security' is a broad one that covers everything from protecting mobile devices from malware threats to reducing risks and securing mobile devices and their data in the case of theft, unauthorized access or accidental loss of the mobile device.

Security Vulnerability

An unintended flaw in software code or a system that leaves it open to the potential for exploitation in the form of unauthorized access or malicious behaviour, such as viruses, worms, Trojan horses and other forms of malware. Also referred to as security exploits, security vulnerabilities can result from software bugs, weak passwords or software that's already been infected by a computer virus or script code injection, and these security vulnerabilities require patches, or fixes, in order to prevent the potential for compromised integrity by hackers or malware.

□

27
Computer Security

Computer security refers to the techniques for ensuring that data stored in a computer cannot be read or compromised by any individuals without authorization. It means the protection of computing systems and the data that they store or access. The internet offers access to a world of products and services, entertainment and information. At the same time, it creates opportunities for scammers, hackers and identity thieves.

Let's find out how you can protect your computer, your information and your online files.

Keep Away from Free Security Scans

It is not a rare case where messages tell you to install and update security software for your computer. You might be tempted by an offer of a free security scan, especially when faced with a pop-up, an email, or an ad that claims 'malicious software' has already been found on your machine. It's likely that you will get a scary message that will claim to find a host of problems, and within seconds, you'll get urgent pop-ups to run an .exe file which promises to fix those problems. In fact, there is nothing to fix, in reality. The worst part is that the program, if installed on your computer, could be harmful. These programs are called 'scareware' because they exploit a person's fear of online viruses and security threats.

Use Security Software that Updates Automatically

The hackers and criminals constantly develop new ways to attack your computer, so your security software must be up-to-date to protect against the latest threats. Most security software can update automatically, which you should set accordingly, and also, set your operating system and web browser to update automatically. If you let your operating system, web browser, or security software get out-of-date, criminals could sneak their bad programs – malware – onto your computer and use it to secretly break into other computers, send spam, or spy on your online activities.

Treat Your Personal Information Like Cash

Don't hand over your credit card numbers, and bank and utility account numbers as they can be used to steal your money or open new accounts in your name. So every time you are asked for your personal information – whether in a web form, an email, a text, or a phone message – think about whether you can really trust the request. In an effort to steal your information, scammers will do everything they can to appear trustworthy.

Check out Companies to find out who you're Really Dealing with

When you're online, a little research can save you a lot of money. If you see an ad or an offer that looks good to you, take a moment to check out the company behind it. Type the company or product name into your search engine with terms like 'review,' 'complaint,' or 'scam.' If you find bad reviews, you'll have to decide if the offer is worth the risk. If you can't find contact information for the company, take your business elsewhere. Don't assume that an ad you see on a reputable site is trustworthy.

Give Personal Information over Encrypted Websites only

If you're shopping or banking online, stick to sites that use encryption to protect your information as it travels from your computer to their server. To determine if a website is encrypted, look for https at the beginning of the web address. Some websites use encryption only on the sign-in page, but if any part of your session isn't encrypted, the entire account could be vulnerable. Look for https on every page of the site you're on, not just where you sign in.

Protect Your Passwords

Here are a few principles for creating strong passwords and keeping them safe:

- The longer the password, the tougher it is to crack. Use at least 10-12 characters.
- Mix letters, numbers, and special characters. Try to be unpredictable – don't use your name, birth date, or common words.
- Don't use the same password for many accounts. If it's stolen from you – or from one of the companies with which you do business – it can be used to take over all your accounts.
- Don't share passwords on the phone, in texts or by email. Legitimate companies will not send you messages asking for your password. If you get such a message, it's probably a scam.
- Keep your passwords in a secure place, out of plain sight.
- Back up your files
- No system is completely secure. Copy important files onto a removable disc or an external hard drive, and store it in a safe place.

Delete Cookies Regularly

A cookie is information saved by your web browser, the software program you use to visit the web. Cookies can be used by companies that collect, store and share bits of information about your online activities to track your behaviour across sites. Cookies also can be used to customize your browsing experience, or to deliver ads targeted to you.

Besides, there are other factors related to security threats.

1. Hacking

Hacking is any technical effort to manipulate the normal behaviour of network connections and connected systems. A hacker is any person engaged in hacking. It is the most popular form of practice in computer security nowadays.

Hacked Email

You might have been hacked if:

- friends and family are getting emails or messages you didn't send.
- your Sent messages folder has messages you didn't send, or it has been emptied.
- your social media accounts have posts you didn't make.
- you can't log into your email or social media account.

A Few Steps that you should follow when you've been Hacked

Update your system and delete malware, if any

Make sure your security software is up-to-date. You can run the security software to scan your computer for viruses and spyware (malware). Delete any suspicious software and restart your computer. Set your security software, internet browser and operating system to update automatically.

Change your passwords

It is probable that someone might get your old password and change it. If you use similar passwords for other accounts, change them, too. Make sure you create strong passwords that will be hard to guess.

Check your account settings

Once you're back in your account, make sure your signature and 'away' message don't contain unfamiliar links, and that messages aren't being forwarded to someone else's address. On your social networking service, look for changes to the account since you last logged in — say, a new 'friend.'

Safeguard your usernames and passwords

Think twice when you're asked to enter credentials like usernames and passwords. Never provide them in response to an email. If the email or text seems to be from your bank, for example, visit the bank website directly rather than clicking on any links or calling any numbers in the message. Scammers impersonate well-known businesses to trick people into giving out personal information.

2. Malware

Malware is short for 'malicious software.' It includes viruses and spyware that get installed on your computer, phone, or mobile device without your consent. These programs can cause your device to crash and can be used to monitor and control your online activity. Criminals use malware to steal personal information, send spam and commit fraud.

Avoid Malware

Scam criminals try to trick people into clicking on links that will download malware and spyware to their computers, especially computers that don't use adequate security software.

- To reduce your risk of downloading unwanted malware and spyware:
- Keep your security software updated. At a minimum, your computer should have anti-virus and anti-spyware software, and a firewall. Set your security software, internet browser and operating system to update automatically.
- Instead of clicking on a link in an email, type the URL of the site you want directly into your browser. Criminals send emails that appear to be from companies you know and trust. The links may look legitimate, but clicking on them could download malware or send you to a spoof site designed to steal your personal information.
- Don't open attachments in emails unless you know who sent it and what it is. Opening attachments — even in emails that seem to be from friends or family — can install malware on your computer.
- Download and install software only from websites you know and trust. Downloading free games, file-sharing programs and customized toolbars may sound appealing, but free software can come with malware.
- Use a pop-up blocker and don't click on any links within pop-ups. If you do, you may install malware on your computer.
- Resist buying software in response to unexpected pop-up messages or emails, especially ads that claim to have scanned your computer and detected malware. That's a tactic scammers use to spread malware.
- Back up your data regularly.

Detect Malware

Your computer may be infected with malware if it:

- slows down, crashes, or displays repeated error messages
- won't shut down or restart
- serves up a barrage of pop-ups
- displays web pages you didn't intend to visit, or sends emails you didn't write

3. Phishing

When internet fraudsters impersonate a business to trick you into giving out your personal information, it is called phishing. Don't reply to email, text, or pop-up messages that ask for your personal or financial information. Don't click on links within them either – even if the message seems to be from an organization you trust. Legitimate businesses don't ask you to send sensitive information through insecure channels.

Examples of Phishing Messages

You open an email or text, and see a message like this:

- "We suspect an unauthorized transaction on your account. To ensure that your account is not compromised, please click the link below and confirm your identity."
- "During our regular verification of accounts, we couldn't verify your information. Please click here to update and verify your information."
- "Our records indicate that your account was overcharged. You must call us within 7 days to receive your refund."

Through all these messages, the senders are phishing for your information so they can use it to commit fraud.

How to Deal with Phishing Scams

- Delete email and text messages that ask you to confirm or provide personal information, like credit card and bank account numbers, social security numbers, passwords, etc. Legitimate companies don't ask for this information via email or text.
- The messages may appear to be from organizations you are familiar with, suppose banks. They might threaten to close your account or take other action if you don't respond.
- Don't reply, and don't click on links or call phone numbers provided in the message, either. These messages direct you to spoof sites – sites that look real but whose purpose is to steal your information so a scammer can run up bills or commit crimes in your name.
- Don't email personal or financial information. Remember that email is not a secure method of transmitting personal information.
- Be cautious about opening attachments and downloading files from emails, regardless of who sent them. These files can contain viruses or other malware that can weaken your computer's security.

4. Using Public Wi-Fi Networks

Wi-Fi hotspots in coffee shops, libraries, airports, hotels, universities and other public places are convenient, but often they're not secure. If you connect to a Wi-Fi network, and send information through websites or mobile apps, it might be accessed by someone else. To protect your information when using wireless hotspots, send information only to sites that are fully encrypted, and avoid using mobile apps that require personal or financial information.

Protect Your Information when using Public Wi-Fi

- When using a hotspot, log in or send personal information only to websites you know are fully encrypted. To be secure, your entire visit to each site should be encrypted – from the time you log in to the site until you log out. If you think you're logged in to an encrypted site but find yourself on an unencrypted page, log out right away.

- Don't stay permanently signed in to accounts. When you've finished using an account, log out.
- Do not use the same password on different websites. It could give someone who gains access to one of your accounts access to many of your accounts.
- Many web browsers alert users who try to visit fraudulent websites or download malicious programs. Pay attention to these warnings, and keep your browser and security software up-to-date.
- Consider changing the settings on your mobile device so it doesn't automatically connect to nearby Wi-Fi. That way, you have more control over when and how your device uses public Wi-Fi.
- If you regularly access online accounts through Wi-Fi hotspots, use a virtual private network (VPN). VPNs encrypt traffic between your computer and the internet, even on unsecured networks. You can get a personal VPN account from a VPN service provider.

Antivirus Software

Antivirus software is a program or set of programs that are designed to prevent, search for, detect and remove software viruses, and other malicious software like worms, trojans, adware and more. Antivirus software may also remove or prevent spyware and adware, along with other forms of malicious programs.

There are several different companies that build and offer antivirus software that offer more or less same basic functions:

- Scan specific files or directories for any malware or known malicious patterns
- Allow you to schedule scans to automatically run for you
- Allow you to initiate a scan of a specific file or of your computer, or of a CD or flash drive at any time.
- Remove any malicious code detected. Sometimes, you will be notified of an infection and asked if you want to clean the file, other programs will automatically do this behind the scenes.

You should be sure that you have the best, up-to-date security software installed to protect your computers, laptops, tablets and smartphones.

Antivirus Software – Free and Paid

Most users are aware that they need an antivirus on their computer. While there is a huge selection of solutions that users can choose from, typically they select free solutions from popular vendors. But you should remember that popular does not always mean better. There are a lot of free antivirus software and free versions of commercial anti-malwares. Free antivirus software generally only searches your computer using signature-based detection which involves looking for patterns of data that are known to be related to already-identified malware.

Paid antivirus software will usually also include heuristics to catch new, or zero-day threats, by either using genetic signatures to identify new variants of existing virus code or by running the file in a virtual environment, also called a sandbox, and watching what it does to see if it has malicious intent.

Virus designers, however, usually test their malicious code against the major antivirus types of malware, specifically ransomware, use polymorphic code to make it difficult to be detected by antivirus software. Besides using antivirus software to keep your computer safe and running smoothly, it is also always a good idea to be proactive: make sure your web browser is updated to the latest version, use a firewall, only download programs from websites you trust and always surf the web using a standard user account, rather than your administrator one.

Here are a few popular antivirus software used widely.

1. Kaspersky Antivirus

2. F-Secure Anti-Virus

F-Secure.

3. McAfee Antivirus Plus

4. Panda Antivirus Pro

5. Trend Micro Antivirus+

6. VoodooSoft VoodooShield 2.0

7. Avast Pro Antivirus

8. AVG Antivrus

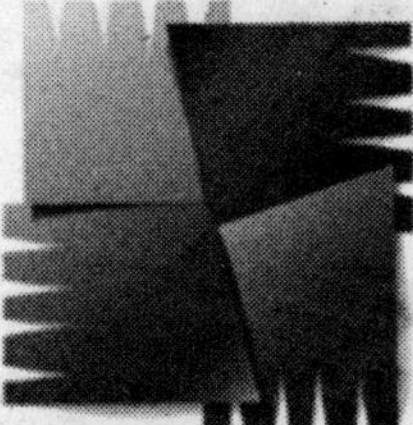

9. ESET NOD32 Antivirus 8

10. G Data Antivirus

11. IObit Advanced SystemCare Ultimate 8

12. Kromtech PCKeeper Antivirus

13. Quick Heal Antivirus

Quick Heal
AntiVirus Pro

28
Applications of Internet

Here we will know about some of the ways in which the Internet is used today, including blogs, social networking, instant messaging, VoIP and media.

Finding Information Online

The most common way to find information online is with a search engine. All you have to do is type in a few words, and the search engine will give you a list of results you can click on. There are many different search engines you can use, but Google is the most popular one.

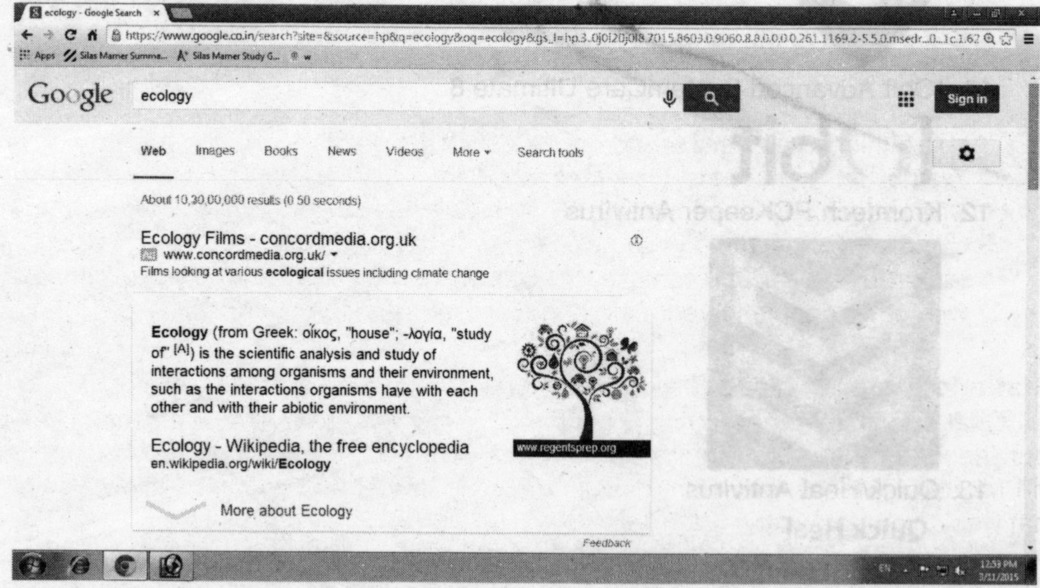

Using the Internet to Communicate

The Internet is not just about finding information. It's also about connecting with friends, family and people you've never met before. Today, there are many different ways to communicate online, including social networking, chat, VoIP and blogging.

Social Networking

Social networking has become one of the main ways people keep in touch.

Here are a few of the most popular social networking sites:

- **Facebook** is used by about 1 billion people. If you have family or friends who live far away, you can use Facebook to keep up with their lives. You can also share things you have found online that interest you.
- **Twitter** lets you share brief messages (or 'tweets') with the entire world or with just your circle of friends. By following people with similar interests, you can discover new things you would not have found otherwise.
- **LinkedIn** is a site you can use for business networking. It allows you to connect with other people in your field and discover new job opportunities.

Chat and Instant Messaging

Chat and instant messaging programmes allow you to have conversations with your friends or just write them a quick note. Two examples are Yahoo! Messenger and Microsoft Messenger. Some sites, such as Gmail and Facebook, allow you to chat within your browser.

VoIP

VoIP (Voice over Internet Protocol) allows you to have telephone service through your Internet connection. Some services also let you do video conferencing, such as Skype and Facebook Video Calling. Many of these services are free or very inexpensive, and some people use them as a replacement for a landline or simply to save minutes on their mobile phones.

Blogs

If you have knowledge or interests you are passionate about, you can create your own blog and share your thoughts with the world.

There are many sites like blogger.com and wordpress.com that let you create a blog for free. You do not need any web design experience – most of the technical stuff has already been created for you, and you can choose a pre-designed template that has the look and feel that you want.

Media on the Internet

TV, radio and the Internet used to be completely separate things, but that is no longer true with today's technology. You can now watch TV shows on your computer, and you can connect to the Internet on many TVs and DVD / Blu-ray players. In addition, you can listen to online radio from all over the world, thus granting you greater access to a more diverse range of media.

Streaming Media

TV and radio on the Internet are examples of streaming media, which means the media downloads while it is playing, so you do not have to wait for it to download first.

But you should note that not all media is streaming. If you have ever bought music via the iTunes Store, you probably had to wait for it to download before you could listen to it.

Media Players and Embedded Media

Media is often embedded in a web page, which means it plays within the web browser. Other times, you will use a separate programme called a media player to play it.

Examples include Windows Media Player and iTunes. An iPod contains built-in media player software that can play various types of files.

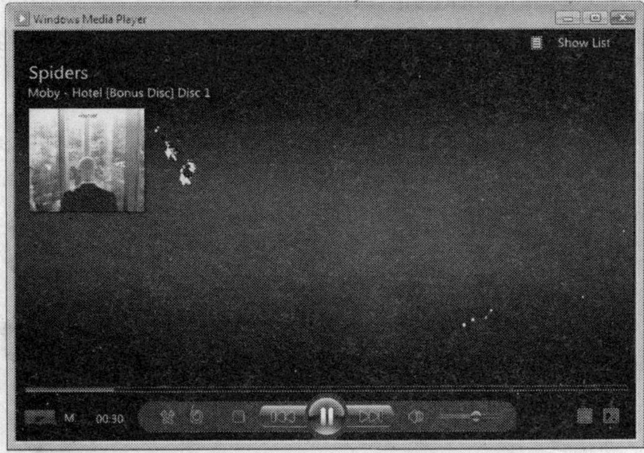

Online Media on Your TV

You can now access online TV shows, movies and music on your TV. Many newer TVs are able to connect to an existing Internet connection. If yours does not have this feature built into it, you can buy a separate digital media receiver, which is a small device that connects to your TV.

Apple TV and Roku are two examples of digital media receivers. Many game consoles, such as the Xbox 360 and PlayStation 3, can also be used to access online content.

E-mail

E-mail (electronic mail) is a way to send and receive messages and content over the Internet.

Advantages of E-mail

E-mail is delivered electronically across the Internet through various servers. E-mail is received online in the inbox of our e-mail service provider, like Gmail, Yahoo, Hotmail, etc.

- E-mail is sent and received within a few minutes if servers are busy.
- E-mail also includes attachments for digital documents, files, images, videos and more.
- E-mail is delivered to our personal and private account with a password required for accessing and viewing e-mails.
- We can send an e-mail to multiple people at once allowing us the option of having a conversation with several people or sending out a message to a hundred.
- You do not have to be at home to get your e-mail. You can access it from any computer or mobile device that gets an Internet connection.
- E-mail is free with Internet connection.

Setting up an E-mail Account on Yahoo

Once you are on the Yahoo! page, you will need to create a user account.

1. Click on the **Create New Account** button.

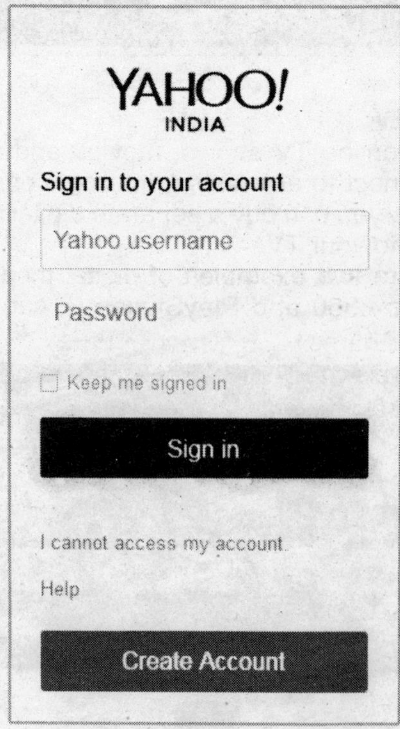

2. When you click on **Create New Account**, it will take you to the registration form shown below.

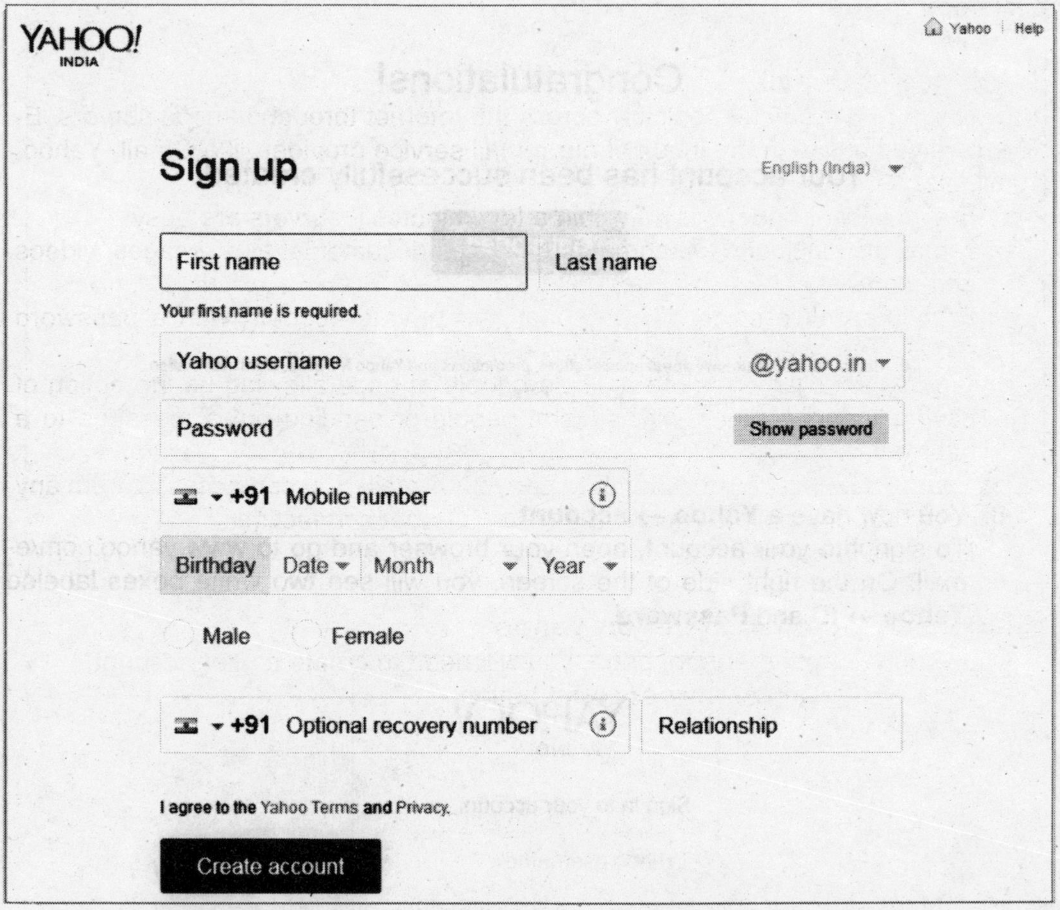

YAHOO! INDIA

Yahoo | Help

Sign up

English (India)

First name | Last name

Your first name is required.

Yahoo username @yahoo.in

Password Show password

+91 Mobile number

Birthday Date Month Year

Male Female

+91 Optional recovery number | Relationship

I agree to the Yahoo Terms and Privacy.

Create account

3. Your **Yahoo ID** and **e-mail** will be the name you use to **log in**, and also the name people will use to e-mail you.
4. Be sure to use a **secure password**. Use a few capital letters and a few numbers. Don't try to use obvious passwords such as 'password' or '12345' or a family member's name.
5. Make sure you write down your **log in name** and **password**.
6. Once you fill out this form, you will be required to submit a verification code.

Verification

Try a new code | Audio code | Help

Enter the code

Submit code

7. Once you have entered the code, click on **Submit code**. You will see the following screen.

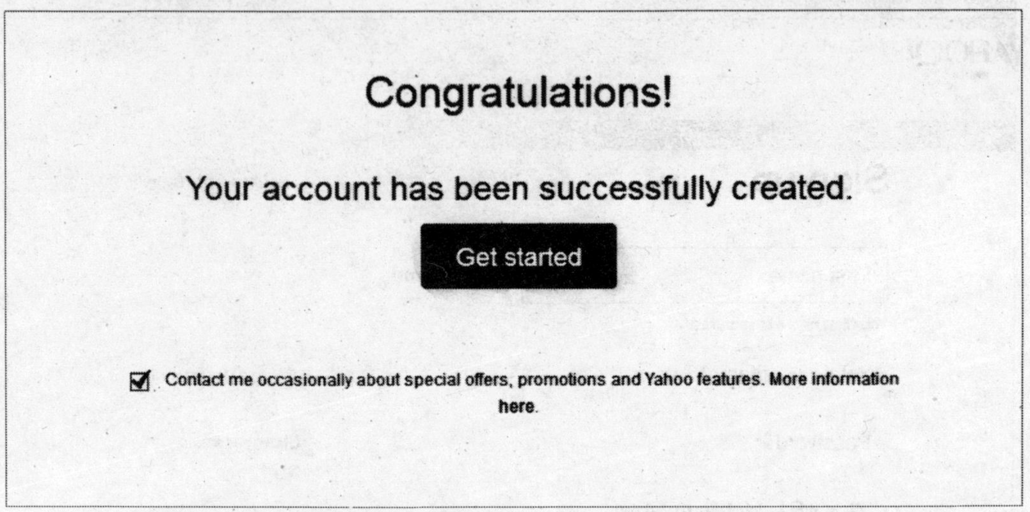

8. You now have a **Yahoo → account**.
   To sign into your account, open your browser and go to www.yahoo.com/e-mail. On the right side of the screen, you will see two white boxes labeled **Yahoo → ID** and **Password**.

Checking E-mail

Once your have set up your e-mail account, you can check your mail from anywhere provided you have access to the Internet. This is how it is done.

1. Connect to the Internet by **double-clicking** on the **Internet Explorer** or **Firefox** desktop icon.
2. Go to the **Yahoo → Mail** site by typing **mail.yahoo.com** into the address bar at the top of the screen.
3. Type your **Yahoo → ID** and **Password** into the box on the right.

4. The next page will show you the number of new messages in your **Inbox**.

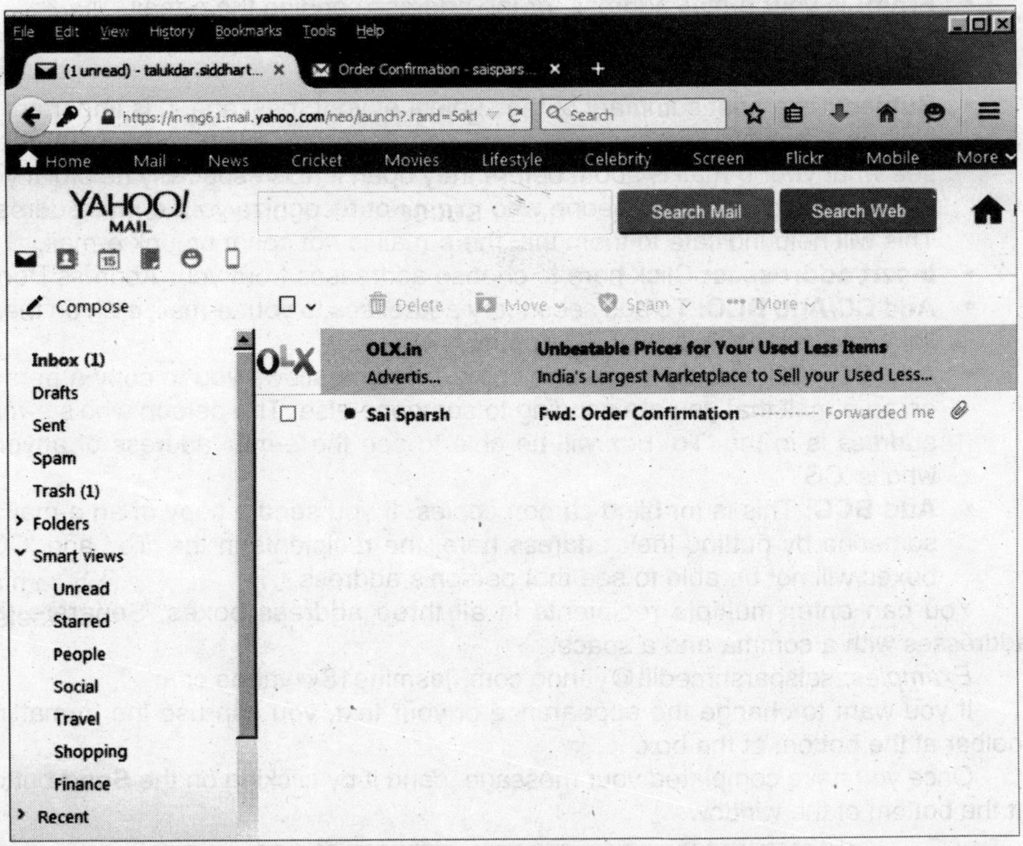

5. Click on the **Inbox** to retrieve your messages. The **Inbox** is where all of your incoming messages are stored.
6. Click on the **Subject** of the message to open and read it.

Composing and Sending Messages

To compose a message, click on the **Compose** button at the top of any screen.

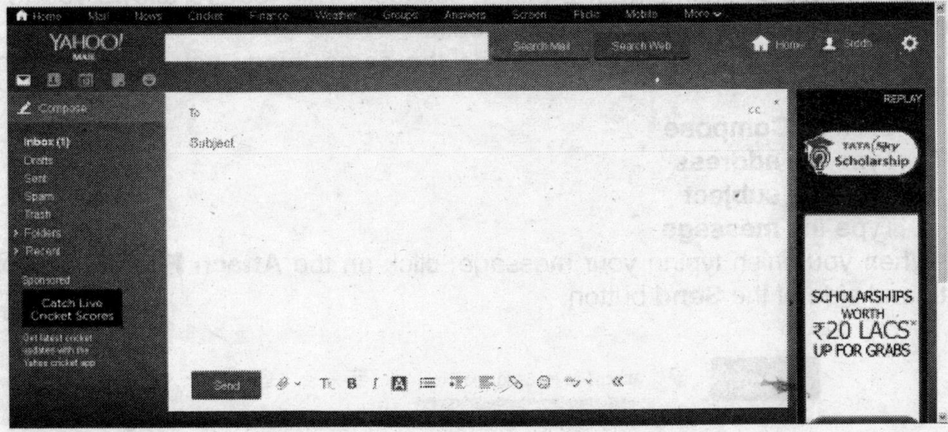

The compose screen is a blank message form which has the following at the top:

- **From:** is your e-mail address, or the address sending the e-mail.
- **To:** is where you type the e-mail address of the person(s) to whom you wish to send the e-mail.
- **Subject:** is a brief summary of the subject of your message. It is important to include a subject line because it will benefit the recipient by allowing them see what your e-mail is about before they open it. It is especially helpful if you are sending e-mail to someone who might not recognize your e-mail address. This will help indicate to them that the e-mail is not spam or junk e-mail.
- **Insert addresses:** Click here to choose addresses from your Address Book.
- **Add CC/Add BCC:** To add secondary addresses to your e-mail, click on these links and additional boxes will appear.
- **Add CC:** 'CC' stands for carbon copy. This box allows you to copy a person on an e-mail that you are sending to someone else. The person who's e-mail address is in the **'To'** box will be able to see the e-mail address of anyone who is 'CC'.
- **Add BCC:** This is for blind carbon copies. If you send a copy of an e-mail to someone by putting their address here, the recipients in the 'To:' and 'CC:' boxes will not be able to see that person's address.

You can enter multiple recipients in all three address boxes. Separate the addresses with a comma and a space.

Examples: saisparshmedia@yahoo.com, jasmine18@yahoo.com

If you want to change the appearance of your text, you can use the formatting toolbar at the bottom of the box.

Once you have completed your message, send it by clicking on the **Send** button at the bottom of the window.

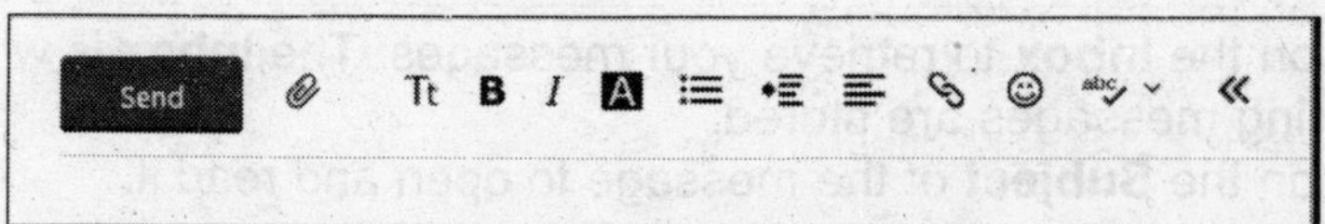

Attaching a File to Your Message

You can attach files to your e-mail messages. This feature allows you to send pictures, documents, videos and other media.

To attach a file, first you need to do the same things you do to compose a message.

1. Click on **Compose**
2. Type the **address**
3. Type the **subject**
4. Type the **message**

When you finish typing your message, click on the **Attach Files** button on the right hand side of the **Send** button.

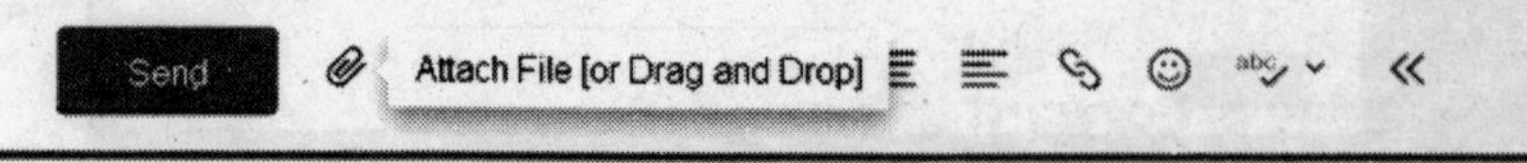

This opens the window from where you can get your file to be attached.

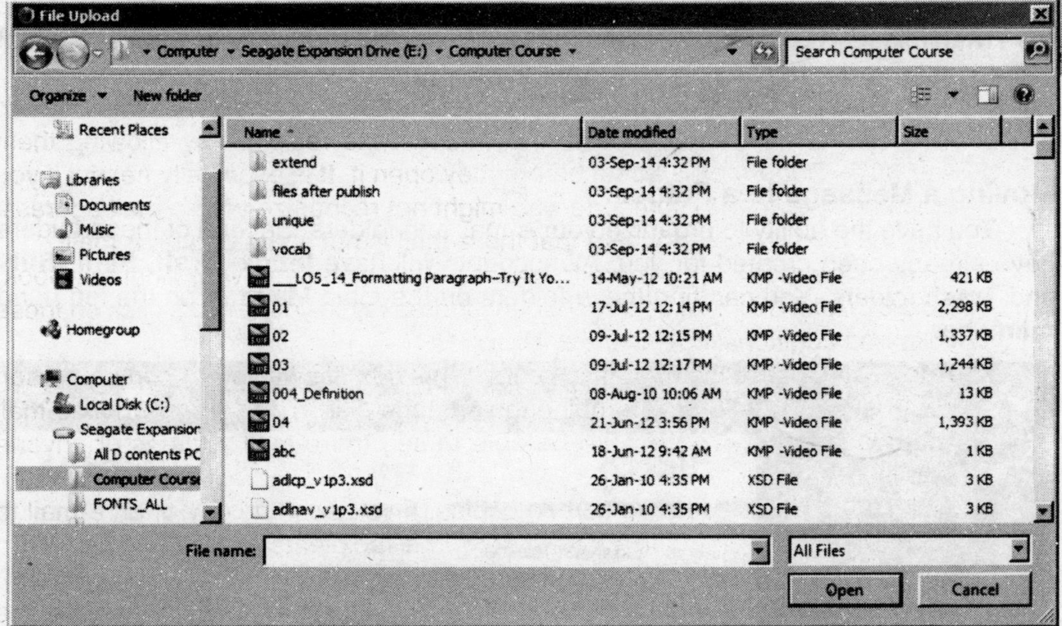

You can attach more than one file.

Receiving and Reading Messages

When you log into Yahoo → Mail, you can get to see a number of new or unread messages in your Inbox.

- Click on the **Inbox** to check your mail.

By default, e-mail messages are viewed in the Inbox. New messages are in bold font. To view your message, click on the **Subject** to open it.

Replying a Mail

If you want to reply to a mail that you have read, you have to just click on one of the arrows given at the top of the mail box.

You will get three options here.

- The first one is **Reply to sender (R)**
- The second one is **Reply to all (A)**
- The third one is **Forward this email (F)**

Deleting a Message

When you click on the **Delete** option, the message you are viewing is moved to the **Trash** folder. The messages in the **Trash** folder are periodically deleted by Yahoo!

Moving a Message to a Folder

You have the ability to organize your e-mail into folders. Several of these folders have already been created for you. All accounts will have **Inbox, Draft, Sent, Bulk** and **Trash** folders. You can find these folders on the main **Mail tab** on the left hand **menu bar**.

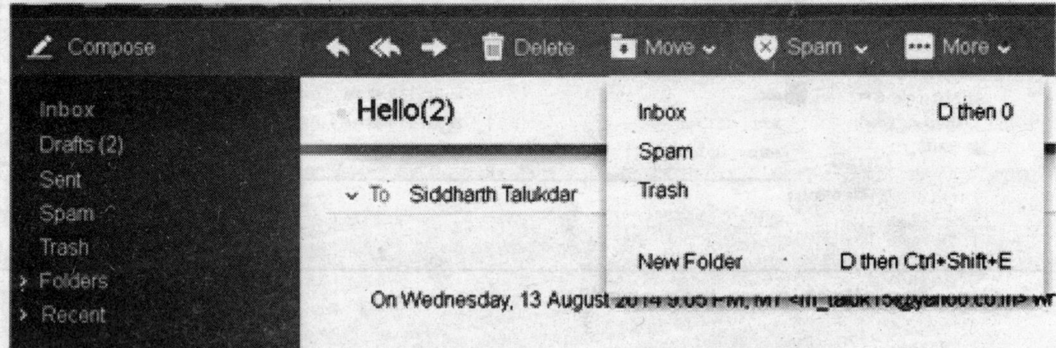

You can create individual folders of your own by clicking on **Folders** and then on **New Folder** option, represented by a '**+**' sign on the left hand **menu bar**.

Messages can be moved to folders by selecting them in the **Inbox**, checking the boxes next to each message you would like to move, then clicking on the **Move menu** button, and selecting the **desired folder**. Or, if you would like to move a message you have opened, simply click on **Move from the message screen**.

Receiving an Attachment

When you receive a message with an attachment, a **paper clip** appears next to the subject of the message in your **Inbox** window.

Click on the subject of the message to open it. At the bottom of the message, you will see a box that lists the attachments.

Norton

Important Links.doc View | Download

Reply, Reply all or Forward | More

Click to Reply All

If you click on the attachment name, Yahoo! will scan the attachment for possible viruses and give you a report.

- Click on **Download Attachment**.

A box will pop up and ask you if you would like to open the file, or if you would like to save it to a disk.

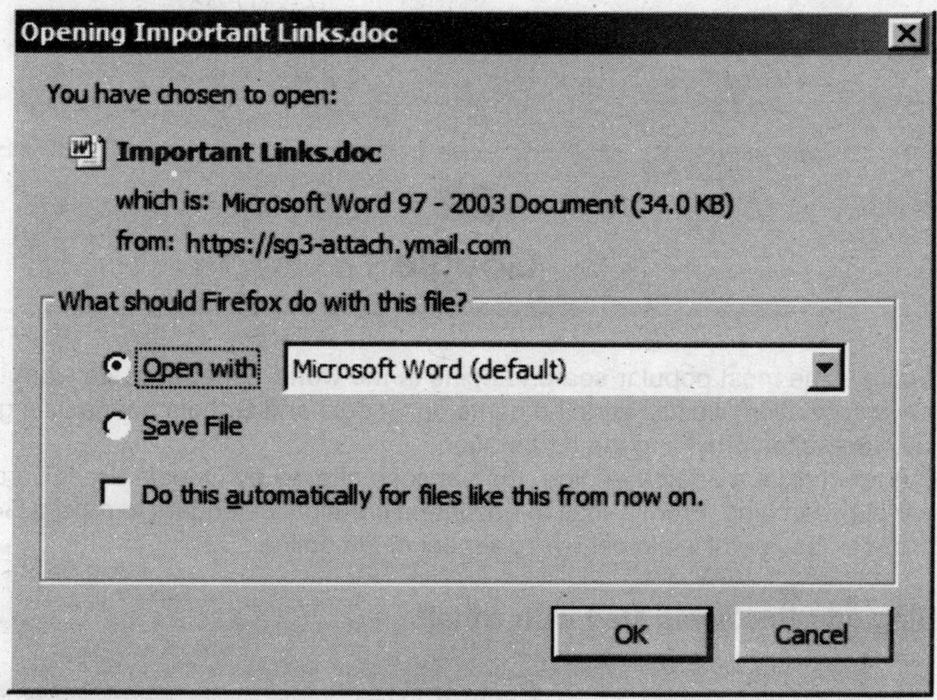

To open the file, select **Open with**, and then click on **OK** button, and the programme that runs this type of file (such as Word) will open the attached file. To save the file to your computer, select **Save File**.

□

29
Google

Google is the most popular search engine in the world. Whenever we want to get any information, we just type the name on Google and Google brings us a galore of related websites providing the information.

But apart from a search engine, the services offered by Google are far broader than simple searching. From e-mail to document creation, calendars to music, Google products can be used for almost every aspect of life online.

Sending and Receiving Mail with Gmail

Log In with Your Google Account

You can access the Gmail home page from the menu bar at the top of the Google search engine. You will need to sign in with your Google account in order to access your Gmail inbox.

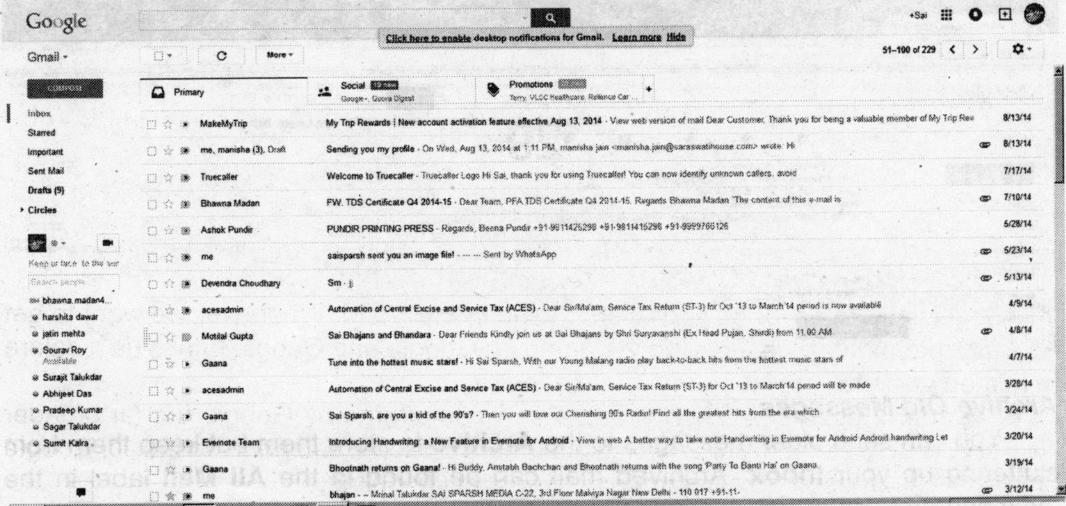

Browse Your E-mails

Your inbox is automatically sorted into tabs. The default tabs are **Primary, Social** and **Promotions**. You can add **Updates** and **Forums** tabs to further sort your e-mail.

- **Primary** are your personal e-mails between people.
- **Social** are e-mails from social networking services, such as Facebook and Twitter.
- **Promotions** are e-mails that you receive from marketing that you have signed up for.

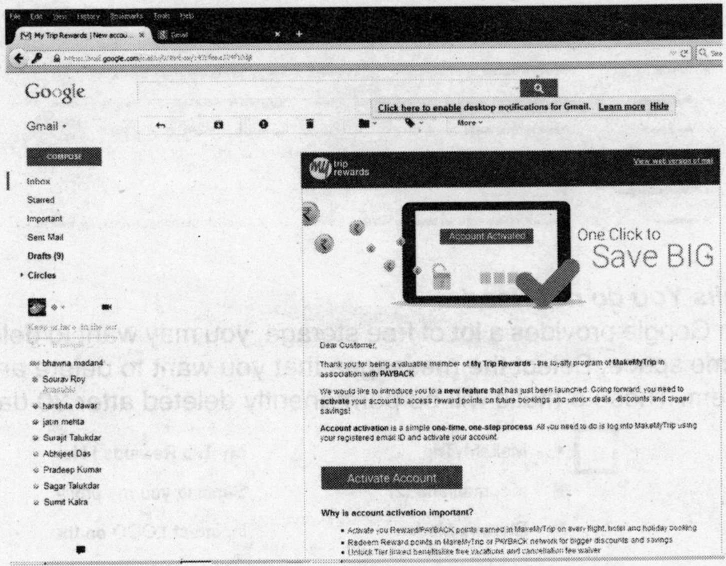

View E-mail Conversations

Any replies to an e-mail are grouped together into a single conversation. The most recent reply will be shown first, and previous e-mails in the conversation can be expanded with the **Expand** icon.

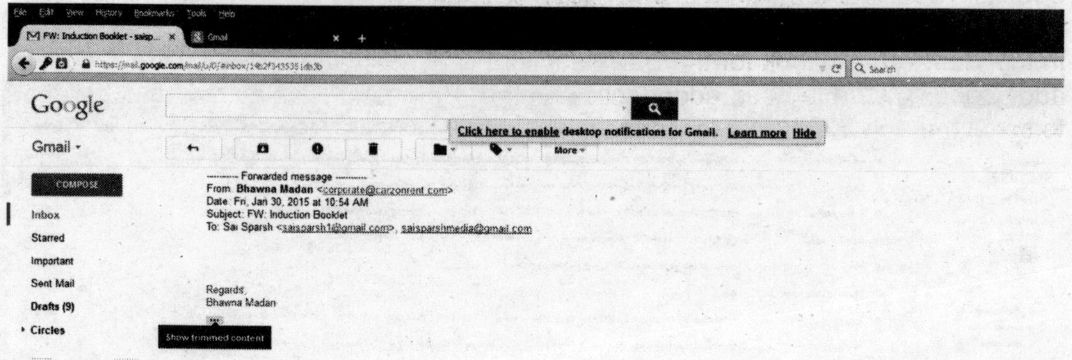

Archive Old Messages

You can send older messages to the **Archive** to store them but keep them from cluttering up your **Inbox**. Archived mail can be found in the **All Mail** label in the left menu.

If someone replies to an archived mail, the conversation will be moved back to your **Inbox**.

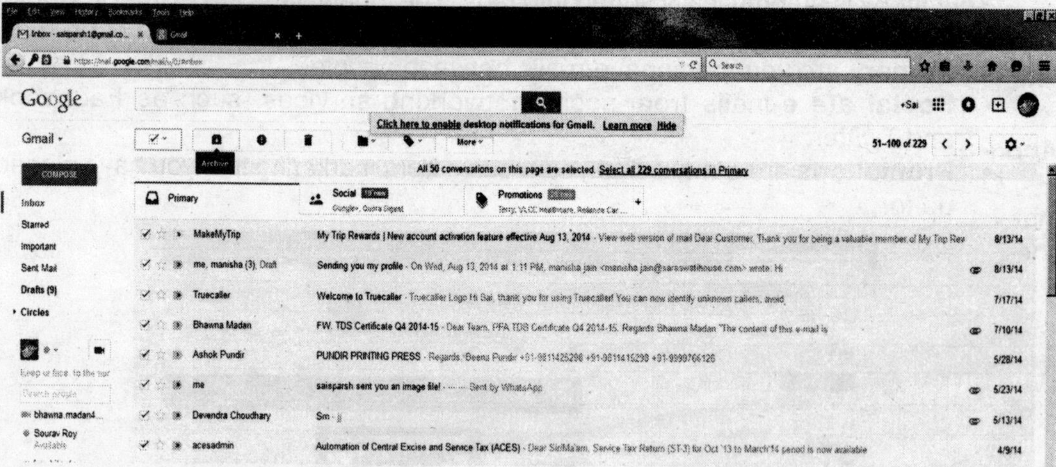

Delete E-mails You do not Need

Although Google provides a lot of free storage, you may want to delete messages to free up some space. Select the messages that you want to delete and click on the **Trash Can** item. These e-mails will be permanently deleted after 30 days.

MakeMyTrip — My Trip Rewards | Nev
me, manisha (2) — Sending you my profile
Bhawna Madan — Incorrect LOGO on the

Star Important E-mails

You can add a **Star** to e-mails that you want to remember for later. This will mark the e-mail with a **Star** icon, and you can use the left menu to browse only your Starred e-mails.

You can add more icons by clicking on the **Gear** menu and selecting **Settings**. In the **General tab**, look for the **Stars** section. Drag icons to **In Use** that you want to add. Once they have been added, click on the **Star** icon multiple times on an e-mail to scroll through the available icons.

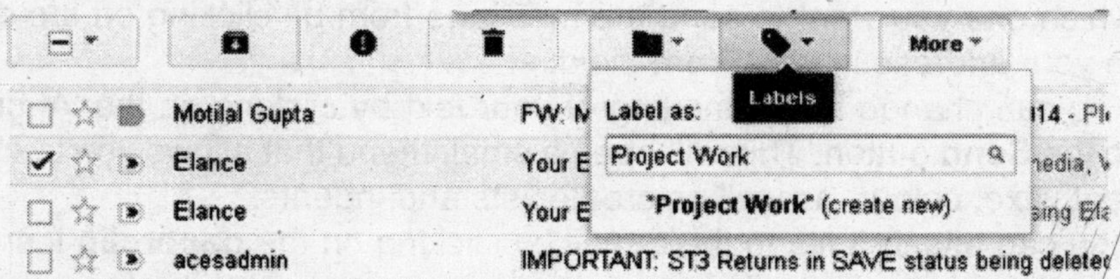

Use Labels to Sort Your Mails

In the **Settings** menu, click on the **Labels tab**. Here you can browse through the pre-existing labels, which will be listed in the left menu of Gmail. Click on the **Create new label** button to create a **new label**.

Click on the **Filters** button to create a rule that will sort incoming mail into the labels you have created. Click on the **Create** a new filter link to set up a new rule.

You can have a filter set by who the e-mail is from, who it is to, words in the subject, and words in the body. Once you have designated your filter, click on **Create filter with this search**.

Apply a Rule to the Filter

Once you have set the filter, check the **Apply the label**: box and select the label that you want. If you want it to go straight into the label and not appear in your inbox, check the **Skip Inbox** box.

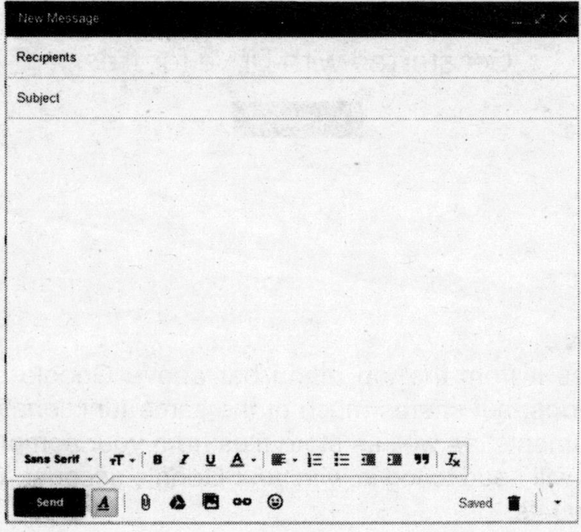

Compose an E-mail

To write an e-mail, click on the **Compose** button at the top of the left menu. A **New Message** window will open. Enter the address into the **'To'** field. If you have the person saved as a contact, you can enter their name and select them from the dropdown menu that appears.

- **'Cc'** will send a copy to another recipient. **'Bcc'** will send a copy to another recipient without any of the other recipients knowing.
- If you have multiple accounts linked to your **Gmail account**, you can choose which one you want to send the message from by clicking on the arrow next to your address in the **'From'** field.
- You can change the formatting of your text by clicking on the 'A' button next to the **Send** button. This will open a small menu that allows you to change the font, size, colour, as well as create lists and indents.
- You can attach a file to the e-mail by clicking on the **paperclip** icon. This will open a window that will allow you to browse your computer for a file to attach. There is a 25MB file size limit for attached files.
- You can send money using **Google Wallet** by hovering over the **+** sign and clicking on the **$** icon. Google will ask you to verify your identity if you have not already.
- You can insert images and **Google Drive** documents into your e-mail by hovering over the **+** sign as well.

Creating and Sharing Files with Google Drive

It is very easy to use Google Drive. But before you start using Google Drive, first you have to sign in with your Google account.

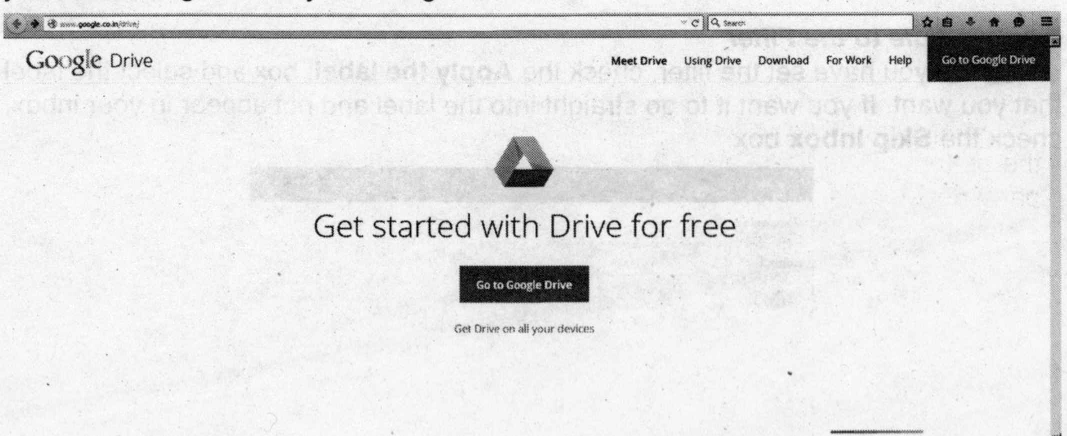

Open Google Drive

You can access it from the top menu bar above Google sites. Google Drive replaced **Google Docs**, but shares much of the same functionality. You can create, edit and share documents, as well as store files from your computer to be accessed anywhere. Just you will need to log in with your Google account. Google Drive is free with all Google accounts.

- To Sign in to Your Google Account, click on the **Sign In** button in the top-right corner to sign in with your Google account. This will help tailor searches to you as well as allow you to save your searching preferences.

Create a New Document

Click on the **Create** button to start a new document. A list will open, allowing you to choose from a word processing document, a spreadsheet, a presentation, or a drawing.

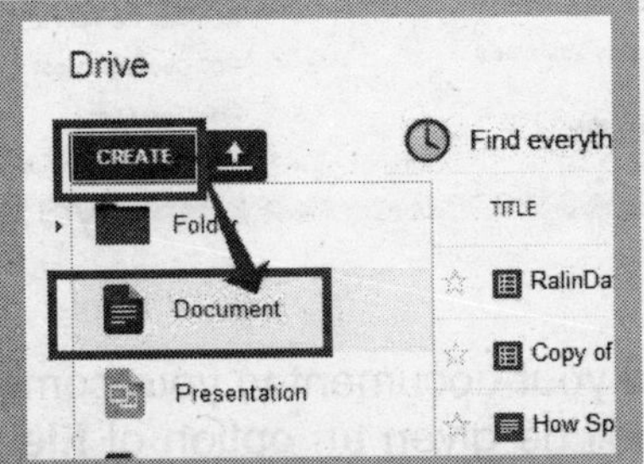

You can add more functionality by clicking on the **Connect more apps** button at the bottom of the list. You can browse other **add-ons** from Google as well as third-party developers.

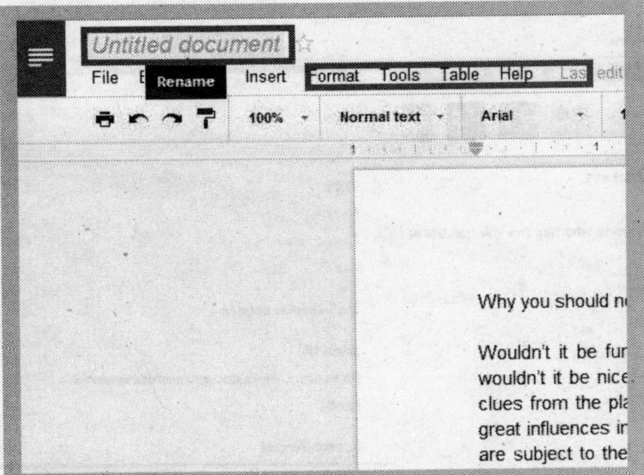

Edit Your New Document

Once you have chosen your format, you can start editing your document. Click on the **title** at the top to change it. Use the **toolbar** to make formatting adjustments.

- The **toolbar** options will change depending on the type of file that you are creating.
- All changes are saved automatically as you work.

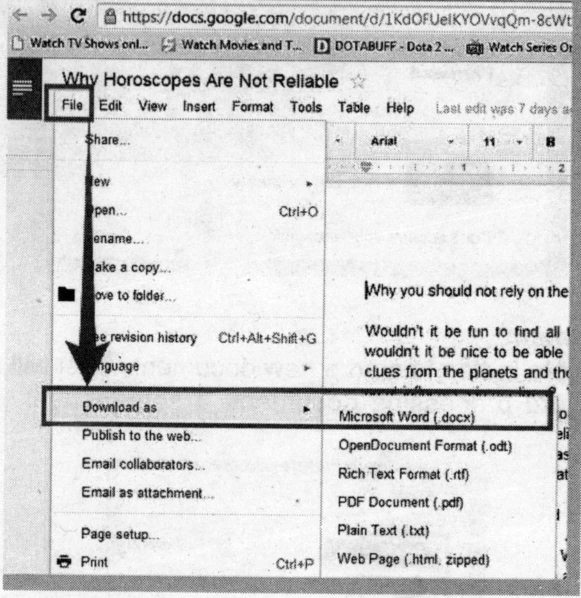

Download the Document

If you want to download your document to your computer, click on **File** and then select **Download as**. You will be given an option of **file formats**. Pick the one that matches the programmes that you use.

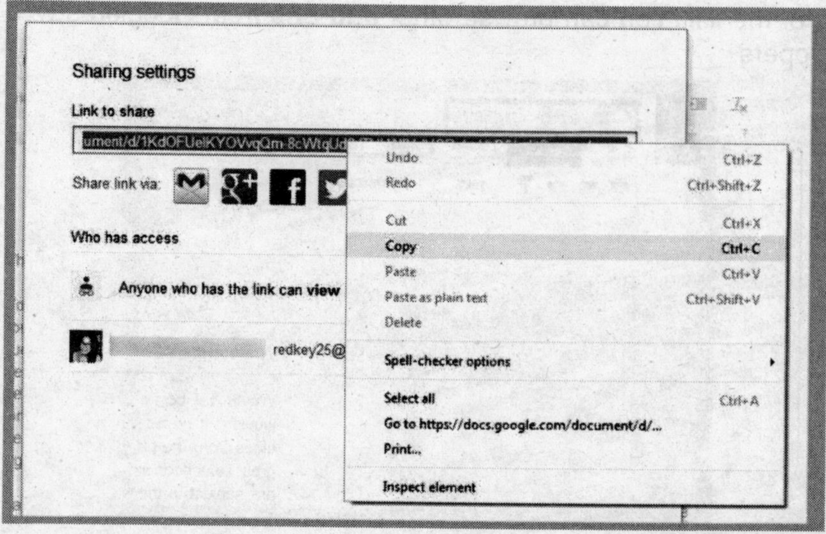

Share the Document

You can share the document with other Google Drive users by clicking on **File** and then selecting **'Share...'** This will open the **Sharing Settings**. Here you can add people to the list of collaborators, as well as link to the document using popular services, such as Facebook and Twitter.

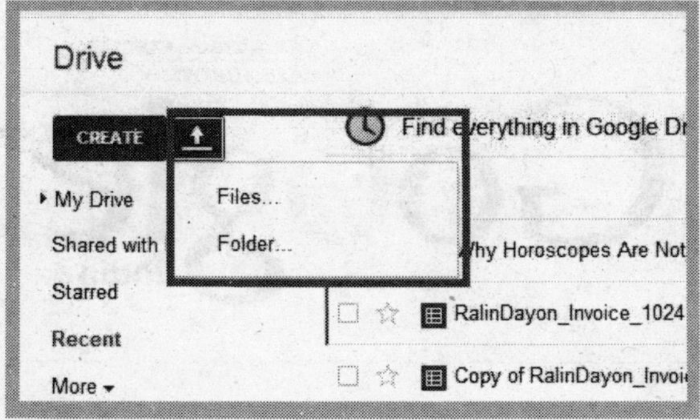

Upload Files from Your Computer

You can upload files that you want to backup from your computer to Google Drive. Click on the **Upload** button next to the **Create** button. You can choose to upload individual files or entire folders.

- Any file type can be uploaded to Google Drive. Certain files, such as Word documents, can be converted into Google documents by clicking on the **Settings** menu in the **Upload window**. Your uploaded documents will be added to your **Google Drive list**.
- You can download the Google Drive programme for your computer that will allow you to create a shared folder that syncs with the Drive automatically. Click on the **Connect Drive** to your desktop button to download it.
- All free Google Drive accounts come with 15 GB of storage (shared across all of your Google services). If you run out of space, delete unwanted files and e-mails, or purchase more storage from Google for a monthly fee.

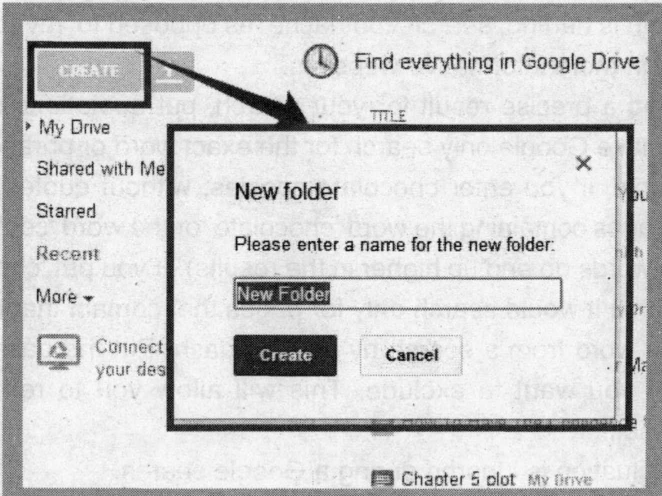

Create Folders to Sort Your Files

Click on the **Add Folder** button at the top of Google Drive to create a custom folder. You can then drag and drop files into the folder, cleaning up your Drive interface.

Searching the Web with Google

Google Search I'm Feeling Lucky

Google.co.in offered in: हिन्दी বাংলা తెలుగు मराठी தமிழ் ગુજરાતી ಕನ್ನಡ മലയാളം ਪੰਜਾਬੀ

Go to the Google Home Page and Type Your Search

Formatting your search in different ways will affect the results that you receive. Try to keep your search terms simple to get the best results. Search using the important words, and leave out the question. The **'I'm Feeling Lucky'** button will take you directly to the first search result.

- Try to use words that the websites that you are looking for will use. For example, if your tooth is hurting, search 'toothache' as opposed to 'my tooth hurts'. This will result in more informative websites.
- If you need a precise result for your search, put quotations mark around it. This will make Google only search for the exact word or phrase in the quotes.
- For example, if you enter chocolate cookies, without quotes, Google would find any pages containing the word 'chocolate' or the word 'cookies' (but pages with both words do end up higher in the results). If you put 'chocolate cookies' in the search it would search only for pages that contain that exact phrase.
- Exclude a word from a search by using a dash. Put the dash in front of the word that you want to exclude. This will allow you to remove unwanted search result.
- Most punctuation is ignored during a Google search.

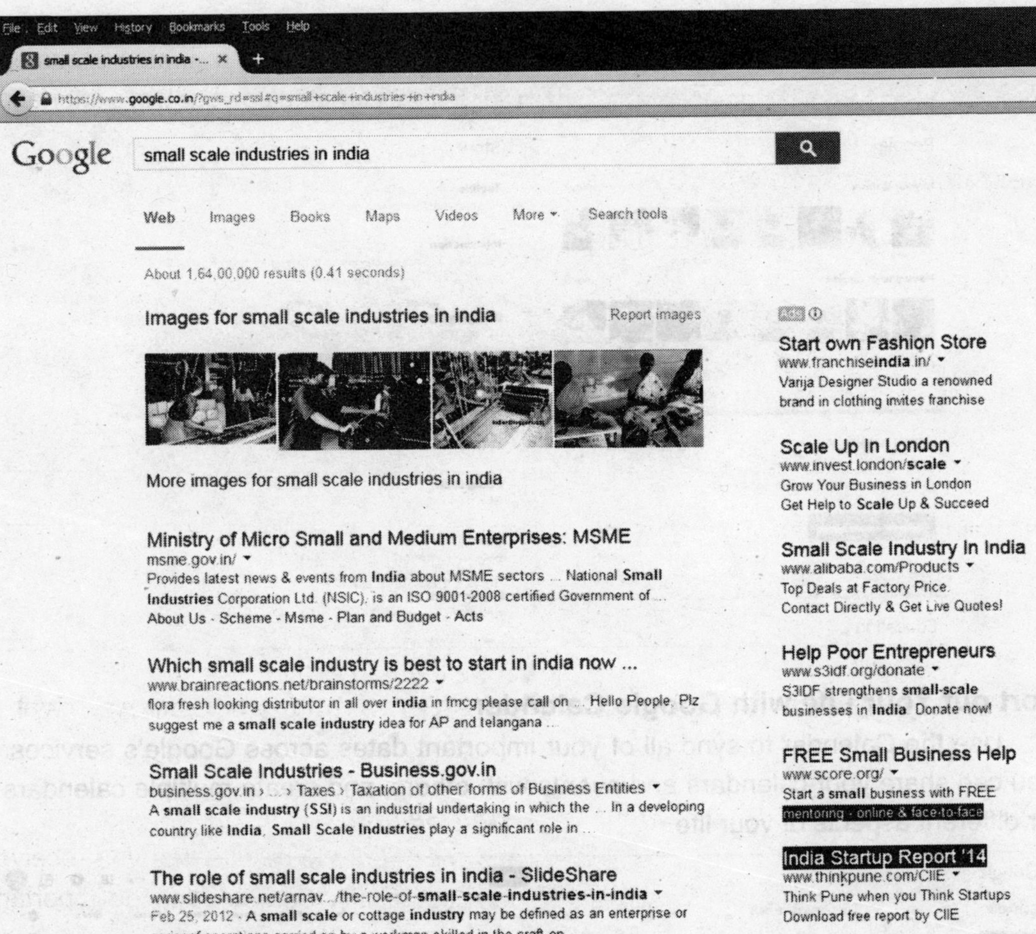

Refine Your Search

You can add specific parameters to your search by opening the **Advanced Search tool**. You can open this by scrolling to the bottom of the search results and clicking on the **Advanced Search link.**

- In the **'Find pages with...'** section, you can specify exactly how you want Google to search for your terms. These can be achieved through the regular search box as well, and the instructions are listed beside each entry.
- In the **'Then narrow your results by...'** section, you can add filters that will hide results that aren't relevant to you. You can set the desired language, region, update date, specific site and more.

Create Your Google+ Profile

Google+ is Google's social networking service. Use it to create an online presence, follow trends and people, and connect with your friends.

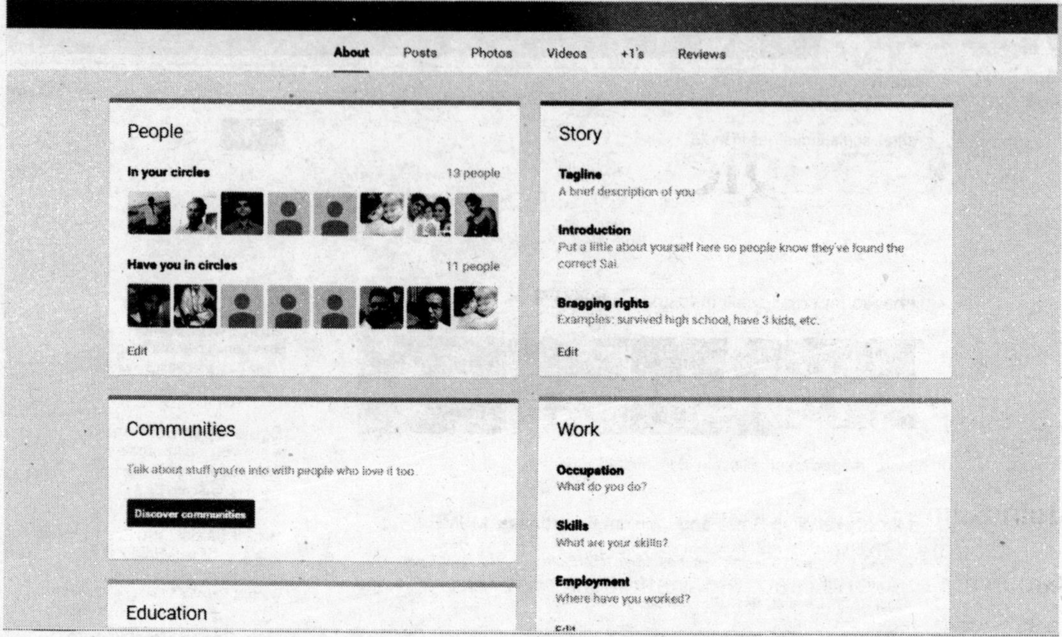

Sort out Your Life with Google Calendar

Use the Calendar to sync all of your important dates across Google's services. You can share your calendars and events with others, and create multiple calendars for different aspects of your life.

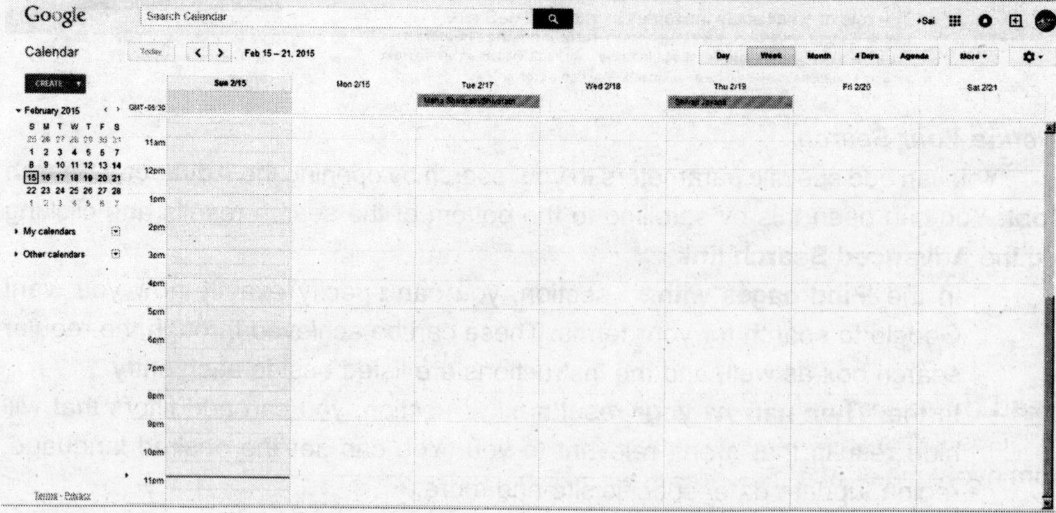

Use Google Scholar to Research Papers for School

Google Scholar will provide search results from peer-reviewed journals and articles. You can use these for research papers and presentations.

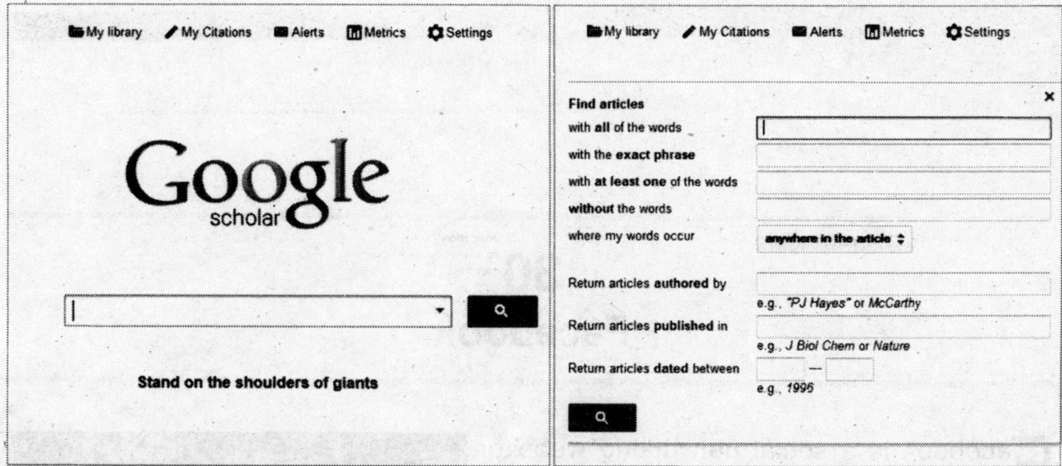

Join Some Google Groups

Google Groups are collections of people that share similar interests. Use the Groups to post and read information relevant to you.

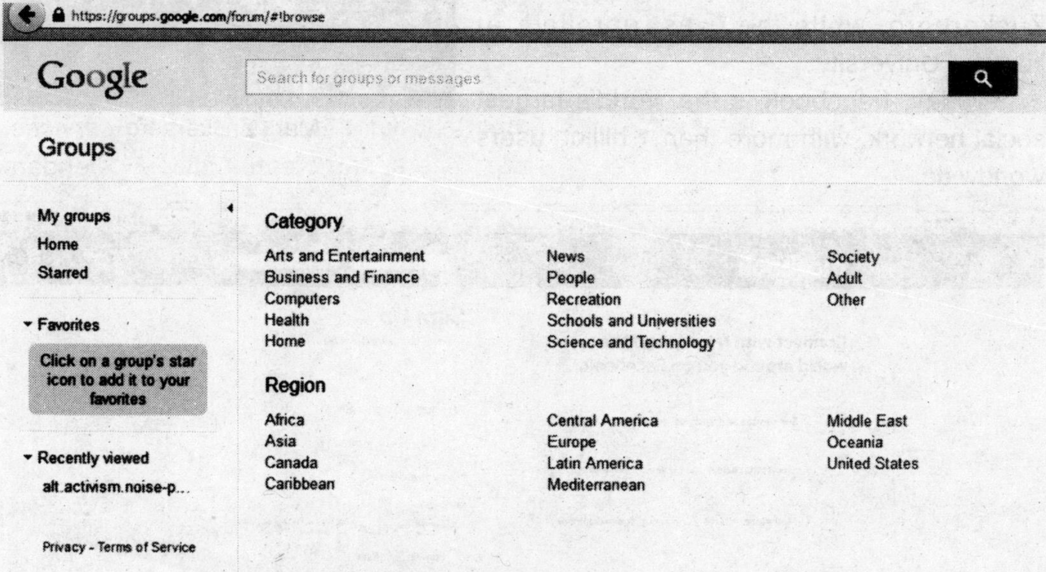

Read the Latest News with Google News

Google News allows you to create a personalized news feed with the latest stories from every major and minor news source.

□

30
Facebook

Facebook is a social networking website that makes it easy for you to connect and share with your family and friends online. Originally designed for college students, Facebook was created in 2004 by Mark Zuckerberg while he was enrolled at Harvard University.

Mark Zuckerberg

Today, Facebook is the world's largest social network, with more than 1 billion users worldwide.

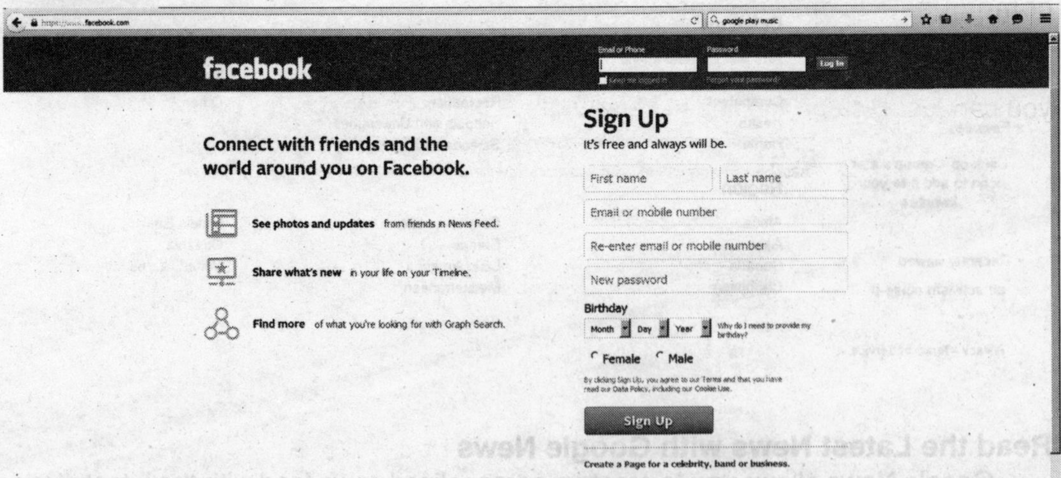

The first step in using Facebook is to sign up and get a new Facebook account. Go to **www.facebook.com** and fill out the **Sign Up** form on the right. You should give your real first and last name along with your e-mail address and the rest of the form. Click on the **Sign up** button at the bottom when you are done.

Facebook will send a message to the e-mail address you provided with a link asking you to confirm your e-mail address.

Find and Connect with Friends on Facebook

After filling out your profile, you can start adding friends by sending them a friend request via an internal Facebook message or to their e-mail address if you know it. If they click to **accept your friend request**, their name and a link to their **profile/Timeline** page will automatically appear on your list of **Facebook friends**.

- Facebook offers various ways to find friends, including a scan of your existing e-mail contact list if you grant access to your e-mail account.

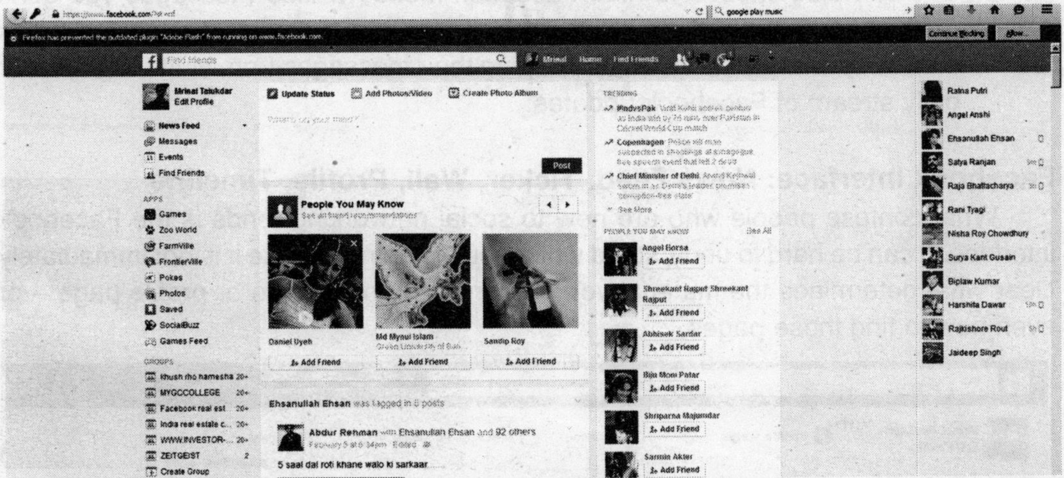

Searching for individuals by name is another option. You can look for people you know on Facebook. As soon as you have a few friends and have 'liked' some companies, comments or products, then Facebook's automated friend recommendation tool will kick in and start showing you links to 'people you may know'. If you recognise their face when their profile image appears on your Facebook page, you can just click on the link to send them a friend request.

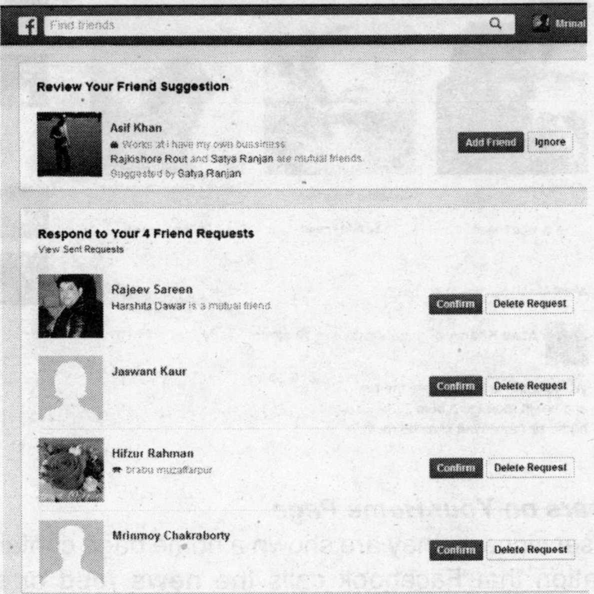

Organize Your Facebook Friends

Once you have a lot of friend connections, it is a good idea to organize your Facebook friends into lists, so you can send different types of messages to different groups.

- The Facebook friends list feature is a great way to manage your friends to accomplish that.
- You can also choose to hide Facebook friends whose messages you don't really want to see. The hide feature allows you to maintain your Facebook friendship with someone while keeping their messages from cluttering up your daily stream of Facebook updates.

Facebook Interface: News Feed, Ticker, Wall, Profile, Timeline

What confuse people who are new to social networking tends is the Facebook interface. It can be hard to understand when you first join because it is not immediately clear what determines the material you see on your home page or profile page – or even how to find those pages.

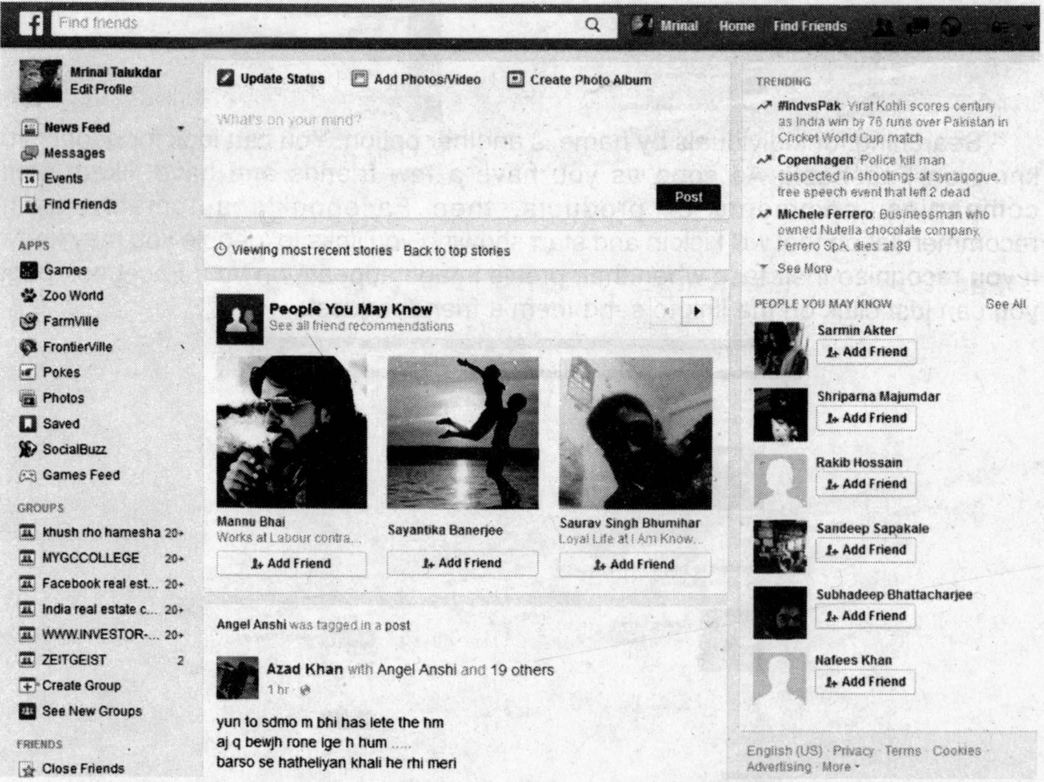

News Feed Appears on Your Home Page

When each user signs in, they are shown a home page containing a personalized stream of information that Facebook calls the **news feed** or **stream**. It is full of information posted by their friends. The news feed appears in the middle column of the home page. You can always return to your personal home page by clicking on the **Facebook icon** at upper left on every Facebook page.

In the news feed are posts or status updates that a user's friends have posted to the network, typically shown only to their Facebook friends. Each user sees a different news feed based on who their friends are and what those friends are posting. The feed can include more than just text messages. It can also contain photos and videos. But the main point is that this stream of updates on your home page is all about your friends and what they are posting.

Ticker Appears on the Right

On the right sidebar of the home page is the **Ticker**, Facebook's name for a different stream of information about your friends. Instead of status updates or posts, the Ticker announces each activity your friends take in real time, such as when someone makes a new friend connection, likes a page, or comments on a friend's post.

Timeline and Profile: All About You

In addition to a home page featuring news from friends, each user has a separate page that is all about themselves. For years, Facebook called this the profile or wall area. But Facebook redesigned and renamed the profile/wall area and started calling it **Timeline** in 2011. You can reach your Timeline page by clicking on your name at the upper right on every Facebook page.

Facebook Communication System – Status Updates, Messages, Chat

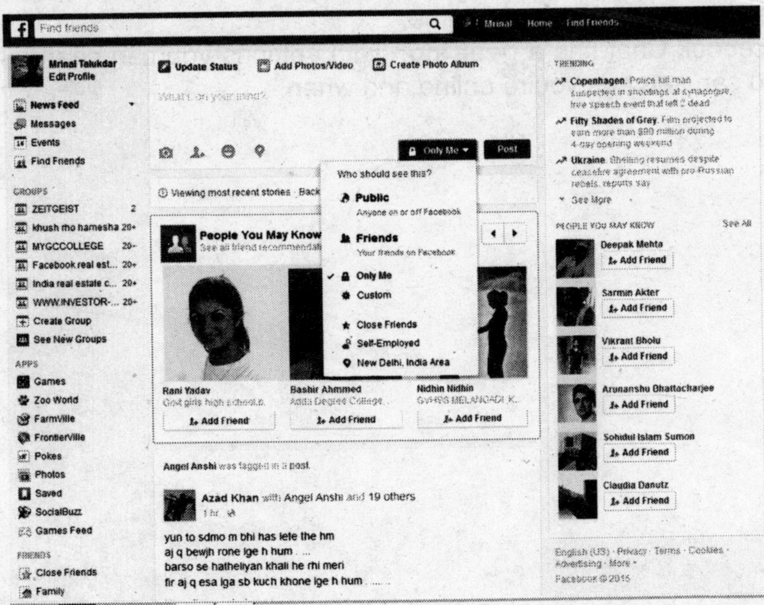

Communication is the heartbeat of Facebook and takes place in various forms, including three major ones.

Status Updates

Status update is what Facebook calls a message that you post via the publishing box that says **'What's on your mind?'** The publishing box appears at the top of both your home page and Timeline page. People use status updates to communicate their activities, post links to news stories, share photos and videos, and comment on life in general.

Internal Messages

Messages are private notes you can send to any friend you're connected with on Facebook. They're viewable only by the person to whom they are sent and do not go into the news feed or ticker for viewing by your network of friends. Rather, each message goes into the recipient's Facebook inbox which functions like a private e-mail address.

- Each user is actually assigned a username@facebook.com e-mail address for this private inbox.

By default, messages also get forwarded to the external e-mail address the user has provided to Facebook.

Live Chat

Chat is Facebook's name for its instant messaging system. You can engage in real-time conversation with any of your Facebook friends who happen to be online and signed in at the same time as you are. The **Facebook Chat box** is on the lower right side of the interface and contains a small green dot next to **Chat**. Clicking on it will open the chat box and show a green dot next to the name of friends who happen to be signed into Facebook at that time.

- Facebook Chat has a **gear icon** with settings you can change to determine who can see that you're online and when.

□

31
Twitter

Twitter is a social network where you post short bursts of thoughts and information. Twitter revolutionized social media by making it simple for the world to communicate in real time.

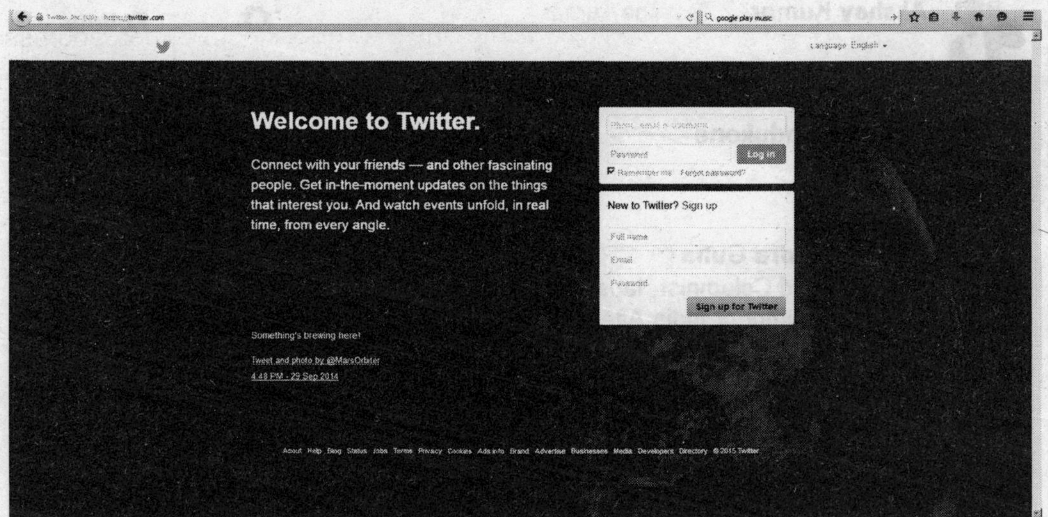

Setting up Your Profile

The first thing you need to do is to set up your profile.

- Click on **Settings** and start filling up your profile.
- The notable areas in here are **URL, bio, picture** and **design**. Put up a link to your site or blog in here along with a brief description. **Upload a picture** to differentiate yourself from the others and then tweak your Twitter design.
- Like any other social networking site, it is important to completely express what you are or what you stand for in your profile.

Find Twitter Accounts to Follow

As a part of the account sign-up process, Twitter will suggest the site's most popular accounts as ones you may want to follow. These are usually celebrities, leaders and leading organizations.

- You can follow them by clicking on the **'follow'** buttons or you can skip this step by clicking on the very small **'Skip this step >>'** link at the bottom of the page.

Who to follow

Follow more people from the suggestions below, tailored just for you.

Search using a person's full name or @username **Search Twitter**

certes **CertesRealty** @CertesRealty
Let's talk Land. Specialists in the domain of Land, with special focus on Delhi MPD 2021
Follow

Akshay Kumar @akshaykumar
Follow

Deepika Padukone @deepikapadukone
Actor
Follow

Ramachandra Guha @Ram_Guha
Historian and Columnist, lapsed Marxist, failed cricketer; author of 'India After Gandhi' and 'Gandhi Before India'. Retweets not necessarily endorsements.
Follow

Naina Ruhail @MissKalosine
Makeup Artist & Blogger. On Insta: Aura181
nainaruhail.com
Followed by Bhaap.com.
Follow

Cchics **Cosmochics** @Cosmochics
Cosmochics is about Fashion, Beauty, Personal Style & Experiences With Products & Places.
#indianblogger #indianblog #beautyblogger #FashionBlogger
Follow

Revathy HnB @RevathyP1
Owner @ Health n Beauty blog
Follow

Narendra Modi @narendramodi
Prime Minister of India
Follow

Finding Twitter Accounts by Category

As a part of the account sign-up process, Twitter will suggest the site's most popular categories, and the most popular Twitter profiles within those categories.

- You can follow these by clicking on the small profile image.
- This will take you to the profile page for that account.
- From there you can click on the **Follow** button.

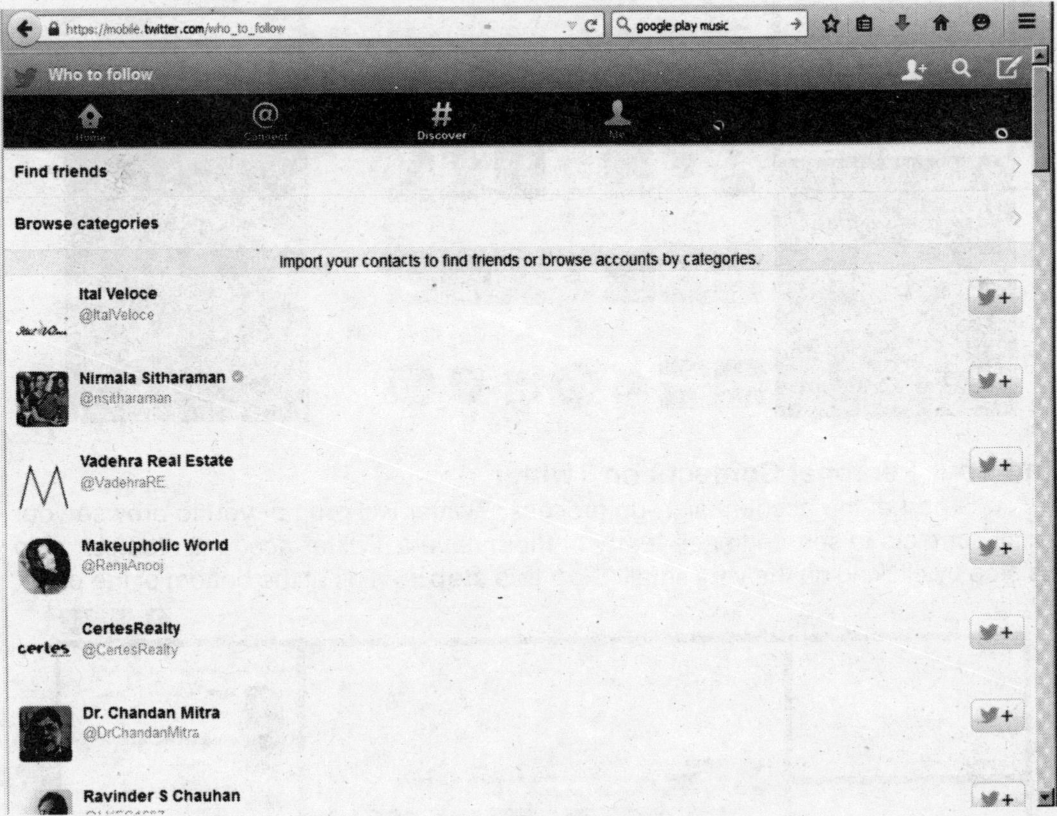

Finding Popular Accounts

You can find Popular Accounts in Twitter through the following steps:

1. On the **Discover** page, click **Popular accounts** from the menu on the left.
2. You'll see a list of topics that may be of interest to you. **Click on a topic** and you'll get a list of relevant Twitter accounts.
3. You can pick and choose which accounts you'd like to follow by clicking the **Follow button** next to each user.
4. After you've explored the list of accounts under one topic, you can return to the full list of categories (click **View all categories**) and select a different interest to find more great accounts to follow.
5. You can also **search by topic** in the search box at the top of the page.

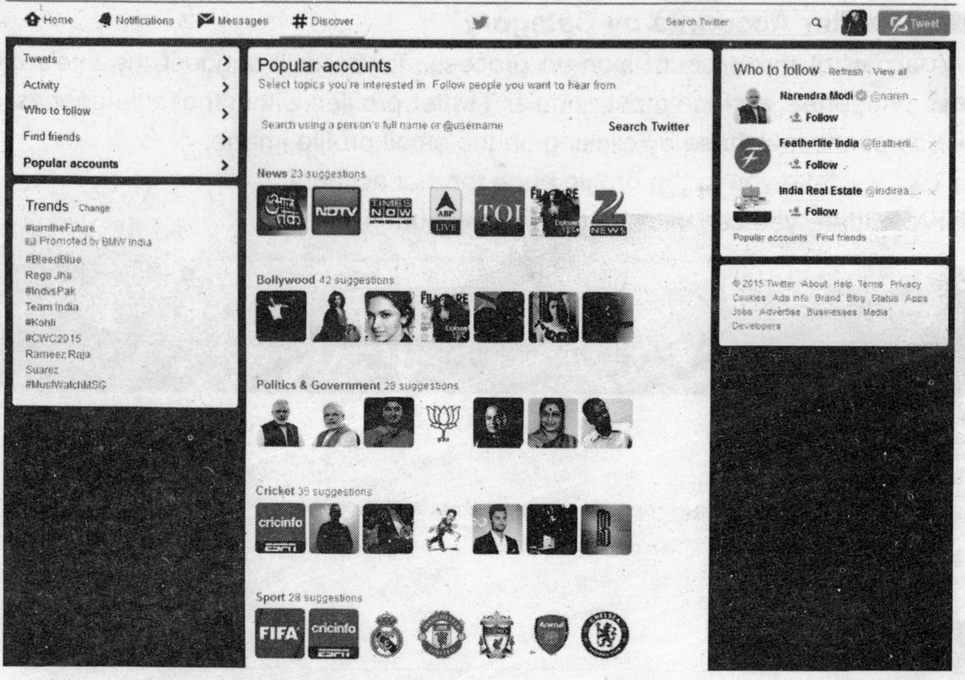

Find Your Personal Contacts on Twitter

As a part of the account sign-up process, Twitter will prompt you to browse your e-mail contacts to search to see if any of them have a Twitter account. You can skip this step by clicking on the very small **'Skip this step >>'** link at the bottom of the page.

Twitter Profile

Your Twitter profile is where you will see your short **bio** and a list of all of the **tweets** you have written. You'll also be able to find who you are following, edit your profile, and find your followers, favourites, lists and images.

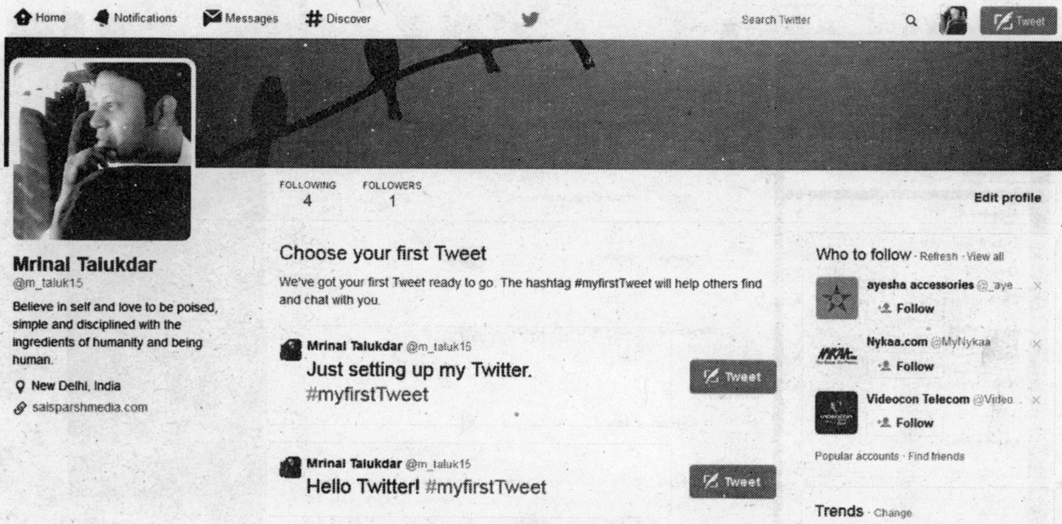

Twitter Home Page

Your Twitter home page is unique to you. It is an activity feed of all the tweets from accounts you follow.

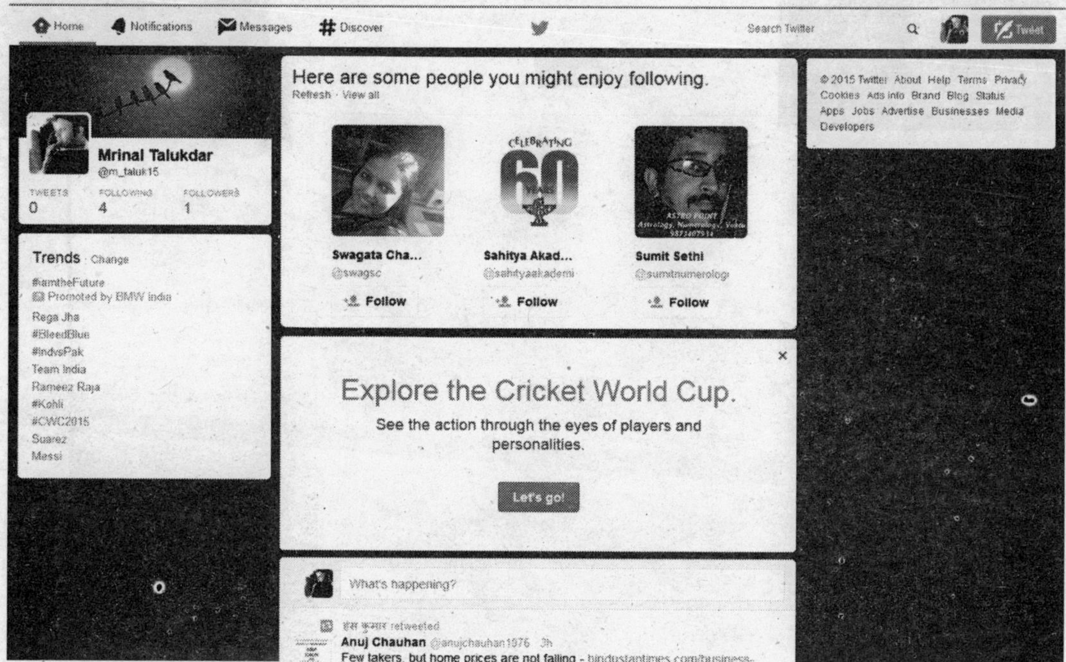

Edit Your Profile, Account Settings

Click on your profile button at the top of any Twitter page and click on **settings** to get to this page. Here you can change your username, e-mail address, language, password, e-mail notification settings, profile, profile background image and design, and more.

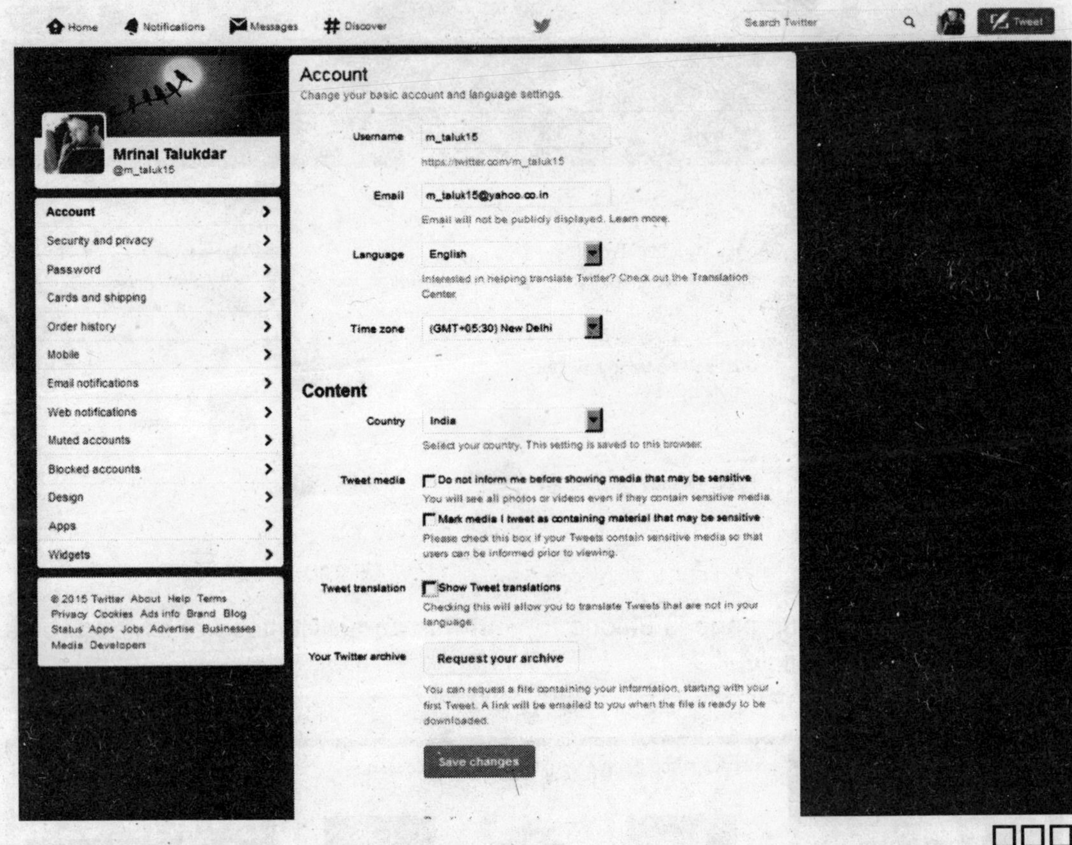

□□□